Imperial Delhi

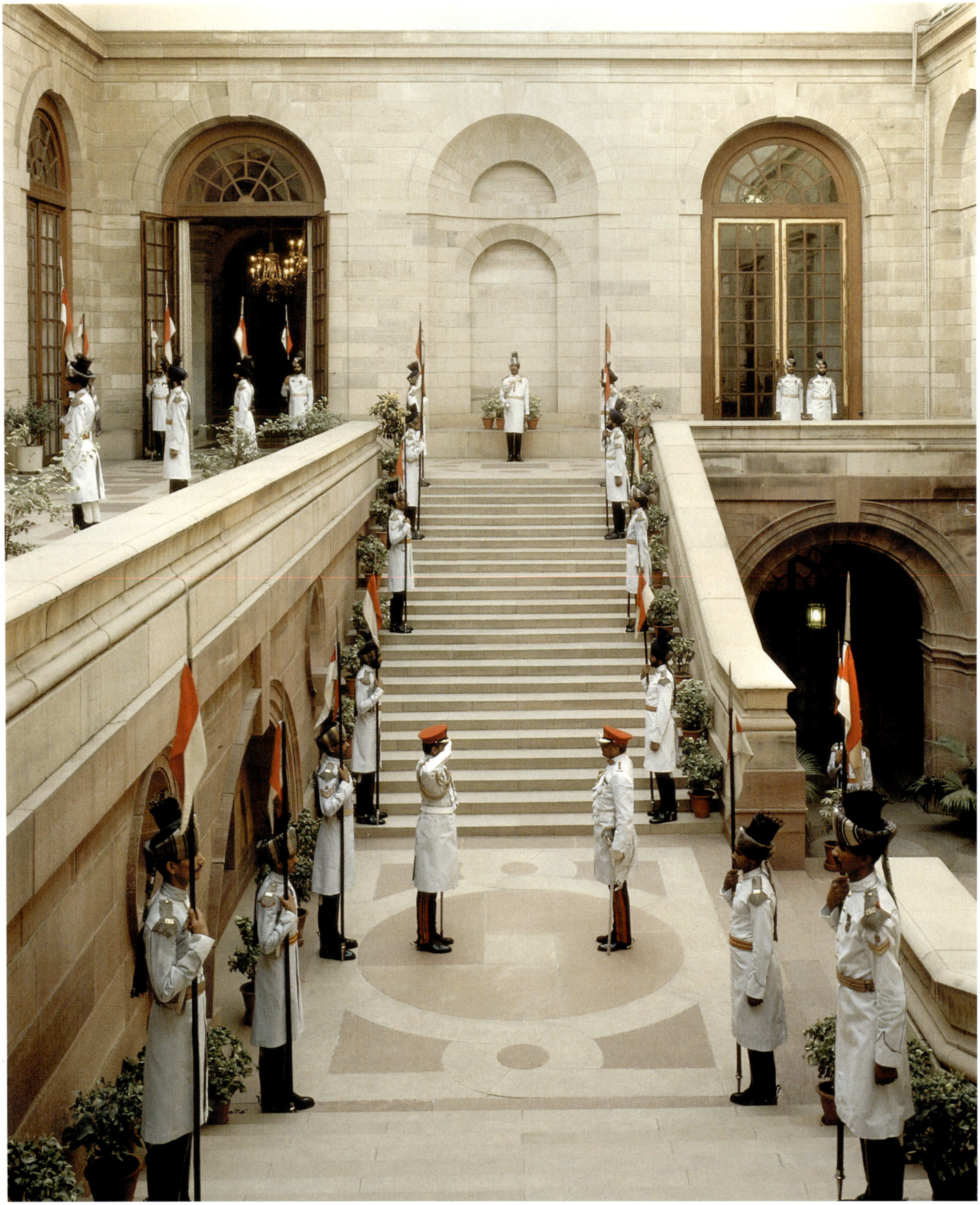

Andreas Volwahsen

Imperial Delhi

The British Capital of the Indian Empire

Prestel

Munich · Berlin · London · New York

To Andrea

Illustration Credits: see p. 301

Front jacket: see pp. 290–91
Back jacket: see p. 134
Frontispiece: see pp. 112–13 (detail)

Prestel Verlag
Königinstrasse 9, 80539 Munich
Tel. +49 (89) 381709-0 · Fax +49 (89) 381709-35

4 Bloomsbury Place, London WC1A 2QA
Tel. +44 (20) 7323 5004 · Fax +44 (20) 7636 8004

175 Fifth Avenue, New York NY 10010
Tel. +1 (212) 995 2720 · Fax +1 (212) 995 2733

www.prestel.com

Prestel books are available worldwide.
Please contact your nearest bookseller or write to any of the above addresses for information concerning your local distributor.

Library of Congress Control Number: 2002112817

The Deutsche Bibliothek lists this Publication in the Deutsche Nationalbibliografie; detailed bibliographic data is available on the Internet at http://dnb.ddb.de

Translated from the German by Sandra Harper, London
Editorial direction by Curt Holtz
Editorial assistance by James Young
Copy-editing by Arjun Gupta, New York
Designed by Iris von Hoesslin, Munich

Origination by Repro Ludwig, Zell am See
Printed by Jütte-Messedruck GmbH, Leipzig
Bound by Kunst- und Verlagsbuchbinderei, Leipzig

Printed in Germany on acid-free paper

ISBN 3-7913-2788-7

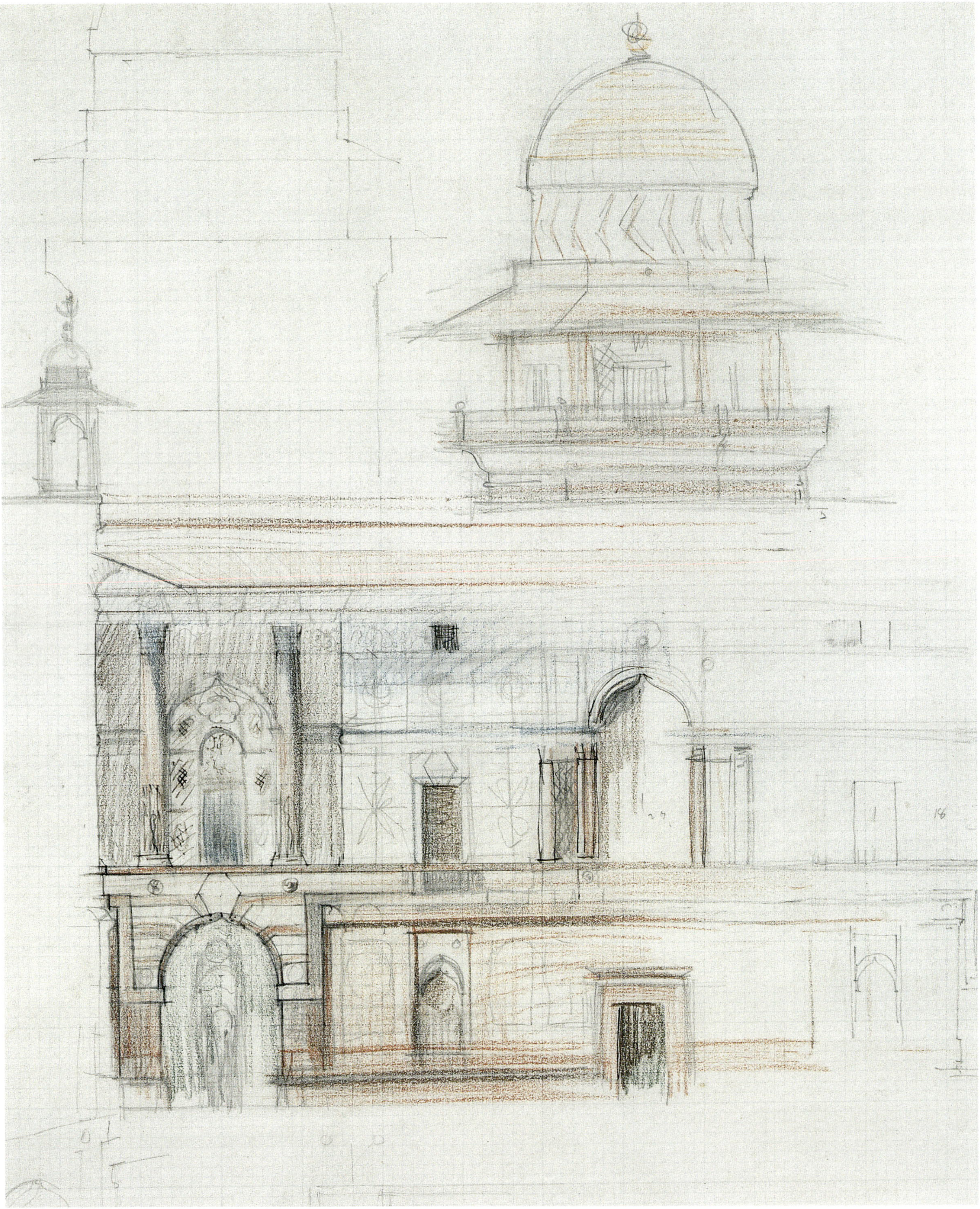

Introduction

In the history of mankind, temples and palaces have been the most important buildings for the representation and protection of cosmic and temporal power. Without these two building types, the founding of empires would have been inconceivable. Moreover, a national identity cannot develop without architectural representations of these sources of power.

Both the temple and the palace required an urban environment, not only during periods of construction, but also in order to function. Thus, after the Persian Wars in the fifth century B.C., Hippodamos founded the town of Milet, General Washington established Washington, D.C. in 1791 as the capital of the new "United States," and in 1911, Britain's King George V, in his capacity as Emperor of India, founded a new capital that was Imperial Delhi.

George V's decision was prompted by a desire to create stability in India by uniting the princely chiefdoms and territories of the subcontinent under his rule. His plan succeeded. The Indian Raj developed a newfound national identity of its own. The maharajas, in dispute with each other for a long time, now considered it an honour to be represented in the new capital by having palaces of their own in Imperial Delhi.

There remained only one small snag for Britain: the British Crown, with its sense of mission and imperial design, was no longer indispensable as a result of the growing national consciousness on the Indian subcontinent – a phenomenon that also emerged in Britain's other dominions around the world.

After nineteen years of construction and another sixteen years of use as the capital of the Raj, the British left when, bowing to pressure from the Indian Congress Party led by Mahatma Gandhi and the will of the Indian people, the Viceroy had to grant India its independence.

It would be a gross simplification to trace this historical development to the building of Imperial Delhi alone. But just how great the significance of the magnificent capital was to the formation of an emergent national consciousness is reflected by the fact that, even after Indian independence, the importance of the capital designed by a defunct colonial power remained intact. The President of the Republic of India moved into the palace of the British Viceroy, and in the Legislative Building there was now a democratically elected parliament.

The architects of Imperial Delhi and the British Viceroy knew exactly how closely interdependent political power was to architectural style. On the one hand, they were certain that British imperial power could only be expressed by Neo-Classical architectural idioms. On the other hand, they were also driven by the certainty that, in the Hindu and Muslim cultural spheres of the Indian subcontinent, buildings of Roman temple architecture might be perceived as farcical. There began a protracted search, with genuine good will and true insight, for an appropriate architectural style. The end result was a capital characterized by an original clarity, but also by a strange monumentality.

The traces of this neither English nor Indian town planning process are slowly being eradicated because of pressures to convert increasing land values into tower blocks and the desire to replace British symbolic forms with Indian ones. Therefore, it is high time to collect all the planning, photographic and textual material from the archives in India and in Great Britain – an essential undertaking if we are to understand one of humanity's most ambitious architectural achievements.

In the new India of the mid nineteen-fifties, independent of the building of Imperial Delhi, there also arose a new capital for the important Indian state of Punjab, called

Fig. 1: In 1914, in order to please the Viceroy, Edwin Lutyens attempted to include Hindu and Islamic elements in the formal repertoire for Viceroy's House. But with every new attempt, he became more certain that, in the framework of Palladian architecture, this was only possible to a very limited extent.

Chandigarh. In his opening speech, the most famous of the architects of Chandigarh, Le Corbusier, referred to a model for his work: "New Delhi, capital of Imperial India, was built by Lutyens over thirty years ago with extreme care, great talent and true success. The critics may rant as they will but the accomplishment of such an undertaking earns respect."[1]

At present, public opinion on important Indian topics such as religious conflict, birth control, economic growth and the retarding influence of the caste system eclipse discussions of town planning. Nevertheless, experts still respond with amazement at the complexity and determination of the plan for an Imperial Delhi. Robert Venturi and Denise Scott Brown, two of the most stimulating architectural theorists of the sixties and seventies, discovered in Imperial Delhi all the contradictions typical of great architecture: "Earlier, one of us, in the context of an architecture of complexity and contradiction, discussed the qualities of paradox, ambiguity and accommodation in Lutyens which have been so stimulating to us as architects. We now go beyond these characteristics of form, space and program because we are beginning to learn as well from the symbolism of his eclectic architecture. Commercial strip architecture *and* Lutyens houses are relevant to an architecture of meaning ... Our greatest lesson from Lutyens is perhaps his tolerance and wit."[2]

Another American architectural theorist expressed similar sentiments in his comment: "The contradictions in Lutyens' buildings, the juxtapositions of the formal and the functional, order and accommodation, the predetermined and the whimsical, symmetry of form and asymmetry of movement etc., which are the basis of his architectural vocabulary, are not unlike the eighteenth-century conception of a Palladian villa set in an English Garden."[3]

Yet, since all theory remains grey if the senses are not appealed to pictorially, in the following chapters we shall attempt to document and cast light on the palaces and churches, the streets and squares, the symbols and monuments, and last but not least, the residences and offices of an elite imperial society.

In the oppressively hot and barren landscape of northern India an English traveller in the first half of the last century approached the British Viceroy's legendary town observing: "The traveller drives out of Old Delhi, past the Pearl Mosque (Jama Masjid) and the Fort. A flat country – brown, scrubby and broken – lies on either side. This country has been compared with the Roman Campagna: at every hand, tombs and mosques from Mogul times and earlier, weathered to the colour of the earth bear witness to former Empires. The road describes a curve and embarks imperceptibly on a gradient. Suddenly, on the right, a scape of towers and domes is lifted from the horizon, sunlit pink and cream dancing against the blue sky, fresh as a cup of milk, grand as Rome. Close at hand the foreground discloses a white arch. The motor turns off the arterial avenue, and skirting the low red base of the gigantic monument, comes to a stop. The traveller heaves a breath. Before his eyes, sloping gently upwards, runs a gravel way of such infinite perspective as to suggest the intervention of a diminishing glass; at whose end, reared above the green tree tops, glitters the seat of government, the sevenths Delhi, four square upon an eminence – dome, tower, dome, tower, dome, red, pink, cream, and white-washed gold and flashing in the morning sun. The traveller loses a breath, and with it his apprehensions and preconceptions. Here is something not merely worthy, but whose like has never been. With a shiver of impatience he shakes off contemporary standard, and makes ready to evoke those of Greece, the Renaissance, and the Moguls."[4]

"Granted the contributions of many other persons, the plan of New Delhi is primarily the fruit of the mind and the heart of Edwin Lutyens. Possessed of a genuine historical perspective, he was at the same time keenly sensitive to the newest developments in the art and science of town planning. The examples of Ebenezer Howard, of Prestwich and Mawson at Port Sunlight, and of Parker and Unwin, underlay his Delhi scheme no less than precedents from the hand of Palladio, Domenico Fontana, Wren, Evelyn, Gabriel, Le Notre, L'Enfant, Haussmann, Burnham and Griffin.

The British vision of the new Delhi had from the first been as eclectic as the assortment of individuals involved, ranging from urban grandeur to rural greenery. The King-Emperor's wishes had embraced an imposing city expressive of 'the power of Western science, art, and

1 Quotation from: D. Scott Brown and R. Venturi: "Learning from Lutyens," in *RIBA Journal*, August 1969, pp. 353, 354.
2 Ibid.
3 A. Greenberg: "Lutyens' Architecture Restudied," in: *Perspecta*, 1969, Connecticut.
4 R. Byron: "New Delhi," in: *AR*, Vol. LXIX, No. 410, January 1931, p. 1.

civilization,' while the Chairman of the Town Planning Committee had declared it essential of the British Raj to dominate the monuments of India's earlier empires."[5]

"Under the powerful inspiration of Lutyens, an 'Indo-British' school of architecture flourished in Delhi in the 1920s and 1930s which was one of the last flowerings of the Classical tradition anywhere."[6] "New Delhi has proved a more successful experiment than that other essay in European cultural imperialism at Chandigarh. Certainly New Delhi is one of the finest things the British have ever done."[7]

5 Robert Grant Irving: *Indian Summer*, New Haven and London, 1981, p. 87.
6 Gavin Stamp: "New Delhi," in: Arts Council: Exhibition catalogue *Edwin Lutyens*, London 1982, p. 41.
7 Ibid., p. 42.

Fig. 2: View of the South Block of the Secretariats with the slope up to Viceroy's House in the foreground.

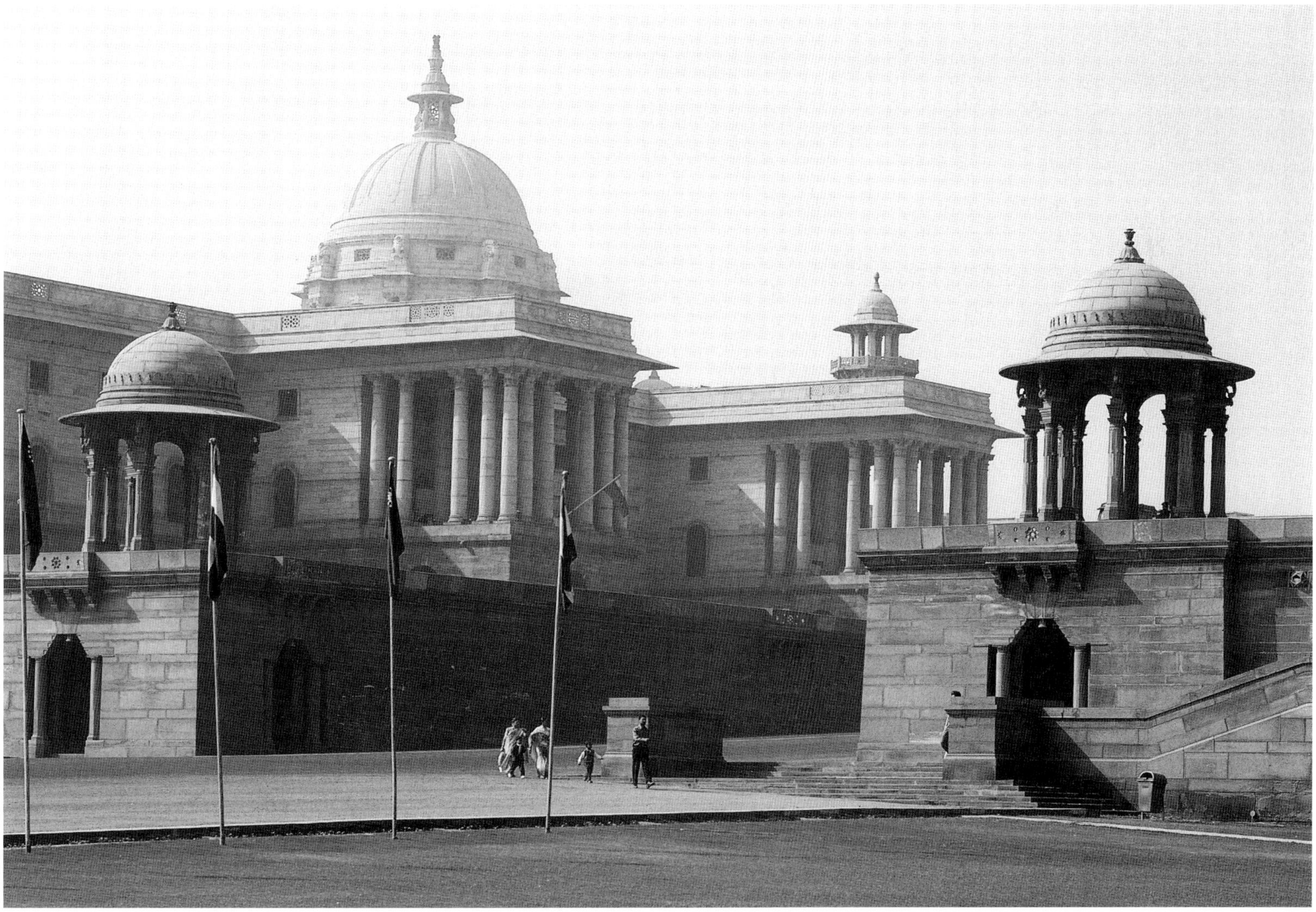

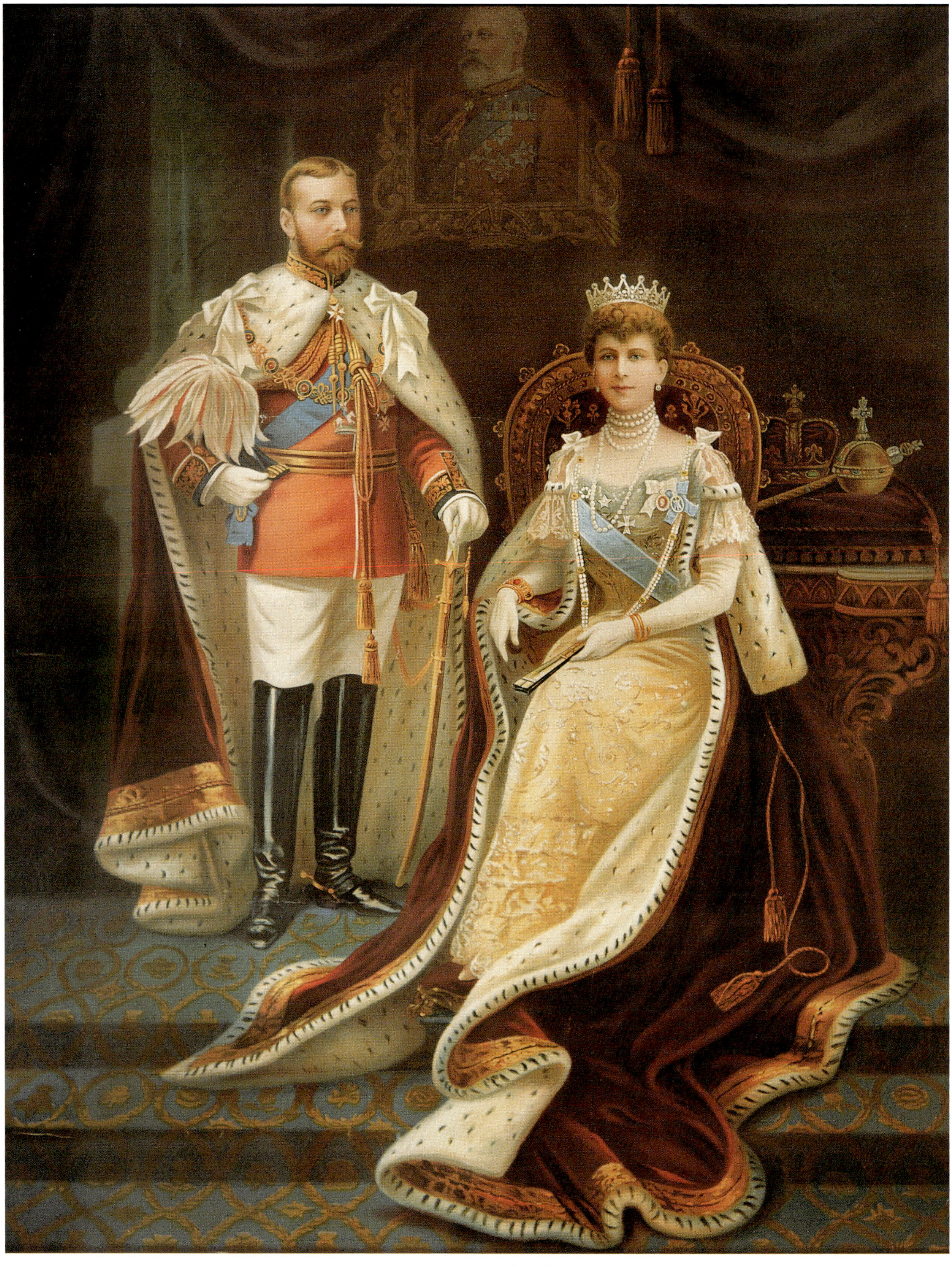

1 Transferring the Capital

The Prince of Wales, later King George V, visited India from 1905–1906. In his conversations with Indian princes and maharajas, they continually pressed to have the capital of the Raj transferred from Calcutta to Delhi. The advantages were – at least from the British point of view – escape from Calcutta's comparatively unhealthy climate and political instability. Moreover, Delhi had played an increasingly significant role over the centuries as a capital for both Hindu and Muslim ruling dynasties.

In 1910, George V wrote to Lord Morley, Secretary of State for India, in preparation for his second visit to India: "Ever since I visited India five years ago I have been impressed by the great advantage which would result from a visit by the sovereign to that great Empire. The events which have unfortunately occurred since 1906 have only strengthened that opinion. I am convinced that if it were possible for me, accompanied by the Queen, to ... hold a Coronation Durbar at Delhi, where we should meet all the Princes, officials and vast numbers of the People, the greatest benefits would accrue to the Country at large. I also trust and I believe that if the proposed visit could be made known some time before, it would tend to allay unrest and, I am sorry to say, seditious spirit, which unfortunately exists in some parts of India."[8]

Fig. 3: King George V and Queen Mary visited India in 1911 in their capacity as Emperor and Empress of India.

The following year, in the middle of 1911, thoughts of a possible transfer were again the subject of discussions between the Viceroy of India, Lord Hardinge, and the members of his council because of a suggestion by Sir Guy Fleetwood Wilson, the Finance Member of the Council. Moreover, the new Secretary of State for India in London, Lord Crewe, promised his full support should there be a corresponding bid from Calcutta. "The King was excited and on August 12 Crewe wired his majesty's approval and that George V would make the announcement at the Delhi Durbar to be held in December." Crewe agreed that "the ancient walls of Delhi enshrine an Imperial tradition comparable with that of Constantinople, or that of Rome itself."[9]

When George V finally came to Delhi in December of 1911, he was surprised at first by the chilly reception given him by the Indian people. But this was the result of a breach of protocol: "... there was the problem of the King-Emperor's entry into Delhi through the ancient gate once used by the Mogul Emperors. An elephant was the appropriate mount for an Emperor of India, but the plans were for a procession headed by high officials on horseback. When King George at last entered Delhi on horseback wearing a field marshal's uniform and topee, and flanked by British officials, the Indian crowds apparently failed to recognise him and his reception was a chilly one"[10] (Fig. 7).

From the point of view of all the participants, however, the ensuing festivities of the Coronation Durbar were a huge success with global impact. Approximately 100,000 Indian princes, officials, British officers, and soldiers gathered outside the old Mughal city on December 12, and by their homage acknowledged the British King as the Emperor of India and Queen Mary as the Empress. The ceremony was documented in great detail, and it was recorded that King George V used the Coronation Durbar to announce the transference of British government in India to Delhi: "Their Imperial Majesties resumed their seats on their thrones and the assembly thought that the great Coronation Durbar was about to be closed. But there was yet to come a momentous and dramatic incident. A little Indian page advanced behind the throne of the King-Emperor with a scroll in his hand. Hesitating, and evidently

8 D. Judd: *The Life and Time of George V*, London 1993, 100–01.
9 Ibid., 101.
10 Ibid.

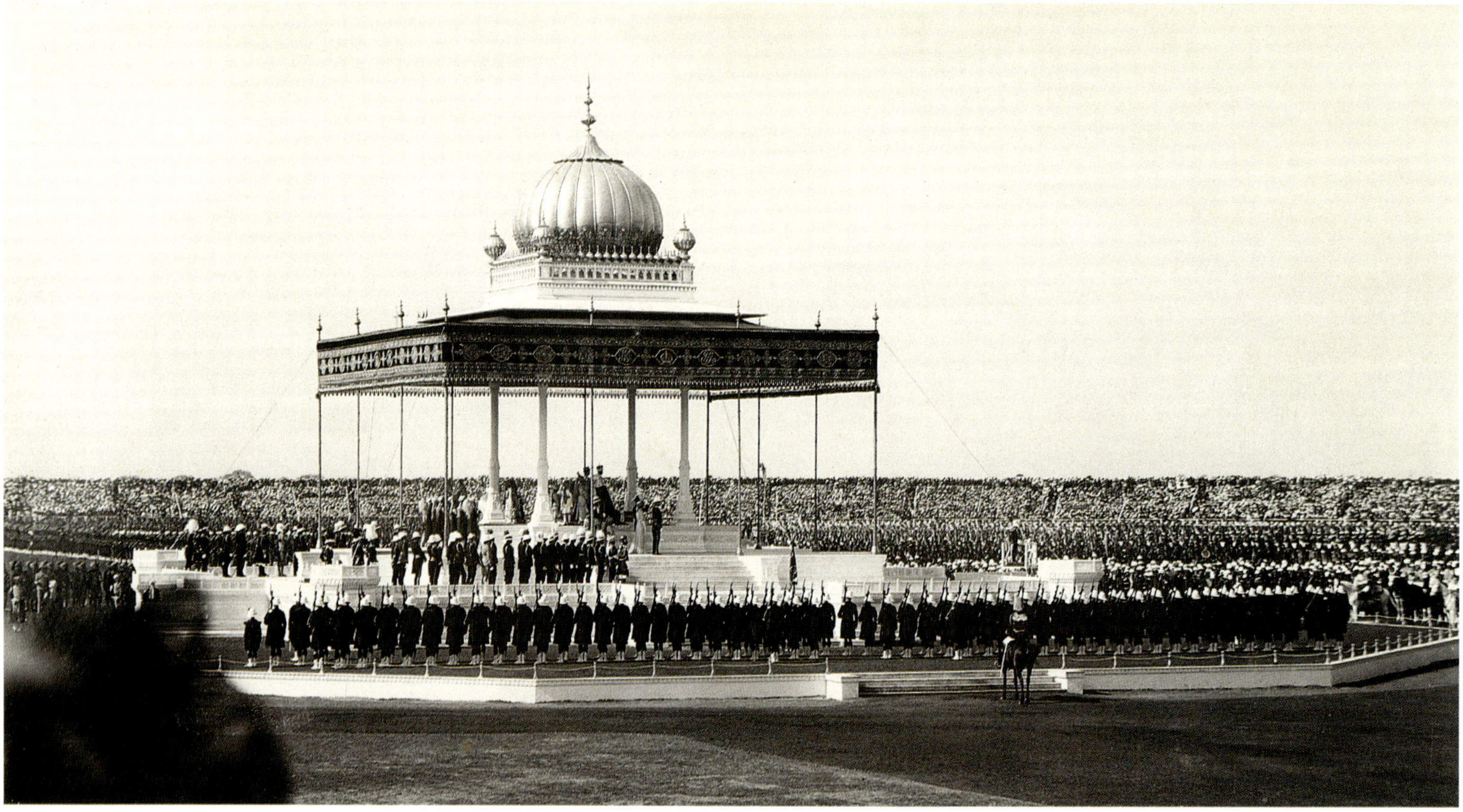

Fig. 4: Approximately 100,000 Indian princes, British officers, and soldiers gathered for the Coronation Durbar of King George V and Queen Mary on December 12, 1911, to acknowledge the British King as Emperor of India.

nervous, the boy looked towards the Governor-General, who beckoned to him to go on. The boy then pushed into the hand of His Imperial Majesty the scroll of paper, and the King Emperor rose and made the following historic announcement: 'We are pleased to announce to Our people that on the advice of Our Ministers, tendered after consultation with Our Governor-General in Council, We have decided upon the transfer of the seat of the Government of India from Calcutta to the ancient capital of Delhi, and simultaneously and as a consequence of this transfer, the creation at as early a date as possible of the Governorship for the Presidency of Bengal, of a new Lieutenant-Governorship in Council, administering the areas of Behar, Chota Nagpur and Orissa, and of a Chief Commissionership of Assam, with such administrative changes and redistribution of boundaries as our Governor-General in Council, with the approval of Our Secretary of State for India in Council, may, in due course, determine.

It is our earnest desire that these changes may conduce to the better administration of India and the greater prosperity of our beloved people.'"[11]

Words such as these conveyed an astonishingly genuine identification of the British Royal Family with their chosen task of promoting order and prosperity in the conquered colonies. In addition, there were other British colonies around the globe. There was no need for the King to pretend in his address. Almost half the world was more or less dependent upon decisions from London. Nevertheless, George V occasionally found the imperial task a little irksome; at any rate, when he had had to wear the gold Crown for several hours at the Durbar in Delhi, he complained about the weight and was looking forward to the next tiger hunt outside the capital (Fig. 5).

"Tigers provided as much trouble as elephants and horses in planning the royal visit, but this time because the King wanted to fit a week's tiger shooting into his already heavy itinerary. George V was an expert marksman, and rifle shooting, together with stamp collecting and sailing, was a keenly pursued hobby. 'The fact is,' wrote the new Secretary of State for India, Lord Crewe, 'that it is a misfortune for a public personage to have any taste so strongly developed as the craze for shooting is in our beloved ruler.' But royal persistence prevailed, and

11 The Imperial Publishing Co.: *The Imperial Coronation Durbar* (Illustrated), Lahore 1911, pp. 6–7.

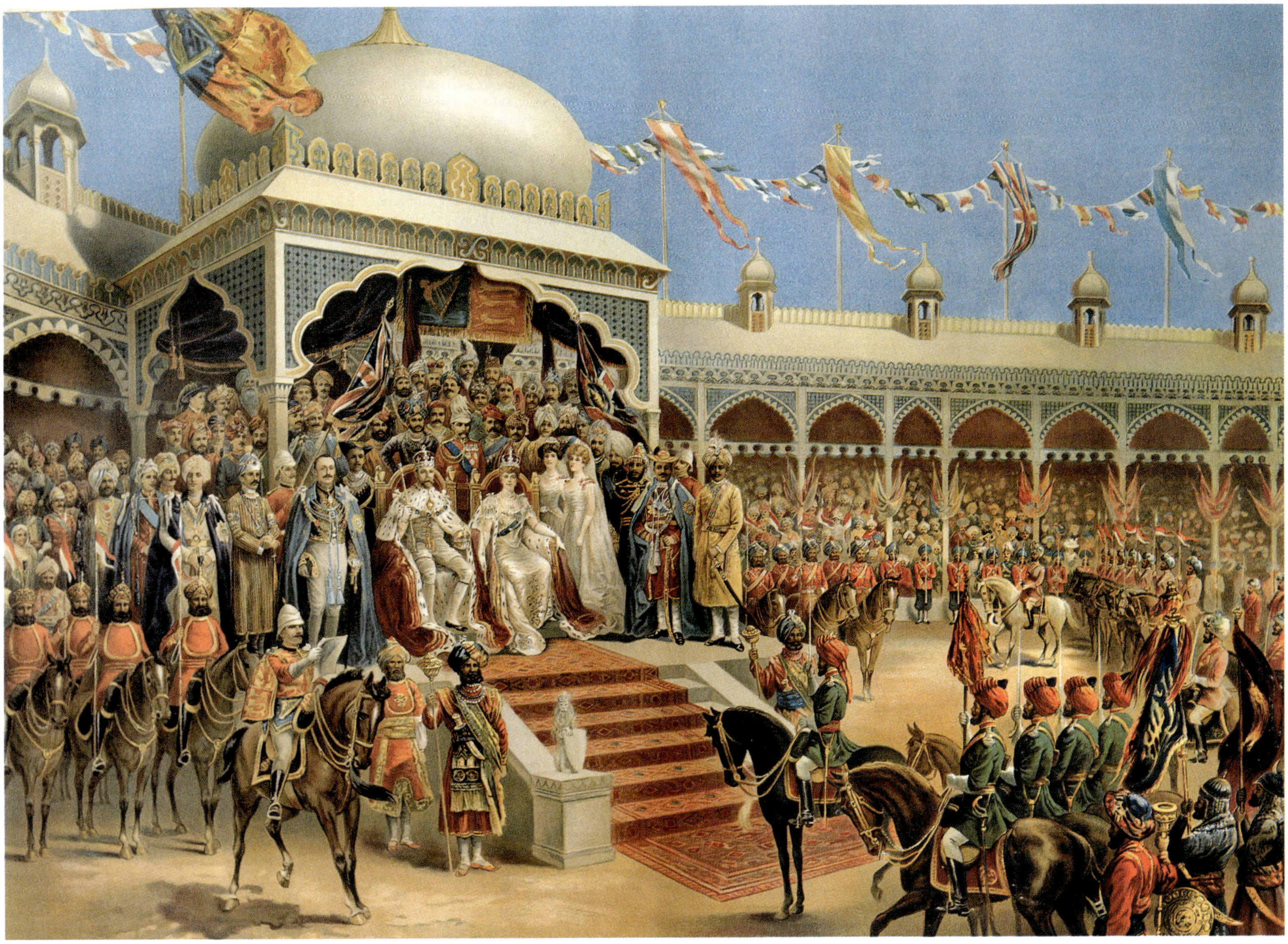

Fig. 5: December 12, 1911, King George V and Queen Mary receive tributes from the Indian princes and maharajas at the Coronation Durbar in Delhi.

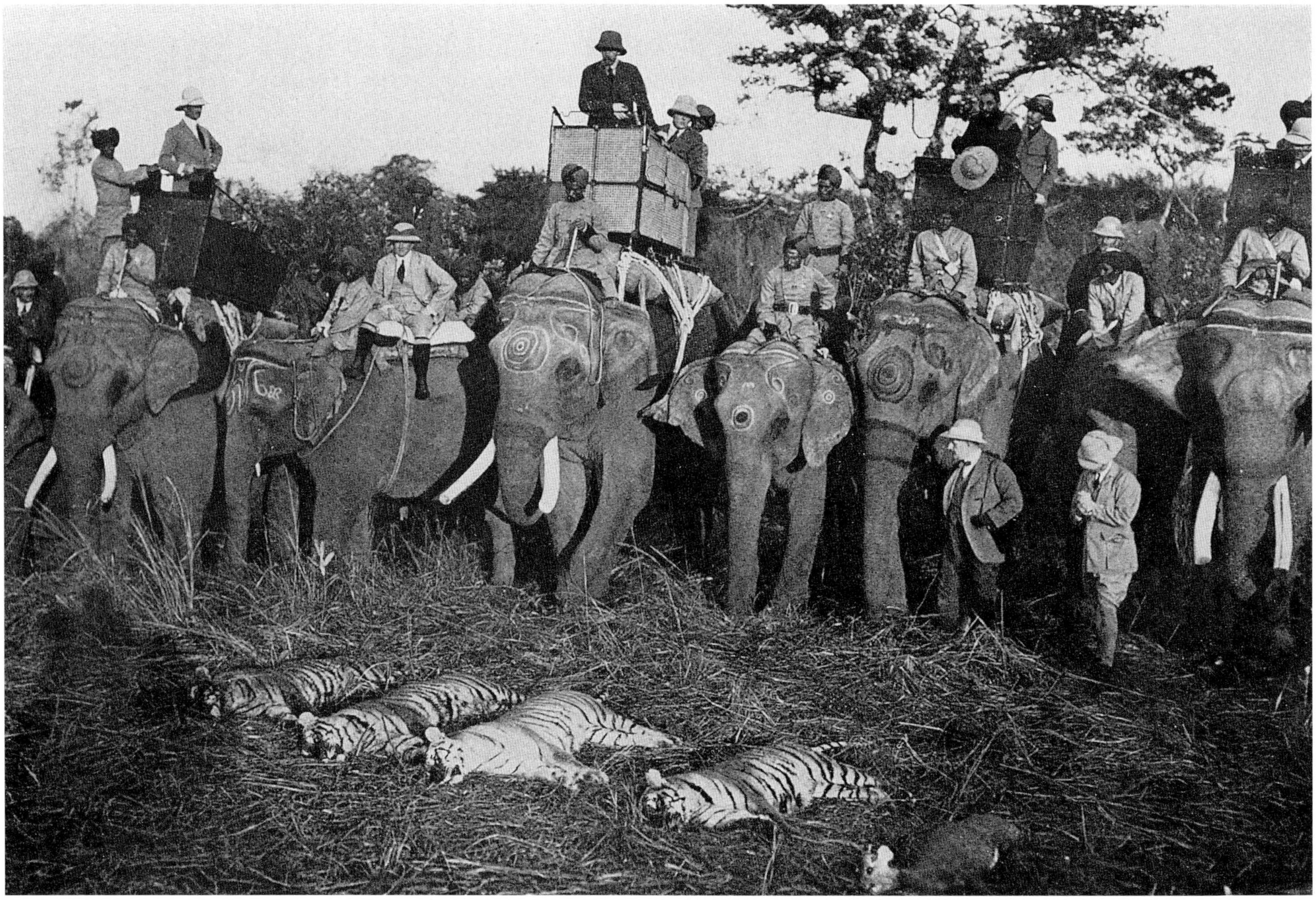

Fig. 6: George V enjoyed tiger hunting outside Delhi much more than court ceremonials and his responsibilities as Emperor.

Fig. 7: During the Durbar celebrations of 1911, King George V rode into the Red Fort on a horse, not on an elephant. This breach of Durbar protocol led the crowd to not recognize him as Emperor of India, thus giving the King, much to his disappointment, a rather cool reception.

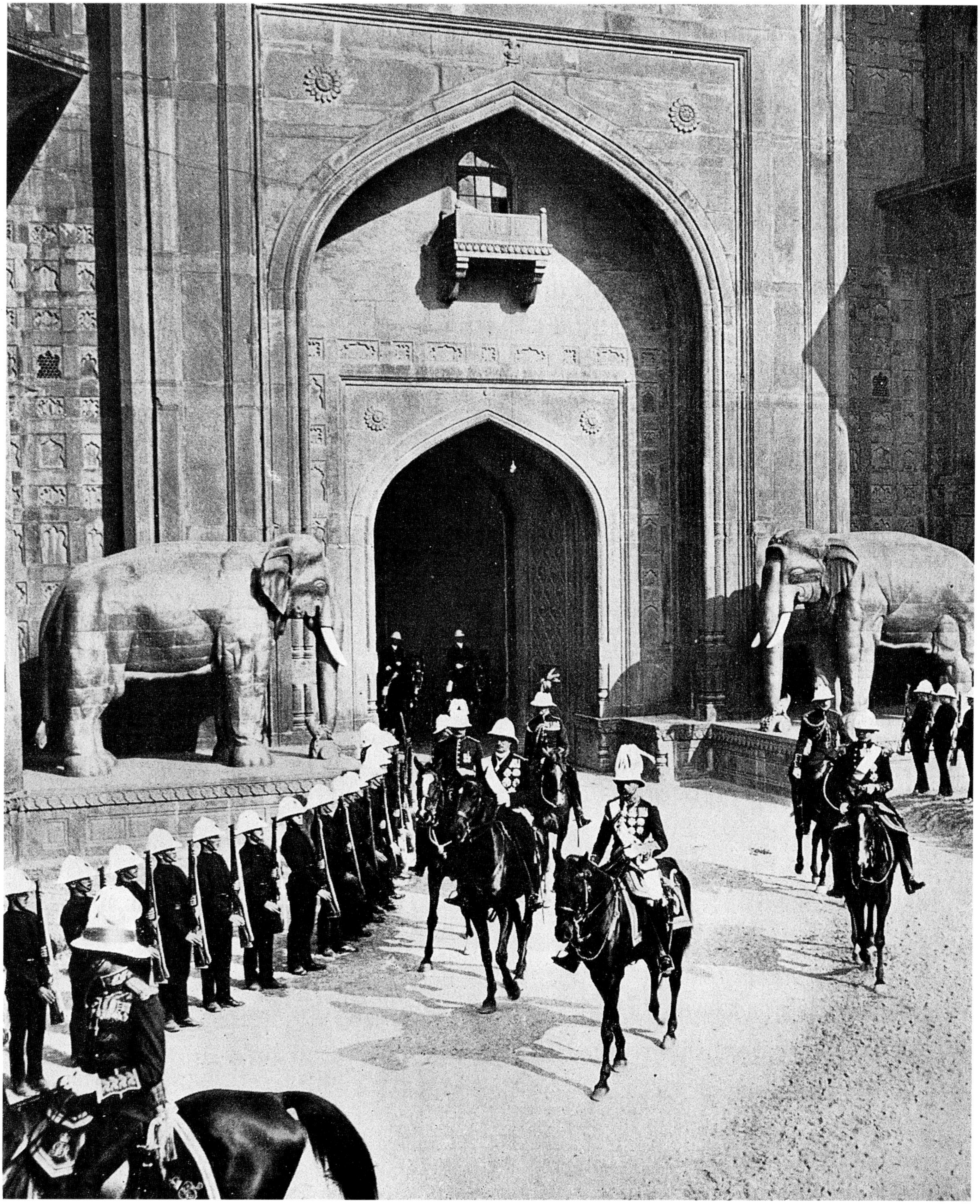

King George went off to bag his tigers, while Queen Mary, who had read a number of serious books to prepare her for her Indian tour, visited Agra and the Taj Mahal"[12] (Fig. 6).

According to Lutyens' biographer, Christopher Hussey: "The decision to build the new city can be regarded as marking the summit of the Edwardian Age's might, the peak of its progress towards the British Commonwealth ideal. The Union Building of the Dominion of South Africa, designed by Herbert Baker, was already established at Pretoria; a competition (won by an American) for the design of that of Australia at Canberra had been launched in the previous April. It was therefore felt, and justifiably, that the new capital of the British Empire in India and eventually of the Dominion of India should be made the occasion for planned architecture of commensurate majesty; an Anglo-Indian Rome. In retrospect, the splendour and political significance of that memorable Durbar, and the impressive suddenness with which so great a project as the building of a new metropolis for a sub-continent was announced, can be seen to have dramatised the undertaking from its inception, lifting it to an emotional plane; heroic indeed but one size larger than life."[13]

The King's decision to transfer the capital of India from Calcutta to Delhi offered him, at the same time, the opportunity for solving another political problem with little fuss and to the satisfaction of the Hindu population: "The 'seditious spirit' which the king acknowledged to exist in India distressed him. Like many others he saw its genesis in the partition of Bengal devised by Lord Curzon in 1905. This well-meant attempt by the Viceroy to reduce the increasingly ungovernable size of Bengal, which numbered 78 million persons, had provoked violent and sustained agitation from Bengali nationalists. For not only was the Bengali-speaking area split in half, but the division also corresponded with communal boundaries. The result was that Eastern Bengal became a preponderantly Muslim province, while Biharis and Oriyas outnumbered the Hindu Bengalis in the province of Bengal itself. Protest meetings and resolutions left Curzon unmoved. His own authoritarian instincts (typified by his alleged motto, 'Never apologize, never explain') suited well the independence he enjoyed as head of a distant and fareflung autocracy, with even the right to overrule a majority of his Council. The Government of India adhered fixedly to the doctrine of efficiency and reasoned that concession to popular outcry would be interpreted as weakness."[14]

The new Viceroy, Lord Hardinge, and the new Secretary of State for India, Lord Crewe,[15] supported the King in his plan to solve this awkward business by merging the two Bengali provinces, thus taking the opportunity to give Calcutta a new role – as a consolation.

12 D. Judd: op. cit., p. 101.
13 Christopher Hussey: *The Life of Sir Edwin Lutyens*, London and New York 1950, p. 237.
14 R.G. Irving: op. cit., p. 18.
15 Both had been in office since 1910.

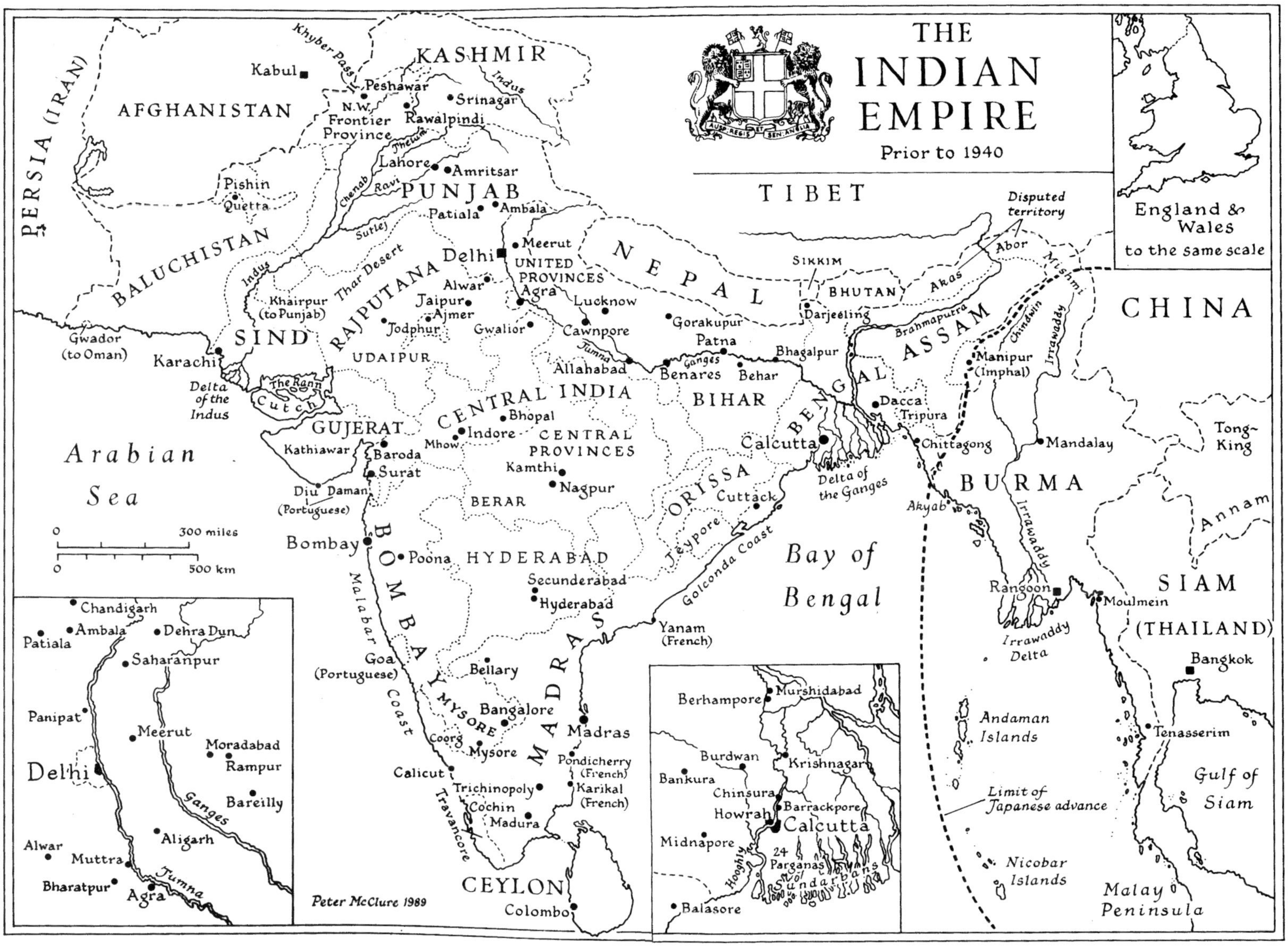

Fig. 8: At the beginning of the twentieth century, the Raj extended from Kashmir in the North to Madras in the South, and from Punjab in the West to Assam in the East.

1.1 Requirements of a Capital for the British Raj

At the beginning of the twentieth-century, English society and particularly the Royal Family perceived the British Empire at the height of international recognition and imperial power. A new capital for the British Raj would not only leave the unpleasant climate and political troubles of Calcutta behind, it would, more importantly, be a clearly visible sign of British rule over the large number of princely states in India. As early as 1904, in a speech in Calcutta, Lord Curzon, Viceroy and Governor-General of India, had ordered: "Make no little plans; they have no magic to stir man's blood and probably themselves will not be realized. Make big plans; aim high in hope and work, remembering that a noble logical diagram once recorded will never die."[16]

In retrospect, viewed almost a century later, it could safely be assumed that: "New Delhi's authors, like the Beaux Arts and Baroque planners before them, assumed without question that the order they created was eternal. Their scale was enormous, for they built for the ages. Ruskin had contended that the glory of a building was its antiquity; how much more so a city! 'It is not a cantonment we have to lay out at Delhi,' declared Sir George Birdwood, 'but an Imperial City – the symbol of the British Raj in India – and it must like Rome be built for eternity.'"[17]

To love the imperial architecture of Rome is one thing, but to build a second Rome was quite another. In British academic circles there began a vehement discussion about possible models and styles. Herbert Baker, having already been advised at this time by his friend Edwin Lutyens of a possible chance to work jointly on building an Imperial Delhi, used the general euphoria to make people aware of his name as a suitable architect through an article in the *Times*: "The King's Decree to build a new capital of India at Delhi brings into prominence the question of the style of architecture to be employed.

It is a question of Imperial as well as of artistic importance; as an event in the history of architecture it may perhaps be compared to the building of Constantinople. The problems of architectural style with which Constantine and his architects had to deal – even if in those days they were conscious of such problems at all – were easy of solution as compared with those which have to be faced today at Delhi. The constructive genius of the Romans had by the fourth century already absorbed all that it required of the arts and artists of the conquered nations. It had fused the characteristics of East and West, of Greece, Western Asia, Egypt and Italy in the new architecture, which remained for all that essentially the offspring of Imperial Rome. The buildings of Constantine's new city were in the direct line of evolution from Hadrian's Pantheon to Justinian's Sophia. Yet the founding of the new capital, in spite of the haste and carelessness with which it seems to have been built, must have given a great impetus to the later developments of Roman architecture which we now call Byzantine."[18]

The prevailing conditions for an architectural plan of previously unknown proportions were favourable. Large areas in the environs of Old Delhi were, in any case, in the possession of the British Crown. Local labour was cheap. An essentially higher and healthier standard of living could be offered to officials of the British government. Most importantly, for the first time in the history of the expanding territories of the Raj, the unity of the British Crown and the Indian people was being moved into full view of the world.

16 *Speeches by Lord Curzon of Kedleston, Viceroy and Governor-General of India*, Vol. 3, Calcutta 1904, p. 437.
17 R.G. Irving: op. cit. p. 90.
18 H. Baker: "New Delhi, the problem of Style," in: the *Times*, October 3, 1912.

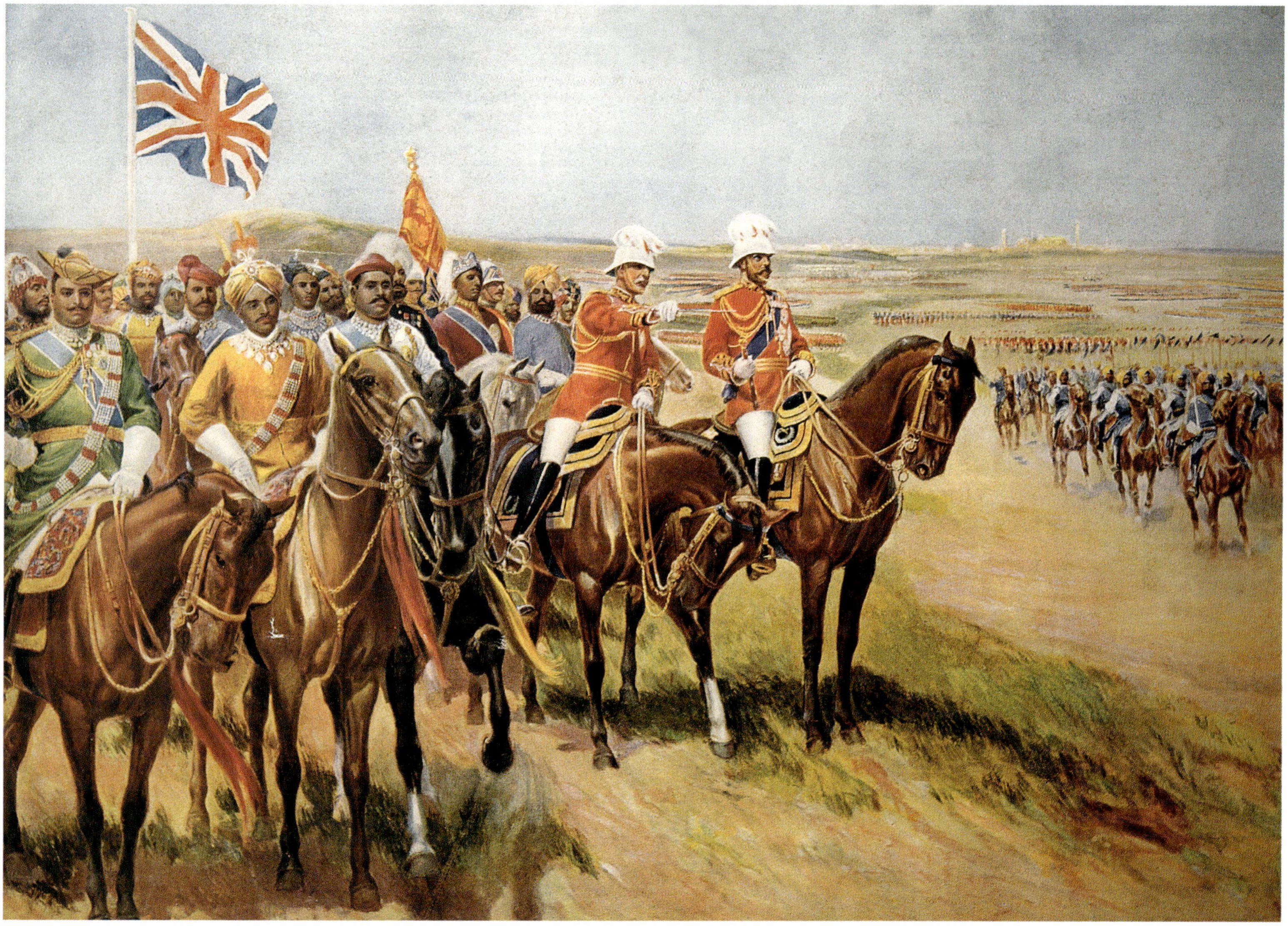

Fig. 9: King George V, Emperor of India, arrives in Delhi with his retinue for the Durbar of 1911.

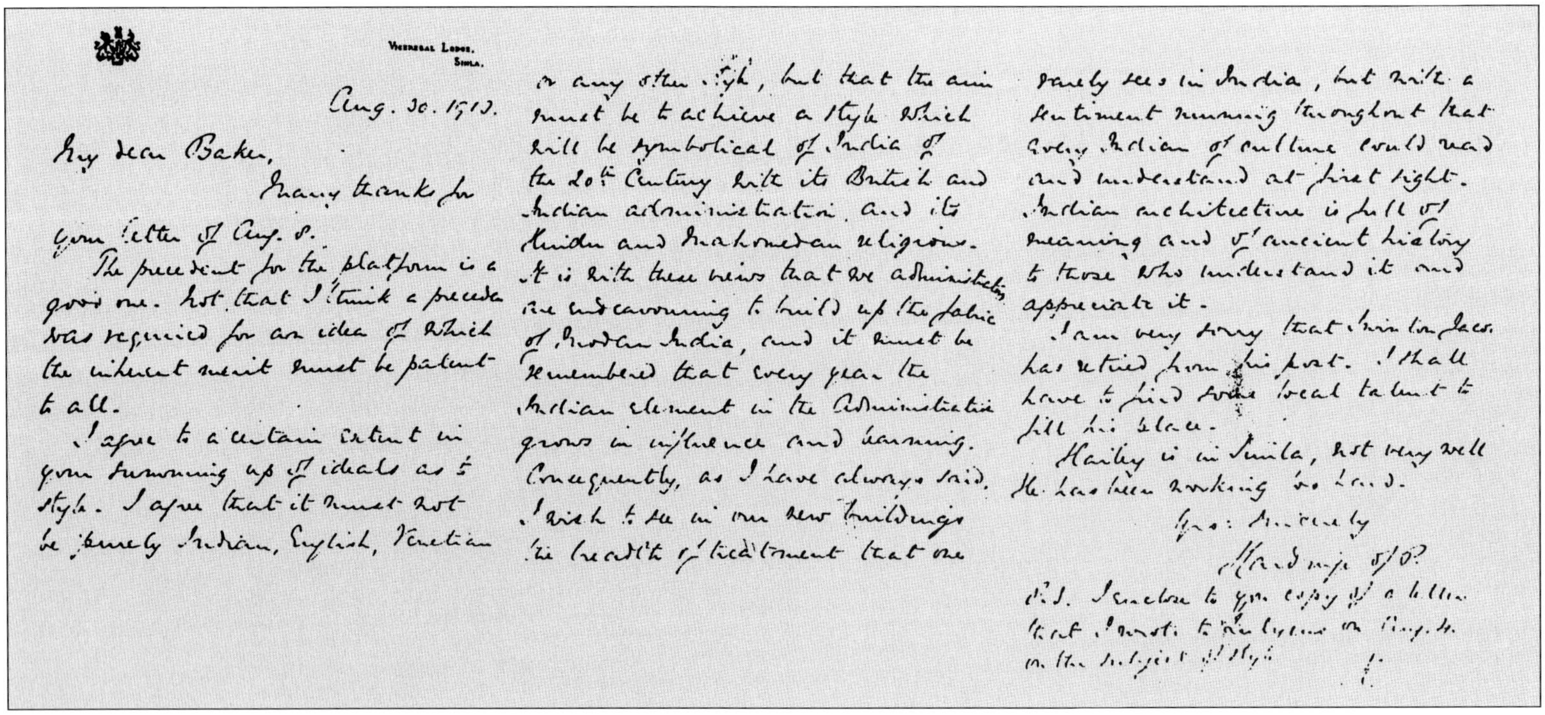

Viceregal Lodge,
Simla.

Aug. 30. 1913.

My dear Baker,

Many thanks for your letter of Aug. 8.

The precedent for the platform is a good one. Not that I think a precedent was required for an idea of which the inherent merit must be patent to all.

I agree to a certain extent in your summing up of ideals as to style. I agree that it must not be purely Indian, English, Venetian or any other style, but that the aim must be to achieve a style which will be symbolical of India of the 20th Century with its British and Indian administration and its Hindu and Mahomedan religions. It is with these views that we administrators are endeavouring to build up the fabric of modern India, and it must be remembered that every year the Indian element in the Administration grows in influence and learning. Consequently, as I have always said, I wish to see in our new buildings the breadth of treatment that one rarely sees in India, but with a sentiment running throughout that every Indian of culture would read and understand at first sight. Indian architecture is full of meaning and of ancient history to those who understand it and appreciate it.

I am very sorry that Swinton Jacob has retired from his post. I shall have to find some local talent to fill his place.

Hailey is in Simla, not very well. He has been working too hard.

Yours sincerely
Hardinge of P.

P.S. I enclose to you copy of a letter that I wrote to Lutyens on Aug. 4 on the subject of style.

Fig. 10: In his letter to Herbert Baker of August 30, 1913, the Viceroy, Lord Hardinge, attempted to tie the architects down to an Indian architectural style: "Indian Architecture is full of meaning and of ancient history to those who understand it and appreciate it."

Fig. 11: The question of a suitable architectural style (e.g. Renaissance or Mughal) for the new capital was taken up by the British Press (*Tribune*, August 21, 1912).

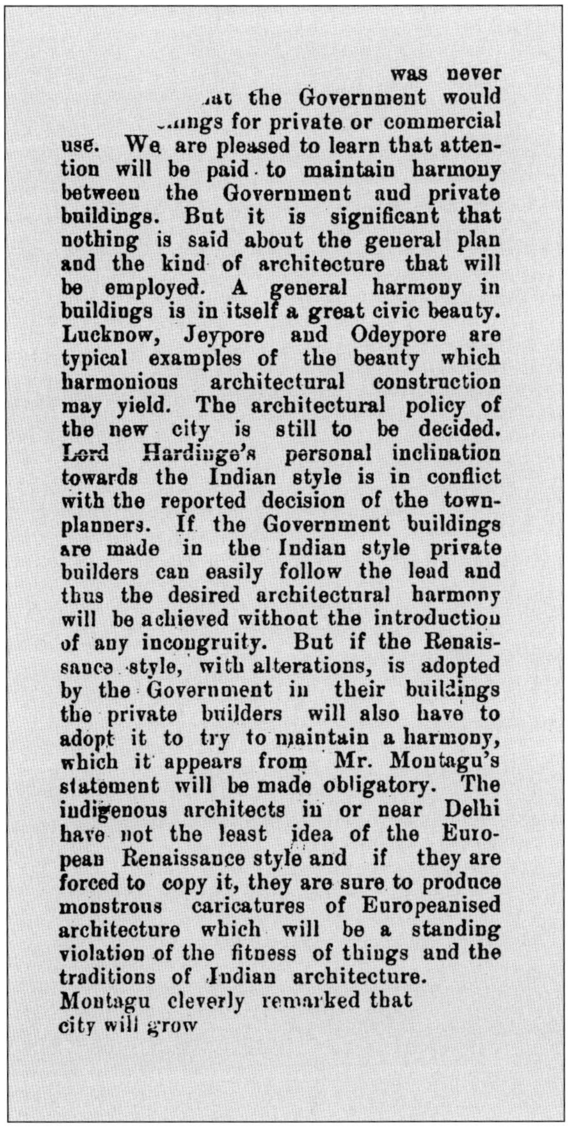

was never ...at the Government would ...ings for private or commercial use. We are pleased to learn that attention will be paid to maintain harmony between the Government and private buildings. But it is significant that nothing is said about the general plan and the kind of architecture that will be employed. A general harmony in buildings is in itself a great civic beauty. Lucknow, Jeypore and Odeypore are typical examples of the beauty which harmonious architectural construction may yield. The architectural policy of the new city is still to be decided. Lord Hardinge's personal inclination towards the Indian style is in conflict with the reported decision of the town-planners. If the Government buildings are made in the Indian style private builders can easily follow the lead and thus the desired architectural harmony will be achieved without the introduction of any incongruity. But if the Renaissance style, with alterations, is adopted by the Government in their buildings the private builders will also have to adopt it to try to maintain a harmony, which it appears from Mr. Montagu's statement will be made obligatory. The indigenous architects in or near Delhi have not the least idea of the European Renaissance style and if they are forced to copy it, they are sure to produce monstrous caricatures of Europeanised architecture which will be a standing violation of the fitness of things and the traditions of Indian architecture. Montagu cleverly remarked that city will grow

1.2 Key Players and Key Issues

The planning and construction of a new seat of government for British colonial rule in India was, even for the British Royal Family and its imperial ambitions, a new and unusual challenge. The announcement of an international town-planning competition was hardly even a consideration, because it would have raised the issue of obligations that were not always in accord with the legitimate interests of the King. After all, George V was not only the King of Britain, but as Emperor of India, he was also ultimately responsible for decisions directly relating to the sub-continent.

Lord Hardinge of Penhurst, an extremely experienced diplomat, was in power as British Viceroy in India. Hardinge enjoyed the complete trust of the Royal Family as well as that of the British Secretary of State for India, Lord Crewe. After the announcement of plans to make the move from Calcutta to Delhi, Lord Hardinge and Lord Crewe remained in constant touch by telegram in order to ensure that the long-prepared move was a success.

Edwin Lutyens

In London, there was now persistent lobbying by architects and town planners interested in the imperial project. Senior officials of the British architectural authorities in India were also calculating their chances of participating in the enormous undertaking. To the amazement of many competitors, the architect Edwin Lutyens held a particularly good hand of cards in this game. Until then, Lutyens had not been able to demonstrate much success in town planning, but he was the favourite and most famous architect of country and manor houses in England at the time.

Lutyens had one more card to play: he was married to the daughter of a former Viceroy of India, Lord Lytton. Lytton, a spirited representative of the Crown in Calcutta, achieved a certain fame when, on January 1, 1877, without any consultation with the government in London – and in a mood of exceptional loyalty – he proclaimed Queen Victoria as "Kaisar-i-Hind," or Empress of India, the "Shah-in Shah Padshah" (Monarch of Monarchs) and heir to the Mughal throne.

The renown of a successful architect of the English nobility, as well as the fame of his wife's family, opened many doors for Edwin Lutyens that, for other applicants, remained closed: "Lutyens was perhaps a surprising, though imaginative, choice. He was not a committee man, he had built no big buildings and he was quite untrained in either the planning of cities or the design of palaces – something that every Beaux-Arts student knew everything about. But he was forty-three, ambitious and the most successful house architect of his generation, and before the Great War decisions of this nature were not made in Whitehall but at country house parties. And in the first decade of this century you would be certain to find at least one satisfied Lutyens client in every political house party."[19]

Against this background, Edwin Lutyens was gradually able to develop his plans for obtaining the commission for Delhi. He had cultivated social contacts and approaches that assured him of his life's ambition. At the same time, he was watchful and was constantly on guard, ready to fend off competitors. For example, there was the architect Henry Vaughan Lanchester, who was experienced in town planning in India, and who was, early in 1912, regarded as an alternative to Lutyens by the India Office. Lutyens had the advantage for Lord Crewe had known him from the time they had worked together on Hampstead Garden Suburb and had been made aware of his unusual talents by various well-known people at the right moment.

"There remained, however, the awkward problem of H.V. Lanchester who had been engaged as an extra consultant. Lutyens had hoped to avoid him entirely, but the Viceroy arranged for them to meet on June 25 in Delhi, when Lanchester would be briefed on the Committee's findings and make any suggestions. Lanchester loomed as an aggressive rival ... Would Lord Crewe support Lanchester to design the buildings? Lutyens' anxiety mounted

19 R. Gradidge: *Edwin Lutyens, Architect Laureate*, London 1979, p. 68.

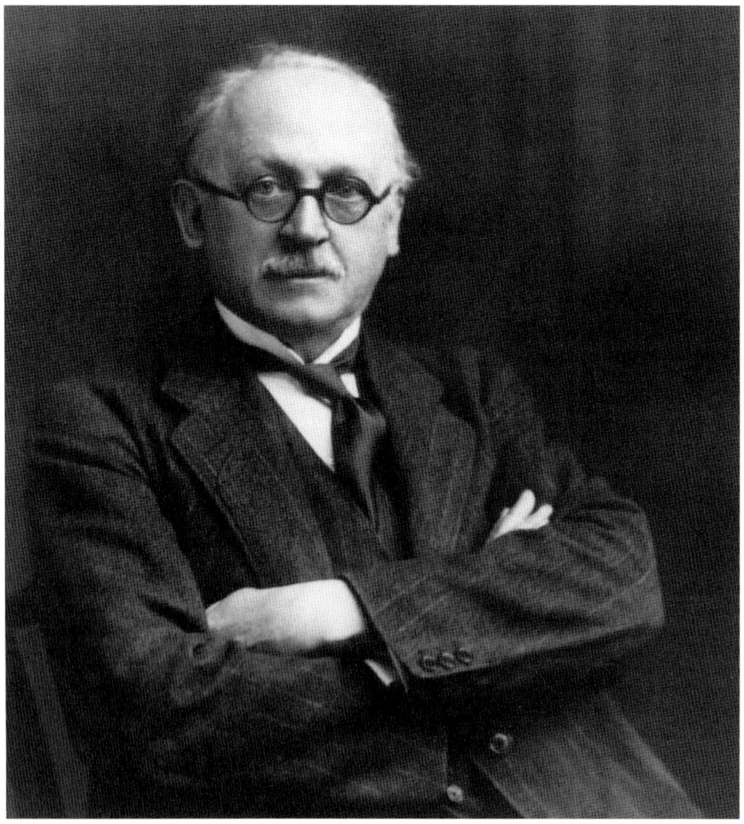

Fig. 12: Edwin Lutyens, better known before 1912 as an architect of English country houses, became a key figure in the design and construction of the new capital at Delhi.

throughout the spring. Admittedly, at the Committee's interview at Buckingham palace, the King had said, 'You are going to do the buildings,' to which Lutyens had promptly replied, 'Yes, sir!' But this was far from the final word of appointment, and Lutyens anticipated that Lanchester would pull for it like the deuce.

By June, Lanchester seemed less formidable. The Viceroy explained that Lanchester's appointment was really the result of a misunderstanding, and Lady Hardinge had said she and her husband would just have to 'be tactful with Lanchester for a month.' More importantly, Lutyens was able to write to his wife, Lady Emily, 'Hardinge has practically given me Govt. House and the big Place.'"[20]

Sir Swinton Jacob was another contender whose designs accurately represented the Indo-Saracenic style in various cities of the Raj. Swinton had built a new reception building for the Maharaja of Jaipur's palace that, to the European observer, looked more Indian than many actual buildings from the Mughal era. The Viceroy would have liked to include him in the team of architects, thereby retaining the prospect of a local building tradition in Imperial Delhi. Jacob had left the Indian Public Works Department in 1896 on account of his age and was now a determined and expert promoter of all things Indian. But Edwin Lutyens was afraid that the old expert on India might collaborate with the Viceroy behind his (Lutyens') back and, in the end, complete Lutyens' dreamed-of imperial architecture with Indo-Islamic facades.

Admittedly, Lutyens was initially concerned about a commission for town planning work ranging from the precision of location to the development of a total town-planning concept. In the end, however, as an architect, Lutyens was primarily interested in concrete second-stage building work.

An old friendship linked Lutyens with Herbert Baker from the days when they worked together in the office of Ernest George in London. Both men despised Bombay's Victorian architecture in which Hindu and Mughal architecture, along with the British Neo-Gothic, competed with one another. Both were convinced of Britain's imperial challenge and of the possibility for architecture to make a contribution in securing British world power: "What struck a chord with Lutyens was not the Indians but the Raj. For him, the Indians, whether

20 R.G. Irving: op. cit. pp. 46, 47.
21 Ibid., p. 228.
22 R. Lutyens: *Sir Edwin Lutyens, An Appreciation in Perspective*, London, 1942, p. 77.

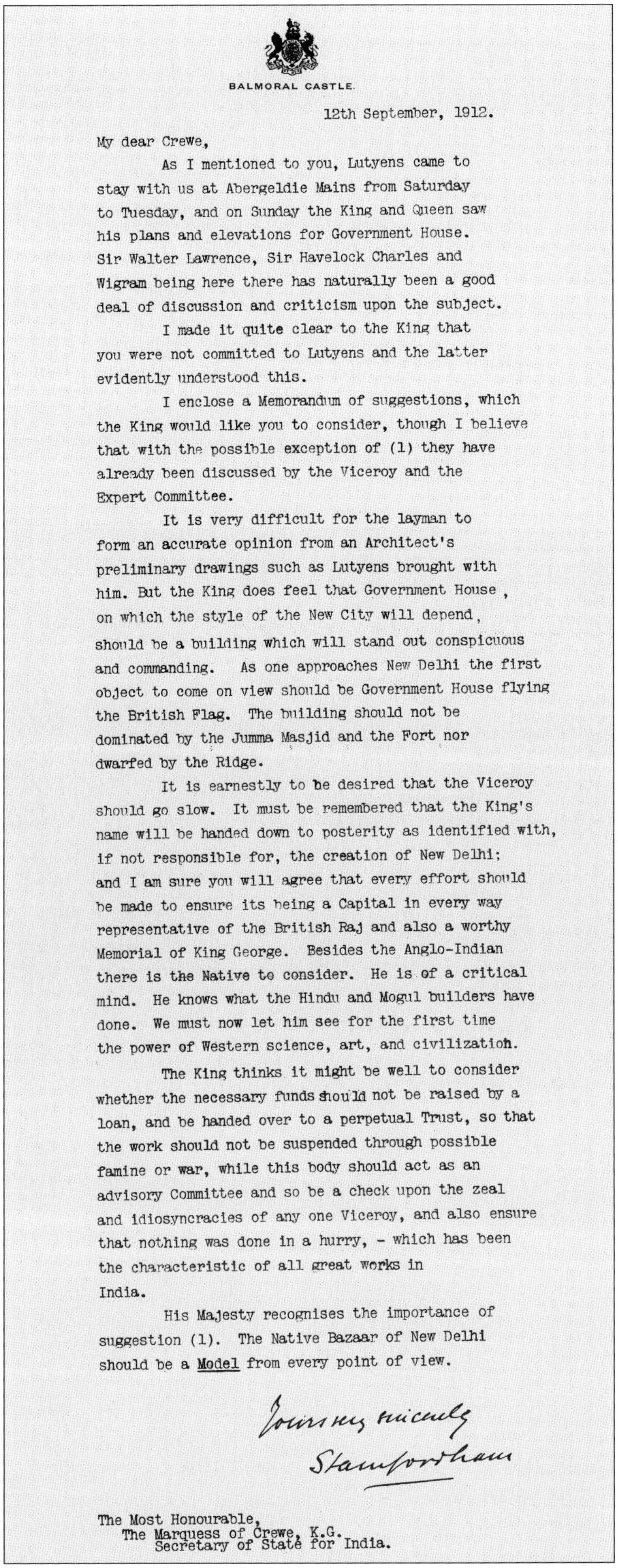

BALMORAL CASTLE.

12th September, 1912.

My dear Crewe,

As I mentioned to you, Lutyens came to stay with us at Abergeldie Mains from Saturday to Tuesday, and on Sunday the King and Queen saw his plans and elevations for Government House. Sir Walter Lawrence, Sir Havelock Charles and Wigram being here there has naturally been a good deal of discussion and criticism upon the subject.

I made it quite clear to the King that you were not committed to Lutyens and the latter evidently understood this.

I enclose a Memorandum of suggestions, which the King would like you to consider, though I believe that with the possible exception of (1) they have already been discussed by the Viceroy and the Expert Committee.

It is very difficult for the layman to form an accurate opinion from an Architect's preliminary drawings such as Lutyens brought with him. But the King does feel that Government House, on which the style of the New City will depend, should be a building which will stand out conspicuous and commanding. As one approaches New Delhi the first object to come on view should be Government House flying the British Flag. The building should not be dominated by the Jumma Masjid and the Fort nor dwarfed by the Ridge.

It is earnestly to be desired that the Viceroy should go slow. It must be remembered that the King's name will be handed down to posterity as identified with, if not responsible for, the creation of New Delhi; and I am sure you will agree that every effort should be made to ensure its being a Capital in every way representative of the British Raj and also a worthy Memorial of King George. Besides the Anglo-Indian there is the Native to consider. He is of a critical mind. He knows what the Hindu and Mogul builders have done. We must now let him see for the first time the power of Western science, art, and civilization.

The King thinks it might be well to consider whether the necessary funds should not be raised by a loan, and be handed over to a perpetual Trust, so that the work should not be suspended through possible famine or war, while this body should act as an advisory Committee and so be a check upon the zeal and idiosyncracies of any one Viceroy, and also ensure that nothing was done in a hurry, - which has been the characteristic of all great works in India.

His Majesty recognises the importance of suggestion (1). The Native Bazaar of New Delhi should be a Model from every point of view.

Yours very sincerely
Stamfordham

The Most Honourable,
The Marquess of Crewe, K.G.
Secretary of State for India.

Fig. 13: On September 12, 1912, the King's secretary, Lord Stamfordham, recommended to the Secretary-of-State for India, Lord Crewe, not to rush decisions about the new royal capital at Delhi, so that they might find a form in keeping with the King's rank.

Muslim or Hindu, were 'children,' their architecture mere joinery in stone, without intellect. In the Raj, on the other hand, he found the ideal of an enlightened imperial despotism, dedicated to public service. Lutyens, who, like many of his generation before 1914, was disillusioned with parliamentary government, found the idea of the Indian Civil Service attractive. But he was appalled by the civil servants' lack of taste and by the buildings erected by the Public Works Department. His ambition to achieve great work was strengthened by a determination to supply the Raj with an architecture fitting its lofty ideals."[21]

Lutyens spared no effort on behalf of these ideals. He even risked the break-up of his marriage and, through a fairly trivial dispute with Herbert Baker, lost his most important ally forever. But the result of his determination, a magnificent Imperial Delhi such as the British Crown never again achieved anywhere else in the world either before or after him, appeared to justify his cause.

Robert Lutyens, the architect's son, later recalled his father observing that: "... he has never taken a day of rest or exercise; music on the whole bores him, and the theatre makes him cry – at the spectacle of tragedy and comedy alike! He smokes a lot of cool pipes which are seldom alight; one of his most personal gestures is tapping out a newly filled pipe on his heel into a waste paper basket. He reads little. He still wears the starched collars of the '90s on all occasions. His beautiful hands are invariably begrimed with pencil dust, and he pares his nails with a pruning knife. When he is not actually working, he plays patience, or else sits absorbed over a jigsaw puzzle. It is difficult to know what he is thinking about in such times. He is invariably silent: not formidable – he is never that; but turned inwards and vaguely unhappy, I suspect, and perplexed by the incontinent demands of the restless and dissatisfied age. He is easily depressed. But his wit is his defence; and his fooling is a means of assault on the stubborn resistance of the unimaginative."[22]

Lutyens' stubbornness in all questions of architectural taste made him many enemies amongst his colleagues. Yet, there is no building and no detail in his plans for India that conveys any stylistic compromise. Thus, he not only convinced the Viceroy in Delhi and the King in London – but also experts in the following decades – of the possibility of realizing a late Classicist dream for the glory of the British Crown on the north Indian plain.

Stamp summarizes the debate on style in the following paragraphs stating: "The employment of an Indian style of architecture at New Delhi was strongly favoured by the Public Works Department of the Government of India – furiously jealous at being passed over in favour of a civilian from back home. An oriental style was also advocated by the Viceroy as being appropriate politically, especially as it was the preference of the native princes. There was also a powerful lobby in Britain, which was opposed to the imposition of a Western style of architecture upon the new capital of India. Prominent in this was the teacher and historian E.B. Havell, who advocated the exploitation of native building traditions and the employment of Indian craftsmen as the only way of reviving the ancient arts of India."[23]

"With his acceptance of the orderliness and dignity of the Western humanist tradition in architecture, Lutyens at first was driven to the other extreme – possibly provoked by the polarized character of the debate. If he had nothing but contempt for the achievements of his compatriots, whether in Bombay or in Simla, he also had little patience with Mogul architecture and was utterly repelled by the apparent chaos and obscurantism of Hindu temples. 'There are no doubt great thinkers and good men'; Lutyens conceded, 'but what proof can I

Fig. 14: The rights and duties of the architects, Edwin Lutyens and Herbert Baker, were laid down in a contract by the Public Works Department, Government of India, Despatch No. 24 P.W. 1913.

Annexure No. 1 to enclosure to Despatch No. 24-P.W. of 1913.

MEMORANDUM.

1. The architects will be jointly responsible for work entrusted to them, and payments will be made to them jointly. The division of work between them will be a matter for their private arrangement; they will, however, intimate to the Imperial Delhi Committee the division of work at which they arrive and the Committee will recognise this division, so far as is compatible with the joint responsibility of the architects. The architects agree that the receipt of either of them for any payment made shall constitute a sufficient quittance.

2. The architects will, in consultation with Sir Swinton Jacob as adviser on Indian architecture and materials, act for so long as required as principal architects and general architectural advisers to the Government of India in all architectural matters connected with the New City and as assessors in any competition for buildings in the New City; provided that this clause shall not be held to preclude Government from acting when it so desires to do so, without seeking the advice of the architects.

3. The architects shall be responsible to, and receive their instructions directly from, the Imperial Delhi Committee, nor shall Government be liable for payment in respect of services rendered, instructions for which have not been communicated to the architects by the Committee. But the architects shall have the right of requiring a reference to the Government of India regarding any order passed or arrangements made by the Committee in respect of designs submitted by them. The Committee shall not make any material alteration in the designs and specifications submitted by the architects without first consulting them.

4. The architects will prepare all designs, and all necessary detail and working drawings, plans and specifications (with such duplicates as it is usual to provide) for such of the buildings enumerated in the annexed schedule, as Government may decide to erect. The Chief Engineer and his staff shall be responsible for all engineering drawings and detail for such buildings and for general supervision.

5. The Chief Engineer and his staff will render all reasonable assistance to the architects when working in India.

6. The architects shall design the internal decoration, fixtures and furniture, of such of the state, public and official rooms and places in the buildings enumerated in the schedule, as are shown in the attached list.

7. The Government shall establish on the work a studio of Indian arts and crafts, for which the architects, with the collaboration of Sir Swinton Jacob, shall be advisers.

8. The architects shall, if they desire, or if the Committee shall so require keep as long as may be necessary, one or more assistants as their representatives on the works. The remuneration of such assistants shall be defrayed by the architects but the committee shall pay their first class steamship fares to and from India, and double first class railway fares in India, but no halting or other allowance shall be payable by the Committee.

9. The architects shall not be expected to make their headquarters in India, but they shall visit Delhi at least once a year, for as many years as the Committee shall so require.

10. For the buildings and work enumerated in the preceding paragraphs, the architects shall receive the following remuneration namely, 5 per cent on the actual cost of the completed works as ordinarily calculated by the Indian Public Works Department, *i.e.*, excluding the cost of tools and plant and supervising establishment. Payment shall be made in the following

2

instalments; 1¼ per cent on receipt of preliminary sketches and designs calculated on the engineer's estimated cost, 1¾ per cent on receipt of general drawings, plans, elevations and sections calculated on the engineer's estimated cost, 2 per cent yearly in accordance with the progress of ascertained expenditure. These payments shall be subject to adjustment in accordance with the actual ascertained expenditure. Advances shall be made from time to time to meet expenditure actually incurred by the architects.

11. In the case of designs of the whole or part of works which have been duly authorised and approved by the Committee, but are not carried into execution, payment shall be made *pro rata* at the rates given in the preceding paragraph.

12. Should the architects be called upon to act as assessors in any competition, they shall each receive the usual R. I. B. A. fee of 30 guineas, *plus* 1/5 per cent of the estimated cost of the design.

13. In addition to the amounts mentioned above, the architects shall receive on account of their visits to Delhi first class steamship fares to and from India, *plus* double first class railway fares for journeys in India. They shall on such occasions travel by such route and with such halts, as the Committee may agree on. They shall each, in addition, receive a subsistence allowance of 30 shillings per day, and a daily fee of 5 guineas, while absent from home; *provided* that for each day of their stay in India, the daily fee shall be enhanced to 10 guineas.

14. The architects shall receive the cost of cables, and out of pocket expenses incurred by them on inspection and supervision of all work which they may be asked to undertake in England, and if such work is outside London they shall in addition be paid the daily fee of 5 guineas provided in paragraph 13 above.

15. Should the architects be called upon to submit designs other than those enumerated in the schedule, they shall be paid on the same basis as that detailed in paragraph 10 above.

16. Should any radical revision be required in any plans or designs drawn up in accordance with instructions received from the Committee, such changes shall be separately paid for *pro rata* with paragraph 10; but the architects shall claim such extra payment before the revision is undertaken.

17. In the event of any dispute arising as to the amounts due under the agreement, the question shall be referred to an arbitrator to be approved by the Secretary of State, and the architects, whose decision shall be final and binding on both parties. A similar procedure shall be followed to assess the compensation due to the architects in the event of complete or partial stoppage of work.

18. If cases arise of professional practice for which the conditions above laid down do not apply, the regulations laid down by the R. I. B. A. shall be followed.

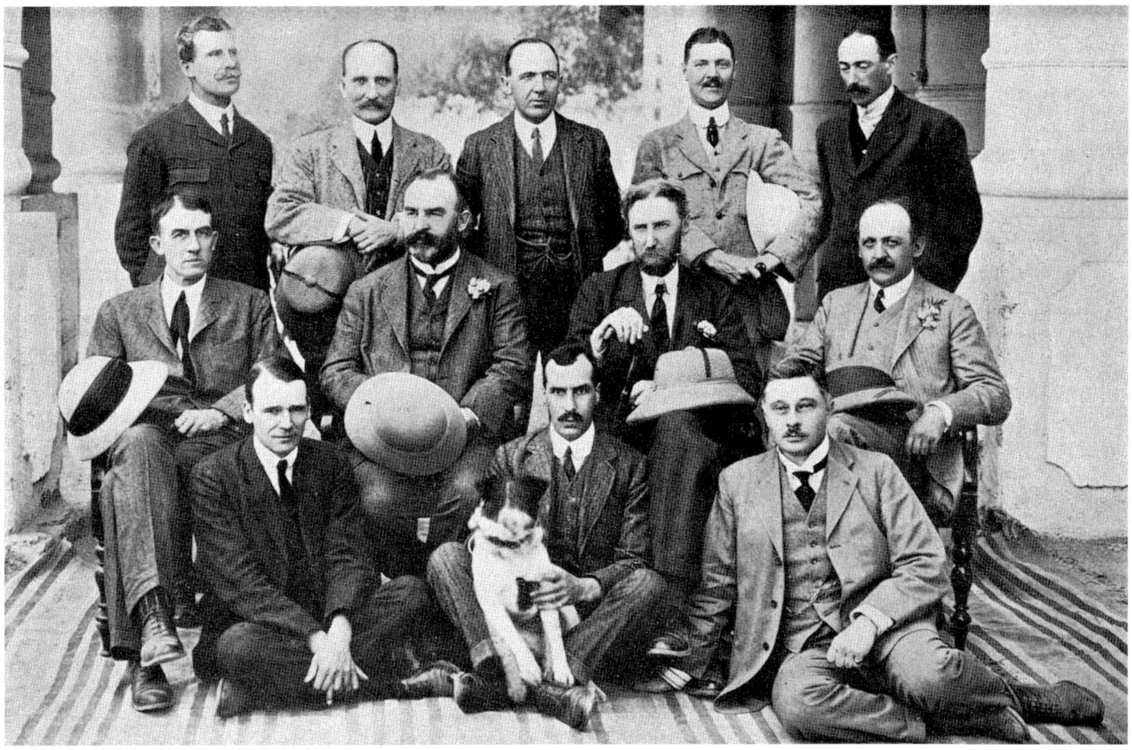

Fig. 15: The New Delhi Planning Committee in 1913. Top row (left to right) Lt.-Col. Ogilvie, I.M.S.; T. Ward, T. Salkield, (Delhi City Engineer), Capt. Sopwith, R.E., G.F. de Monmorency. Middle Row: Herbert Baker, J. Brodie, Capt. George Swinton, E.L. Lutyens. Front Row: S.H. Evans (assistant to E.L.L), Capt. Roberts, R.E., Amman (assistant to Brodie).

find that their thoughts are not as unfinished and as slovenly as the work of that other half of India that offends and distresses the eye at every turn, everywhere, wherever I have been in Native States or British territory? There is no trace of any Wren. Is there an Isaac Newton? I doubt it. Without the one you cannot have the other ... Personally I do not believe there is *any* real Indian architecture or any great tradition. There are just spurts by various mushroom dynasties with as much intellect as there is in any other art nouveau.'"[24]

Occasional critics had difficulty finding the right arguments against Lutyens. After all, the success of Imperial Delhi was absolutely impossible to ignore. "When Patrick Geddes arrived at New Delhi in 1915, Lutyens records: 'a certain Professor Geddes ... a crank ... talked rot in an insulting way.' The Raj was concerned with extending the writ of Whitehall, not social planning."[25]

If we are to attempt to paint a just portrait of Edwin Lutyens' personality, then we have to note his efforts to maintain a fair or even a friendly relationship with his colleagues. He never tried to display his superiority, maintaining instead a solid grasp of loyalty and a sense of humour: "All this time he would have one of his pockets full of little pipes sticking straight out from his front teeth but probably not alight; this matter of keeping his pipes going was very expensive in matches and on the comparatively rare occasions when he came into the drawing office – he was somewhat shy of his men – and leaned over your board, his hand would slowly close over your box of matches and that was the last you saw of it. This led to the ruse of taking the matches out of their case and pinning the case to the table and then replacing the matches; when the questing hand closed over the box it was unable to move it and a slow smile spread over his face; it was the kind of joke he thoroughly appreciated."[26]

Lutyens' daily hopes and fears, as well as the special pleasures and troubles during his regular stays in India have been preserved for us in the hundreds of letters written to his wife, Lady Emily. He illustrated his regular descriptions of comic events affectionately with hand-drawn sketches (Fig. 18), thus painting a lively picture of his work in India for his children.

23 G. Stamp: op. cit. p. 36.
24 Ibid., p. 37.
25 C.M. Chipkin: "Lutyens and Imperialism," letter to the RIBA Journal, July 1969, p. 263.
26 Henry Medd in a broadcast on 29.3.1969 (Lutyens' birthday) on All-India Radio.

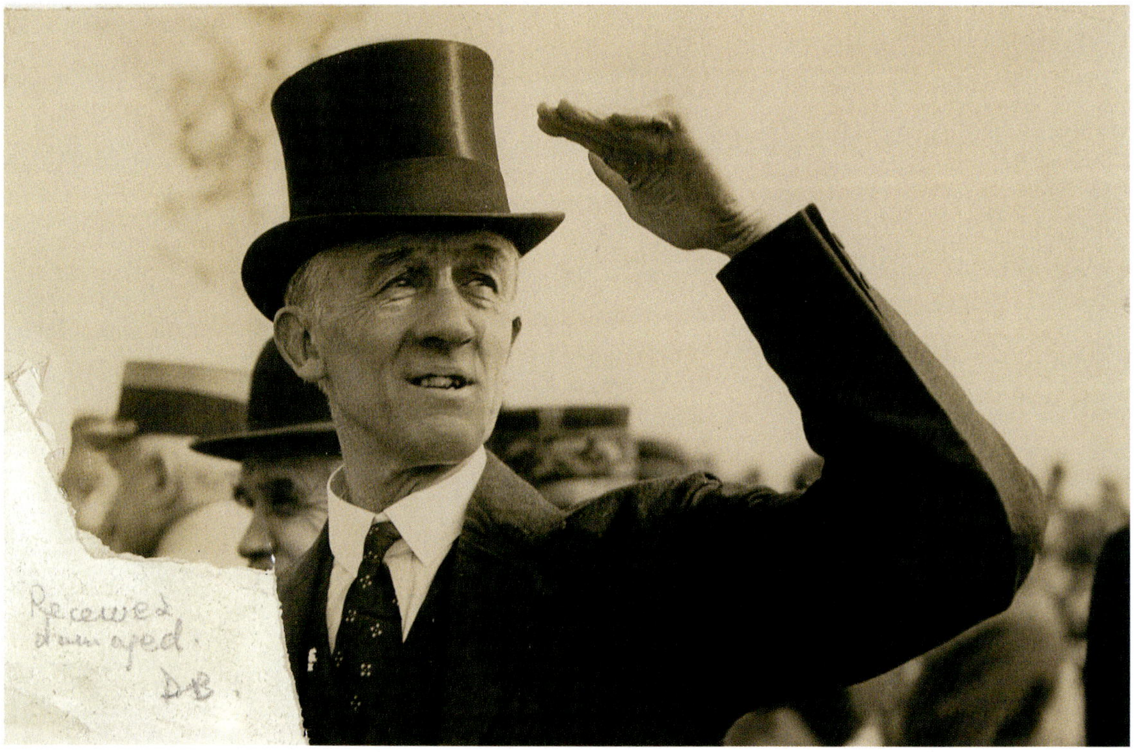

Fig. 16: Sir Herbert Baker, a good friend of Lutyens, became a rival and an opponent in the course of their joint planning for Imperial Delhi

Herbert Baker

In 1913, on Lutyens' recommendation, Herbert Baker joined the architect as an equal partner to work on the British government's commission. Baker described the story behind this partnership in his memoirs: "It was with great excitement that I opened in Rome a telegram from the India Office asking whether I would collaborate with Lutyens in designing New Delhi. When I was in Africa I kept in touch with my old friend by correspondence, illustrating our letters with our designs and their problems. His talent for expressive sketches made his letters of great interest. And whenever I went home I saw much of him and of his work. I had the highest opinion of his ability and natural intuition, and had long hoped that some day these talents would be devoted to some national work of greater importance than the delightful country houses for which he has won lasting fame ... In day-dreams I sometimes fancied how splendid it would be if we would work together on some imperial theme. So my delight can be understood at this providential fulfilment of my imaginations."[27]

Herbert Baker's appointment came as no surprise. On October 3, 1912, during the period of general wrangling over a slice of the new capital's architectural-cake, Baker had taken part in a public debate through an article – a long letter in the *Times* – entitled "New Delhi, the Problem of Style." His previous experience in the construction of the government building in Pretoria qualified him for a comparable new task. His article in the *Times* found widespread agreement in Whitehall, reflecting the consciousness of the London elite: "The new capital is not merely the shrine of the glory of India, but is to be the living centre of the administration. First and foremost it is the spirit of British sovereignty, which must be imprisoned in its stone and bronze. The new capital must be the sculptural monument of the good government and unity which India, for the first time in its history, has enjoyed under British rule. British rule in India is not a mere veneer of government and culture. It is a new civilization in growth, a blend of the best elements of East and West. The effect of this will remain even should British sovereignty ever depart from the shores of India."[28]

In retrospect, the strong sense of harmony shared between Lutyens and Baker during those first years in Delhi can be attributed to their usefulness to each other. Ultimately, however, their ideals were too divergent: "Lutyens' vision of an ordered, humanistic architecture

27 H. Baker: *Architecture and Personalities*, London 1944, p. 64.
28 Ibid.

Fig. 17: The Delhi Town Planning Committee appointed by the British Viceroy and the India Office originally consisted only of George Swinton, Edwin Lutyens and John Brodie. The Committee's first task was to find a suitable piece of land for the capital outside the old Mughal capital of Delhi.

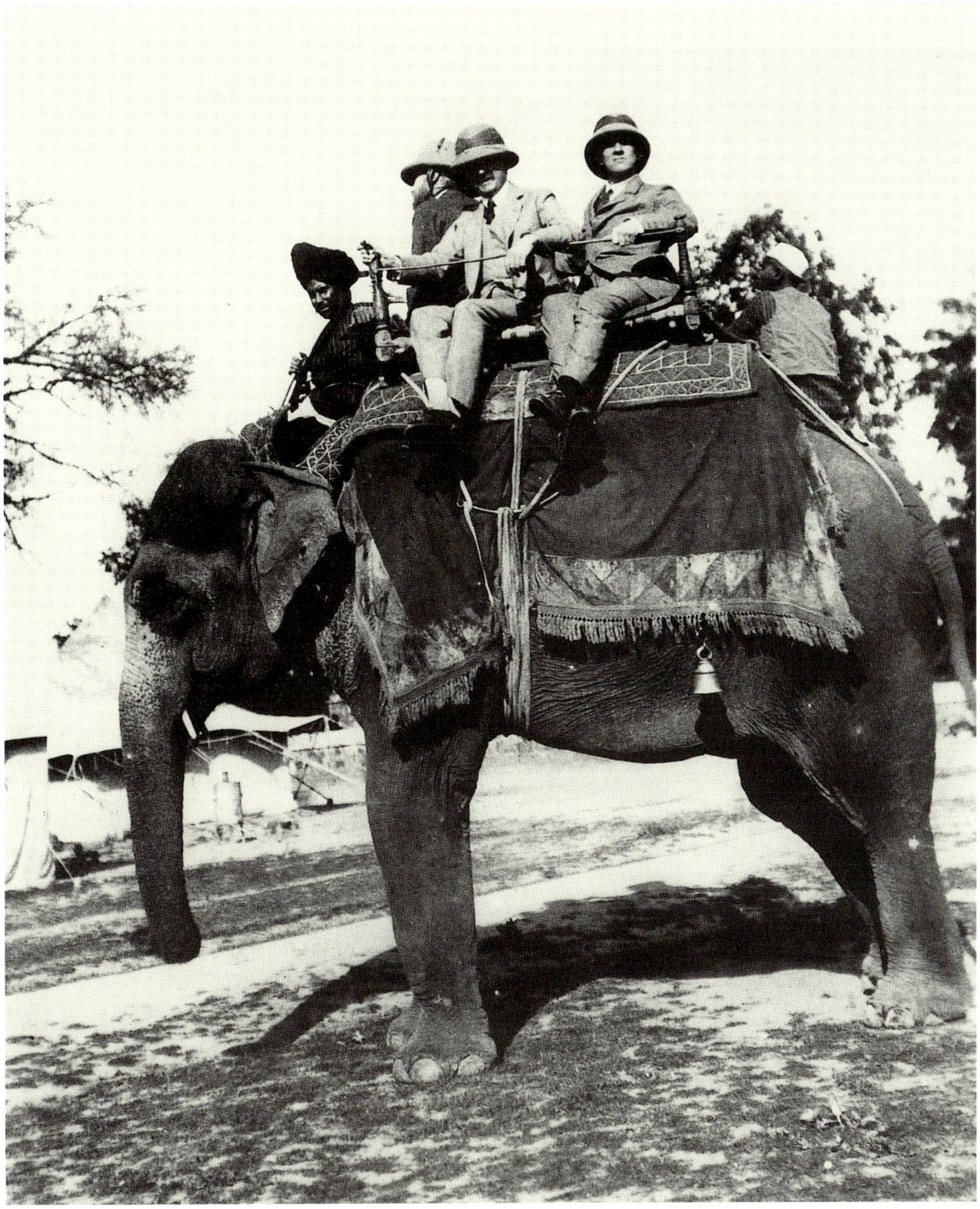

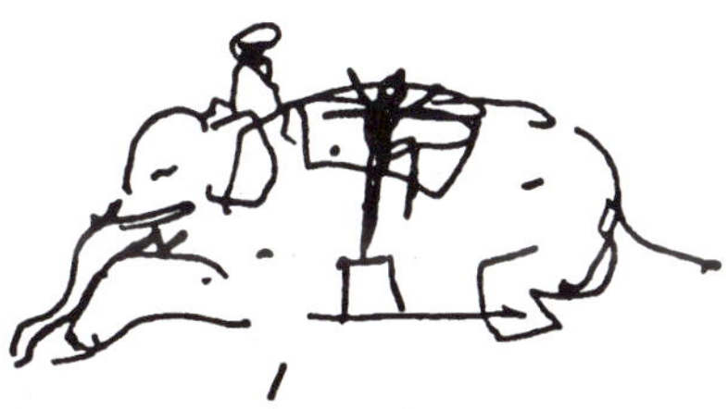

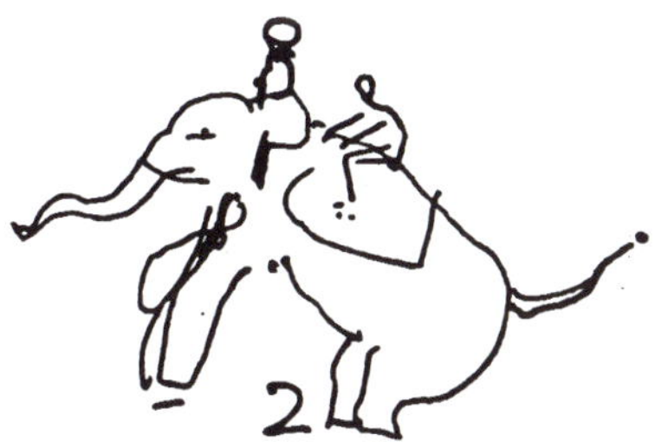

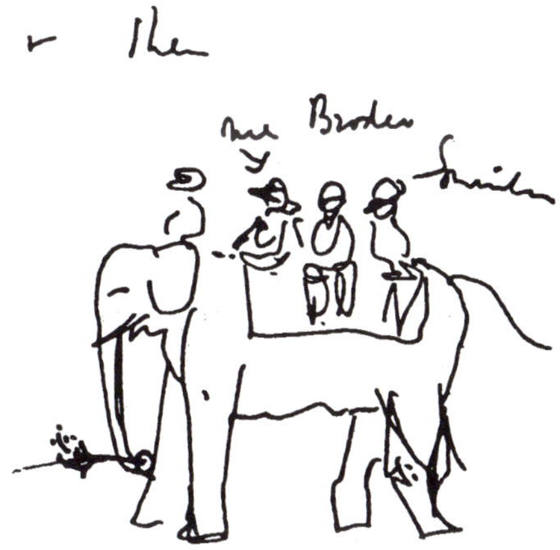

Fig. 18: In letters to his wife, Lutyens described the difficult reconnaissance trip by elephant when searching for the most favourable location for the new capital of the Raj. Members of the Delhi Town Planning Committee were allocated elephants in the absence of streets passable for vehicles.

Tuesday night April 23.12.

Another long day. 5.45 we started and motored out to where we were to find the elephant. Mrs Brodie came too to snap-shot us. Swinton got on first and then Brodie. He weighs 16 stone 11 lb. The elephant, and it is a large one, laid down in a ditch and yet the pad was a good 6 foot above the ground. Brodie took a run and jumped on coming tummy down. The shock made the elephant trumpet and he nearly got up to run away but the mahout whacked him and talked to him as though he was a bad child and it laid down quietly again – for me! Think of my feelings and how gently I got up! We had a very long morning and went miles on the top of this fearful and beloved creature and we went over very rough ground and there were some awful moments going up and down into nullahs.

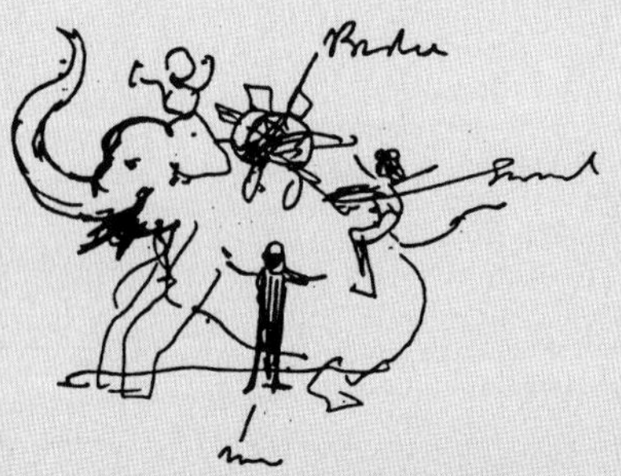

We got home to breakfast about 10.30 and then 11.30 to the office where discussions and reports took place until 3. We were all dead tired and vowed to sleep but we got talking again until it was time to start out in motors again at 5. We explored the east banks of the Jumna and saw many odd sights. Indians fishing, a wedding party in bullock wagons, monkeys, jackals etc., etc. and back at 7.30.

I think we are settling on a site. We are all agreed at present that we may come home earlier but nothing will be settled till we see Lord Hardinge[1] next week. He comes for the day on his way to Simla. The reports we are receiving are voluminous and in quantity. When we can begin to do constructive work seems far off yet.

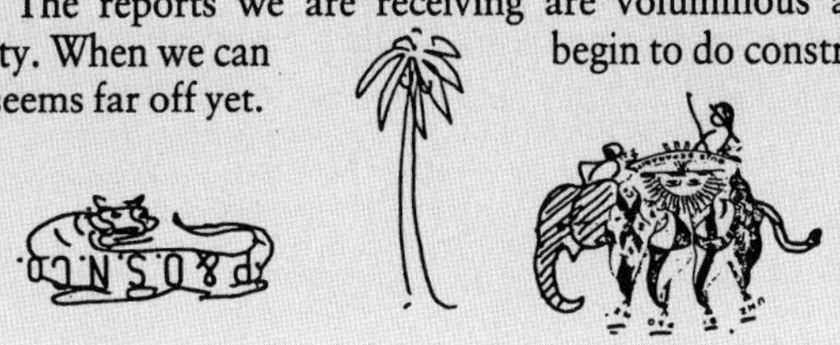

April 25.12.

Another elephant bout this morning and it was rather awful going along canal banks with overhanging trees. The ground looked rotten and you could not see the path on which Elephas walked.

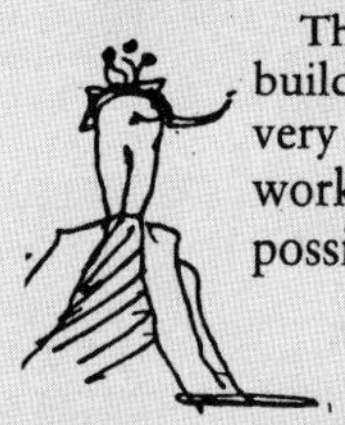

The Mogul architecture is cumbrous ill-constructed building covered with a veneer of stone or marble and very tiresome to the Western intelligence. Some of the work is lovely, but then it is from some outside and possibly Italian influence. To fit it you must squat on your haunches covered with jewels, and little else in the way of clothing.

rather differed from that of his collaborator in New Delhi, Herbert Baker. Baker's ideas were, indeed, more typical of Britain at the optimistic, arrogant summit of the Empire; they were nationalist and imperialist, symbolic and ceremonial. His architecture was much more literally dependent upon tradition, yet he could write to Lutyens upon hearing of the New Delhi commission that, 'It really is a great event in the history of the world and of architecture – that rulers should have the strength and sense to do the right thing. It would only be possible now under a despotism – some day perhaps democracies will follow ... I wonder what you will do – whether you will drop the language and the classical tradition and just go for surfaces – sun and shadow. It must not be Indian, nor English, nor Roman, but it must be Imperial.'"[29]

Both architects were aware of their differing perspectives. "Sir Herbert revelled ... in heraldic ornament while Lutyens, as his colleague puts it, 'concentrated his extraordinary powers and his immense industry and enthusiasm on the abstract and geometrical qualities to the disregard and consideration of human and national sentiment and their expression in his art.'"[30]

Lutyens' and Baker's different ideas were also expressed in the partners' tactics concerning the continual pressure of the Viceroy to include as many Indo-Islamic architectural elements as possible in their designs, particularly the keel arches of Mughal buildings. Lutyens implored Baker, both orally and in writing, not to make compromises on such a central issue. He wrote to Baker about the matter on August 29, 1913: "The letter received from his Excellency is very disappointing. I should like to ask him to what country the rainbow belongs! One cannot tinker with the round arch. God did not make the Eastern rainbow pointed to show His wide sympathies. Point your round arch ever so little, it ceases to be round and its quality goes. If you once let an error of that sort creep in with folk like Indians you will keep no definite control – and why start errorising?"[31]

On September 26, Baker replied: "My dear colleague who *can* write so nicely, I like your being outspoken – when it helps the cause. But don't when fighting an enemy, and when annoyed, turn and rend your friend. I, by taking a rather less obdurate attitude, and recognizing the standpoint of sentiment and politics, can help to fight the arch – the devilish ones – best. You must recognize the political standpoint in a political capital, or, if you don't, the reasonableness of politicians, our master, in doing so. And you get your way best by doing so, and showing that there are more vital things than the mere accidental shape of an arch."[32]

Fig. 19: In April 1912, in a letter to his wife, Lady Emily, Edwin Lutyens described the reconnaissance trip captured in the photograph and sketched the difficulties of mounting an elephant.

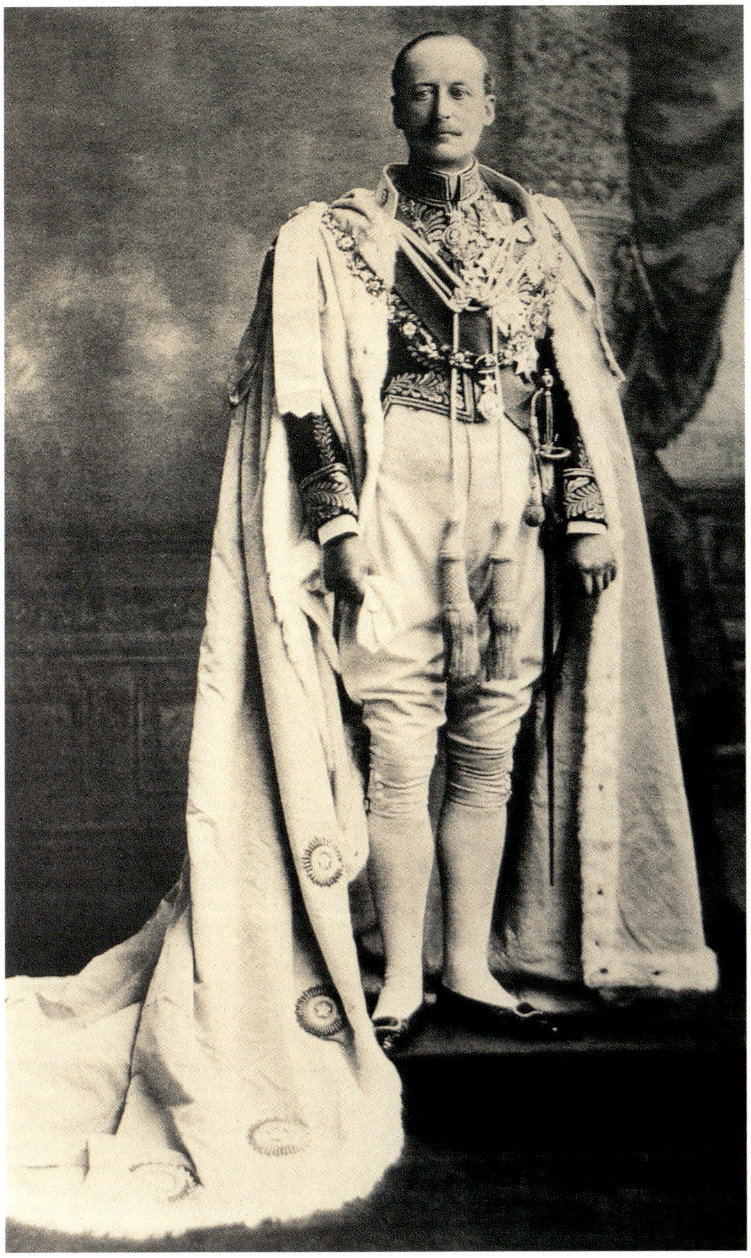

Fig. 20: Lord Hardinge of Penhurst, Viceroy of India (1910–15), was responsible for choosing the location of the new capital, Delhi, and was charged with settling on a suitable town plan, appropriate architectural style and, above all, with keeping to the budget set in London (a maximum of £ 6,113,600 set in 1914) for an estimated construction period of six years.

Lord Hardinge of Penhurst, Viceroy of India

In London, the responsibility for the plans for Imperial Delhi lay with the Secretary of State for India, Lord Crewe, but in India it was with the Viceroy, Lord Hardinge of Penhurst. Lord Hardinge was responsible for all decisions relating to the selection of a suitable location for the new buildings. He also bore the responsibility for the plan of the town and its appropriate architectural style. His budget for the construction of Imperial Delhi was fixed in London at £ 6,113,600 at an estimated period of construction of six years.

Along with his promotion to Viceroy of India in 1910, an old dream was realized by the career-minded diplomat to follow in the footsteps of his grandfather, the first Viscount Hardinge, as Governor-General of India. He confidently embarked upon the greatest architectural project his country had ever undertaken. After all, he was personally involved in the preparation of George V's decisions. He agreed with Lord Crewe that the building of a new capital was to be seen as a sign of "unfaltering determination to maintain British rule in India." In addition, this "would support the permanency of British sovereign Rule over the length and breadth of the country."[33] "Delhi is still a name to conjure with. It is intimately associated in the minds of the Hindus with sacred legends which go back even beyond the dawn of history ... To the Mohammedans it would be a source of unbounded gratification to see the ancient capital of the Moguls restored to its proud position as the seat of the Empire."[34]

Prior to his posting in Delhi, Lord Hardinge had gained experience as a diplomat in London, Constantinople, Berlin, Sofia, Bucharest, Paris, Teheran, St Petersburg, and Washington, D.C. (1885–86). He had first-hand experience of the planning and history of the construction of the American capital and he repeatedly adopted Pierre Charles L'Enfant's and George Washington's ideas as a yardstick for comparable decisions in the design and construction of Imperial Delhi. His self-confident commitment, also in matters of architectural taste, was often in Lutyens' opinion not sensitive enough. Thus, there were clashes similar to those centuries ago between Michelangelo and Pope Julius II: "The Viceroy changes his mind every time I see him. I am afraid he will make work very difficult. He has no idea how to get things done and to get to work. And all he will think about (is) what the place will look like in three years time. Three hundred is what I think of. I mentioned ten years in regard to something and he said it was so far ahead not worth considering! This is the building of an Imperial City!"[35]

Lord Hardinge was in a hurry to construct Imperial Delhi and as a result, as early as 1912, he was pressing the Secretary of State for India to give Lutyens a contract for the construction of the Viceroy's palace without delay, and then to take his time in announcing a competition for all other important buildings. In February, after Lord Crewe himself had

29 M. Lutyens: *Sir Edwin Lutyens*, in the exhibition catalogue of the Arts Council, 1981.
30 A.S.G. Butler: *The Architecture of Sir Edwin Lutyens, The Lutyens Memorial*, London 1950, p. 29.
31 Quoted from: Christopher Hussey: op. cit., p. 296.
32 Ibid., p. 296
33 R.G. Irving: op. cit., p. 27.
34 Ibid., p. 29.
35 Letter from Edwin Lutyens to his wife, Lady Emily, written January 7, 1913.

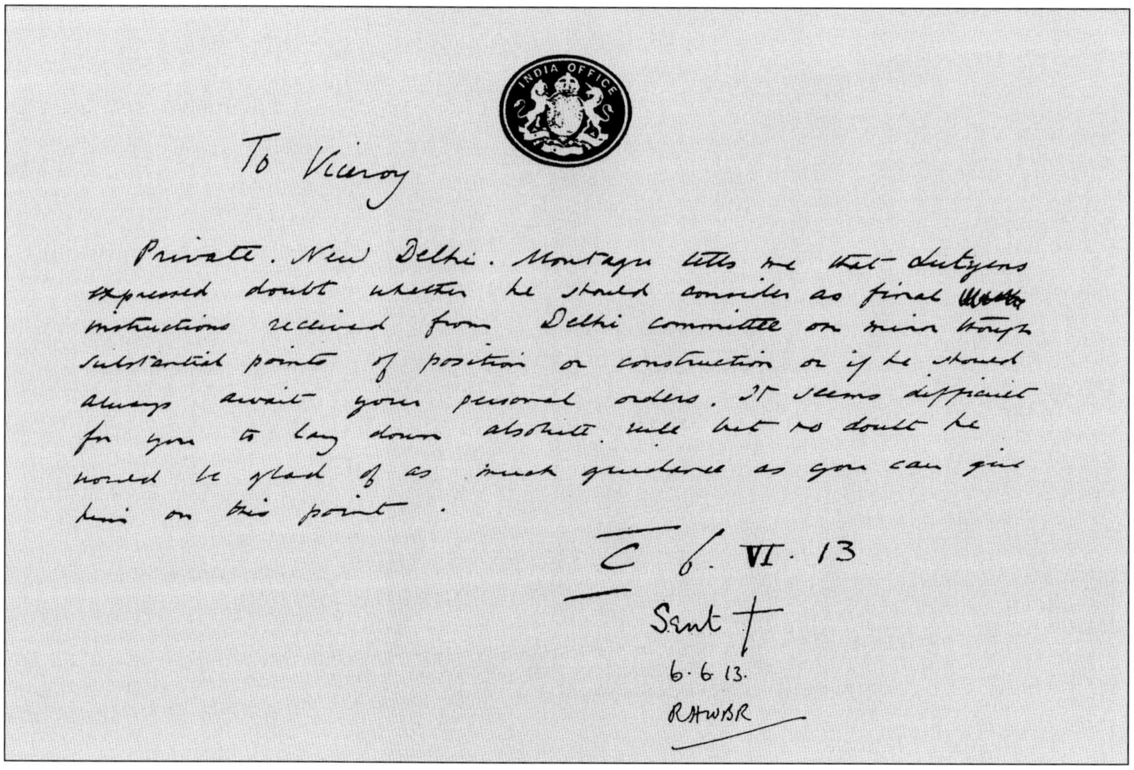
To Viceroy

Private. New Delhi. Montagu tells me that Lutyens expressed doubt whether he should consider as final instructions received from Delhi committee on minor though substantial points of position or construction or if he should always await your personal orders. It seems difficult for you to lay down absolute rule but no doubt he would be glad of as much guidance as you can give him on this point.

C 6. VI. 13

Sent + 6.6.13.

RHWBR

Fig. 21: Lord Crewe of the India Office in London and the Viceroy, Lord Hardinge, come to an agreement on all the questions of content and organization regarding the plans in Delhi.

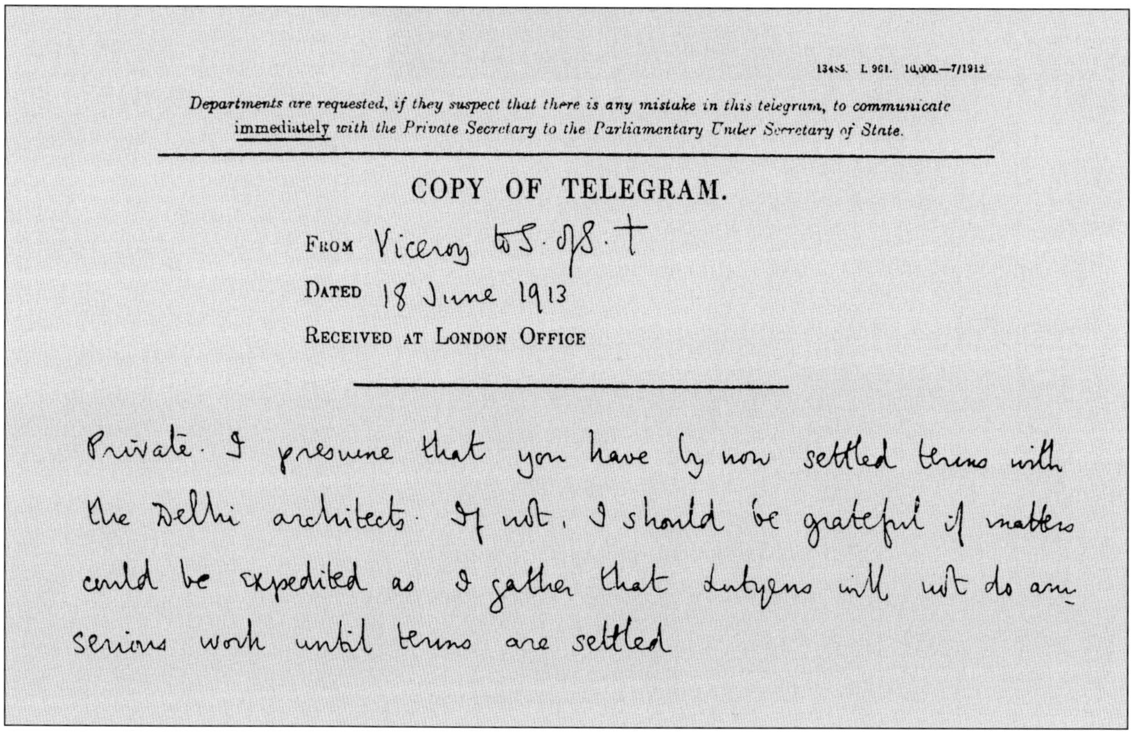
13485. L 961. 10,000.—7/1912.

Departments are requested, if they suspect that there is any mistake in this telegram, to communicate immediately with the Private Secretary to the Parliamentary Under Secretary of State.

COPY OF TELEGRAM.

FROM Viceroy to S. of S. +

DATED 18 June 1913

RECEIVED AT LONDON OFFICE

Private. I presume that you have by now settled terms with the Delhi architects. If not, I should be grateful if matters could be expedited as I gather that Lutyens will not do any serious work until terms are settled

Fig. 22: In a telegram to the Secretary of State for India, Lord Crewe, the Viceroy, Lord Hardinge, supports Lutyens' efforts to secure a contract from the India Office in London for the planning of Imperial Delhi.

recommended to the Viceroy the services of Edwin Lutyens, Lord Hardinge did not wish to lose time in embarking upon his life's work.

Collaboration between Lord Hardinge and Edwin Lutyens, notwithstanding mutual respect, was never simple since both men came from very different backgrounds. "It was difficult to reach a common basis for discussion. I do not think Lord Hardinge yet realises what great architecture might be and should express. It must be constructive. Architecture will always find her noblest expression in stone. Every different material will influence that expression. Though Lord Hardinge has great taste and is certainly what one would call artistic, I do not think he realises the use of ornament in relation to construction, where it should begin and end, and what is integral and what applied. He begins with ornament instead of construction – and it waylays me. In all great styles you will find the constructional purpose is clearly defined. The system adopted is carried throughout the whole fabric, according to the logical demands of the material used. Architecture, more than any other art, represents the intellectual progress of those that are in authority. You can decorate, and the tendency has ever been, as a style develops, to increase the decoration until it encroaches on and mutilates the initial lines of construction, whereupon the style becomes debased. It has occurred over and over again. You see it here in India – travesties of wood construction in stone – and here they have never had the initial advantage of those intellectual giants, the Greeks, who handed the torch to the Romans, they to the great Italians and on to the Frenchmen and to Wren, who made it sane for England. A ray too reached India. I should have liked to have handed on that torch and made it sane for India, and Indian in its character. To express modern India in stone, to represent her amazing sense of the supernatural, with its complement to profound fatalism and enduring patience, is no easy task.

This cannot be done by the almost sterile stability of the English classical style; nor can it be done by capturing Indian details and inserting their features, like hanging pictures on a wall! In giving India some new sense of architectural construction, adapted to her crafts, lies the great chance of creating what may become a new and inspiring period in the history of art. Lord Hardinge takes my sketch and inserts windows of some particular type. This cannot be done – it is not the window I object to but an insertion, which disturbs the adjacent spaces and their proportions and their relation to the whole. The whole must needs be reconsidered and designed anew. It means beginning again, which of course I do not mind, but if Baker is to work with me I should rather wait for his arrival, so as to work together. By this you will see where I am fearful of a Viceroy's arbitrary insistence on features and insertions. He, as I can well understand, is fearful of my obstinacy. I have no wish to be obstinate, but only to serve the Viceroy, and so India, to the best of my ability."[36]

36 Quotation from a letter to Lady Emily in: Christopher Hussey: op. cit., p. 280.

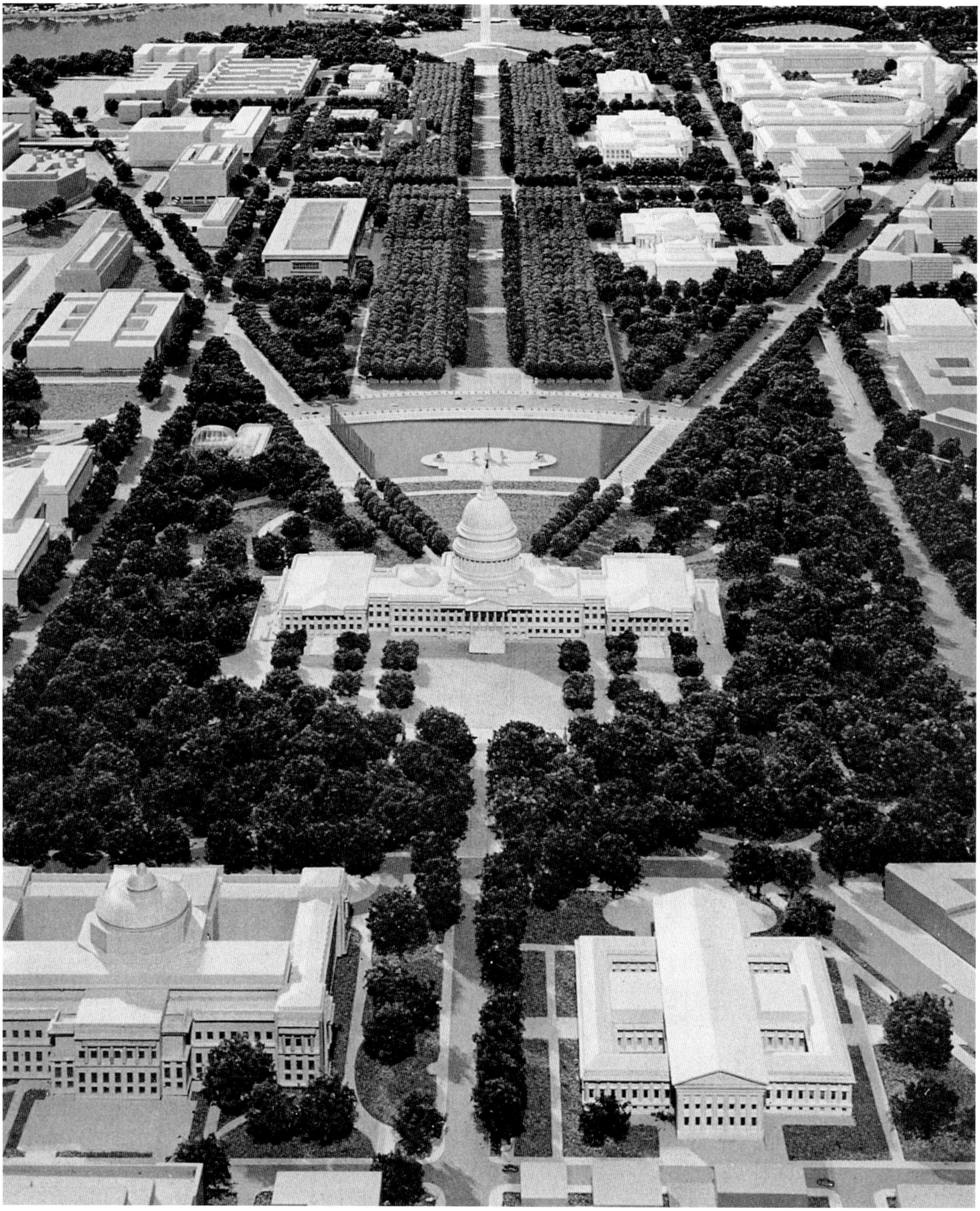

2 Models and Inspiration for the Plan of Imperial Delhi

The research material on Imperial Delhi reveals no shortage of references to models, both potential and actual, for the design of the town and its individual government buildings. The clear, geometric layout of the town stems from Edwin Lutyens' pen, and an examination of his various models is helpful to recognize more clearly his intentions for the plan and its relation to contemporary town planning in other continents.

Unlike his contemporary, Frank Lloyd Wright, Lutyens was firmly rooted in the architectural traditions of ancient Rome, the Italian Renaissance, the British Georgian style, and the Classicism of continental Europe. At the beginning of the twentieth century, Lutyens and his British colleagues did not see any reason to abandon or even supersede these established visual idioms of form and meaning, especially since this formal canon accorded so splendidly with the imperial objectives of international British foreign policy.

In the context of apparently limitless military power and assumed cultural superiority, only monumental architectural representations, such as Haussmann's plan of Paris with the Champs Elysées, Christopher Wren's unrealized plan for London after the Great Fire, or the new capital of Washington, D.C. in the United States of America, were worthy of consideration as models for the capital city of the Raj. Thus, it might not have been surprising if the visitor to Imperial Delhi (1912–31) imagined himself to be now in the French, the English, or the American capital.

Additional models came from Great Britain: Lutyens played an active part in the planning of Hampstead Garden City, and this experience prompted him to adopt the concept of a garden city for the residential areas of the new administrative city. In the search for suitable models for the business centre of Imperial Delhi, his colleagues used a layout from Bath – the Round Circus that had already been copied often and successfully in England.

Finally, imperial Rome offered town planning and architectural models, that imperial Britain wanted to appropriate. On the occasion of the World Exhibition in Rome in 1911, Lutyens designed and built an exhibition hall for his country. More importantly, he became acquainted with the capital as a basic form for the seat of government and the Pantheon as the most sublime assembly space in history.

For members of the Delhi Town Planning Committee, confronted by the rich history of examples of noteworthy European architectural models, the issue was not so much the question of an appropriate plan for an Indian town. Instead, in the particular political context of imperial Britain, it was a matter of which motifs, perspectives and spatial orders most effectively illustrated the British Crown's claims to leadership.

Only one of the decision-makers in Delhi, the Viceroy Lord Hardinge, recognized the arrogant and tentatively dangerous position of his architects. He repeatedly urged them to incorporate local Hindu and Muslim architectural forms into their imperial architectural designs. He was supported in his efforts by some of the most important architectural historians of the age, such as E.B. Havell who, "... in a letter to the *Times* shortly after the Durbar, denounced the 'bastard Gothic and emasculated Italian Renaissance' edifices of Calcutta, suggesting to the Public Works Department as models the Mughal works of Delhi, Agra, and Fatehpur Sikri. In 1912, Havell pressed his attack. In a lecture before the East India Association at Caxton Hall, Westminster, on October 21, later published in the *British Architect* and circulated privately to persons of importance, he excoriated the *Times* and other proponents of

Fig. 23: Many elements of the design for Imperial Delhi allude to L'Enfant's plan for Washington, D.C. (here in the form of a model with the Capitol in the centre).

Renaissance architecture. If adopted for Delhi, he protested, it was a style, which spelled 'the ruin of Indian craftsmanship, the intellectual impoverishment of the educated classes, and the strangling of Indian art.' The public buildings of the Government of India exercised a potent influence for good or evil, for Indian craftsmen and aristocratic Indian patrons alike looked to them for models of taste and fashion. In 1913, Havell reserved the entire last chapter of his monumental volume, *Indian Architecture,* for an impassioned polemic against a 'make-believe' capital city of Renaissance or, equally, British-designed Indo-Saracenic architecture. He suggested that intelligent patronage of the indigenous heritage of India, following the example of Akbar, could prove a bridge between the cultures, and as 'a means of reconciling racial and religious differences.'"[1]

2.1 Paris: Haussmann's Plans for the City Based on Versailles (1862)

At the beginning of the nineteenth century, Napoleon Bonaparte already had concrete plans to rebuild Paris into a glittering capital with magnificent streets and monuments placed in its squares and at its road junctions. But Napoleon's officials convinced him that, for instance, the completely inadequate supply of safe drinking water was a more urgent issue for the inhabitants of the city. A cholera epidemic broke out in the city during the thirties, and the most immediate priority was the need for a better sewage system.

Not until the second half of the nineteenth century did Paris, under Napoleon III, undergo fundamental changes in its urban development under the direction of Georges-Eugène Haussmann,[2] prefect of the Département de la Seine. These changes were accompanied by a new increase in trade – especially with the large new department stores – and a forced evacuation of the less well-to-do social groups into eastern areas of the city and its peripheries. This was the result of a radical redevelopment policy whose aim was an improved traffic infrastructure with imperial vistas and generously laid-out squares.

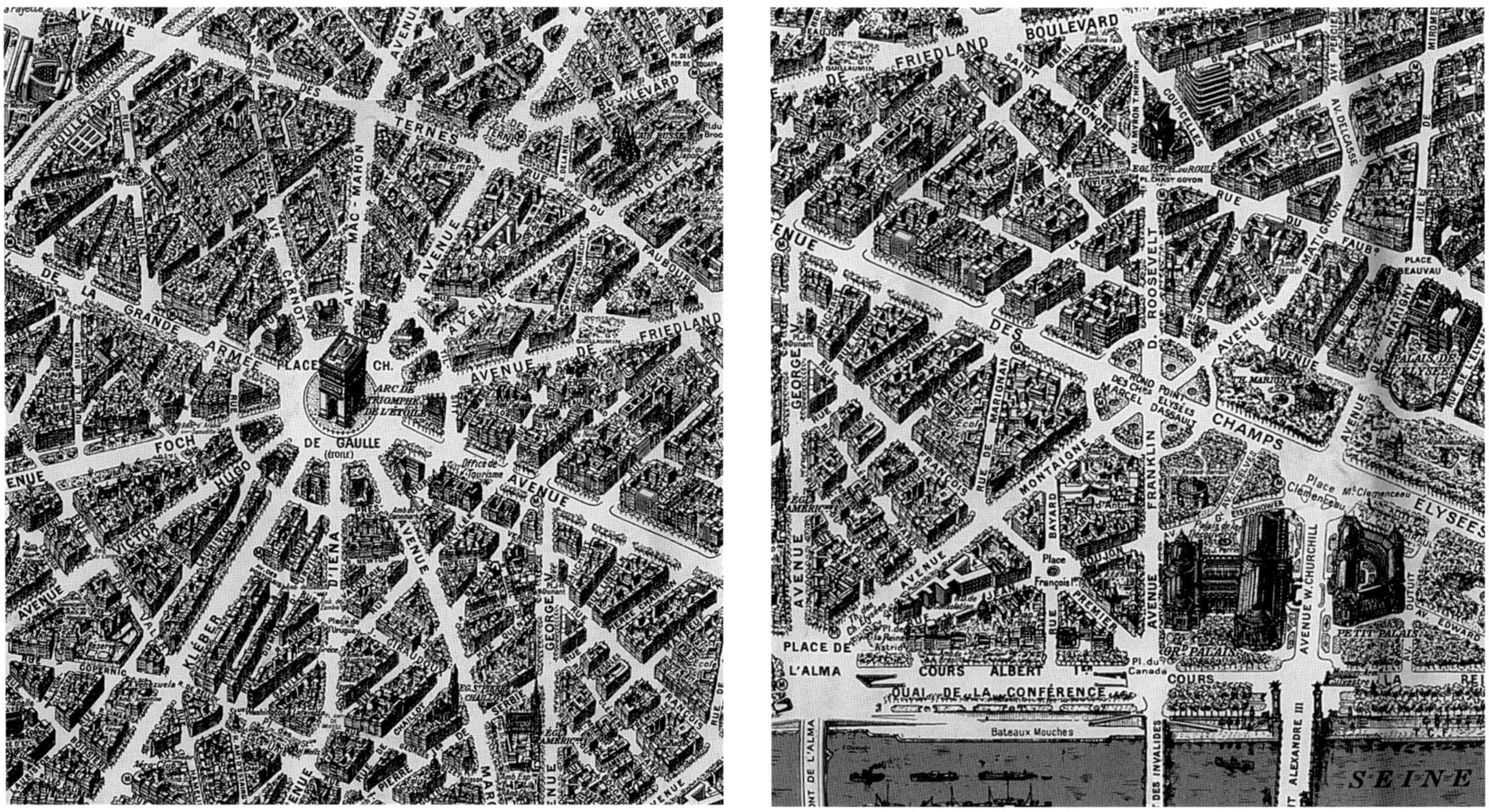

Fig. 24: The Arc de Triomphe in Paris with the twelve avenues radiating out from it (left) was the model for the layout of the All India War Memorial (now the All India Gate); the hexagonal street pattern around the Avenue des Champs Elysées (right) was the model for the layout of King's Way (now Raj Path) in New Delhi.

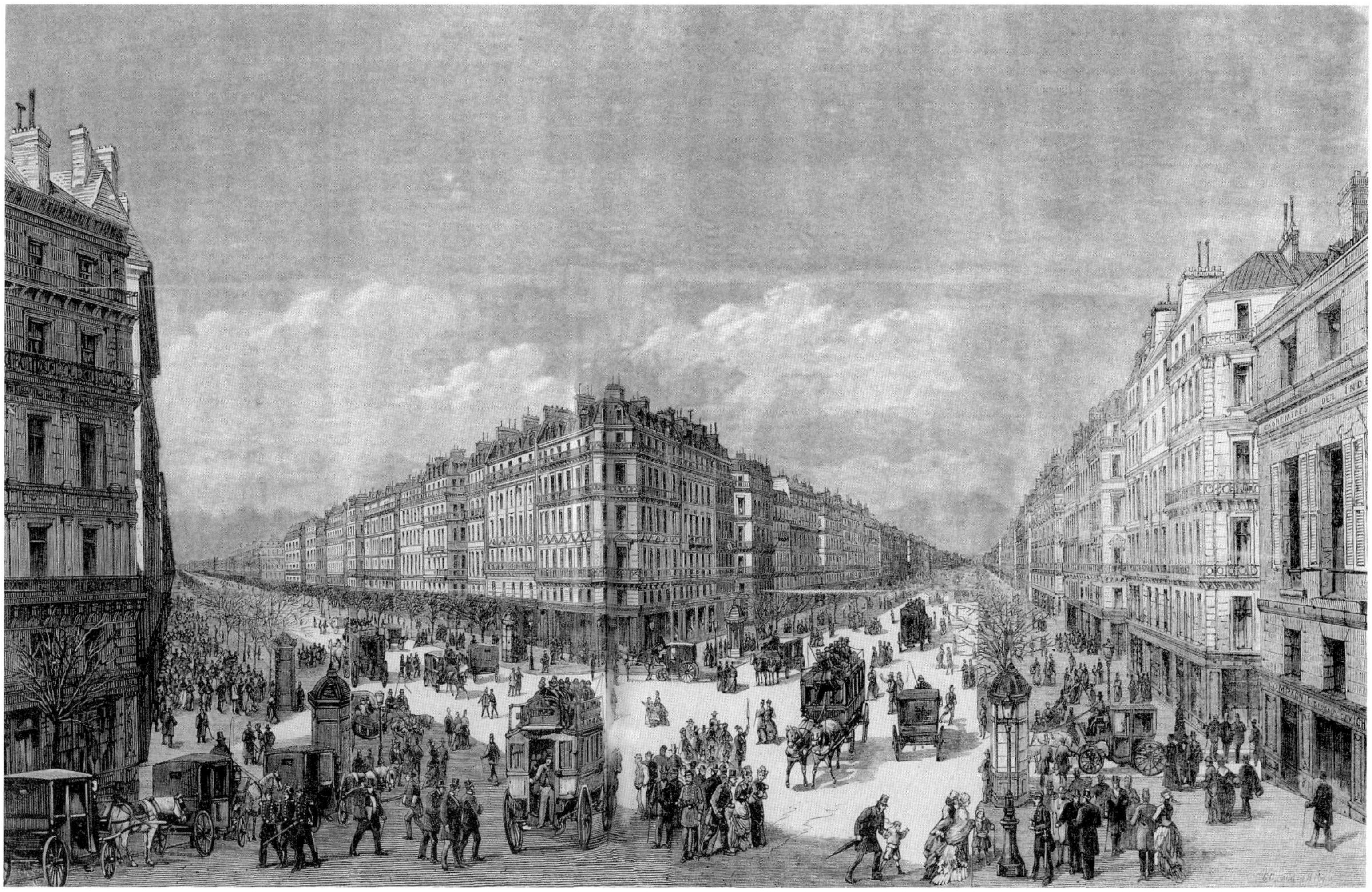

Fig. 25: The model of the Parisian boulevards with shops and apartments on both sides was not carried out exactly in Imperial Delhi because the density of its population in relation to Paris was too low and did not have sufficient buying power to sustain such services.

In the history of town planning there is no prior example that reflected the magnitude of the alterations, the radical nature of the architectural solutions, and the accompanying financial trickery. Haussmann and Napoleon III invented and built in a single massive economic and employment-related political act of power the very same splendid metropolis that Napoleon Bonaparte had once dreamed of.

In 1870, the Second Empire of France may have collapsed in its war against Prussia, but the rebuilding of Paris continued in light of the increasingly successful economic boom. It reached a climax in the nineties with the building of a new public transport system, the metro.

Justice is not done to the usefulness and far-sightedness of the alterations to the plan of Paris if they are regarded simply as a transfer of the radial avenues and streets from Versailles. Not only was the entire technical infrastructure – water, sewage, road transport, metro – raised to a technically exemplary standard, but a new type of city was created whose essential features and elements were copied in many countries around the world. The repeated emulation of this plan elevated Paris to the status of one of the most beautiful cities, and also as one of the most economically successful centres in the world.

The Parisian example was clear to Edwin Lutyens when, in 1912, he and his colleagues in the Delhi Town Planning Committee worked out various new options for the British Viceroy of India to the town plan for a future Imperial Delhi. Lutyens was also aware of the restrictions in adopting one of the most successful city models of all times: in Paris the spending power of one of the richest nations in Europe was increasing. In Imperial Delhi on the other hand, the spending power of the British colonial government was so small by comparison, that there would be no shops, or dance-halls and theatres lining the avenues, but a range of particularly large and quick-growing native trees.

1 R.G. Irving: *Indian Summer*, New Haven and London 1981, p. 104.
2 1809–91, from 1853 Prefect of the Département de la Seine.

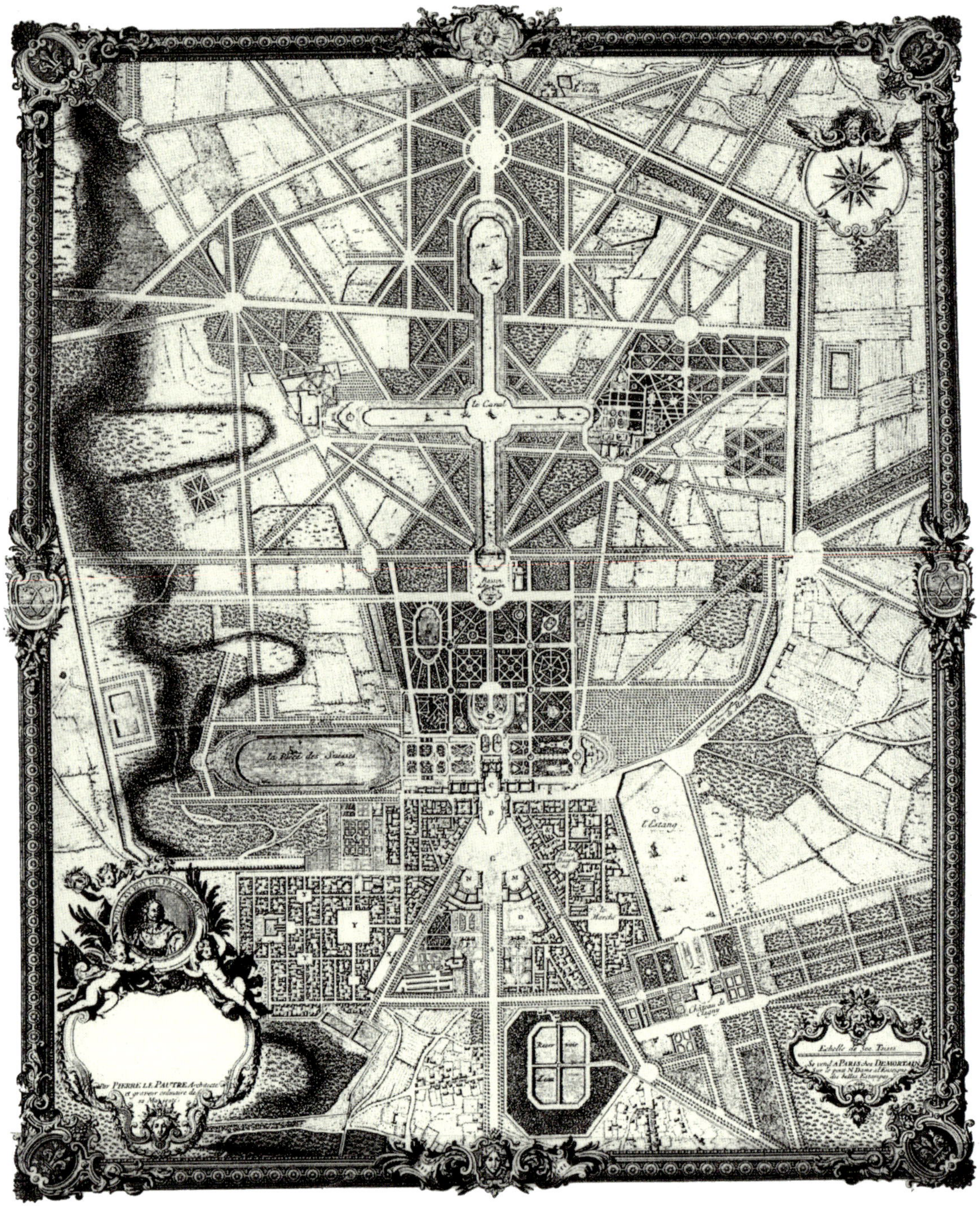

Fig. 26: Both Baron Haussmann's plans for Paris and all the boulevard networks in other countries derived from that system are based on the pattern of radial streets and avenues at Versailles.

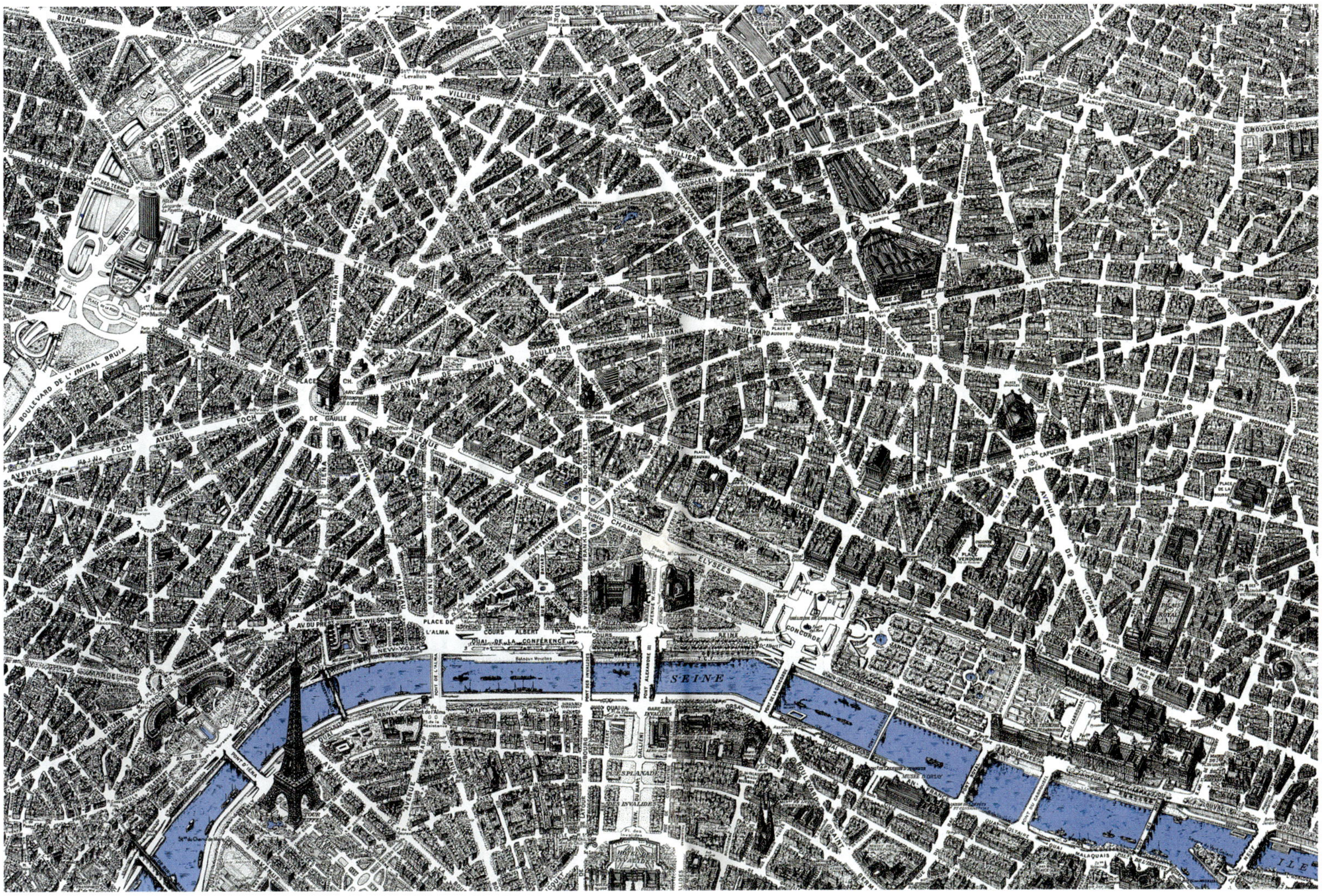

Fig. 27: The sequence of palace (at right, the Louvre), triumphal column (obelisk in the Place de la Concorde), and triumphal arch (at left, the Arc de Triomphe) are models for many grand imperial town-planning concepts, including the Great Axis for Berlin by Albert Speer.

Nevertheless, Lutyens and his colleagues had such high consideration for the model of the Champs Elysées as an exemplary axis for linking the palace, victory column and triumphal arch as indispensable to the plan – and incomparable in its symbolic and formal perfection – that they did not shrink from building (cf. Chapter 3.2) an imitation of the celebrated avenue in Imperial Delhi. Both avenues – the Champs Elysées in Paris and King's Way in New Delhi – do justice to their imperial status on their respective national holidays when their countries' armed forces display the power and the glory of the homeland to the multitudes of curious onlookers.

2.2 London: Christopher Wren's Plan After the Great Fire (1666)

Only once in the long history of the British capital has there been an opportunity to create a system of wide avenues affording better light to residences, a modern water supply and a sewage system within the maze of exceptionally narrow streets, traditional land laws and extremely unhealthy conditions of the city. This opportunity for reconfiguration followed the Great Fire of 1666 that had destroyed almost the entire city centre of London consisting of about 13,200 houses.

This fateful opportunity for an improved design was not seized because of conflicting interests. A number of town plans, especially those by John Evelyn, Christopher Wren,[3] and Valentine Knight, reveal how advantageous it would have been for the capital to take this opportunity for development following the plans of Paris and Rome.

Nevertheless, Christopher Wren and Inigo Jones were highly regarded models for Edwin Lutyens and he was well acquainted with Wren's plans for the city of London. Wren had not simply suggested an abstract framework of a radial street pattern, but proposed an overarching network of radial arterial roads similar to the Roman pattern of axial roads at the Piazza del Popolo, and supplemented by a rectangular system of secondary residential streets.

The position of the main arterial roads was developed logically by connecting the city gates with the most important buildings in the plan, namely the Royal Exchange, St Paul's Cathedral, and the Guildhall. Several large squares were planned in accordance with the

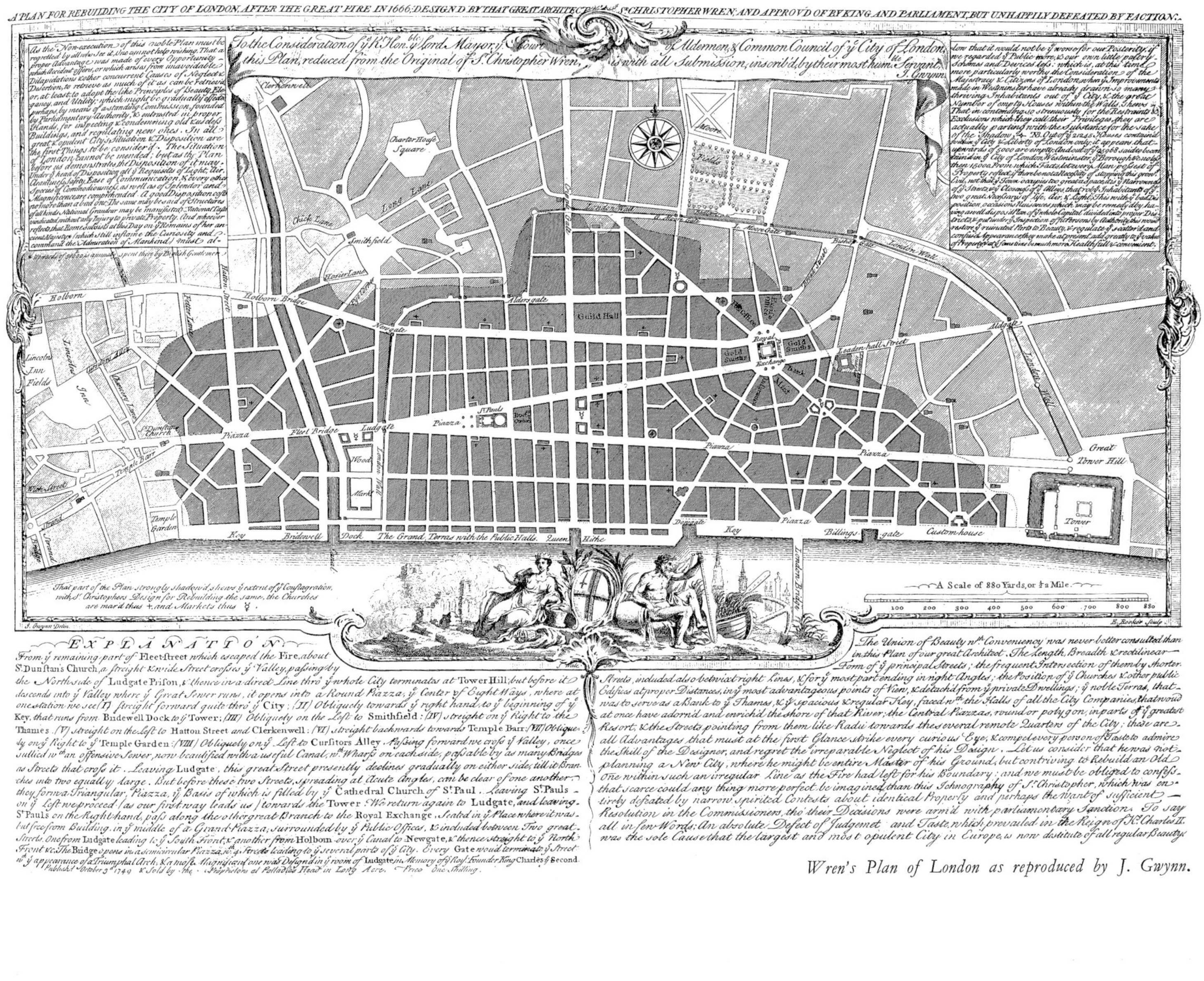

Fig. 28: Christopher Wren's plan for rebuilding London after the Great Fire of 1666 also adopted the town-planning elements of the Parisian model.

layout of a new axis between Ludgate in the west and Tower Hill in the east. West of the straightened, now navigable Fleet with its many bridges was planned an octagonal urban sub-centre. The same octagonal motif would be adopted again around the Royal Exchange. One of the streets radiating from the exchange led directly to London Bridge.

Like John Evelyn's town plan, Christopher Wren's plan also accurately reflected the tradition of Baroque town planning. It was only many years later that Wren was able to realize a small part of his plan in the design and construction of St Paul's Cathedral. Wren himself commented on the collapse of his extensive plans stating: "The Practicability of the whole Scheme without loss to any man, or Infringement of any Property, was at that time demonstrated, and all material objections fully weighted and answered; the only, and as it happened, insurmountable difficulty remaining, was the obstinate averseness of the great part of the Citizens to alter the old Properties and to recede from building their Houses again on the old ground and Foundations, as also the distrust in many, and unwillingness to give up their Properties, though for a time only, into the hands of Publick Trustees, or Commissioners, till they might be Dispensed to them again with more advantage to themselves than otherwise was possible to be affected; for such a method was proposed that by an equal distribution of ground into Buildings, leaving out Church yards, Gardens, etc. (which were to be removed out of the Town), there would have been sufficient room both for the Augmentation of the Street, Disposition of the Churches, Halls and all Public Buildings, and to have given every proprietor full Satisfaction, and although few Proprietors should happen to have been seated again, directly upon the very same Ground they had possessed before the Fire, yet no man would have been thrust any considerable distance from it, but been placed at least as conveniently, and sometimes more so, to their own Trades, than before.

By these means the opportunity was lost of making the new City the most magnificent, as well as Commodious for Health and Trade, of any on Earth: and the Surveyor being thus confined and cramped in his design, it required no small labour and skill to model the City in the manner it has since appeared."[4]

2.3 Bath and its Masonic Symbols (1754)

The town plan for Imperial Delhi contained countless references to, and direct borrowings from, the architecture of the European Renaissance and the Classical canon. The eclecticism of the first two decades of the twentieth century was not an indiscriminate combination of motifs from some old historical junk-room, but a carefully wrought combination of cherished mainstream ideals. Therefore, it is worthwhile pursuing the individual forms back to their presumed sources. This search for historical antecedents provides the prospect of gaining a better understanding of architectural intentions, but it also raises the possibility of mistaking sources.

In the search for the conceptual origins of the circular commercial centre of New Delhi, Connaught Circus, there is little danger of error. The British tradition of the round or oval shapes for plazas goes back via John Nash's Park Crescent in London to John Wood's Circus in Bath, built in 1754.

In the eighteenth-century Bath was *the* place for social climbers and therefore the city in which the process of adopting prestigious symbols by the upwardly-mobile bourgeoisie found its most concentrated expression. How society in eighteenth-century Bath appeared is revealed by an extract from Smollett's letter-novel *The Expedition of Humphrey Clicker* (1771): "All these absurdities (i.e. the arrangement of the town) arise from the general tide of luxury, which hath overspread the nation, and swept away all, even the very dregs of the people. Every upstart of fortune, harnessed in the trappings of the mode, presents himself at Bath, as in the focus of observation ...; men of low birth, of no breeding, have found themselves suddenly translated into the state of affluence, unknown to former ages; and no wonder that their brains should

3 1632–1723.
4 Christopher Wren: *Parentalia*, Farnborough, Hants 1965.

be intoxicated with pride, vanity, and presumption. Knowing no other criterions of greatness, but the ostentation of wealth, they discharge their affluence without taste or conduct ...; all of them hurry to Bath, because here, without any further qualification, they can mingle with the princes and nobles of the land ... they may hobble country-dances and cotillions among lordlings, squires, counsellors and clergy ... Such is the composition of what is called the fashionable company at Bath."[5]

In this unusual market for speculative house building, the Woods – father John Wood the elder and his son John Wood the younger – decided to offer the well-to-do clientele of bourgeois social-climbers terraced housing for rent or re-sale that came with a distinctive aura about them. The architectural forms of the round Circus, the semi-oval of the Royal Crescent, and the rectangle of Queen's Square are full of overt allusions to a grand architectural style. But most people today are still unaware that the Circus, for example, also contains a number of Masonic symbols.

Not until the last two decades did new research in architectural history reveal that John Wood the elder might have been a Freemason himself.[6] Moreover, the strict geometric forms in the ground plan of Bath could be directly attributed to Masonic concepts of geometry that represented an image of the "Great Architect of the Universe." The fact that, without exception, all the metopes of the Doric order on the ground floor depict Masonic symbols (cf. Fig. 31),

5 I. Smollett: *The Expedition of Humphrey Clicker*: London 1771/1967, quoted in Loosen-Frieling, I.: *Architektur zwischen Norm und Geschmack*, Hildesheim, Zürich, New York 1992, p. 164.

6 A. v. Buttlar: *Der Englische Landsitz* 1715–60, Mittenwald 1982, p. 118.

7 Loosen-Frieling: op. cit., p. 251.

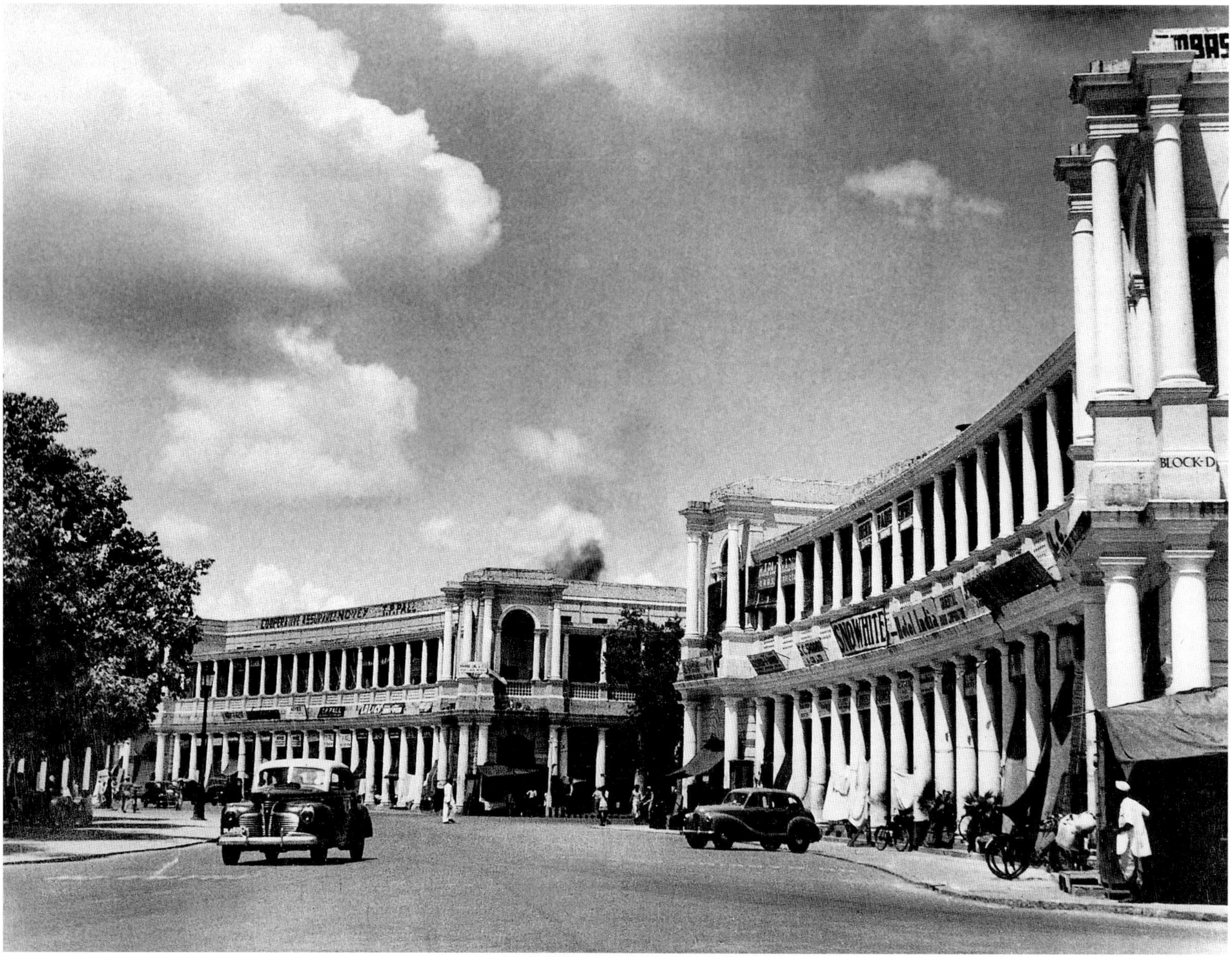

Fig. 29: The plan for Connaught Circus in New Delhi by Robert Tor Russel closely followed the models of the Circus in Bath and Park Crescent in London.

supports the assumption of their derivation. In the context of Masonic symbolism, the round shape of the Circus is a symbol of eternity, and the three entrances in the layout form an equilateral triangle representing the symbol of the Godhead.

For his three-storied facade, Wood chose pillar capitals in the three Neo-Classical styles, coinciding with the Masonic canon that refers to them in their literature as the three pillars of wisdom (Doric), strength (Tuscan), and beauty (Corinthian). The choice of double pillars was probably related to the two pillars of Jachin and Boaz at the entrance to the temple.[7]

Along with the Masonic references in the architecture of the Circus, the circular architecture of the plaza has, since its construction, been linked with the Coliseum in Rome and was even sarcastically referred to as such by the inhabitants. The reference remained not only because of the ground plan, but also due to the classical superimposition according to the Roman pattern. The architects consciously encouraged such comparisons by promoting associations with classical sports stadia.

Summerson traced the obvious connections with the Coliseum in Rome – though with the outside turned inward in Bath – to an unusual lack of concern on the part of John Wood in handling historical models: "Had Wood been less of a scholar he would never have been inspired to build a circus at all. Had he been more of a scholar, an exact knowledge of the extent and the nature of the Roman Coliseum would probably have extinguished the suggestiveness

Fig. 30: The eighteenth-century accommodation built in Bath made use of an ambitious historical formal canon. Only the most recent research in architectural history shows that the squares designed by John Wood the Elder and John Wood the Younger were not only amatter of an easily marketable town-planning concept, but a complex system of Masonic geometry highly regarded at that time.

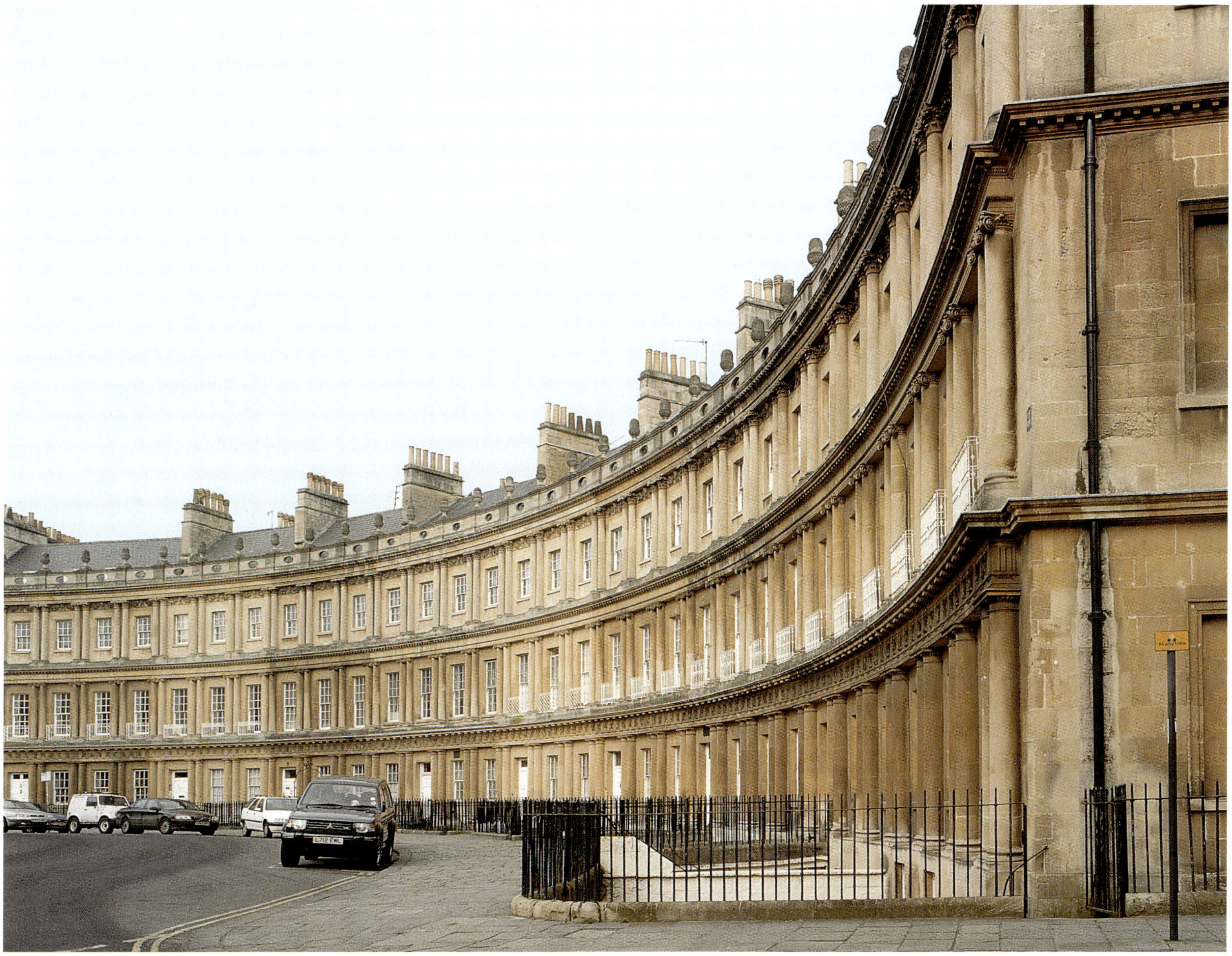

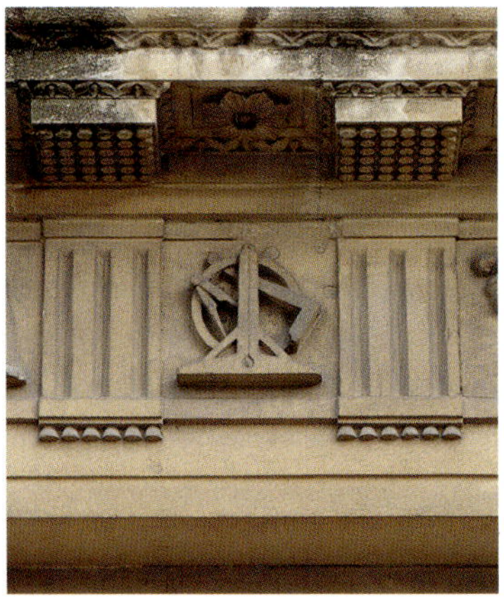

Fig. 31: The reliefs in the metopes on the facade of the Circus depict many Masonic symbols.

of the romantic half-knowledge which was his inspiration."[8] Despite such criticism, the general enthusiasm of contemporaries and of English town planners for the original creations of squares in Bath led to a great tradition of circular and semicircular plazas. Connaught Circus in Imperial Delhi represents both the high point and the end of individualistic re-interpretation of the Coliseum as a motif in town planning on a grand scale.

There was, however, no lack of prominent critics who disagreed with what they perceived as the impudent adaptation of monumental architectural concepts for residential building. First and foremost, in 1809, the architect John Soane made the criticism that, although the Circus "may please us by its prettiness and a sort of novelty, as a rattle pleases a child ... the area is so small the height of each order is so diminutive that the general appearance of the entire building is mean, gloomy and confined."[9]

English architects took this criticism to heart. The semicircular and later, round versions of the Circus and the Royal Crescent became increasingly larger. In the example in New Delhi, the double circle of Connaught Place and Connaught Circus finally becomes so large that the observer loses track and finds it difficult to recognize the regularity of the basic geometric shape (Fig. 207).

A quick look at the conceptual sources for the layout of the squares in Bath is useful for a later examination of Connaught Place and Connaught Circus in New Delhi (cf. Chapter 4.3.4). Roman formal plans on the one hand, as well as the ideas of the Freemasons on the other, were held in especially high regard at the time of the founding of Imperial Delhi, and these two sources fuse together into forms that are unique in both cases.

8 J. Summerson: *Architecture in Britain* 1530–1830, London 1953, p. 233ff.
9 J. Soane: *Lectures on Architecture*, London 1809.

Fig. 32: The Colosseum in Rome (seen here as part of an engraving by G.B. Piranesi, *View of the Flavian Amphitheatre*) was reversed in the design of the Circus in Bath.

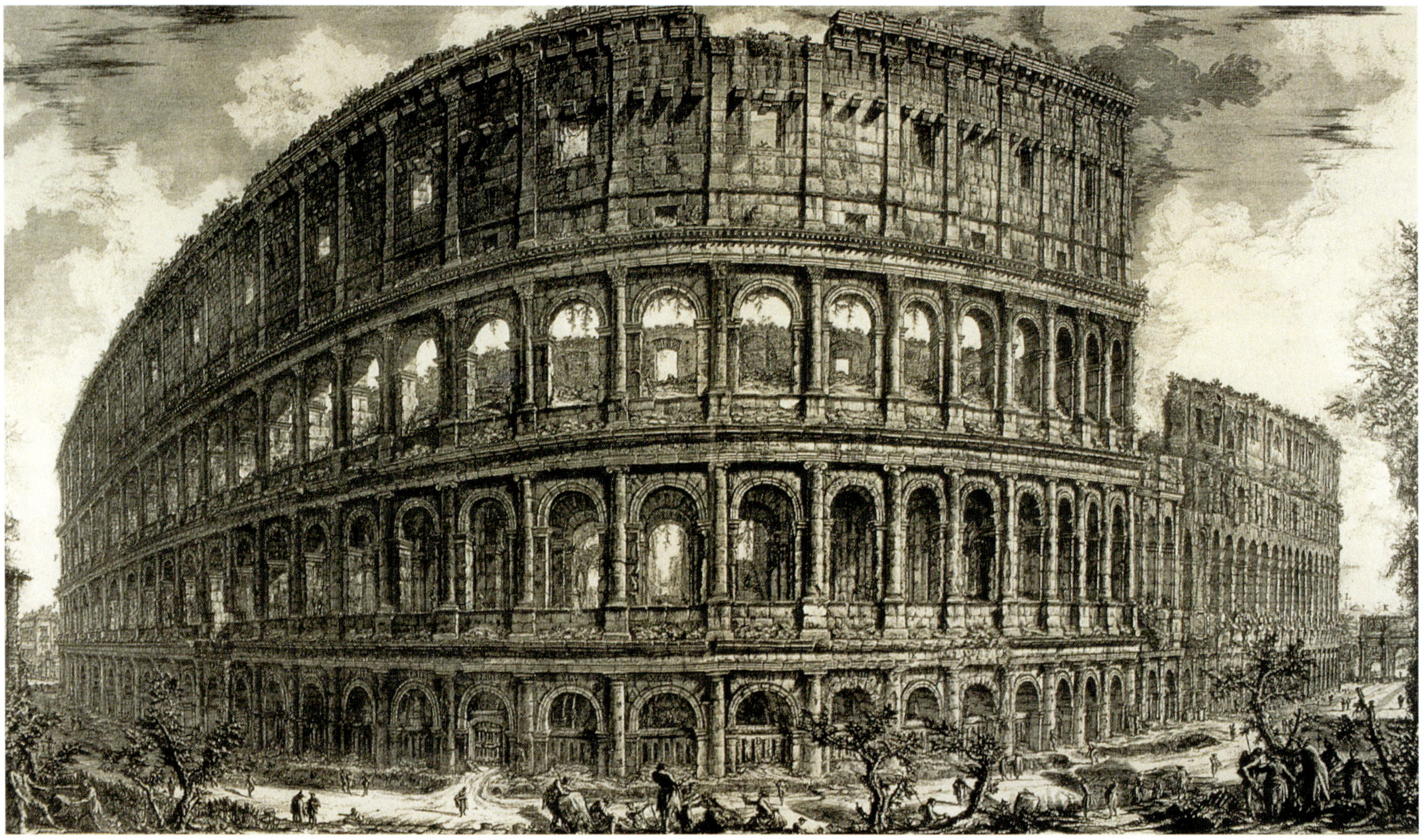

2.4 Washington, D.C.: The Freemasons' City (1791)

An examination of the town plan of Imperial Delhi with its hexagonal system of wide boulevards and the important historical or new buildings at the intersections inevitably recalls the similar plan of the American capital, Washington, D.C.

After fierce debate, the American Congress had chosen a site directly by the Potomac River for the capital of the United States that was subsequently approved by President Washington on July 16, 1790. Pierre Charles L'Enfant delivered a plan on the basis of elements from the models of London, Madrid, Paris, Amsterdam, Naples, Venice, and Florence. His plan for the "Federal City" was realized without any essential changes and remains intact in the American capital today: "Most important for the future beauty and artistic effect of the city was the selection and location of building, statuary and monument sites. Washington, L'Enfant and Ellicott, who was doing the field work, went over the ground together, and 'carefully,' as a note on the margin of the map informs us, selected the sites of the 'grand edifices' where they would command the greatest prospect, and be susceptible of the greatest improvement ... Although the most prominent feature in the landscape, the hill on which the Capitol is built is not of sufficient height to lift the building entirely above its surroundings. This gives the

Fig. 33: Pierre Charles L'Enfant's plan for Washington, D.C. is based on the model of the Avenue des Champs Elysées in Paris with an axis (at a right angle) comprised of the President's House, the Washington Memorial, and the Capitol.

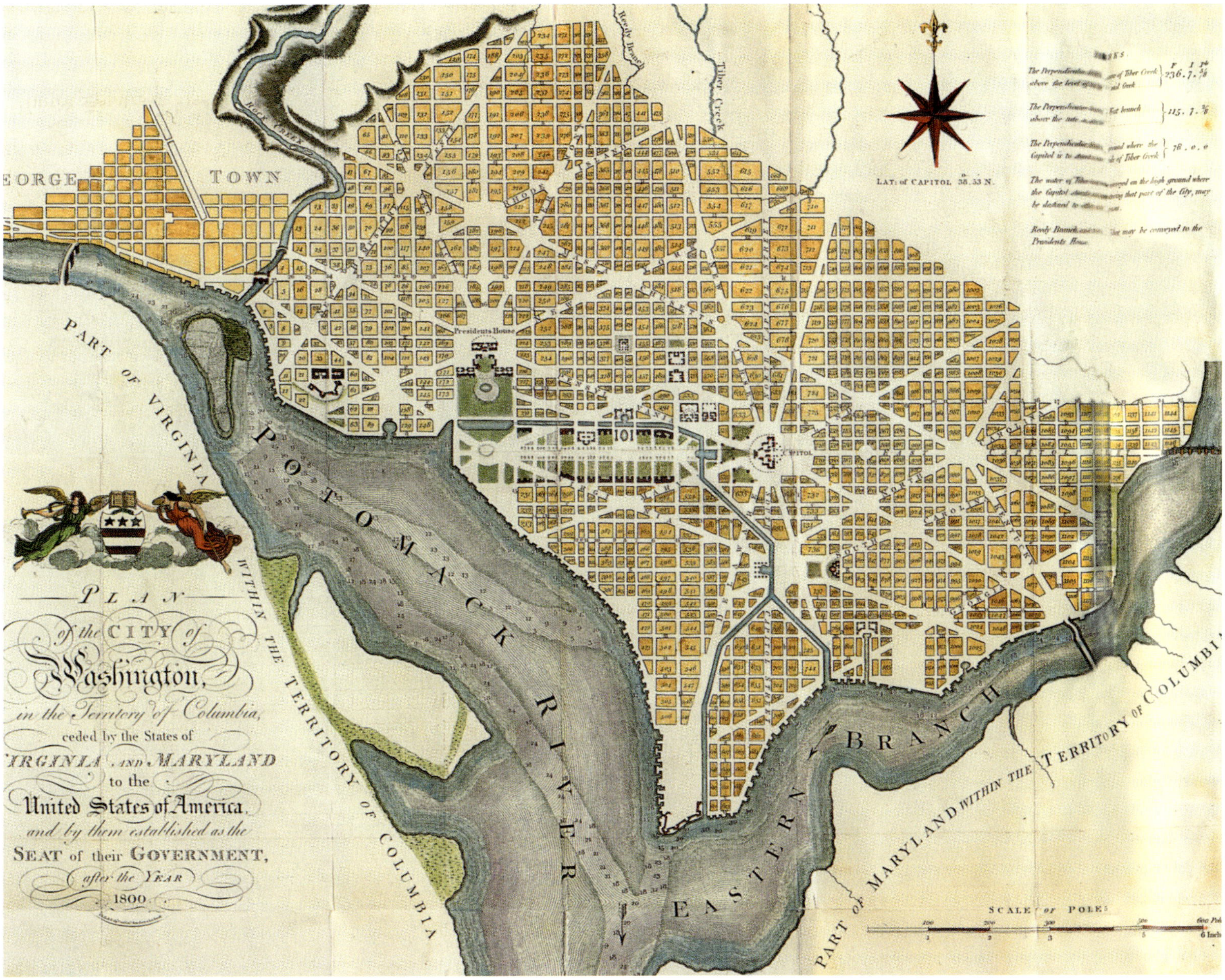

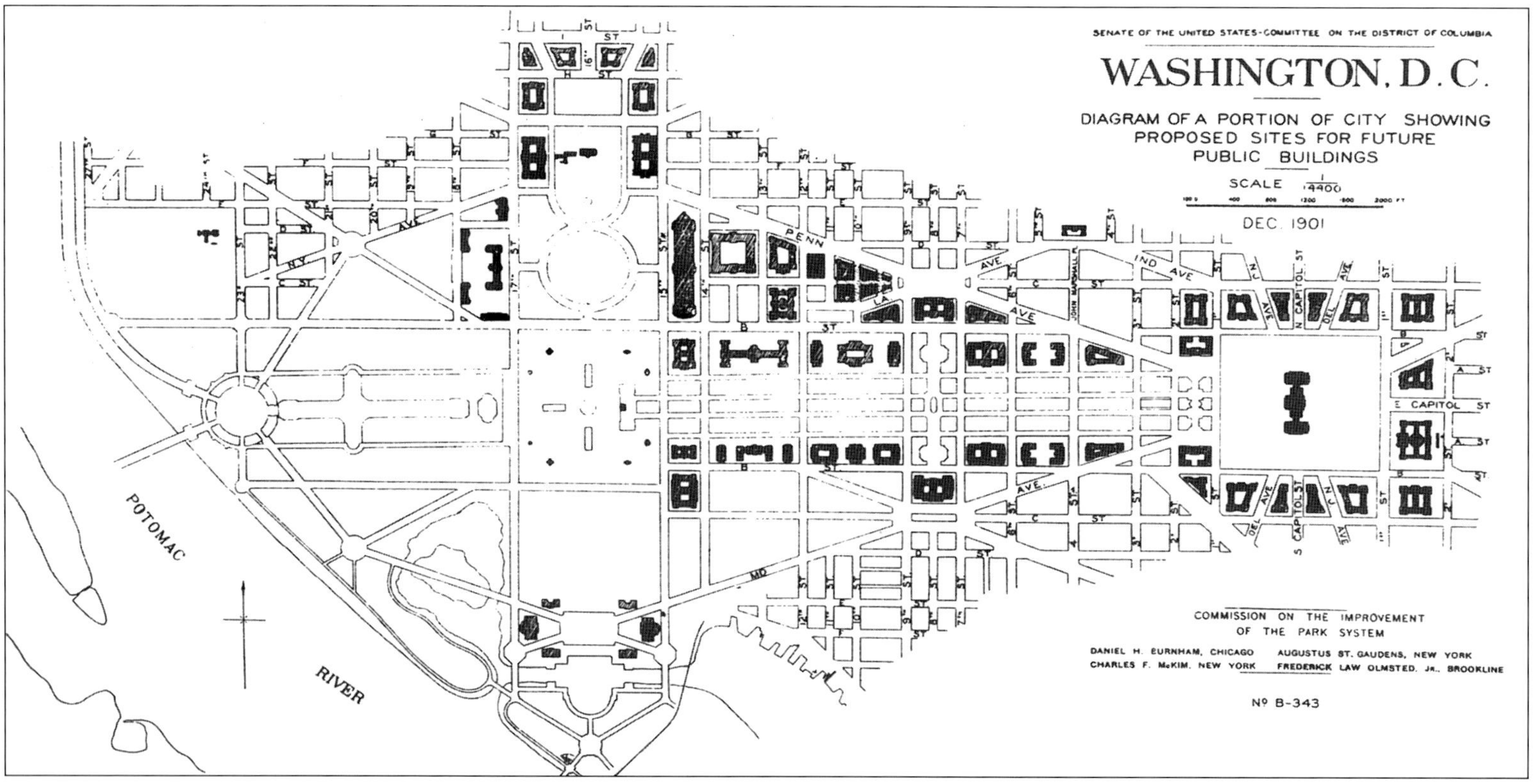

Fig. 34: In the plan of the Senate Park Commission of 1902 an attempt was undertaken to continue the axis of the Capitol to the Washington Memorial farther up to a triumphal arch.

background of hills which, in connection with the sky and the changing colors which the foliage undergoes with the seasons, adds to the charm of this white pile."[10]

The history of the founding of Washington, D.C. and the reasons behind its geometric ground plan were familiar to all those involved in the founding of Imperial Delhi. It was a Freemasons' city that embodied their concepts of geometry as being illustrative of the notion of harmony in the universe. Led by George Washington, on April 15, 1791, the foundation stone was laid, and the builders used the symbols of the setsquare and apron, thus recording the connection between the founding of the city and freemasonry.

The town planners of Imperial Delhi, however, were not all Freemasons. Nevertheless, the Royal Family and London society as well were clearly influenced by Masonic ideals. The functional and visual advantages of a city designed according to the model of the prosperous city of Washington, D.C. were obvious apart from any geometric preferences. Thus, L'Enfant's work became one of the most important sources for the British town planners in Delhi in 1912 and 1913: "Had L'Enfant's layout (or its twentieth-century revival) influenced the Delhi planners in 1913? Certainly Herbert Baker, so closely involved in the Delhi Town Planning Committee's deliberations over a layout in 1913, had four years earlier expressed his estimate of L'Enfant's scheme as 'at once original, practical, and beautiful,' and had lamented that it had not been adopted by the American Government, to serve as 'an ideal and stimulus' for all future efforts. Washington's layout, with its 'wonderful vistas,' had 'greatly' impressed Lord Hardinge while posted there (1885–86) as a young diplomat. Nearly thirty years later, during the conception of New Delhi, 'the first thing' he did, in his words, 'was to send for plans of Washington and Paris.' Lutyens had himself explicitly linked the American and Indian cities when he described Delhi's hexagonal plan as 'a sorry nuisance' to those persons whose minds could not 'embrace the intelligence of L'Enfant at Washington.' On visiting the American capital in 1925, Lutyens told his wife frankly and without false modesty that he thought the plan 'not as good as Delhi or as fine,' but confessed that the buildings, the bulk of them in marble, were 'far better.'"[11]

The similarities between Washington, D.C. and Imperial Delhi are astonishing. As early as 1792, when the first published version of Washington's town plan appeared, the following

10 G. Brown: *History of the United States Capitol*, New York 1970, p. 2.
11 G.R. Irving: op. cit., p. 83.
12 G. Brown: op. cit., annex.

entries of *Observations Explanatory of the Plan* could be applied equally to the town plan of Imperial Delhi: "I. The positions of the different grand edifices and for several grand squares or areas of different shape as they are laid down were first determined on the most advantageous ground commanding the most extensive prospects, and the better susceptible of such improvements as the various intents of the several objects may require.

II. Lines or avenues of direct communication have been devised to connect the separate and most distant objects with the principal, and to preserve through the whole a reciprocity of sight at the same time. Attention has been paid to the passing of those leading avenues over the most favourable ground for prospect and convenience.

III. North and South lines, intersected by others running due east and west, make the distribution of the city into streets, squares, etc., and those lines have been combined so as to meet at certain given points with those divergent avenues, so as to form on the spaces 'first determined' the different squares or areas, which are all proportioned in magnitude to the number of avenues leading to them."[12]

The parallels between Washington, D.C. and Imperial Delhi become even more striking when we take into account the modifications of L'Enfant's ideas suggested by the McMillan Commission from 1901–02. Lord Hardinge and his Delhi Town Planning Committee were also certainly familiar with these new considerations.

The McMillan Commission essentially suggested:

- Lengthening the Mall westwards to a Triumphal Arch.
- Lengthening the axis running from the White House vertically to the Mall southwards.
- For the sake of preserving symmetry throughout the layout, completing Pennsylvania Avenue with a symmetrically placed avenue south of the Mall.
- Emphasizing the intersection of the two main axes situated perpendicularly to each other by the placement of prominent buildings.

Basically all the guidelines for the geometry of the town plan of Imperial Delhi were laid down accordingly. In addition, a detailed examination of the Mall clearly shows how closely Edwin Lutyens, in his plan of King's Way (now the Raj Path), adheres to the model in the United States (cf. Fig. 35 and Fig. 36):

"The more the scheme laid out by Washington and L'Enfant is studied, the more forcibly it strikes one as the best. It is easy to imagine the magnificence of a boulevard 400 feet wide,

Fig. 35: In the master plan of Washington, D.C., the site of the Capitol and the avenues radiating outwards from it, especially the Mall (in the centre of the picture), anticipates the essential elements in the plans for Imperial Delhi.

Fig. 36: Only once, in the long history of the British Empire, did the powerful Crown succeed in creating a truly imperial town plan: the city of New Delhi.

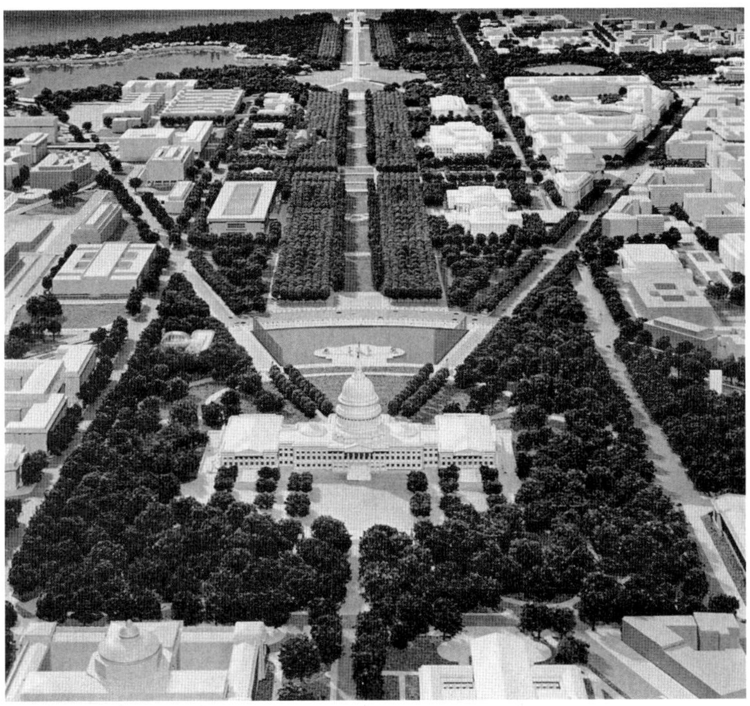

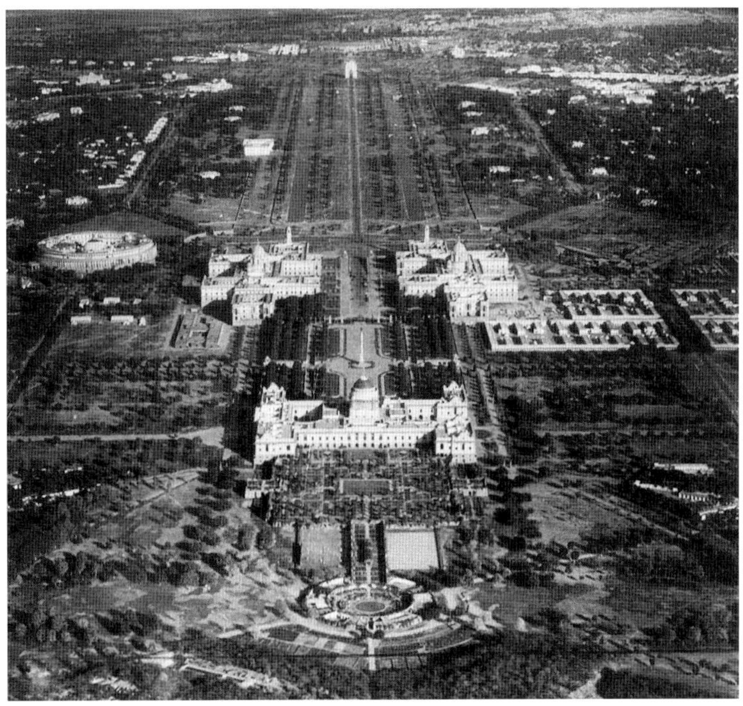

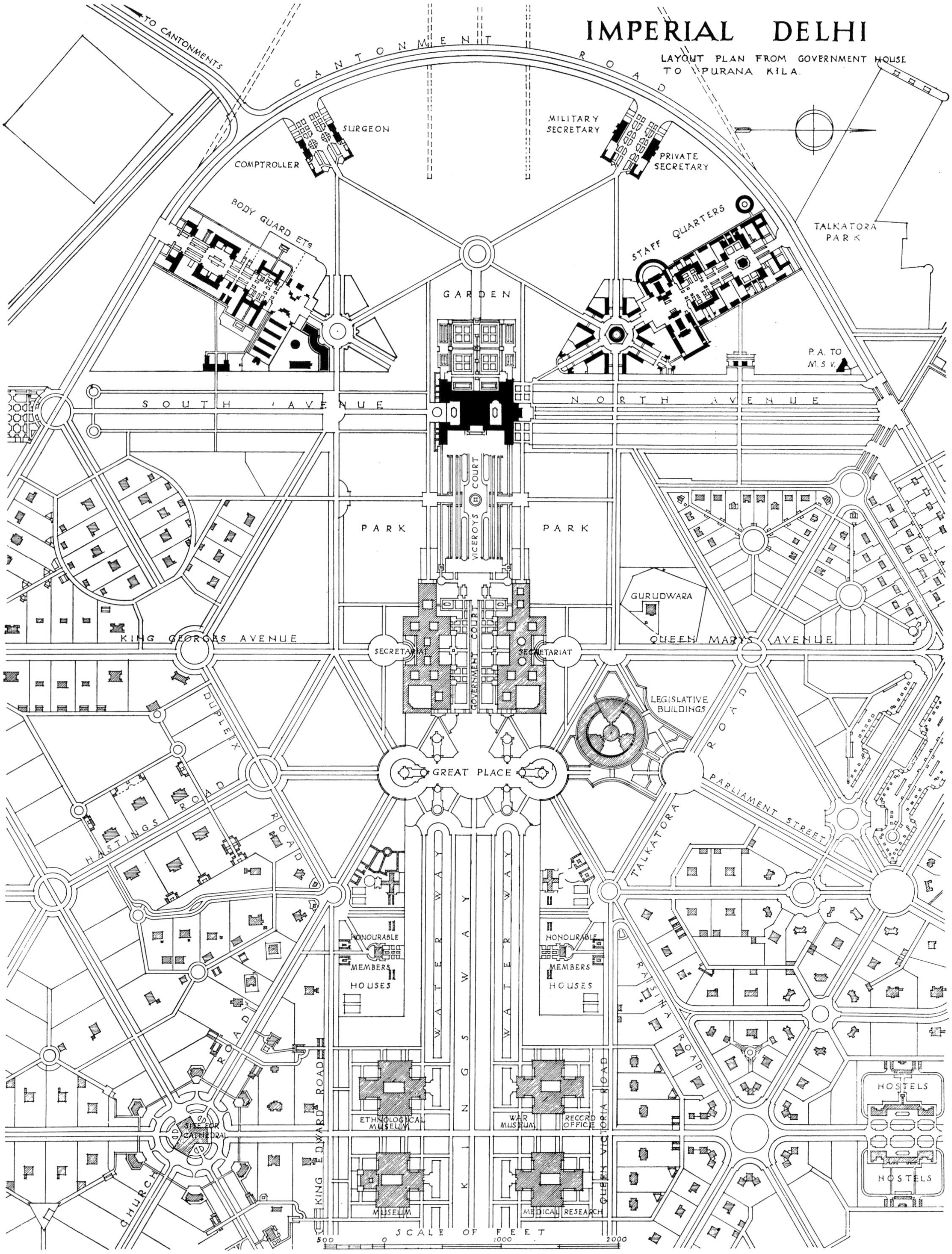
IMPERIAL DELHI
LAYOUT PLAN FROM GOVERNMENT HOUSE TO PURANA KILA.
TO CANTONMENTS
CANTONMENT ROAD
SURGEON
COMPTROLLER
MILITARY SECRETARY
PRIVATE SECRETARY
BODY GUARD ETs
STAFF QUARTERS
TALKATORA PARK
GARDEN
P.A. TO M.S.V.
SOUTH AVENUE
NORTH AVENUE
VICEROYS COURT
PARK
PARK
GURUDWARA
KING GEORGES AVENUE
QUEEN MARYS AVENUE
SECRETARIAT
SECRETARIAT
GOVERNMENT COURT
LEGISLATIVE BUILDINGS
DUPLEX ROAD
GREAT PLACE
TALKATORA ROAD
PARLIAMENT STREET
HASTINGS ROAD
HONOURABLE MEMBERS HOUSES
HONOURABLE MEMBERS HOUSES
WATER WAY
KINGS WAY
WATER WAY
RAISINA ROAD
HOSTELS
ETHNOLOGICAL MUSEUM
WAR MUSEUM
RECORD OFFICE
SITE FOR CATHEDRAL
KING EDWARD ROAD
QUEEN VICTORIA ROAD
HOSTELS
CHURCH
MUSEUM
MEDICAL RESEARCH
SCALE OF FEET
500 0 1000 2000

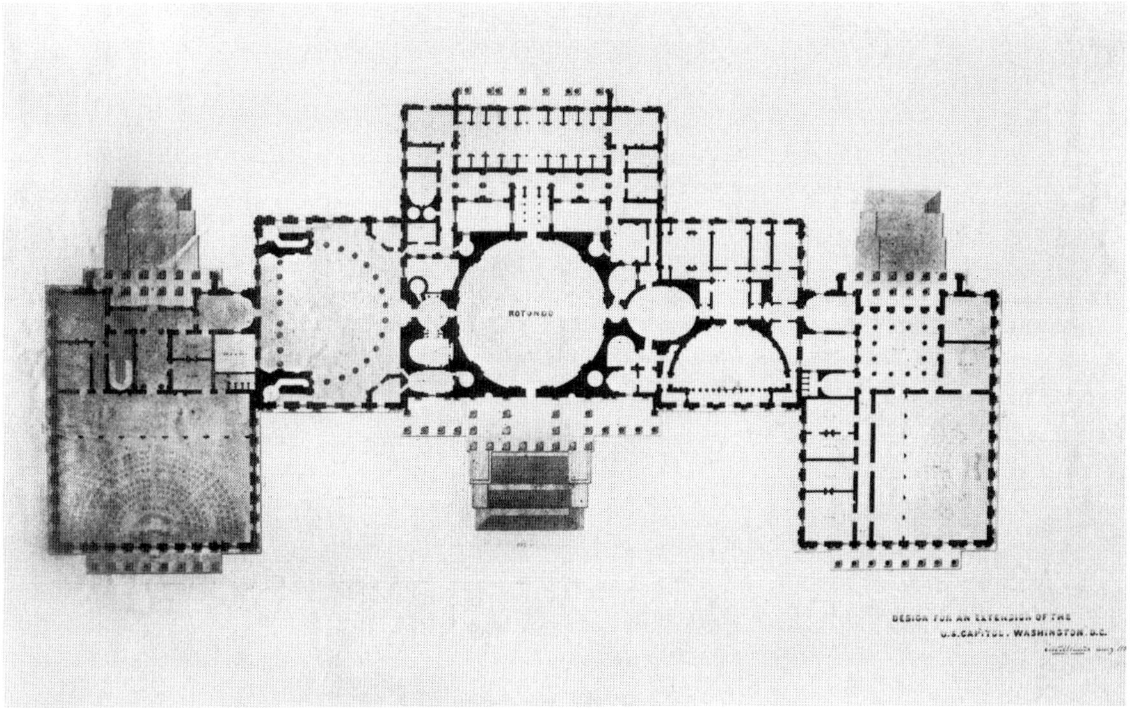

Fig. 38: In the central section of the ground plan and elevation of the Capitol in Washington, D.C. (architect: Walter, 1851), there are strong similarities with the spatial disposition found in the Viceroy's Palace (now Rashtrapati Bhavan) in Delhi.

Fig. 37: Edwin Lutyens' town plan for the centre of New Delhi replaced the Capitol in Washington, D.C. with the Viceroy's Palace and the Mall with King's Way.

beginning at the Capitol and ending with the Monument, a distance of nearly a mile and a half, bounded on both sides by parks 600 feet wide, laid out by a skilled landscape architect and adorned by the work of capable artists. Looking from the boulevard across the park, a continuous line of beautiful buildings was to have formed the background. They were not to have been deep enough to curtail either the natural or artistic beauties of the park, or to encroach upon the people's right to an air space. By this time such an avenue would have acquired a worldwide reputation, if it had been carried out by competent architects, landscape artists, and sculptors consulting and working in harmony with each other. The parked portion of the Champs Elysées, which is approximately 1,300 feet wide and three-quarters of a mile long, would not have compared with it in magnitude or grandeur."[13]

Last but not least, the Champs Elysées in Paris, the Mall in Washington, D.C. and King's Way in New Delhi also share the trait of being used by their respective populations, probably more than was ever intended, as an inner-city recreation area: "The Central Vista (King's Way) was enthusiastically used as a park from the outset. Its riding paths afforded a lengthy canter, and the alternate quick-growing temporary and slow-growing permanent trees created intimate shady spaces within the attractive sweep of greensward. On his last trip to Delhi in 1938, Lutyens happily recorded that the King's Way had become "very popular" for evening walks by the Indians, and twenty years later architect Henry Medd used the same words. Use steadily increased, and by 1968 a resident town planner reported a "very large number" of persons congregated along the avenue every evening, and on Sundays and holy days he noted that it was very common to see the Central Vista "packed with people" from one end to the other. In fact, concern existed about overuse of the space. A children's playground and boating on the waterways were welcome additions, but certain activities and groups threatened the amenity: ubiquitous student drivers created a nuisance, a nearby regiment used the park as a parade ground at all hours, local colleges and high schools made the lawns their daily playing fields, and events at the National Stadium brought temporary car parks and hawkers' booths."[14]

Imperial Delhi's reference to Washington, D.C. as a model was not confined to the layout of the town. Lutyens placed the city in high regard for the plan of Viceroy's House in Delhi (the palace of the British Viceroy of India). In Viceroy's House, a mighty staircase leads to a high portico and behind the portico in the American Capitol there is a central rotunda,

13 Ibid., p. 3.
14 R.G. Irving: op. cit., p. 251.

repeated in Viceroy's House as the circular Durbar Hall. In both seats of government the central building is also flanked by wings and in both places, symmetrical halls with pillars mark off the front and the back.

Lutyens would not have dreamt of copying another country's seat of government; particularly in the case of Washington, D.C., the capital of a government that had turned against the British Crown in the War of Independence. Nevertheless, the imperial atmosphere, and the absolute claim to power of both nations had hardly changed in the half-century which separated the building of Washington, D.C. and New Delhi. As a result, the town plan and architectural concepts for both cities bear a strikingly close resemblance.

2.5 Hampstead Garden Suburb (1908)

An attempt to find models for Imperial Delhi not only leads to large city sites such as the boulevard systems of Paris and Washington, D.C., it also points to Edwin Lutyens' most un-imperial undertaking, the design and construction of the English garden city, Hampstead Garden Suburb near London. Here, Lutyens designed the town centre at Central Square for the two planners Barry Parker and Raymond Unwin.

The ideals behind the English garden city had, since Ebenezer Howard's writings,[15] been equally concerned with social reform and town planning. For Lutyens, the artistic task stood somewhere in between these two issues. He designed and built – wholly in the tradition of Howard's axial diagrams of the city (Fig. 39) – a centre with residential streets radiating outwards. At the intersections, however, there was no palace or Arc de Triomphe, but a small town hall and a church (Fig. 44). With the aid of hindsight we might liken this plan to a composer's small finger exercise before he created his great symphony in India, possessing the same melody – three of the street axes lead to the centre of worldly power – yet without the monumental quality of imperial British ambition.

Fig. 39: In Ebenezer Howard's suggestions for an ideal Garden City, geometric structures are combined with a way of life that appeared to be closer to nature.

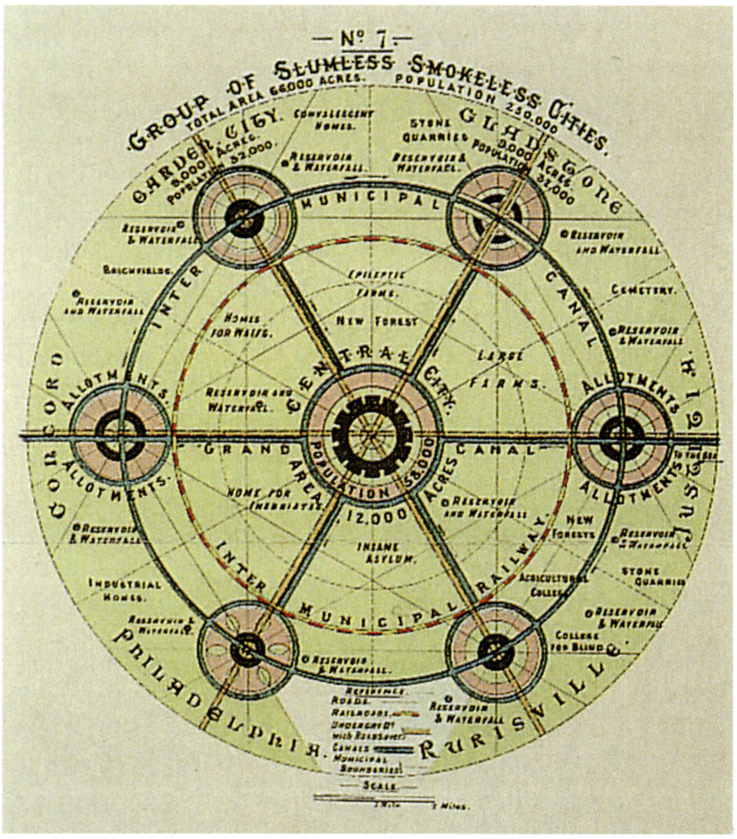

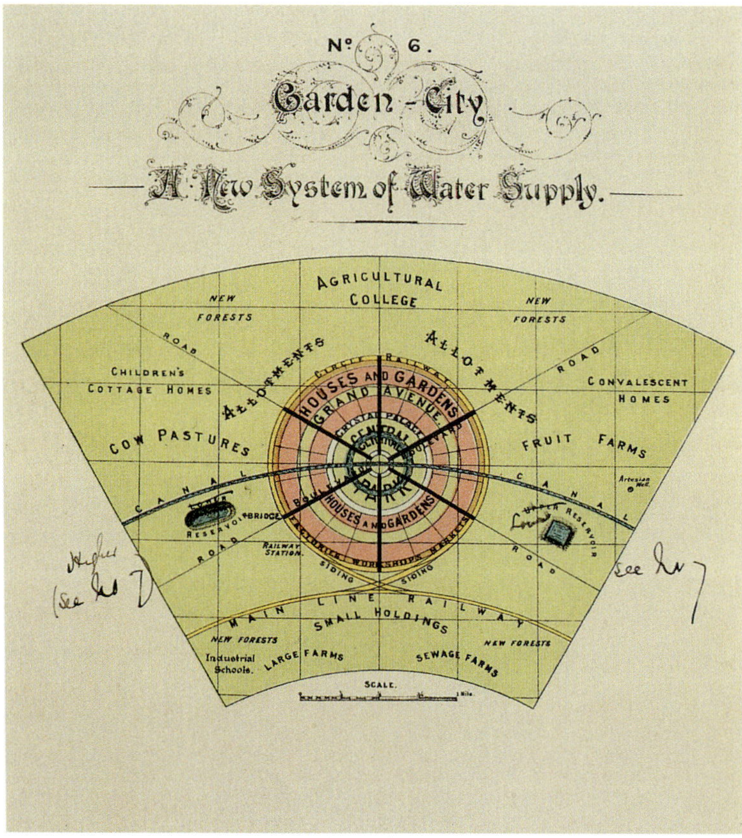

15 E. Howard: *Tomorrow: A Peaceful Way to Real Reform*, London 1898. New edition: *Garden Cities of Tomorrow*, London 1902.

Fig. 40: At left: New Delhi still appears today as a subtropical garden city with a Roman-style centre at its highest location. The intended similarity with Renaissance Rome reflects the British Crown's claim to power; the garden city extending around the palaces reflects Lutyens' experience gained from his planning of Hampstead Garden Suburb.

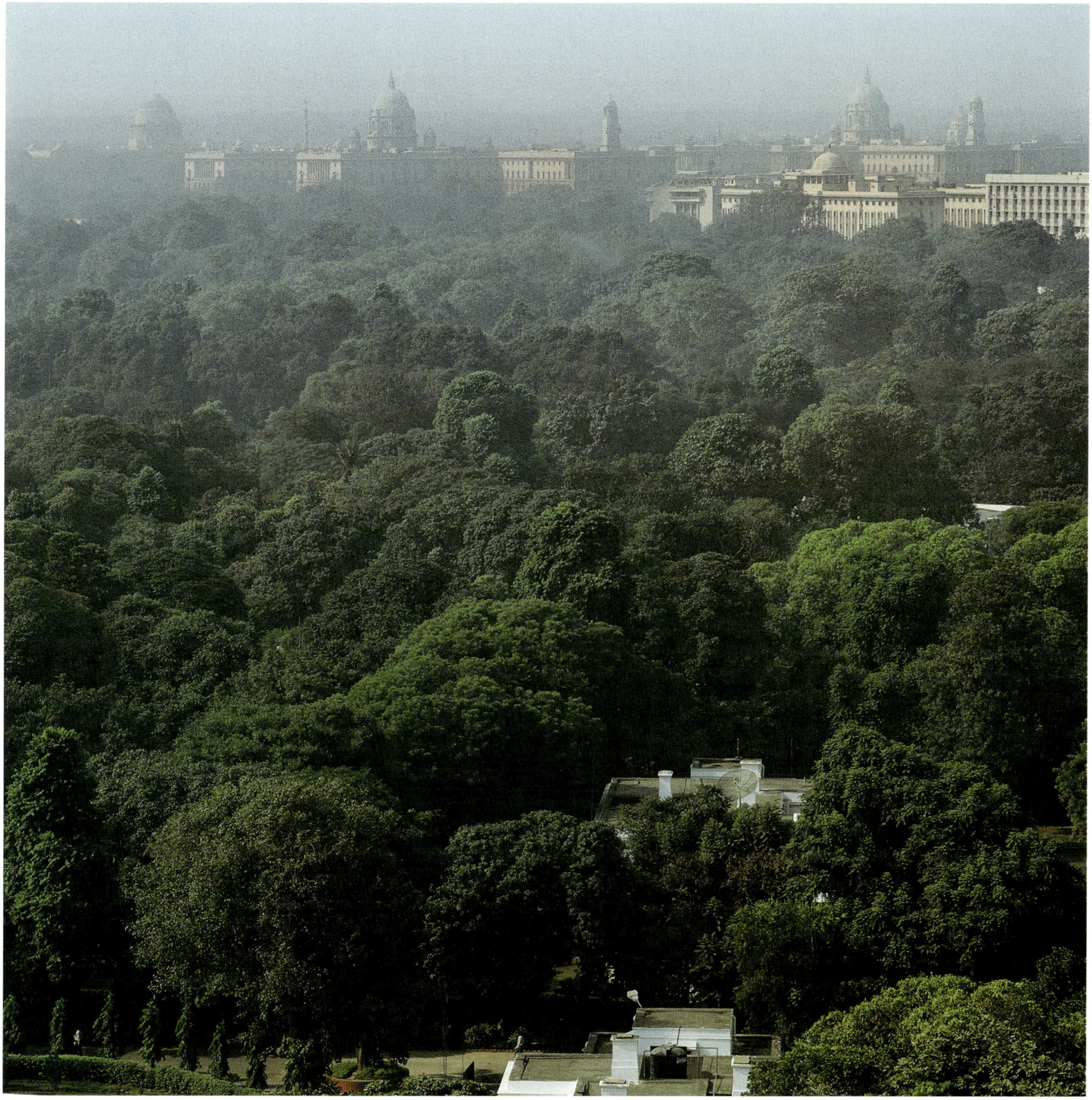

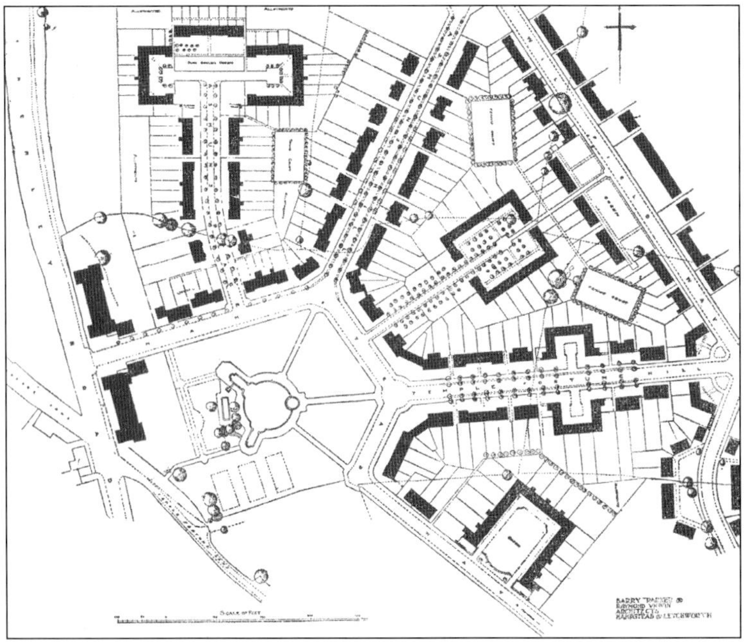

Fig. 41: Hampstead Garden Suburb, on the edge of London, was designed and built by Parker and Unwin as one of the first garden cities. City-centre and green residential areas complement one another.

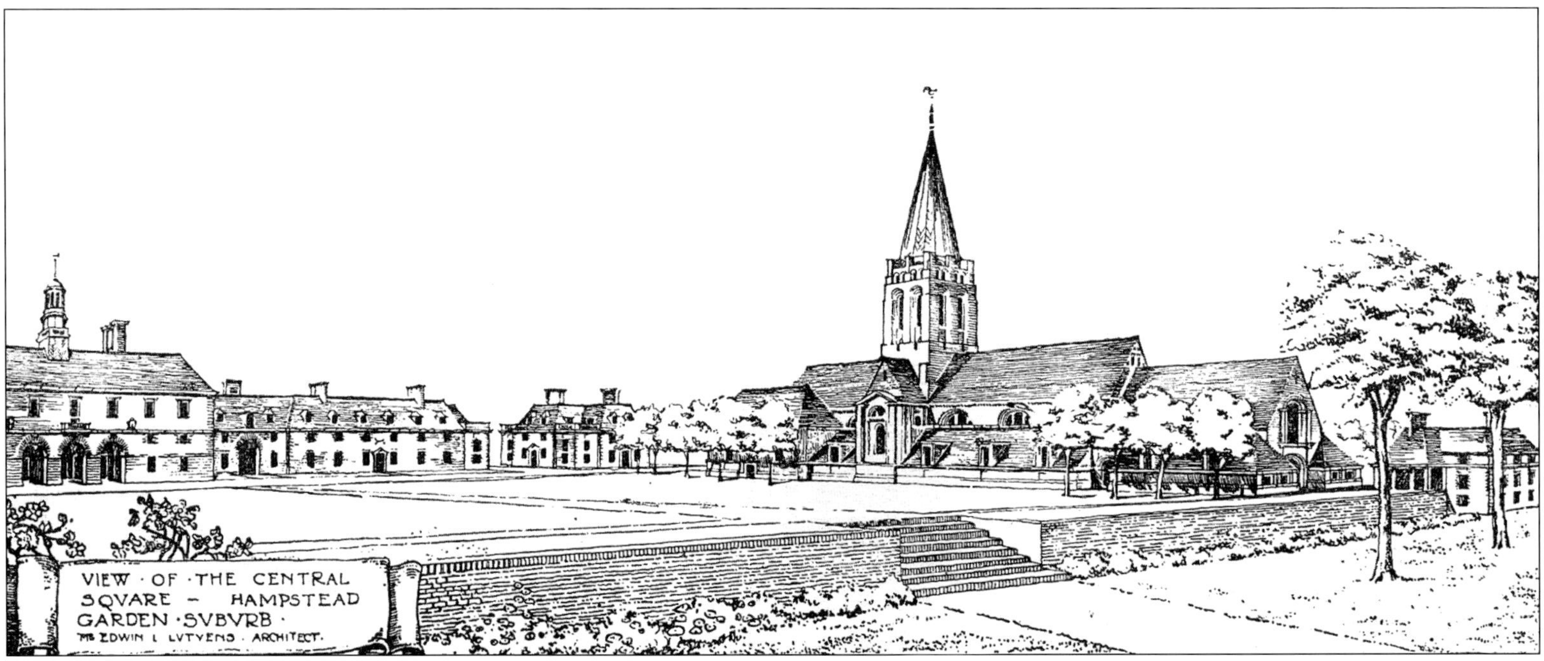

Fig. 42: As a young architect, Lutyens designed the development at Central Square in the raised centre of Hampstead Garden Suburb.

Lutyens' decision to lay out the living accommodations of the British and Indian staff of the colonial government in Imperial Delhi as a garden city, around an acropolis of the Viceroy's office and administrative buildings, is still recognisable today in the ground-plan and aerial view of the city (Fig. 40). It has often been criticised for not having links with the socio-political utopias of its models.

The planners of Imperial Delhi had hardly any other option than to decide, finally, on a very free residential development and one single shopping centre at Connaught Circus. Quite simply, the potential 50,000 inhabitants had insufficient spending power for grand boulevards with shops, cafés and restaurants. On the other hand, the town's almost unlimited space allowed the employees of the colonial government to be allocated generously laid out plots of parkland with grand bungalows.

The maharajas who would have liked their residences built directly on King's Way would, at most, have provided a touch of big-city luxury. Yet, to the Viceroy, that intention seemed inappropriate, even presumptuous. So the greatest of all the avenues in Imperial Delhi was not lined with residential or commercial property, but with large trees specifically selected for that purpose. Thus, the largest of all garden cities was not built in England, but in the India of the Raj.

The town's characteristic blend of garden city with acropolis in the centre has continually attracted criticism of New Delhi. In 1968, Stan Nilsson wrote the following about the town plan of the capital: "The street plan of the city is not successful either. It is a confusing web of triangles stacked in hexagons with a roundabout at each junction. Its debt to the Garden City makes it less of a city than a giant cantonment. Its bungalows stand isolated on large plots, and its streets are empty of people and urban vitality. Even after sixty years (and a considerable growth in the population) parts of it retain a suburban tranquillity: at night, dogs come out of the houses to sleep in the streets where they are guaranteed an undisturbed peace. King's Way (now Raj Path) was always purely ceremonial, for it leads nowhere that anyone wants to go, and except during Republic Day parades, it is lifeless."[16]

2.6 Canberra (1912)

In the two decades before and after the turn of the century the British Crown increasingly needed to reorganize its continually growing colonial possessions in all parts of the world, providing them with a unified judicial system, and allowing them their own identity while retaining their required loyalty to the Crown. Here, the purpose was not a renunciation of Britain's imperial claims, but a clever calculation intended to stabilize a global empire that could hardly be more varied in its parts.

It was a part of this British strategy to build new capitals with magnificent architecture in its most important Crown possessions. Almost simultaneously there arose:

- An administrative centre for the recently unified South African colonies in the monumental Union Buildings of 1910 to 1913 for Pretoria by Herbert Baker.
- A new seat for the Indian Viceroy as part of an axial plan for Palladian Imperial Delhi from 1912 to 1931.
- A bourgeois capital for the relatively independent Australia from 1912, with the new capital, Canberra, situated away from all the important trading centres.

In his manual on urban design, one of the planners of the new Imperial Delhi, H.V. Lanchester, later described the simultaneous plans for Canberra stating: "When it was decided to provide a new capital for Federated Australia, and Canberra was chosen as an appropriate location, the site was generally acclaimed as presenting good opportunities for development, and it was the more unfortunate, therefore, that the conditions of the competition for a plan were not such as could be accepted by British designers, who declined to enter. However, a number of plans were prepared in America and on the Continent, and that by Mr W.B. Griffin, of Chicago, which was

16 S. Nilsson: *European Architecture in India*, London 1968.

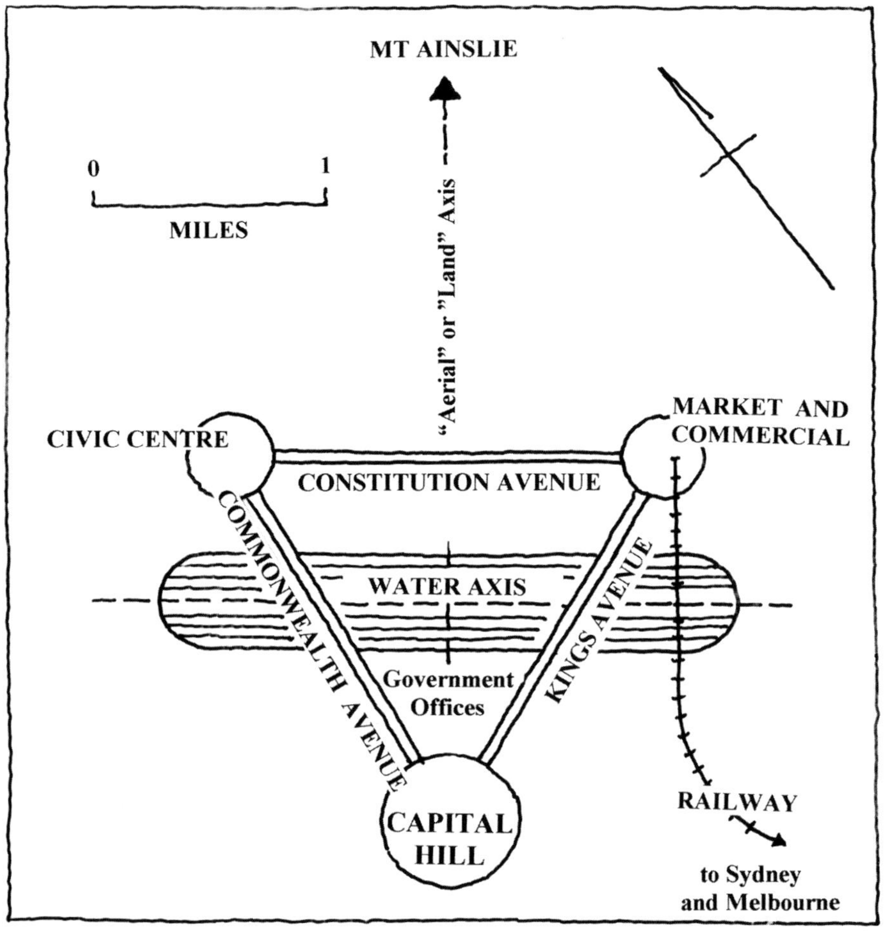

Fig. 43: Contemporaneous to Lutyens' plan for New Delhi, W.B. Griffin emerged as winner of an international competition for the new Australian capital, Canberra. It was similar to the plan of Imperial Delhi and the century-old plan of Washington, D.C.

selected, is of marked distinction and displays many points of originality. While carefully considered as regards the allocation of areas for various purposes, the scheme binds these together by a well-devised system of axial routes, and the whole gains firmness by the orientation of the plan on a main axis linking up two summits. As this axis crosses the principal valley at right angles the degree of symmetry thus secured allows for many minor variations in detail which give interest to the plan without allowing it to fall into confusion."[17]

Lanchester made a critical comparison between Canberra and the layout for the new Delhi which was eventually developed without his collaboration: "The outline of the scheme follows the Renaissance tradition of triangulations with focal points. The main axes N. to S. and E. to W. have good terminal features, but some of the subsidiary vistas are badly related to them and are aligned awkwardly on the principal buildings. The prepossession in favour of the equilateral triangle has involved the designers in a series of problems that are imperfectly resolved."[18]

Griffin's design for Canberra was distinguished, especially in comparison to all other participants in the competition,[19] by a simple geometric linking of a street network in the Beaux-Arts style[20] with the most important focal points in the landscape. In retrospect, this concept was closer to hand than the other due, in part, to the very dynamic plans, of E. Saarinen and the Baroque competition designs also presented by Schanfelberg, Rees and Gummer.

The *New York Times* devoted a whole page to the plan on June 2, 1912, and quoted the planner as follows: "I do not know if I shall be called to Australia in order to supervise the construction of the new town. I hope so. I even expect it. It would only be right. For nobody in the world can realise my ideas better than I myself.

I do not know which architectural direction I am to take. I have planned a town which resembles no other town in the world. I conceived it in a way which I assumed at the time to be unacceptable to any government in the world. I designed an ideal town – a town that corresponds to my ideal of a town of the future.

17 H.V. Lanchester: *The Art of Town Planning*, London 1925, p. 200.
18 Ibid., p. 204f.
19 Cf. David Van Zanten: *Walter Burley Griffins Plan für die australische Hauptstadt Canberra*, Munich 1988, p. 322ff.
20 The so-called Beaux-Arts style in town planning developed especially in the USA following the World Exhibition of Chicago in 1893. Important examples are Daniel Burnham's concluding plans for Washington, D.C. and his plan for Chicago at the beginning of the century.
21 *New York Times*, June 2, 1912
22 David Van Zanten: op. cit., p. 322ff.

I am what one might call a naturalist in architecture. I do not believe in any school of architecture. I believe rather in an architecture which is the logical result of the environment in which it is to be realised. I have built houses in Chicago which ought to do justice to the requirements of the place. They do not accord with the usual types of houses ... I took care to adapt them to the climatic and topographical conditions of Chicago.

Naturally it is difficult to describe such buildings. They are not like the buildings of any school ... Our national architecture after all has to be first developed. When it has been formed it will be an architecture that corresponds to the climatic conditions; it remains to be seen on which principles it is oriented.

I have never been in Australia, but I have an idea of the Australian climate and thus I also have a vague idea what sort of architecture I should recommend for the future Australian capital. But I am not yet in a position to expound all the details. Australia is a newer country than the USA. It has no architectural tradition. Its architectural ideals are not yet influenced by any imported schools ... I believe that in such a country free from traditions I ought to be in a position to develop a very beautiful architectural type which is in accord with the climatic peculiarities and harmonizes with its typography. I would very much like to try that."[21]

In 1912, Lord Hardinge, the British Viceroy in India, had sent copies from London of the plans for Canberra in connection with his task of building a new capital for British India: "How curious they must have seemed to him! ... The initiative for the Australian federation had stemmed from the Australians themselves. They had selected Canberra's architects through open competition – derided by the British experts – and won by a clever young Yankee. The architects of Pretoria and New Delhi on the other hand had been determined by the colonial administration with the approval of the London experts. And naturally that was reflected in the results. The Pretoria plan was an optimistic symbol of the Anglo-Boer Union, seemingly spontaneous, in reality however imposed by military power. And the plan for New Delhi was the proud expression of British rule over a foreign race."[22]

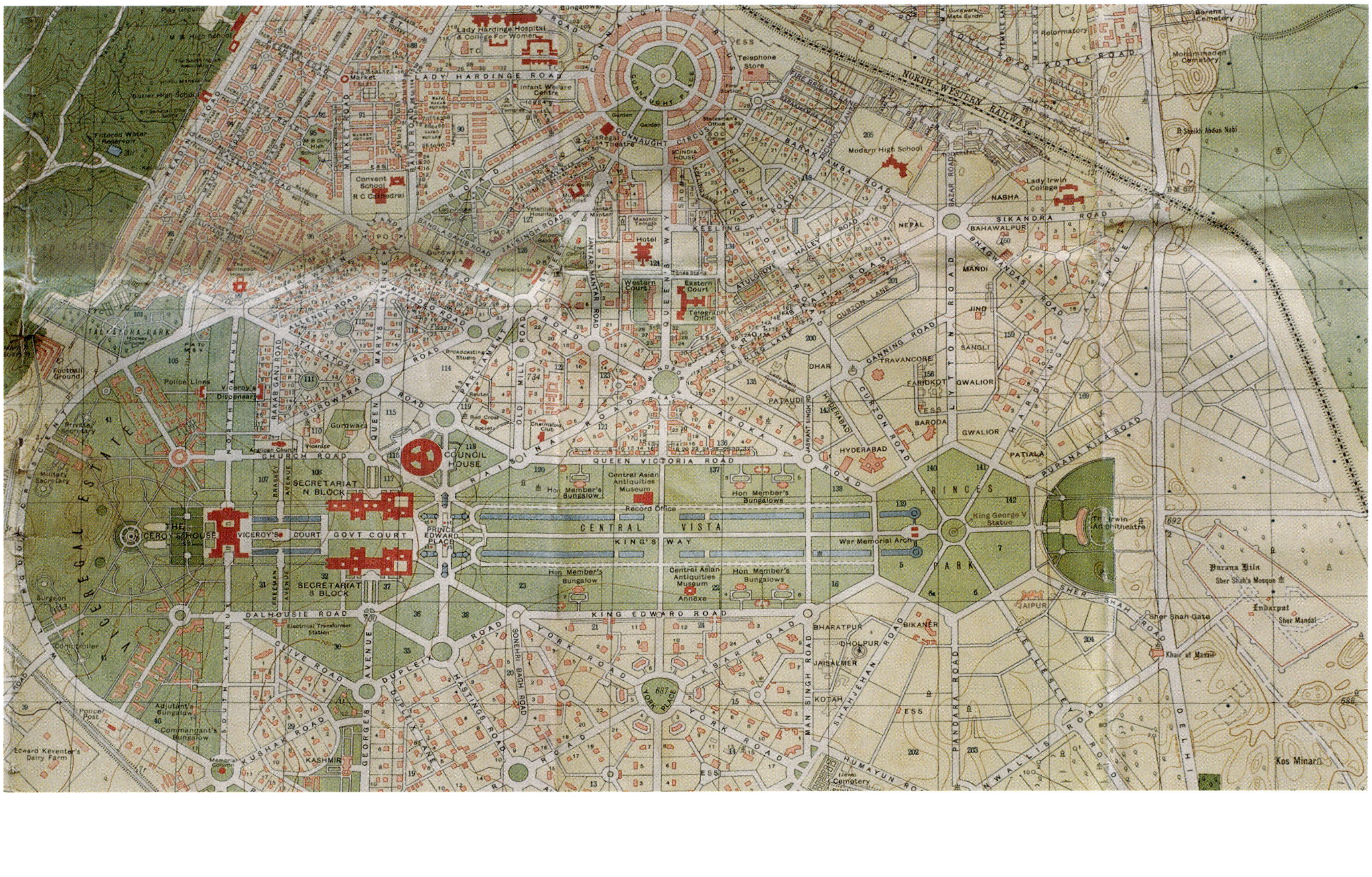

Fig. 44: In the plan for Canberra, the three important functions Capitol Hill, the Market, and the Commercial Centre are grouped together in the Civic Centre, whereas in the plan for Imperial Delhi, a triangle links the Viceroy's Palace, the commercial centre of Connaught Circus and King George V Memorial.

Fig. 45: Hexagonal and octagonal systems of avenues are oriented on important natural and architectural features in Canberra's plan.

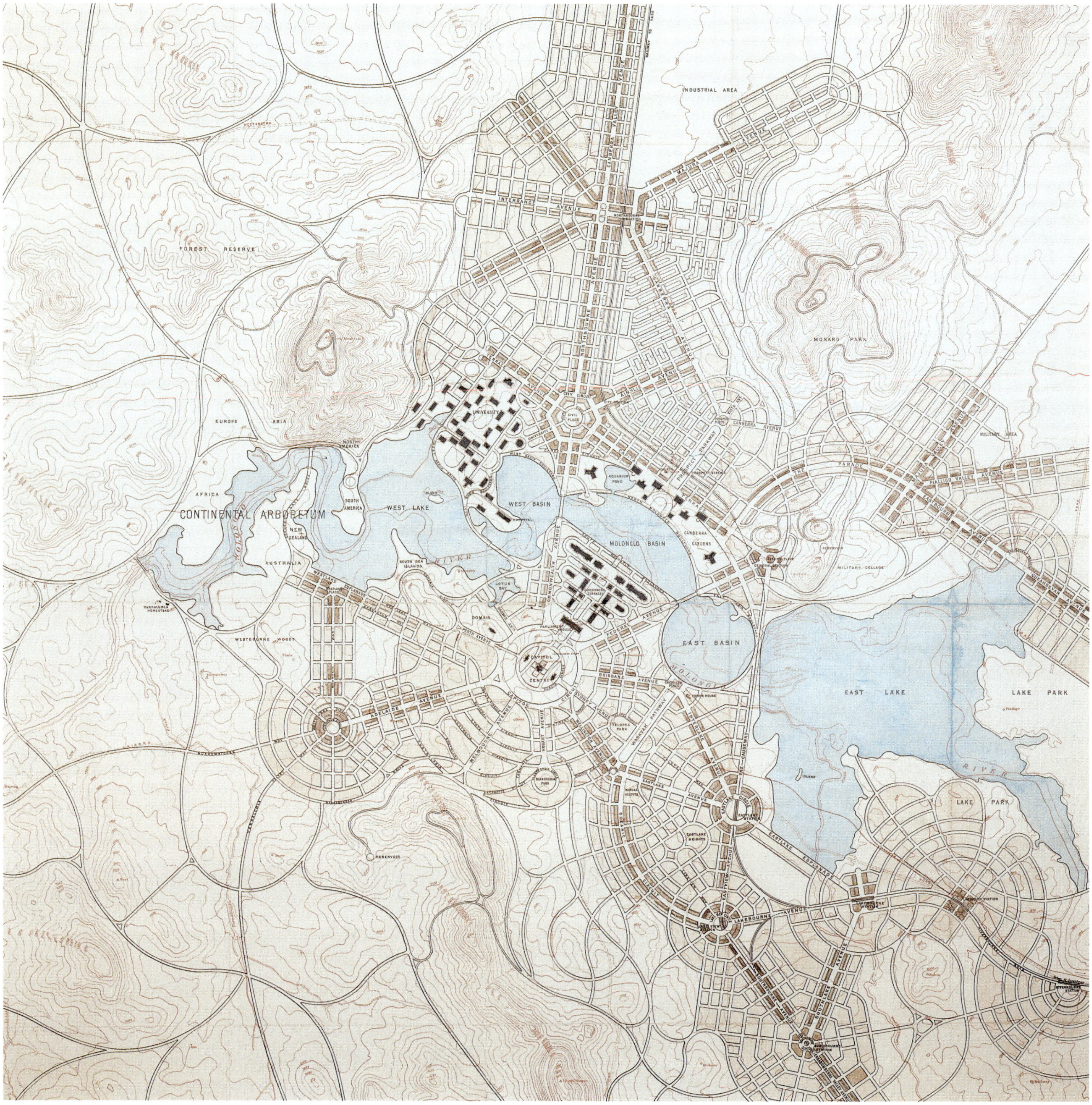

2.7 Berlin: A Last Attempt at an Imperial Design (1937)

23 A. Speer: *Architecture 1932–1942*, Brussels 1985, p. 45.
24 Ibid., p. 46.

Edwin Lutyens' architecture in India is not only to be viewed as the remarkable achievement of an architect-personality possessed of a creative desire, but also as an architecturally logical phase at the end of a late Neo-Classicism fostered by the designs of the empire. It is a phase that adopts Roman, French and American symbols and shapes so as to fuse them into a new imperial spirit. It is not only possible to reconstruct this process in the imperial architecture of New Delhi, but also in its forerunners such as in the architecture of Washington, D.C., capital of the United States of America (cf. Chapter 2.4).

Let us leave the antecedents of Imperial Delhi and look forward in time, toward possible successors or imitators of the Raj's capital. This approach would inevitably lead to the architectural concept that attempted to combine many features of the imperial architecture of the last two thousand years expressed in Albert Speer's plan for a large axis in Berlin, a plan that, fortunately, never came to fruition: "On the 30th of January 1937, Hitler informed the Reichstag about his modernization plan for the German capitals. On the same day, he named Albert Speer to the post of Inspector General of Buildings for the Renovation of the Federal Capital, bestowing upon him the powers and authority of a secretary of state. At the age of thirty-two, the young plenipotentiary inspector established the offices of the G.B.I. (General Bau Inspektor) in the former Academy of Fine Arts next to the Brandenburg Gate. From that moment on Berlin was planned to become the capital of Europe, an area that would stretch from the Atlantic Ocean to the Ural Mountains, and be dominated, politically, economically and culturally by the new Germany. The city would take on the functions of a continental metropolis, and Speer was to lay the foundations of monuments, palaces and squares which would form the focus and symbolic centre of a centralized, industrialized and mobilized continent."[23]

The north-south axis was planned to be located in the centre of Berlin, a Champs Elysées of a size previously unknown. Ministries and administrative buildings were lined along this axis – the headquarters of the Armed Forces, the Secret Service, the Foreign Office, the Ministry for Propaganda, and others, however, large business enterprises such as Krupp and Siemens, were also to be included: "Dominated on its Northern end by the cupola of the Great Hall and extending South to the distant Süd-Bahnhof, this avenue of superlatives was to unfold its granite facades, its gardens and parades, fountains, monuments and colossal triumphal Arch on a five-kilometre stretch. It was not a mere rectilinear corridor. The grand axis was an articulated suite of seven differentiated monumental spaces."[24]

A plaza with a gigantic triumphal arch formed a high point in the succession of buildings, monuments and open spaces: "The plaza was to be crowned by Hitler's great arch or 'Arch of Triumph,' as he only occasionally called it. Napoleon's Arc de Triomphe on the Place

Fig. 46: Design for the Great Hall on the north-south axis in Berlin, photographic model, architect: Albert Speer, 1939.

Fig. 47: The capitals on the New Reichskanzlei (Reich Chancellery), designed by Albert Speer. Like Edwin Lutyens' capitals for Viceroy's House in Delhi, Speer's capitals represent an attempt to introduce new ideas into traditional architectural forms.

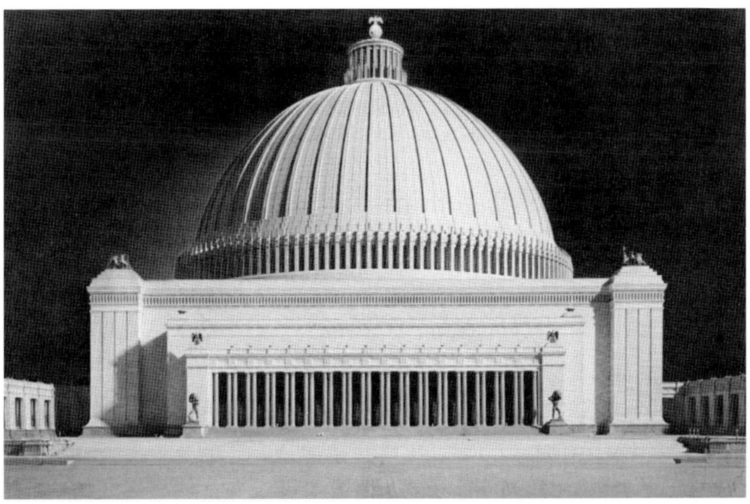

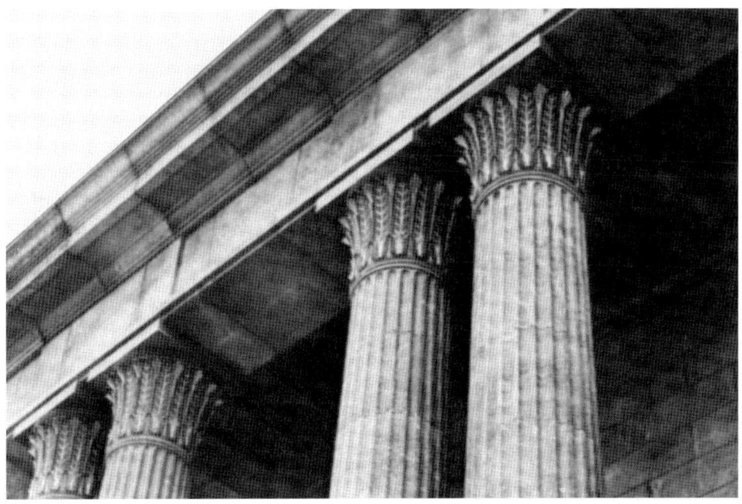

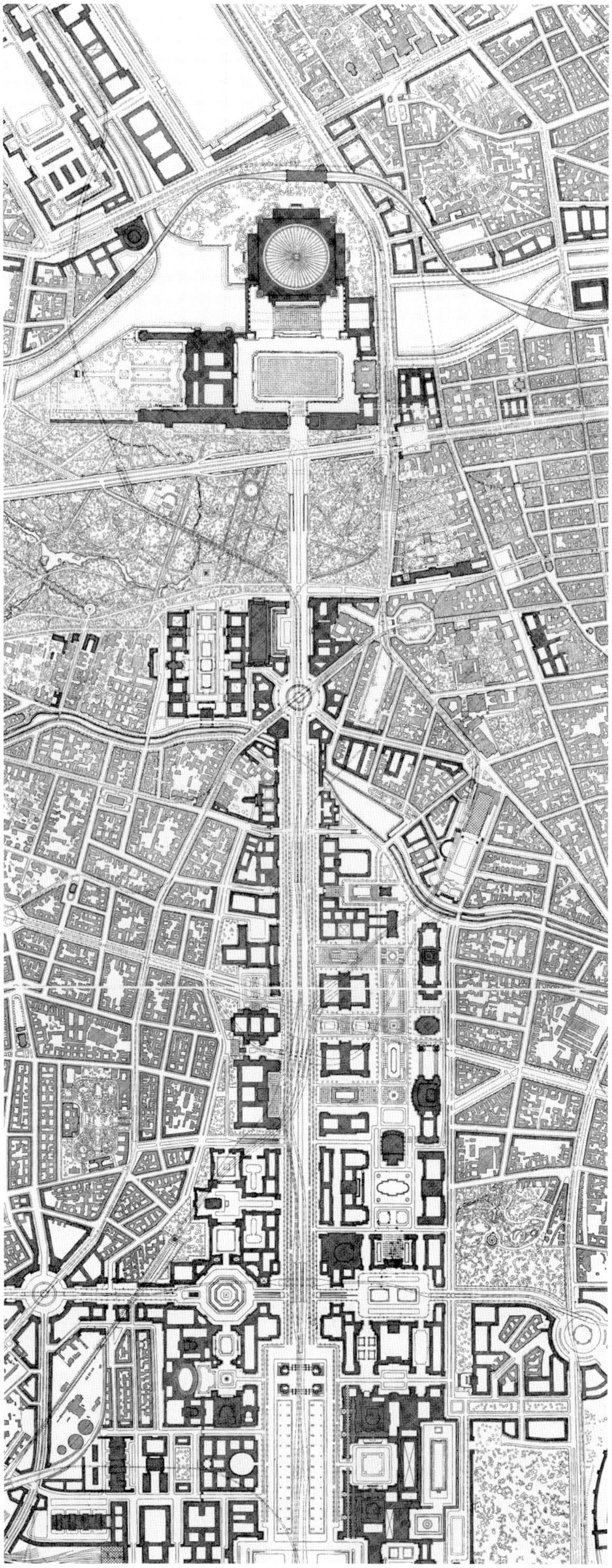

de l'Etoile, which is one hundred and sixty feet high certainly presents a monumental appearance and provides a majestic terminus to the Champs Elysées. Our triumphal arch, five hundred and fifty feet wide, three hundred and ninety-two feet deep, and three hundred and eighty-six feet high, would have towered over all the other buildings on this southern portion of the avenue and would literally have dwarfed them."[25]

At the other end of the north-south axis the Great Hall formed a high point: "This structure, the greatest assembly hall in the world ever conceived up to that time, consisted of one vast hall that could hold between one hundred and fifty and one hundred and eighty thousand persons standing ... In a sense the Pantheon in Rome had served as our model. The Berlin dome was also to contain a round opening for light, but this opening alone would be one hundred and fifty-two feet in diameter, larger than the entire dome of the Pantheon (142 feet) and of St Peter's (145 feet). The interior would contain sixteen times the volume of St Peter's.

Designs of such a scale naturally indicate a kind of chronic megalomania, which is reason enough to dwell on these grandiose plans. Yet that broad boulevard, those new railroad stations with their underground communications, are not so excessive by present-day standards when skyscrapers and public buildings all over the world have reached similar proportions. Perhaps it was less their size than the way they violated the human scale that made them abnormal. The great domed hall, Hitler's future Chancellery, Goering's grandiose ministry, the Soldier's Hall and the triumphal arch – I saw all these buildings with Hitler's political eyes. Once, when we were contemplating the model city, he took my arm and with moist eyes confided: Now do you understand why we are building all this on such a scale? The capital of the German Empire – if only my health were good ..."[26]

"Speer avoided the vacuity of its monumental counterparts in Chandigarh, Brasilia, New Delhi and Washington, where giant buildings were dwarfed by the immensity of their surrounding spaces. He cannot be accused of having badly used the means of his art or of having muddled the elements of his plan."[27]

Despite our perplexity today when confronted by this intended limitless demonstration of power in Berlin, the example is extremely useful as a non-polemic, and also for a critical recognition of Edwin Lutyens' achievements in town planning some twenty-three years earlier. Essentially, what marks the difference between Lutyens and Speer is that the one had the good fortune to work for a great King, while the other had the misfortune to serve Adolf Hitler.

There is no lack of interesting parallels between the architecture of Lutyens and Speer. To recognize and thus reveal all of them would focus too heavily on one architect at

Fig. 48: The north-south axis for Berlin planned in 1937.

the expense of the other. It is important to note one further detail: in Imperial Delhi, Lutyens took pains to crown the pillars in the Viceroy's palace with a specially designed "Indian" capital (Fig. 165). Latrobe had similarly done so about two and a half centuries earlier in the capital at Washington, D.C. (Fig. 164). Now Speer, also, was trying to embellish the shape of the capitals on the New Imperial Office (Reichskanzlei) in Berlin with some new ideas (Fig. 47).

For a balanced judgement of the strengths and weaknesses of related planning and architectural concepts such as those of Washington, D.C., New Delhi and Berlin, we have, until today, simply lacked the necessary historical distance. In the past, a separation of the architecture from its corresponding political background appeared neither possible nor even desirable.

25 Ibid., p. 46.
26 Albert Speer: *Inside the Third Reich*, London 1971.
27 Albert Speer: op. cit., p. 49.

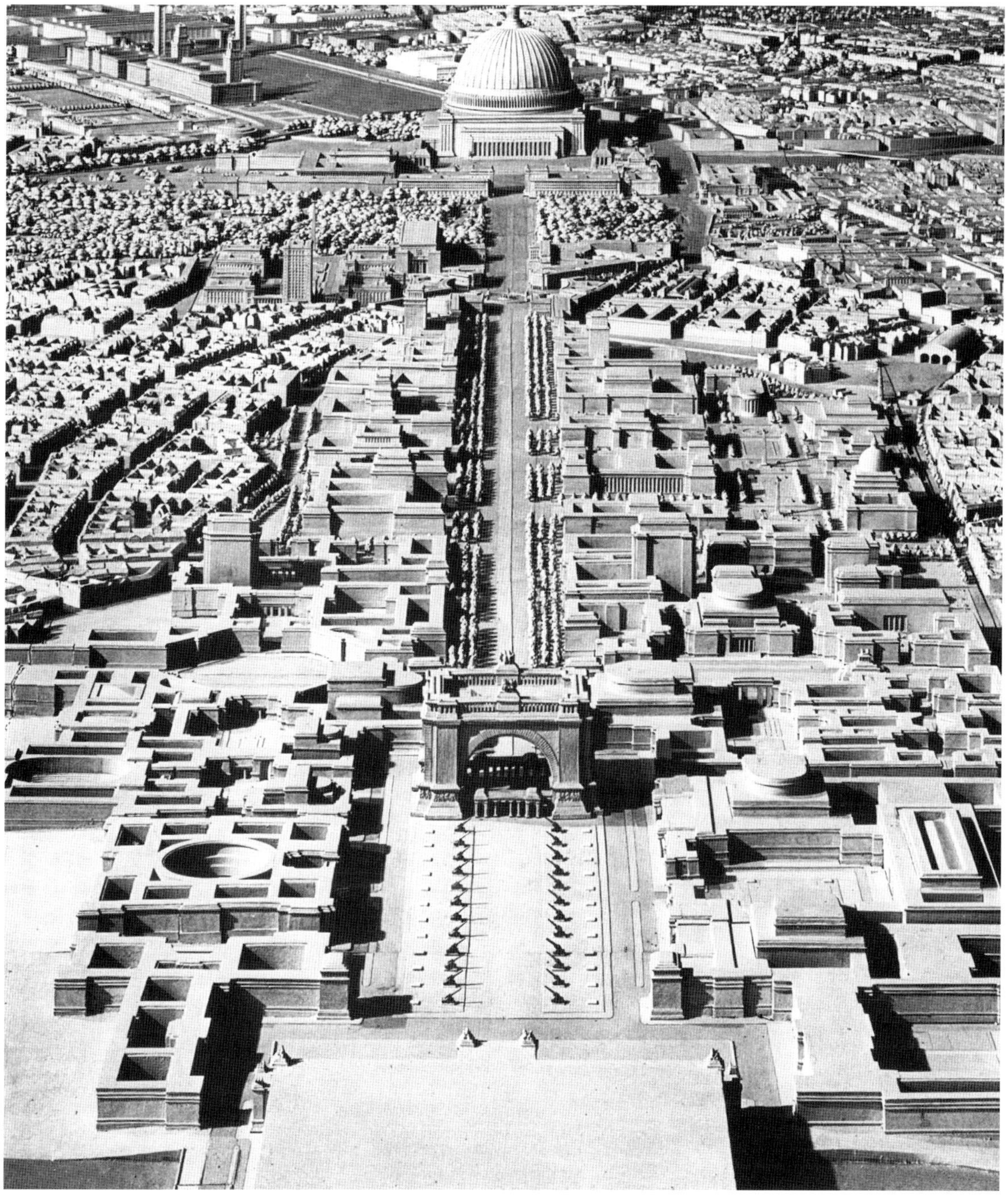

Fig. 49: Design for the north-south axis in Berlin, architect: Albert Speer, 1939.

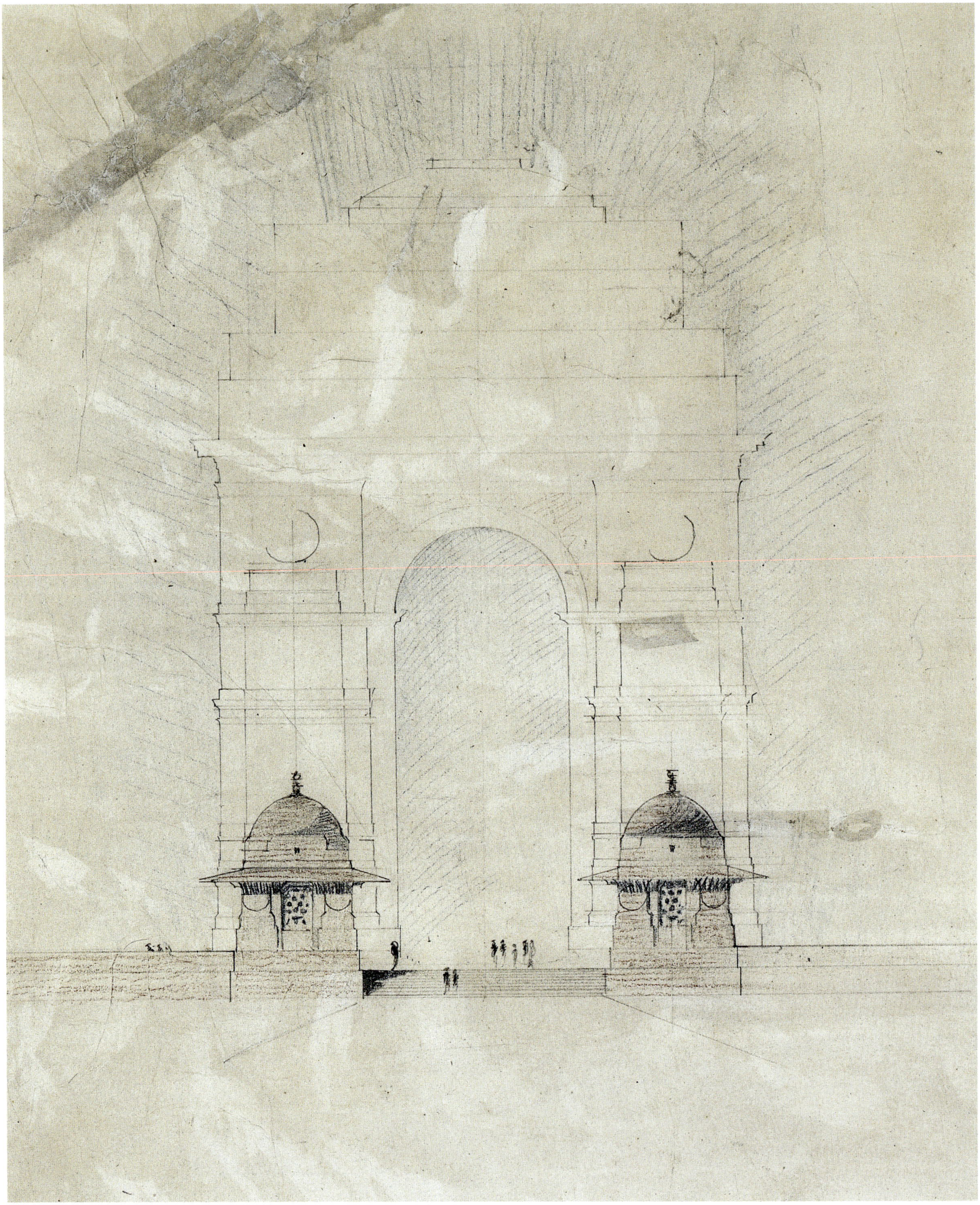

3 Elements and Symbols for Imperial Delhi

Fig. 50: Lutyens' second plan for the All India War Memorial has two chattris (Mughal-style pavilions) in front of the triumphal arch. (To quote from Lutyens: "Chattris are stupid useless things," September 16, 1913.)

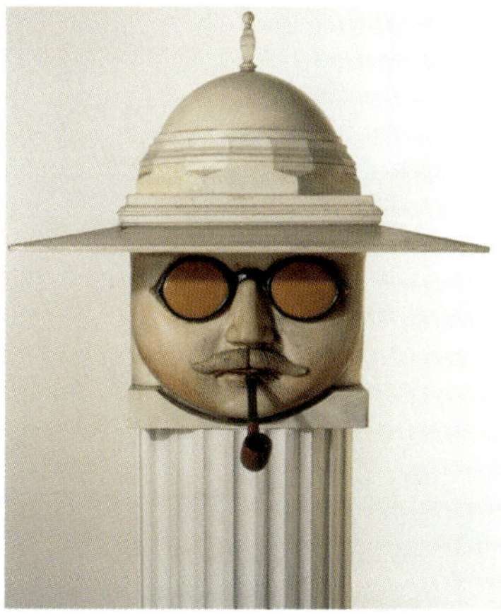

Fig. 51: Caricature bust of Sir Edwin Lutyens in the RIBA library with a hat in the form of the Indian cupola on Viceroy's House in New Delhi.

When Edwin Lutyens received the commission to design a new capital city for the British Raj, he was very well aware of the complexity of the task. For Lutyens, the adoption of well-known architectural patterns did not come into question because there was a lack of monumental examples marked by imperial ambitions.

Town plans such as those for Milet in Asia Minor of the fifth century B.C., or for New York in the eighteenth century, with their regular street patterns, were acceptable as models for a military cantonment, a type that already appeared in many tedious examples throughout India at the beginning of the twentieth century. Alternatively, concentric town plans such as those of thirteenth-century Peking, or Karlsruhe in the eighteenth century hardly came into question because they expressed an absolute world order and system of government.

The spirit of urban planning in the early twentieth century was linked to a series of complex geometrical town plans such as those of Washington, D.C. and Canberra. These plans made it possible to illustrate a strongly differentiated system of meanings, symbols and shapes. From this stage, a long process of decision-making (see Chapter 4.2) led, decisively in the case of Imperial Delhi, to a town plan that was similarly full of references to the geometry of British freemasonry, Hindu mandala geometry, non-figurative Islamic ornament and, most importantly, to the axial and symmetrical self-consciousness of the British royal tradition.

Both the King in London and the Viceroy in Delhi would have preferred to see a capital for India that was directly linked to the architecture of the great Islamic Mughal tradition. In this sense, the cityscapes of Calcutta and Bombay were stamped with a blend of English Gothic and Islamic domes and keel arches. The architects of New Delhi despised these patterns, but on the other hand, they could not and did not want to rid themselves completely of Indian influence. Alongside typical European symbols such as the obelisk, column, urn, round arch, and dome, the buildings for British India introduced Indian motifs such as the keel arch, lotus-blossom, snake, elephant and stupa.

In retrospect, this blend was attractive because of an obviously successful synthesis that was comparable to the combination of Chinese and European stylistic elements at the beginning of the twentieth century in European art and architecture. It also had the advantage, though certainly not intended, in that the architecture of Imperial Delhi proved to be entirely acceptable to the new Indian national government after the withdrawal of Great Britain.

All the architectural symbols of Imperial Delhi were ultimately chosen or newly designed by Edwin Lutyens by 1931. There was a single important criterion for the choice – each case had to make a formal contribution to the representation of the superiority and legitimacy of British world power. Contributions to the representation of an imperial order were drawn from a large variety of models but most can be traced back to ancient Rome. The graphic work by Giovanni Battista Piranesi (1720–78) proved to be a rich store of quotations for Lutyens.[2]

Imperial Delhi's town-planning elements, its palaces, ministries (or secretariats), avenues, historic buildings, and residences, fit together to form a network of sight lines, traffic axes, geometrical plazas, and parkland according to the principles of the "City Beautiful" and Beaux-Arts town plans in America at the beginning of the twentieth century. Because the Viceroy was also dreaming of a garden city on the model of Raymond Unwin's plan,[3] there arose, in the arid plain south of the old Mughal city of Delhi, a unique blend of the town-planning ideals of that age.

1 Cf. Chapter 4.2.
2 Cf. for example Figs. 72, 149.
3 Cf. Raymond Unwin: *Town Planning in Practice, an Introduction to the Art of Designing Cities and Suburbs*, London 1911.

3.1 Triangle and Hexagram: Masonic Symbols, Hindu Cosmology or Mughal Geometry?

No city in the world has derived its plan structure from the geometric shapes of the equilateral triangle and the hexagram or hexagon as consistently as New Delhi. These forms apply as much to the town plan (Fig. 56), as to the individual buildings (Fig. 79), and to a certain degree even the furniture, the fountains (Fig. 107), and the structuring of the facades (Fig. 86). Upon closer examination, however, the consistent repetition of forms only applies to Edwin Lutyens' contributions. His colleagues and successors, H. Baker, H.A.N. Medd and R.T. Russel, were less decisive in their choice of a formal canon or proportional system.

Lutyens' use of triangle, hexagon and hexagram, might be explained by membership in a Freemason's lodge, or by Jewish descent. On the other hand, the explanation provided by his contemporaries, that it was a geometric or mathematical fad, is certainly too superficial.

Influences of Masonic geometry

Admittedly, a careful examination of the attendance list at the Freemasons' lodge in Delhi reveals that neither Lutyens nor any of his colleagues took part in any event at the local lodge. Had they been active Freemasons they would have been duty-bound to attend.

Jewish descent is ruled out in the case of Lutyens. His family, which moved from Holland to Hamburg in the eighteenth century and then in 1740 to England, was Protestant and deeply religious. Therefore it was not the Star of David which determined the structure and architecture of Imperial Delhi.

If one stops to reflect on the marked associations that the English educated upper classes had with freemasonry, and that the Royal Family was also actively engaged in its Masonic lodges in London during the nineteenth century (see Fig. 55), then this link may explain how the triangle and hexagram, at the beginning of the twentieth century in Great Britain, represented a geometric abbreviation for an elite tradition of thought and social consciousness.

Since 1897, Lutyens had been married to Lady Emily, a daughter of the first Earl of Lytton, and was a welcome guest amongst the English nobility, but not just because of his wife's lineage. Her parentage, however, admitted him into the best homes in the country and

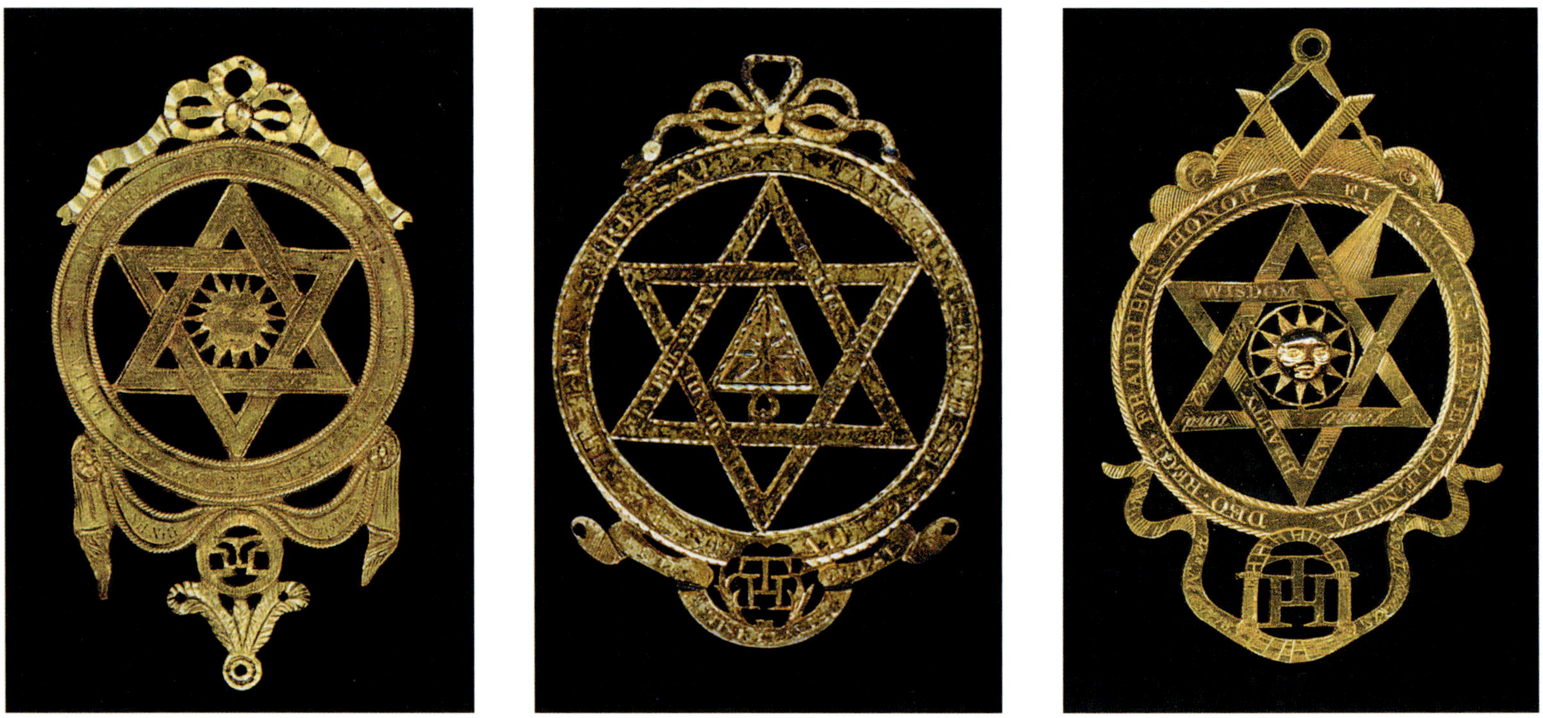

Fig. 52: Since the eighteenth century, members of the Royal Arch of English Freemasons have worn the hexagram in a circle as their jewel. Since most members of the Royal Family during Edwin Lutyens' time were Freemasons, the hexagram was presumably not a coincidental choice for the basic pattern of Imperial Delhi's town plan.

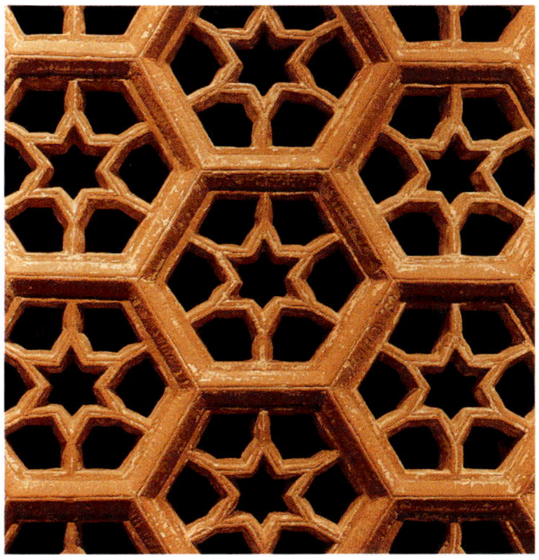
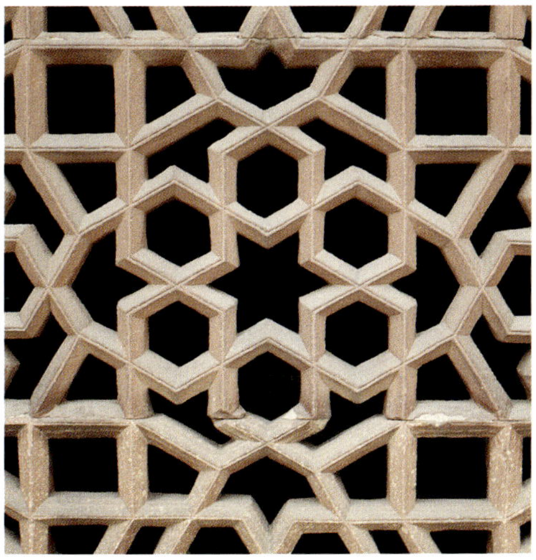
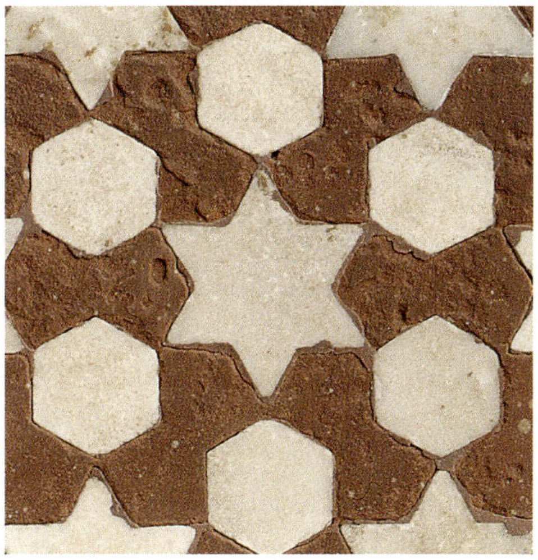

Fig. 53: Hexagram and hexagon are also elements frequently used in Indian Mughal architecture. Lutyens' plan for Imperial Delhi was clearly intended to demonstrate a link between the crown and the past splendour of the Mughals.

provided him with both an interesting and an affluent clientele for English country houses. When the King himself finally commissioned Lutyens to design Imperial Delhi the symbolism of geometry in freemasonry was probably close at hand.

The most elite of the London lodges, the Royal Arch, had the hexagram in the circle as its centrepiece (Fig. 52). The star was produced by two triangles, one pointing to heaven and the other to earth. It was the symbol of omnipotence that Freemasons describe as the "Great Architect of the Universe."

Lutyens was also aware of the significance of geometry in freemasonry as the explanatory pattern of the universe: "Geometry, the first and noblest of sciences, is the basis on which the superstructure of Masonry is erected. By geometry, we may curiously trace Nature through her various windings, to her most concealed recesses. By it we may discover the power, the wisdom, and the goodness of the grand Artificer of the universe, and view with amazing delight the beautiful proportions, which connect and grace his vast machine. By it we may discover how the planets move in their different orbs, and mathematically demonstrate their various revolutions. By it we may rationally account for the return of the seasons, and the mixed variety of scenes which they display to the discerning eye. Numberless worlds are around us, all framed by the same Divine Artist, which roll through the vast expanse, and are all beautiful proportions which connect and grace his vast machine, and are all conducted by the same unerring law of Nature. How must we then improve? With what grand ideas must such knowledge fill our minds; and how worthy is it of attention of all rational beings. A survey of Nature, and the observation of its beautiful proportions first determined man to imitate the divine plan, and to study symmetry and order. This gave rise to societies, and birth to every useful art. The architect began to design, and the plans which he laid down, improved by experience and time, produced some of those excellent works which will be the admiration of future ages. Thus, from the commencement of the world, we may trace the foundation of Masonry."[4]

Another possible link between Lutyens and freemasonry should be mentioned. He was a casual acquaintance of Pandit Motilal Nehru, the father of the first Prime Minister of India. Pandit Nehru was a well-known Indian Freemason. "Lutyens liked the friendly old Nationalist, enjoyed his wit, and took him over to the buildings. He said that if Gandhi had been here, he would certainly have brought him too, though Gandhi deplored the waste of money on architectural piles. I said it was all Indian work, and much better worth doing than spinning; that India, where she once led in the fine arts, is now deplorably behind the times, with half-baked statesmanship and agitation the only live thing. I told him of our search for Indian materials that would wear, and the hopelessness of it. He said he had not thought of building as an education to the Indian mason craftsman. So I hope to get him interested. He wears a black coat and white jodhpurs, on which I drew buttons, so that he looked like an English bishop – and told him that was all he was fit for if he did not help India in her material needs."'[5]

4 W. Preston cit. in C.F.W. Dyer: *Symbolism in Craft Freemasonry*, London 1976.
5 Christopher Hussey: *The Life of Sir Edwin Lutyens*, London 1950, p. 426.

With all these historical, social and intellectual guidelines it was not surprising that Lutyens, perhaps in moments of fantasy, or better, genius, made use of a formal canon which was immediately understood by English society and the Indian upper classes.

There is one other possibility of interpreting Edwin Lutyens' great love of the triangle and hexagram – at least in theory – by exploring the meaning of these shapes in Hinduism. Similarities between the geometric symbols of the Hindus and the English freemasons forcibly struck English travellers to India at the beginning of the twentieth century. L. Vilbert wrote about the Indians and about the freemasons in India: "... they (the Hindus) have a definite symbolism of the circle and triangle. Thus the triangle, point downwards, symbolizes Shiva, the destroying fire; point upwards it is Vishnu, the preserving water; and the two conjoined in the circle of Brahma form the symbol known as the Chakra, the magic weapon of Vishnu. But this is our Royal Arch Jewel."[6] Nevertheless, Lutyens' interest in Hinduism was admittedly slight since his judgement about Hindu temple architecture was anything but flattering: "Veneered joinery in stone, concrete and marble on a gigantic scale there is lots of, but no real architecture ... Personally I do not believe there is any real Indian architecture or any great tradition. There are just spurts by various mushroom dynasties with as much intellect in them as any other art nouveau."[7]

Influences of Mughal architecture

It only remains for us to examine the formal language of Mughal architecture as another potentially influential factor for Edwin Lutyens' geometric designs of the city and its buildings. The theological ban on anthropomorphic portrayals (as blasphemous to God) in Islam also led to extremely inventive geometric ornamentation and ground plan arrangements in Mughal India. The Viceroy sent the architects of Imperial Delhi, who showed little interest in Mughal design, on two study tours of the most important Mughal buildings.

In this formal visual language of Mughal forms, hexagonal shapes occupied as important a place as octagonal ones. Upon the very plain chosen for the new capital of the Raj, between the Jumna River and The Ridge (cf. plan in Fig. 60), there are at Humayun's tomb the most impressive examples of hexagonal inlay work in red sandstone and white marble. Both of the facings on the Humayun tomb appear almost to anticipate the town plan of Imperial Delhi (Fig. 57). Had the Viceroy not expressly wanted British India to make reference to the conquered empire of the Islamic Mughal emperors?

For Lutyens and his colleagues, the Viceroy's desire for the inclusion of Indo-Islamic architectural elements was an abomination. Moreover, nothing was further from the minds of the town planners and architects, with their notions of Neo-Palladian stylistic elements and British imperial building traditions, than borrowing from the local building traditions.

If Mughal architecture was hardly used as a direct model for the absolutely hexagonal plan of New Delhi, just as the hexagonal symbolism of Hinduism or the geometry of contemporary Freemasons' lodges, then there is little room to make plausible lateral connections to any of these traditions.

6 L. Vilbert: *Freemasonry in India*, manuscript, London 1920, Library of Freemason Hall.

7 C. Percy, J. Ridley: *The Letters of Edwin Lutyens to his Wife Lady Emily*, London 1985, p. 223.

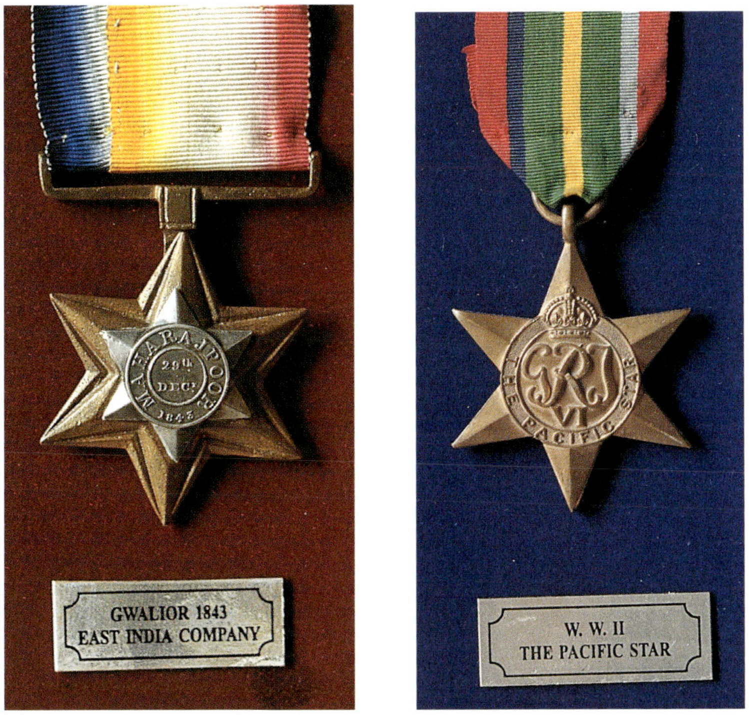

Fig. 54: The hexagram appeared in the nineteenth century on the medals of the East India Company, and then in the twentieth century in India, as a military decoration of World War II.

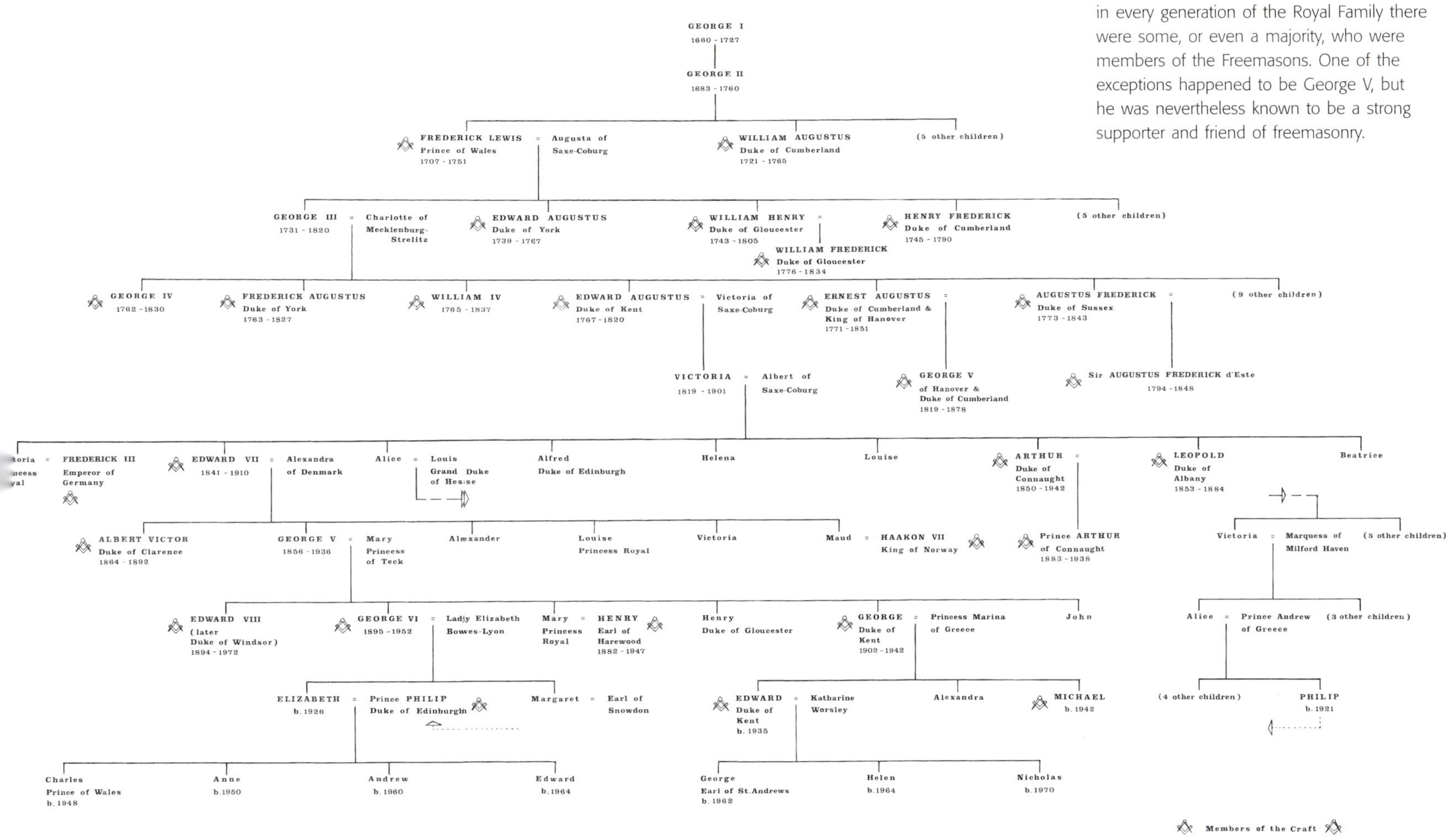

Fig. 55: From the eighteenth century onwards, in every generation of the Royal Family there were some, or even a majority, who were members of the Freemasons. One of the exceptions happened to be George V, but he was nevertheless known to be a strong supporter and friend of freemasonry.

The spirit of the age as a synthesis of different formal influences

Either the age was one of synthesis or we are looking for inappropriate models for the plan. If we assume that it was syncretic, then we believe this historical moment to be a decisive moment, similar to those of other historical epochs. Often the spirit of the age concentrates formal experiences and preferences without the availability of appropriate detailed research into their sources.

In the case of Edwin Lutyens' hexagonal design patterns it is quite conceivable that:

- The architect, in his private and professional life in London, was constantly exposed to the theories of the socially predominant Freemasons and continued to be influenced by them for a long time thereafter.
- Through his wife, Lady Emily, who was sympathetic to the Theosophical Society, Lutyens was familiar with Hindu symbolism and geometry.
- As an exceptionally educated cosmopolitan architect, Lutyens was not, in the end, totally resistant to the Viceroy's desire for Mughal elements.

Of all these possibilities, the first appears to be the most probable. Lady Emily's membership with the Theosophical Society was, in fact, a constant irritation to Lutyens and, for over twenty years, it led to an increasing estrangement between them and even to talk of a possible separation. His consideration for the purely politically-based preferences of the King and the Viceroy for the architectural style of the Mughal emperors was so restricted that he could hardly have intended to introduce a Mughal motif throughout the British royal capital.

By synthesizing these life experiences and deliberations and, also influenced by the plans for Washington, D.C., Canberra and Paris, all exemplary in Lutyens' eyes, the architect drew up an extraordinarily strict ground plan of the town by combining the best suggestions of Henry Vaughan Lanchester's early work (cf. stages in the town planning in Chapter 4.2).

The centre of power, consisting of Viceroy's House, the two Secretariats and the four archives and museums, was defined by a hexagram. In the main axis of the town running from east to west, triangles derived from this axis along with a triangle surrounding the star formed almost all the important points of the town, whether they were the commercial centre of Connaught Circus, the site of the All India War Memorial (which was not added until later), or the site of three planned churches.

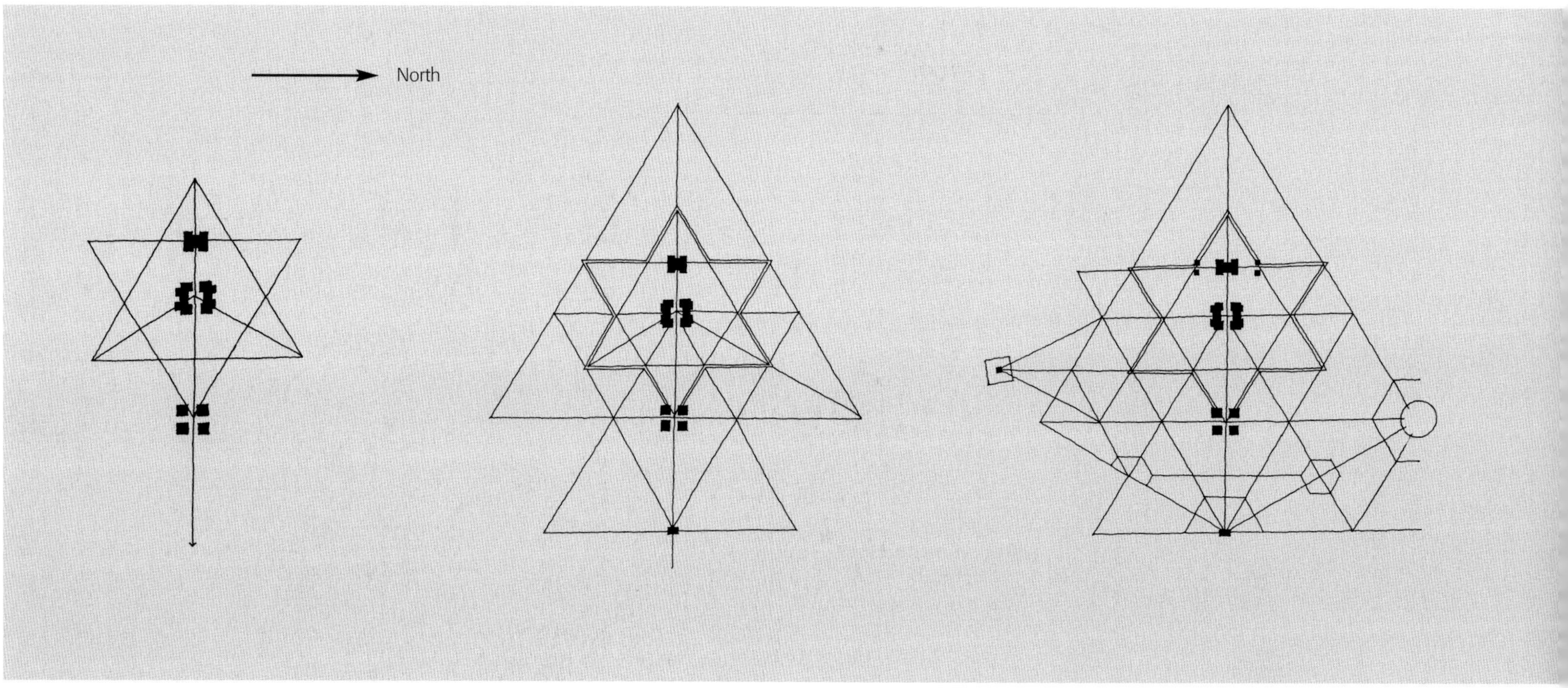

The abstract geometric shape of Imperial Delhi's plan was hardly diminished anywhere to take account of the topography. For instance, Raisina Hill was really too steep and too restrictive to hold Viceroy's House and the Secretariats along with a reasonable amount of space around them. It was not, however, the building programme that was altered, but the shape of Raisina Hill. The top was levelled off and banks of earth placed around the edges even allowed the creation of a large and level Mogul garden to the west of Viceroy's House.

In 1912, before the plans for Imperial Delhi could take a decisive step forward, Lutyens had to induce the King in London, as well as the India Office and its Secretary of State for India, Lord Crewe, to give a definite commission in addition to general declarations of intent: "Lutyens returned to London from India in July, 1912 ... Lutyens' first concern in July, 1912 was to secure his appointment as architect of New Delhi. Though he had the backing of Lord Hardinge, Lord Crewe, the Secretary of State, remained unconvinced and there was still talk of a competition. The autumn of 1912 found Lutyens energetically lobbying, interviewing India Office Officials and paying court to his patrons at Balmoral and Crewe House. It was partly in order to facilitate his own appointment that Lutyens pushed for Herbert Baker's engagement – the work involved was anyway far too great for one man – and in October, 1912 Baker agreed to collaborate. By November, 1912, when he left for India, Lutyens' appointment with Baker was virtually in the bag, and it was officially announced in January, 1913. At the same time it was agreed that Lutyens was to design Viceroy's House and Baker the Secretariats."[8]

From January 1913 onwards, all those involved in the decision-making processes in Imperial Delhi knew that, although the final decisions lay with the Viceroy, no decision would be made without the approval of Edwin Lutyens. The unusual amount of power the architectural star possessed is inconceivable today, however. Our contemporary monitors of such celebrity were, to a large extent, non-existent in Lutyens' time. Thus, ideal preconditions were created for a speedy and uncompromising realization of the planning concept once it was decided and later on even recorded on the pedestal of the Jaipur Column (Fig. 58).

Lutyens himself often complained that, lacking a normal schooling, he had not been endowed with the negotiating and diplomatic skills enjoyed by Herbert Baker, and that he always instinctively gave the Viceroy precedence in all crucial decisions.

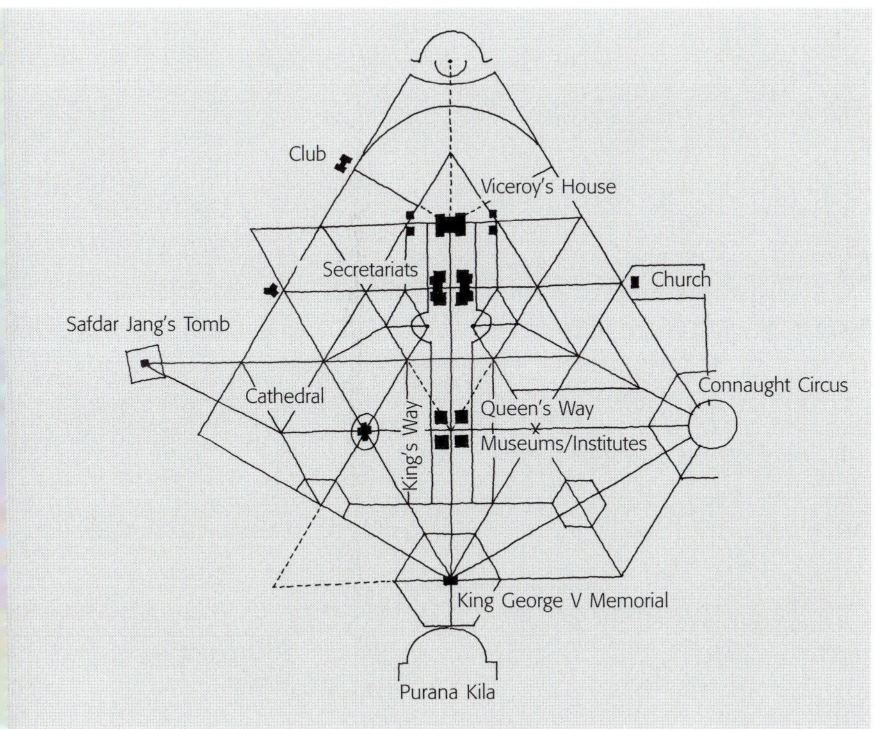

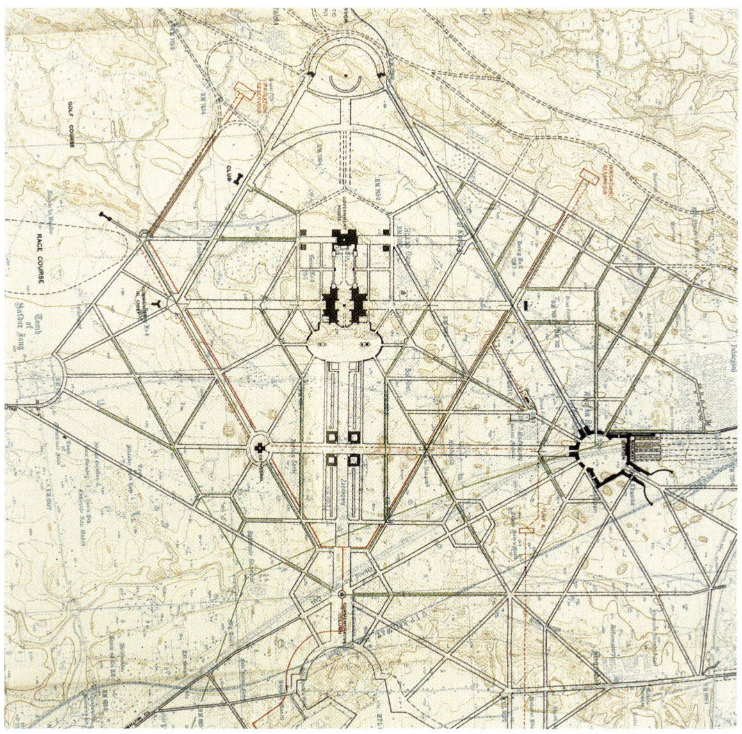

Fig. 56: Stages in the development of the town plan for Imperial Delhi based on the hexagram and the triangle. In the first stage of the plan, Viceroy's House (above), the Secretariats (centre), and four planned museums (below) form the hexagram. Its main axis, leading from the Viceroy's Palace, is oriented on the east, exactly along the old town (Purana Kila) on the Jumna River. In this diagram, east is at the bottom of the image).

With its "Final Report on the Town Planning of the New Imperial Capital,"[9] the members of the Delhi Town Planning Committee finally presented a plan on March 20, 1913 that did justice to supply routes, waste-disposal, traffic and landscaping requirements. In addition, it combined a hexagonal town plan[10] typical of its time with a network of sight lines that included numerous old monuments from the Mughal period.

The Delhi Town Planning Committee concerned itself expressly with the following monuments: "Looking from the centre of the site towards the river there is Shah Jehan's Delhi on the left, following the river frontage is Ferozshah's Delhi, Indrapat and Humayun's tomb fill the outlook in front, while outside the site itself Tughlakabad, Siri, Jehanpanah, Kila Rai Prithora, Lal Kot and the Qutb complete the panorama. Isolated buildings such as Safdar Jang's tomb, the Lodi mausoleums, and the observatory of Jey Singh are within the site itself."[11]

Lutyens' determined use of the hexagon and the triangle in the ground plan of the town led to numerous interpretations and much speculation, beginning with notes by Henry Vaughan Lanchester about Lutyens' "prepossession in favour of the equilateral triangle."[12]

We encounter this predilection for geometric shapes such as the triangle and hexagon throughout the history of architecture, even outside baroque urban architecture and Beaux-

8 Ibid. p. 249.
9 Cf. Chapter 4.2.
10 Cf. for example the town plan of Canberra on p. 54.
11 *Final Report of the Delhi Town Planning Committee,* London 1913, page 59.
12 H.V. Lanchester: *The Art of Town Planning,* New York 1925, p. 204f.

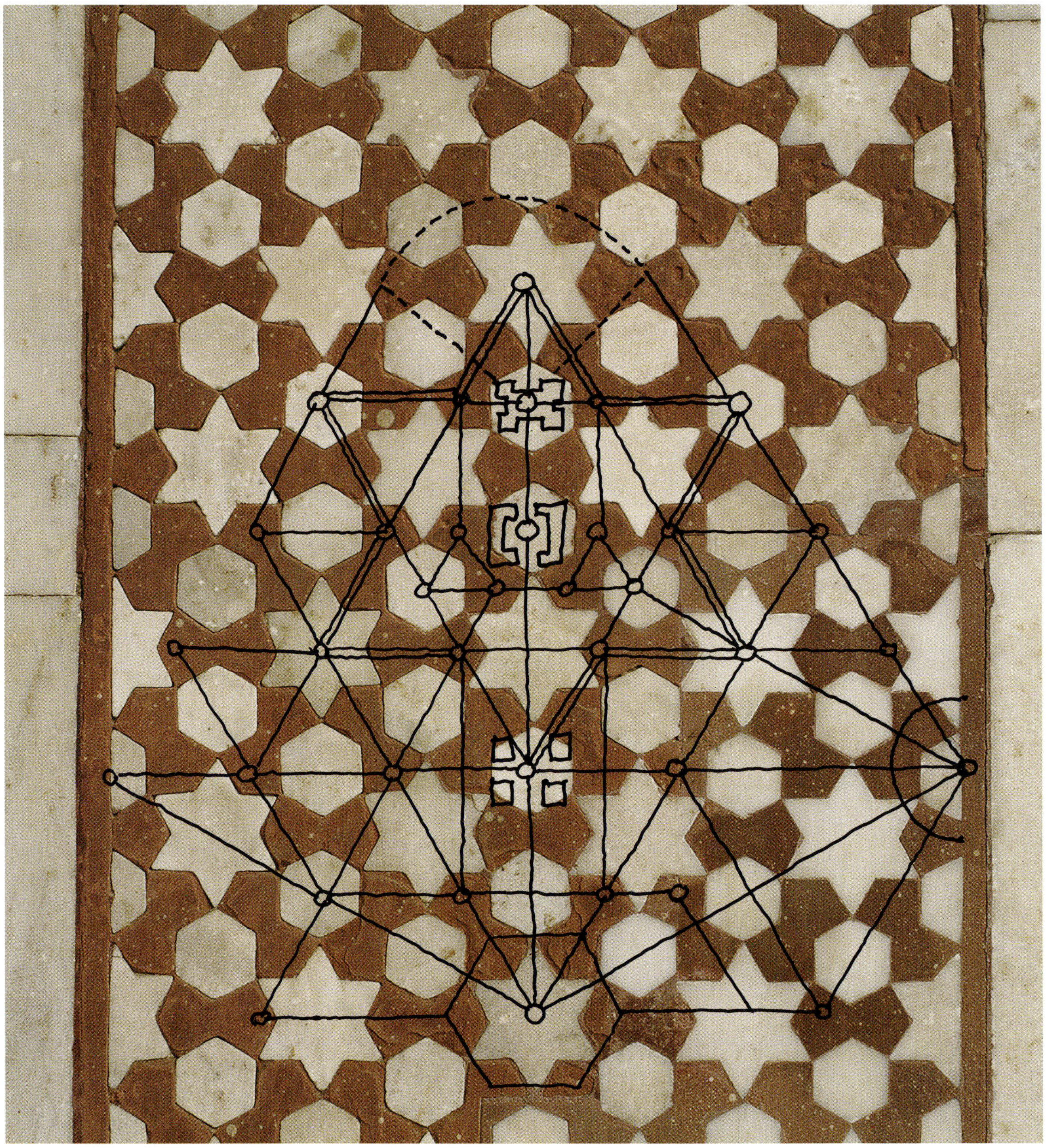

Fig. 57: The hexagonal inlay work on Humayun's tomb appears, when superimposed on the town plan, to reflect the latter right down to its very details. Yet, there is little to support the idea that Lutyens wanted to include the patterns of the Mughal age in his plan for Imperial Delhi.

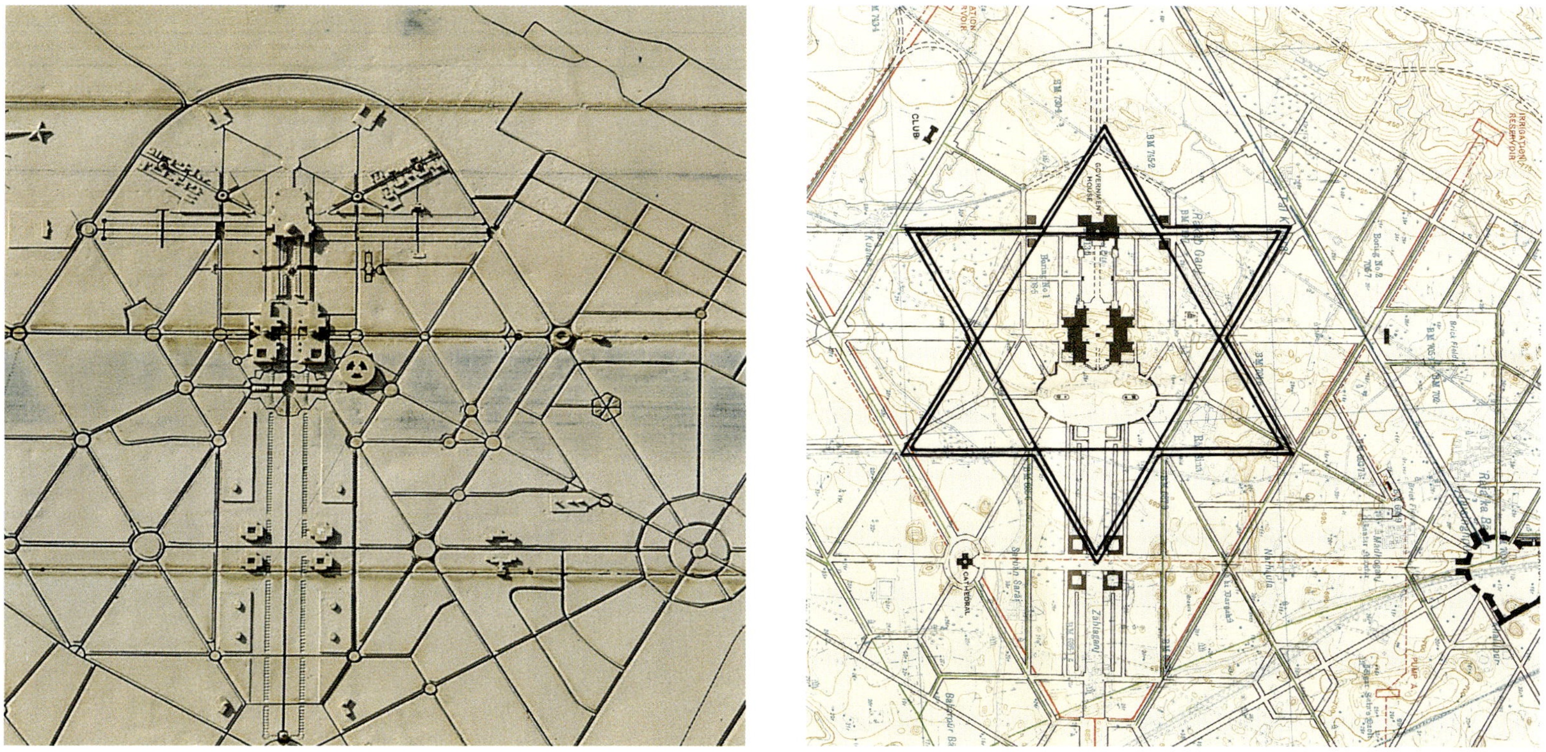

Fig. 58: The hexagram in the town plan. At left, the town plan on the base of the Jaipur Column is not oriented towards the north, as is usually the case, but rather to the west. Only then is a normal hexagram produced as the basic pattern of the town. One triangle "points to heaven, the other to earth." At right, "the hexagram is produced by two triangles, one pointing to heaven, one to earth. It is the symbol of the Almighty, whom the Freemasons call 'The Great Architect of the Universe.'"

Arts town planning. To name only two examples, it appears in the geometric definitions of the Ashrafiyya Madrasa in Cairo from the fifteenth century and in Cologne Cathedral from the fourteenth century. Both of these structures are situated far from London and New Delhi in time and space. One reason why these forms remain important in the architectural imagination is as a function of the land survey: the coordinates of a ground plan or elevation can only be determined with particular precision if they are combined into a system of equilateral triangles. Nevertheless, there is often also a cultic reason for the utilization of equilateral triangles in art and architecture.[13]

The development of the ground plan of the town proceeded in an unusually intensive dialogue with Viceroy Lord Hardinge, and Lutyens later confirmed this, stating: "The New City owes its being to Lord Hardinge, whose Statue now stands surveying the length of the Central Vista, and has inscribed upon its pedestal, the right, proper and proud word FOUNDER. His patience and courage in times of great stress, personal and political, his even temper in the midst of diverse discussion, remain in my memory as being parallel only with the greatness of his conception.

His command that one Avenue should lead to Purana Kila, and another to the Jumma Masjid, was the father of the equilateral and hexagonal plan. A sorry nuisance to all whose thoughts could not merge beyond the right angles of New York, nor embrace the intelligence of L'Enfant at Washington."[14]

13 A.G. Walls: *Geometry and Architecture in Islamic Jerusalem*, Buckhurst Hill 1989.

14 Sir Edwin Lutyens on 2.2.1933 in a speech at the India Society in London.

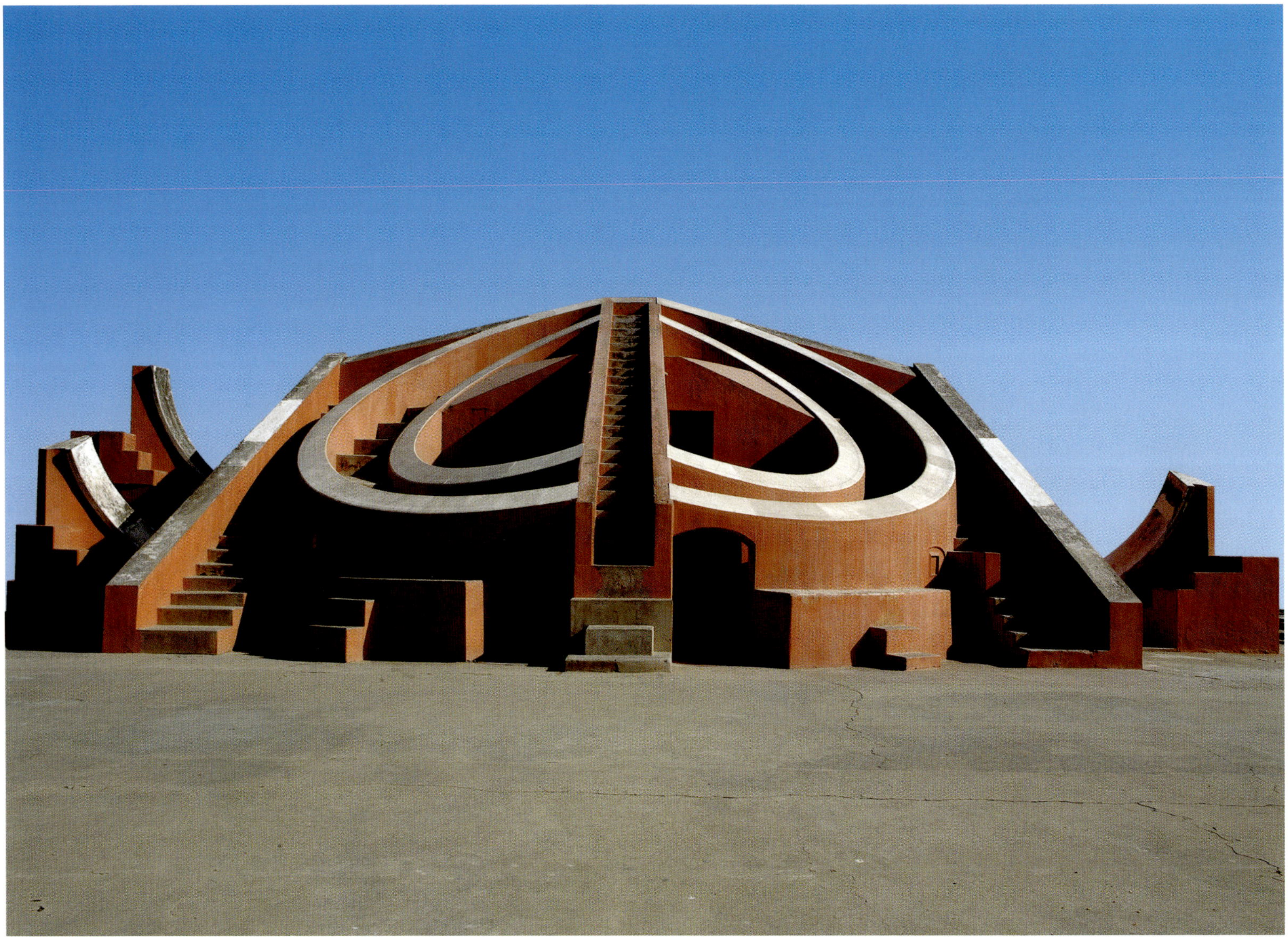

Fig. 59: A large number of historic buildings made it difficult for the Delhi Town Planning Committee to adapt the strictly hexagonal town plan to existing structures. One of the focal points taken into consideration was the eighteenth-century observatory of Jantar Mantar.

Fig. 60: In its "Final Report on the Town Planning of the New Imperial Delhi" (presented to both Houses of Parliament by Command of His Majesty) the Delhi Town Planning Committee put forward on March 20, 1913 the town plan that was finally realized.

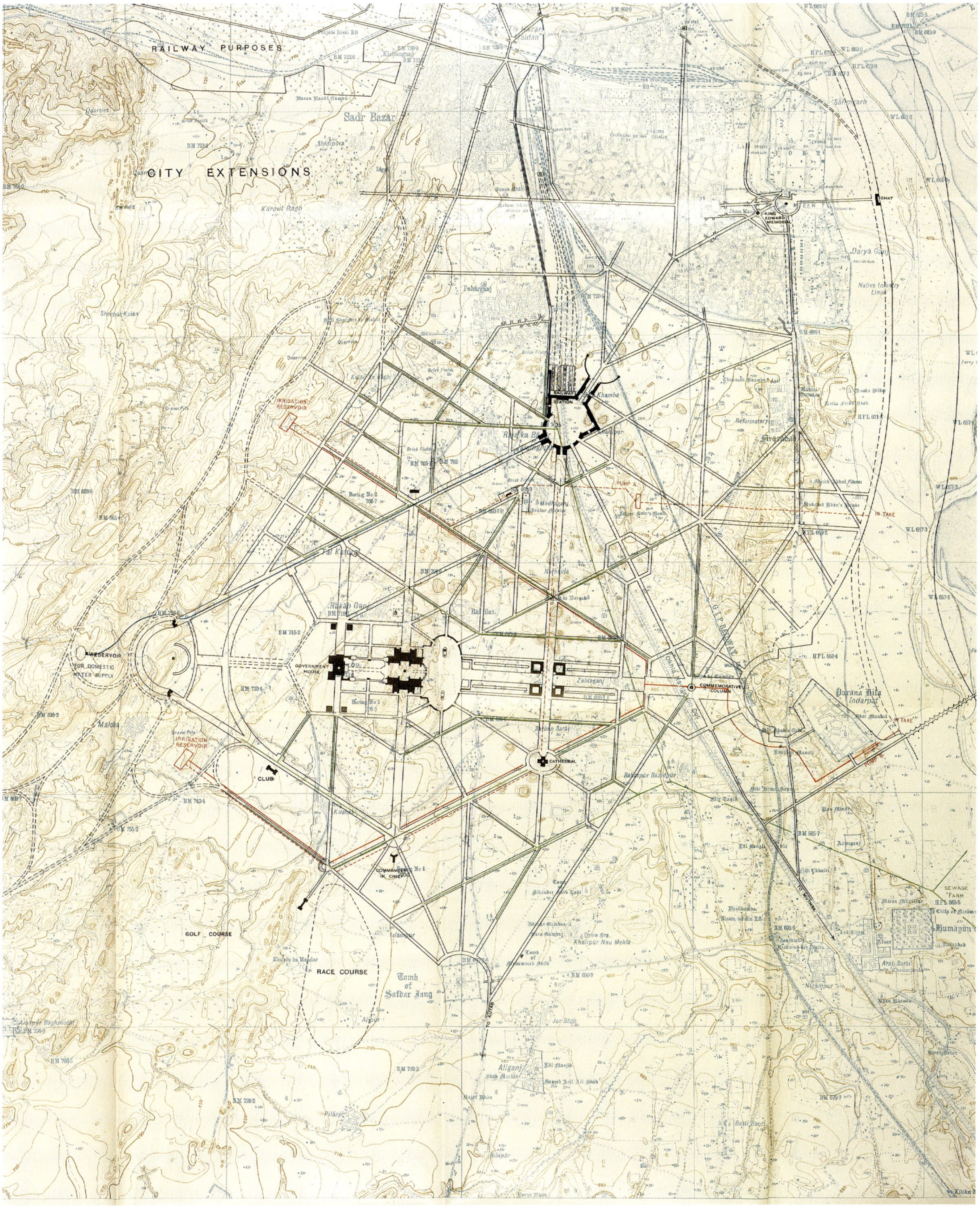
RAILWAY PURPOSES
CITY EXTENSIONS
Sadr Bazar
KING EDWARD MEMORIAL
RAILWAY STATION
IRRIGATION RESERVOIR
RESERVOIR FOR DOMESTIC WATER SUPPLY
GOVERNMENT HOUSE
COMMEMORATIVE COLUMN
CATHEDRAL
CLUB
COMMANDER IN CHIEF
GOLF COURSE
RACE COURSE
Tomb of Safdar Jang
Purana Qila
SEWAGE FARM

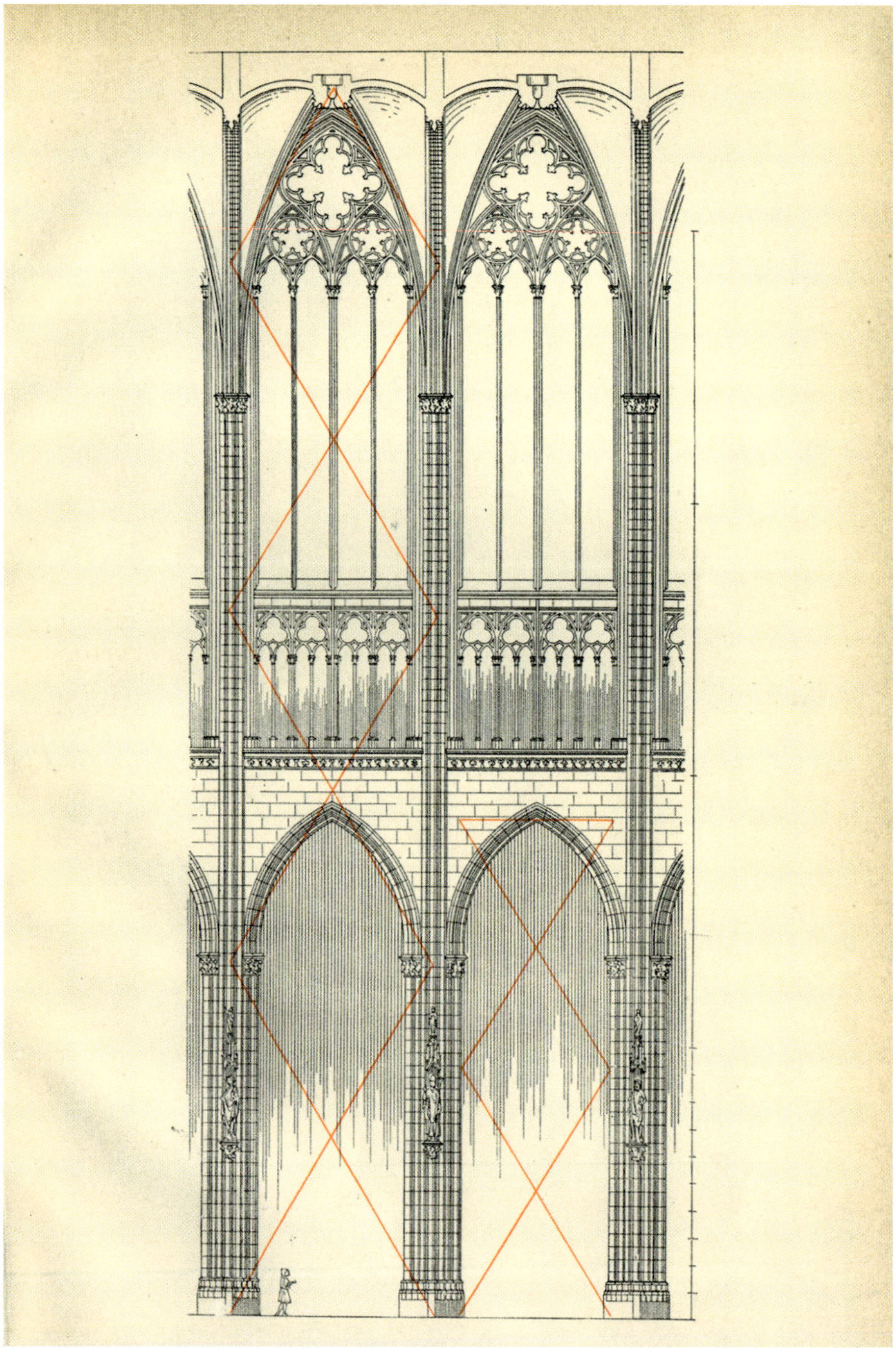

Fig. 61: In many cultures, the equilateral triangle is the geometric key to the ground plans and elevations of sacred buildings. There are cultic as well as surveying reasons for this. Some examples include the fifteenth-century Ashrafiyya Madrasa in Cairo (left), and the fourteenth-century Cologne Cathedral (right).

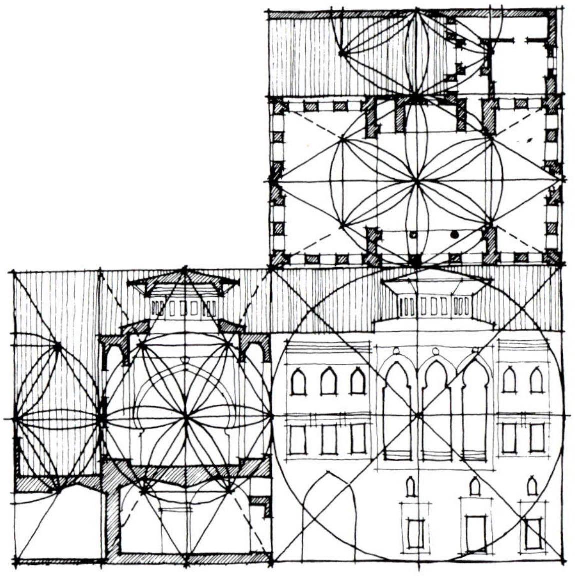

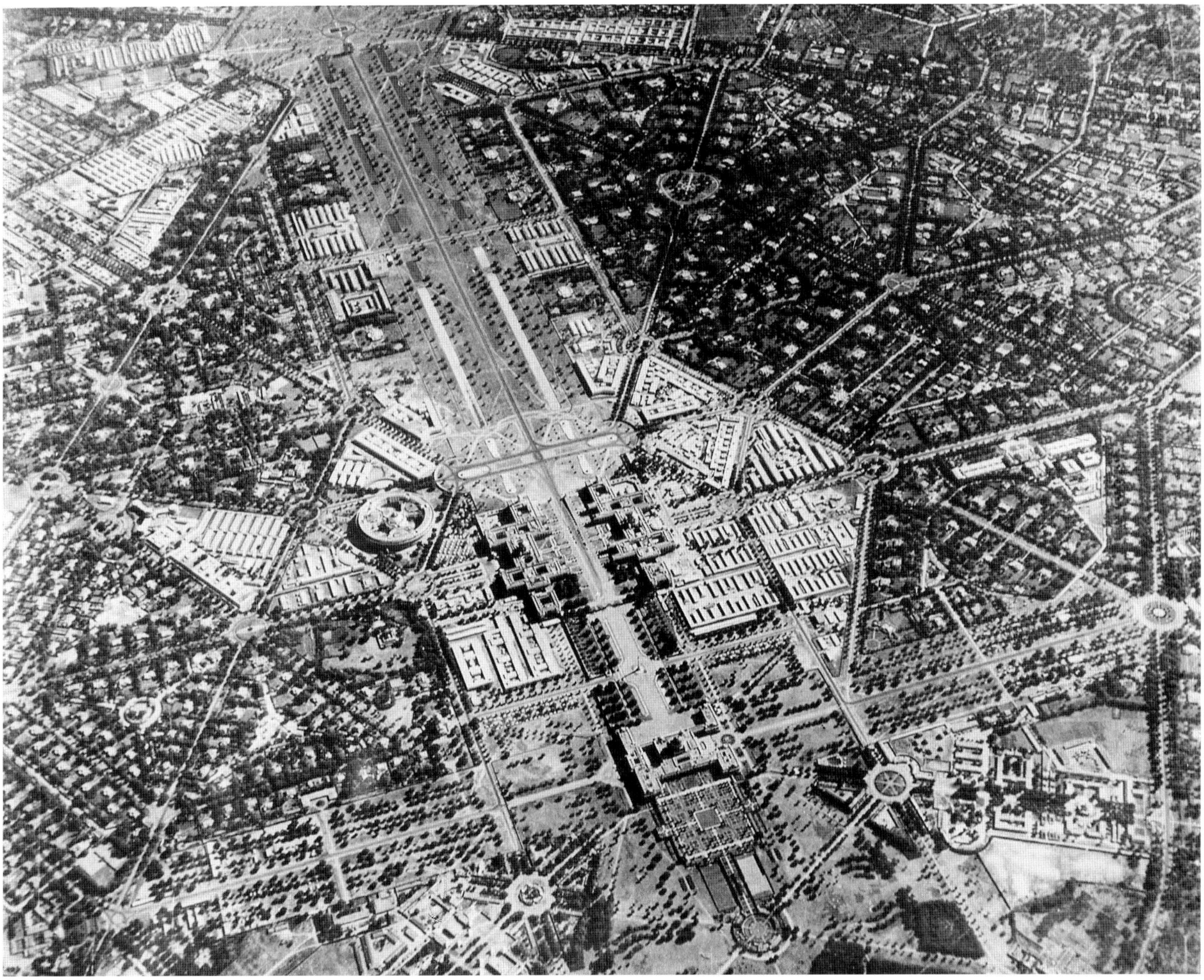

Fig. 62: An aerial photograph from the 1930s shows the uncompromising way in which Edwin Lutyens' hexagonal town plan was put into practice. In the centre of the picture lie Herbert Baker's two Secretariats; below them is Viceroy's House with its square Mughal Garden.

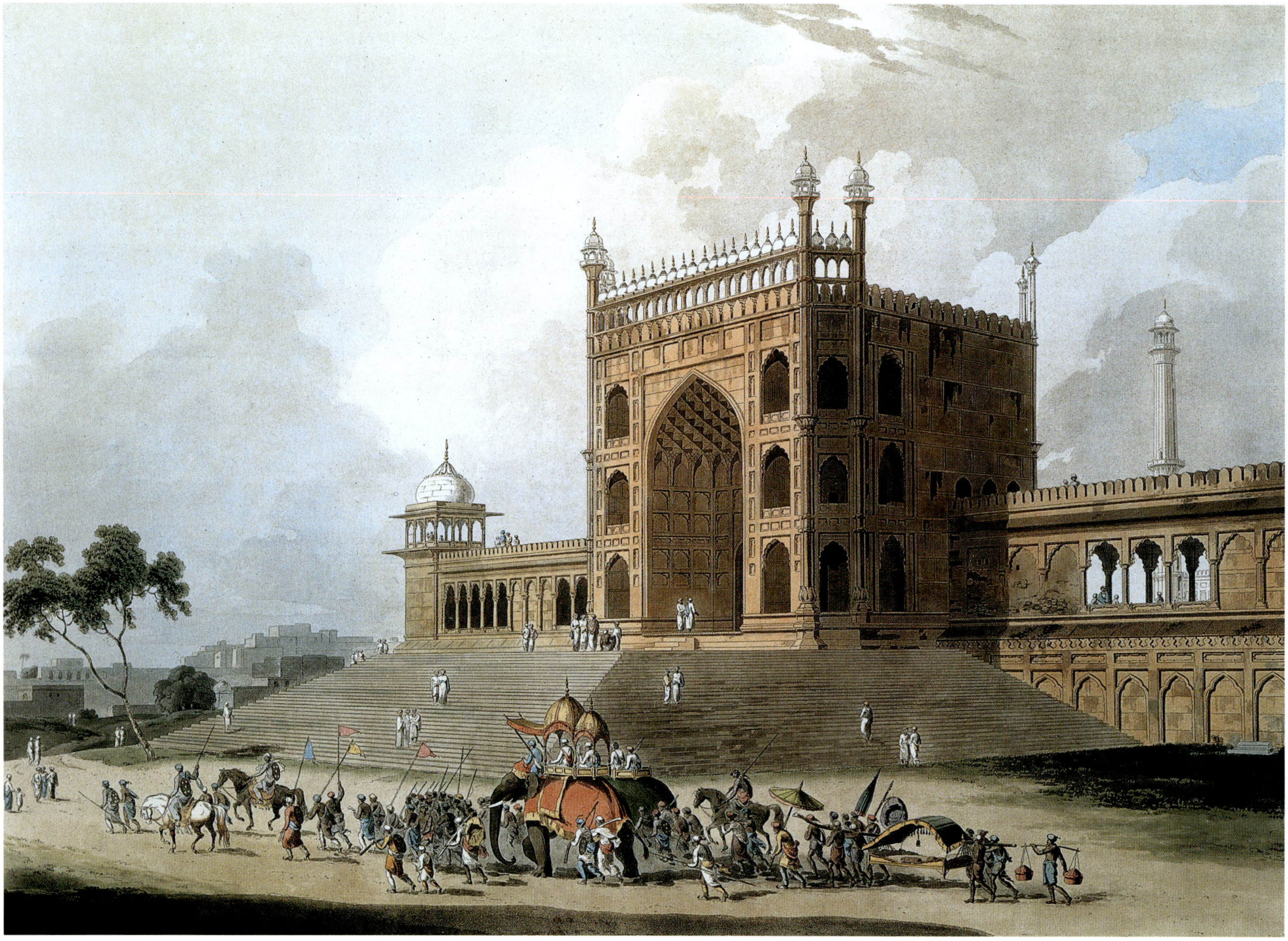

Fig. 63: *Eastern Gate of the Jummah Musjid at Delhi*. Aquatint by Thomas Daniell, 1795.

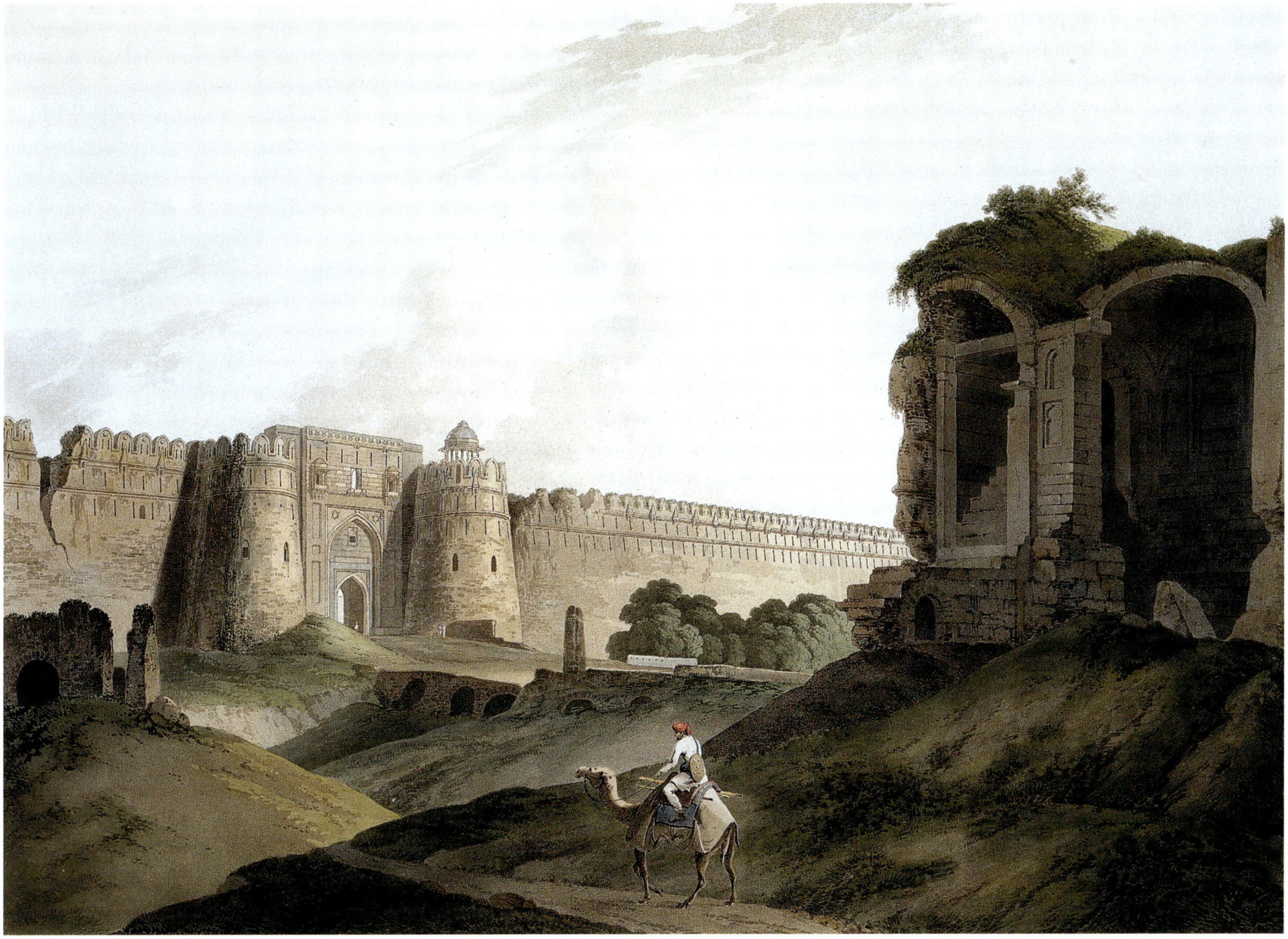

Fig. 64: Purana Kila, the earliest foundation of Delhi in Thomas Daniell's *The Western Entrance of Shere Shah's Fort*, 1796.

3.2 The Imperial Axis: Palace, Obelisk and Triumphal Arch

In the history of town planning, there is no shortage of examples of grand axial avenues laid out either for religious, military or prestigious reasons. The most important model of an avenue in nineteenth- and twentieth-century major town planning – in a long series of historical models – is the Champs Elysées in Paris (Fig. 65) with its three fixed points: the palace (Louvre), obelisk and triumphal arch. This symbolic trio of power also held a particular attraction for the architects of Imperial Delhi, but in the densely built-up areas of central London, the Crown's builders never succeeded in constructing a series of buildings as prominent and rich in symbolism.

In Imperial Delhi, they built a Neo-Classical imperial axis known as King's Way that was initially built in stages, and not according to a preconceived plan. There was also no obelisk but a column like that of Trajan's between the palace and the triumphal arch. It was not until about a decade after the great east-west axis had been planned (1912) that the triumphal arch was added to King's Way. The outcome was that the individual additions were brought together in exactly the same sequence established at the Champs Elysées – the order of palace, obelisk and triumphal arch. Indeed, even the Rond Point half way between the Arc de Triomphe and the Place de la Concorde was duplicated in Imperial Delhi as a planned plaza half way between the All India War Memorial and the Jaipur Column.

Amidst all the similarities between King's Way and the Champs Elysées it is important to note one difference in the sequence of architectural fixed points: at the point in the broad plain of Delhi which marks the start of the slope up to Raisina Hill, as part of the axial concept, there is Prince Edward Place, a square later named Great Place. While this square is part of the strict hexagonal structure of the town, it is also part of the rectangular forecourt of the main axis: "The great place, or present Vijak Chauk, forecourt to the entire palatine acropolis at Raisina, was equally unambiguous as a statement of imperium. Within its geometric bounds Lutyens tamed the limitless plain, uniting indigenous and alien forms in a symmetrical plaza where the martial might of British India could parade in awesome splendor. Red stone Sanchi railings screened either end, recalling the plait that girdled the dome of Viceroy's House, while six rhubarb-red obelisk fountains evoke at once memories of the piazzas in Renaissance and baroque Italy."[15]

15 R.G. Irving: *Indian Summer*, New Haven and London, p. 250.

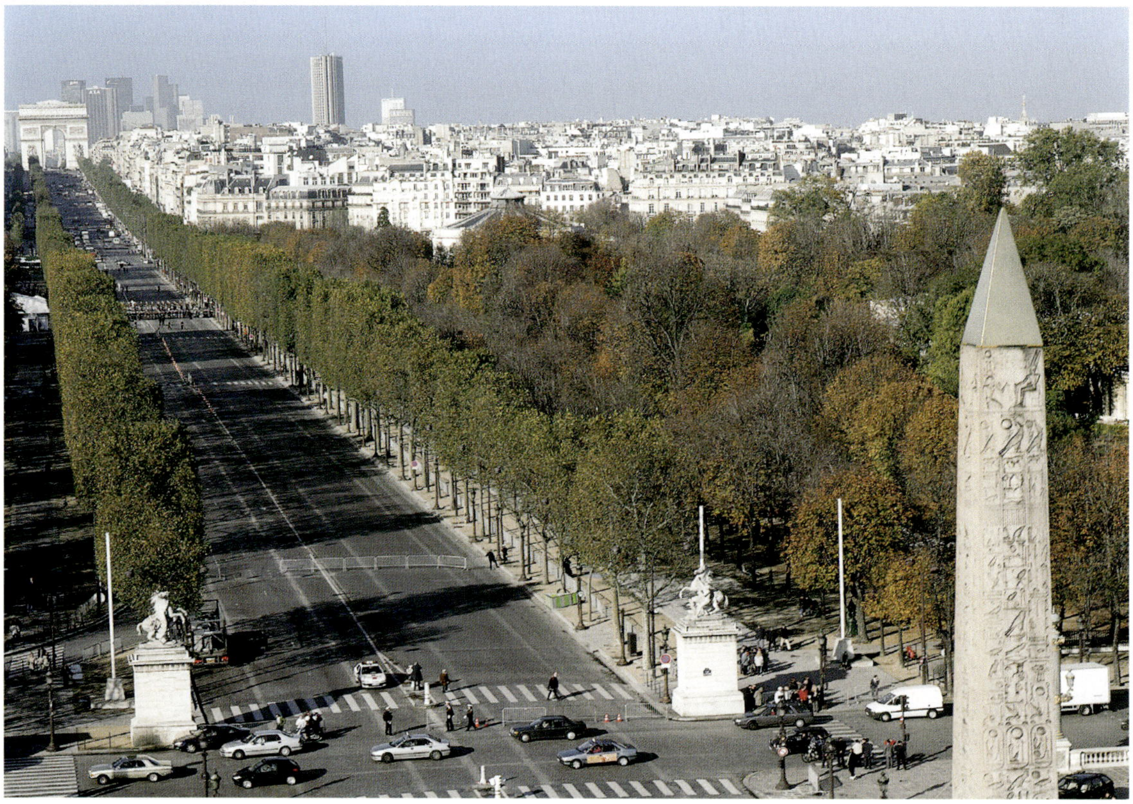

Fig. 65: From the Louvre to the Arc de Triomphe via the Place de la Concorde with its obelisk, the Champs Elysées in Paris has become a world famous model for the representation of an imperial claim to rule, whether in Washington, D.C., New Delhi, or Berlin.

Figure 116 shows the view from the roof of Viceroy's House down to the axis of King's Way, with the Jaipur Column in the foreground and the All India War Memorial in the background. Although familiar to Europeans since the Baroque era, a series of buildings such as these were not intended for everyday use, and must have had a confusing or, at least, a surprising effect on the Indians. Hindu and Buddhist processions usually revolved around a holy site. In addition, the military triumphal processions of the Islamic conquerors that had invaded India from the northwest since the eleventh century did not connect the memory of their triumphs with an architectural axis.

In 1936, the British architects of Imperial Delhi finally completed the monumental axis with one final element, namely the King George V Memorial in memory of the deceased founder of British Delhi (cf. Chapter 3.2.4). Thus, thousands of kilometres away from the real centre of British world power, a monumental idealized image of imperial power was created, carved in stone that, ironically, only fulfilled its intended function for a few years.

In European history, the representation of power, or the military demonstration of power, has often been a fundamental reason for designing large axes in town plans. Nowhere else does that become clearer than on July 14 (Bastille Day) on the Champs Elysées in Paris or on January 26 (Republic Day) on King's Way in New Delhi (Fig. 66). The idea behind the design of these magnificent streets only becomes clear through military parades and flags waving in patriotic celebration.

In many large cities, the imperial axis is modelled on Paris with its combination of palace, victory column and triumphal arch.

Paris:	Louvre	Obelisk	Arc de Triomphe
Berlin:	Stadtschloss	Brandenburg Gate	Victory Arch
Munich:	Residence	Obelisk	Propylaen
Washington, D.C.:	Capitol Hill	Obelisk	White House
Nancy:	Place Stanislas Palais	Arc de Triomphe	Memorial
New Delhi:	Viceroy's House	Jaipur Column	All India War Memorial

Fig. 66: King's Way (Raj Path) in Imperial Delhi leads from the Viceroy's Palace to the All India War Memorial. Parade on Republic Day, January 26, 2001.

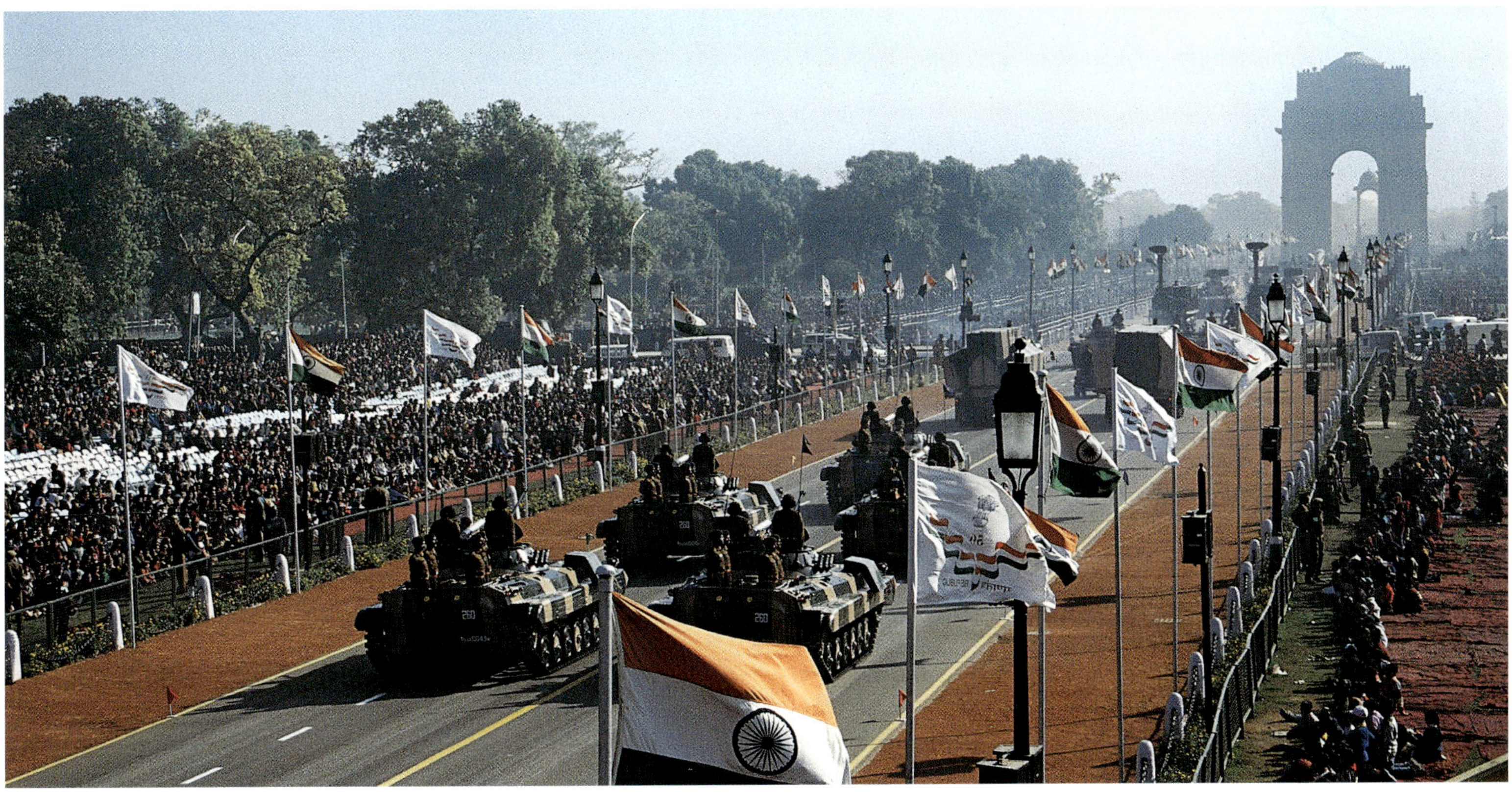

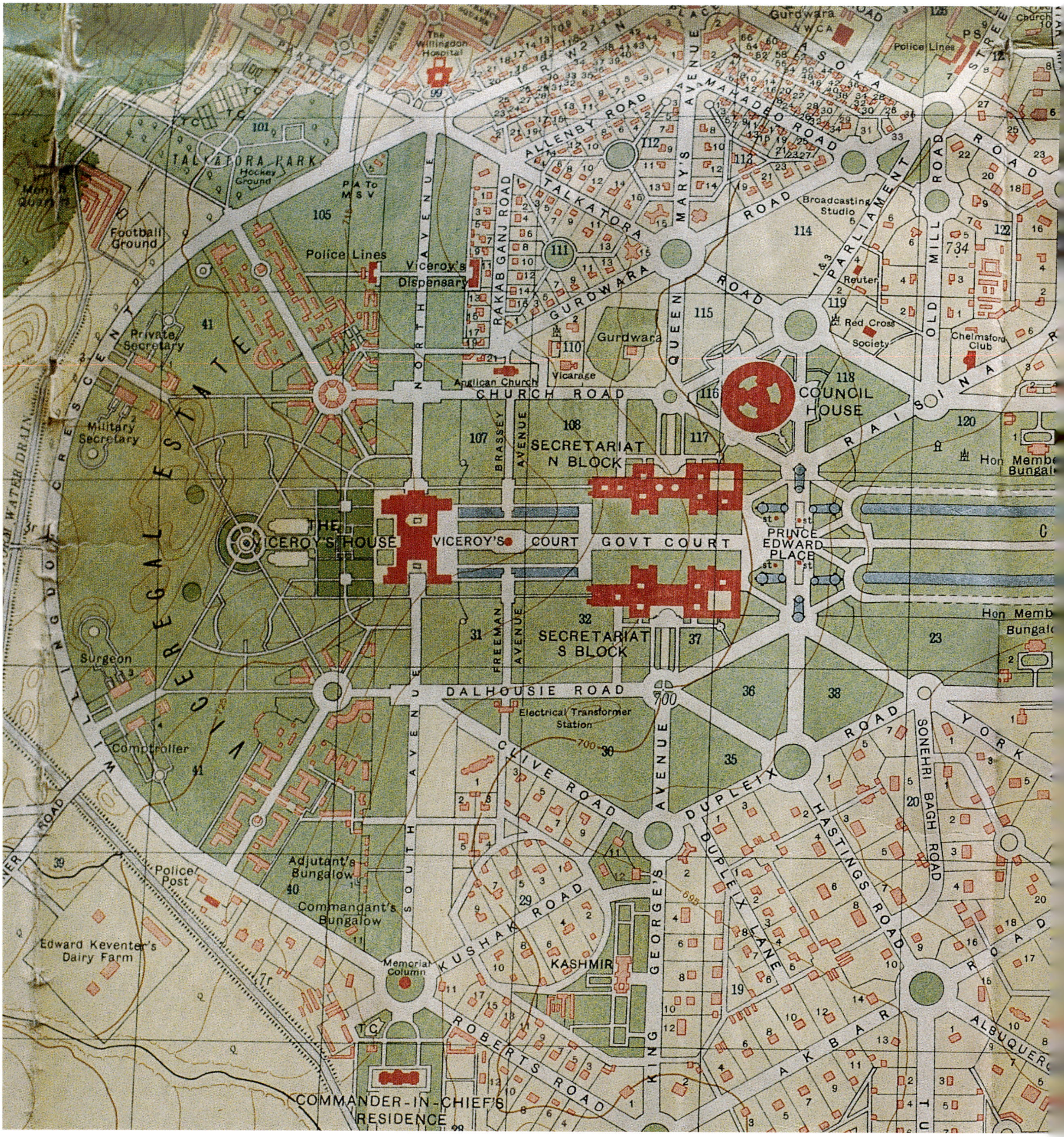

THE VICEROY'S HOUSE
VICEREGAL ESTATE
VICEROY'S COURT
GOVT COURT
SECRETARIAT N BLOCK
SECRETARIAT S BLOCK
COUNCIL HOUSE
PRINCE EDWARD PLACE
CHURCH ROAD
DALHOUSIE ROAD
CLIVE ROAD
DUPLEIX ROAD
DUPLEX LANE
HASTINGS ROAD
SONEHRI BAGH ROAD
YORK ROAD
AKBAR ROAD
ALBUQUERQUE
ROBERTS ROAD
KUSHAK ROAD
KING GEORGE'S AVENUE
QUEEN MARY'S AVENUE
NORTH AVENUE
SOUTH AVENUE
BRASSEY AVENUE
FREEMAN AVENUE
RAKABGANJ ROAD
GURDWARA ROAD
TALKATORA ROAD
ALLENBY ROAD
IRWIN ROAD
ASOKA ROAD
MAHADEO ROAD
PARLIAMENT STREET
OLD MILL ROAD
RAISINA ROAD
WILLINGDON CRESCENT
TALKATORA PARK
Hockey Ground
Football Ground
Police Lines
Viceroy's Dispensary
Anglican Church
Vicarage
Gurdwara
Broadcasting Studio
Reuter
Red Cross Society
Chelmsford Club
Private Secretary
Military Secretary
Surgeon
Comptroller
Adjutant's Bungalow
Commandant's Bungalow
Police Post
Edward Keventer's Dairy Farm
Memorial Column
KASHMIR
Electrical Transformer Station
COMMANDER-IN-CHIEF'S RESIDENCE
The Willingdon Hospital
Hon Members Bungalow

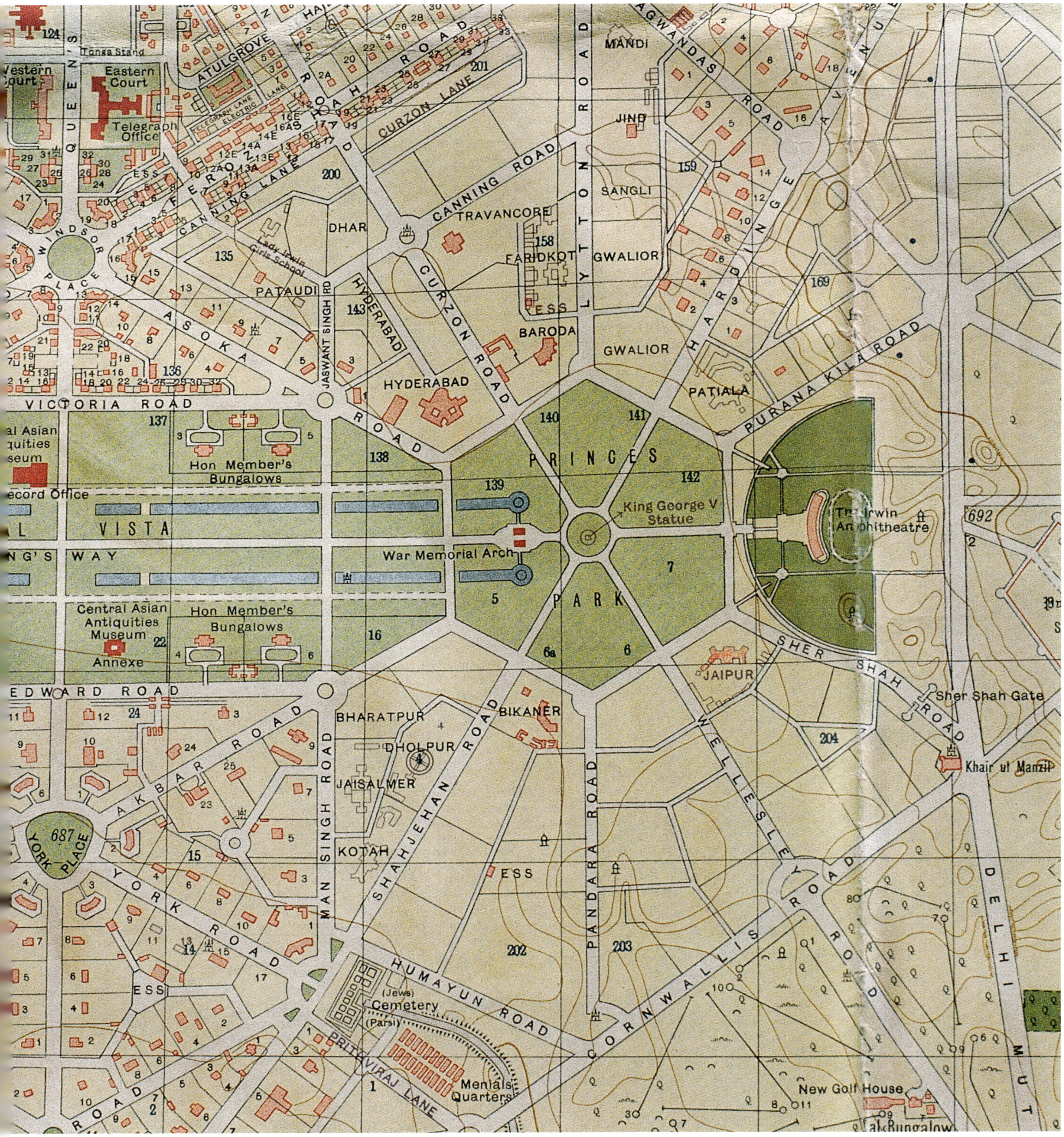

Fig. 67: King's Way (now Raj Path) forms the main axis of Imperial Delhi with Viceroy's House at the west end, the War Memorial Arch and the statue of George V at the east.

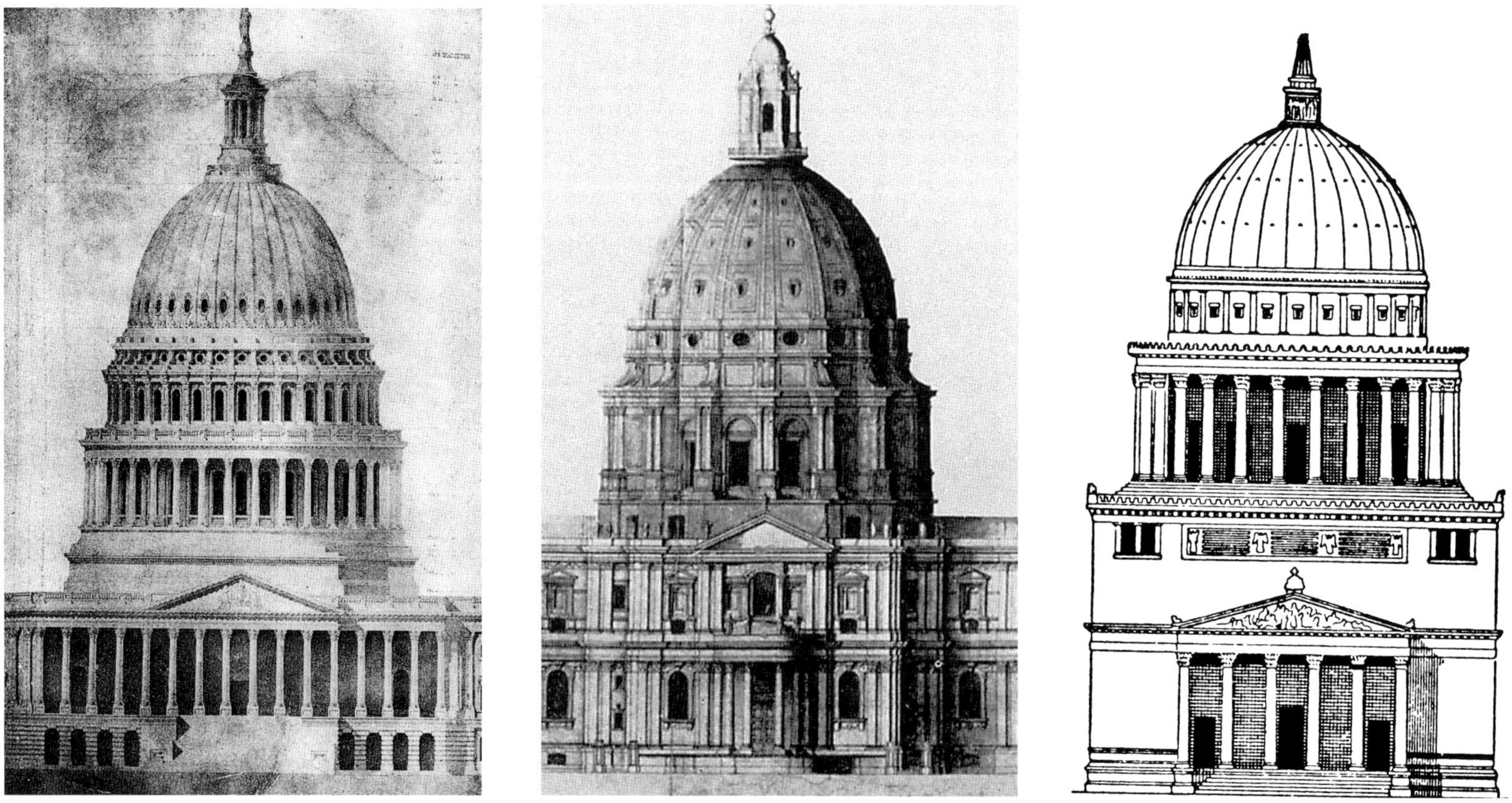

Fig. 68: One of Edwin Lutyens' early sketches for the Viceroy's Palace (following page) closely follows the well-known patterns of the Capitol in Washington, D.C., St Paul's Cathedral in London, and the St Nicholas Church in Potsdam, Germany.

3.2.1 Viceroy's House, now Rashtrapati Bhavan (Architect: Edwin Lutyens), 1914–1929

The British Empire needed an impressive focal point on the Indian subcontinent for the safeguarding of its valuable colonial possessions. The largest economic and military power in the world no longer looked sufficiently impressive or grand in Calcutta. The new palace for the Viceroy of India in Imperial Delhi would be an impressive symbol of the actual power structure for the partly subject and partly independent princely fiefdoms of the more than 500 Indian maharajas.

Never before in the history of mankind had there been a comparable concentration of power. Only the architecture of ancient Rome was able to provide the necessary formal models. Edwin Lutyens was aware of the unique nature of the task at hand. It also coincided perfectly with his dreams of cathedrals, palaces and lordly residences, which he had been unable to fully realize in designing country houses for his affluent English patrons.

The moment was ripe for his ambitions, and Lutyens acquired the approval of the King in London that he should have the sole responsibility for the design and construction of the palace in Imperial Delhi. There was to be no competition and no opposition in Imperial Delhi! His friend and partner Herbert Baker, so indispensable for the task of conjuring an entire capital, would not dispute his right to this royal task. Lord Hardinge, the British envoy in India, in light of the positive preliminary decisions in London and also because of the support of Lutyens by his wife, the Vicereine, would not become involved in any further contentious matters.

Architectural models

At best, the task was comparable to designing and building Buckingham Palace itself – yet this royal residence was more imperial since the empire of His Majesty, King George V was many times larger and more powerful than that of Queen Victoria, the young patron of Buckingham Palace during the first half of the nineteenth century. In any case, there was no

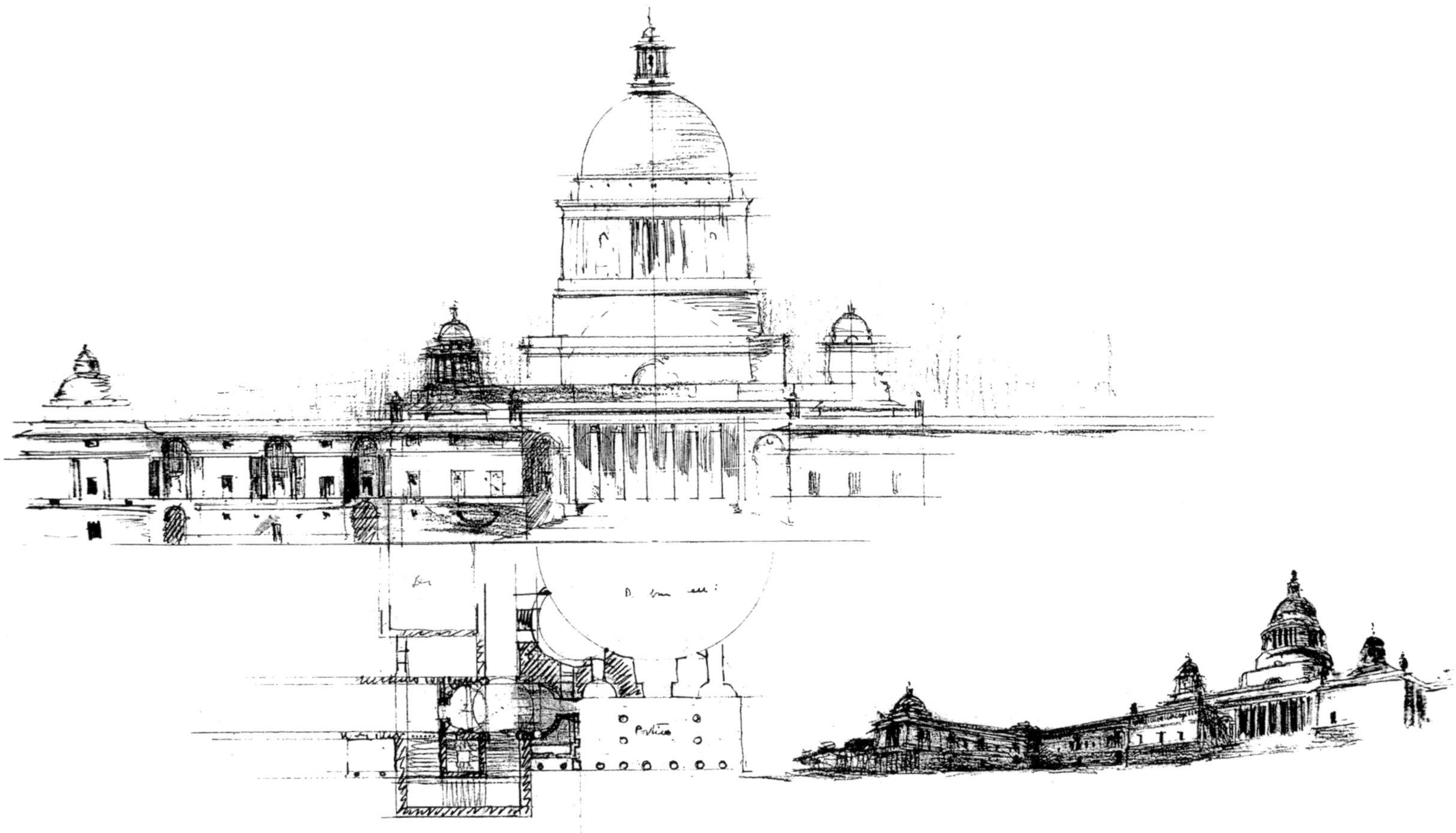

Fig. 69: The models on the opposite page led Lutyens to design a dome on a high tambour for the central section and Neo-Palladian wings on either side.

question of copying Buckingham Palace. Finally, a British King-Emperor only appeared once in a lifetime and for a short while, if at all, to India. Nevertheless, parallels to Buckingham Palace might be pleasing to the Viceroy. So it was no coincidence when Lutyens made the length of the facade of Viceroy's House exactly the same length as the facade of Buckingham Palace: 630 feet.

In designing Viceroy's House, alongside the architectural models of Rome, there arose another series of architectural styles that were familiar to Lutyens from personal examination, or at least from specialist literature. The capital of Washington, D.C. by Thomas Walter was a symbol of the rapidly increasing world power of the United States (Fig. 68, left). St Paul's Cathedral in London, by Christopher Wren, was a symbol of the magnificent reconstruction of London after the Great Fire of 1666 (Fig. 68, centre). Finally, there was the Church of St Nicholas in Potsdam (Fig. 68, right) designed by Karl Friedrich Schinkel in a strict Neo-Classical style. All three united references to the world of Palladio and ancient Rome that were so dear to Lutyens' heart.

Thus, it was no coincidence that one of the plans for Viceroy's House closely resembled the elevation of St Nicholas' Church (Fig. 69). It was characterized by a dome on a tall tambour along Schinkel's model, flanked by Indo-Islamic pavilions suited to Lord Hardinge's taste and linked together by a Neo-Palladian plinth course. Eclecticism was no stopgap here, but for the time being, a powerful synthesis of the fundamental ideals and stylistic elements of the last Neo-Classical phase in the history of European architecture.

The Viceroy in Imperial Delhi and Lord Crewe, the responsible official in the London India Office, both understood each of these architectural styles. Moreover, beyond the ongoing budgetary discussions, the architecture of Edwin Lutyens was in accordance not only with the taste of the Royal Family, but more importantly with the spirit of a pre-World War I Britain as characterized by a sense of mission and arrogance.

Fig. 70: Viceroy's House in New Delhi. North-south section (above). Ground plan of the main storey (below).

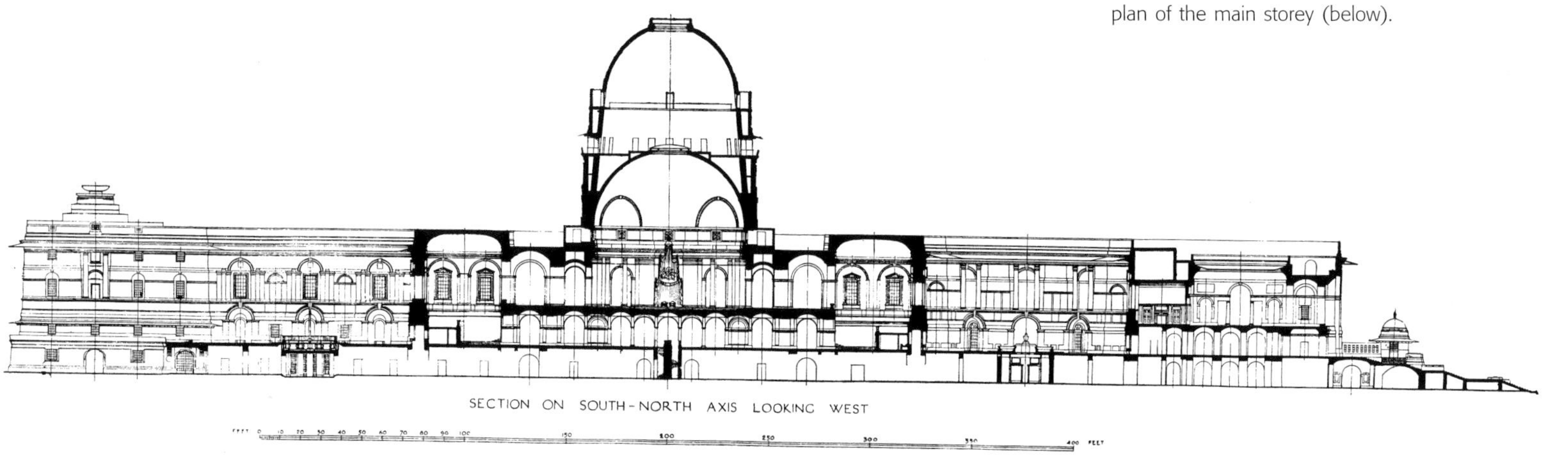

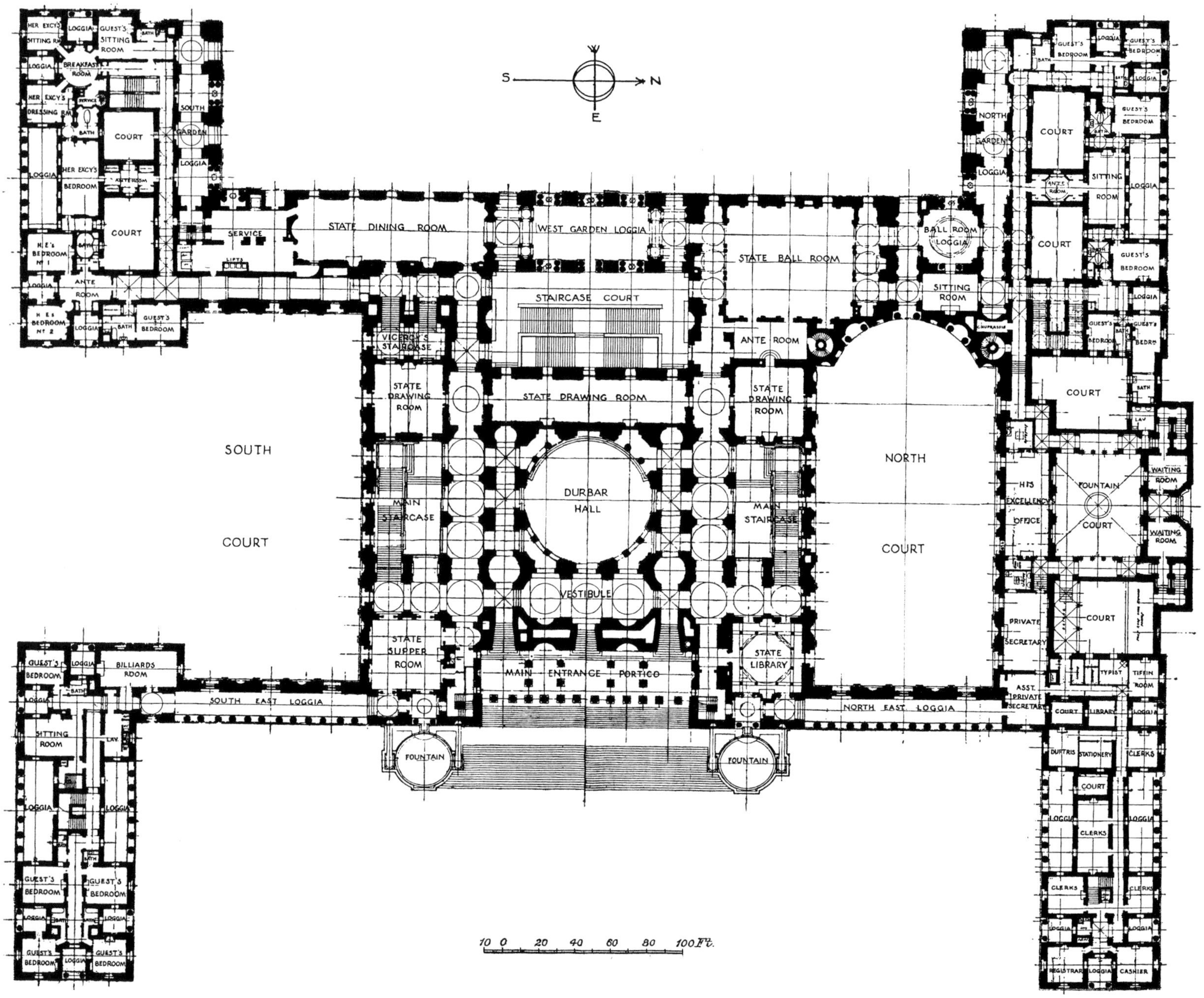

Alternatives to the design

After his appointment as a Member of the Delhi Town Planning Committee in 1912, Lutyens' thoughts had turned to the question of an appropriate architectural style for the British Viceroy's palace. In one of his hand-drawn sketches (Fig. 71) Lutyens designed a solution in the style of St Peter's and Bernini's colonnades in Rome. Two columns at the rounded corners of the square, at each side of the palace, contain the handwritten description "Trajan Column." Along the curves of one side of the palace is a cathedral; on the other side is the Viceroy's Secretariat. In this early stage of the plan the Viceroy's palace already had an H-shaped ground plan with a domed Durbar Hall in the centre.

Fig. 71: Edwin Lutyens' first hand-drawn sketches for Viceroy's House already depict an H-shaped ground plan with a dome over the central section.

In another hand-drawn sketch (Fig. 73) the H-shaped ground plan was given inner courtyards for improved lighting of office and reception areas, and had pillars placed along each side to emphasize four huge pavilions on the first upper storey. This architectural motif was

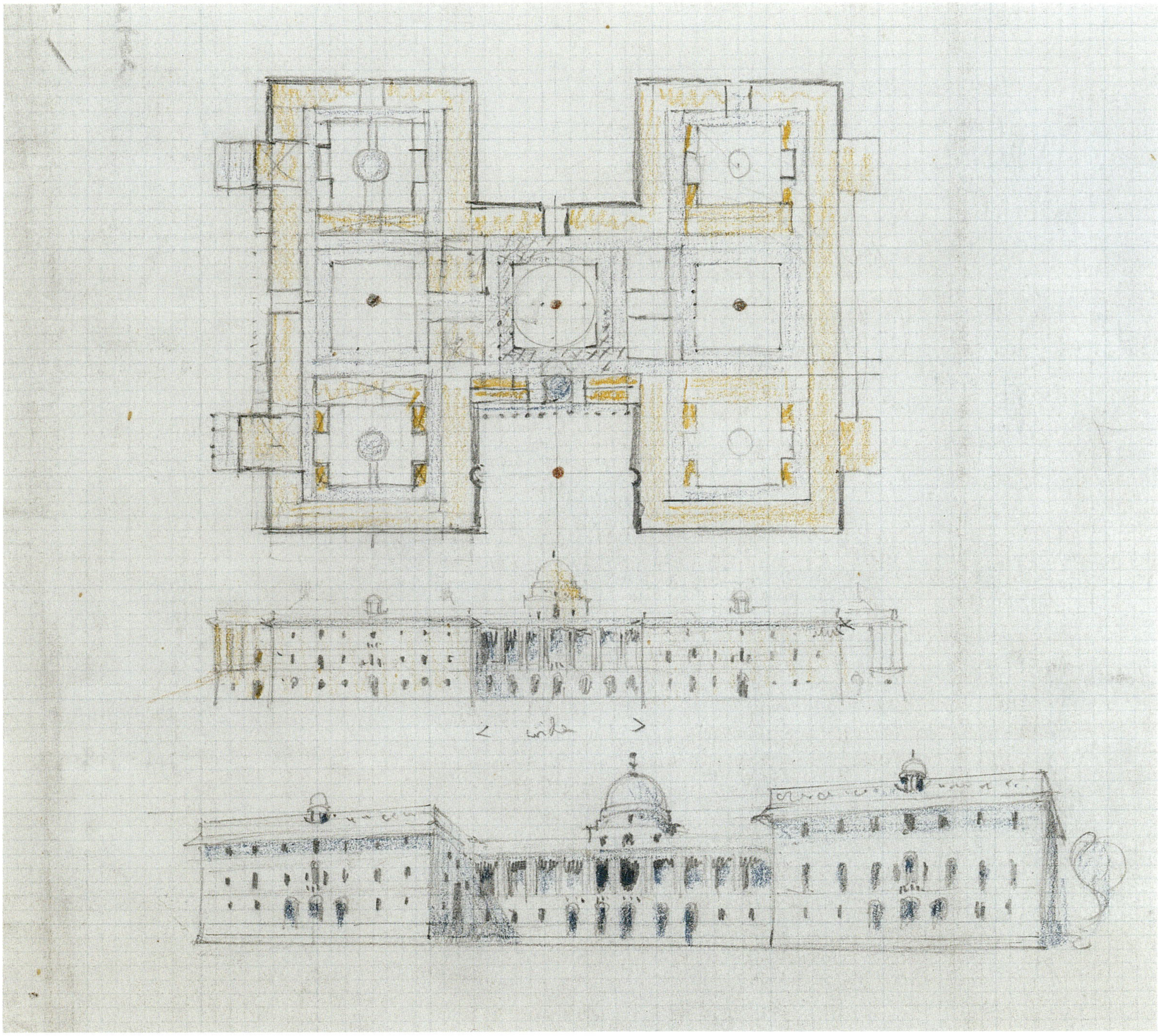

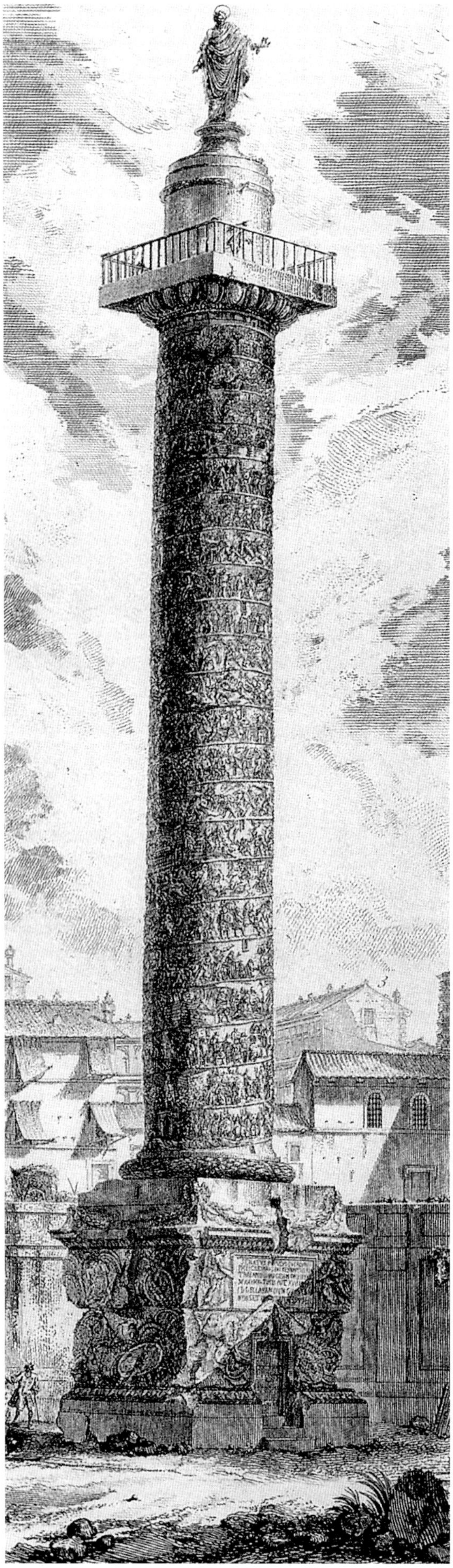

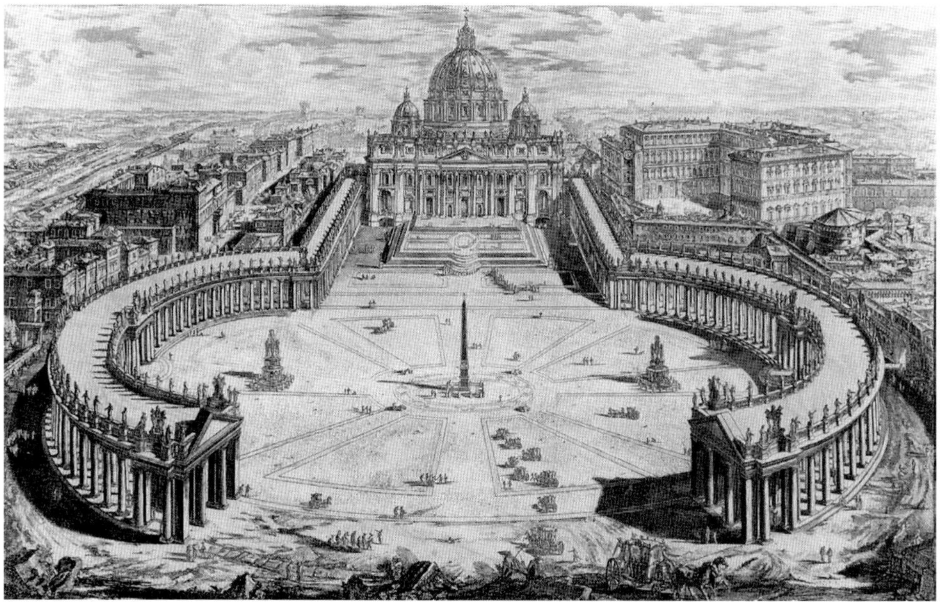

Fig. 72: Trajan's column and Bernini's colonnades for St Peter's Square in Rome (two engravings by Piranesi) were models for Lutyens' initial plan for the courtyard in front of Viceroy's House.

Fig. 73: A hand-drawn sketch by Lutyens from June 14, 1912, provided for a large square in front of Viceroy's House with colonnades à la Bernini and two columns in the transverse axis (handwritten entry: Trajan Column); west is on top.

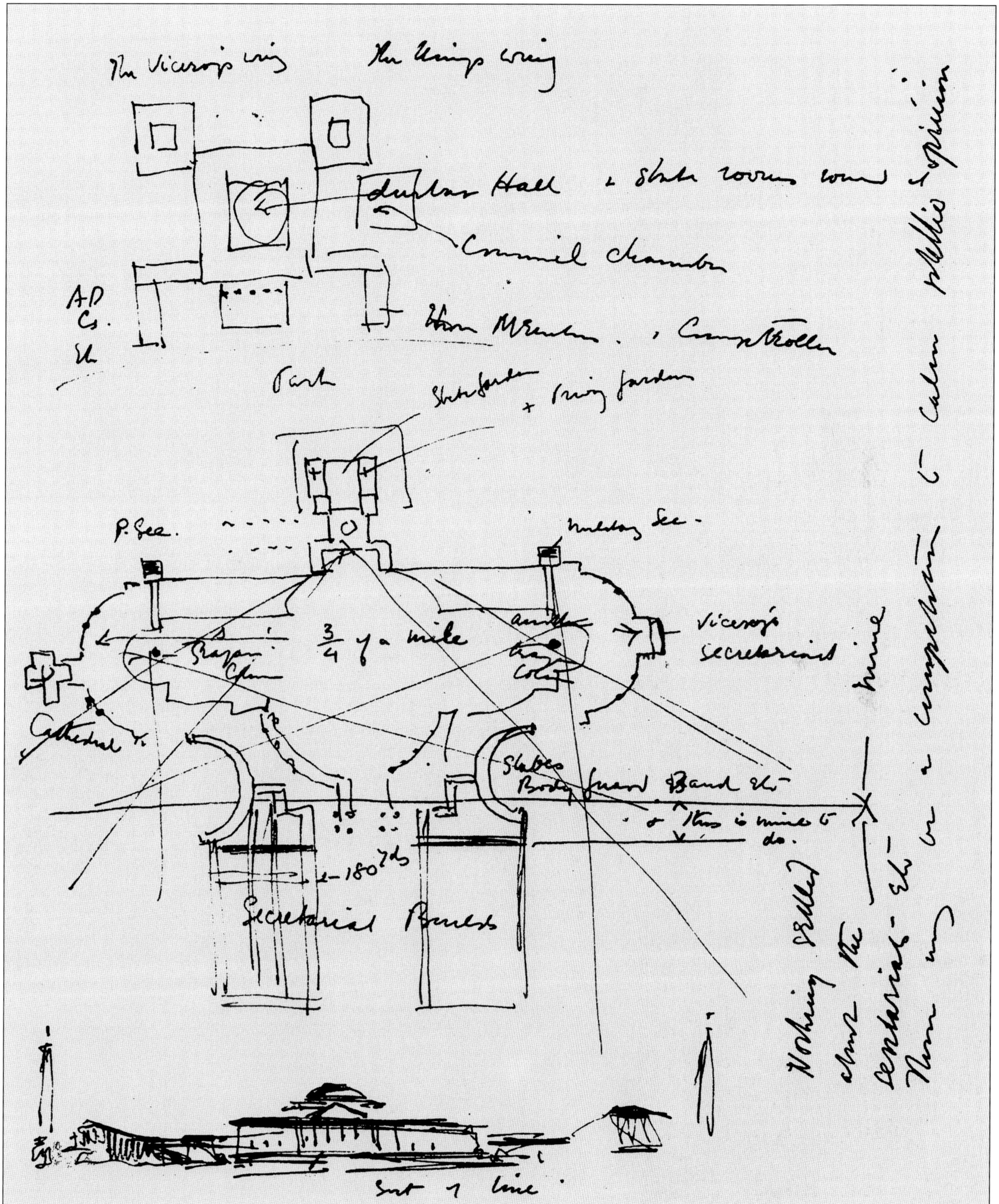
The Viceroy's wing
The Kings wing
Durbar Hall & State rooms round
Council chamber
AD
Cs.
Hon Members . , Comptroller
Park
State garden
+ Privy garden
P. Sec.
Military Sec.
3/4 of a mile
Viceroy's Secretariat
Cathedral
Stables
Body Guard Band etc
Secretariat Barracks
Sort of line

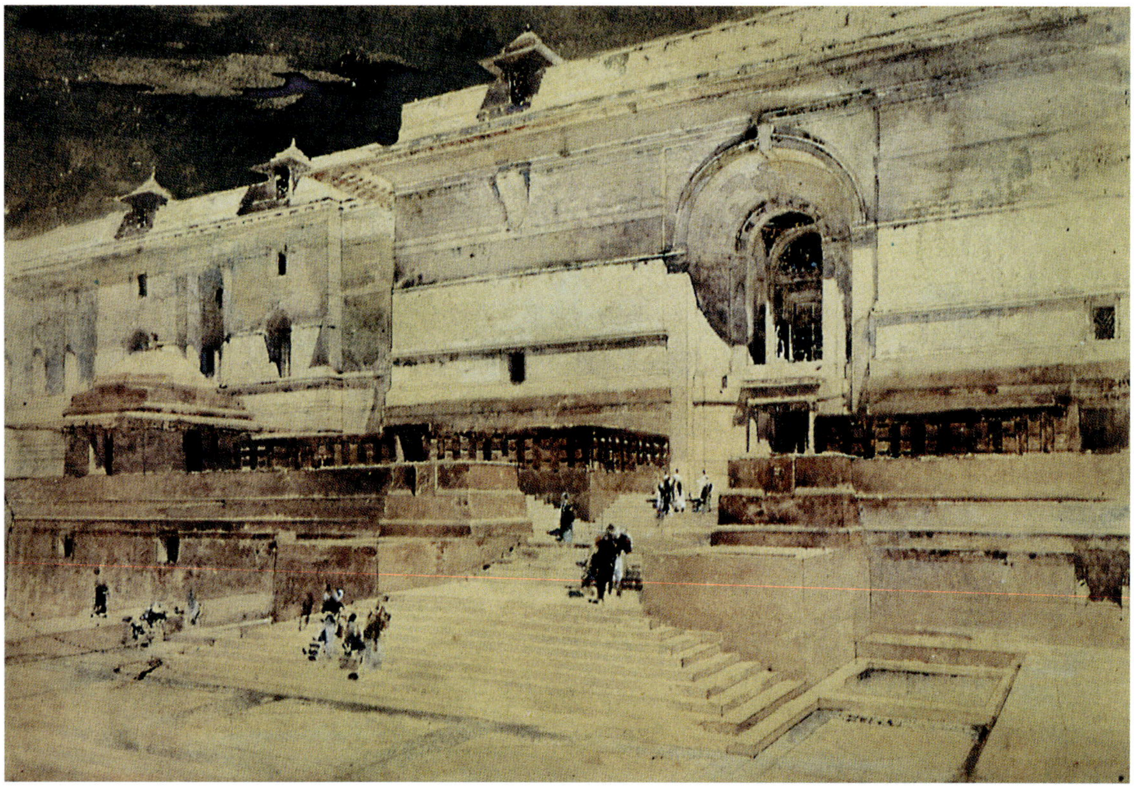

Fig. 74: A watercolour by William Walcot from 1914 depicts the northern entrance of Viceroy's House, designed by Edwin Lutyens. All the facades, courtyards, and steps were introduced to the Viceroy according to their architectural effect by a series of watercolours.

omitted in Lutyens' final plan, but appeared again in Herbert Baker's plans for the Secretariats, where it was implemented (Fig. 129).

In a preliminary sketch of the future Viceroy's House, Lutyens referred directly back to the Villa Rotonda near Vicenza (Fig. 78). Although Palladio was one of Lutyens' greatest models, he rejected this particular model because of the impossibility of fitting all the necessary living and office accommodation into such a compact building type. In the end, the Villa Rotonda did find its way into the plans for Viceroy's House, in the central area of the circular Durbar Hall, and in the portico at its front.

Like other patrons, the Viceroy, Lord Hardinge, wanted to include some of his own ideas. Consequently, the increasing size of the building exceeded the budget set by London. A process of cuts and restrictions, equally painful to architect and patron, was introduced.

The Viceroy gradually accepted a plan that was finally realized (Fig. 75). In spite of all the suggestions for alterations, a palace was built which, in the clarity of its spatial order, was not inferior to Buckingham Palace and exceeded it in its total area. In addition, through the consistent axial alignment of the largest and most important room, the Durbar Hall, there was a clear division of offices.

To the west of the Durbar Hall were the three important official rooms with prospects out to the Mughal garden, namely the State Dining Room, the West Garden Loggia, and the State Ball Room. In the adjoining southwest wing were living accommodations for the Viceroy and his family; symmetrical to these sections were suites for the Viceroy's guests in the northwest wing. To the east of the Durbar Hall, on one side of the huge open-air staircase, was the administration wing for the Viceroy's officials and on its opposing side, an additional guest wing.

Comparisons with Frank Lloyd Wright's architecture

The strict geometry and symmetry of the ground plan and elevation has always led architects and architectural historians to consider to what extent and by what principles form and function stand in relation to each other. Perhaps, particularly striking is a comparison by

A. Greenberg, who, in 1969, referred to parallels with the architecture of Frank Lloyd Wright. On Wright's logic about the disposition of the ground plan Greenberg wrote: "The similarity to the organization of Lutyens' plan is startling: the use of a preconceived geometric plan form, cross axes occupied by a solid mass, asymmetrical circulation within a plan of symmetrically disposed rooms, the interweaving of circulation and axes, and the development of sequences of spaces. The differences stem from Wright's preference for the cruciform plan, one room thick, which allows a direct interior-to-exterior relationship. The circumferential circulation can then be tied to the core and complemented by the radial vistas out on the axes to the exterior."[16]

There was no direct relationship between contemporaries Frank Lloyd Wright and Edwin Lutyens. Despite the parallels in spatial disposition they were divided not only by continents, but also by different models and a different clientele. The one looked back to the splendour of imperial traditions in Europe; at the same time, the other laid the foundations for a new epoch in the history of architecture. Of course, both were aware of the other's buildings, but there was no pressing need or desire for an exchange of ideas.

In retrospect, the stages of the plan or different plans for the Viceroy's palace can only be reconstructed with some uncertainty. Common to all of them was the aim of making a monumental domed room modelled on the Pantheon as the central point of a symmetrical building modelled on the Villa Rotonda at Vicenza. For example, in Lutyens' plan of June 14, 1912, this was brought about (see Fig. 73, above) by extending the central building reserved for official functions through a wing in the east (west is on top in Fig. 73), for the administration, and the square extensions in the west for living accommodation.

Spatial disposition

In the final plan, these architectural and functional components were altered in shape in accordance with an ambitious spatial concept, and more importantly, in accordance with Lutyens' preference for a geometric code. In so doing, a larger amount of road surfaces impinge on the eye. This is not attributable to any supposed incompetence in the rational arrangement of the ground plan. Rather, the ceremonial significance of the movement towards the centre of imperial power inside the palace has been properly thought out in the same way as the ceremonial significance of the seemingly interminably long Raj Path from the Jumna River to Viceroy's House.

The great open staircase along the axis of Viceroy's House, together with the added portico and an enormous vestibule, no longer had the function of respectfully receiving large numbers of visitors. Only heads of state were allowed to use this axial entrance. VIPs drove in their coaches or cars from north to south, to the central staircase court through tunnels in the upper basement that appeared to be underground. From there, they walked via an enormous open staircase (see Fig. 98), through the Staircase Court – a stairwell open at the top – up to the level of the Durbar Hall. Even then, they only reached the hall after making a half turn because the Staircase Court had been intentionally placed, not at the front, but at the back of Durbar Hall.

In his comparison with Frank Lloyd Wright, Allen Greenberg summed up the distinctive features of many of Lutyens' ground plans as follows: "There is an almost symmetrical disposition of rooms within a square or a symmetrical H plan. This order is emphasized by the symmetry of the exterior massing, the fenestration, and the placement of the chimneys and the entrance ... Superimposed on this plan is an independent and circumambulatory circulation pattern. Neither the formal and symmetrical massing, nor the elevations express the intricacy of the interior plan. Almost all of Lutyens' houses conform to this scheme. The plan of Viceroy's House, for example, is a variation of that of Nashdom. The portico and Durbar Hall are enlarged and domed versions of the latter's entrance porch and circular courtyard ... The interplay of axes and the independent circulation system implies that movement itself, as distinct from axial or visual linkages, is the main element of continuity.[17]

16 A. Greenberg: "Lutyens' Architecture Restudied," in: *Perspecta*, 1969, Connecticut, p. 145.

17 Ibid., pp. 129, 130.

Fig. 75: Lutyens' preliminary drafts were often covered with calculations about important proportions. It was the task of his team to draw up a clean plan taking great care to include all this information.

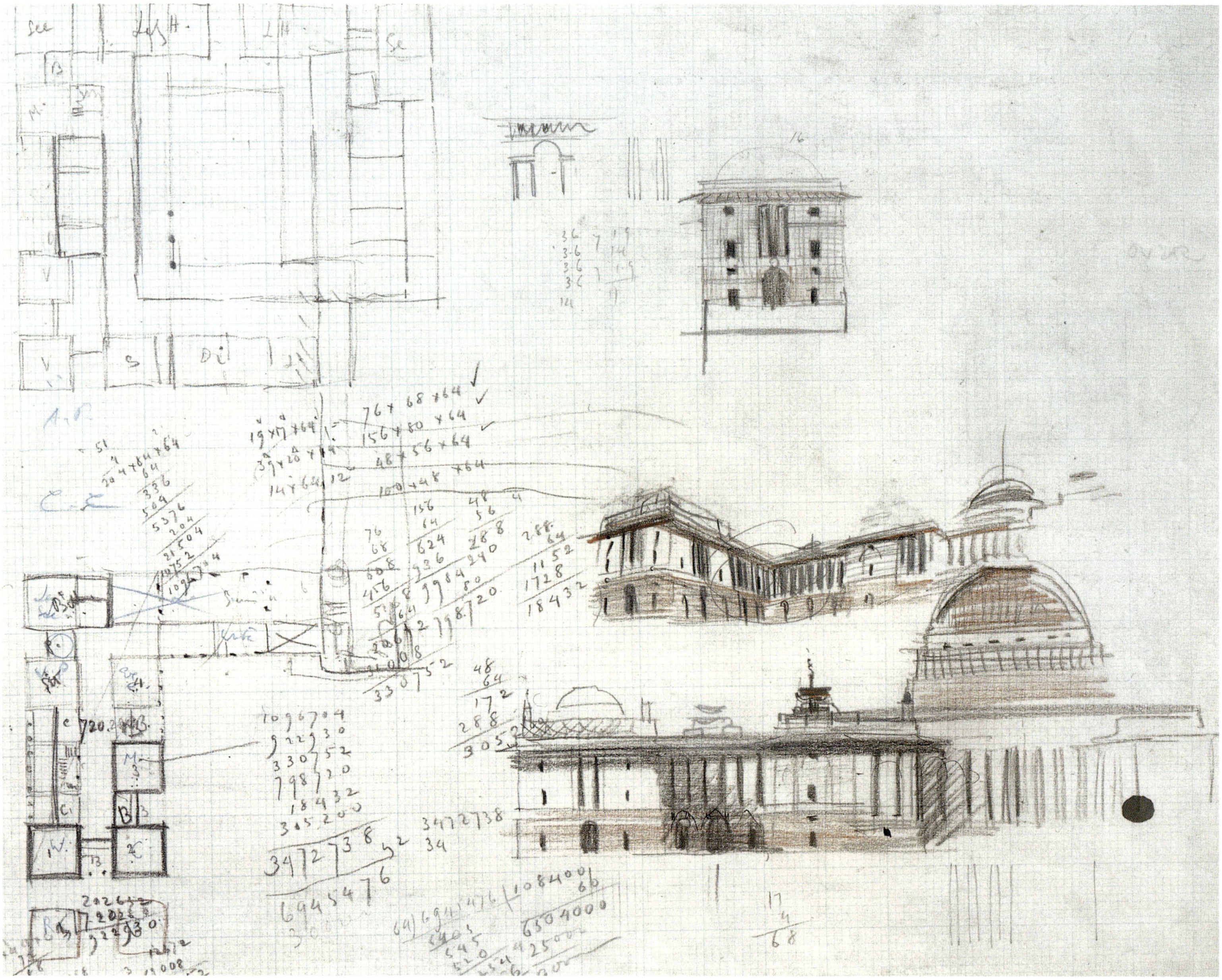

Fig. 77: In 1922, William Rothenstein drew a portrait of Lutyens, then a successful, forty-three-year-old London architect.

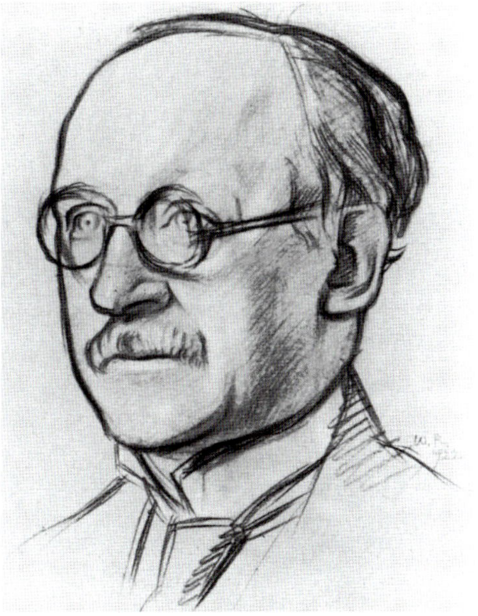

Fig. 76: In 1914, in order to please the Viceroy, Lutyens attempted to include Hindu and Islamic elements in the formal repertoire for Viceroy's House. But with every new attempt, he became more certain that in the framework of Neo-Palladian architecture this was only possible to a very limited extent.

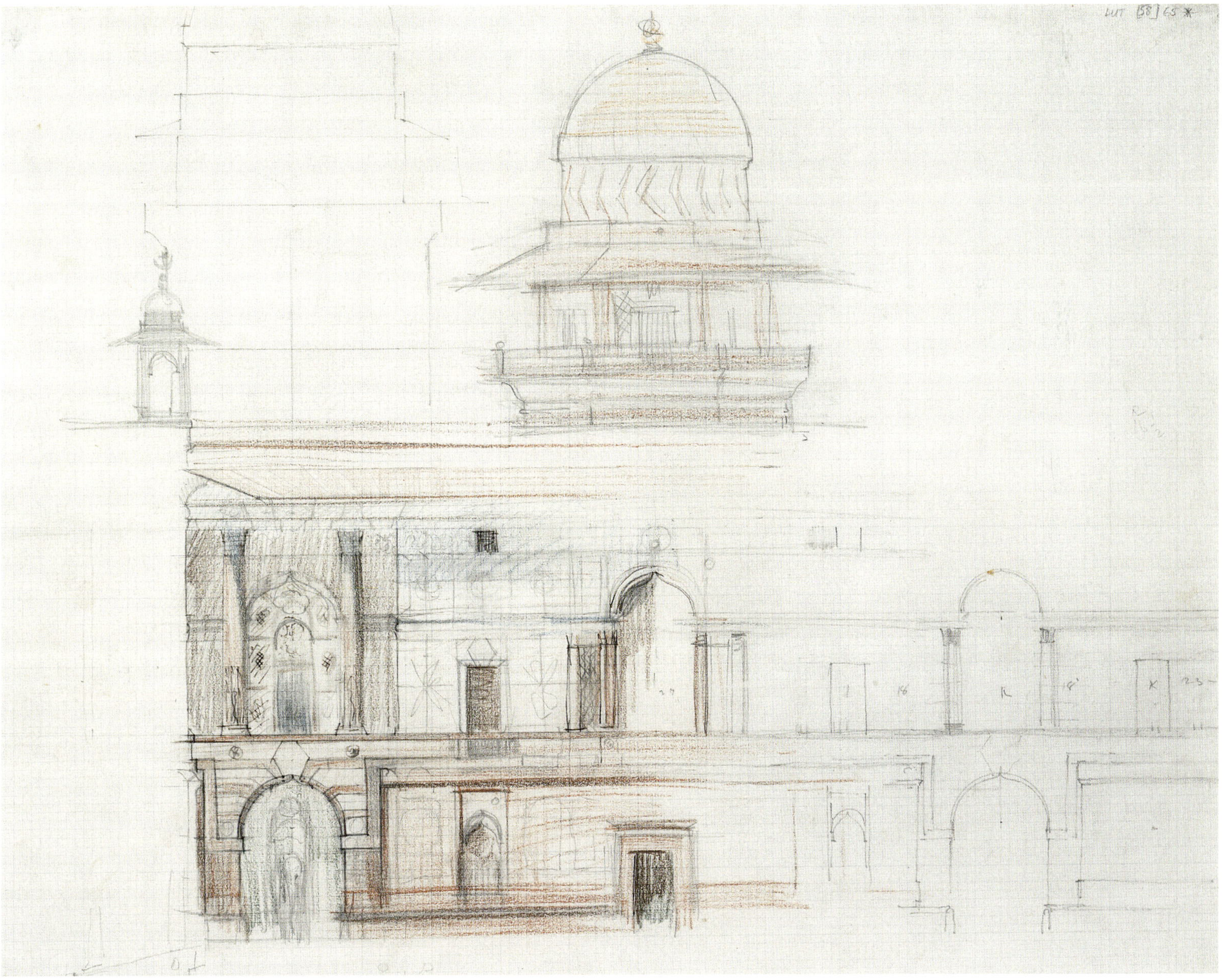

Fig. 78: Lutyens experimented untiringly in both his Delhi and London offices, and on the long sea voyages between the two, with geometric ground plans for the Durbar Hall in Viceroy's House. The primary models were the Pantheon in Rome and Palladio's Villa Rotonda in Vicenza, whose ground plan and elevation he adopted in one of the alternative plans, including details of the shape of the roof and dome, and the window arrangement.

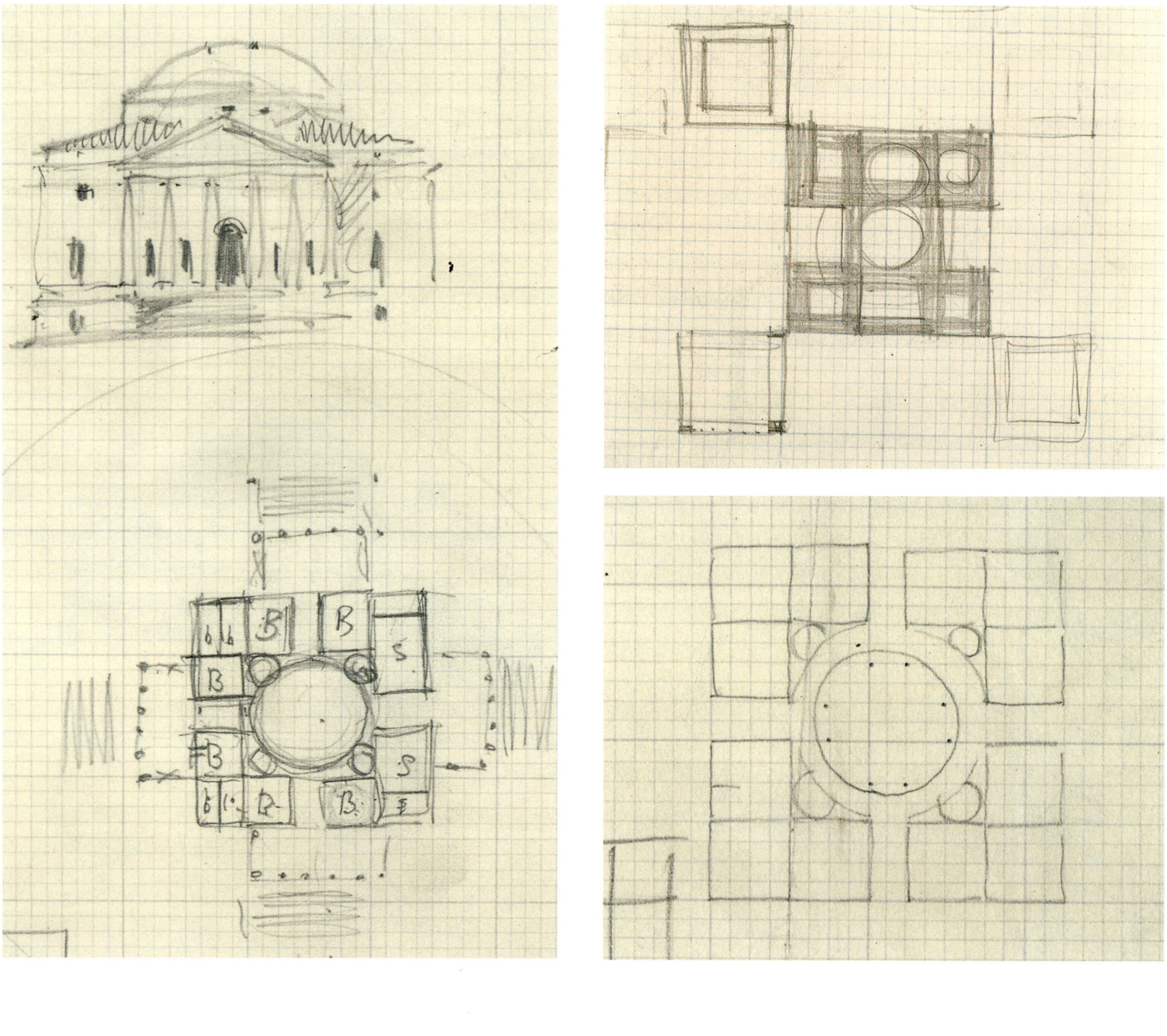

Geometry

Just as Edwin Lutyens' functional developments were planned in a complex and detailed way, his sketches were so filled with complex mathematical and geometric instructions concerning the proportions of every architectural element (see Fig. 75). A comprehensive analysis of these has yet to appear. Individual basic forms and proportions, since they constantly recur, permit us to make a rough reconstruction of the geometry of his plans for Viceroy's House.

The starting point for the ground plan was the so-called "ideal rectangle" that Lutyens had also used in other buildings (step 1). The length and breadth of the 'ideal rectangle' are obtained from two adjacent equilateral triangles. The longer sides of the rectangle run from north to south, and the shorter ones from east to west.

A circle inscribed in the "ideal rectangle" (step 2) not only defines the central square of the whole plan, but also the axes of the two large courtyards to the south and north of the Durbar Hall (cf. step 4). At the same time, a second circle inscribed in the original equilateral triangles defines the position and size of the four wings.

The initial geometric shape of the four wings was, in every case, a square that was added directly on to the central square (step 3). The diagonals of the resultant five squares and the original triangles of the "ideal rectangle" together defined all the spatial proportions and axes of the buildings.

Apart from the rather pointless question as to which precise way Lutyens conceived the ground plan of Viceroy's House, the much more interesting question about its significance remains unexplained. Even Lutyens' contemporaries had little to say about the matter.

W.A.S. Lloyd, who worked in Lutyens' office in London, commented on his boss' love of mathematical rules in his plans: "He worked entirely by relations of parts, thereby involving all in extraordinary mathematical fractions. A notorious instance was the diminishing rustication blocks on the Midland Bank, Poultry, each of which was to be a fraction less in height than the one below it and involved a diminution by 0.273 recurring of an inch. He would admit of no approximation. 'About! I don't know what you mean by about!' he would say."[16]

Because Lutyens made no mention of the subject of mathematical and geometric regularity in his numerous letters, this aspect of his planning appears to us today, probably correctly, to be a jealously guarded and mysterious secret that, in its complexity, was never shared with any other human being. Only once did he explicitly draw on his sketching pad the geometric basis of so many of his plans, namely, the motif of the hexagon, as a circle of spheres on the edge of the plan (Fig. 80). Unlike Vitruvius or Palladio, he obviously had no interest in passing on all of his personal ideas of the beautiful or sublime as a guiding principle, or of even discussing such matters with his colleagues and pupils.

One of the many demonstrable geometric rules we should mention is the angle of just under 60° that Lutyens refers to as AN. It appears again and again in, among other places, the cross-sectional plans of ceiling profiles, architraves, and cornices: "First, at the top left-hand corner, what is labelled The Angle refers to one variously described as 54° 45' or 54 $^{3}/_{4}$°. Its exact inclination is not so important as the fact that this is one formed by the diagonal of a rectangle of which the long side is one formed by the diagonal of a square on its base. It is the angle which Lutyens discovered, some years after commencing in practice, made a cornice turning an outside right-angle appear – for geometrical reasons – to be at 45° in section on the mitre. It had the same valuable effect on the hips of roofs; and, as he discovered that the results of a use of this angle pleased him to look at, he adopted it as a self-imposed regulation."[19]

In our attempts to decipher at least some of Lutyens' geometric secrets, we not only come across the constantly recurring combination of square, circle, and equilateral triangle as the basic geometric shapes in the ground plan, but also in all the elevations of Viceroy's House. In this, Lutyens followed the tradition of Francesco Borromini and Christopher Wren. In 1634, Borromini had developed the plan for his little church of S Carlino alle Quattro Fontane in Rome from the equilateral triangle (Fig. 85, left), and Christopher Wren followed the same geometric path in his plan of St Paul's Cathedral in London in 1666 (Fig. 85 right).

18 Christopher Hussey, op. cit., p. 491.

19 A.S.G. Butler: *The Architecture of Sir Edwin Lutyens*, Vol. III, London and New York 1950, p. 21.

Step 1

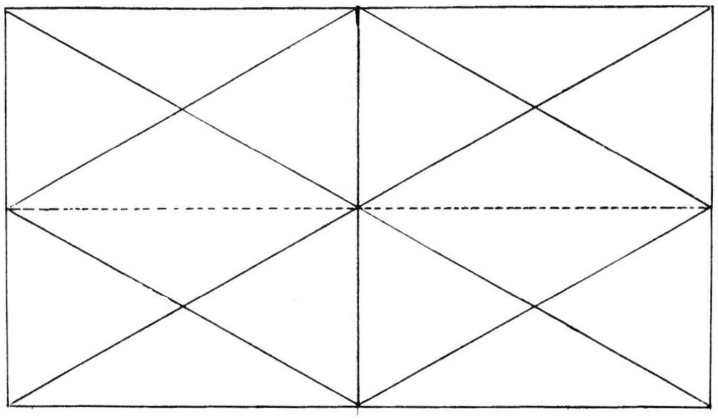

Step 2

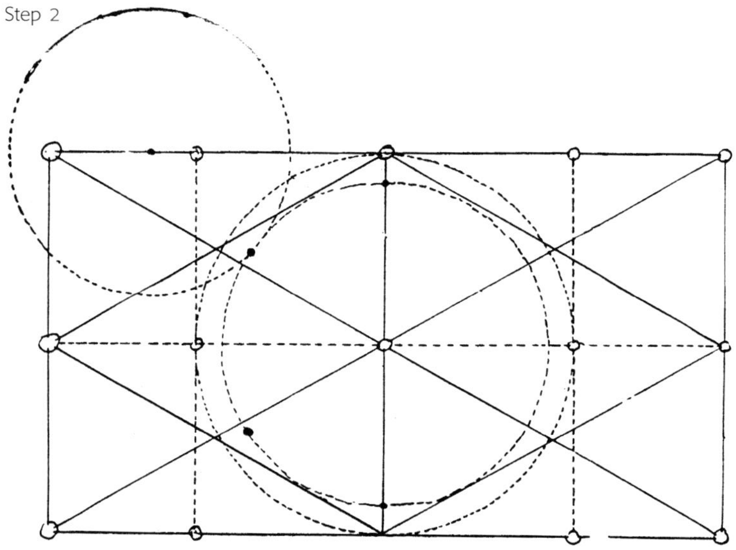

On a section of the facade of the northern entrance to Viceroy's House, the link with geometry can be reconstructed with certainty because of an original drawing from Lutyens' office (Fig. 86) published by Robert Byron in 1931.[20] The monumental round arch of this entranceway stretching over two storeys is defined by two circles with the diameter of d1. Two circles d2 with a diameter of half the size are placed on top of each other in the lower circle. Again, two circles d3, now only with diameters of a quarter the size of d1 lie inside these, i.e. d3 = d1/4.

D3 is the basic measurement for the development of the height of this facade, and also defines the width of the gateway. Next, there is an equilateral triangle that lies on the lowest circle (d3) and has a height of 7d1. The length of the side of the triangle determines the position of the windows on both sides of the gate.

Such geometric interpretations of this kind run the risk of over-interpretation, as well as arriving at an interpretation that may not be adequate. Therefore, it is fortunate that, as in the case sited above, part of the geometric interpretation was given to us by the architect.

Another example of the geometric development of the facades at Viceroy's House worth mentioning is the west side of the northwest wing (Fig. 87). Here, we no longer have an original plan with the architect's instructions on the logic of its proportions, but the system of circles and squares is obvious and can be reconstructed as follows without the danger of over-interpretation: A large square representing the width of the northwest wing, divided into five equal vertical strips, forms the basis of the main axis of the facade below the roof-fountain. These strips determine the position of the window axes and also the width of the gaps between the pillars of the top storey. In developing its height, the large square of the facade is not divided into five equal strips, but in the proportion of 1: 1.5 : 1.5 : 1 into four strips. All the important points of the facades are then defined by either the unit 1, the unit 1.5, or the unit 0.5.

20 R. Byron: "New Delhi," in: *AR*, Vol. LXIX, No. 410, January 1931, p. 26.

Step 3

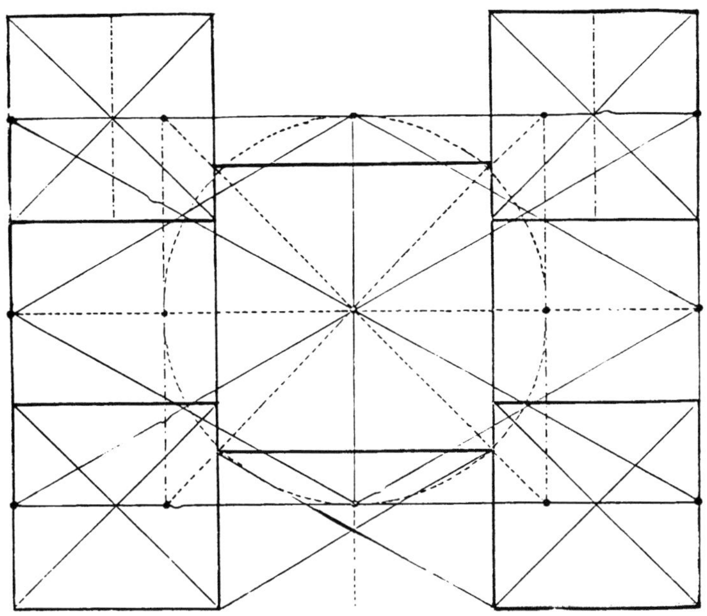

Step 4

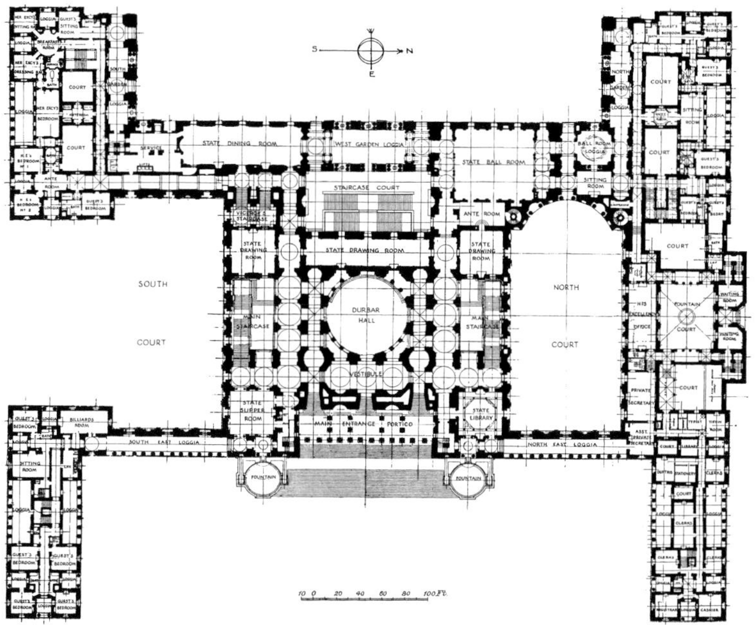

Fig. 79: The plan for Viceroy's House (now Rashtrapati Bhavan) is derived from the so-called "ideal rectangle" on which Lutyens, among others, based his plan for the All India War Memorial. It is derived from two equilateral triangles placed against each other. Another geometric element for the plan was the square with its diagonals.

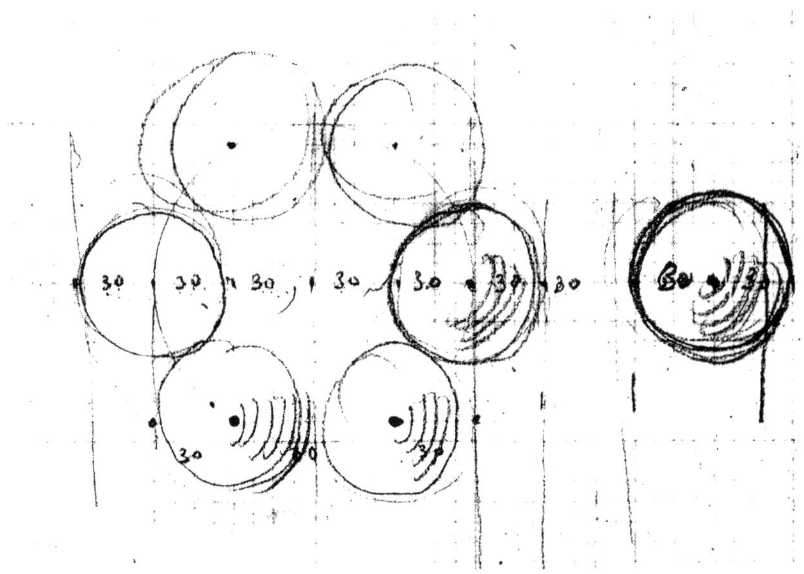

Fig. 80: Lutyens' preference for the geometric motif of the hexagon and hexagram also appears in his hand-drawings.

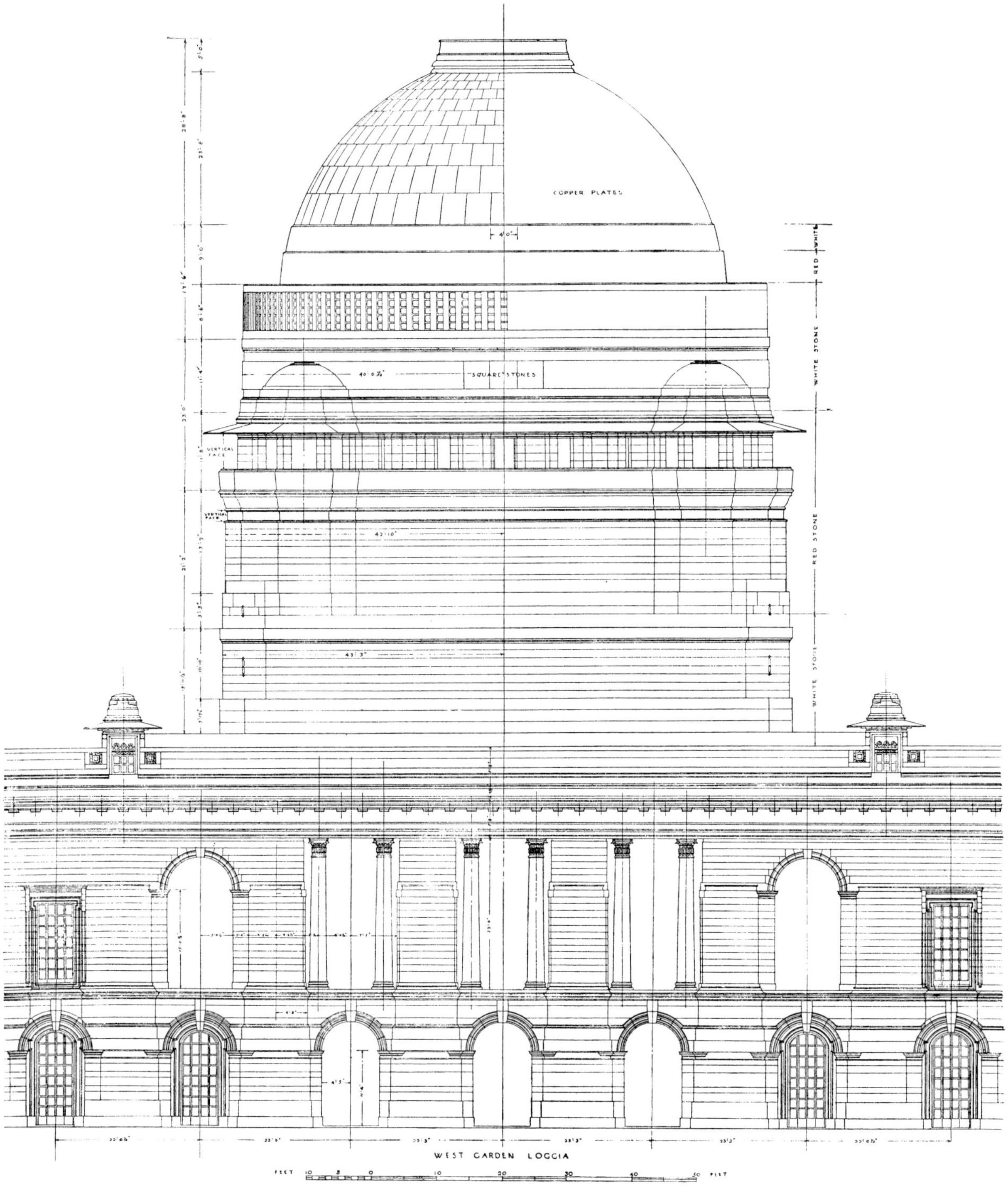

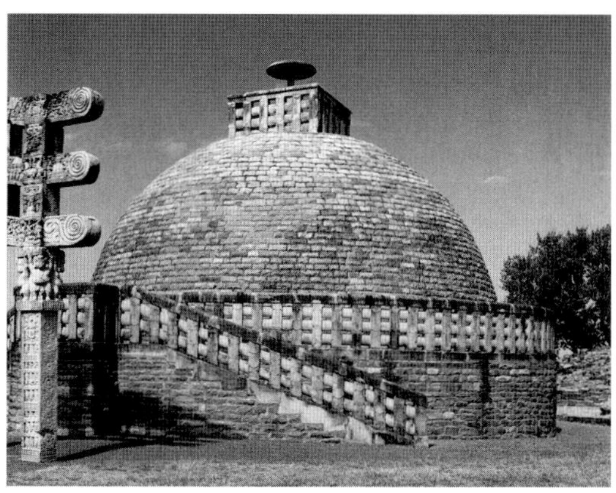

Fig. 81: Ultimately, the design of Viceroy's House in Imperial Delhi followed the models of the Capitol in Washington, D.C. and the Pantheon in Rome much less closely. In the tambour, Lutyens adopted the form of the chattris, not a favourite form for the architect (cf. Fig. 50), and the stone railings around early Buddhist shrines.

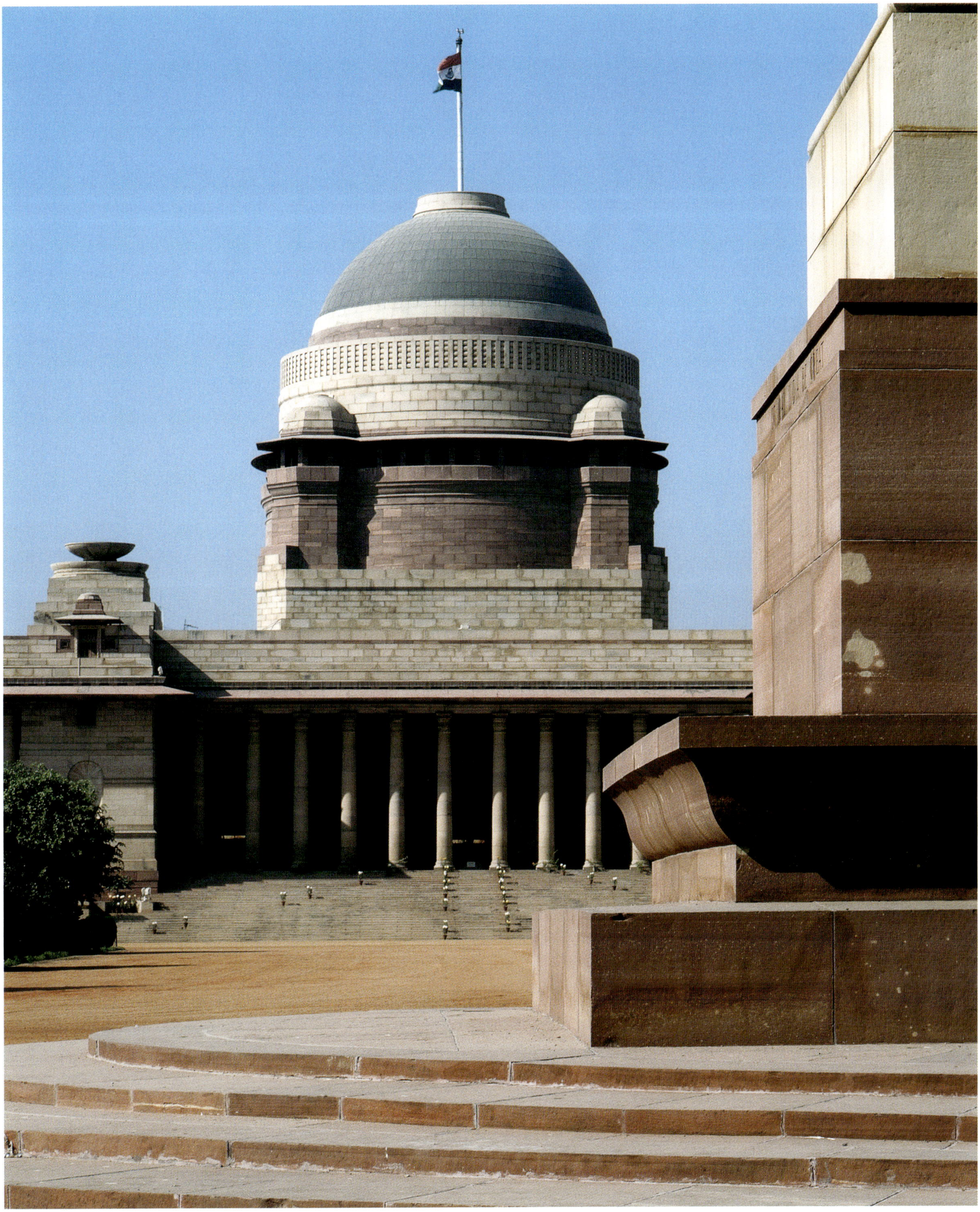

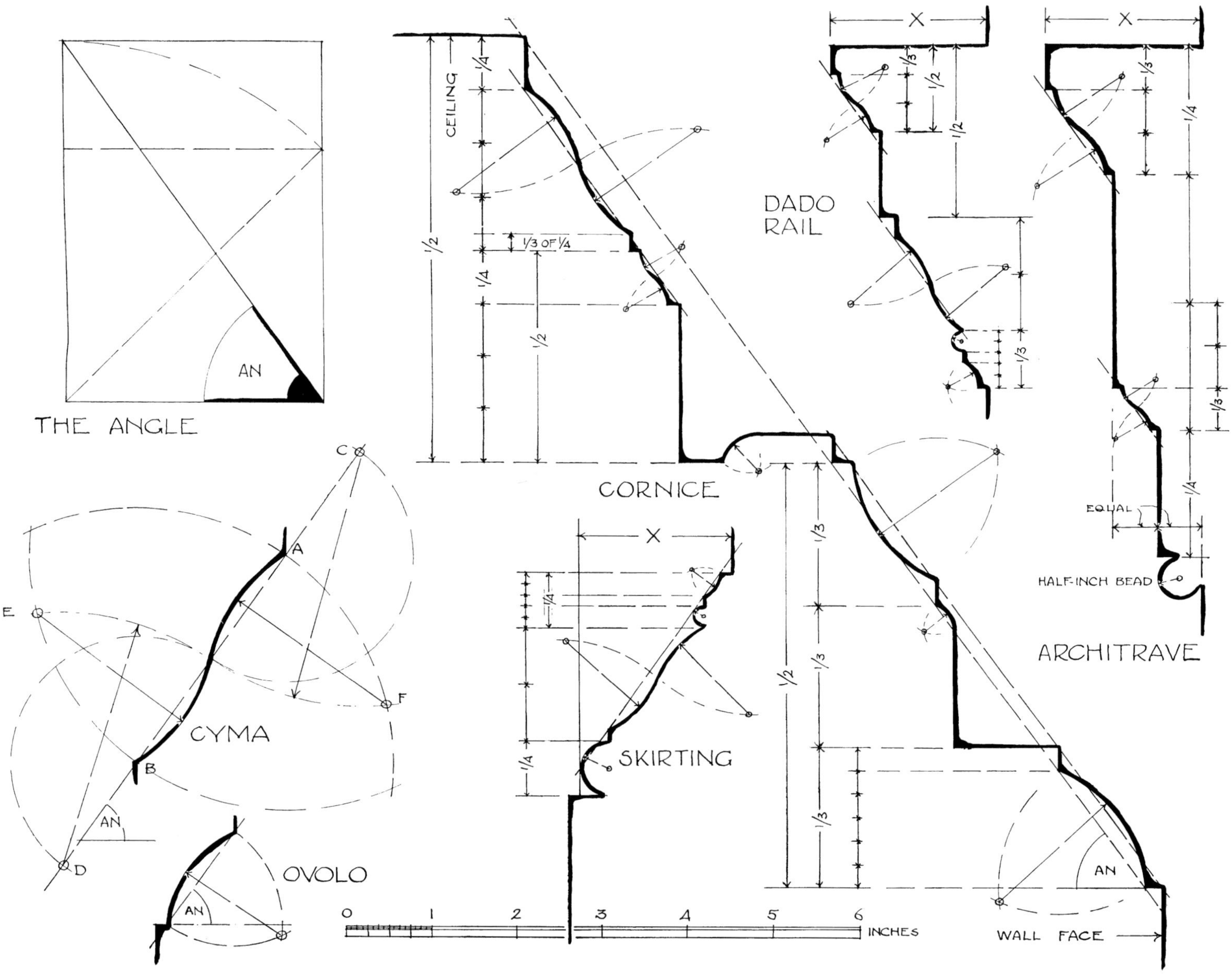

Fig. 82: Lutyens insisted on geometrically or numerically defined rules for all architectural details. Thus, the angle described by him as AN acquired a special significance. This angle is derived by using a compass stroke with the diagonal of a square.

Fig. 83: The Great Staircase in the Staircase Court at the time of construction (cf. Fig. 98).

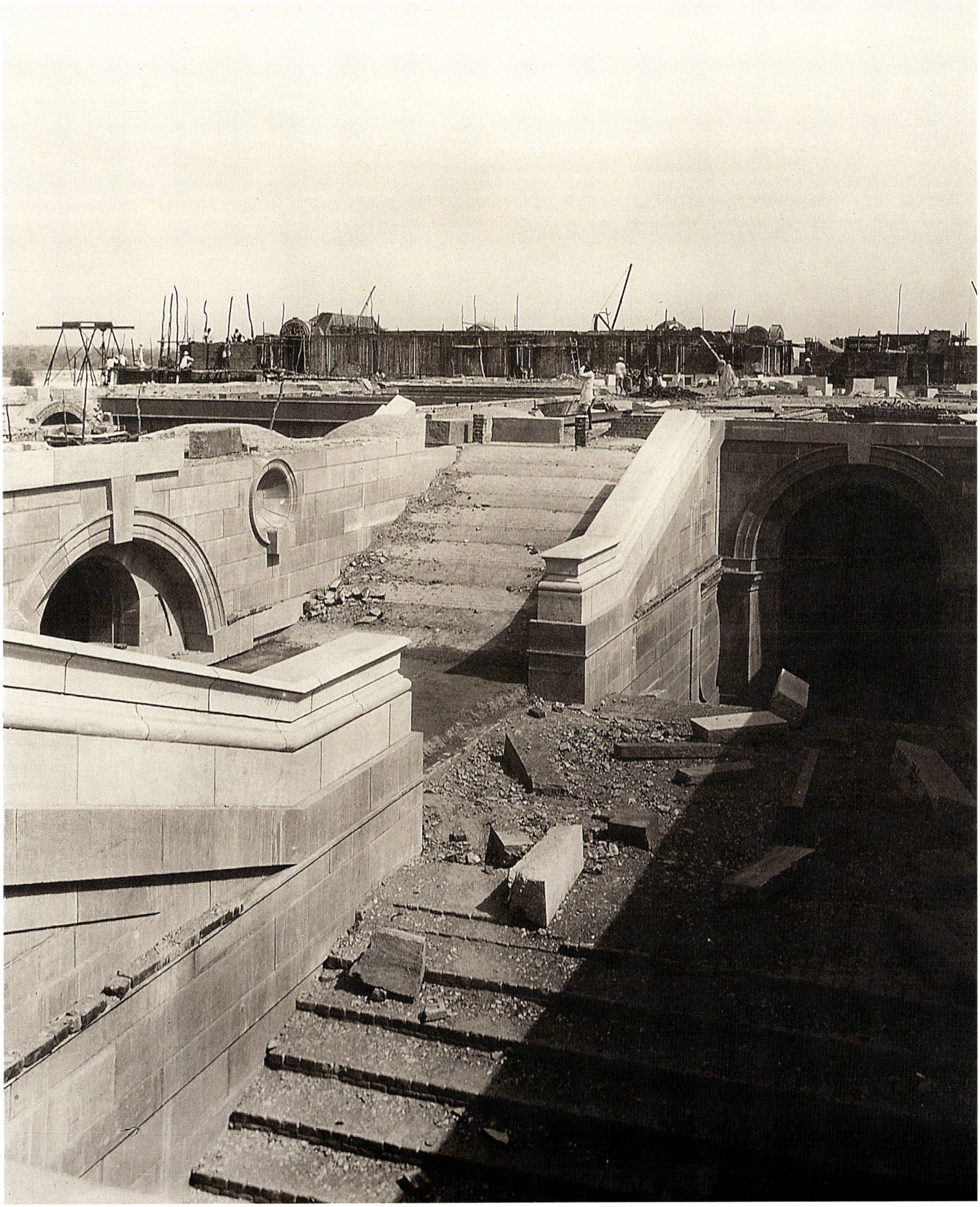

Such interpretations are certainly useful for reconstructing the development of a design, but they do not reveal a basic statement about the starting points and intentions of a definite formal canon. As early as 1895–96, Lutyens had already taken a playful interest in the formal canon of imperial architecture. In his sketchbook "Castle in the Air," he painted a fantasy watercolour, *Château d'Ease, en Air, sur Fleuve des Rêves,* to amuse an invalid lady, Mrs Robert Webb of Milford House, near Godalming. The Chateau is on the river and is only accessible by water. The entrance, the "Porte Fluviale de Circonstance," is in the Romanesque style. A light green copper dome hangs over the grand facade. Margaret Richardson writes, "Drawn from the Renaissance and Byzantine sources that were inspiring architects during the 1890s, the sketchbook is full of ideas that were expressed much later in Lutyens' designs for the Viceroy's House, the Dublin Bridge, and Liverpool Cathedral."[21]

21 Margaret Richardson: *Sketches by Edwin Lutyens,* RIBA Drawings Monographs No. 1, London, 1994.

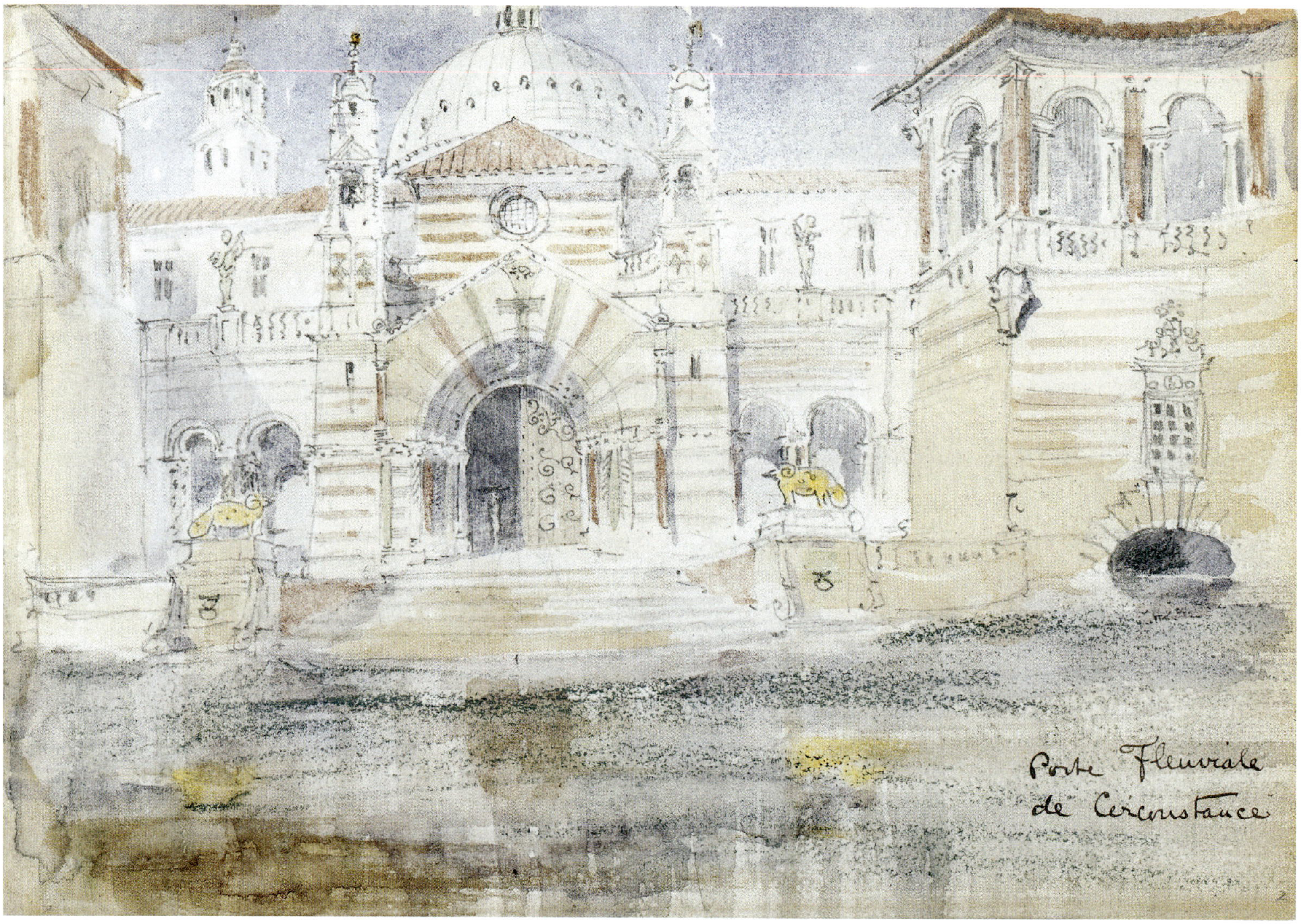

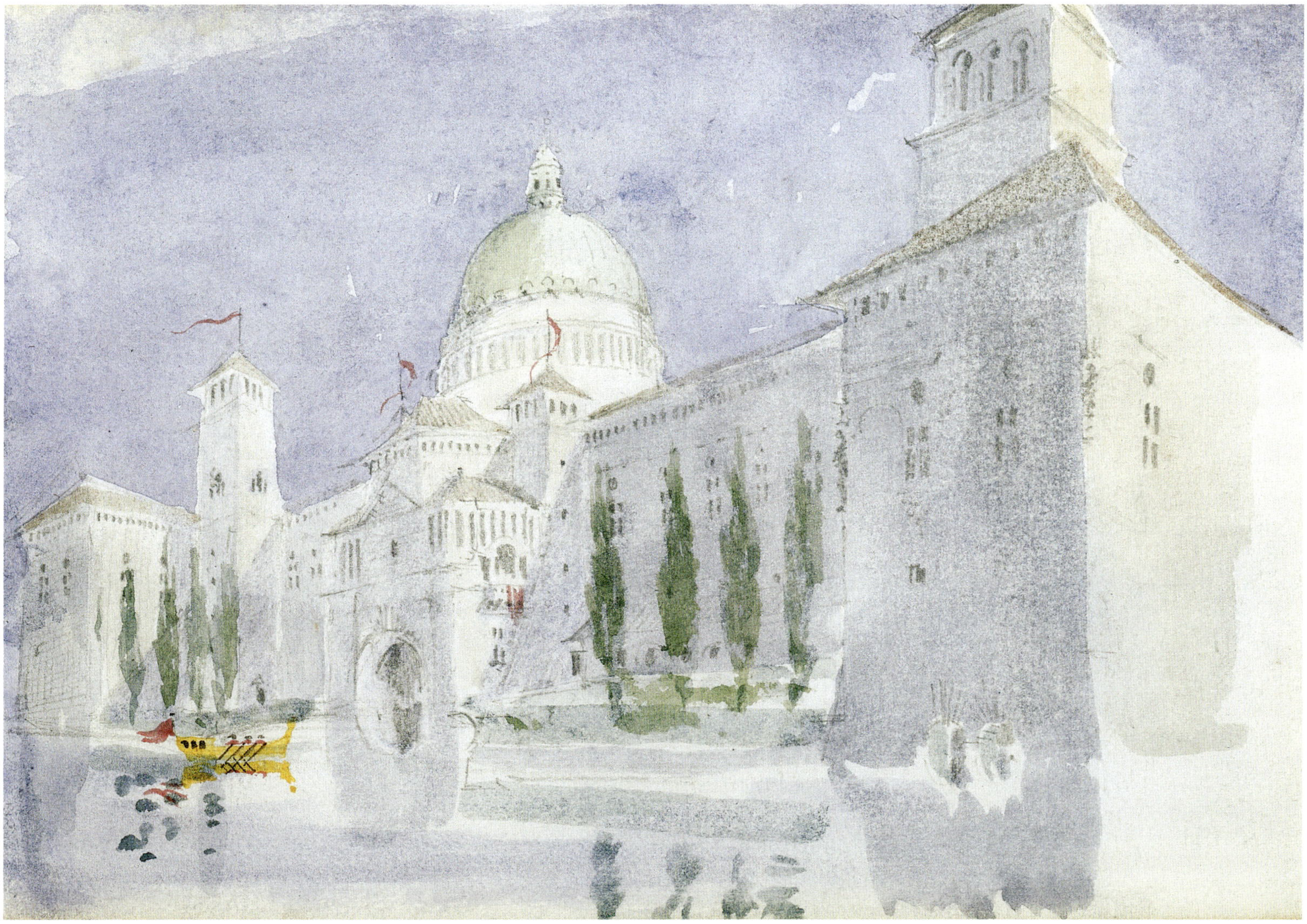

Fig. 84: Early watercolours by Edwin Lutyens for a fantasy castle, *Château d'Ease, en Air, sur Fleuve des Rêves*, already foreshadow the character of Viceroy's House and its central Durbar Hall. *Porte Fleuviale de Circonstance* (at left). *Port d'Amour* (at right), painted between 1893 and 1896.

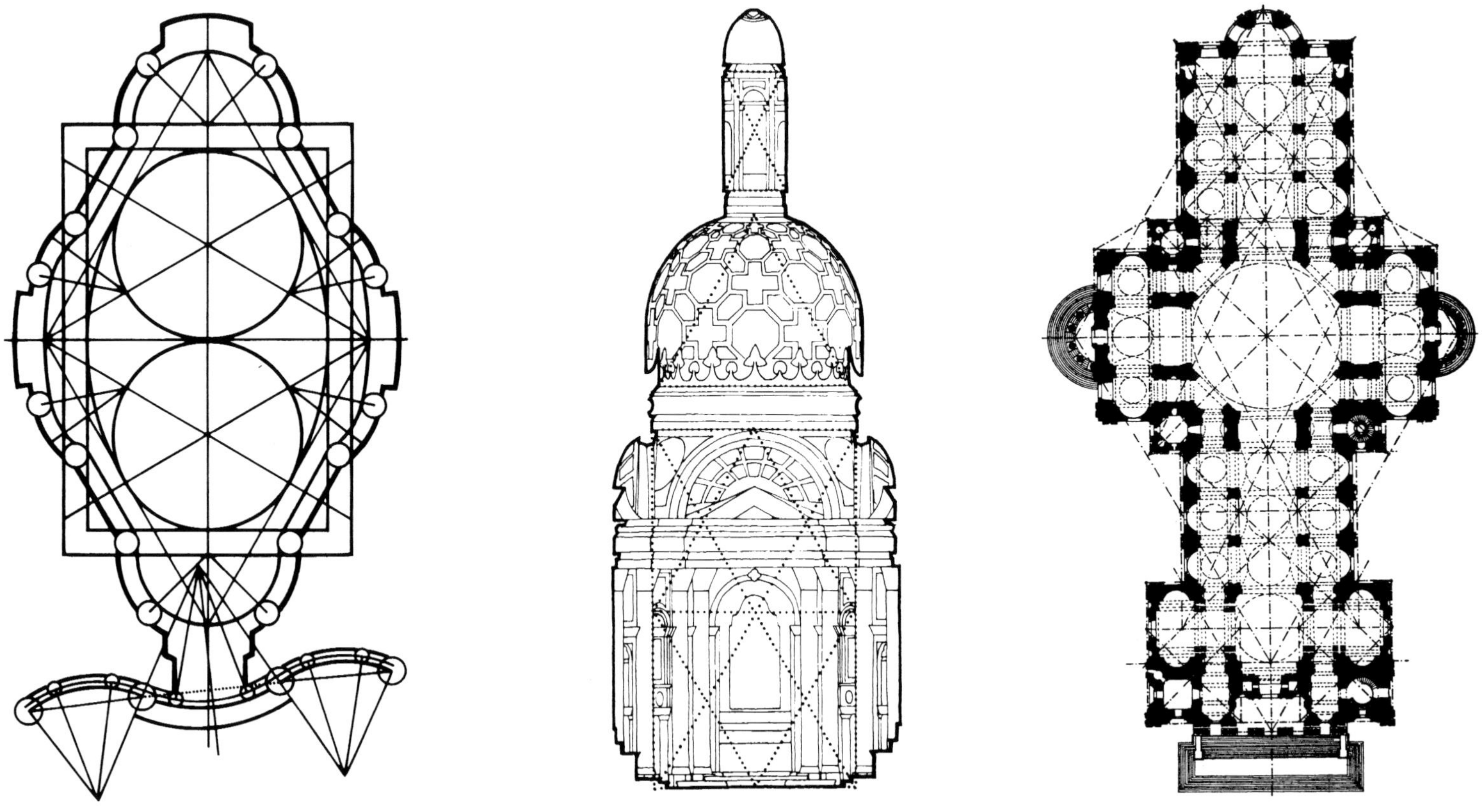

Fig. 85: Francesco Borromini's plan for S Carlino alle quattre fontane in Rome, and Christopher Wren's plan for St Paul's Cathedral in London were both based on the equilateral triangle as geometric pattern. These models strongly influenced Lutyens in his search for an appropriate geometry for Viceroy's House.

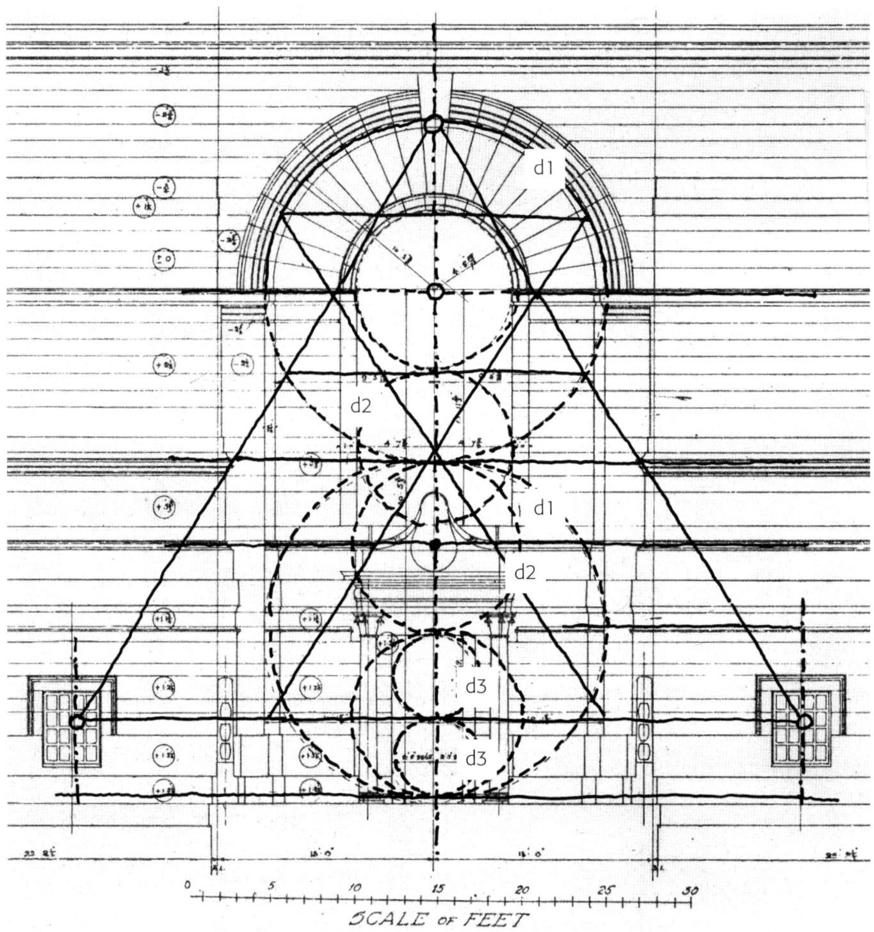

Fig. 86: All the details of the facades of Viceroy's House are subject to a geometric canon embracing the elements of the equilateral triangle, the square, and the circle.

Fig. 87: The elevations of Viceroy's House were planned by Lutyens entirely on the basis of simple geometrical forms, i.e. square and circle.

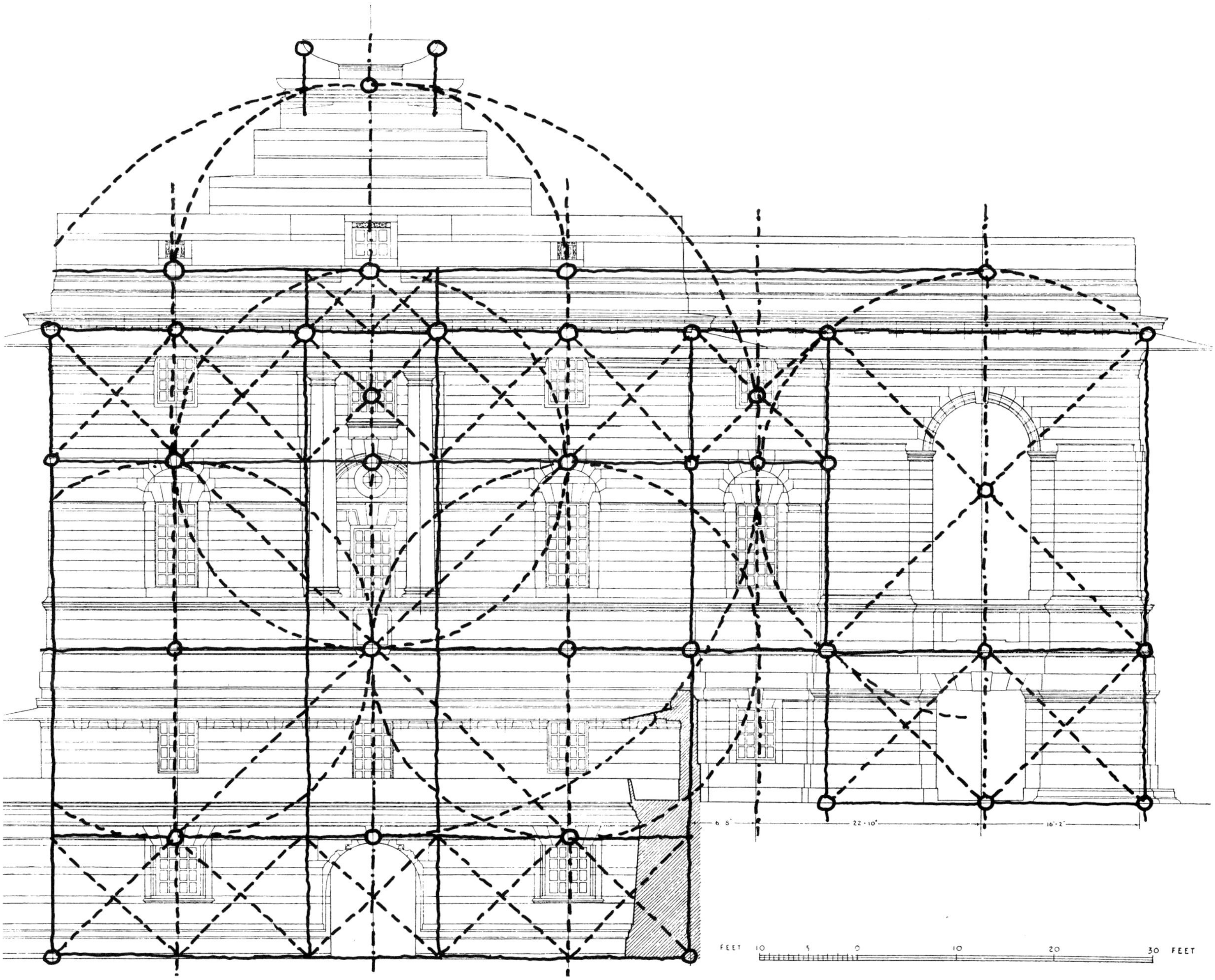

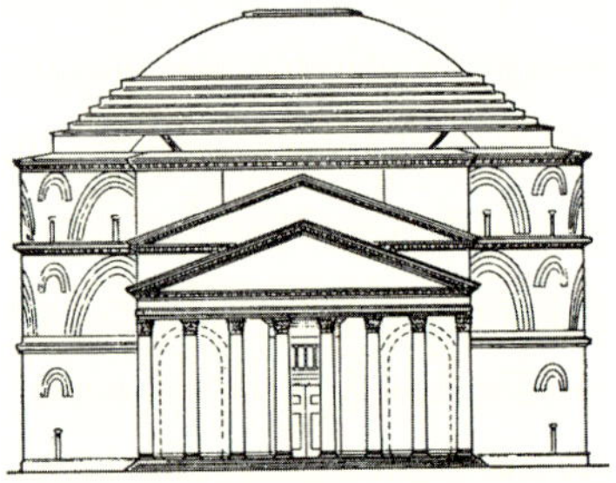
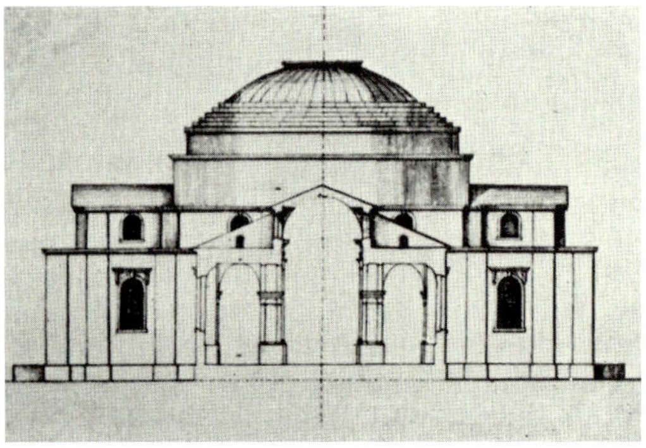
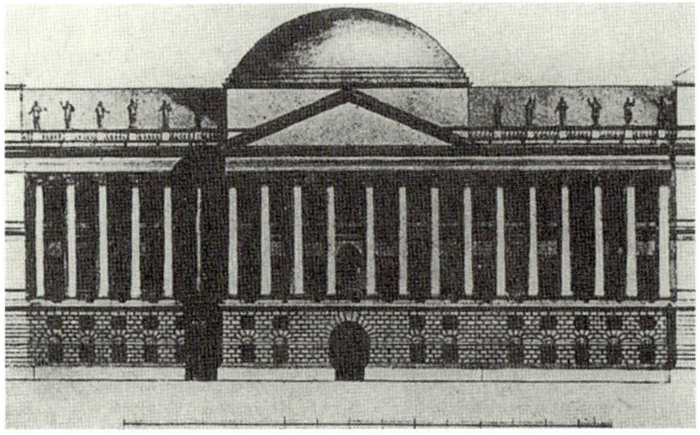

Fig. 88: Lutyens' earliest plan for Viceroy's House (following page) adopts a building style that reappears in a sequence modelled on the Pantheon in Rome, at the beginning of the second century (left). This style is represented in an early plan by Christopher Wren for St Paul's Cathedral in London at the end of the seventeenth century (centre), and in William Kent's plan for Parliament House in London in the middle of the eighteenth century (right).

Renaissance or Mughal style?

It is important to remember the difficulty that Lutyens faced designing the first stages of the plan for Viceroy's House: "Lutyens' initial preference had been for pure classicism. This was what he had envisaged on his first visit to India, and his first designs for Viceroy's House, made in 1912, were strongly Renaissance in character. The Viceroy, on the other hand, pressed for an Indian style, and in particular for the Indo-Saracenic – that loose amalgam of Mogul and Gothic elements that had characterized the architecture of the Raj since the Mutiny of 1857.

Hardinge's reasons were as much political as aesthetic. To stamp the new capital with an alien, Western style would be to negate the entire political purpose of the move to Delhi: the conciliation of Indian, and particularly Muslim, opinion. The virtue of Indo-Saracenic was that it expressed the Raj's aspiration, in the aftermath of the Mutiny, to work in harmony with the old native elites."[22]

On August 30, 1912, Lutyens wrote to his wife, "I am rather nervous too about the King who wants Mogul architecture, etc. Fancy Shakespeare being asked by Elizabeth to write an ode in Chaucerian metre, etc."[23] On September 6 he adds, in another letter, "I do hope all goes well and I shall be able to satisfy the King's Mogul taste."[24]

On December 16, Lutyens, in a statement typical of the ethnocentric views of imperial Britain, added: "Hardinge and Chirol[25] both say that the opinion of the Princes in India is almost entirely in favour of an Indian style. But I say what on earth can an Indian Raj know about architecture and its ethics."[26]

Lutyens was a serious Neo-Classicist who suffered from his political associates' poor understanding of the principles of Palladio and Piranesi. For the architect, their ideas and works possessed absolute value. Sometimes he gave free rein to his displeasure as in the sketches in his letter to Lady Emily on September 6, 1912 (see Figure 89). He even went as far as to give specialist lectures for the Viceroy and Vicereine. The Viceroy was no simple conversation partner. He not only had a broad education, but also occasionally made reference to his good taste in art, for his father was a highly regarded amateur artist in English society.

22 C. Percy, J. Ridley: *The Letters of Edwin Lutyens to his wife Lady Emily*, London 1985, p. 256.
23 Ibid.
24 Ibid.
25 Valentine Chirol (1852–1929), author and foreign editor of the *Times* 1899–1912, was a member of the Royal Commission on the Indian Public Service from 1912 to 1914.
26 C. Percy, L. Ridley: op. cit.

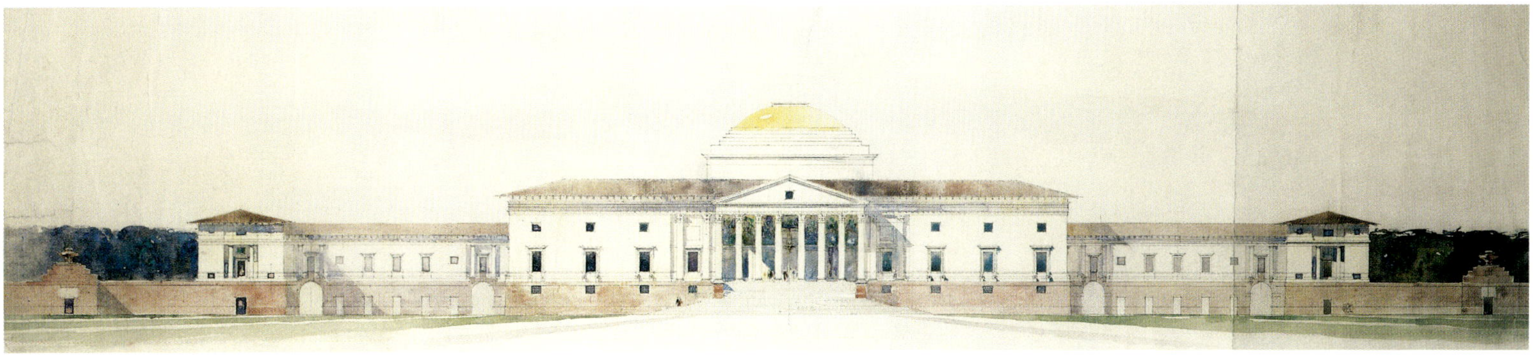

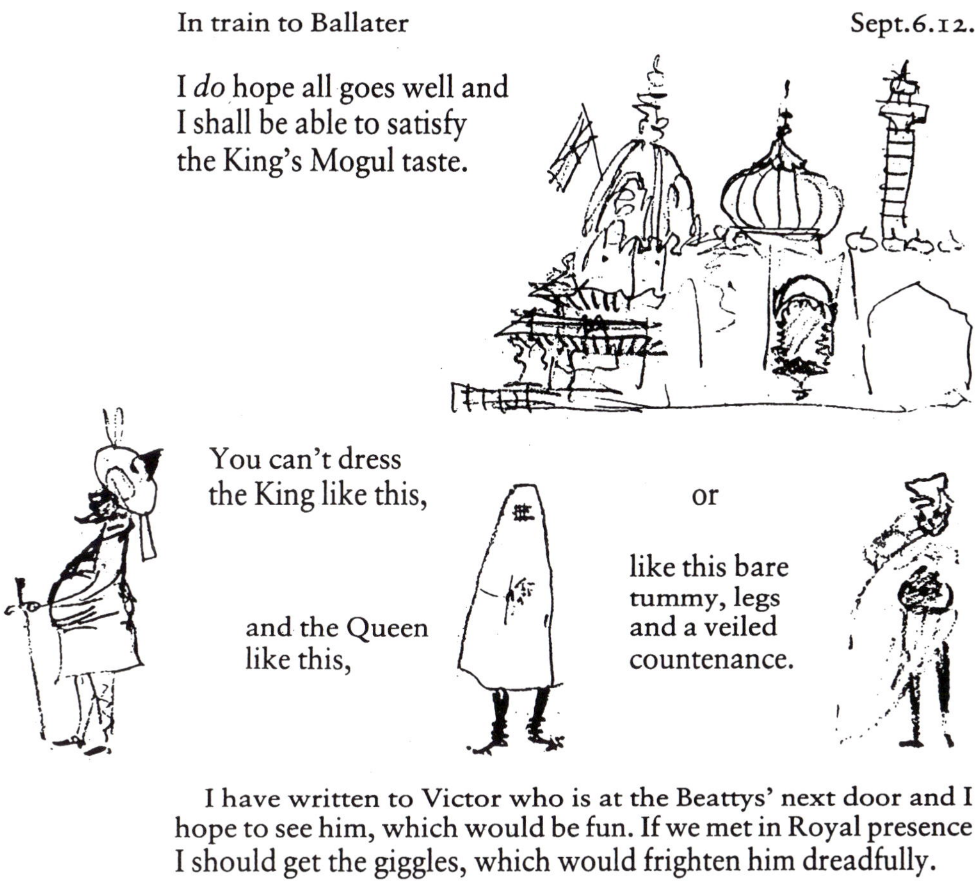

In train to Ballater

Sept.6.12.

I *do* hope all goes well and I shall be able to satisfy the King's Mogul taste.

You can't dress the King like this,

and the Queen like this,

or

like this bare tummy, legs and a veiled countenance.

I have written to Victor who is at the Beattys' next door and I hope to see him, which would be fun. If we met in Royal presence I should get the giggles, which would frighten him dreadfully.

Fig. 89: In a letter to his wife dated September 6, 1912, Lutyens employs amusing diagrams to explain the apparently unsolvable problem of combining imperial Neo-Palladian architecture with elements of Indian architecture.

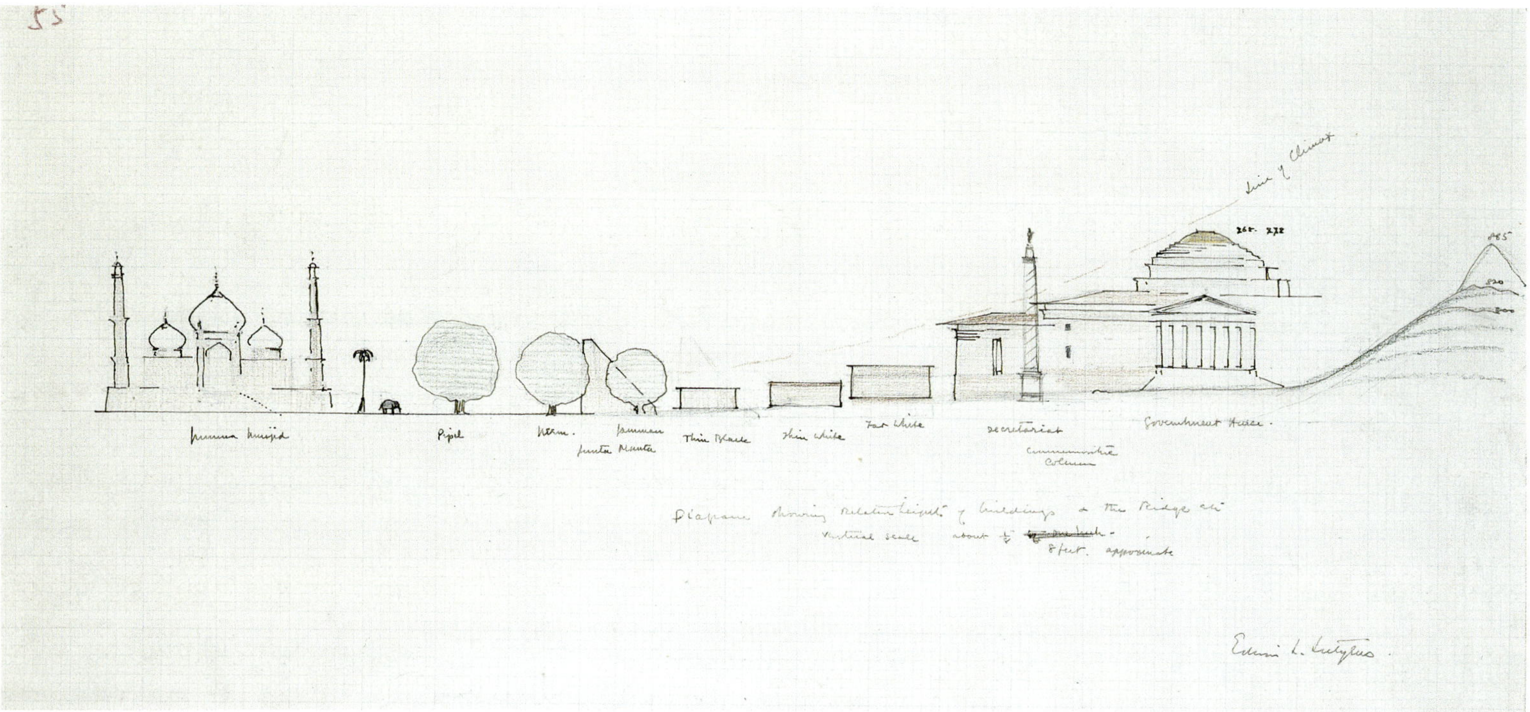

Fig. 90: As early as 1912, in the first months of his search for an appropriate form for the Viceroy's Palace, Edwin Lutyens sketched an abbreviated longitudinal section for the proportions for the Palace with a Trajan's Column (right), the Jama Masjid (left), and the Jantar Mantar observatory with the Secretariats (centre).

The blending of Neo-Classical and Indian formal elements

A conflict between Lutyens and most of his professional colleagues appeared inevitable, and both the King in London and the Viceroy in Delhi did not side with the architect. Nevertheless, gradually the gap between the two sides closed. In the Viceroy's case, Lutyens had the Vicereine, whom he had won over with his well-known charm as an important supporter. In addition, his attempts to anchor Hindu and Indo-Islamic elements in his classicist architecture were both serious and successful.

The Buddhist stupa at Sanchi (first century, A.D.) did not look like a foreign body when Lutyens placed it as a simple dome on the Durbar Hall. The marble inlay work in the Durbar Hall could have been derived from Mughal architecture (Fig. 103). The chattris, i.e. stone pavilions, following models in Delhi and Agra, fit harmoniously with the dome above Viceroy's House (Fig. 94). The capitals of the portico were modelled on the Jaina temple at Modbidri (Fig. 165). The walling-in of the furthest reaches of the administrative area with monumental stone walls in the style of Buddhist vedikas heightened the desired atmosphere of sanctity. Finally, the Mughal Garden on the west side of Viceroy's House, with its strict geometry, was in no way inferior to that in Srinagar (Fig. 111).

The blending of Classicist and Indian formal elements probably succeeded because both formal repertoires were used with an extremely restrained severity. Thus, an architectural style emerged which Herbert Baker, for all his rivalry with Edwin Lutyens, described as "a noble development of the germ of L'Enfant's plan of Washington and Wren's rejected design for the City of London."[27]

In the first phase of the plan of 1912,[28] situation, size, form, and orientation of Viceroy's House did not of relate to the All India War Memorial planned later in 1921. Yet it succeeded together with the Secretariats (Fig. 7) in front, the Jama Masjid in Old Delhi and, because of its unusual size, the Jantar Mantar observatory[29] built by Maharaja Jai Singh II of Jaipur. In a sketch from 1912, Lutyens depicted all the above-named buildings to scale. An elephant and a palm next to the Jama Masijd show clearly the change in scale made by Lutyens from the largest mosque in India to an essentially much larger palace for the representative of the British Crown. At the beginning of the twentieth century, an imperial gesture seemed unconvincing without a dramatic change in scale.

27 Herbert Baker: *Architectural Design: Symbolism in Stone and Marble*, London 1930.
28 Cf. Chapter 4.2.
29 Cf. A. Volwahsen: *Cosmic Architecture in India*, op. cit. The observatory was constructed in 1728 on a broad plain outside Delhi. The Delhi Town Planning Committee selected this very plain for the building of the new Imperial Delhi. Therefore the observatory is now situated in the centre of New Delhi.

Rooms and furnishings

There are approximately 285 rooms of varying functions in the different wings of Viceroy's House (cf. section and ground plan of the main storey). The main floor plan shows a clear functional division of five large areas. The central section with the Durbar Hall, the state dining room, the state ballroom, and three state drawing rooms are used exclusively for official purposes. In order to guarantee sufficient light in such a large floor area, the Staircase Court was laid out as both a stairwell and a light-well.

The four wings, along with the central section, were linked only by comparatively narrow sections. The southwest wing formed a self-contained English-style country house with living, sleeping, and guest rooms, divided into three storeys and with direct access to the Mughal Garden. The outer northwest wing, identical in shape to the southwest wing, consists of three storeys incorporating approximately twenty single rooms and suites for the Viceroy's guests with views over the surrounding gardens. Inner courtyards and shady loggias maintain a pleasant temperature in the rooms and were probably intended to increase cross-ventilation.

In the narrow wings to the right and left of the great portico in front of the Durbar Hall, the rooms are, for the most part, offices for the Viceroy's personal staff, and adjacent to these are more guestrooms for less important guests.

Today, the visitor to Viceroy's House might wander at a loss through an endless series of small and large courtyards on the north side of the palace, between the northwest and the northeast wings. Lutyens had originally envisaged a large meeting room here for the Viceroy's

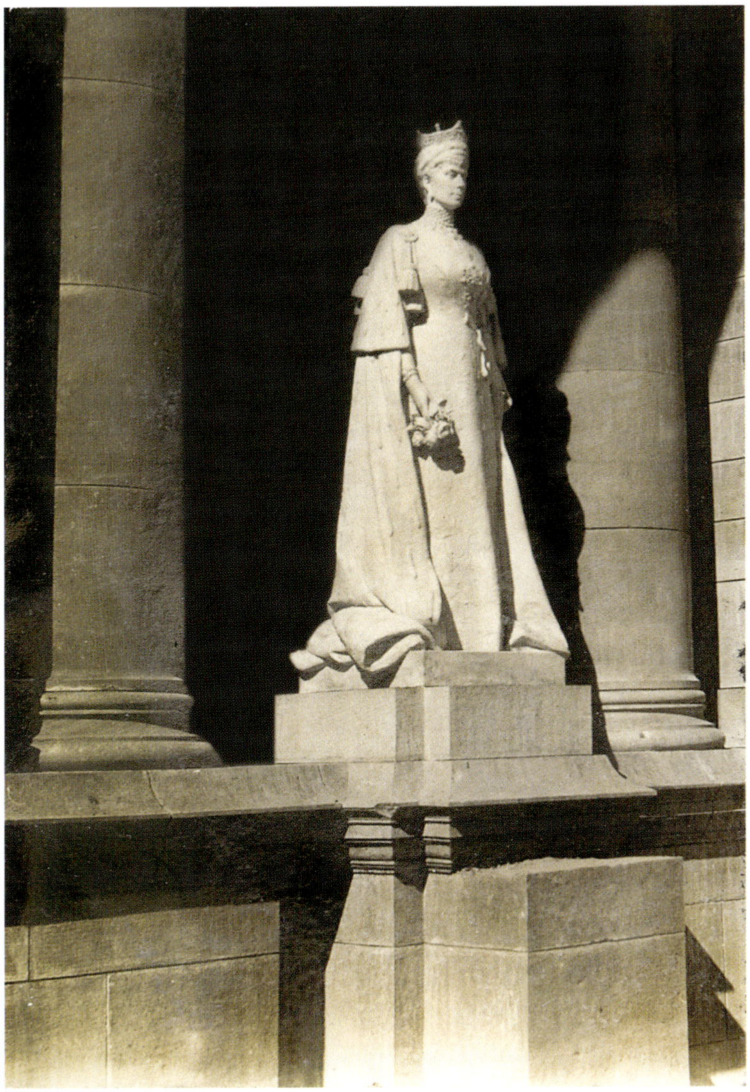

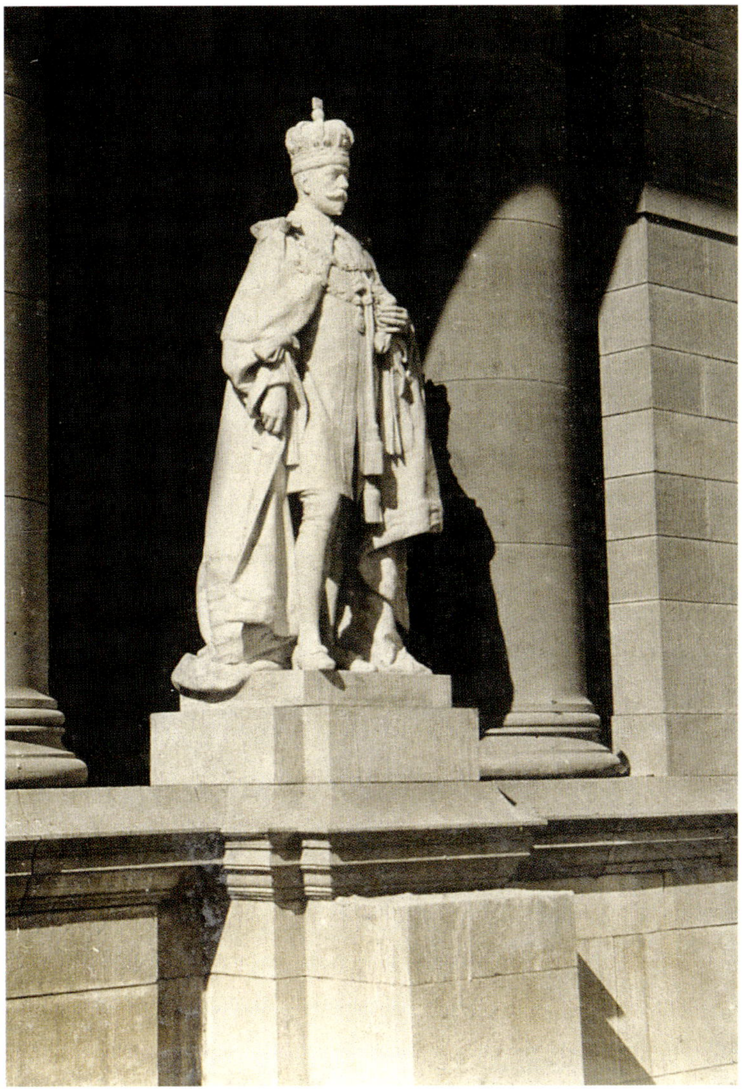

Fig. 91: At either side of the staircase to Viceroy's House were marble statues of Queen Mary and King George V. Both statues were removed in 1949 after Indian independence.

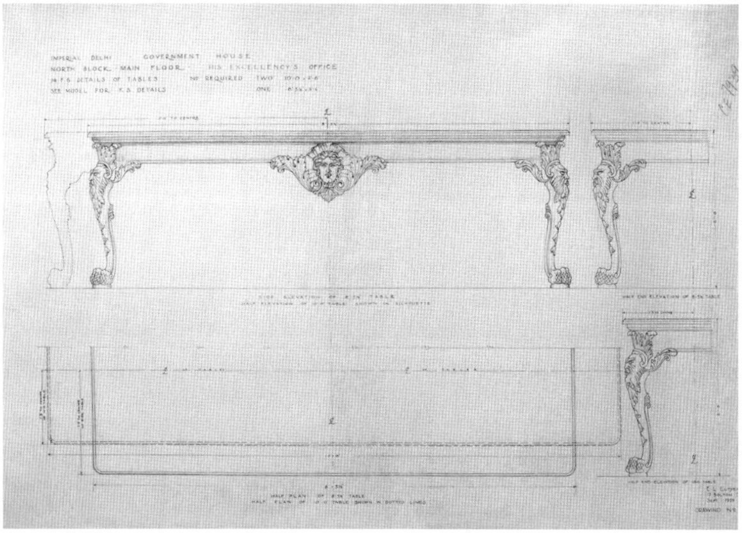

Fig. 92: Lutyens had a comprehensive understanding of his task, from the planning of the street network for Imperial Delhi and the construction of individual buildings, to the provision of sculptured ornaments on the Viceroy's desk. Owing to a stroke of good fortune, hundreds of detailed drawings have been preserved in the Planning Archive of the Central Public Works Department in New Delhi.

Council. In 1920–21 this was abandoned after the Chelmsford-Montague reform had necessitated a separate legislative building with three chambers.

The visitor may also be baffled on occasion because of the sheer size of all the architectural elements: "In all respects the Viceregal establishment was appropriately imperial in scale. At the close of British rule in 1947, over two thousand persons served Lord Mountbatten at Viceroy's House in New Delhi: aides and clerks, soldiers and police, and a veritable army of servants and staff throughout the palace and its grounds, stables, garage, post office, and dispensary. Including families and other dependents, altogether more than six thousand persons had permanent housing in the Viceregal compound at Raisina, and over a thousand more lived at Simla and Calcutta."[30]

In furnishing Viceroy's House, Lutyens found himself faced by apparently unsolvable problems. The furniture designed by him for almost all of the rooms did not usually survive the extreme yearly variations of humidity in India. During the hot, rainy period both imported and local wood swelled up. Ready-made furniture from England was also not successful since it did not weather the extremely dry months or the extremely damp months of the monsoon: "The extremes of humidity and temperature in Delhi were particularly hard on the English antiques which fell to pieces almost as soon as they arrived."[31]

The furniture in Viceroy's House today is, to a large extent, not original from when the House had opened. One fortunate coincidence is that, alongside countless architectural drawings, hundreds of detailed drawings of the original pieces survived almost undamaged in metal containers discovered in the planning archive of the Central Public Works Department of New Delhi (cf. example in Fig. 92). Thus, one could presumably be able to reconstruct the furniture, despite the loss that occurred because of natural causes and neglect.

The furniture drawing in figure 92 shows two different desks in the Viceroy's office along with their dimensions. The tables are of particular interest in so far as they do not reflect the formal innovative power of Lutyens' architecture in Imperial Delhi, but reflect the markedly conservative formal elements of the late Louis XIV style (around 1700) as found, for example, in boulle furniture and its associated English versions of the eighteenth century.

The elements consist of satyr masks (at the corners of the tables), lion monopodes (on the table legs), and Daphne masks (as the central motif in the middle of the table). These motifs recur as symbols of power in the history of furniture design and Lutyens inserted them deliberately, not from a whim or a lack of ideas, but in order to display to every visitor the power and magnificence of British rule over India.

30 R.G. Irving: op. cit., p. 227.

31 Mary Lutyens: *Edwin Lutyens, by his Daughter*, London n.d., p. 238.

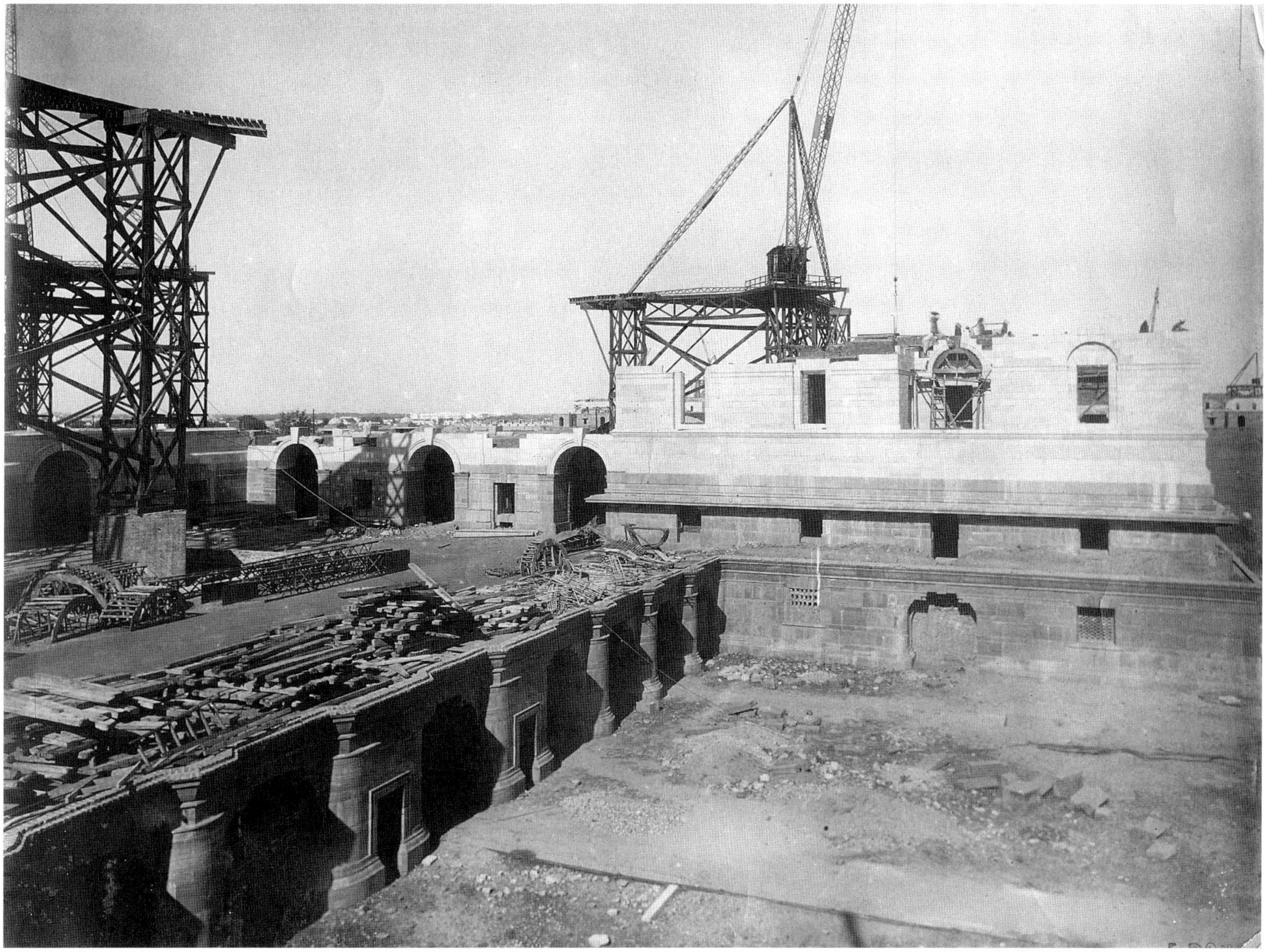

Fig. 93: The construction at Viceroy's House almost came to a standstill during World War I. This historic photograph shows the building's progress on May 9, 1924, presenting a view into the courtyard on the south side with an already completed lower storey.

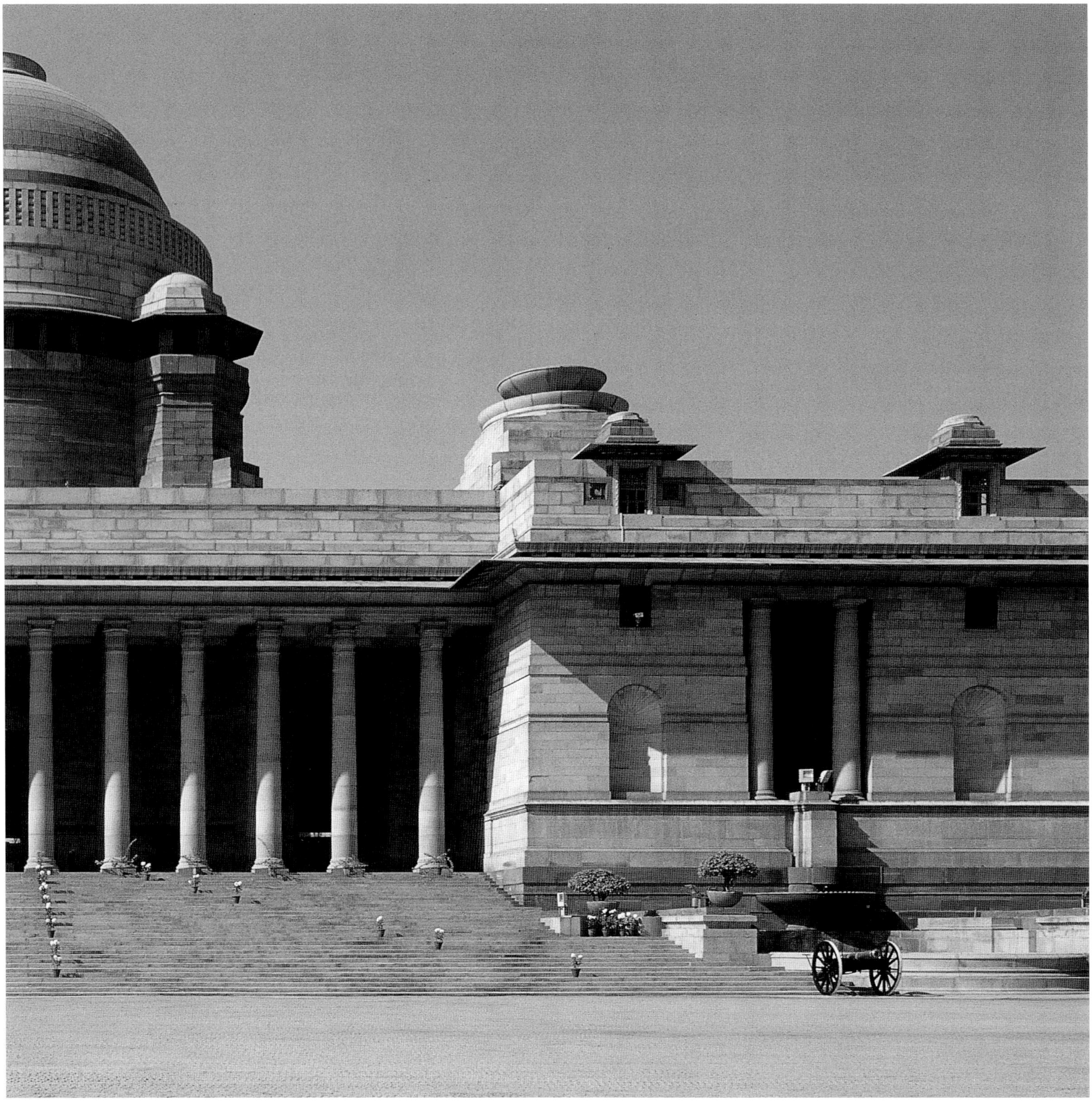

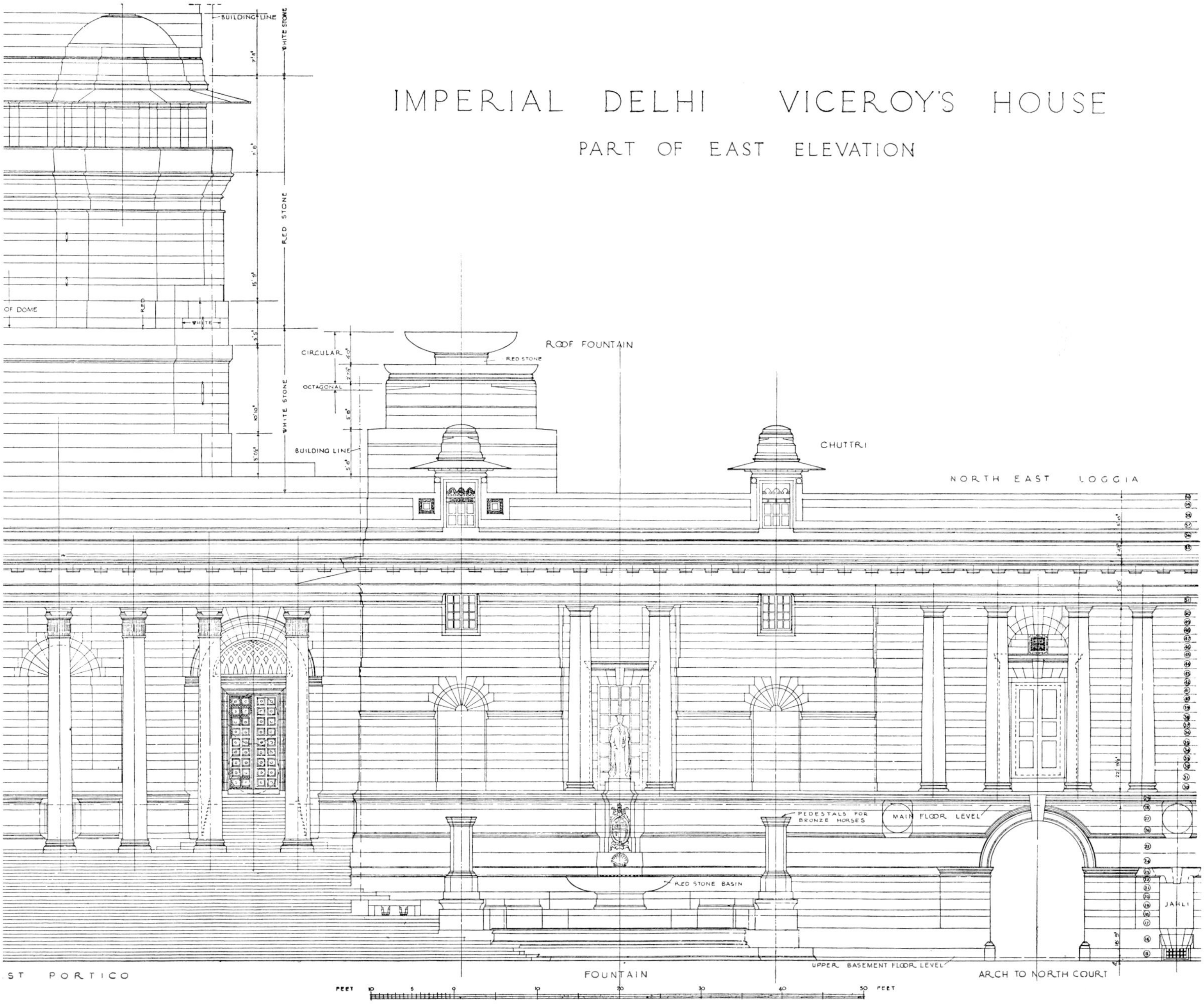

Fig. 94: Photograph (left) and plan (right) of a section from the east facade (the main facade) of Viceroy's House with the tambour of the dome (left in the photograph), one of the roof fountains (centre, top) and the statue of Queen Mary (centre in the east elevation).

Different entrances for different social groups

An examination of the functions of the lower and upper basements also allows us to discern a peculiarity in the ground plan and elevation of Viceroy's House that today might appear very difficult to understand. The design carefully planned for different ways of entering the palace depending upon the social status of the visitor. Official visitors and guests at celebrations drove their coach or car in from the south via the South Avenue into the upper basement of Viceroy's House. Here, the visitors got out of their vehicles and walked to the main floor or ground storey by means of an unusually wide staircase in the Staircase Court (Fig. 98).

The difference between the sparsely lit upper basement and the Staircase Court, which was flooded with light, was a clear indication to every visitor from a lower social background or profession that he was now ascending into the well-lit world of the highest earthly power in India. The large stairway in the Staircase Court may not have had a normal ceiling above its massive wall cornice – just the open sky as its ceiling – but this was not just a pretty architectural idea, but a carefully thought-out demonstration of protocol and power expressed by the ruling British government. Even today, the Indian government continues to use this most unusual space for the impressive monumental statement it makes: "A particular delight is the Staircase Court, in which the stairs rise from one of the cross-tunnels in which guests are dropped from their cars; the visitor rises into a great, stone room, but above the coved cornice there is no ceiling, only sky and through this space can be seen that strange, imperious dome."[32]

The other no less symbolic entrance to Viceroy's House was reserved only for the most important government representatives and state visitors. These VIPs drove past the row of lions (Fig. 151), across the Viceroy's Court directly to the large open staircase in front of the Durbar Hall, thus taking the quickest route to the palace's banquet halls and offices (Fig. 151).

As a rule, the Viceroy received his important guests on the long open staircase. Protocol determined how many steps he walked down to greet the guest and this depended on his

Fig. 95: The internal structure and the provision rooms of the lower basement of Viceroy's House are connected by a network of tunnels and corridors (photographs 1924–27 during the period of construction).

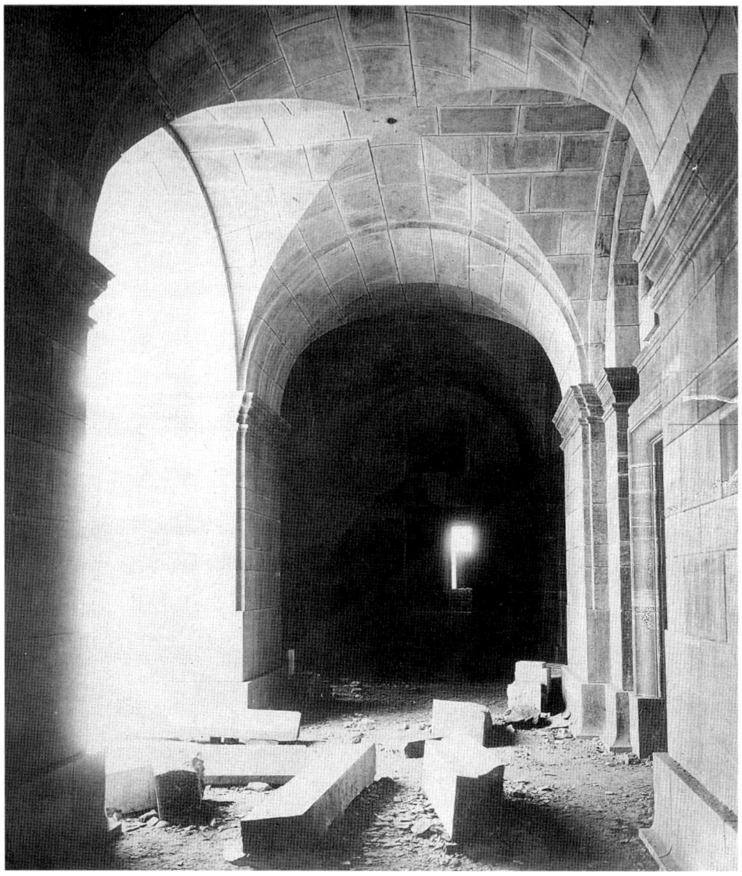

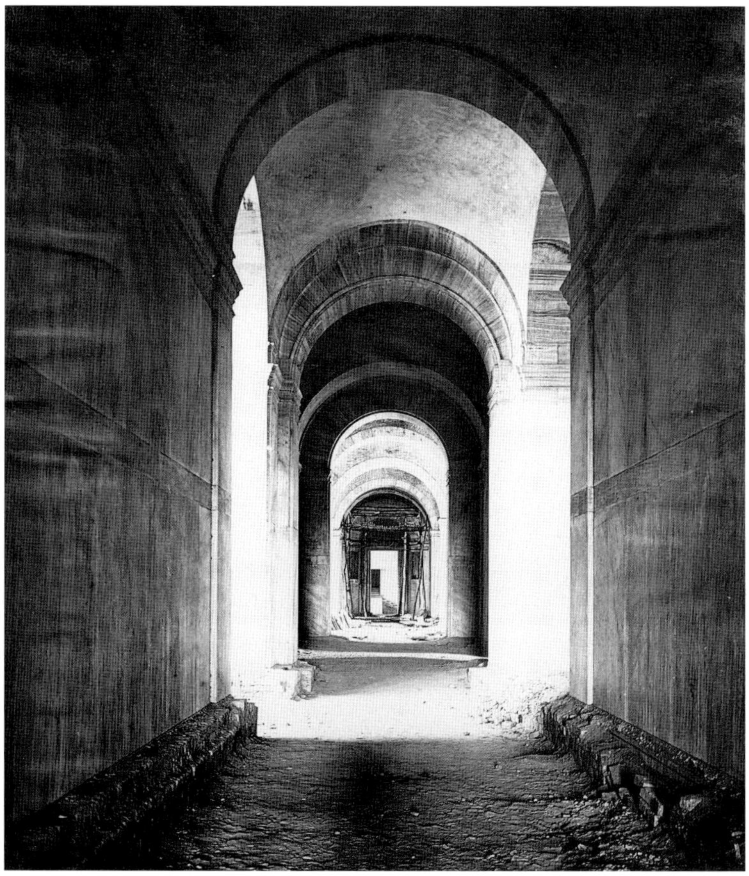

social status and political significance. Ironically, Mahatma Gandhi was not received on the staircase by the Viceroy.

"Never has a palace been entered by stairs of such majestic invitation; nor has the house of a King's representative been fronted with such immaculate nobility. This is architecture *in excelsis* – a supreme composition of lines in plan, section and elevation, made with such art as to need no further enriching, no pinned-on ornament nor pious filigree. The very placing of the lines gives the thing its glory. Only the addition of the four prancing bronze horses on the pedestals in front is needed to give final point to the niches in the wall behind and, by their glowing animalism, to emphasize the chastity of the background."[33]

A magnificent opening

In 1931, when Lady Emily came to Delhi with her husband for the official opening of the new capital, she too was surprised by the size and splendour of Viceroy's House. "She described the thrill of driving up the great King's Way and seeing the House appear. 'All is so changed in the last years that it is like a dream – the trees grown, the wonderful Arch up.' But, now that all was finished, the 'great crime' – as every Lutyens must hold the slope between the Secretariats to be – was the more glaring. Seeing it now, she more fully understood: 'Father's rage at the spoiling of his life's great work by the silly slope. Nevertheless, and 'despite the niggling economies' of the Government of India, this remains a colossal and most wonderful achievement and should make Father's name go down in history as one of the great architects of all time. Hudson is so moved that he can hardly keep from tears. He said to me yesterday 'Poor old Christopher Wren could never have done this!'

The union of eastern and western sensibilities was most remarkable, 'yet all is original, nothing copied.' For Lady Emily, the grand simplicity of the place was the most outstanding quality of all, though with such a wealth of beautiful detail, everything seemed appropriate to its setting, 'And everything – furniture, fire-backs, clocks, door handles – designed by the

32 G. Stamp: "New Delhi," in: *Exhibition catalogue of the Arts Council*, London 1982, p. 40.

33 Andrew S.G. Butler: op. cit., p. 35.

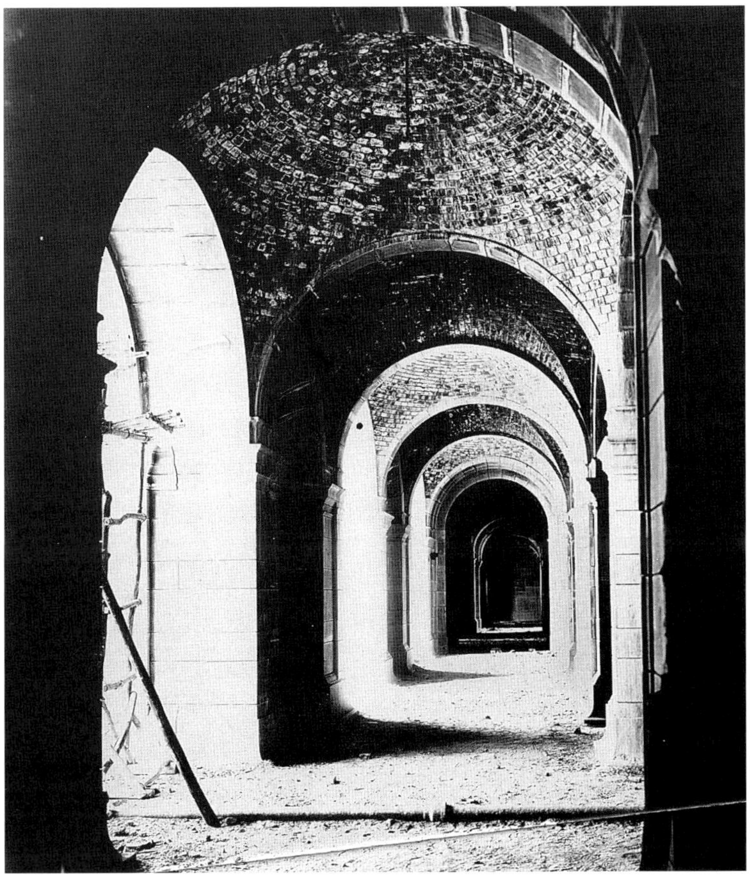

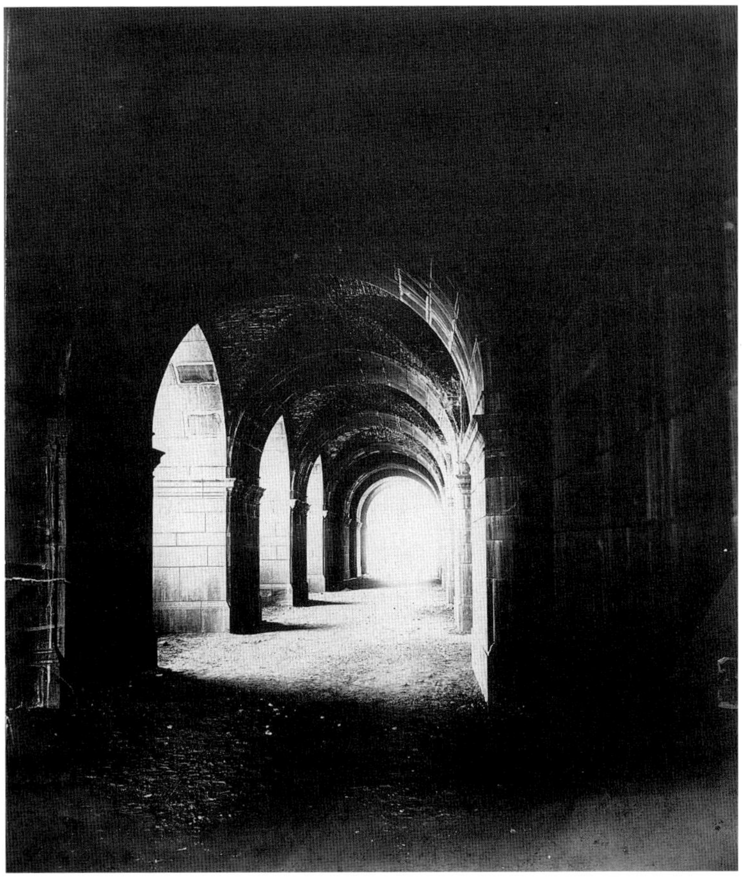

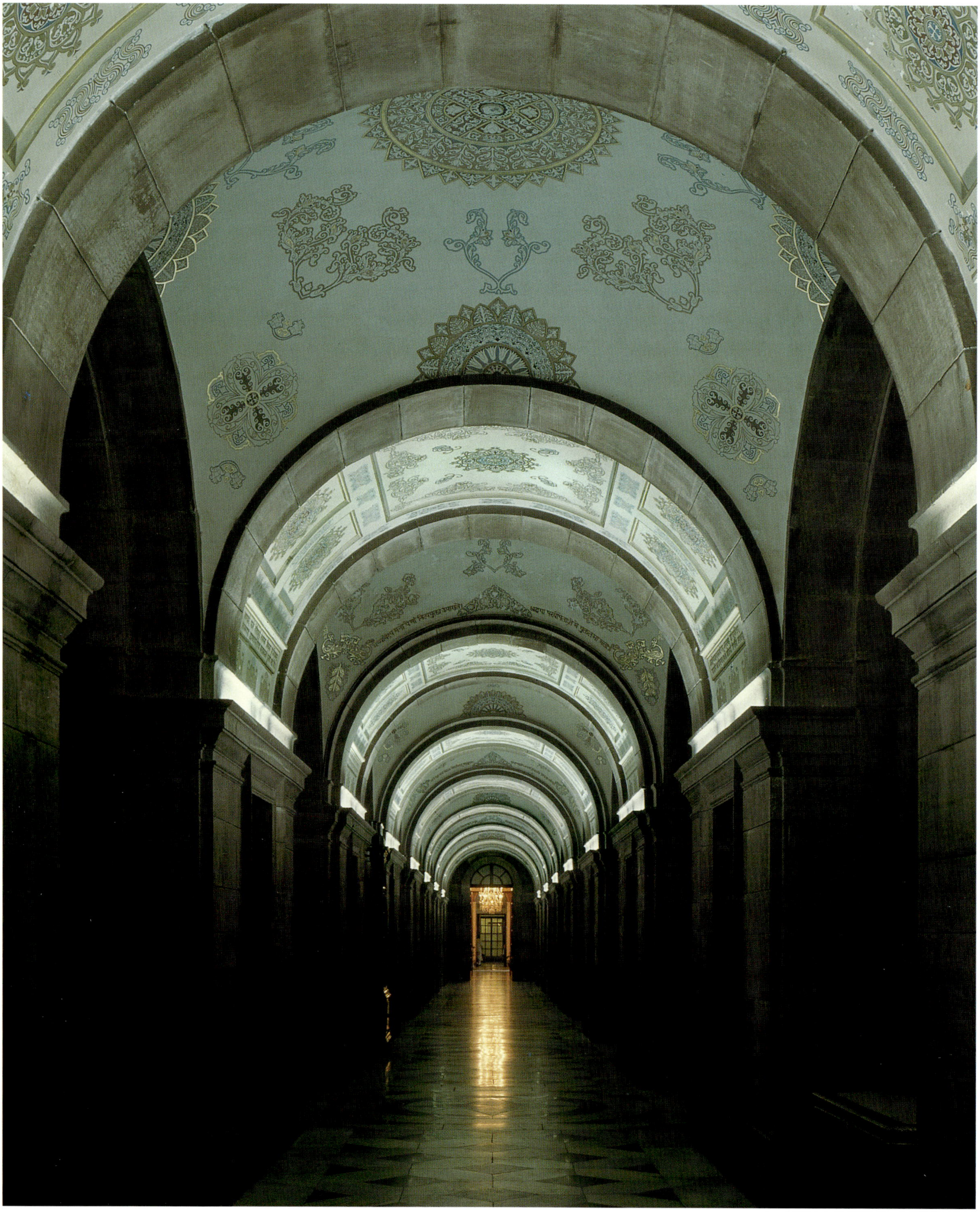

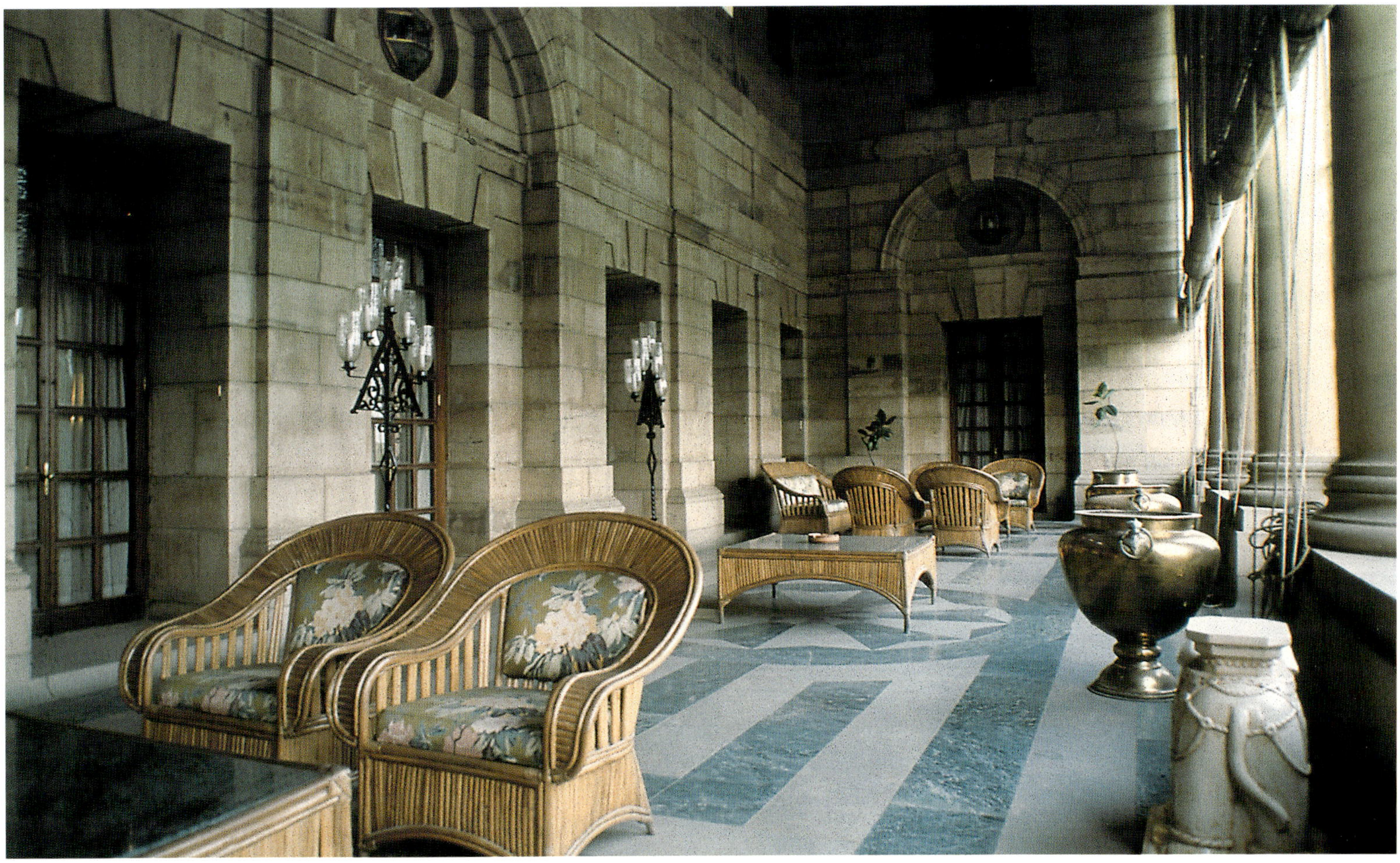

Fig. 97: The verandah in the Guest Wing of Viceroy's House maintains a pleasant temperature even on the hottest summer day because of its shade and cross ventilation.

Fig. 96: In the long corridors of Viceroy's House the originally planned marble wall linings were eventually replaced by plaster for financial reasons.

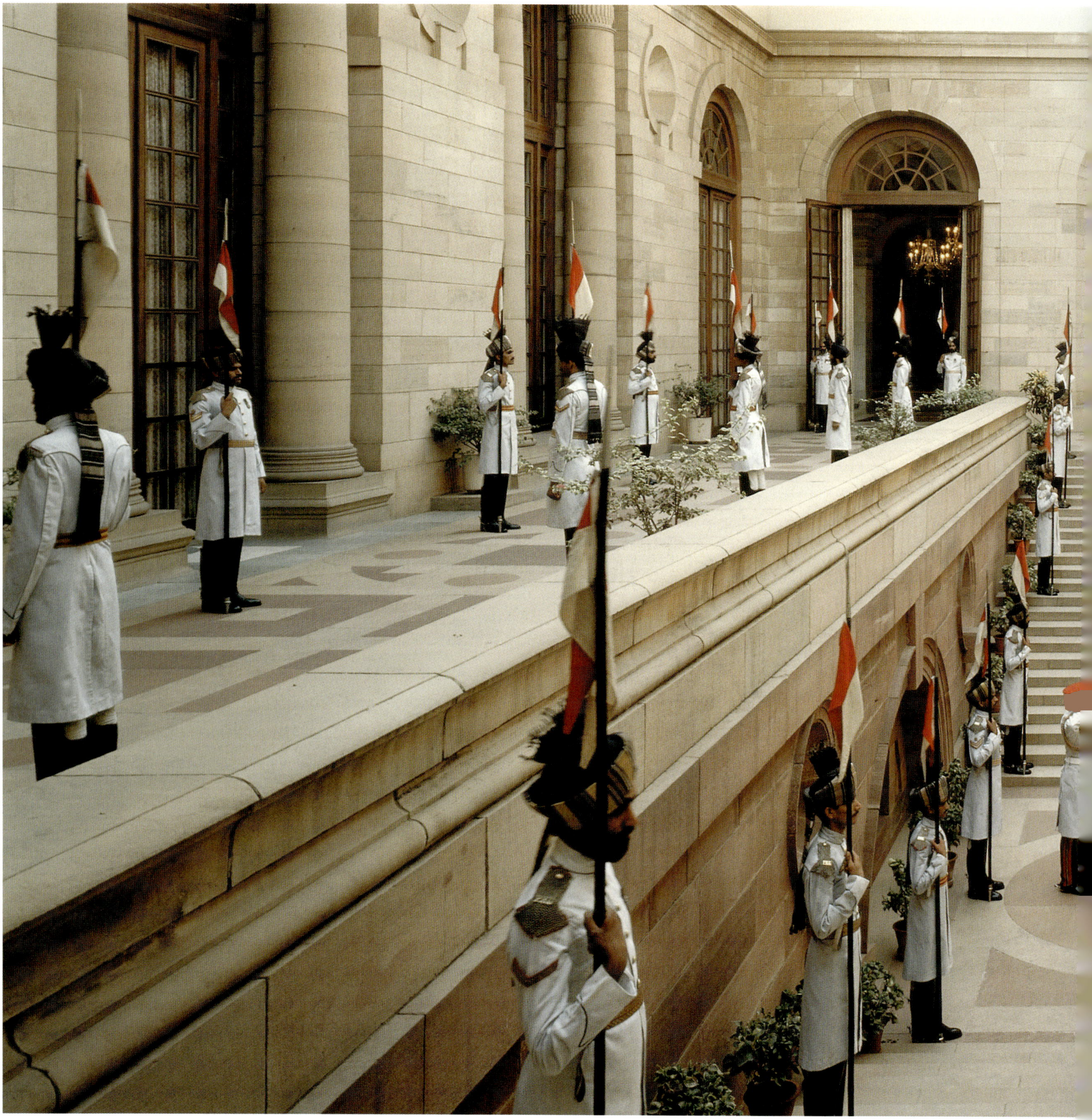

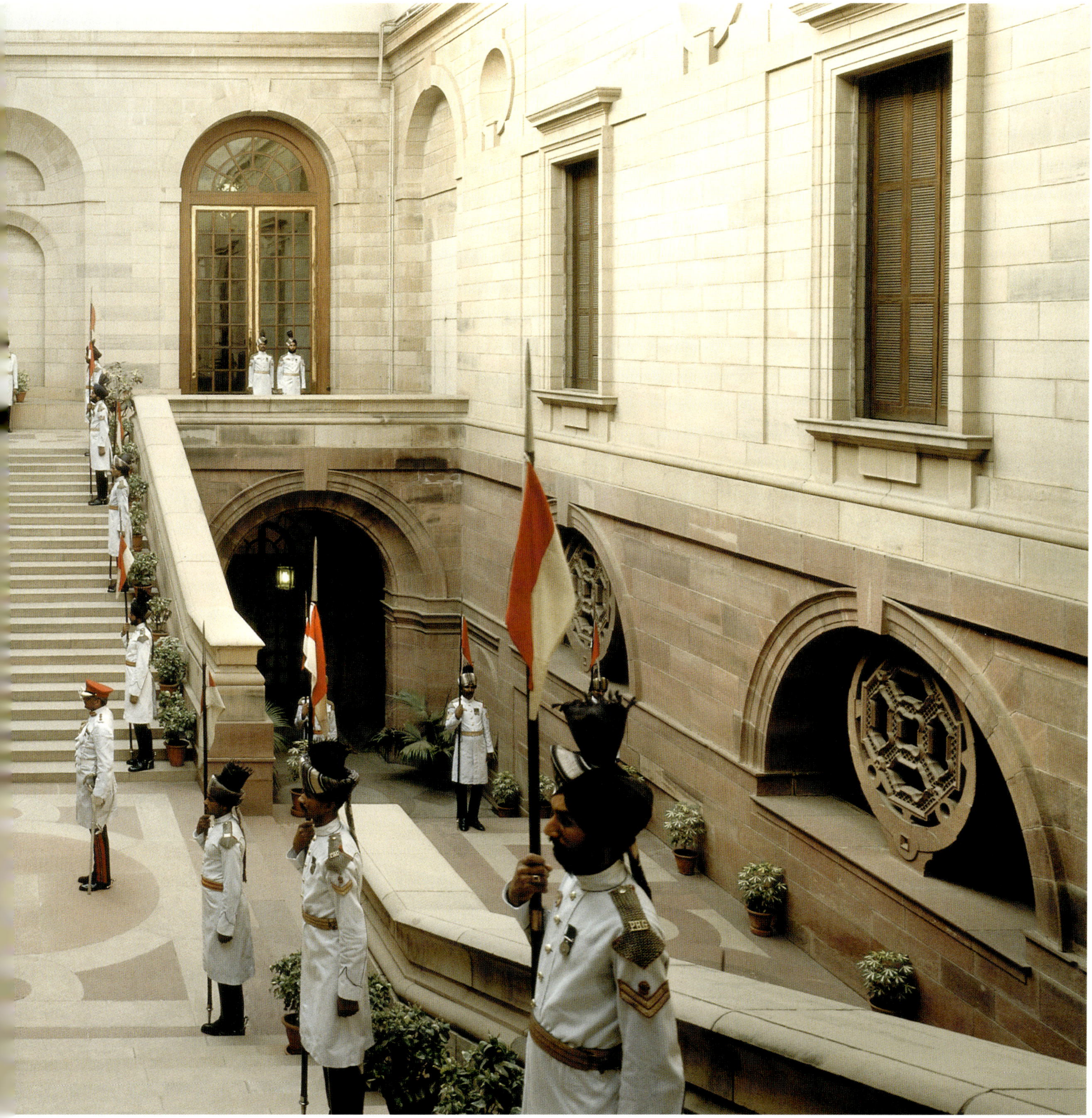

Fig. 98: The Great Staircase in Staircase Court is still used today on festive occasions by the President's guard (formerly the Viceroy's guard) for the roll-call.

single mind.' As for the garden, it was a paradise: 'Though so formal, yet everything has grown up so quickly, and flowers are set in such masses, producing a riot of colour and scents, that, with the fountains playing continually, there is not the least sense of stiffness.'"[34]

The year of the official opening of Imperial Delhi was not only a glittering success for the British Crown, but also for the architects. Captain George Swinton stood in bewilderment before the palace whose site he had chosen nineteen years earlier with his colleagues of the Delhi Town Planning Committee: "... for there has now risen before us in all its majesty – Viceroy's House! It is very rarely that one sees a great building, indeed anything, which is so thoroughly satisfactory that all criticism ceases. In this case, though one may wonder how others estimate value, for oneself there is nothing to be said. One looks – one accepts – one marvels. Why is the great building which rears itself up in front of us so satisfactory? Why have our critical faculties suddenly ceased to function? No man worth his salt is not critical. Of course Sir Edwin had had a mighty opportunity. It was to be a regal building. Unquestionably he has succeeded. The Viceroy's House would seem to express the perfect architecture which takes its stand on proportions alone. That is its decoration."[35]

The State Ballroom

The most important room in Viceroy's House is, without doubt the Durbar Hall, but for English society in Imperial Delhi the favourite room was the exceptionally splendid State Ballroom. One reached the State Ballroom from the Durbar Hall by the magnificent North Corridor: "The North Corridor is prolonged to the Garden Front as a lobby to the ballroom from which it is separated by three arches repeated beyond the dancing floor by those of a counterpart. Here, guests could meet separated from the dancers whose dresses and uniforms looked the brighter against the walls of white marble and old English mirrors beneath the glow of six crystal chandeliers (Fig. 99). The walls above the marble, left plain to strengthen this contrast, were subsequently enlivened by misplaced painted decoration.

At either end, the Ballroom gives into loggias in the west front. That to the north is square, with an eye to the sky in its coffered roof, and affords possible access to the Guest's wing through the North-west Garden Loggia. But the sensational moment here is when, from a short corridor that we have crossed unnoticed, we suddenly catch a glimpse inwards, across the North Court, through an answering aperture in its east end, along one of the tanks of Viceroy's Court aligned transversally on the loggias of the Secretariats in the distance. That exact and tremendous perspective is one of the datum lines over which Lutyens and Baker sweated blood in the earliest months of Delhi: not merely so as to give this peep, but to ensure the perfect architectural adjustment of their spheres of which this is an almost incidental aspect."[36]

The later painting of the walls, criticized by Christopher Hussey, goes back to one of Lady Willingdon's ideas in the thirties. Prasad writes that Lady Willingdon, "has some other decorations and changes also done, and a later Viceroy, Lord Linlithgow, invited Lutyens to revisit the building and have a look at the ornamentation. Lutyens was happy to do away with most of the 'vagarious vagaries,' as he termed them, of Lady Willingdon. But the ones on the ceiling of the dance hall were allowed to stay. They are not outstanding as art, but serve well as decoration. Matching the lushness of the ceiling of the Dance Hall is a huge Persian pattern carpet on the floor. It was wholly woven in India. Six chandeliers suspended from the high ceiling and six more around the hall and eleven candelabra on the walls light up the hall. More light comes from five windows which look down on the Mughal Garden. The wall and the pillars are of pale grey marble, enhancing the sense of formality. The far wall has a loft for the orchestra."[37]

34 Christopher Hussey: op. cit., p. 522.
35 George Swinton, in: *The Empire Review*, May 1931.
36 Christopher Hussey, op. cit., p. 509.
37 H.Y. Sharada Prasad: op. cit., p. 68.

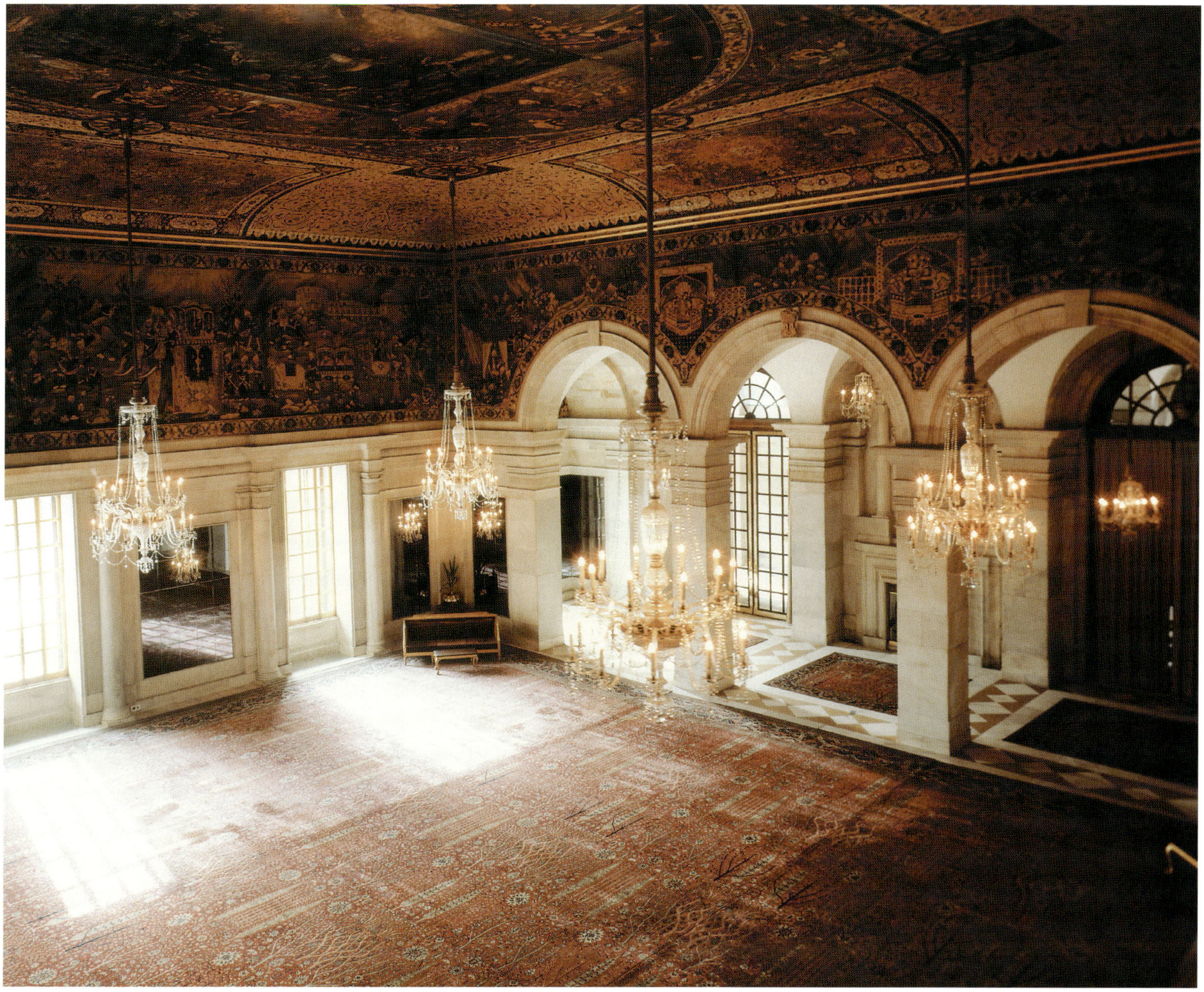

Fig. 99: For formal receptions the State Ballroom still offers a particularly festive venue today.

Durbar Hall

The central point of Imperial Delhi was Viceroy's House. And the central point of Viceroy's House was the Durbar Hall.[38] It served the Viceroy as a stage for official receptions. The most important reception for an Indian prince or emperor was certainly the Durbar, a ceremony of honouring and pledging one's loyalty to the ruler.

Every maharaja assured himself of the loyalty of his most important officials and administrators in the festive atmosphere of a Durbar held in his principality. The emperor of India, following the model of the Mughal emperors, held an audience for his generals, princes, maharajas, visiting officials, and the heads of his administration.

In this sense, the Durbar Hall roughly corresponds to the throne room in European castles. A courtly ceremony comparable to the Indian Durbar, however, does not exist in the princely and royal houses of Europe.

For the Durbar Hall in Viceroy's House, Edwin Lutyens chose the richly symbolic form of the Pantheon in Rome. In doing so, he placed it in the impressive group of Mannerist and Classicist buildings with round domes, beginning with the Villa Rotunda of Andrea Palladio, continued by Friedrich Schinkel with the Altes Museum in Berlin, an unrealized plan by Leo von Klenze for the Hall of Fame in Munich, and the Rotunda in the United States Capitol by Thomas Walter: "Today's visitors of the Durbar Hall find their delight in non-pictorial features. The chief ornament of the room consists in its proportions and the colorful events it still houses. The prefect geometry of circles and squares – articulated in cylindrical and hemispherical volumes, diametrical axes, giant exedrae, and emphatic paving patterns – implies an empire of ordered unity and permanence, of effective laws, and of universality transcending the local and sectarian. As sunshine streams through the outer and inner oculus, it suffuses the domed hall with its extraordinary brilliance. Heaven's rays, arrogated to human purpose, bathe the raised thrones with a dramatic intensity never enjoyed even by the

Fig. 100: View from the roof of the Secretariat, North Block, to Viceroy's House in the year of its dedication, 1931.

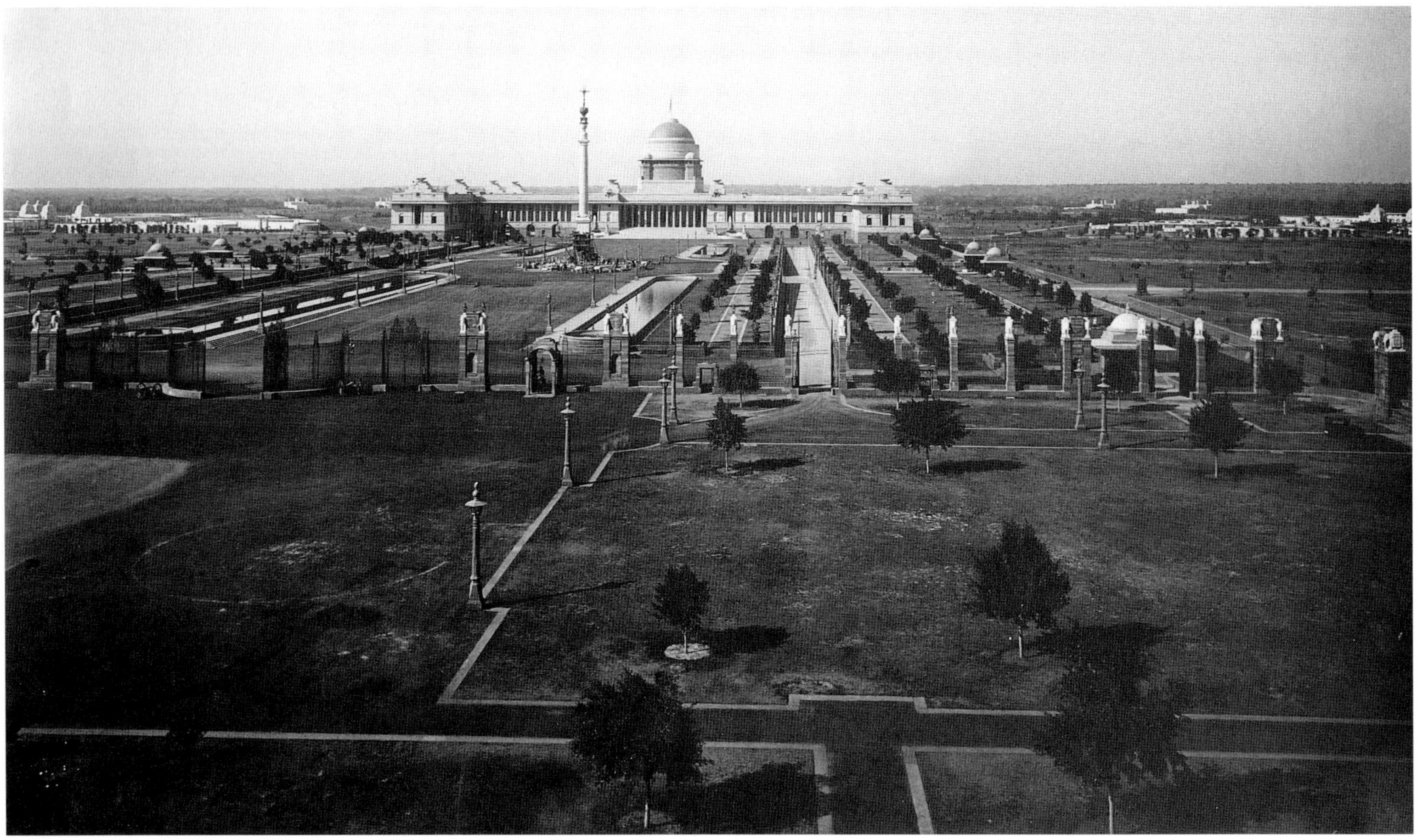

Sun King at Versailles. The tangible and ethereal, the manmade and natural, are here inextricably linked in a setting for human action. Surely the Durbar Hall is no less than the image of a man-centred cosmos: to use Palladio's description of the Pantheon, it bears in its plan and dome 'the figure of the world.'"[39]

"In both Rome and Delhi, today's traveller can thrill to the same electric pleasure, the visual and emotional impact of a lofty soaring space, lit dramatically from high above, and radiant with colour and glittering marble. If he stands beneath the great oculus at Raisina Hill and ponders the purpose of those who built there, he may recall John Davidson's lines, written scarcely a decade before the initial designs for Imperial Delhi:

It is with nations as with men:
One must be first. We're the mightiest,
The heirs of Rome."[40]

Lutyens was not the first to find the Pantheon in Rome the most important monumental space of the western world. It was already being drawn, painted and imitated in building at the time of the Renaissance, during the baroque and classical eras. An interior view of the Pantheon, painted around 1750 by G.P. Pannini (Fig. 104), vividly foreshadows how, at the beginning of the twentieth century, Lutyens and Lord Hardinge imagined the Durbar Hall as the centre of humanist learning, British social order, and imperial power.

The elevation of Durbar Hall was altered many times from the initial plans to achieve the structure that was finally built. In this connection, the following conflict was central to the

38 Durbar is an old Persian word which means "levee" as well as "court."
39 R.G. Irving: op. cit., p. 195.
40 Ibid.

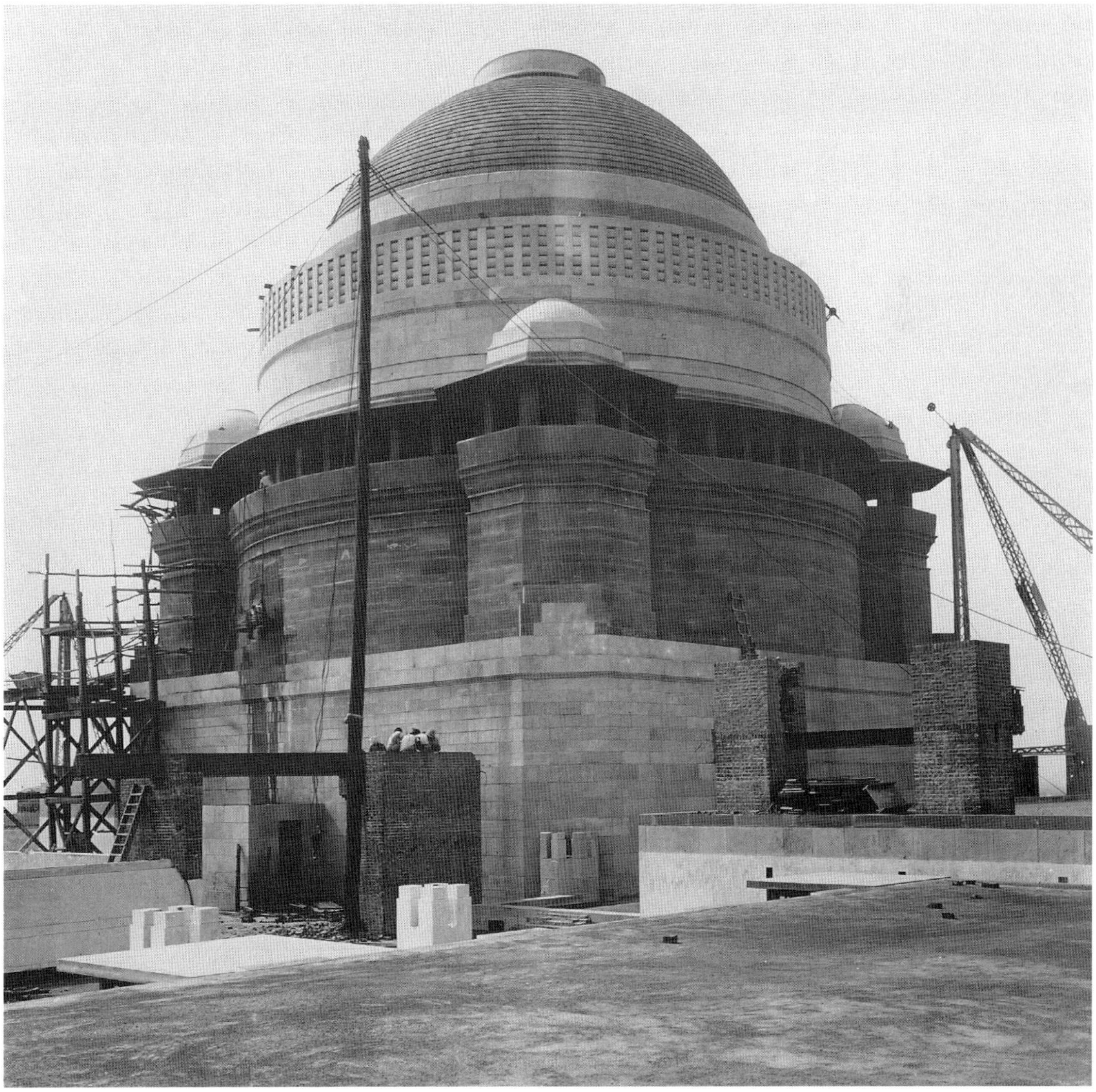

Fig. 101: The Durbar Hall and its dome under construction.

considerations of the outcome: As in the Pantheon, the interior space of the Durbar Hall was intended to present an intelligible portrayal of absolute harmony. Therefore, it should follow its model and form the exact shape of an imaginary sphere (Fig. 105). In its exterior view this goal led to a dome that was hardly visible in the city's silhouette, and Lutyens decided – certainly with a heavy heart – to depart from the noble model. Just as his revered model, Christopher Wren, did not hesitate to provide St Paul's Cathedral with a double-layered dome on a high tambour, so Lutyens now chose a no less elongated three-layered dome on a high tambour (Fig. 106) for the Durbar Hall.

Each of the originally foreseen three layers of the dome had its own function: The innermost dome, built of brick, serves only to limit the interior space and, like the model in Rome, is provided with an oculus for festive illumination. The middle and very steep layer of the dome – also with an oculus – serves to take the weight of the tambour. A reinforced concrete ceiling at the height of the lowest oculus heightens this effect and simultaneously acts as a ring anchor. Finally, the third and outermost layer – where unfortunately today, the oculus has been blocked – is a hemisphere of reinforced concrete with a very slight, if at all perceptible, horizontal thrust. This engineering solution determines the external appearance of the Durbar Hall as it appears in the cityscape of Imperial Delhi.

In light of the formal and constructional complexity, some questions remain unanswered: Did economic considerations drive Lutyens to choose such a difficult construction? Is there not a need on the part of the architect to balance interior space and exterior effect to the best possible formal proportions that can be realized?

After many statistical calculations and considerations the decision was made to build a two-layered and not a three-layered construction.

Christopher Hussey states in *The Life of Sir Edwin Lutyens*, "The outer dome was not begun till 1928. A very valuable economy in its construction, worth some £ 7,000 which could therefore be expended elsewhere, was due to the initiative of J.L. Sale, Superintending Engineer. Lutyens had designed a brick cone, of the type used by Wren for St Paul's, to carry the apex of the outer dome. Sale prepared a drawing demonstrating the possibility of doing without the cone. The drum of the dome consists of an inner and outer wall or skin. He proposed a reinforced concrete deck roofing the drum, tied to the inner dome, and also tying the skins of the drum together. The weight of the outer dome would rest on the inner skin of the drum (inclined slightly inwards) but also to be distributed to the outer skin by means of the reinforced decking. Lutyens, after exhaustive examination, adopted the system."

The work on the most important part of Viceroy's House was now accelerated and finally completed on April 6, 1929 (Fig. 112).

Hussey continues, "The copper casing of the dome, however, was not laid till the following year. During the ensuing heat of 1929, the under surface of the inner dome was rendered and the final polishing given to the marbles of its walls and floor. The last stone of the eye of the outer dome was laid in April, 1929, eighteen years from its genesis and seven months before the appointed day, by Lord Irwin in the presence of a select company who had been hoisted aloft for the short but vertiginous ceremony. Lutyens was not present, having already returned to England.

But we may imagine ourselves perched on that vantage point, one morning in December, 1929. Our situation was almost identical when we supposed ourselves suspended from Lord Hardinge's ballroom at this very point in 1913, surveying the arid contours of Raisina Hill. But, where then a wilderness of rock and scrub and spoil heaps are nor acres of roofs and courts and canals, eighty miles of tree-planted roads, the living garden of a Moghul's garden, numberless offices, bungalows, and the appurtenances of the Indian capital radiating about aor eminence. From Viceroy's Court below us, through Government Court and then beyond the fountains of the Great Place, the 800 feet wide perspective of Kings Way stretches eastward to the Memorial Arch beyond which the antique wall of Purana Kily, now surrounded by the beginnings of a considerable park, overlook the waters of the Jumna."

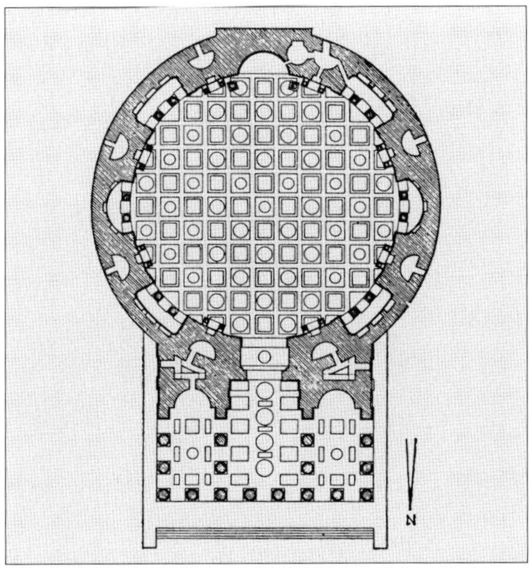

The Pantheon, Rome

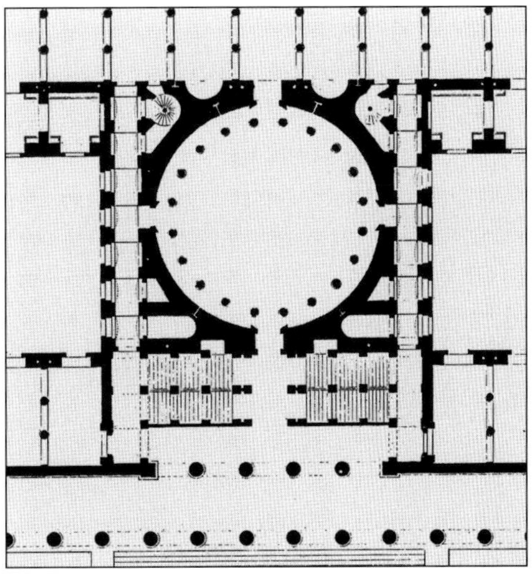

Altes Museum, Berlin

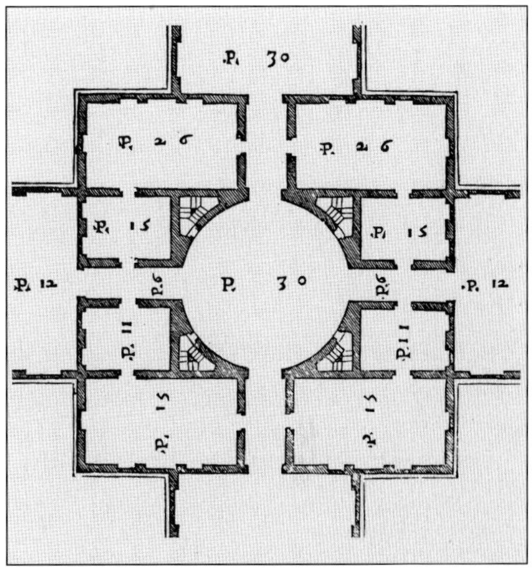

Villa Rotunda, Vicenza

Fig. 102: The Pantheon in Rome was a direct model for the plan of the Durbar Hall. In addition, the Altes Museum in Berlin by Friedrich Schinkel and the Villa Rotunda at Vicenza by Andrea Palladio were possible secondary models to Lutyens' plan. The similarity of the layout of the ground plan to an unrealized plan by Leo von Klenze for a Hall of Fame in Munich is also of interest.

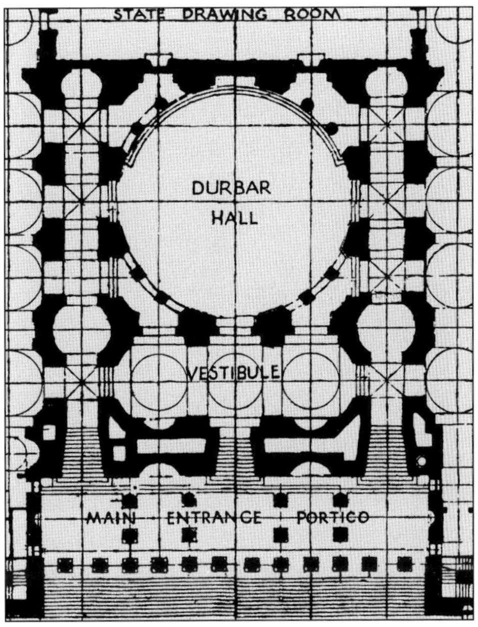

Durbar Hall

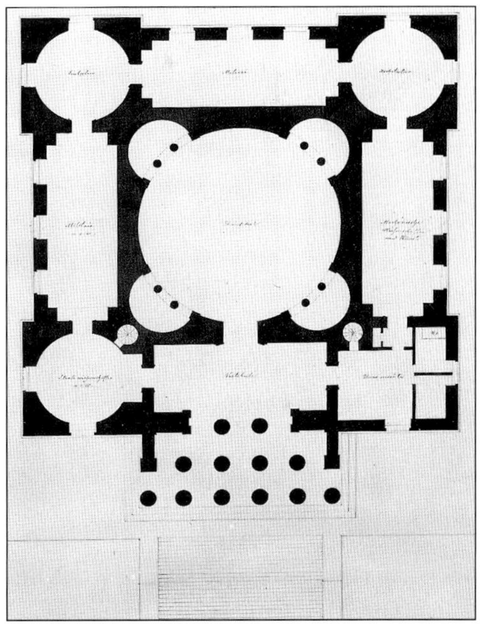

Hall of Fame, Munich

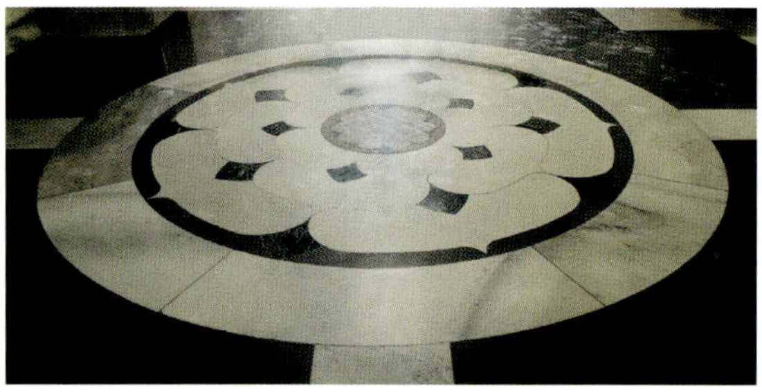

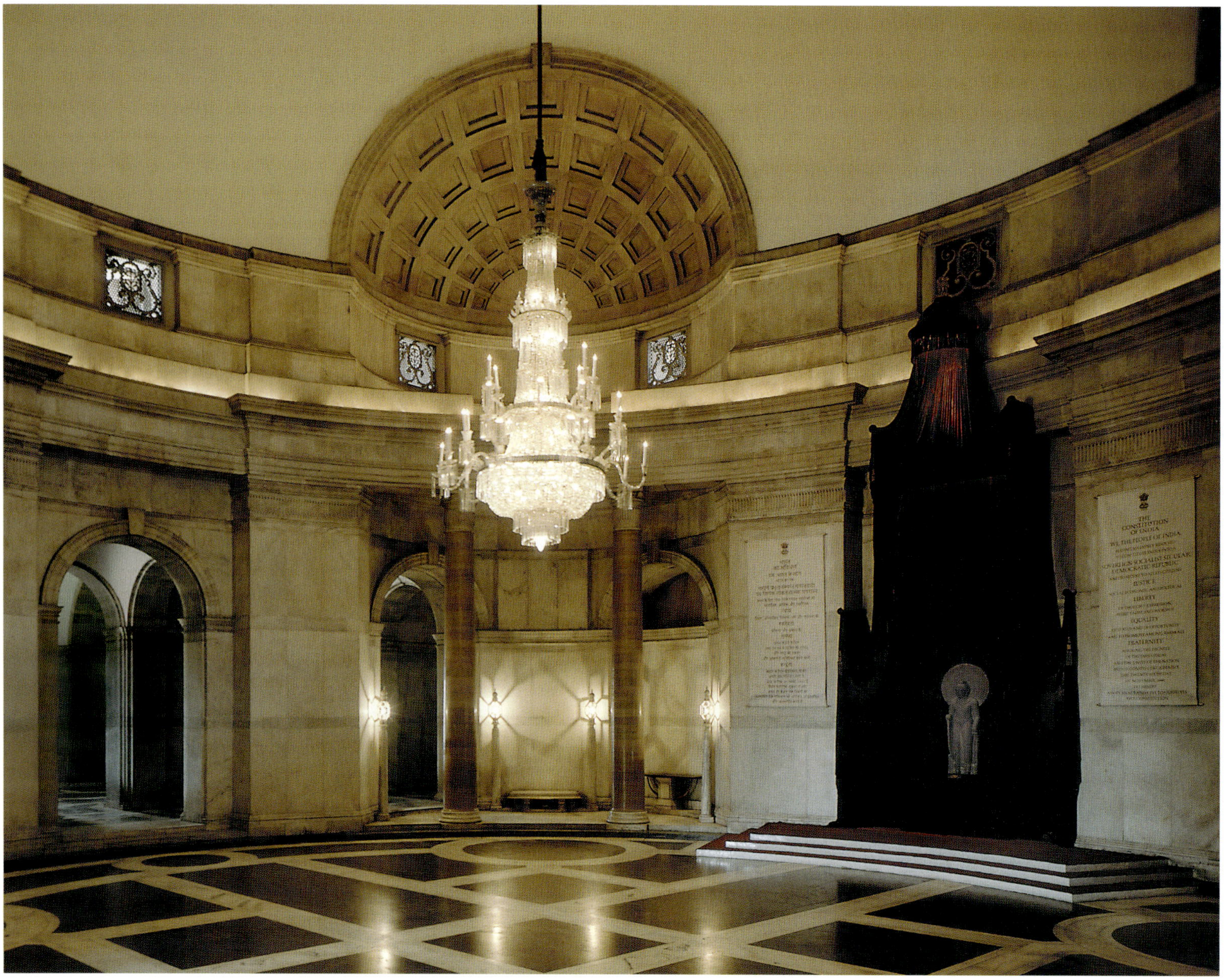

Fig. 103: Diagonal view into the Durbar Hall of the corner solution in the style of the Pantheon in Rome. In the vestibule of the Durbar Hall the inlay work in marble depicts a five-petaled lotus flower (above). Only rarely did Edwin Lutyens use the pentagram and pentagon in his designs.

Fig. 104: Lutyens was not the first to proclaim the Pantheon in Rome as the most important monumental space in the world. Painted around 1750 by G.P. Pannini, *Interior of the Pantheon* vividly foreshadows how Lutyens and Lord Hardinge imagined the Durbar Hall as the centre of humanist learning, British social order and imperial power.

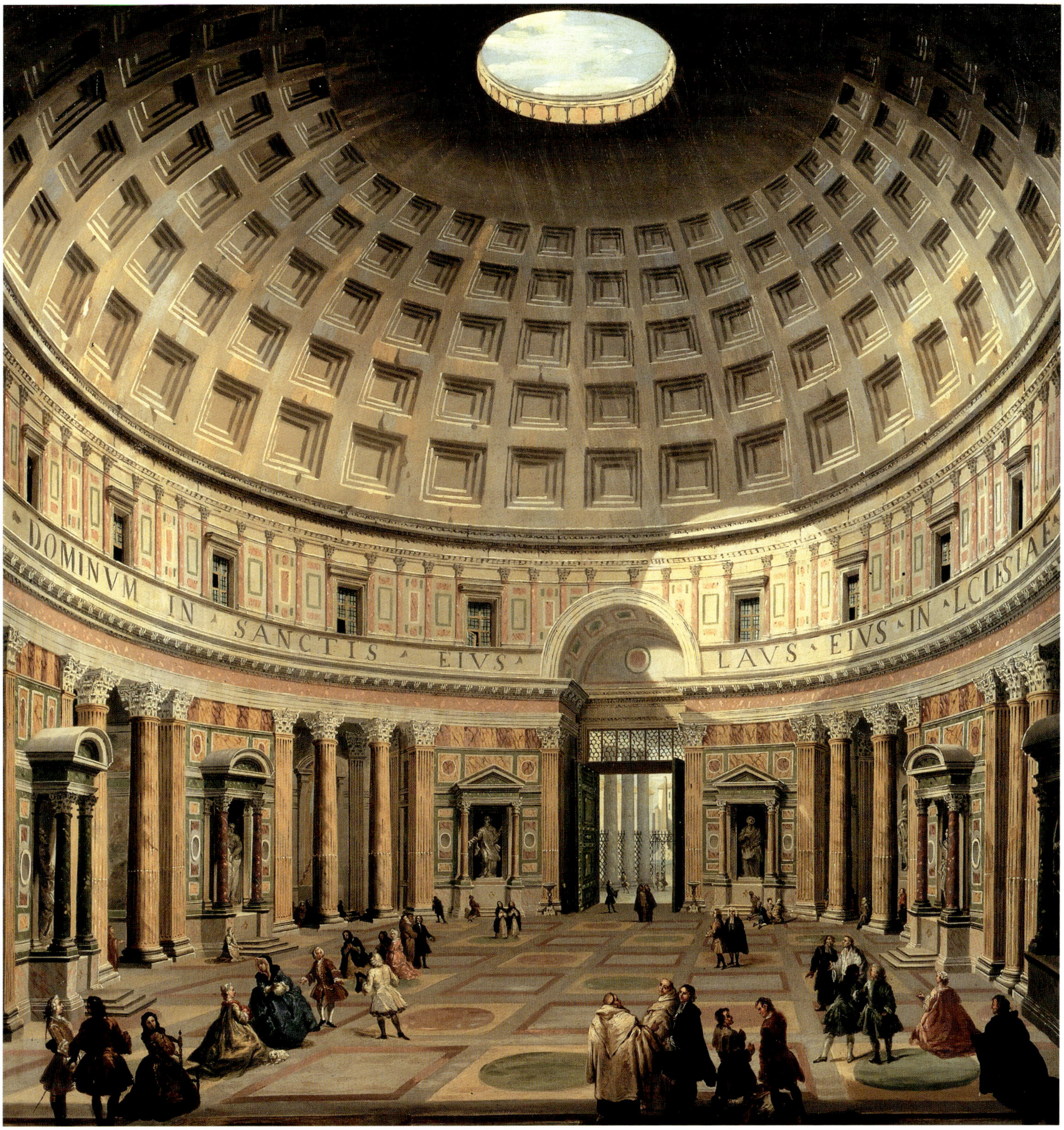
DOMINVM IN SANCTIS EIVS LAVS EIVS IN ECCLESIA

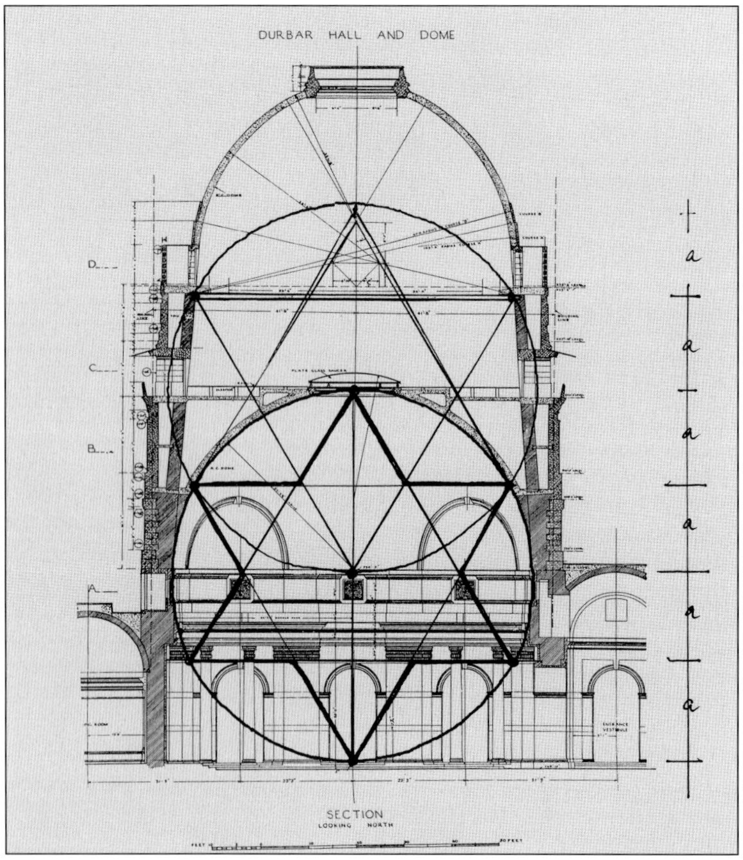

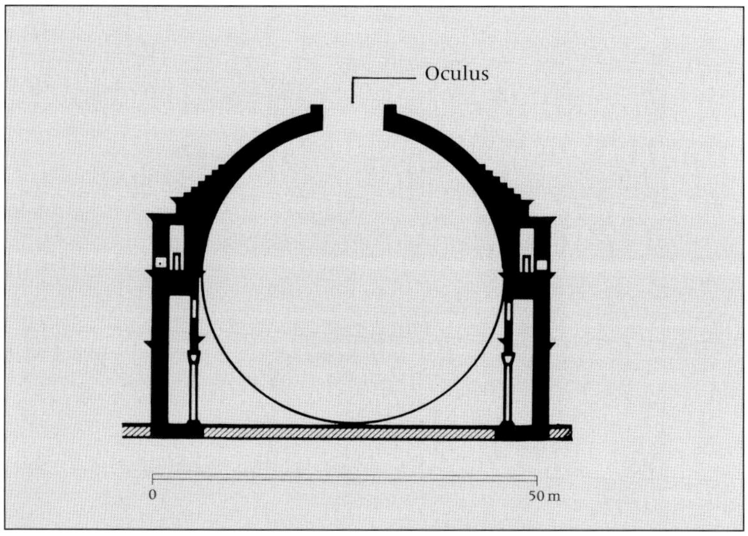

Fig. 105: The interior space of the Durbar Hall (left) encloses an imaginary perfect sphere after the model of the Pantheon in Rome (right).

Fig. 106: The architectural plan of July, 1926 for the dome above the Durbar Hall reveals an unusual three-layered construction composed of an inner layer (pink) made of brick, a steep middle layer also of brick (pink), and an outer layer of concrete (green). The enormous tambour takes the horizontal thrust of the inner dome with its great weight. The natural stone elements are marked in blue.

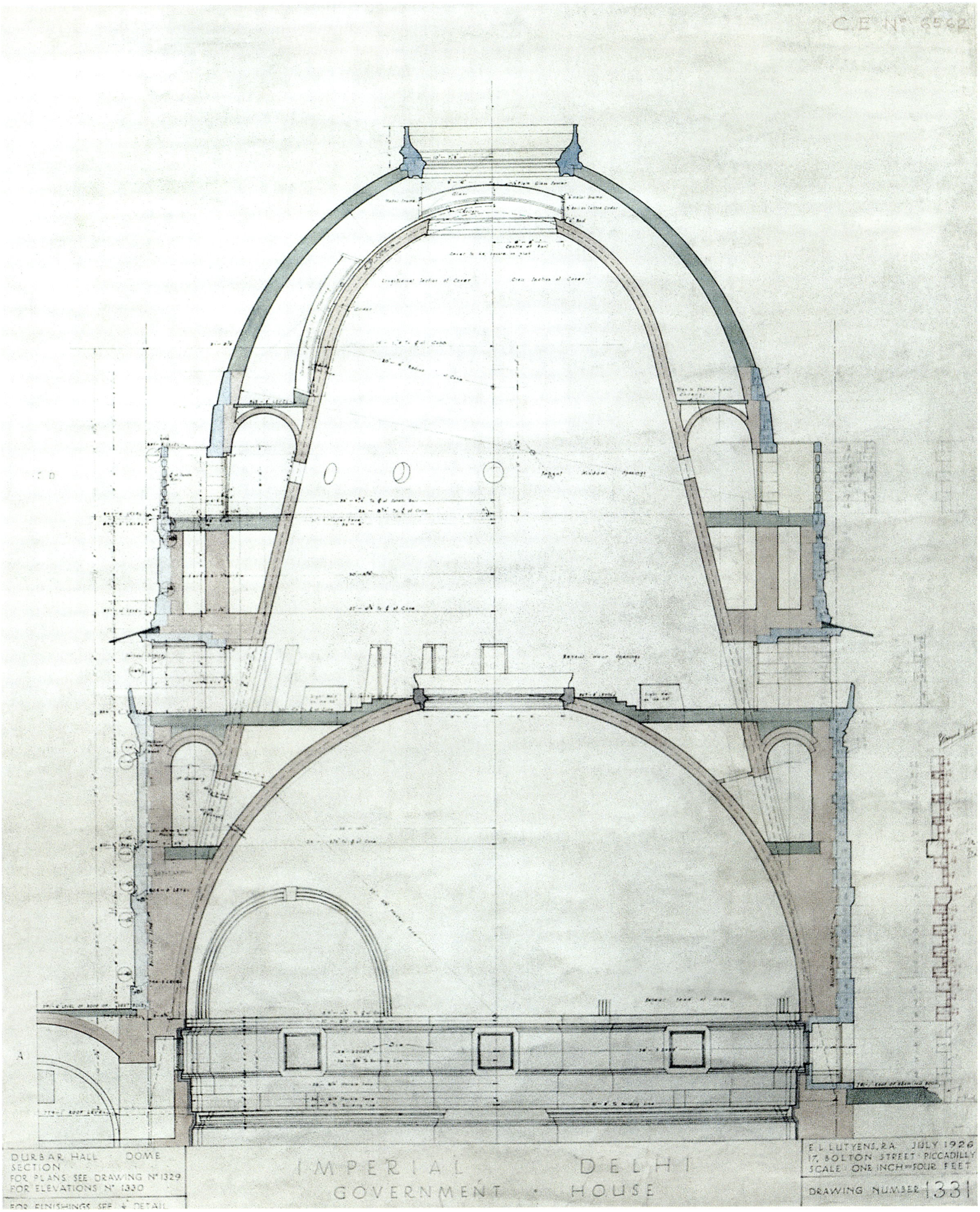
C.E. Nº 6562
DURBAR HALL DOME
SECTION
FOR PLANS: SEE DRAWING Nº 1329
FOR ELEVATIONS Nº 1330
FOR FINISHINGS SEE ¼" DETAIL
IMPERIAL DELHI
GOVERNMENT · HOUSE
E L LUTYENS. R.A. JULY 1926
17, BOLTON STREET · PICCADILLY
SCALE ONE INCH = FOUR FEET
DRAWING NUMBER 1331

The Mughal Garden

As is frequently the case in European palaces, directly behind Viceroy's House on the west side, there is a geometrically laid-out garden and further west, a circular pool. In Kashmir, Edwin Lutyens had become acquainted with the gardens of the Mughal emperors, and in the old towns of Delhi and Agra with the grounds of the forts and the gardens around important funeral monuments.

In deference to the local building tradition, he conceived the garden of Viceroy's House in this tradition of Mughal design. In the dry and hot climate of Delhi there was no possibility of anything other than an artificially watered garden. Moreover, Lutyens knew how much the Viceroy valued the adoption of Indian traditions and symbols.

One of his models is a square garden that is part of the Shalimar Bagh (Garden of the Halls of Love) from Srinagar in the seventeenth century. In Srinagar, capital of Kashmir, it is called the "Garden of the Women." At its centre, in a water-basin, lies the pavilion in which the ladies of the harem spent their leisure time. A circle of three concentric fountains cooled the air in the pavilion. In the centre of the Mughal garden there is also a square island and on its lawn a marquee is always erected for festivals.

The geometry of the Mughal Garden at Viceroy's House is certainly impressive (Fig. 111), but the geometric rules of its layout have not yet been clarified. This is all the more surprising considering the walled paths, the straight canals, and the symmetrical layout lead one to expect an overall unified plan.

In 1931, Lady Emily lavished particular praise upon the Mughal Garden on her visit to Delhi for the official inauguration: "Though so formal, yet everything has grown up so quickly, and flowers are set in such masses, producing a riot of colour and scents, that with the fountains playing continually, there is not the least sense of stiffness. The round garden beyond beats everything for sheer beauty and is beyond words."[41]

The fountains in the Mughal Garden deserve special attention (Fig. 108). The Garden's ground plan, like so many elements in Lutyens' architecture, is derived from the hexagram. Admittedly, this derivation becomes enigmatic when one joins up the points of overlap in each plane of the Victoria Regina lily which, when stylized, resembles an exact copy of the jewel of the Royal Arch of Freemasons (cf. Figs. 107, 52) mentioned earlier in the town plan (Fig. 56). This fountain shape, unknown until then, was such a success in Imperial Delhi that Lutyens used it about a decade later for the Mughal Garden of Hyderabad House.

Another novelty is the pergola, combining the square Mughal Garden with the round pool to the west of it (Fig. 110). Lutyens, according to oral tradition, was not able to obtain any stone beams sufficiently long for the red sandstone pergola. Thereupon he conceived a statically balanced system of short beams that were held in balance by decorated stone weights.

41 E. Lutyens: *Candles in the Sun*, London 1957.

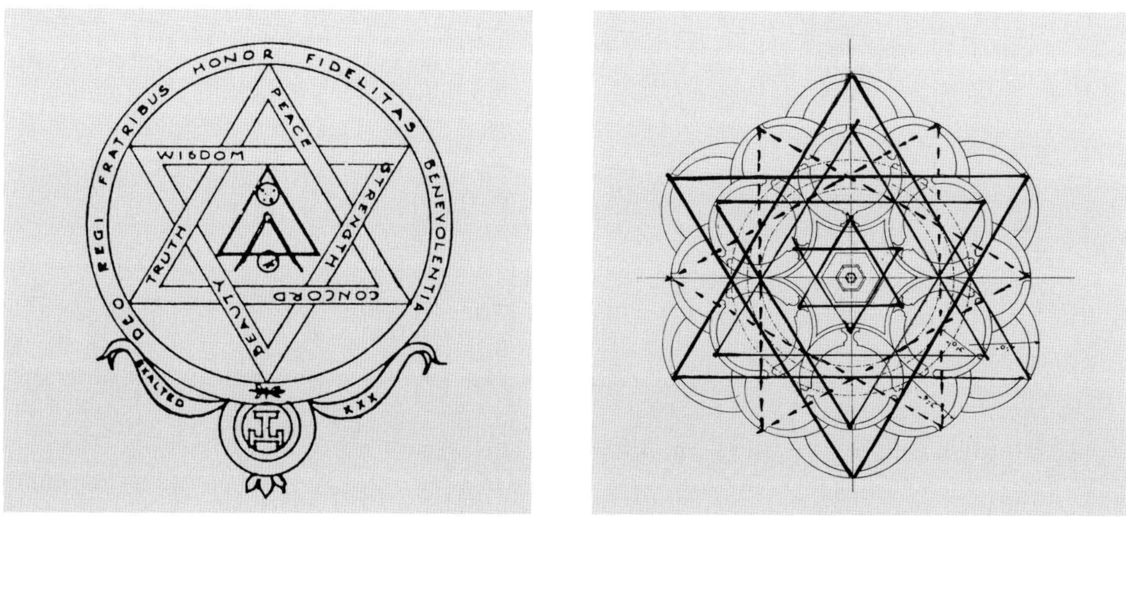

Figs. 107: The basic geometric structure of the fountains in the Mughal Garden bears a close resemblance to the jewel of the Royal Arch Freemasons, as well as the basic structure of the town plan of Imperial Delhi (cf. Fig. 56).

"The Mughal Garden is at its most glorious in the early months of the year. It is thrown open to the public in February/March and thousands troop in to admire its well-groomed elegance and the wealth of flowers in all imaginable hues and forms ... Unlike other gardens which grow a limited variety of roses but in large masses, the Mughal Garden has probably the largest range of rose varieties in one place – more than 250 – and these include Benkinsian, believed to be the parent of all the strains. The garden also grows sixty of the 101 known kinds of Bougainvillaea ... Trees which grow slowly and gracefully and live long figure prominently in the list of 600 varieties selected – mango, neem, jamun, peepal, banyan. These attract a large wealth of

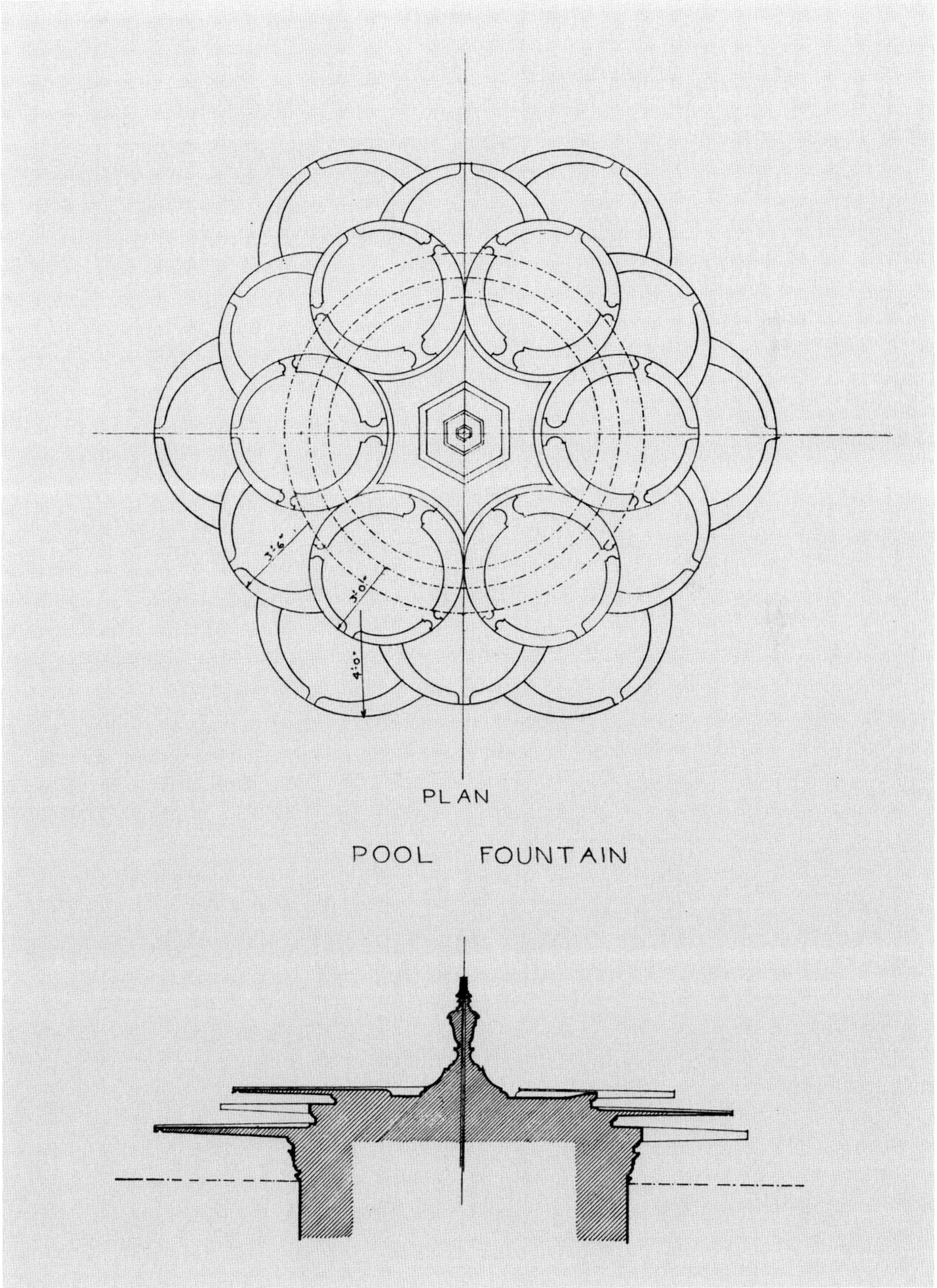

Fig. 108: Ground plan and section of the hexagonal fountain in the Mughal Garden of Viceroy's House.

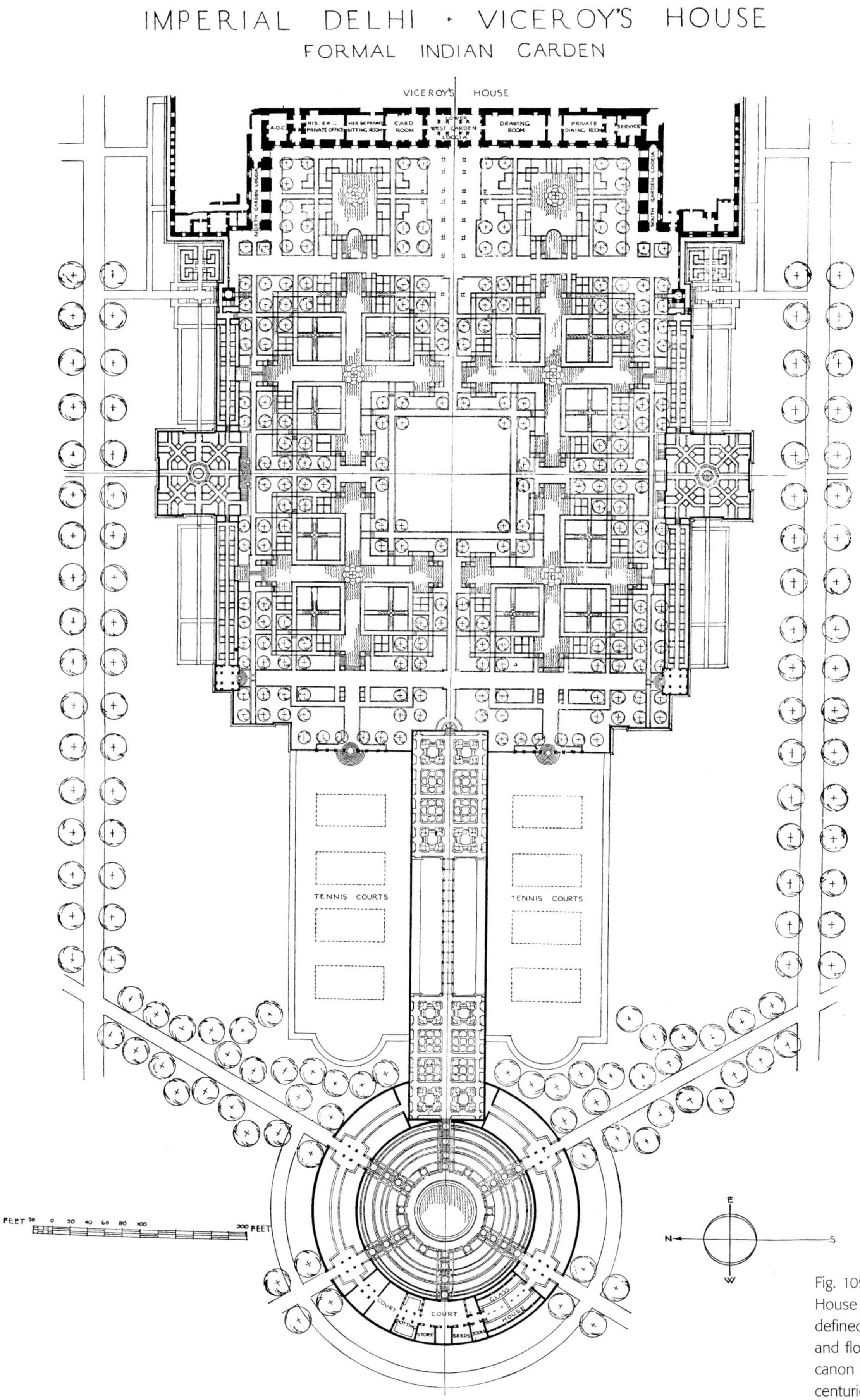

Fig. 109: The garden behind Viceroy's House with its strict geometric layout defined by low walls, paths, water areas, and flower beds adopts the formal canon of Mughal gardens from previous centuries.

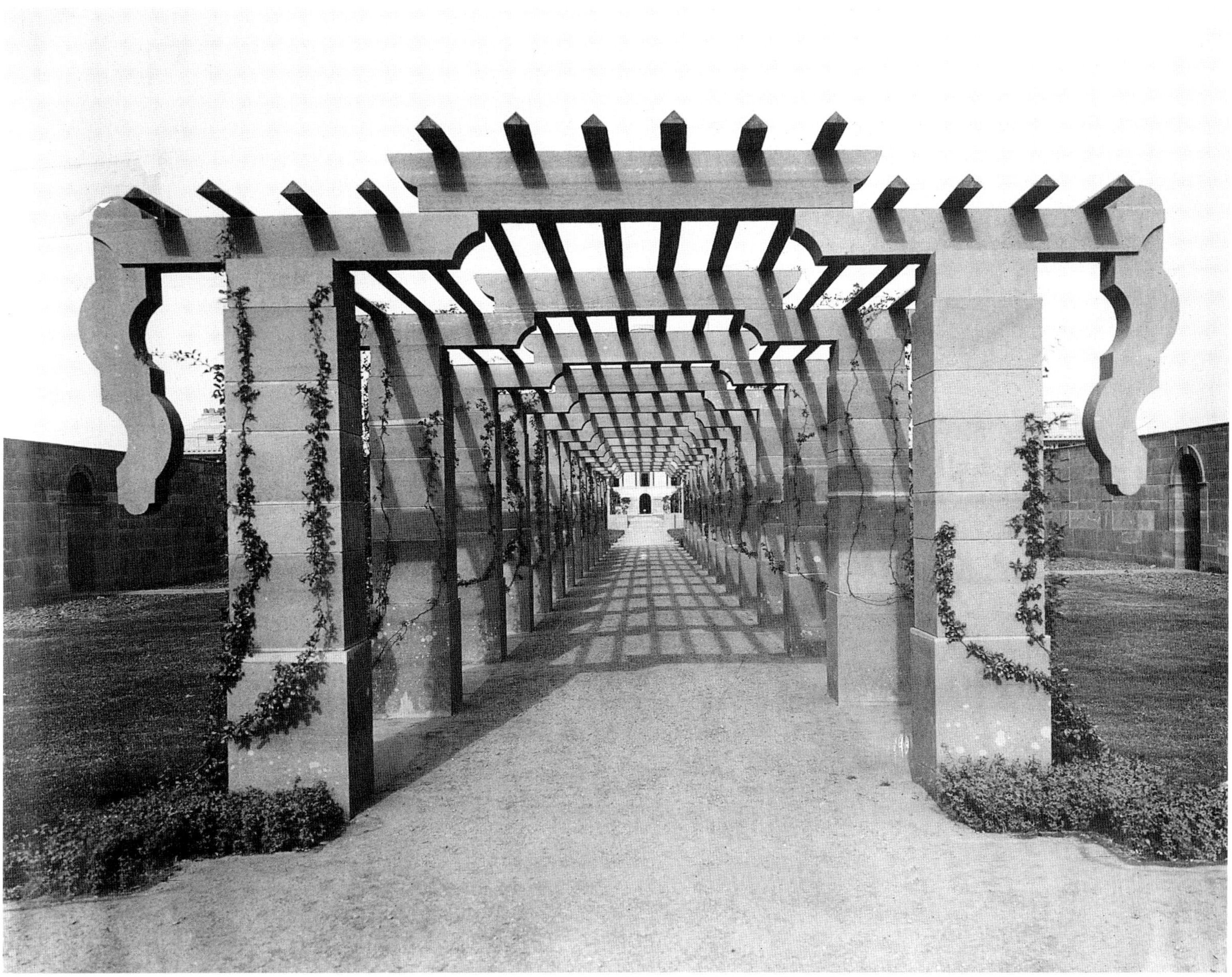

Fig. 110: In the main axis of the so-called Mughal Garden, red sandstone pergolas covered with plants provide shade for walking. Historic photograph c. 1930.

birdlife. It is not unusual to come across dancing peacocks during the day and hear the howl of jackals at night."[42]

The Mughal Garden owes its overwhelming effect also to the contrast with the surrounding dry landscape: "The patterns of water, color, and symmetry from Lutyens' hand were in marked contrast to the arid, drab wilderness outside the estate. The formal palace edifice and its geometric garden, juxtaposed against the untamed Delhi Ridge, was meant to be telling affirmation of power and of passionate British resolve to bring order to India – tangible proof, to use poet John Davidson's words, of the 'ruthless obligation ... to be despotic for the world's behoof.'

The fifteen acres of bright hues and bold patterns fashioned west of the palace by Lutyens and W.R. Mustoe, Director of Horticulture, were but a small fraction of the extraordinary 250-acre grounds. A handful of British estates might possess a comparably impressive park of specimen plantings, but how many also had a swimming pool, squash court, cricket ground, nine-hole golf course and eight tennis courts? None could boast a garden staff of 418, of whom fifty devoted themselves largely to scaring depredatory birds and another twenty, entirely to flower arrangements. Within the Viceregal compound a 'utility garden' alone comprised sixteen acres, providing abundant cut flowers for the palace, seasonal vegetables and citrus fruits for its kitchens, and rose bushes sufficient to replace three thousand each year."[43]

42 H.Y.S. Prasad: *Rashtrapati Bhavan, The Story of the President's House,* New Delhi 1992.

43 R.G. Irving: op. cit., p. 226.

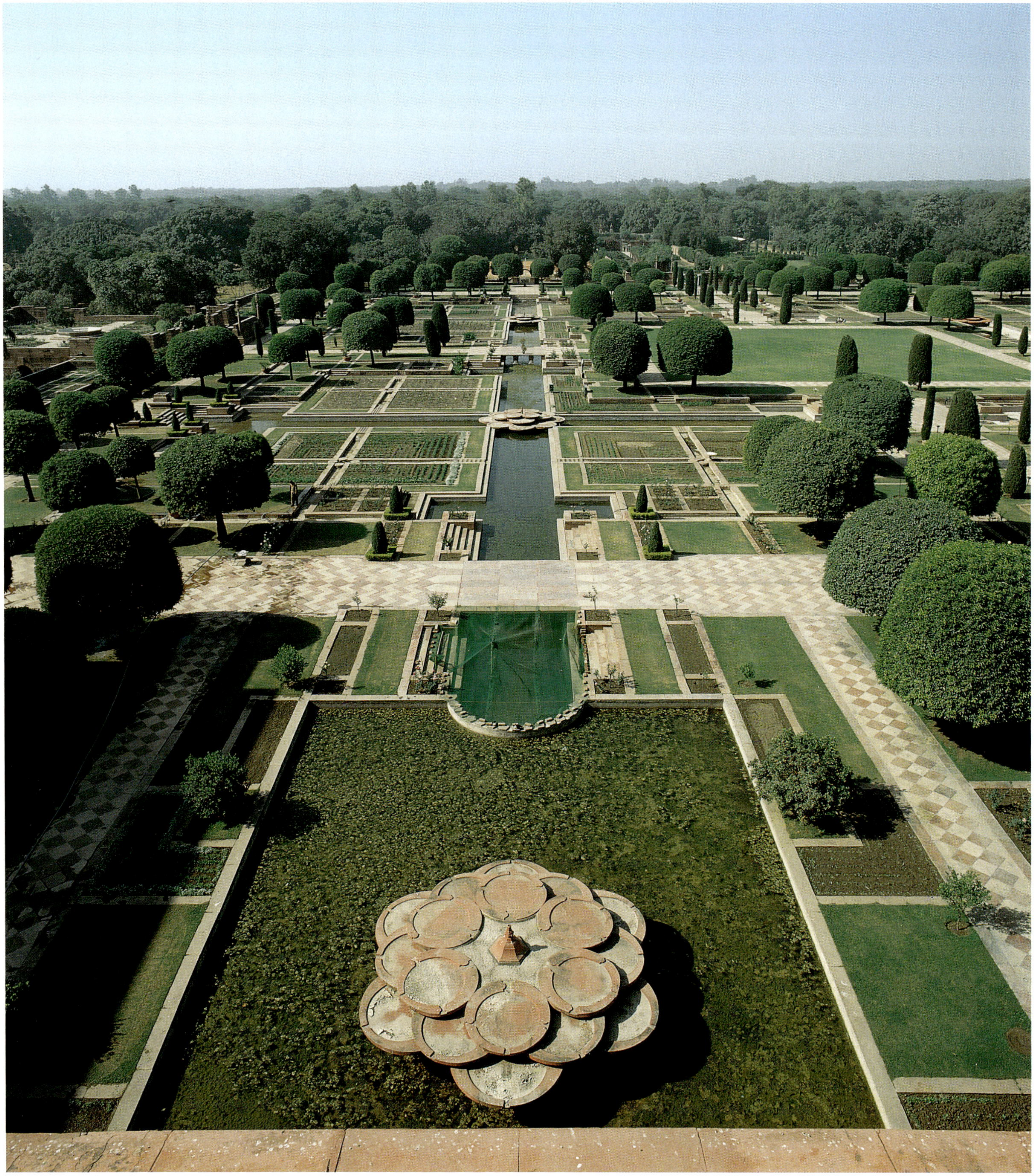

Fig. 111: View from the roof of Viceroy's House into the Mughal Garden. There are fountains with a basic hexagonal structure at all the intersections of its path.

44 Robert Byron: *New Delhi, Architectural Review*, Vol. LXIX, No. 410, January 1931, p. 28.

One of the first times the Mughal Garden was ever mentioned was in Robert Byron's article about New Delhi in 1931: "Of the garden itself, some twelve acres in extent – of its maze of grass squares, flower beds, and bridged waters at different levels, all framed in red stone; of its fountains like heaps of pennies; of its exquisite red and white gazebos, whose pierced panels are repeated in the water beside them; of the terraced battlements of flowers that rise like bastions on either side: of the stone Eiffel towers at the ends, bound in flashing brass and awaiting the growth of trees inside then; of the stone hoops all along the further boundary; of the stone pergola in the corridor beyond; and of the final circular enclosure attached to the corridor as a racquet to its handle – many pages could be written, and will be elsewhere. The general effect, at present, is bare; but in ten years the existing trees will have become a forest. The design, like the elaborate and formal water systems of the Moguls and the Italians, is strictly architectural, and is thus made the instrument of a logical transition between the great house behind and the rough landscape overlooked. But this process is not accomplished by that alone. For out in the landscape lie, on one side, the Viceroy's stables, and on the other, the Viceroy's bodyguard lines: complicated and symmetrical groups of buildings, having towers at their ends, and so planned, diamond-wise, as to accentuate their diagonal relation to the central axis – the axis which persists from the Memorial Arch at the foot of King's Way to the centre of the garden's final pond in the circular enclosure beyond the corridor. Thus, if the Viceroy steps out to pick a rose, he can look up to find the very horizon in deferential alignment with himself. Such is a proper setting for a ruler. But the architect has given his heart to the pansies as well. Throughout every detail of the garden is visible the same consummate manipulation of stone as distinguishes the whole city. And even the flowers responded to their environment of perfection."[44]

Fig. 112: On April 6, 1929, Sir Alexander Rouse (Chief Engineer), Teja Singh Malik (Chief Engineer of the Public Works Department) and the Viceroy, Lord Irwin (shown at centre), celebrated the completion of the dome above the Durbar Hall and the completion of the construction of Viceroy's House.

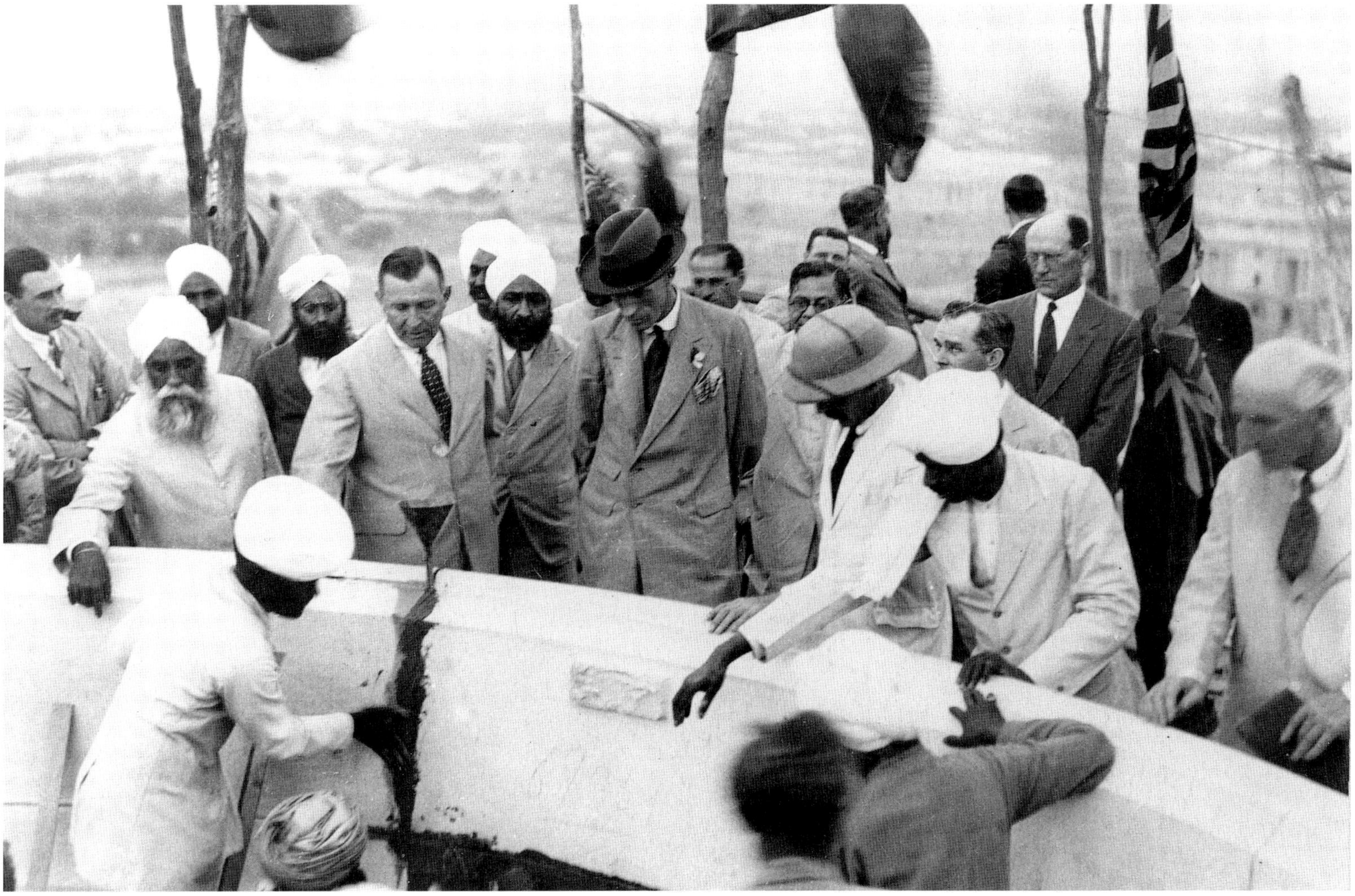

3.2.2 Jaipur Column (Architect: Edwin Lutyens), 1915

Ever since Pope Sixtus V's plans for Rome in the sixteenth century and Haussmann's system of boulevards for Paris in the nineteenth century, an imperial town plan has hardly been conceivable without a system of triumphal arches, obelisks and victory columns as fixed points in the arrangement.

In 1915, a fortunate coincidence led to Maharaja Sawai Madho Singh of Jaipur donating the sum of around £ 14,000, so that the foundation of the new capital would be commemorated by a column at a prominent place in the cityscape of Imperial Delhi. Lutyens decided that the most suitable location for this column was the Viceroy Court directly in front of Viceroy's House: "A germinal sketch for Delhi by Lutyens in June 1912 had depicted a spacious forum with two pillars, each labelled 'Trajan Column' (Fig. 73), and a sketch in September had shown a single shaft with distinctive spiral markings and crowned by a human figure. In June 1915, William Walcot executed a pair of alternative perspectives of the pillar, one capped with the figure of King George, the other with a lotus finial. Later that month, Lutyens urged the second design upon Lord Hardinge; marble statues of the king and queen, commissioned in 1913, eventually adorned the State Entrance of Viceroy's House.

The allusion to Trajan could be read as a compliment to King George: the Roman emperor had been a masterly administrator at the climax of Rome's military power, a ruler who set a premium on the welfare of his imperial subjects ...

The south relief displayed the heraldic arms of Britain, while the east face bore the plan of Imperial Delhi, carved at Lutyens' direction in the style of 'the diagram on the obelisk in the Place de la Concorde."[45]

The column, fitted together from various elements of stone and bronze, gave Lutyens particular problems with regard to static equilibrium. Its stability could only be assured by a technical trick: "The monument, 144 feet high, has a white sandstone shaft of only seven feet (average) diameter, which is spined with a drawn steel tube to give additional support to the crystal star and bronze lotus surmounting it and weighing five tons. This tube is anchored to the reinforced concrete core of the base. The exquisite elasticity of the structure is indicated by

45 R.G. Irving: op. cit., p. 246.

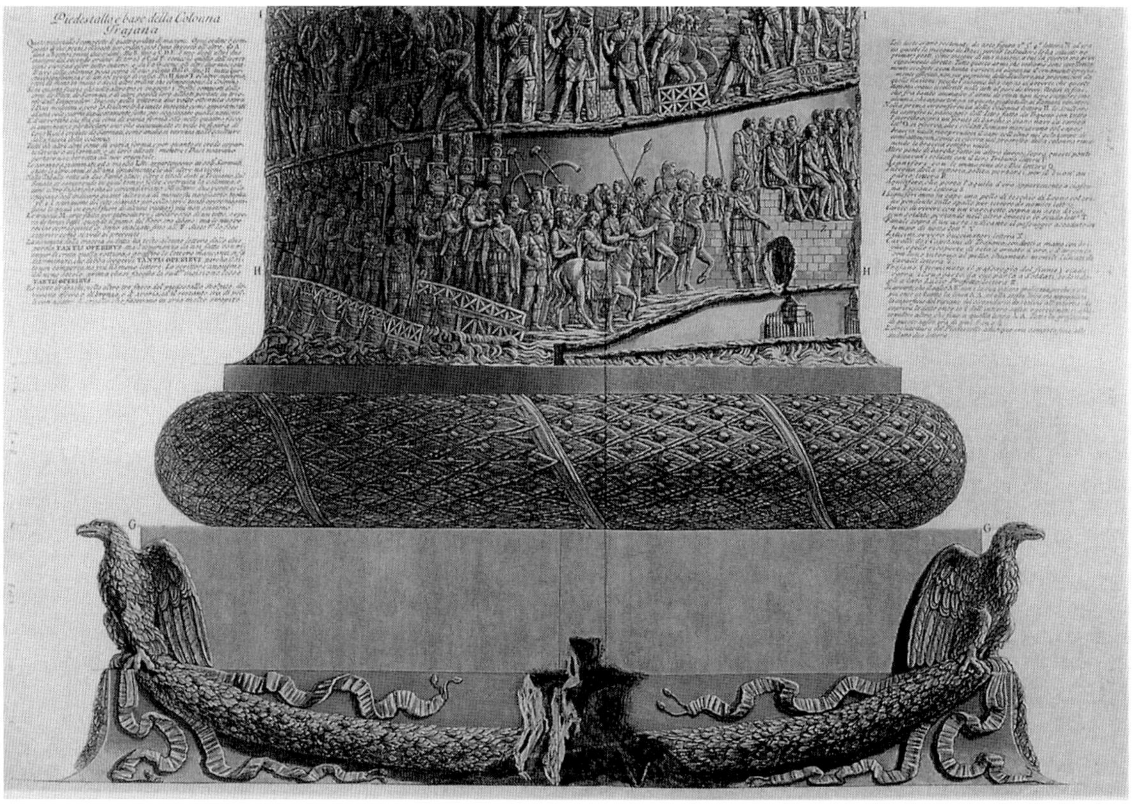

Fig. 113: Pedestal and base of Trajan's Column (engraving by Piranesi) are the direct models for the pedestal and base of the Jaipur Column in the courtyard of Viceroy's House.

the observation that the tip of the star is liable to oscillate up to six inches in a stiff breeze. In 1929, the temperamental carver Giudicci was still cutting the bas-reliefs on the base, which C.S. Jagger had modelled. The star was not put in position till 1930."[46]

The Jaipur Column is especially significant for our historical examination of Imperial Delhi thanks to the town plan being recorded in a bas-relief on the pedestal. Its orientation is unusual since west is depicted at the top. Only in this position is the hexagram in the town plan recognizable. This is the hexagon associated with the beloved geometry of the Freemasons, Hindu symbolism and, finally, with the designs of Mughal architecture (cf. chapter 3.1).

The details of the Jaipur Column were a matter of very great concern for Lutyens. For his model, he adopted motifs from Trajan's Column right down to the last detail of a laurel wreath and a laurel garland, at whose edges royal eagles keep guard (Figs. 113, 114). But to adorn the pillar drums, as in the case of Trajan's Column, with relief scenes depicting the life of the victorious emperor would have been too expensive. British oak-leaves presented a more inexpensive variant.

"The slender pillar, assisted by a pedestal set on a double base of red, rises to a height of 100 ft. Upon it rests a white egg from which, secured by a brass hoop, burgeons a bronze lotus. Finally the calyx of this flower balances on its very tip a six-pointed star of glass, diurnal reminder of the Indian orders of chivalry. The star is 15 ft. in diameter and 148 ft. above the ground."[47]

The plinth of the Jaipur Column also offered the most concise opportunity for Lutyens to combine his concepts of imperial British virtues with the destiny of the Raj:

Endow your thought with faith
Your deed with courage
Your life with sacrifice
So all men may know
The greatness of India.

46 Christopher Hussey: op. cit., p. 505.
47 R.G. Irving: op. cit., p. 243

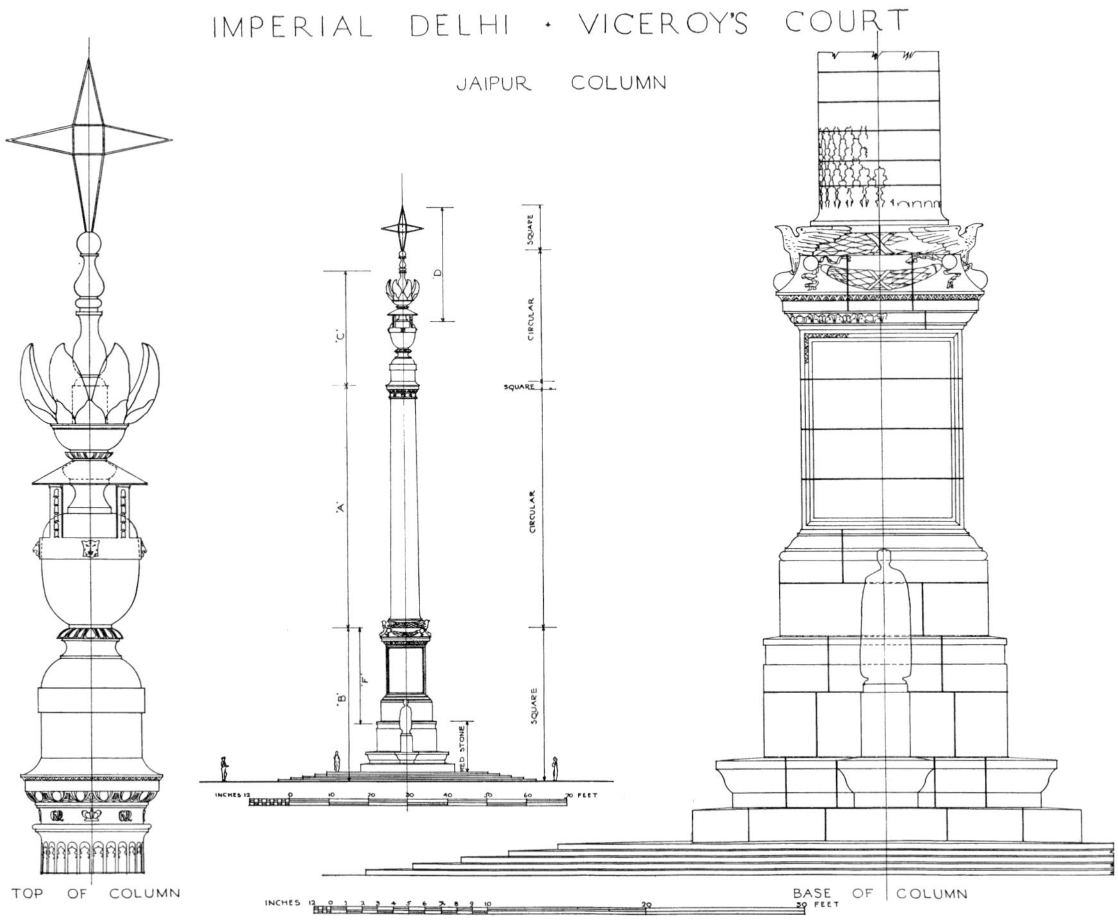

Fig. 114: In the wide courtyard in front of Viceroy's House stands the Jaipur Column donated by the Maharaja of Jaipur. The column's models are Trajan's Column in Rome and the obelisk in the Place de la Concorde in Paris.

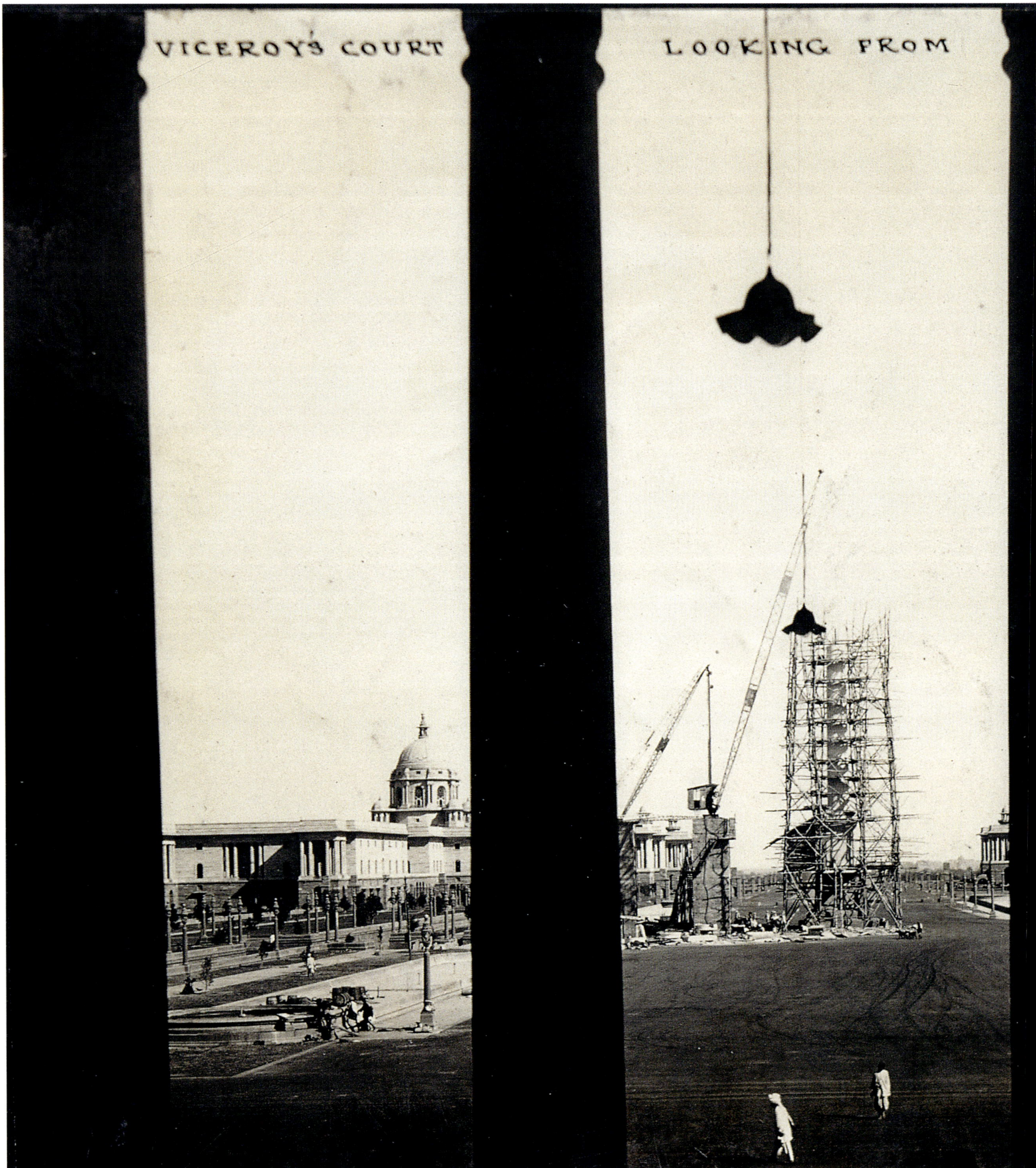
VICEROY'S COURT
LOOKING FROM

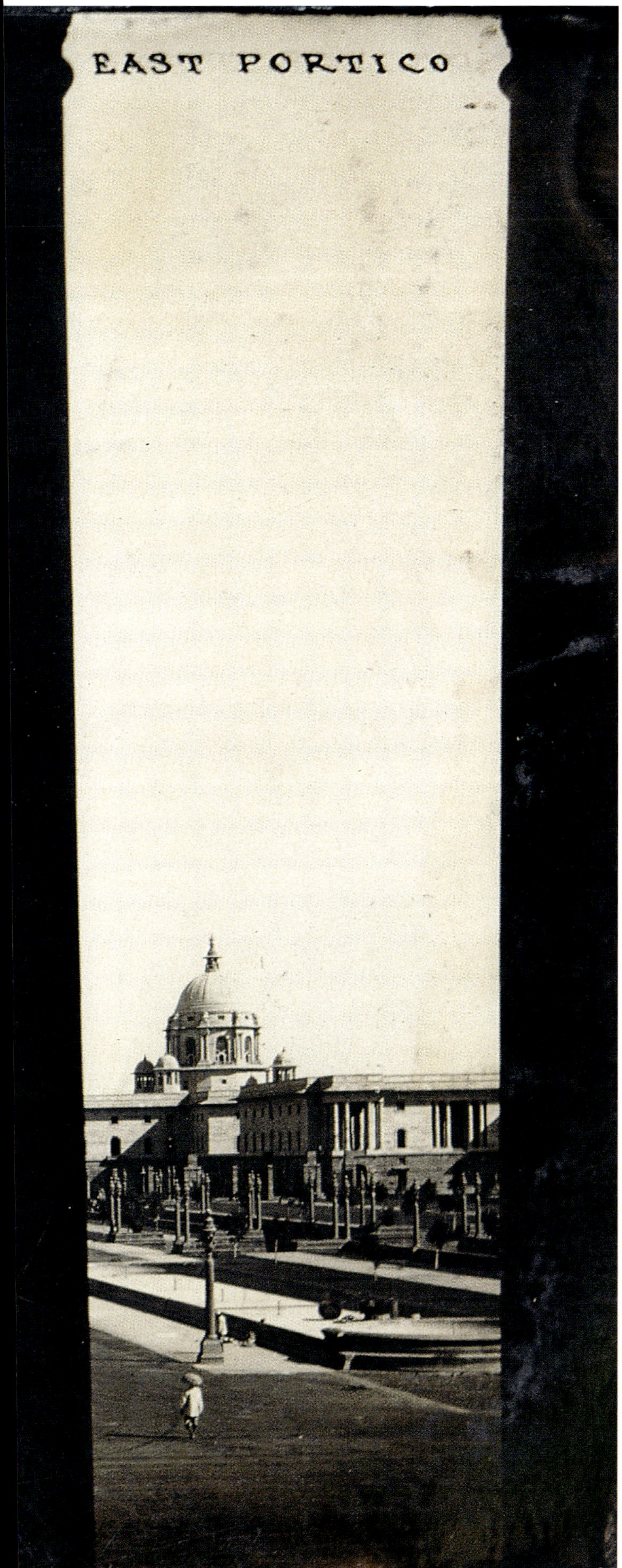

Fig. 115: View from the portico of Viceroy's House to the Jaipur Column during its construction. To the right and left of the column are the two Secretariats.

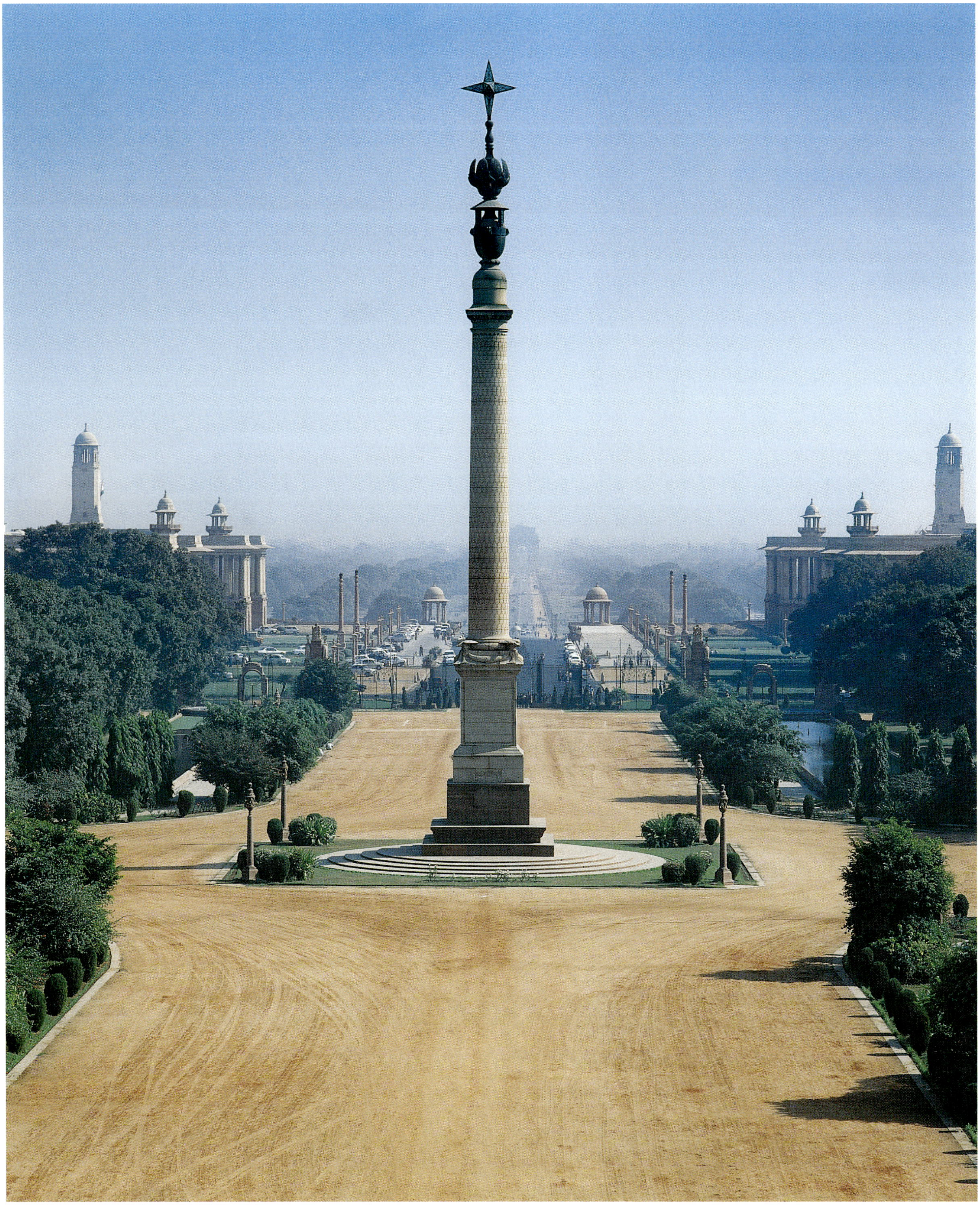

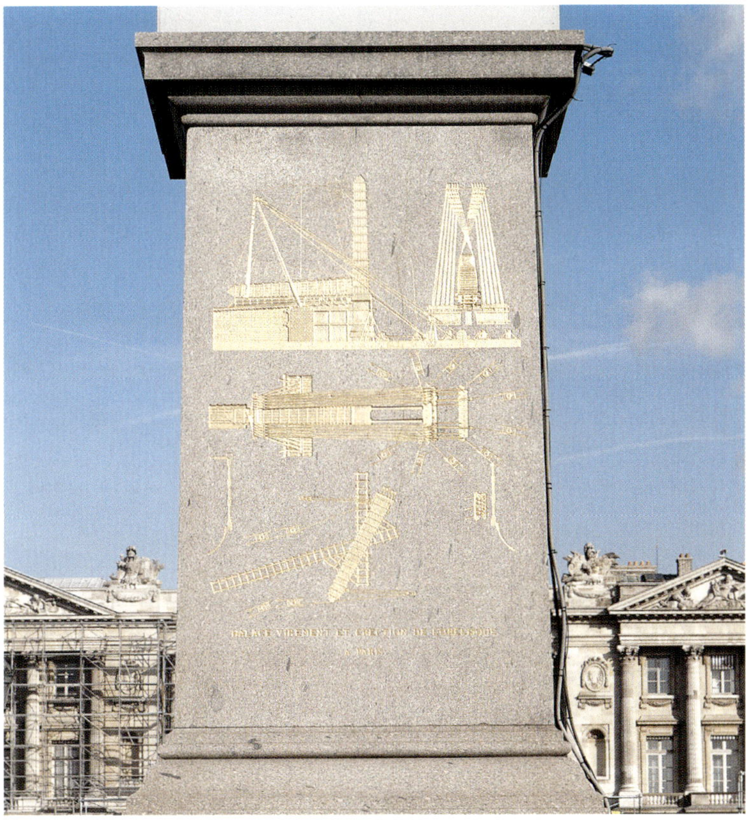

Fig. 117: The documentation of the building of the obelisk on the Place de la Concorde is on its plinth. The following inscription "Balance, virement et erection de l'obelisque a Paris" attests to this too.

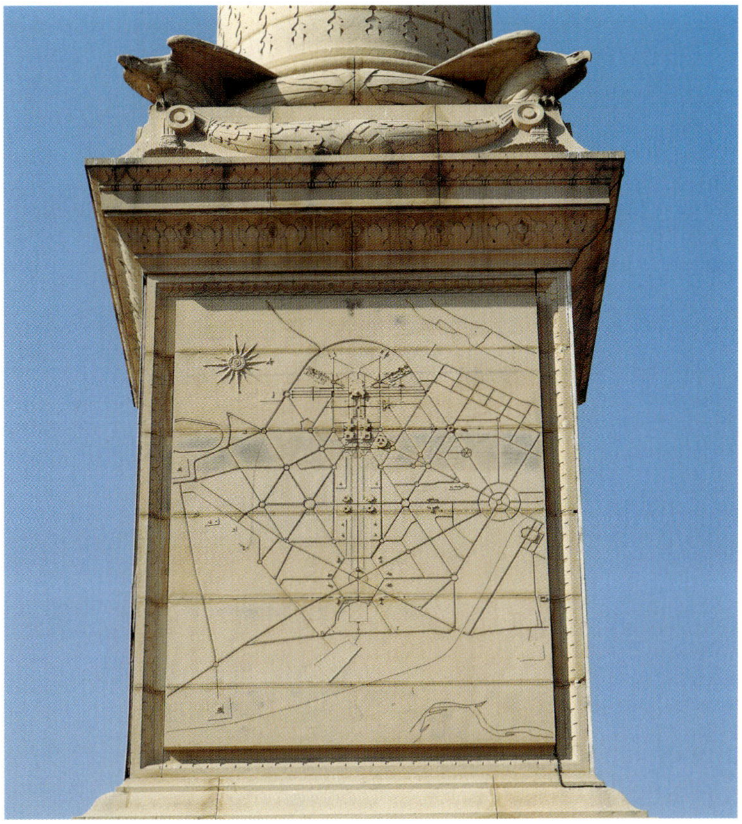

Fig. 118: The plinth of the Jaipur Column displays a building principle borrowed from the depiction on the plinth of the obelisk in Paris; principle for the erection of an obelisk in Paris and, in the latter, the draft plan for Imperial Delhi. No contemporary or later town plan shows more authentically the hexagonal plan with the most important public buildings at its key points.

Fig. 116: View from the roof of Viceroy's House east, past the Jaipur Column, to the All India Gate at the end of King's Way (now Raj Path).

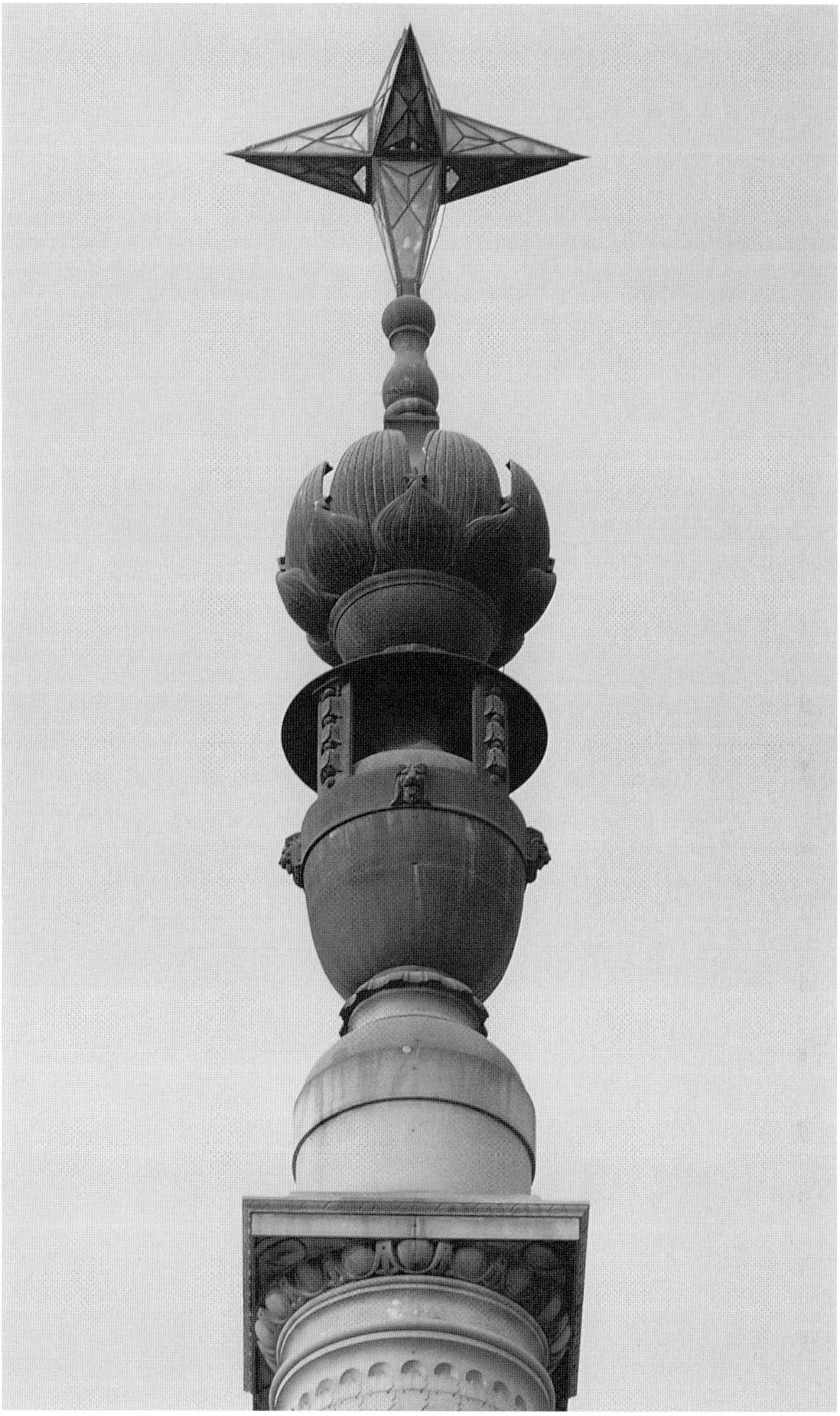

Fig. 119: At the top of the Jaipur Column, the imperial orb, lotus flower, and hexagram point to the six orientations of the world (above, below, north, south, west, east).

Fig. 120: High on Raisina Hill, at the grand wrought-iron gate to Viceroy's House, the public part of the great axis of King's Way ends. The gate also marks the border agreed upon by Edwin Lutyens and Herbert Baker in the plans for boundary between Viceroy's House and the Secretariats.

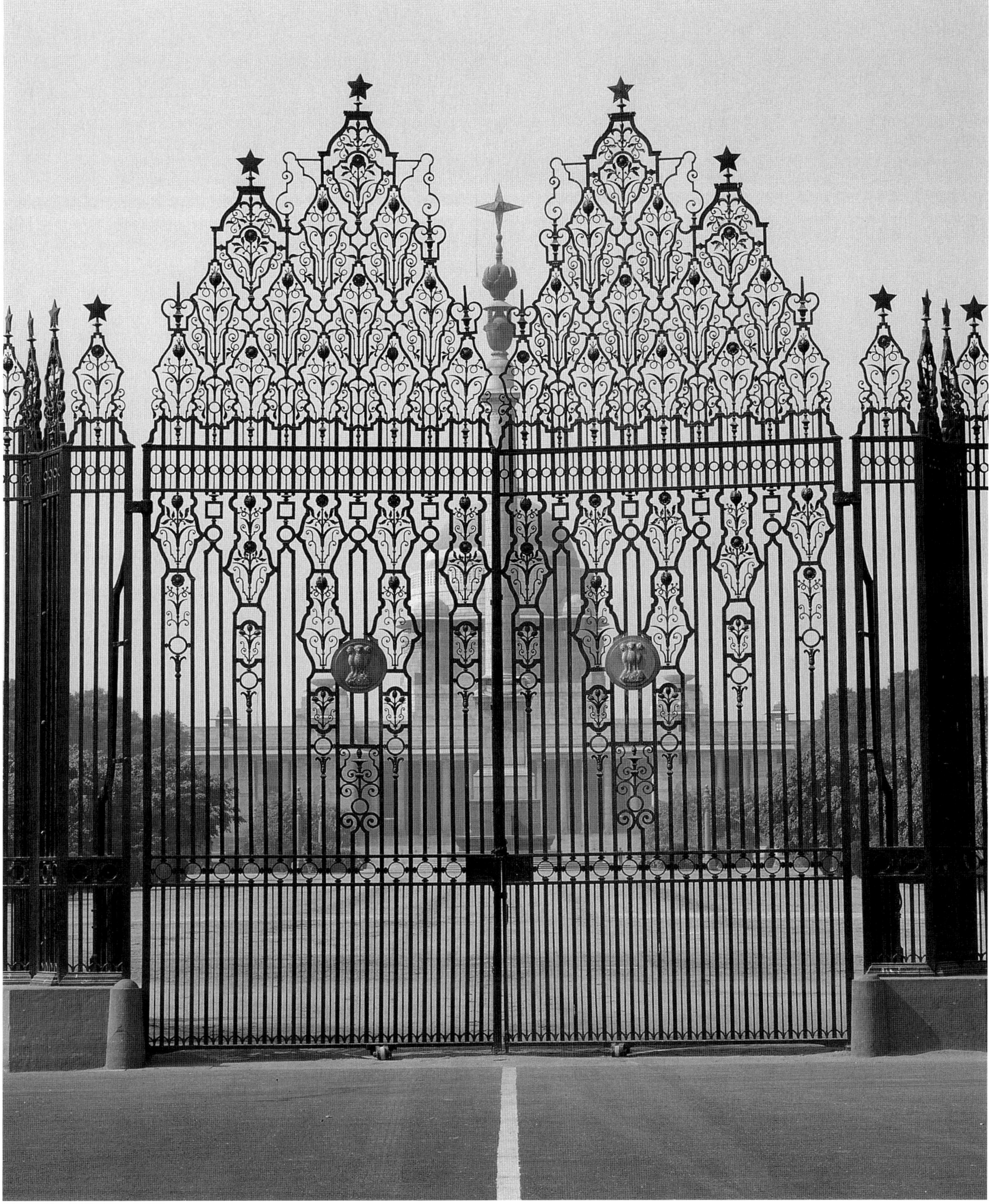

3.2.3 The Secretariats (Architect: Herbert Baker), 1914–1927

At the beginning of their collaboration in Imperial Delhi, Herbert Baker and Edwin Lutyens came to an agreement with the then Secretary of State in the India Office about their respective responsibilities. Lutyens took the responsibility for the town plan and for the Viceroy's palace, Viceroy's House. Baker received the commission for the two Secretariats and the Legislative Building.

To his task, Herbert Baker brought his rich experience as the architect of the government building in Pretoria, South Africa. "Unlike Lutyens, whom he thought concentrated his intellectual talents on abstract and geometric qualities to the neglect of human and national sentiment, Baker felt that content in art was the most important priority. Therefore, in building New Delhi, English Neo-Classical architecture in the manner of Inigo Jones and Wren should be adopted in order to fearlessly 'put the stamp of British sovereignty' on the subcontinent of India.

Drawing an analogy with the Roman Empire, Baker quoted his friend William Morris: 'Only Rome in her greatest days did what England has been doing, as a matter of course, for one hundred years!' Baker felt that architects, with their allied artists and craftsmen, had an opportunity 'to immortalize through their arts' the law and order that British administration had 'produced out of chaos.' Like Alexander the Great or the Romans, the British might put 'their own impress on the arts, which they had at first absorbed.'

In a paper entitled 'Architecture of Empire' prepared for the Round Table, Baker underlined the value he attached to the principles of classical architecture, the 'dearly bought experience of over 2,000 years' culminating in the language and style of Jones and Wren and their eighteenth-century followers. He saw parallels between architecture and British colonial rule itself."[48] He also liked to refer to the ideas of Christopher Wren, for whom architecture in the public realm had, above all, the political task of promoting national identity and patriotism.

It is in this context also that we should view Herbert Baker's desire to build the Secretariats near Viceroy's House, thus forming a unity in town planning and symbolism on Raisina Hill. Imperial Delhi was to be directly linked to the prominent government centres of Persepolis and Babylon, and also with the sacred regions of Agrigentum and Segesta.

After the decision was taken to bring together all the offices or ministries into two monumental administrative buildings that were externally identical, the architects turned to the square before Viceroy's House, described by Baker as a "sacred plaza," and designed one of the greatest building complexes of this age, three storeys high and extending over an area of 1,200 x 1,300 feet.

Imperial architecture for Pretoria and Delhi

In the interior of these mighty buildings, courtyards vary in the style of the Renaissance palaces of Florence and Rome, with wide stairwells, circular buildings, and high office and assembly rooms that command respect.

Herbert Baker borrowed many details that he took from his recently completed Union Buildings in Pretoria, such as the towers that crown each Secretariat (Fig. 127), the protruding columned porticos at each corner and axis of the buildings, and finally, in the raised position of the buildings, on a plinth course accessible by wide and long flights of steps (Fig. 129). Baker knew that it was his successful work in Pretoria that now qualified him for Delhi: "In the early autumn of 1912, when the Pretoria buildings were nearly completed (except for the east block, which was a repetition of the west), I had hints that I might be asked to go to Delhi as joint architect with Edwin Lutyens for the new Capital. I knew that on the strength of my Pretoria buildings, my appointment had been recommended by Lord Hardinge, but on great pressure from home, he, rightly, appointed Lutyens. When he was out there, however, the Viceroy decided that Lutyens must have a collaborator, and then I also was appointed. I had written a letter to the *Times* on the controversial problem of the style of architecture which would not only satisfy Indian sentiment, but would embody the high ideals of our rule in India ... I advocated that

48 R.G. Irving: op. cit., p. 278.

Fig. 121: Herbert Baker termed the columned porticos in front of the minister's offices on the first floor of each Secretariat "temples."

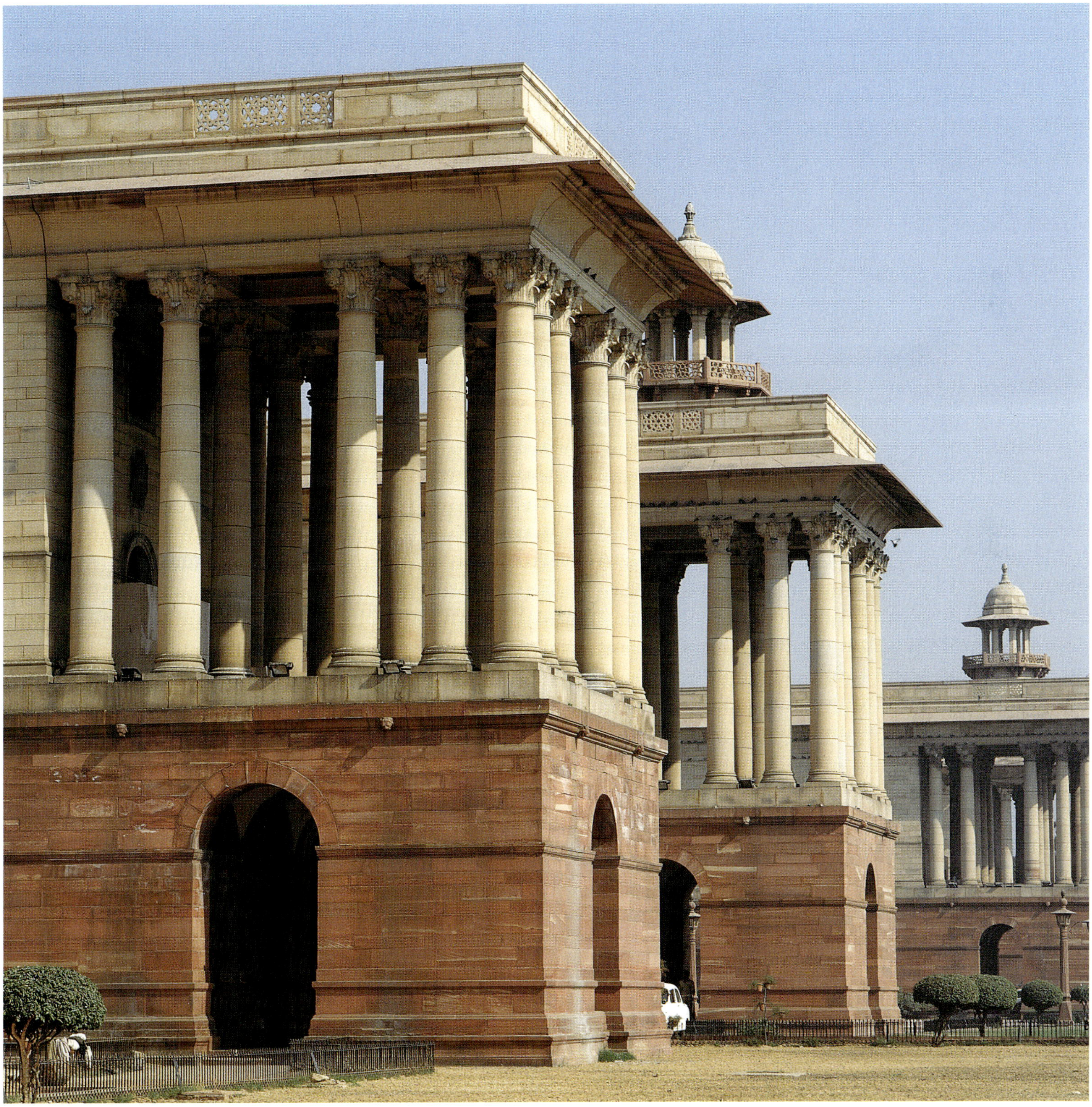

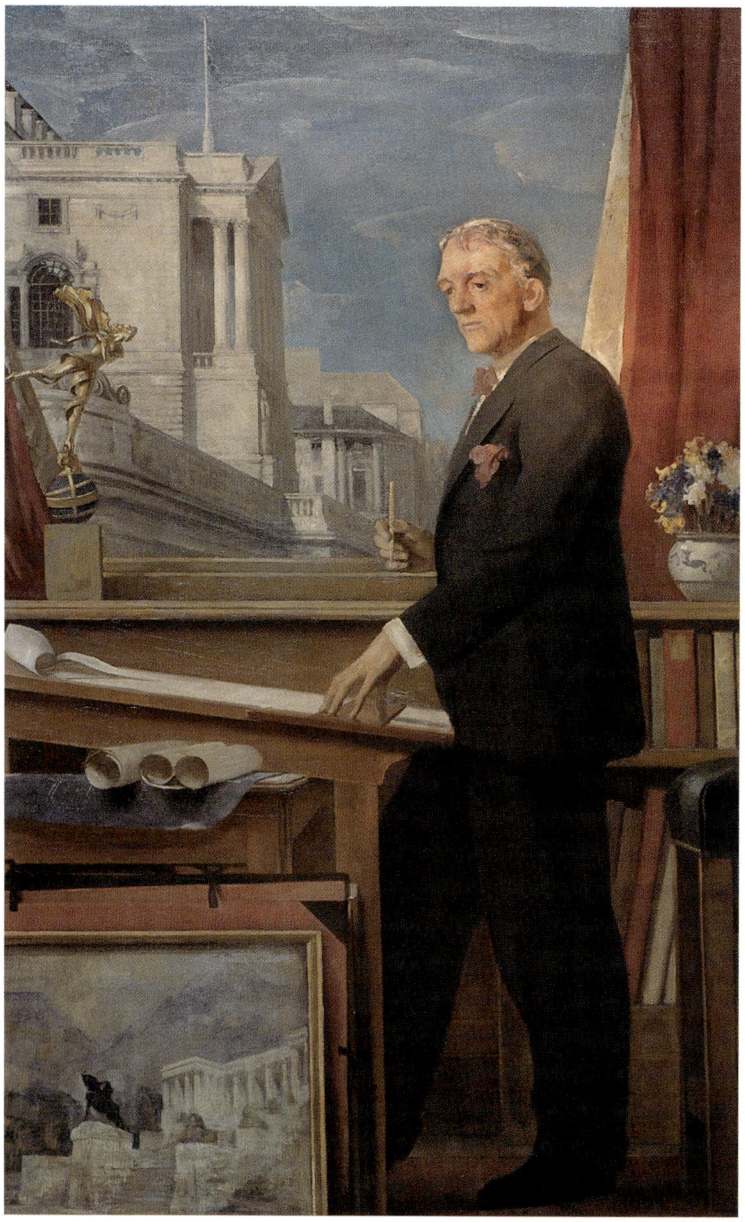

Fig. 122: Herbert Baker, the architect of the Secretariats, prefered having himself portrayed along with Neo-Classical paintings.

there should be no direct imitation of Indian styles of building, nor the following of any orthodox classical period. The aim should rather be, I contended, to build according to the great elemental qualities and traditions, which have become classical, of the architecture of Greece and Rome, which grew out of the needs of a southern climate; and to graft thereon structural features of the architecture of India as well as decoration expressing the myths, symbols and history of its people. With this possibility in mind I went home in the autumn, and on to Italy to refresh my memory at the home of the Mother of the Arts. An architect can best derive inspiration in an hour or two spent in meditation and adjustment of his scale to big things under the vast dome of the Pantheon."[49]

With Herbert Baker, as with Edwin Lutyens, the source of architectural conceptions was England's awareness of its mission. In an explanation of his own view of the world, he quoted a colleague from the year 1910: "So long as the consciousness of civilized man recognizes government as the noblest task of the race, so long by administering India is our pride of place unquestioned. No nation in modern times has done the like or can aspire to do it. To hold India, with its hundreds of races and religions and languages, and castes and customs, to be possessed of such a heritage of history, learning and romance is an achievement for which the world's records show but one parallel. Thothmes and Sennacherib, Alexander and Napoleon, never did the like. Only Rome in her greatest days did what England has been doing, as a matter of course, for one hundred years. We in India have found out and taught a modern world how to govern a continent incapable of the task itself, and when the future annals of a steadily shrinking world are written, the achievement will rank higher than the broadest-minded decrees of the Senate or the most generous edicts of the Caesars."[50]

The columned porticos of the Secretariats

A striking architectural peculiarity of the Secretariats are the columned porticos added to the building on all sides: "The offices of the Ministers, or Honourable Members as they are called in India, and some Chief Secretaries have, opening from them large columned porticoes – not porticoes strictly speaking, being on an upper floor, but 'pavilion' sounds too weak a word. I like to think of them as 'temples,' as I had in my thoughts in designing them, both there and for the Government Buildings at Pretoria, Rhodes' way of taking men with narrow minds out to look up at the 'mountain': at Delhi Ministers might 'lift up their hearts' not 'to the hills,' but over the far ruinous sites of the historic cities of the Hindu and Mohamedan dynasties to the new Capital beneath them that unites for the first time through the centuries all races and religions of India.

The four 'temples' in front that look down the Central Vista, or King's Way, stand fifty feet above the general level of the city; between the two on either side rise the high towers.

49 H. Baker: *Architecture and Personalities*, London 1944, p. 63.
50 Ibid.
51 Ibid., p. 69.
52 Ibid., p. 71.

They and the 'temples' on the great podium seem the guardians of the Processional Way up the Acropolis, and may suggest the attributes of majesty which distinguished the rock platform and stairways at Persepolis."[51]

Peculiarities of the climatic conditions

In the treatment of the facades and in respect of the necessary consideration of the climatic peculiarities of Northern India the Secretariats differ clearly from Viceroy's House: on the one hand Lutyens provided wherever possible shady verandas, and on the other hand he minimized the depth of each wing in order to facilitate cross-ventilation.

Baker follows a different strategy of air conditioning: "The Secretariats were built without continuous verandahs or other such outside protection as is usual in India from the heat of the sun. They have instead very thick hollow walls into which the windows are deep-set, so that the high rays of the sun cannot shine on and heat the glass. Against the low sun of morning and evening they are protected by teak latticed shutters. By this means the lighting of the rooms can be better regulated and the offices are not so gloomy in the cooler weather; the sun-baked walls also sooner radiate during the cooler nights their heat, which usually clings to the stuffy verandah."[52]

Fig. 123: For Herbert Baker, architect of the two Secretariats, Rome was also an important formal model for an imperial architectural style, in particular the dome of St Peter's (here, a wooden model from the Vatican).

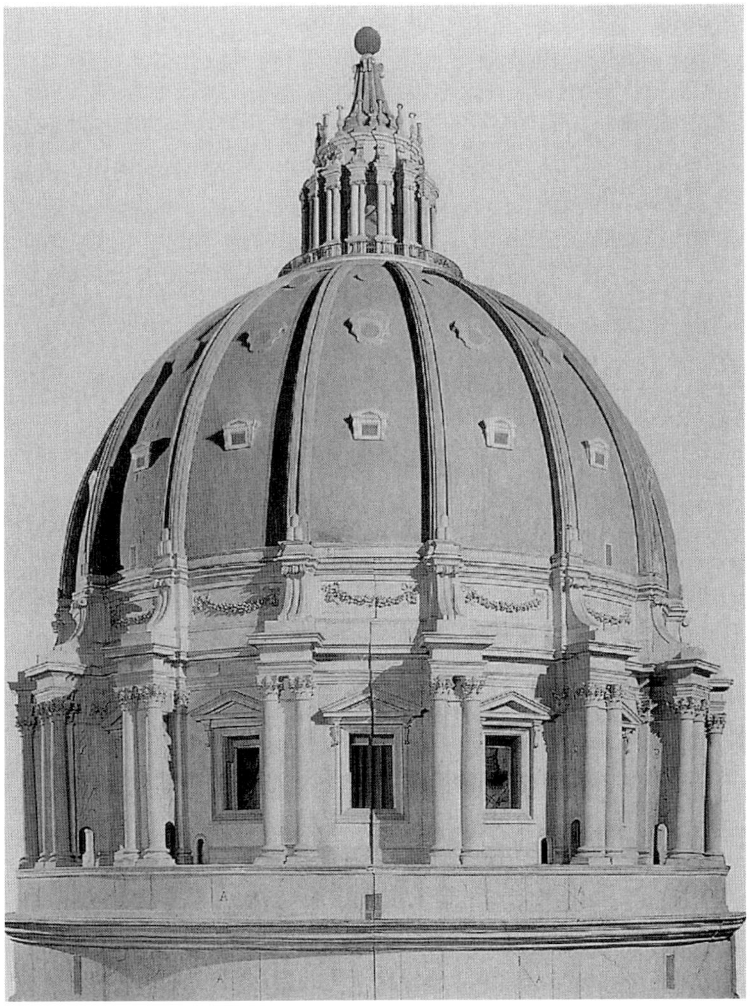

The columns of the four dominions

In the wide courtyard between the two Secretariats stand four columns whose bases bear coats of arms: "It was a great satisfaction to me when Lord Irwin finally agreed that four columns should be set up as symbols of the Dominions of the Empire, in the Court of the Secretariat: They were shown there in my original plan, but had acquired a greater significance when the Dominions signed independently the Peace of Versailles, and when they were granted full Dominion status. These columns are similar in form to the columns which the emperor Asoka set up throughout India, inscribed with the edicts of his united Empire, in size and unity equal only in India to the empires of Akbar and the British. The best examples are the fallen drums and capitals, carved with Greek excellence, at Sarnath and the standing pillar in the ruins of Feroz Shah's city in Old Delhi. The ancient iron pillar at the Kutab, of some mysterious alloy that never rusts, which has weathered to many hues, is similar in design. At an earlier stage I suggested to Amery, the Colonial secretary, that it would be a good gesture of Imperial unity, and a mark of the gratitude of the Empire for the services of India in the German war, if each Dominion gave a column to the new Capital in Delhi. He asked Edward Grigg, who went with the prince of Wales on his progress round the Empire, to make the suggestion to the Dominion Governments. But they were not then unanimous in favour of the gift.

The circumstances were more propitious at the time when the buildings were completed; and when I reopened the

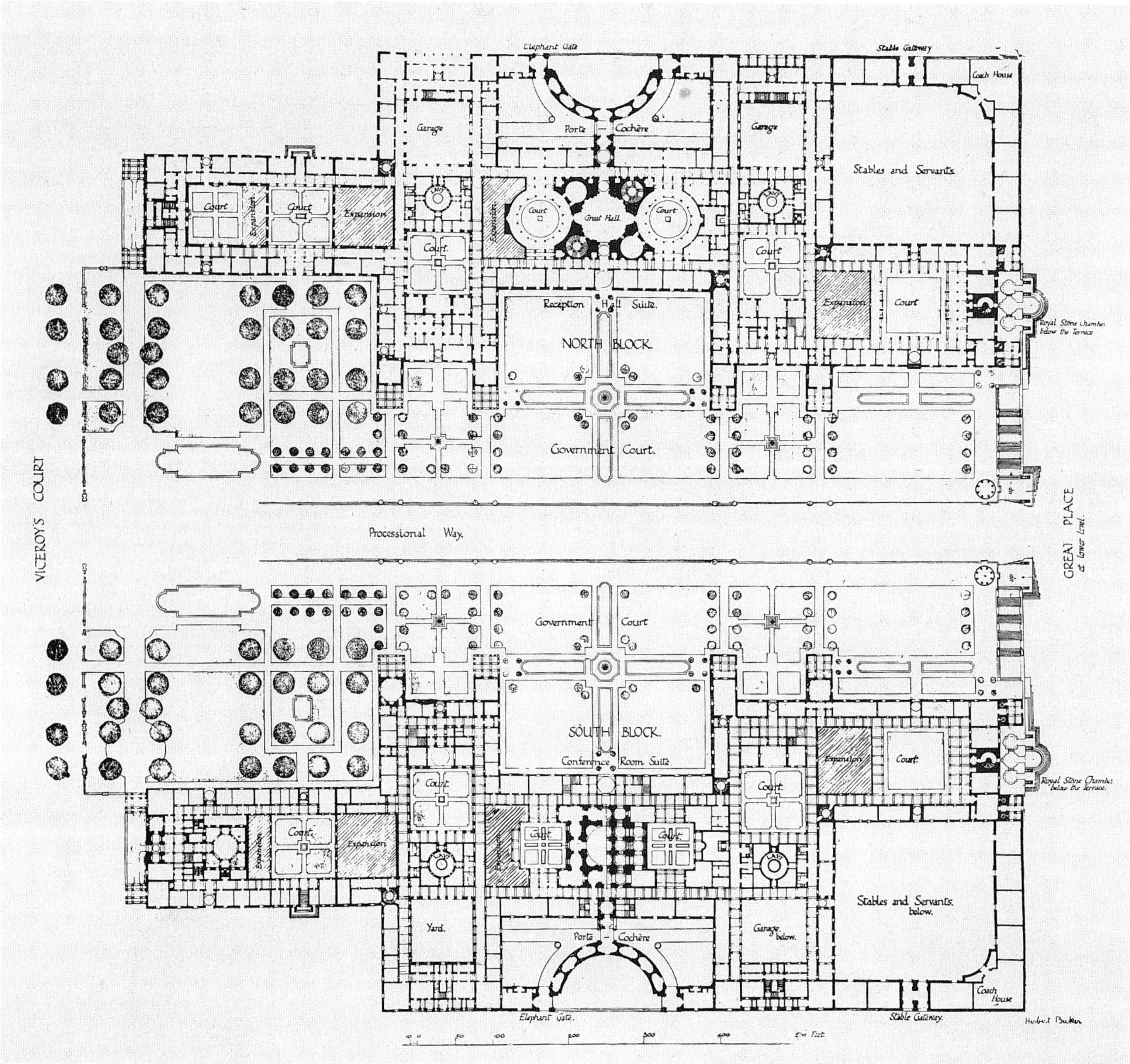

Fig. 124: Ground plan of the two Secretariats with Government Court situated in between.

idea to the Viceroy, Lord Irwin, the gift of the columns, communicated through the Home Government to the Prime Ministers of the Dominion, are surmounted by a full-rigged ship, symbol of the ocean-link of Empire, and on each is inscribed in English and three Indian languages: 'to India in token of their common loyalty to the King-Emperor, MCMXXX.'"[53]

The setting of British sovereignty over India on Raisina Hill, not far from the capital of the Mughal emperors and replete with references to the Acropolis in Athens, the Capitol in Rome, and the Palace of Persepolis, also carries a tragicomic note: "The government officers who peopled the Secretariat Buildings were leading actors in the symbolic drama of Imperial Delhi, a chosen few perched by day on a rocky mount in an enclave as artificial as any Himalayan hill station. The Raisina acropolis was a majestic stage set for the spectacle of the Indian Civil Service, the tiny corps who were governors over a quarter of the human race. Normally of long tenure, members of this exalted cadre were known in common parlance as the 'heaven-born' and enjoyed a reputation for matchless integrity and scrupulous fairness."[54]

Matchless integrity and scrupulous fairness were only one side of the British Raj. Political arrogance and racist pride characterized the other. Surveillance of the media[55] and the arresting of leaders from the independence movement[56] were an inevitable consequence. So after only two decades, the pages of history turned remorselessly in imperial India. For the British Empire, only an expertly trained Civil Service remained preserved on the Indian subcontinent and, of course, the architecture of Imperial Delhi.

The conflict over the slope on Raisina Hill

Another conflict involving the architecture of Imperial Delhi was the violent professional and ultimately personal conflicts between Edwin Lutyens and Herbert Baker about the approach from Prince Edward Place (later Great Place) up to Raisina Hill, i.e. to Viceroy's House.

The two architects unanimously agreed to propose to the Viceroy, Lord Hardinge, that the area on Raisina Hill was the best site for the two Secretariats, i.e. directly next to, or in front of Viceroy's House. Hardinge accepted the proposal. Only later did Lutyens notice that, because of the unavoidable slope, the direct view to the palace was briefly blocked to the view of the approaching visitor. Lutyens wrote indignantly to Baker who, understandably, was not troubled by this deficiency. Lutyens felt the working relationship was at a critical point, stating, "This is not satisfactory collaboration. There is yet time to avoid these grave defects, so that the original idea we agreed and expressed in your own perspectives is maintained."[57] His indignation was understandable inasmuch as the watercolours being prepared at that time by William Walcot reflected a different impression of the intended building measures. In Walcot's images, Viceroy's House was clearly visible from Great Place sitting in between both Secretariats!

Herbert Baker did not agree with Lutyens' suggested alterations. His reasons are clearly stated in his memoirs: "Another criticism was that, on approaching the great platform with the arcades and colonnades of the Secretariats on their high walled terrace, Government House (later called Viceroy's House) is partially hidden from view. But this was the inevitable result of setting both buildings up on the raised platform. The same thing has happened on other famous sites. On ascending the great flight of steps to the Acropolis at Athens the porticoes of the Propylea are seen in their full glory, but the colonnades of the Parthenon are for a while hidden. The high porticoes of the Secretariats are Delhi's Propylea! Another example is the old Capitol at Rome; there, as one climbs the great stairway by the Lupercal, the beautiful building attributed to Michelangelo, at the end of the court, is partly hidden by the steps, and the eye rests on the two great statues at the top of the steps, the noble Horses led by the Great Twin Brethren, Castor and Pollux.

In planning the Acropolis I had in mind that, as Perroit and Chipiez write in their *History of the Art in Persia* the object of Darius in building his stupendous platform at Persepolis was to lift up a privileged enclosure in enjoyment of the view and air above the city spread out on the plain below ...

53 Ibid., p. 74.
54 R.G. Irving: op. cit., pp. 279, 280.
55 R. Darnton: "Un-British Activities," in: *The New York Review of Books*, Vol. XLVIII, No. 6, April 12, 2001, p. 84.
56 Cf. J. Nehru: *The Discovery of India*, Calcutta 1946 and New Delhi 1999.
57 Quotation by Lutyens, in: Christopher Hussey: op. cit., p. 351.

There was a further advantage in the plan adopted, that the raised garden court between the two blocks of the Secretariats, with its flower-beds, fountains, dedicatory columns, and the statuary yet to come, would provide enjoyment of the highest value not merely to the official occupants of the Secretariats but also to the visiting public of India ... I like to think of this pleasant raised garden court as the 'temenos' where dwells the genius loci of the Government of India."[58]

The Viceroy too, addressed several times about this matter by Lutyens, did not understand his indignation. In a letter of March 13, 1916, to the President of the Delhi Committee, Sir Hailey, he wrote: "You and I rode to the top of Raisina Hill and decided that that was the site for Government House. My idea had always been that it alone should be on Raisina Hill, the Secretariats on the lower ground. The architects however conceived a scheme which they thought better ... and that Government House should be thrown further back and thus share with the Secretariats the dominant position in the new city. I remember pointing out that this would be the result; but the architects pressed their scheme, and as I considered it to be a fine one from the architectural point of view, I accepted their views. From that moment, the idea that the Government House (later Viceroy's House) should be seen from every part of the city vanished ... The idea that it should be seen without interruption along any particular road was never raised, and I remember that it was perfectly obvious to me, as to everyone else, that the crest of the hill would naturally obscure the view of Government House on the processional road for a space of rather less than half a mile from the foot of the hill. This to me was of trivial importance, once the idea of the visibility of Government House from every side had been surrendered."[59]

And now Herbert Baker went on the offensive because a gentler and therefore longer slope would cut in two his Government Court between the Secretariats: "Whether the Acropolis idea of our original conception was right or wrong, now it is there, it appears to me inconceivably unwise to cut the raised court in two by a continuous deep cutting or to cut it away in endless and useless steps. To do so would have 'mistake of conception' and 'change of plan' writ large over it for all time."[60]

58 H. Baker: op. cit., p. 67.
59 Cf. Christopher Hussey, op. cit., p. 355.
60 Ibid., p. 352.

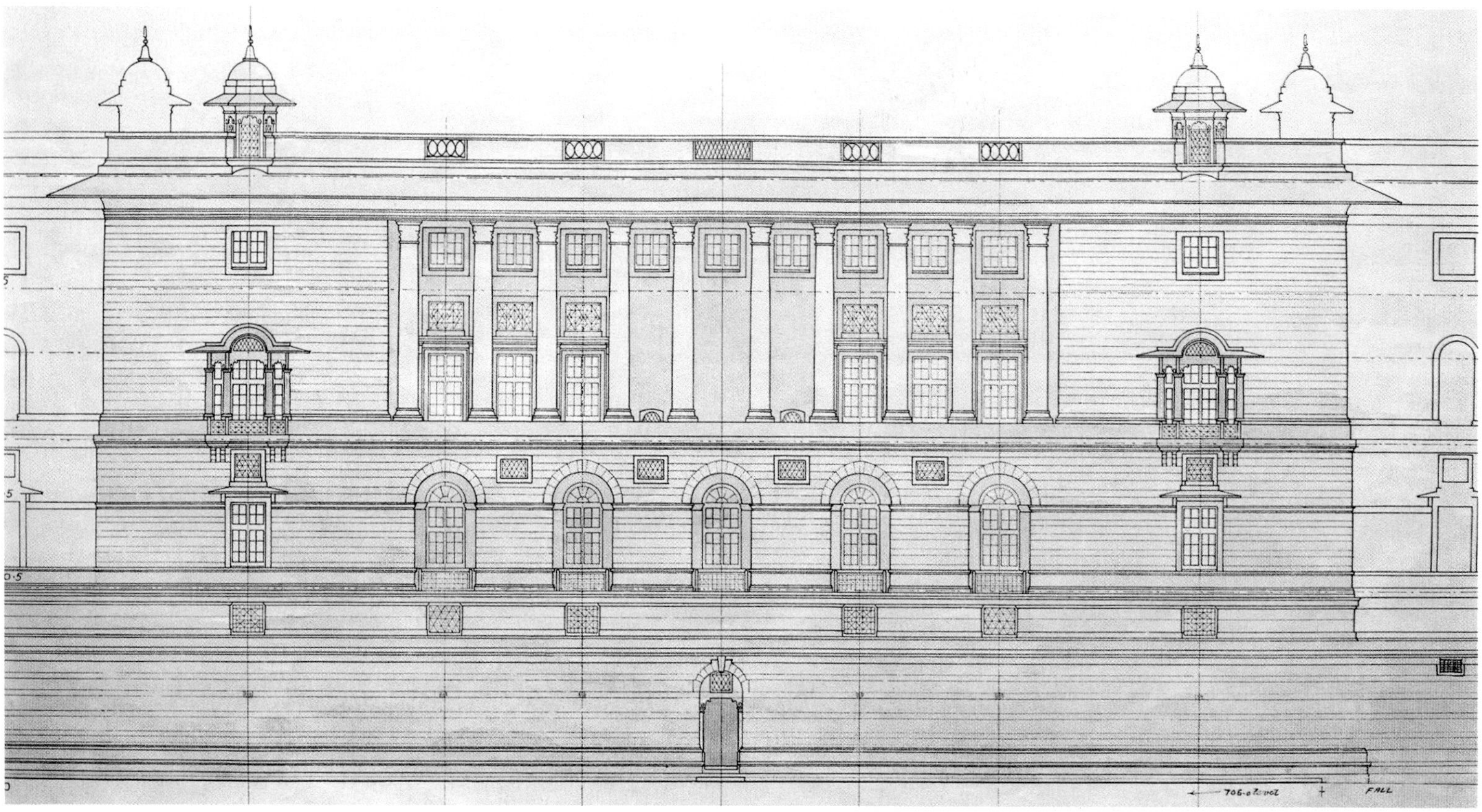

Fig. 125: The Secretariats, South Block, view from the south (detail).

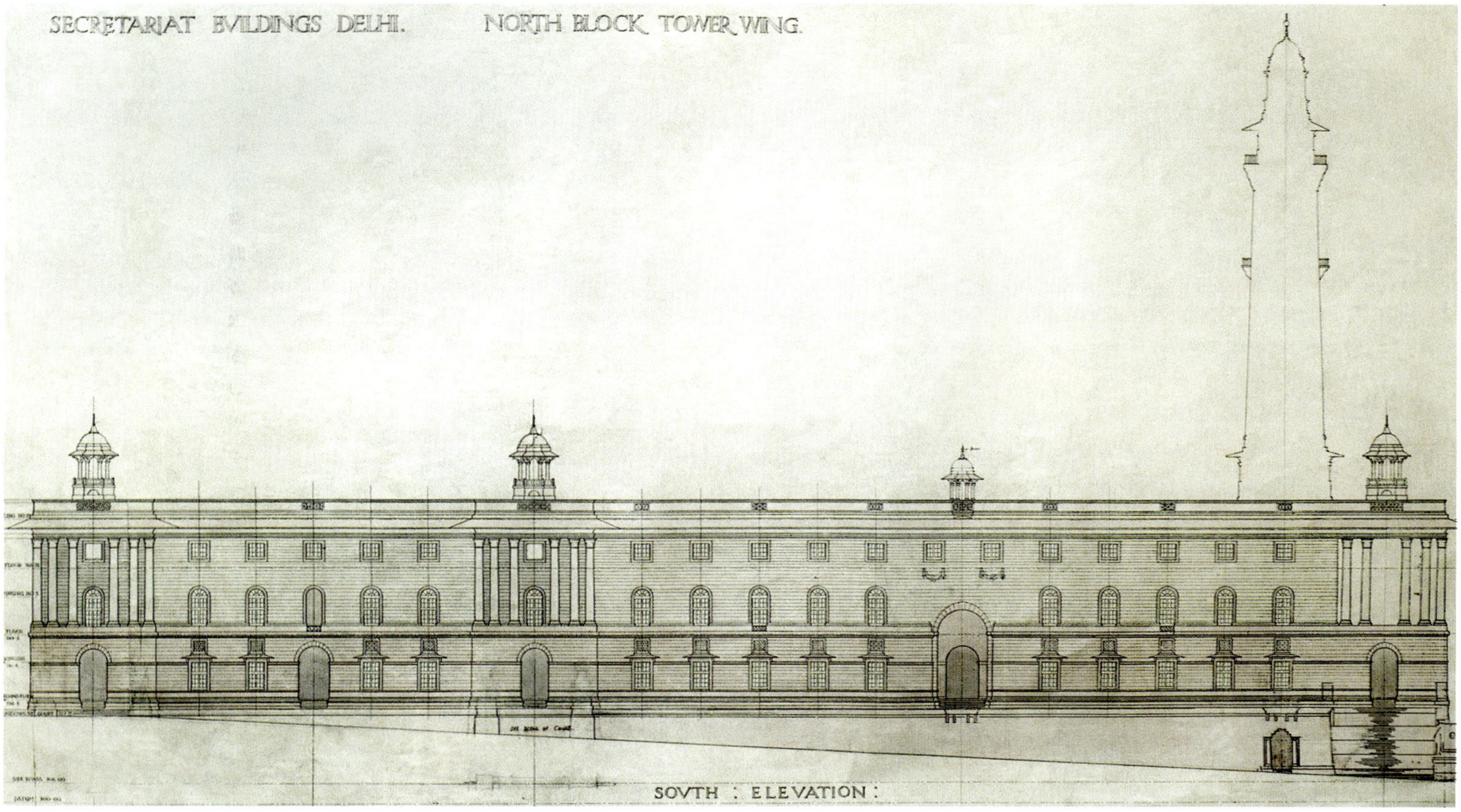

Fig. 126: (Above) Secretariats, North Block, view from the south and a section through the slope of the Great Place to Raisina Hill. (Below) Secretariats, view from the east with the slope in the middle.

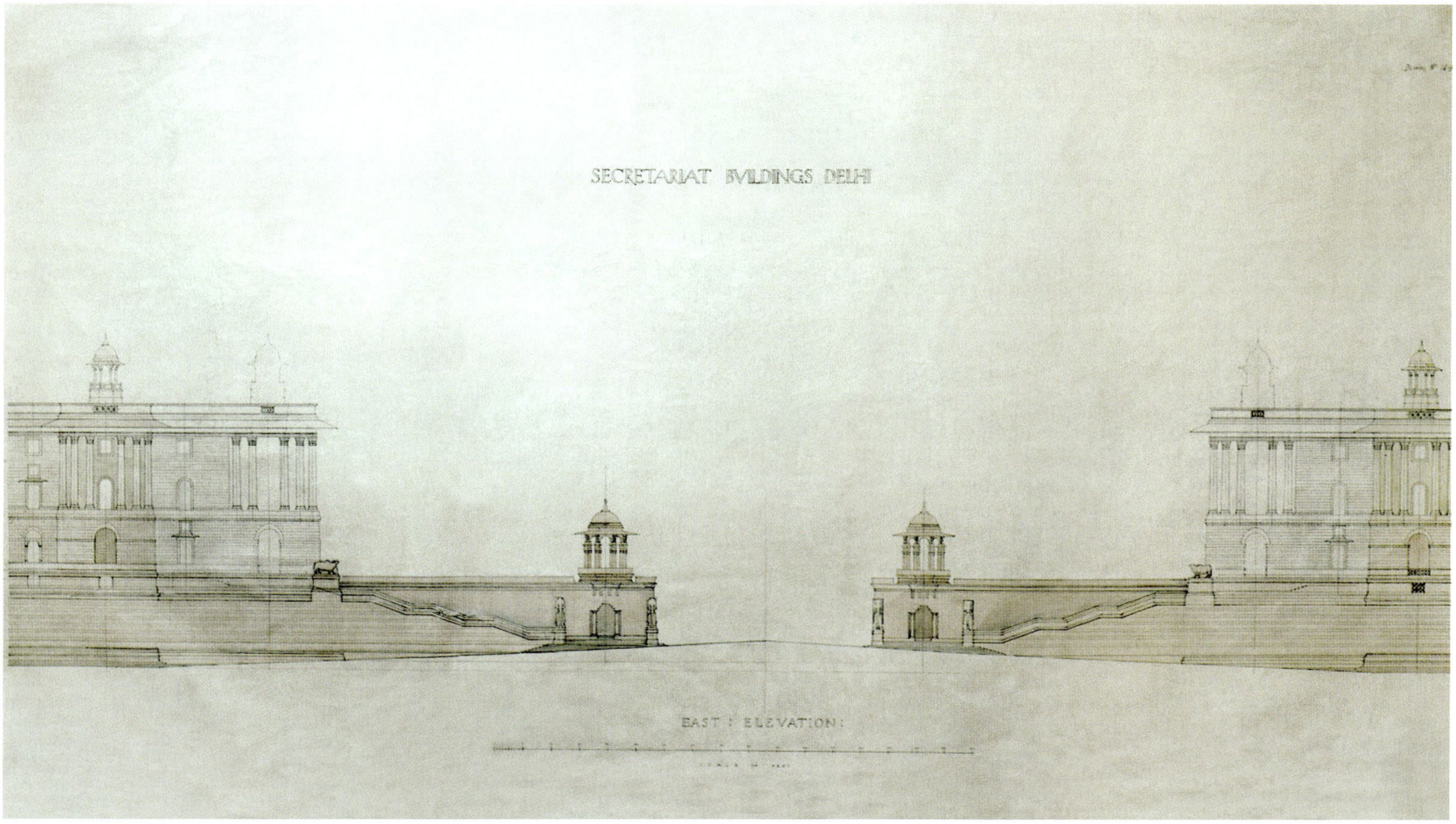

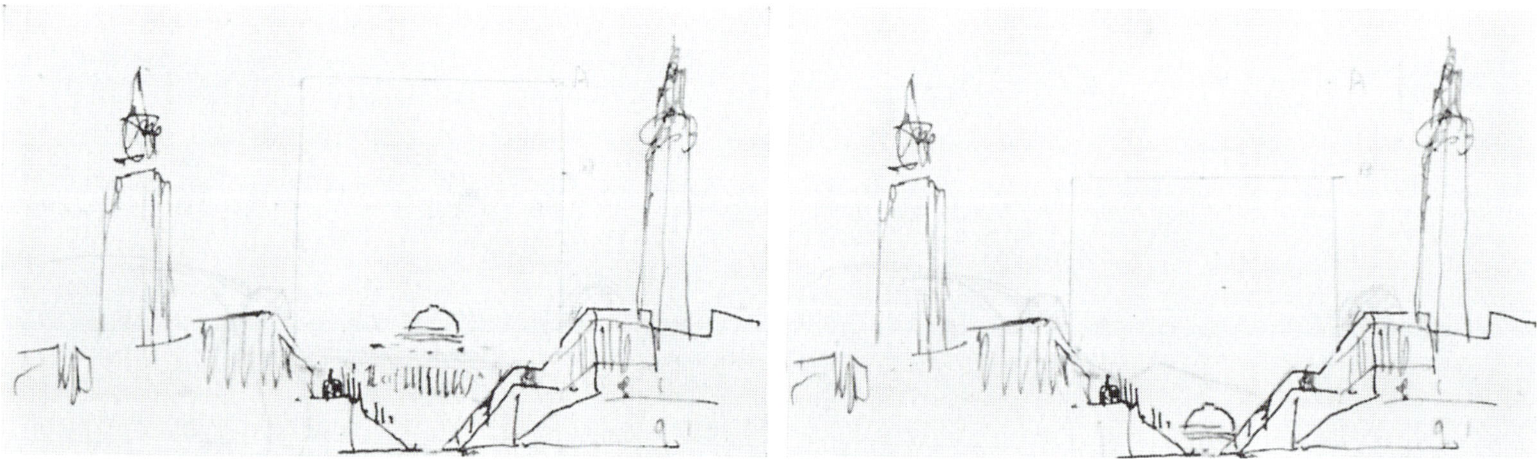

Fig. 127: With the help of two vertically adjustable transparent drawings from March 10, 1916, Edwin Lutyens tried, in vain, to convince the Viceroy, Lord Hardinge, of the disadvantages of a steep slope between the two Secretariats.

Fig. 128: On driving up from King's Way to Viceroy's House, the broad sweep of Viceroy's House disappears for a short while because of the incline of the slope. Thus, only the dome of the Durbar Hall remains visible.

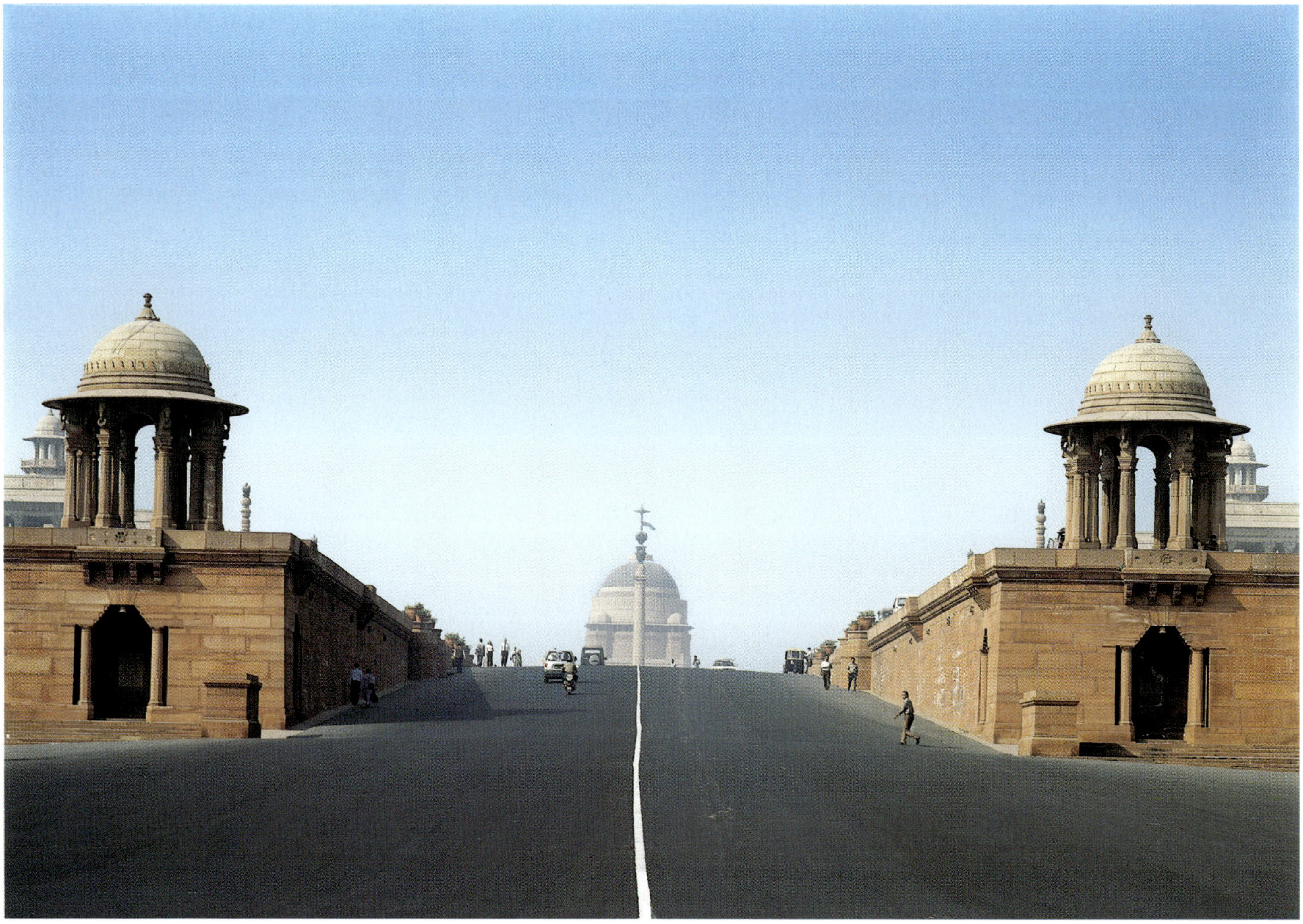

Fig. 129: A wide flight of steps, double and triple pillars, and a solid base are elements of imperial pretension in Herbert Baker's Secretariats.

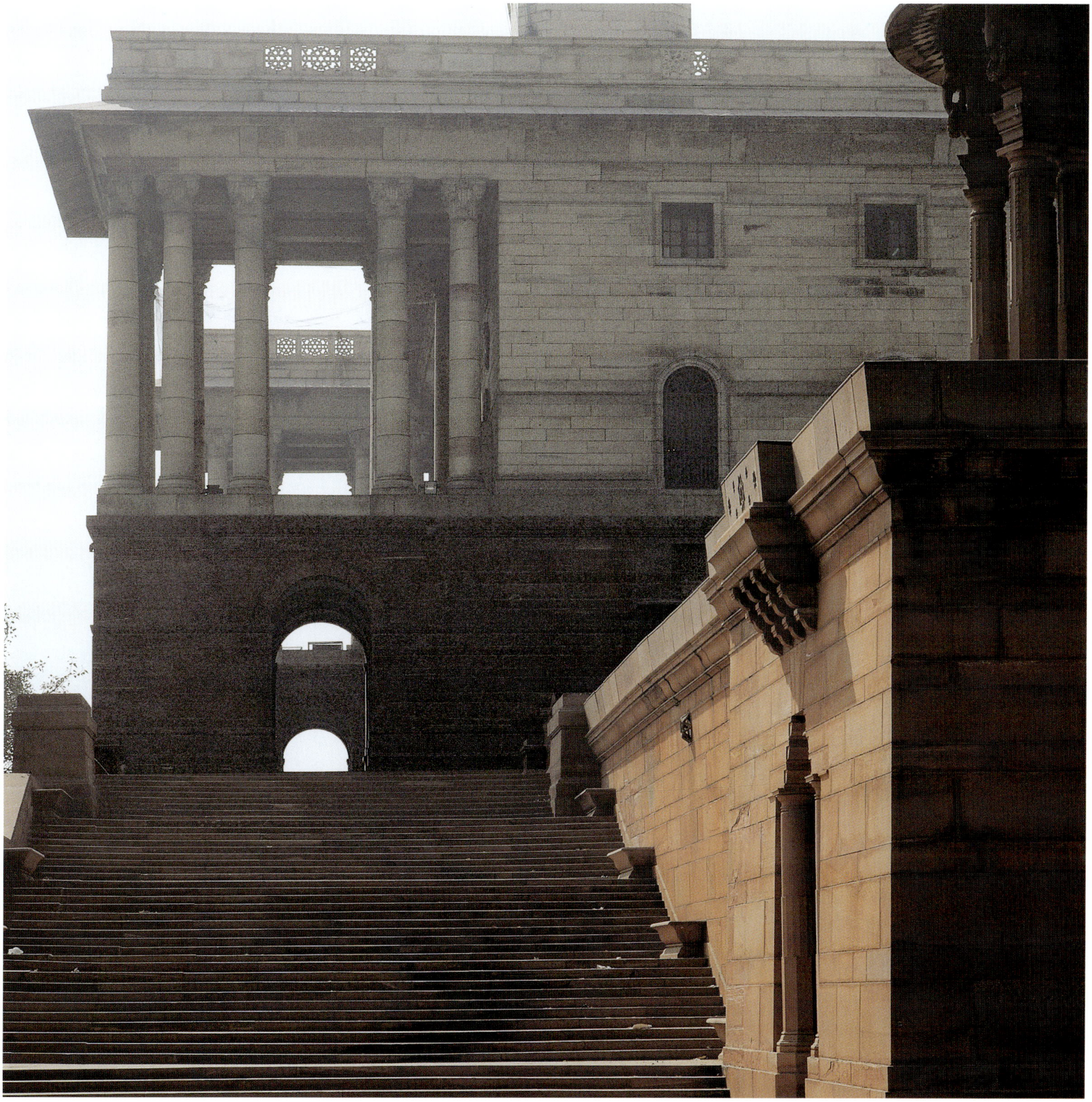

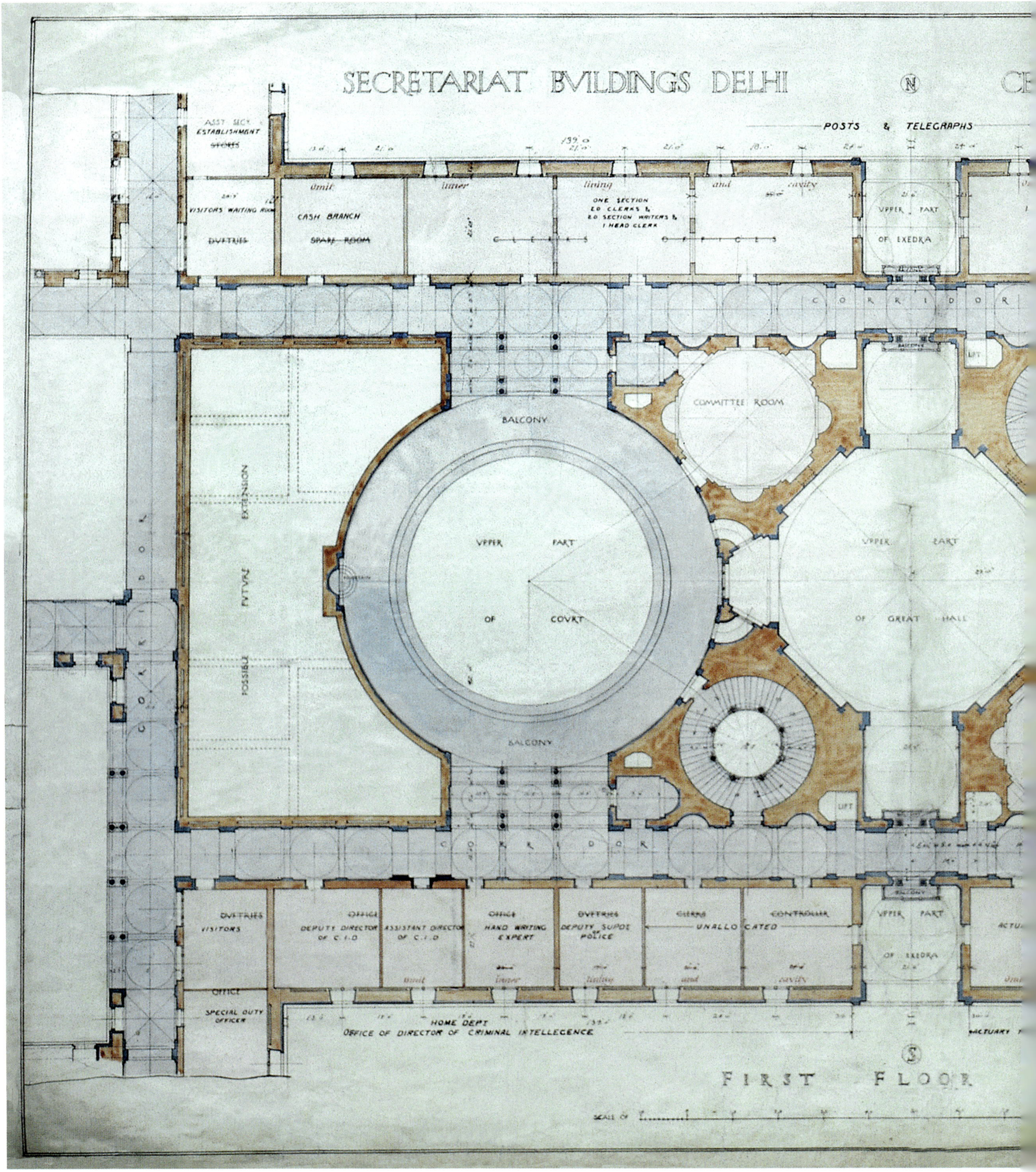
SECRETARIAT BVILDINGS DELHI
POSTS & TELEGRAPHS
CASH BRANCH
CORRIDOR
COMMITTEE ROOM
BALCONY
VPPER PART
OF COVRT
POSSIBLE FVTVRE EXTENSION
OF GREAT HALL
UPPER PART OF EXEDRA
LIFT
HOME DEPT
OFFICE OF DIRECTOR OF CRIMINAL INTELLECENCE
FIRST FLOOR

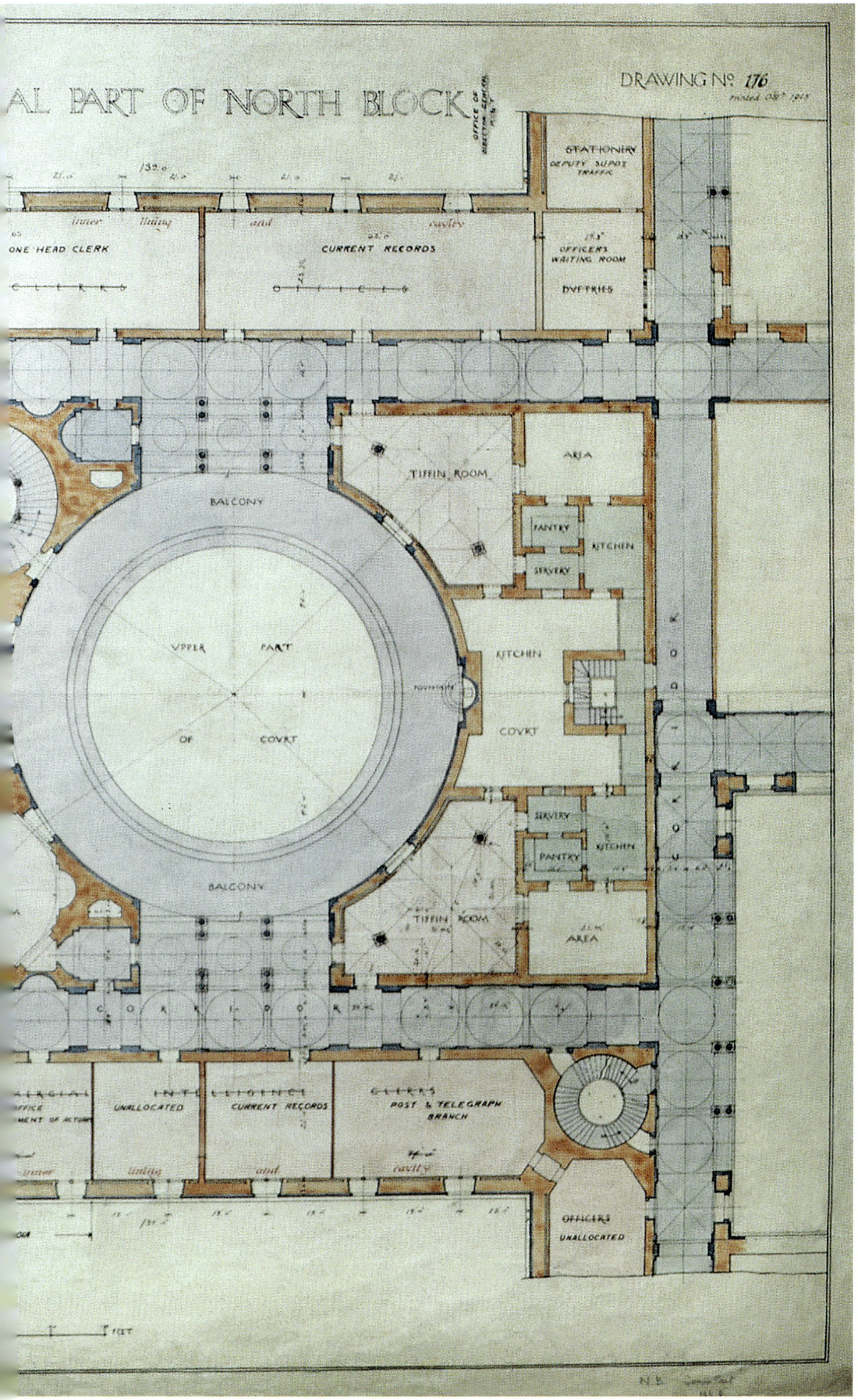

Fig. 130: The Secretariats, North Block, ground plan of the middle section.

The deciding vote of the Delhi Committee did not follow Edwin Lutyens' arguments: "The Committee took the view that Lutyens' proposal involved a departure from accepted plans 'carrying the termination of the slope back to a little east of the railings dividing Government Court from Viceroy's Court'; whereas Baker was claiming that 'the pitch of the road is inherent in the nature of the raised platform which was agreed to as a basis of the plan for the central buildings in 1913'; and that 'in a two mile vista a prospect which for part of the distance hides and then reveals itself again is rather an attraction than otherwise.'"[61]

61 Christopher Hussey: op. cit., p. 353.

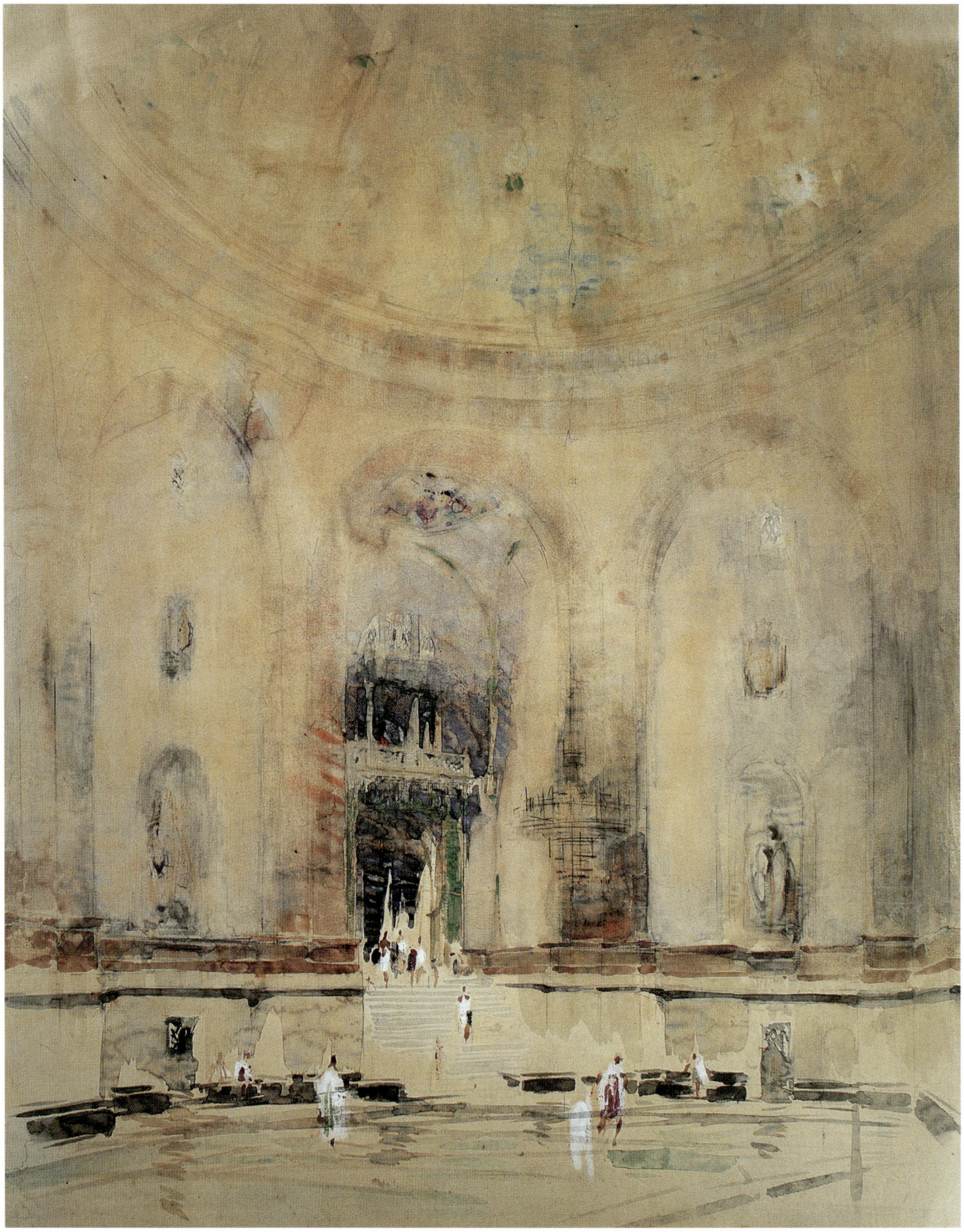

Fig. 131: According to the customs of the time, in an attempt to explain his plans for the Secretariats, Herbert Baker had about nineteen watercolours painted by William Walcot; shown here, a view into the central hall of the Secretariats.

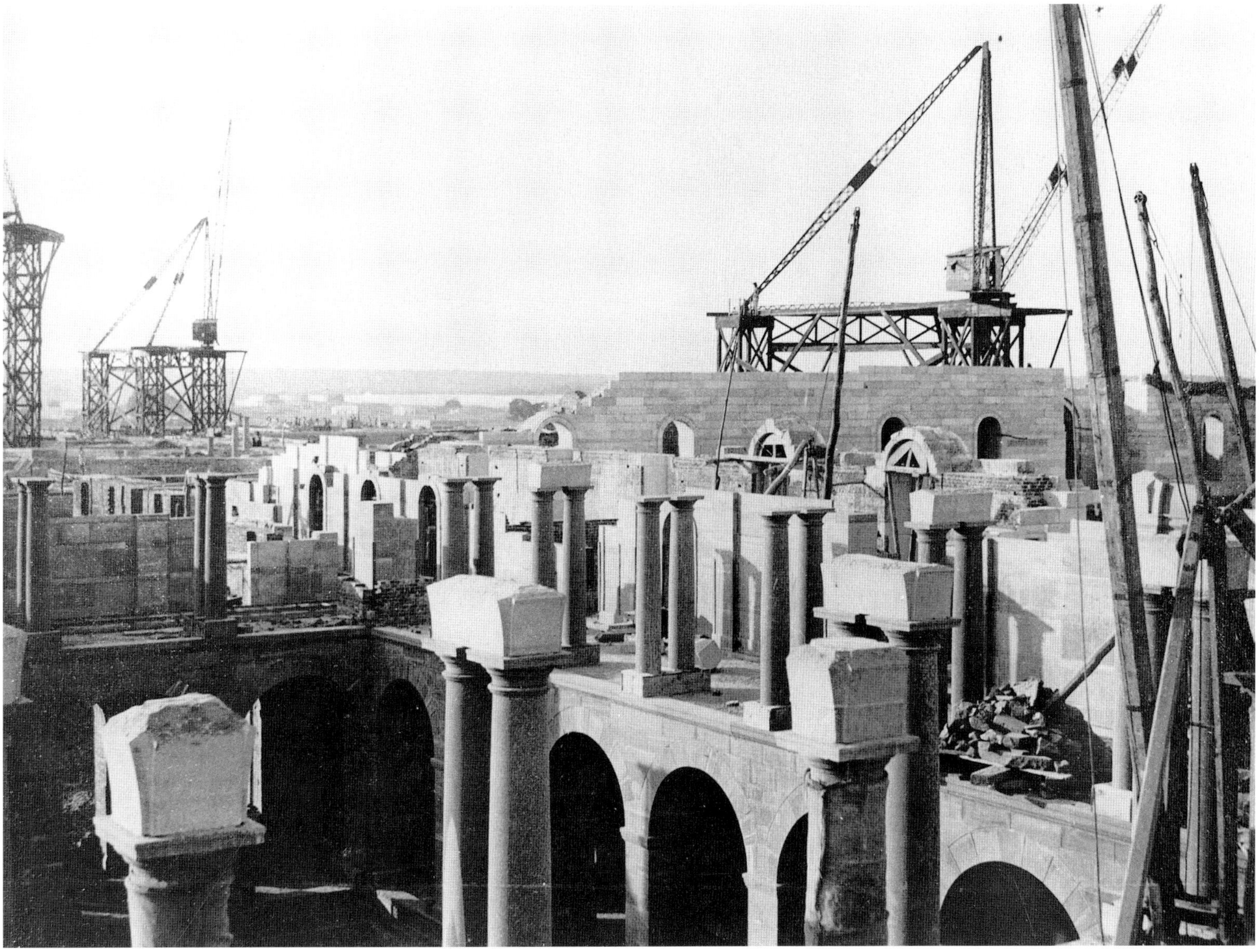

Fig. 132: View into one of the courtyards of the Secretariats during their construction, c. 1920.

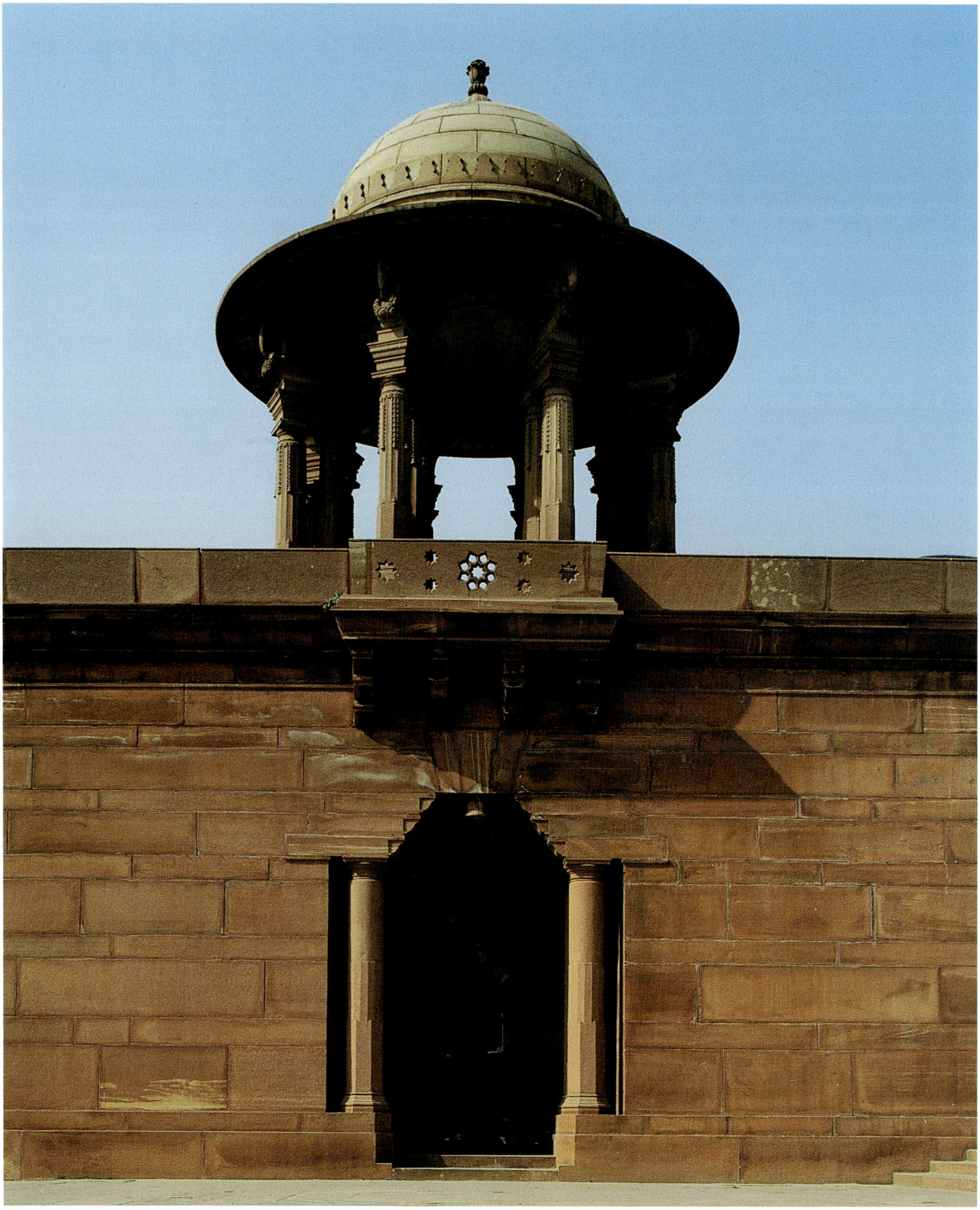

Herbert Baker's designs for coats of arms

A particular concern of Herbert Baker's was the design of appropriate coats of arms for the Indian provinces. Lutyens reported that Baker was: "... very busy making out emblems for India, Provinces, and indeed all the Dependencies of the British Empire – the Rose, Leek, Five Rivers of Punjab, etc. I maintain that an architect should always design in three dimensions. It is his job. That is why I want to give the star of India (on Jaipur Column) six points, since five won't be seen from all views as an entity; and yet it can be applied to a coat or shield. Any Animal (except a flea or a sole) is all right. In Europe, you can always use a figure and emblazon your bearings on a shield, but an allegorical figure is not possible in India.

Architecture should begin where literature (words) leaves off, each depending on the other. It always has in great periods.

Baker says it (designing the symbols) is very difficult. I fear it is, and all the more worth the doing. It wants a Shakespearean wit to ordain symbols which will hold the people to them and hold water too.

It is certainly the duty of the architect to go the one better and stick to his three dimensions, and let the painters and writers do the others. I would rather see an orb, which means power, surmounted by a star of six points (which can be drawn flat or round)."[62]

Herbert Baker's assessment

In his memoirs, Herbert Baker made the following assessment of all his architectural efforts in Pretoria and Delhi: "There must be no conscious straining after invention or originality, to which sincerity in following the true and natural laws alone can give birth. There must be good building and a frank acceptance of modern methods and materials. The controlling mind must heat and weld into his orderly conception all that India has to give him of subtlety and industry in craftsmanship. And lastly, he must so fire the imagination of the painters, sculptors, and craftsmen of the Empire, that they may, interfusing their arts with his, together raise a permanent record of the 'history, learning, and romance' of India.

If these fixed stars are kept clear in the vision of the architect, he should, by following the precedents of the best traditions of English architecture, and keeping an open mind for the needs and requirements of India and its Government, satisfy both the demands of the new Delhi and go far to develop a new style of architecture, which should have spontaneous growth throughout India and in the tropical dependencies of the British Empire. English art at its highest should at least bring no harm to India. Our best architects and artists, inspired by the character and genius of Wren, and the great teachers of the last century, are engaged in establishing historical records that can say for England, as Pericles said of the Greeks, 'We are lovers of the Beautiful, yet simple in our taste: and we cultivate the arts without loss of manliness.'"[63]

62 Ibid., p. 346.
63 H. Baker: op. cit., p. 222.

Fig. 133: Herbert Baker combined gateways with overhanging arches in the Hindu style, Neo-Palladian inset pillars, and Mughal-style pavilions to emphasize the base in local red sandstone with the Secretariats towering above.

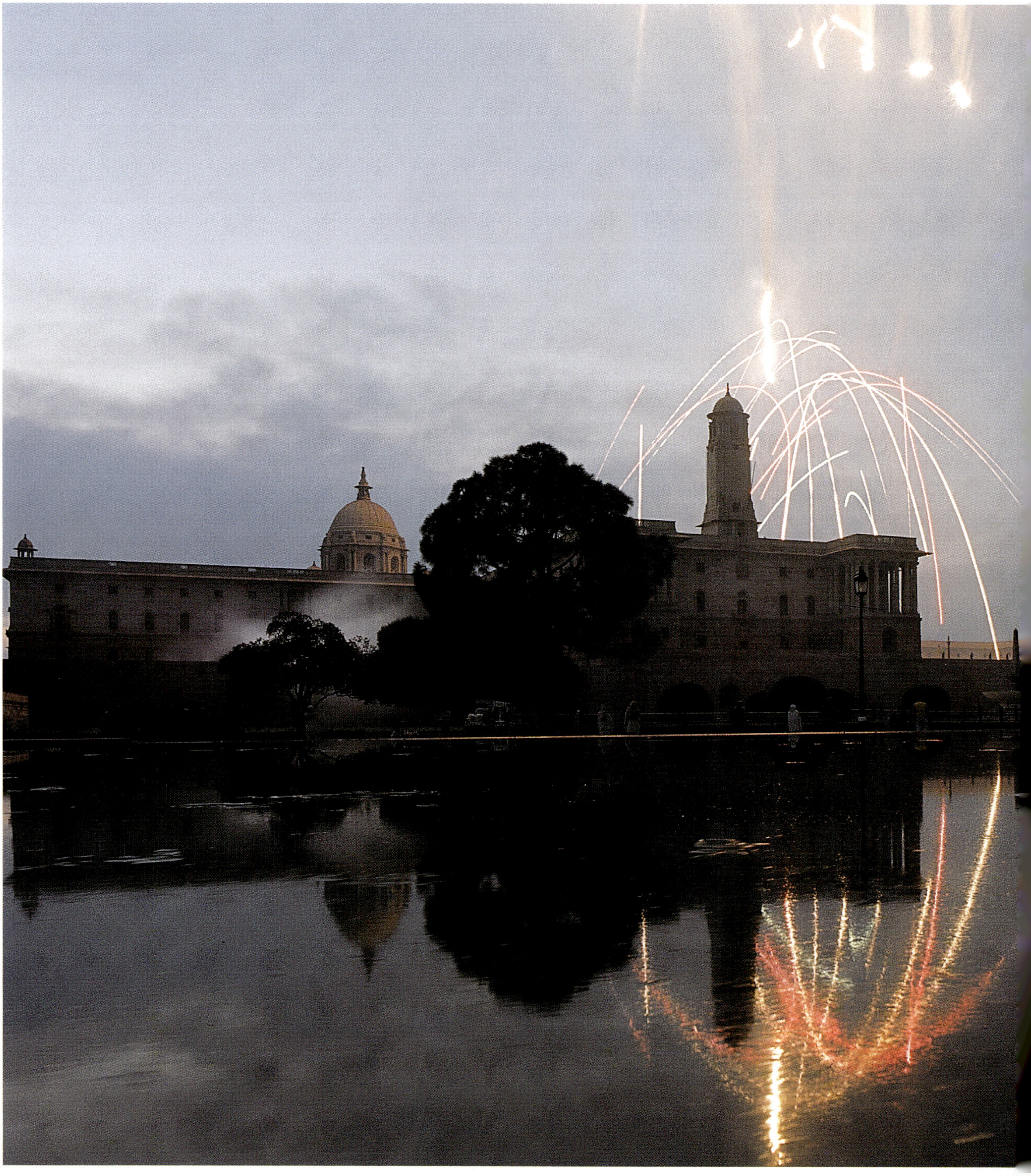

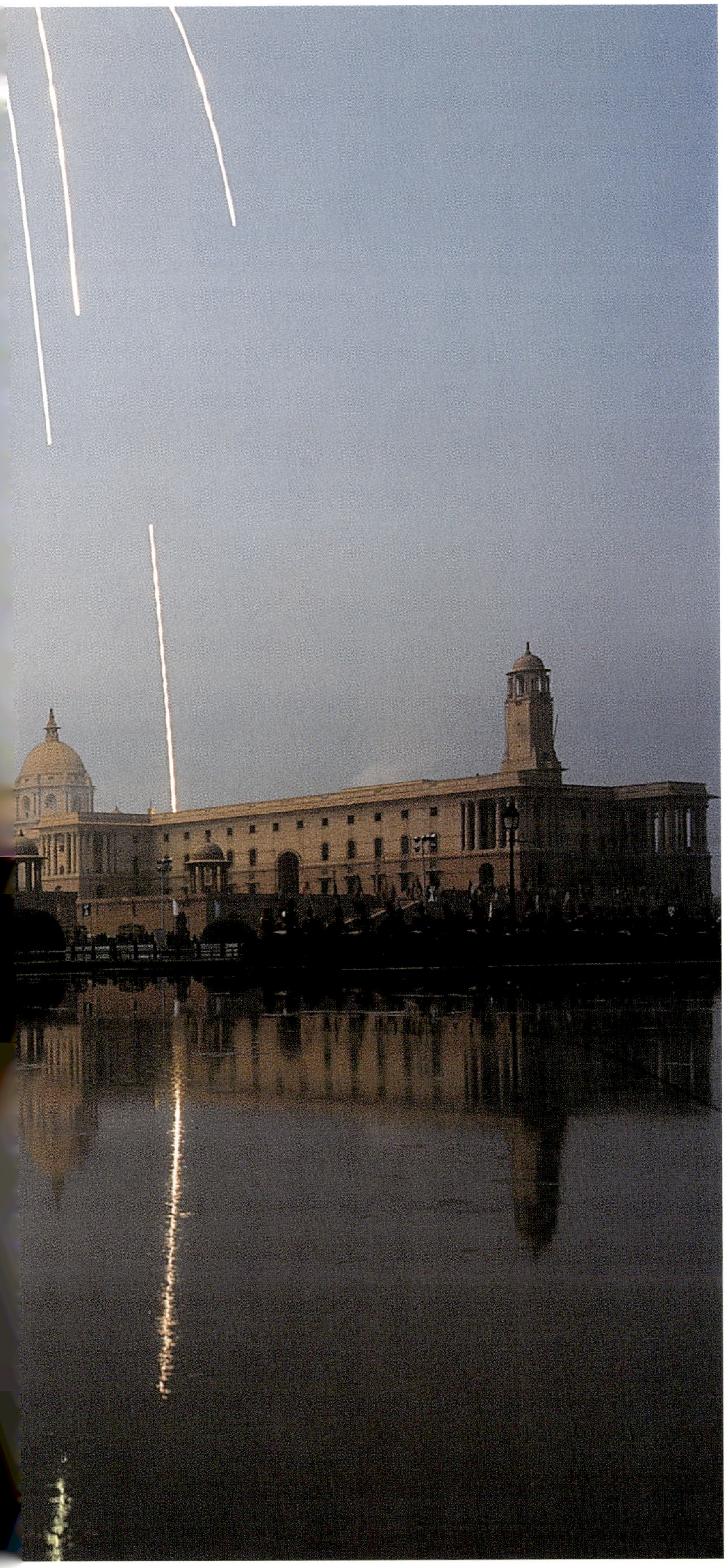

Fig. 134: At the firework display on Republic Day, the Secretariats are reflected in the fountains at Prince Edward Place (later Great Place).

3.2.4 All India War Memorial Arch, 1921–1931 and King George V Memorial, (Architect: Edwin Lutyens), 1936

The main axis of the town plan is the showpiece thoroughfare of Imperial Delhi. It runs from the eastern end of the city, without any architectural sign, to the sandy banks of the Jumma river. The original idea of this street being aligned with the walls of the Purana Kila was impossible to execute within the strict geometry of the road network. Naturally, the result was totally unsatisfactory to Edwin Lutyens whose concept of town planning was in accordance with that of imperial Rome.

During World War I, it became clear that a monument to the large number of Indians who had fallen in battle for the British Empire was politically desirable. As early as 1917, an initial plan by Lutyens confronted this need and envisaged, at the end of King's Way, a square with colonnades à la Bernini, and within this axis a triumphal arch (Fig. 135).

In the year after the war had been won, opinion solidified about the need for such a commission. Lutyens wrote to Lord Stamfordham: "As regards the proposed War Memorial, I hear it is suggested that it should take some utilitarian form. This, I think, will be a great opportunity missed. Utilitarian objects should be provided in any case in due time as a duty. But to

Fig. 135: Preliminary draft by Edwin Lutyens for the All India War Memorial Arch.

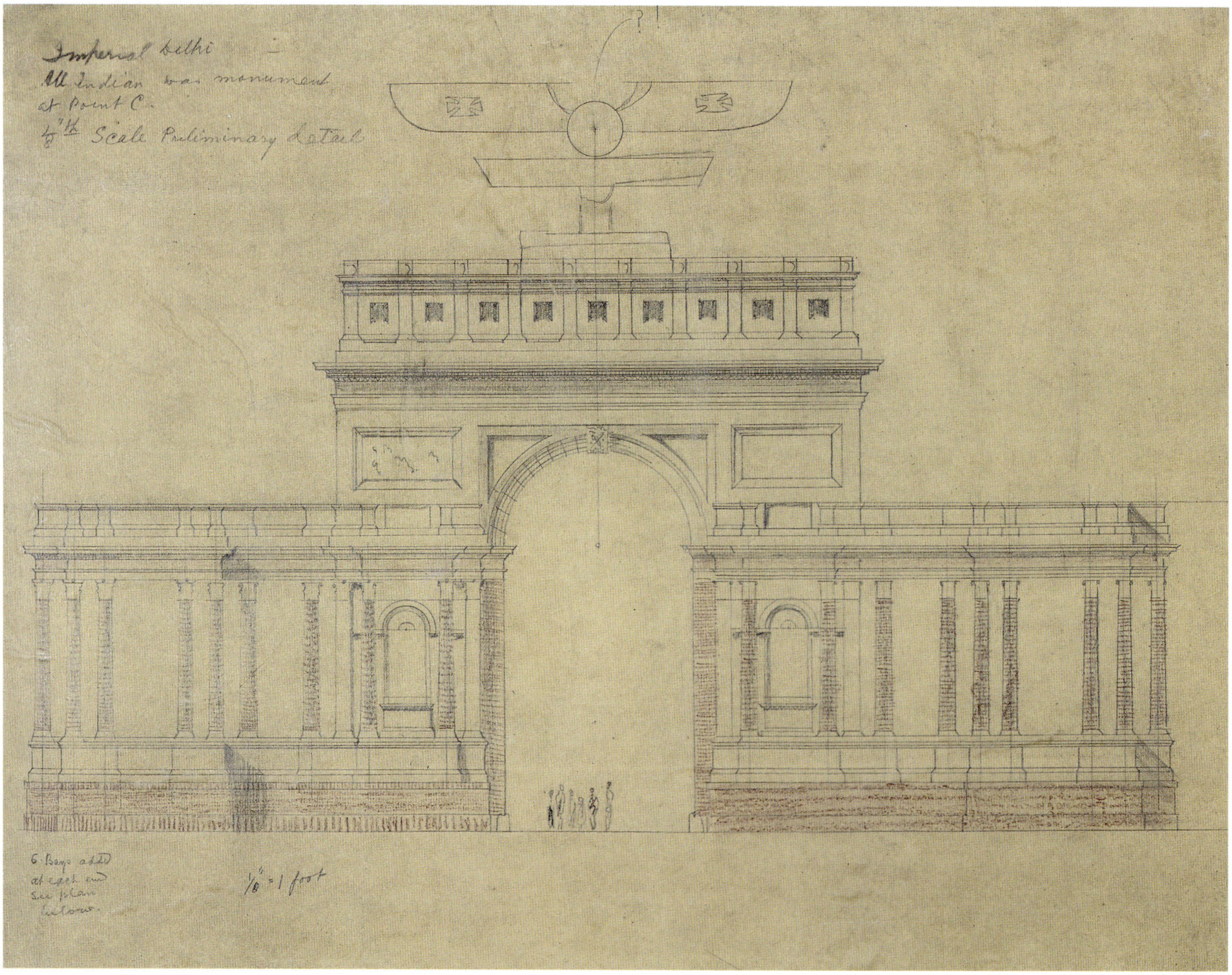

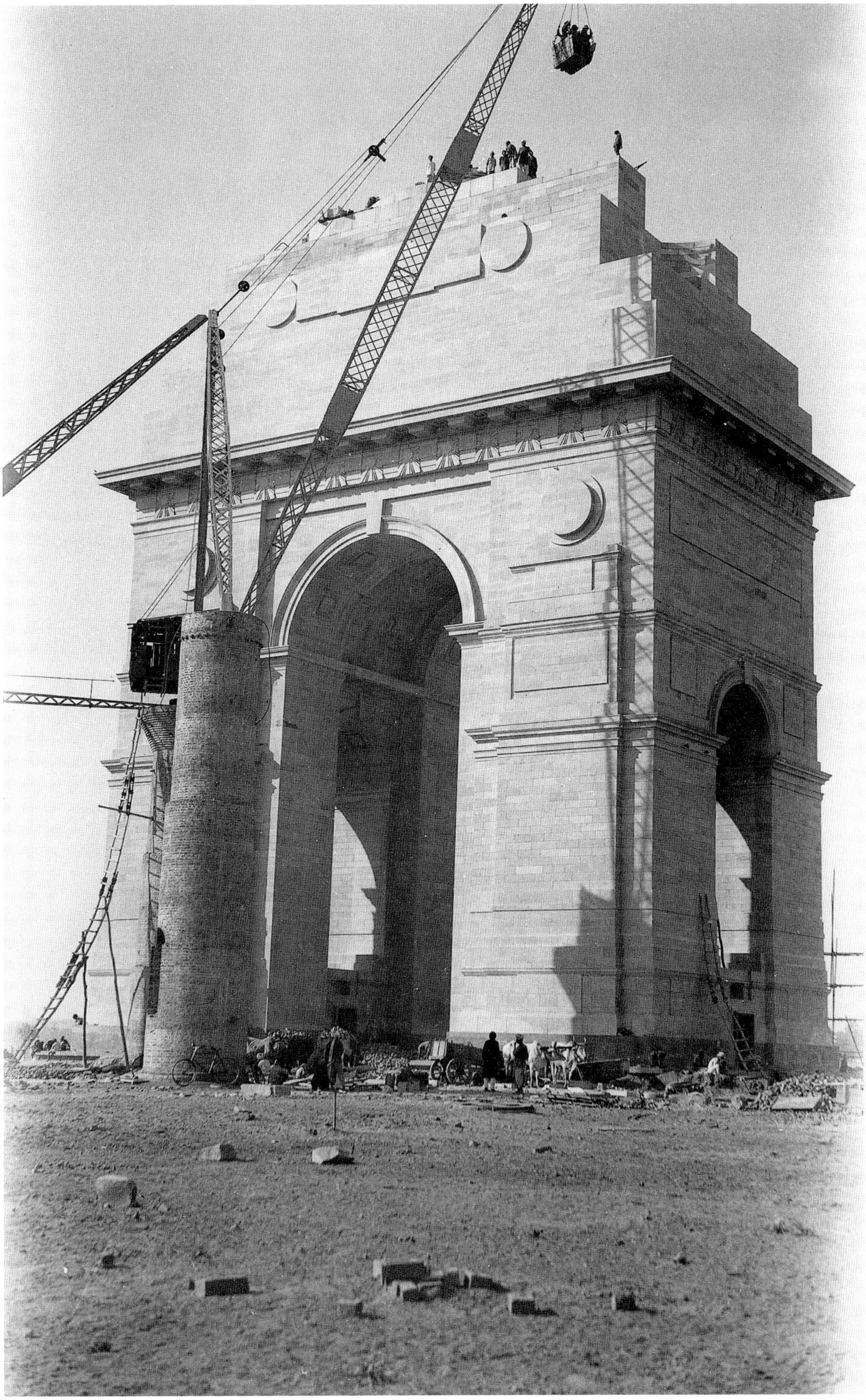

Fig. 136: In 1931, construction of the All India War Memorial Arch was nearing completion.

commemorate this Great War a structure should be erected where, independent of creed and caste, all India may commemorate her great men, who have served their King-Emperor and Country, now and for all time.

It would surely do more to give pride of country, unity of service, than the erection or endowment of a scheme that can only appeal to a limited class – as against all India.

This is a question if I may venture to say so, that His Majesty should decide and in his name call for subscriptions which, judging from the success of the Queen Victoria Memorial at Calcutta, should be very large."[64]

Imperial consciousness in the British Empire was still untroubled by dissent, and the loyalty of the Indian princely houses remained beyond question. The last point comes as no surprise – after all, the power and riches of the maharajas had become solely dependent on the benevolence of the colonial power. This dependence became painfully clear to the princes when, at the handover of rule to the government led by the Congress Party at Independence in 1947, Indian royals lost their rights to govern, as well as a large part of their often legendary riches.

"Duty, discipline, unity, fraternity, loyalty, service and sacrifice: these were the meanings which the All-India arch was meant to convey to a country witnessing renewed political agitation and turbulence. Small wonder that the King's uncle, mindful of a world 'dark with trouble,' called upon Indian soldiers to be worthy heirs of those who had faithfully served the Raj. Like a huge noticeboard, the arch honored by name cherished comrades, as well as extolling exemplary fidelity to common values, encouraging continued partnership in the established order, and celebrating the 'ideal and fact of British rule over India.'"[65]

Erected over a decade from 1921–31, the Triumphal Arch is based on Lutyens' second plan, and was realized only after omitting the chattris in the Mughal style, an element that had been included only out of a sense of duty: "The Delhi Monument honoured 60,000 Indian soldiers who died overseas and recorded on its walls the names of 13,516 British and Indian officers and men of no known grave who fell fighting on the North-West Frontier and in the Third Afghan War of 1919."[66]

A comparison with models from Paris is imperative. The Arc de Triomphe from the nineteenth century and the Porte St Denis from the seventeenth century derive their structures from a square divided into three horizontal and vertical sections. In the central section of the resulting nine elevation squares, an inscribed circle serves as a model for the position and size of the round arch. Lutyens also chose the square divided into three horizontal and vertical sections as the basic geometric form for the All India War Memorial Arch. Lutyens moved the round arch up only by one arch-radius. That is, by the proportion of 2.5 to 1 diameters of a circle

64 Letter from E. Lutyens to Lord Stamfordham in the winter of 1918/9, quoted in Christopher Hussey: op. cit., p. 369.
65 R.G. Irving: op. cit., p. 259.
66 Ibid., p. 258.

Arc de Triomphe, Paris 1836

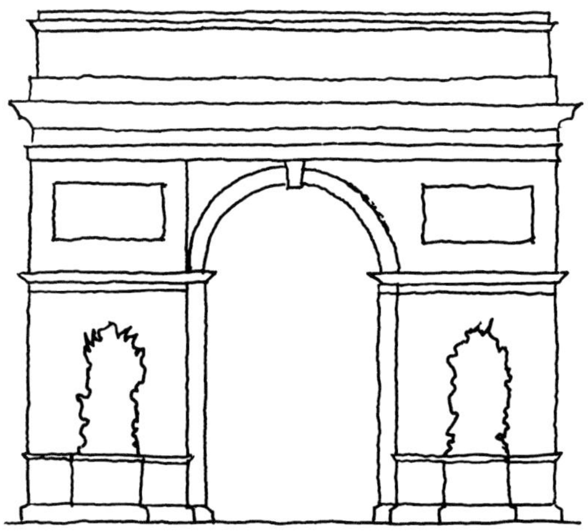

Titus Arch, Rome c. 90 B.C.

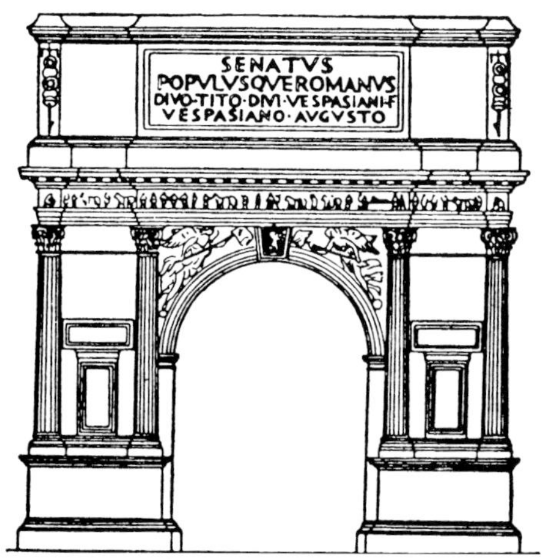

Porte St Denis, Paris 1673

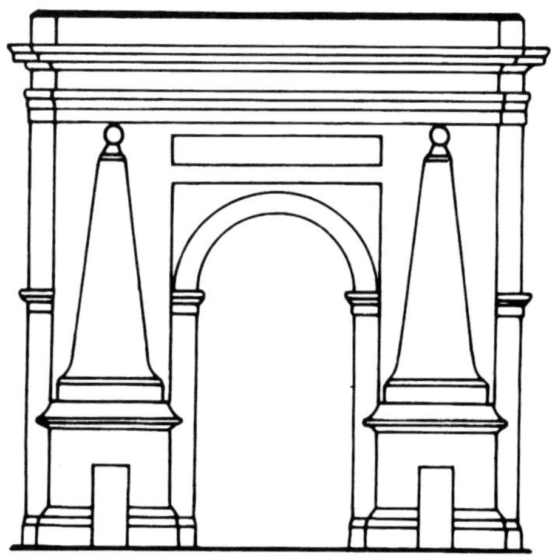

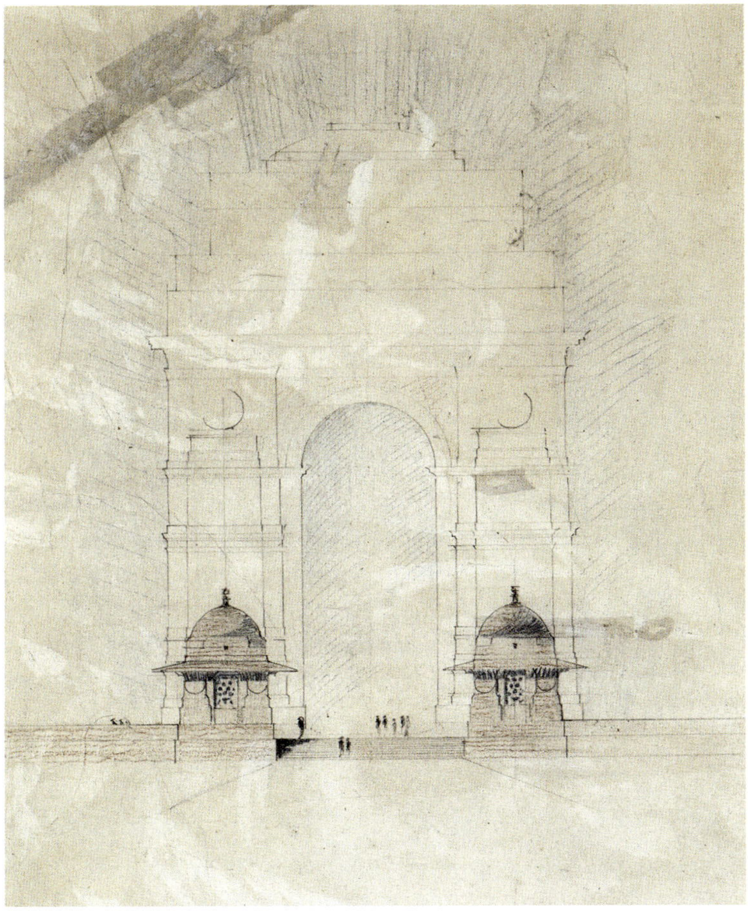

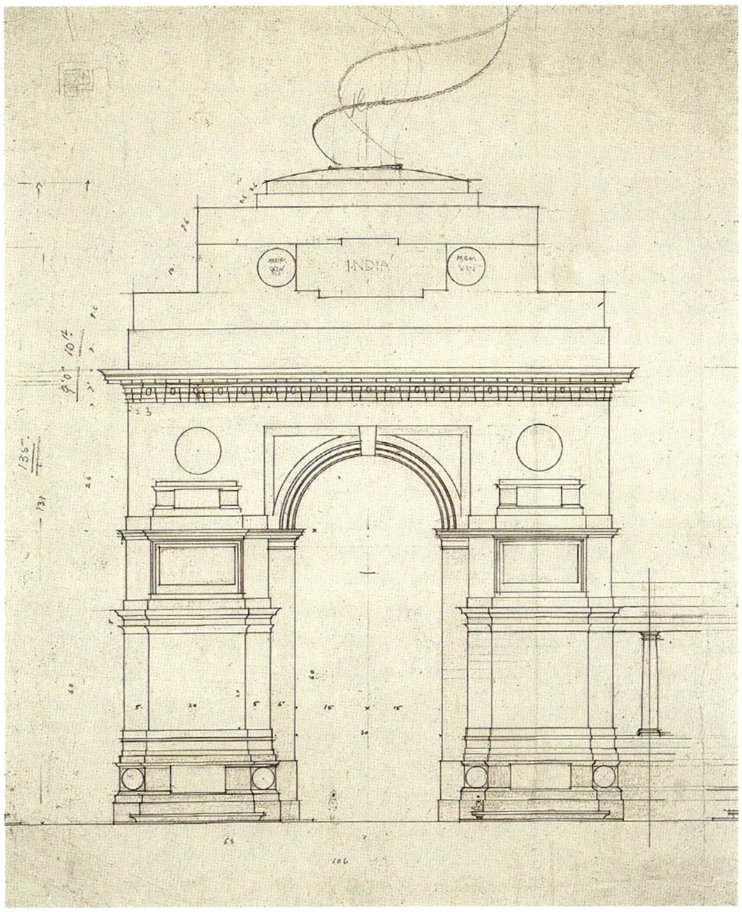

Fig. 137: The plan finally realized for the All India War Memorial Arch (above) had its formal origins in the Arc de Triomphe in Paris, the Titus Arch in Rome, and probably also the Porte St Denis in Paris (left). In an intermediate solution, Lutyens explicitely followed the Viceroy's suggestion to incorporate Mughal chattris in front of the memorial.

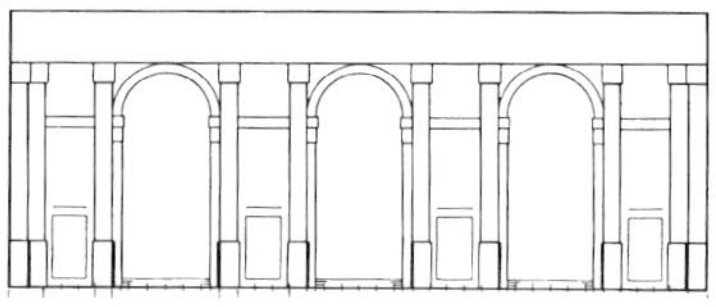

For gateway arches and throughfares, Edwin Lutyens very frequently used an elongated form that is produced geometrically from 2.5 diameters of the circle. The same proportion is also found in Alberti's church of S Andrea in Mantua (1472).

repeatedly encountered in many of his buildings for entrances, gateways, and windows. He had come to love this elongated archway in Italian architecture, a form modelled on Alberti's design of the church of S Andrea in Mantua dating from the fifteenth century.

Lutyens' triumphal arch for Imperial Delhi is especially striking in that he dispensed with figural decoration, pillars, and Indo-Islamic ornamentation in the design. This was a step in the direction of architecture that impresses by its proportions and weight, and in its next stage led, in 1929, to the clear shapes of St Martin's church by Arthur Shoosmith (cf. Chapter 4.3.6.) and, after World War II, to Louis Kahn's plans for the government buildings in Dhaka, Bangladesh.

The overall plan for the All India War Memorial is one great geometric jigsaw. Every axis and every corner is defined by a system of squares built one on top of the other. The ground plan on the other hand, is derived from two or four equilateral triangles inserted into each other (see Fig. 140). Through this arrangement of triangles, the rectangle that frequently recurs in Lutyens' work takes shape. This is the so-called "ideal rectangle" that also determined, geometrically, his Memorial to the Missing in Thiepval, Belgium.

At first glance, the two gigantic stone urns of the All India War Memorial Arch, both standing in the cross passageways of the arch, appear puzzling to the viewer; equally gigantic pine cones grow out of them (Fig. 143). Both symbolic shapes are foreign to the Indian formal language and originate in the European world of heroic symbolism.

The urn symbolizes heroic death and has its origin in the Roman formal repertoire. The pine cone symbolizes birth and rebirth. Lutyens was familiar with the gigantic pine cone from the Cortile della Pigna in the Vatican (Fig. 144). He combined urn and pinec one in a representation of the cycle of death and life.

"Imperial duty and Dominion fraternity were solemn keynotes of the commemoration ceremony held on February 12, (1931) at Lutyens' War Memorial. As the pale winter sun dropped behind the domes of Raisina, the Viceroy stood bareheaded, wreath in hand, before the monument arch that not only paid tribute to common imperial sacrifice but also formed a symbolic gateway to the new Delhi. A special guard of honor of much-bemedalled soldiers, men who had ridden the cobbled streets of France and filled its sodden trenches or fought on Himalayan frontiers, framed the scene to perfection, while red and white pennons of the Central India Horse proudly brightened King's Way. A 'fire of remembrance' blazed on the summit of the arch, and a single bugler sounded the Last Post, whose sad refrain seemed as much a final salute to the Indian Empire as to her recent war casualties."[67]

There were also secondary reasons for situating the All India War Memorial Arch on the Raj Path: The main axis of the town, from Viceroy's House leading eastward to the Jumna river, becomes lost to view in the seemingly endless plain. In connection with the inaugural celebrations of the capital, Robert Byron described it in 1931, stating: "The monumental Roman arch can be a futile object, particularly when it happens to be Roman. Here, Sir Edwin Lutyens' adaptation of it supplies a definite need. An axis so spacious as the King's Way, leading to an architectural complex of such size and splendour as the Viceroy's House and the Secretariats,

Fig. 138: The Arc de Triomphe and the Porte St Denis in Paris display a similarly strict Geometric structure. Both were models for Edwin Lutyens' design for the All India War Memorial in New Delhi.

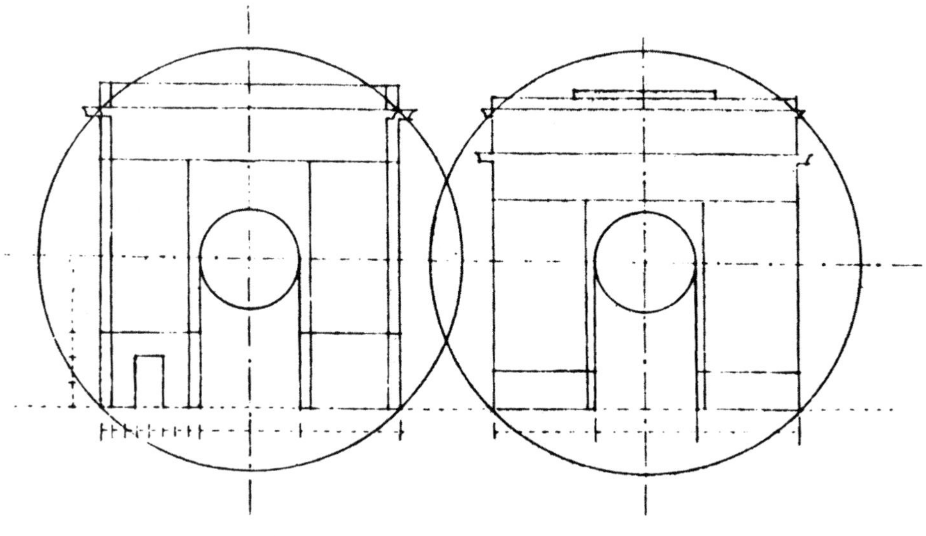

demands an ostentatious beginning. The height of the arch is 138 ft.; but this is increased optically by the system of steps on the roof and the utter flatness of the surrounding plain. Its chief character derives from the fact that the arch of the main opening, although 75 ft. high, springs from a point less than half way up the whole building; so that the arch, as an arch, has something to support, and is therefore invested with a kind of life, a quality which the Arc de Triomphe, for example, lacks."[68]

The great Triumphal Arch in New Delhi was highly praised in the contemporary academic press. Even Herbert Baker, long since in dispute with Lutyens at the time of the construction and the dedication of the All India War Memorial Arch, had only words of praise for this architectural achievement: "Vivid still in my memory are two pictures when Nature seemed to bless New Delhi with propitious omen. In the early days before the opposition to the new site had died down, I went with Ramsay MacDonald and Herbert Fisher, later Warden of New College, to the rock-hillock which the architects had planned should be the very centre of the city. We were looking down on what Lord Curzon had described as 'the deserted cities of dreary and disconsolate tombs,' and wondering how a beautiful city could arise from such an unprepossessing landscape, when a brilliant rainbow formed a perfect arch over what was destined to be the great vista, where Lutyens' Memorial Arch now stands. We acclaimed the good omen. When, after many laborious years, Lord Irwin opened in state the memorial, crowned with an altar-bowl on which burns the Sacred Fire, a flaming crimson sunset was seen through the arch as we looked up the vista to the Capitol."[69]

67 R.G. Irving: op. cit., p. 347.
68 R. Byron: op. cit., p. 16.
69 H. Baker: op. cit., p. 77.

Fig. 139: Reconstruction of the various stages in the plan of the All India War Memorial in New Delhi. Its derivation was a square divided into three both vertically and horizontally.

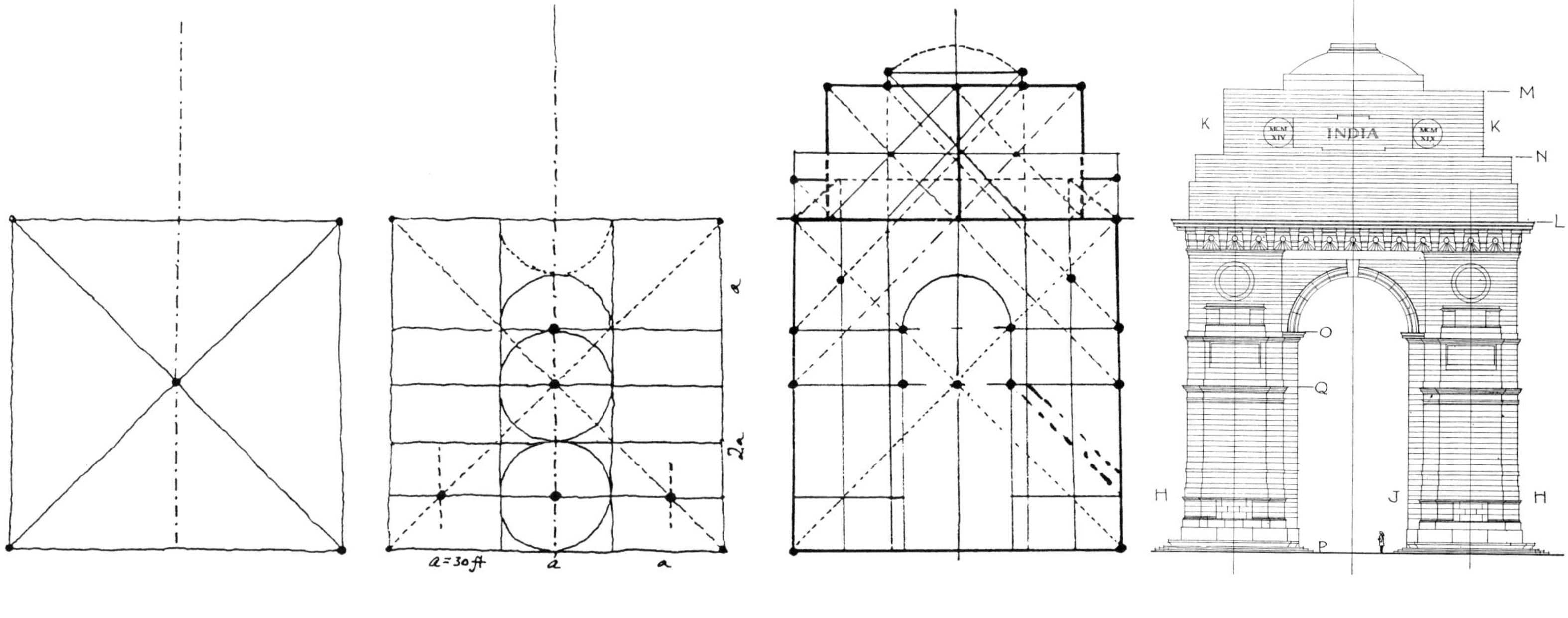

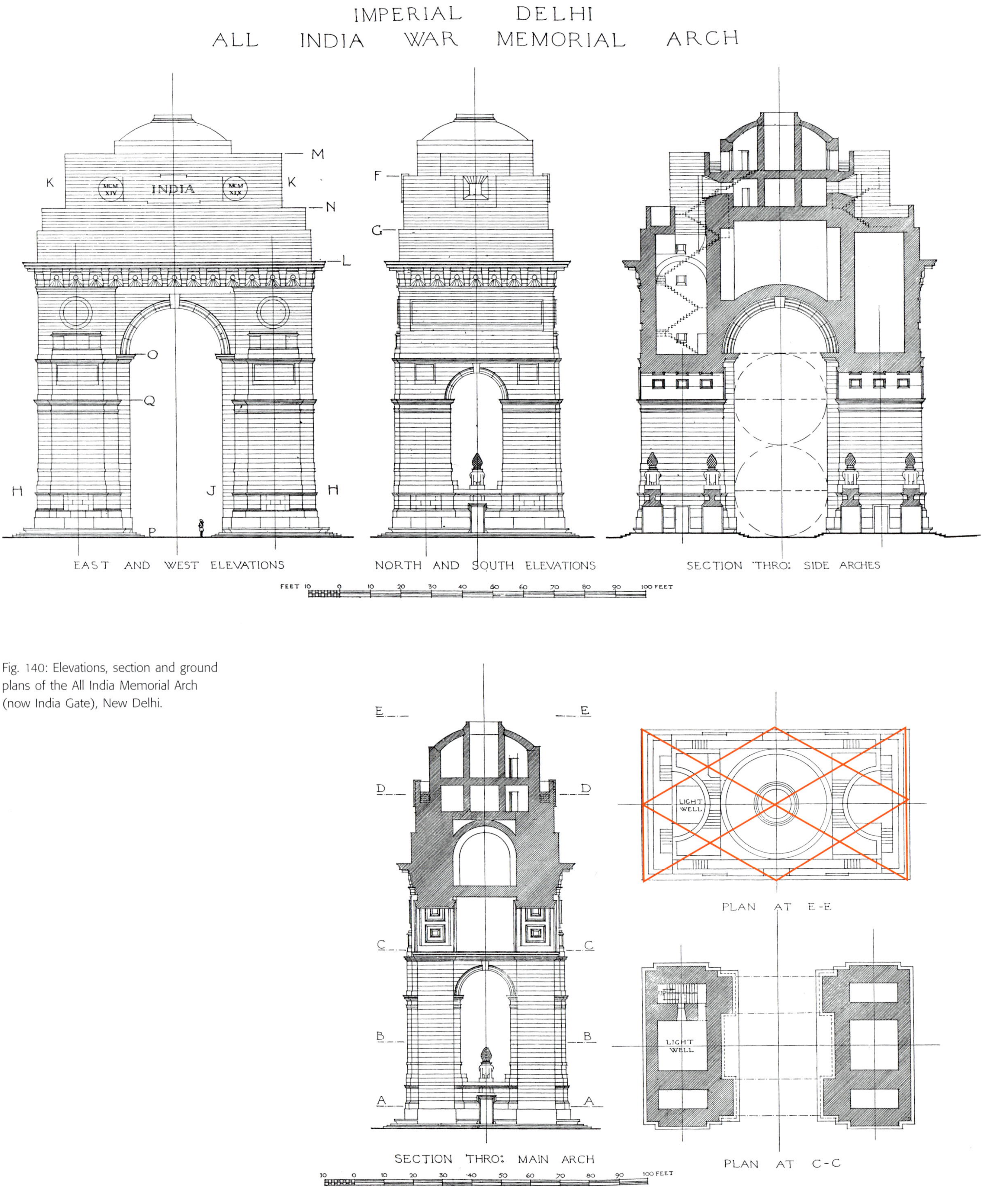

Fig. 140: Elevations, section and ground plans of the All India Memorial Arch (now India Gate), New Delhi.

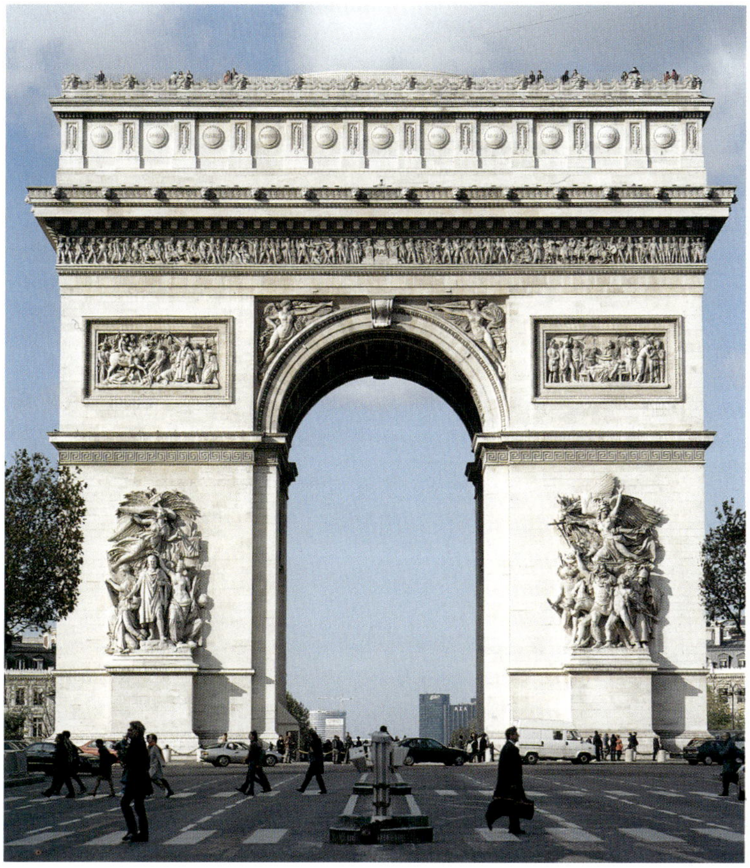

Fig. 141: The Arc de Triomphe at the end of the Champs Elysées in Paris became the prototype of the imperial triumphal arch for architects in the nineteenth and twentieth centuries.

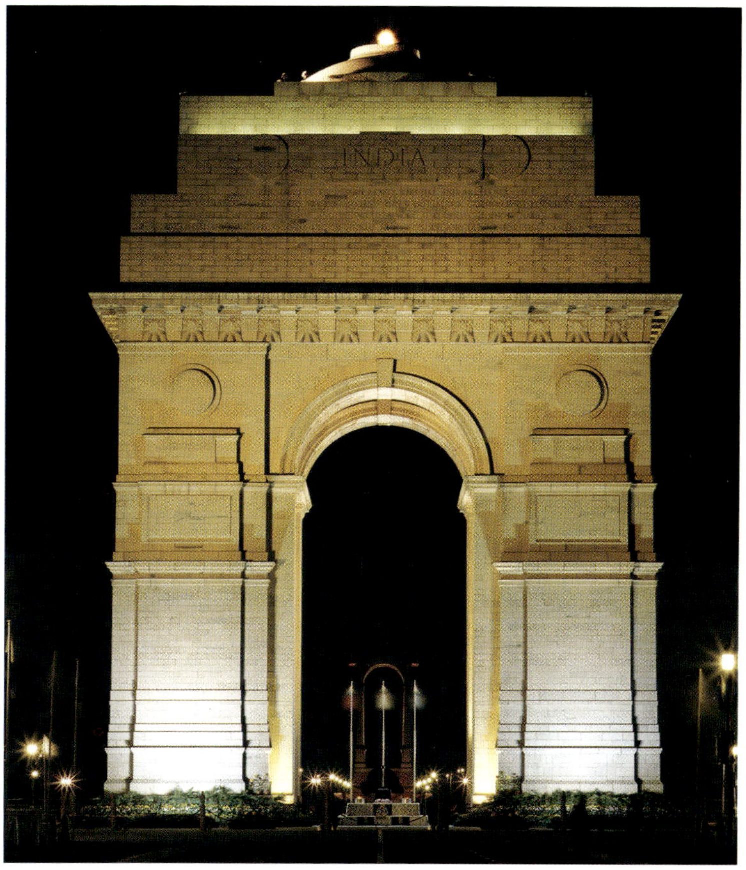

Fig. 142: The All India War Memorial Arch (Edwin Lutyens) was constructed between 1921 and 1931 in memory of the Indian and British soldiers who fell in World War I and in the Third Afghan War of 1919.

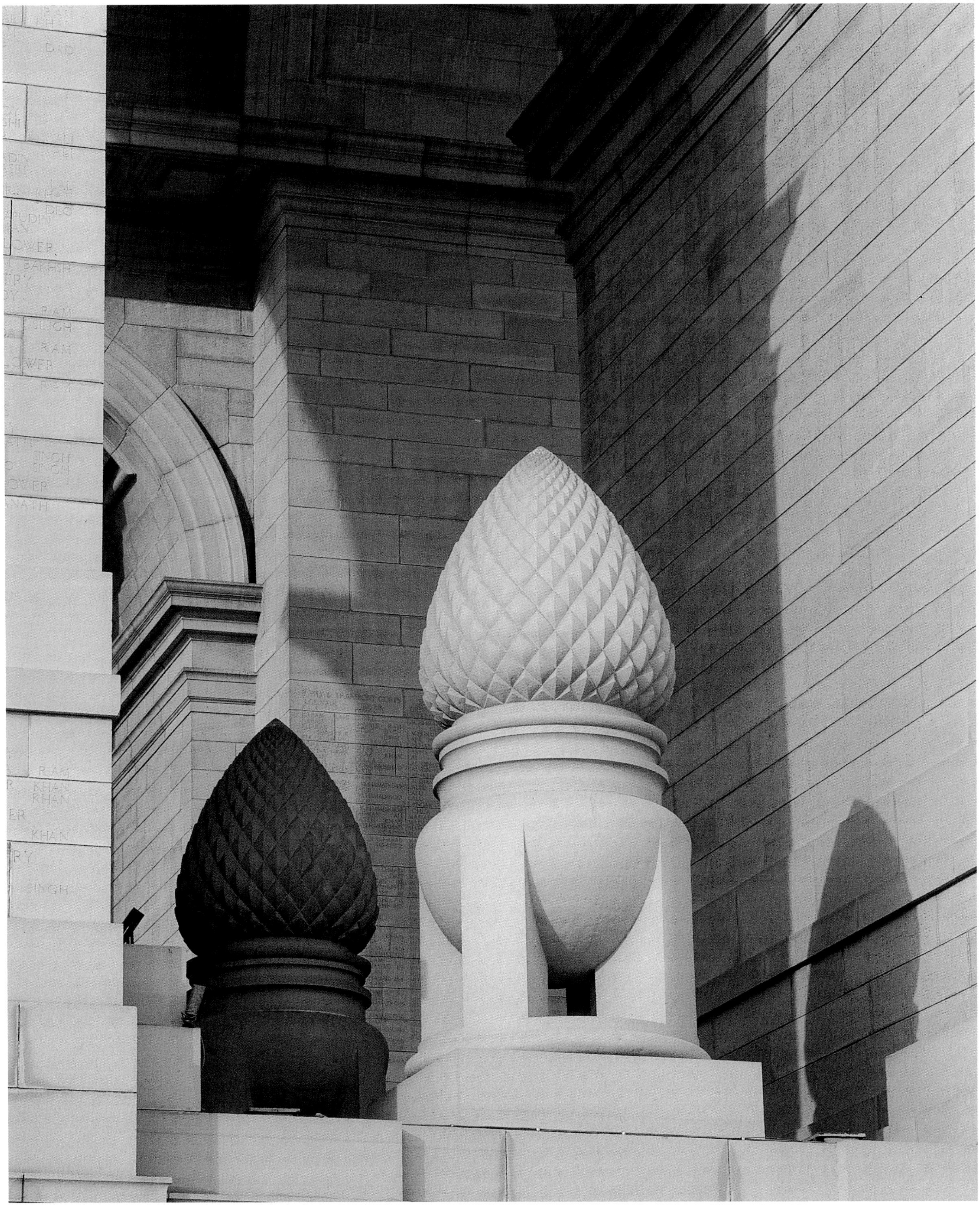

Fig. 144: During his architectural activity in Rome from 1910 to 1911, Lutyens became familiar with a gigantic pine cone from antiquity in the Cortile della Pigna of the Vatican, originally cast in bronze for a fountain in Rome.

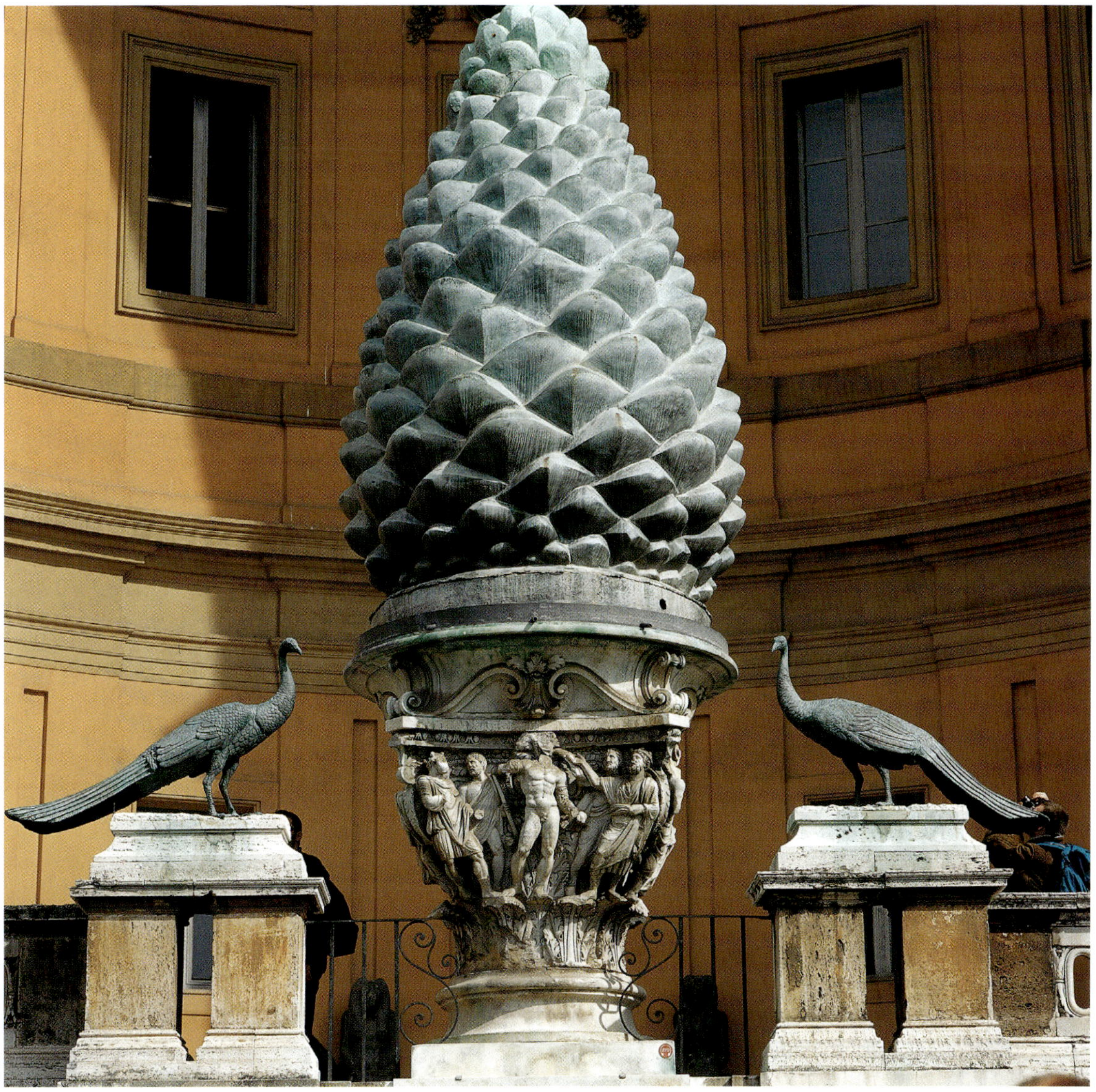

Fig. 143: Lutyens placed into the side openings of the All India War Memorial Arch gigantic urns and pine cones, i.e. symbols of death and birth since Roman antiquity. The idea of combining both motifs presumably came to him a long time before the plan of the All India War Memorial, i.e. during his time in Rome.

The fountains

A brief look at the fountains of Imperial Delhi is helpful in conjunction with the All India War Memorial Arch since the triumphal arch is framed on both sides by large fountains (Fig. 146). The fountains form the terminal points of two long waterways on both sides of King's Way which, for their part, are fed by six large fountains in Prince Edward Place (also called Great Place).

The fountains at the All War India Memorial Arch adopt the hexagonal structure of the town plan (see right edge of the elevation-drawing in Fig. 145), and the twenty-four drainage channels in the lower stone plinth are also based on this geometry. In lieu of any recorded explanations by the architect, we can only surmise that he wanted to give the same basic proportional framework to other architectural details as in the plan of some triangular tables for the Palace of the Viceroy, or in the development of the palace ground plan from the equilateral triangle (Fig. 79).

The basic geometric shapes of the triangle and the hexagon appear again in the King George V Memorial (see site plan in Fig. 146). The outer limitation of the fountain basin there is defined by two equilateral triangles and the site plan of the surrounding Princes Park describes a hexagon.

There are numerous fountains in the main axis of Imperial Delhi:

- four fountains on the roof of Viceroy's House (Fig. 94)
- six fountains on Prince Edward Place or Great Place (Fig. 134)
- two fountains to the right and left of the All India War Memorial Arch (Fig. 145)
- the fountain area of the King George V Memorial (Fig. 147)

All of these fountains are derived from two conceptual and formal origins. The first is the Place de la Concorde in Paris, and the second is the well-known system of roof-fountains that the Mughal emperors used to cool their garden-palaces. Admittedly, the fountain area of the King George V Memorial forms an exception. The stone shells inserted into the diagonals symbolize the notion of Great Britain ruling over the oceans.

In 1931, Robert Byron commented in *The Architectural Review* on the six fountains in Prince Edward Place, or Great Place: "At either end of the Place are set three fountains, each 240 feet in length and consisting of two circular sheets of water joined by an oblong on a slightly lower level. In each of these triple groups, the fountains are set in right-angles to one another, the centre one laterally, pointing outwards along the length of the Great Place, the other two parallel with King's Way and exactly in line with the flanking waterways, with which one of them actually connects, while its opposite number lies across the Place immediately beneath the end-facades of the Secretariats. The circular sheets at either end of the fountains are of different sizes: the larger placed outermost in each case, and sprouting a stone obelisk, altogether 30 feet high, from a double basin on a pedestal; the smaller and inner decorated only with a tiny curling jet. All six fountains are executed in the red stone, which their blow spray turns a rich rust colour."[70]

The unusual luxury of a system of fountains linked by wide waterways between Great Place and King George V Memorial only becomes clear in the hot, dry climate of New Delhi. The Indian government closed down the four fountains on the roof of Viceroy's House several years ago, because the link with the tradition of the Mughal emperors was no longer in accordance with a democratic and, at the same time, impecunious seat of government.

70 R. Byron: op. cit., p. 6.

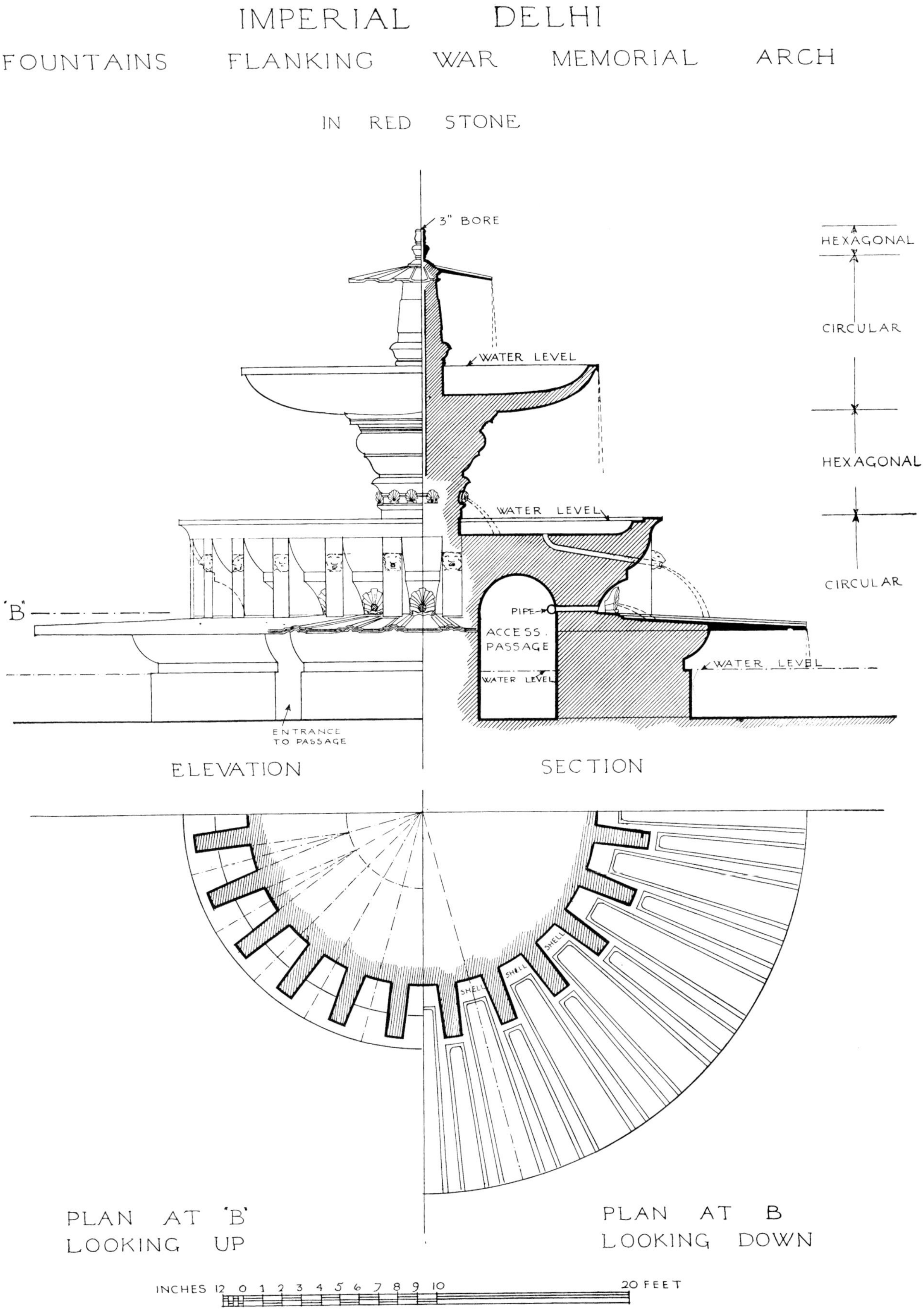

Fig. 145: The large fountains on both sides of the All India War Memorial reflect the geometric shapes of the hexagon and circle that recur in Edwin Lutyens' architecture.

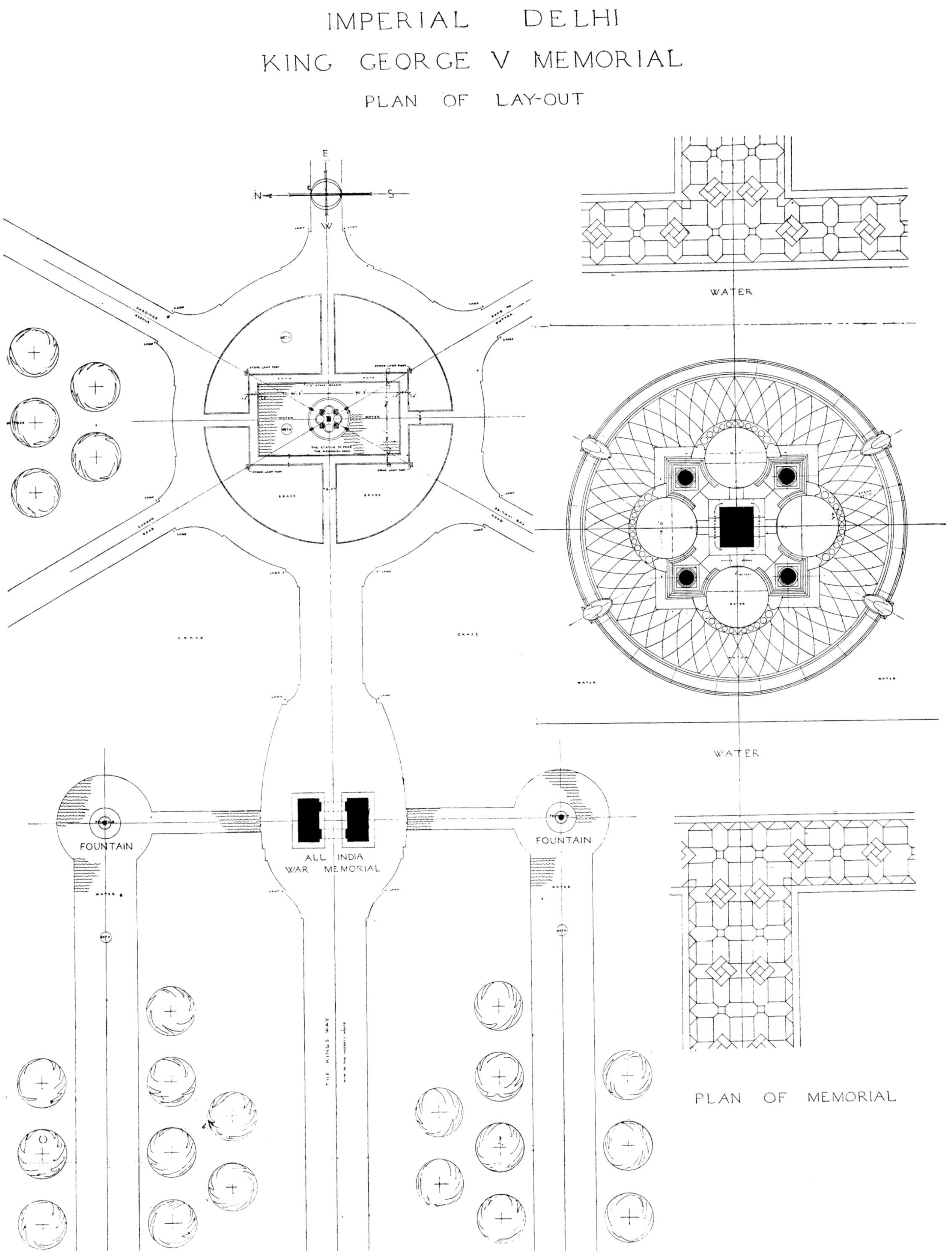
IMPERIAL DELHI
KING GEORGE V MEMORIAL
PLAN OF LAY-OUT
E
N
S
W
WATER
FOUNTAIN
ALL INDIA
WAR MEMORIAL
FOUNTAIN
PLAN OF MEMORIAL

The King George V Memorial

Directly behind the All India War Memorial stands the King George V Memorial designed by Edwin Lutyens in 1936. The King died the same year and it appeared appropriate, indeed imperative, to all those involved in the construction of Imperial Delhi to erect a monument to the founder. This seemed especially necessary considering how the construction of the city had progressed without friction and was crowned by successes.

The basic formal idea of the memorial is the representation of the King-Emperor beneath a baldachin. There were models found not only in Hadrian's Villa in Tivoli and in London (the Albert Memorial), but also in India itself. For example, in Mahaballipuram a comparable stone baldachin for the protection of small bronze statues of gods is still preserved today. This Indian baldachin appears as Thomas and William Daniell recorded it at the end of the eighteenth century in their aquatints "Oriental Scenery" (see Fig. 148).[71] We may assume that Edwin Lutyens was also familiar with this famous series of aquatints.

The architectural construction of the stone baldachin made particular demands on the architects. A simple stacked construction on the model from Mahaballipuram was ruled out because its statics did not coincide with modern principles of stable construction: "Architects will wonder how Lutyens dealt with the thrust from the arches carried by the slender columns of the Delhi Order.[72] Working drawings explain that he built a reinforced concrete arch as a strong core behind the visible *voussoirs*; that the deep setting of the chujja stones rested on this and then, one course above the top, a solid reinforced concrete raft – a foot thick and fourteen feet square – bound the structure together. We should add that the domed ceiling is built in brick, four and a half inches thick and finished with Cunam plaster. The outer dome is constructed of stone on the top; and the crown – nearly 3 feet high – is made of gilt bronze."[73]

The statue of King George V was, like its plinth, worked in marble. Charles Jagger and Edwin Lutyens were responsible for the initial design of the statue. After Indian independence, the statue was removed and the entire site lost much of its original dignified, imperial quality along with its focal point. "Ornamental use of water in the royal memorial, complementing a tissue of symbolic meanings and associations, tempered and enlivened the severity of the abstract geometric patterns. The plan of the Baldachin and its site in a circular basin recalled the complex medley of convex and concave curves in Hadrian's island villa or Maritime Theater at Tivoli as well as the elaborately curvilinear fountain at the centre of the private wing in Domitian's imperial residence on the Palatine. A sketch plan by Lutyens, early in the conception of Viceroy's House, exhibited striking similarities. Both alien and native heritage were fused in explicit symbols which emphasized the majesty of the King-Emperor's person and of his proconsuls and servants. Emblems of kingship abounded: the British imperial crown, orb, and robes, the chivalric star of India, the baldachin, and even the water itself evoking ancient oriental traditions of a divine monarch as mystic giver of the waters of life. Sculptured nautilus shells implied British dominion of the seas and conjured memories of the sovereign's oceanic pilgrimage for his coronation durbar. The baldachin was not only an image of kingship but also of the heavens, of that abode of the divinities and cosmic canopy which compassed the whole British Empire. With unintentional irony the monument – the very embodiment of an order now mortally challenged – faced directly into the setting sun."[74]

71 Th. and W. Daniell: *Oriental Scenery*, London, 1807.
72 On the development and significance of the Delhi Order see Fig. 65.
73 A.S.G. Butler: op. cit., p. 45.
74 R.G. Irving: op. cit., p. 262.

Fig. 146: The plan of the layout for the King George V Memorial shows the combination of geometric elements of triangle, square and hexagon typical of Edwin Lutyens' work.

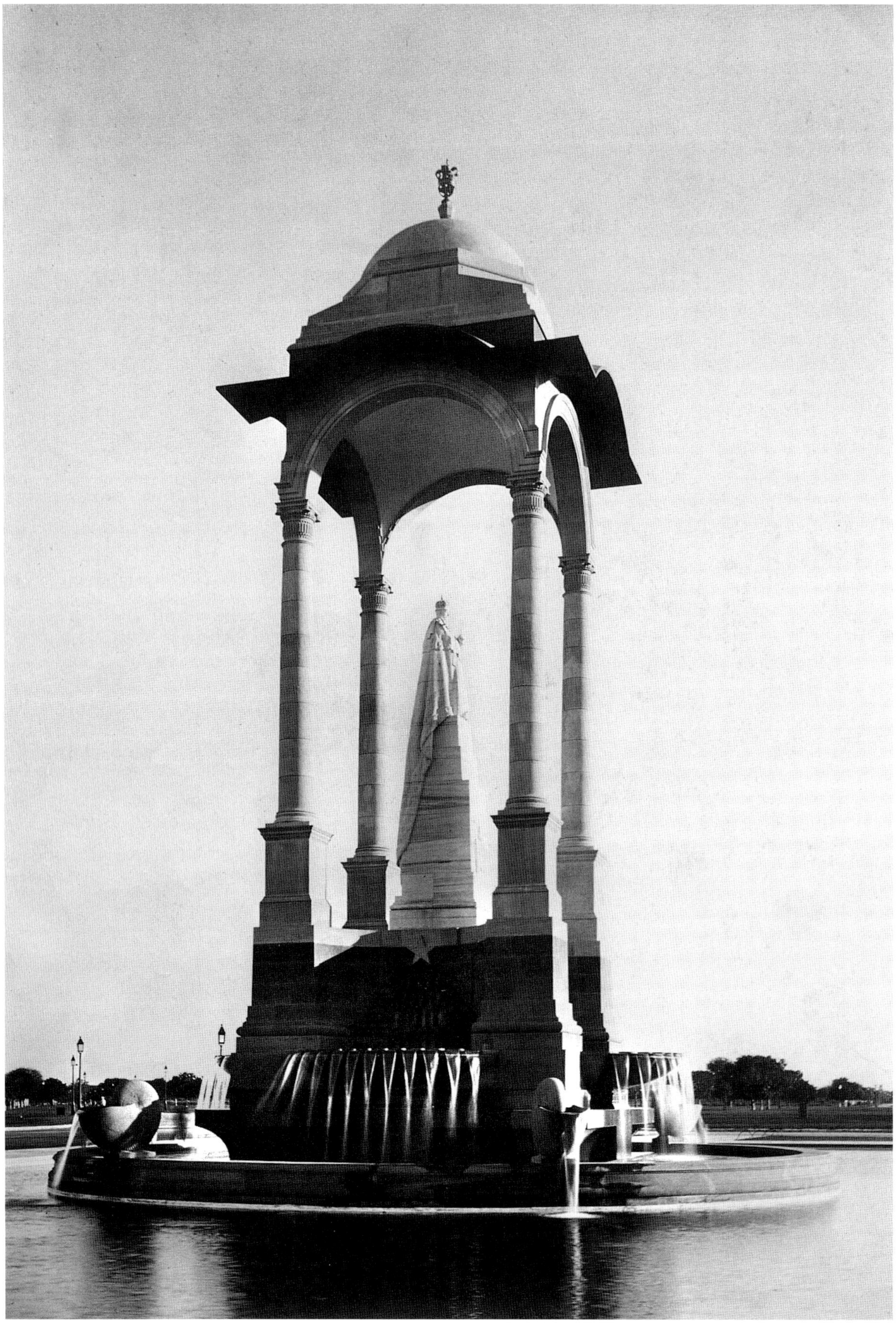

Fig. 147: Photograph from the thirties of the King George V Memorial. The statue was removed after Indian Independence in 1947/48.

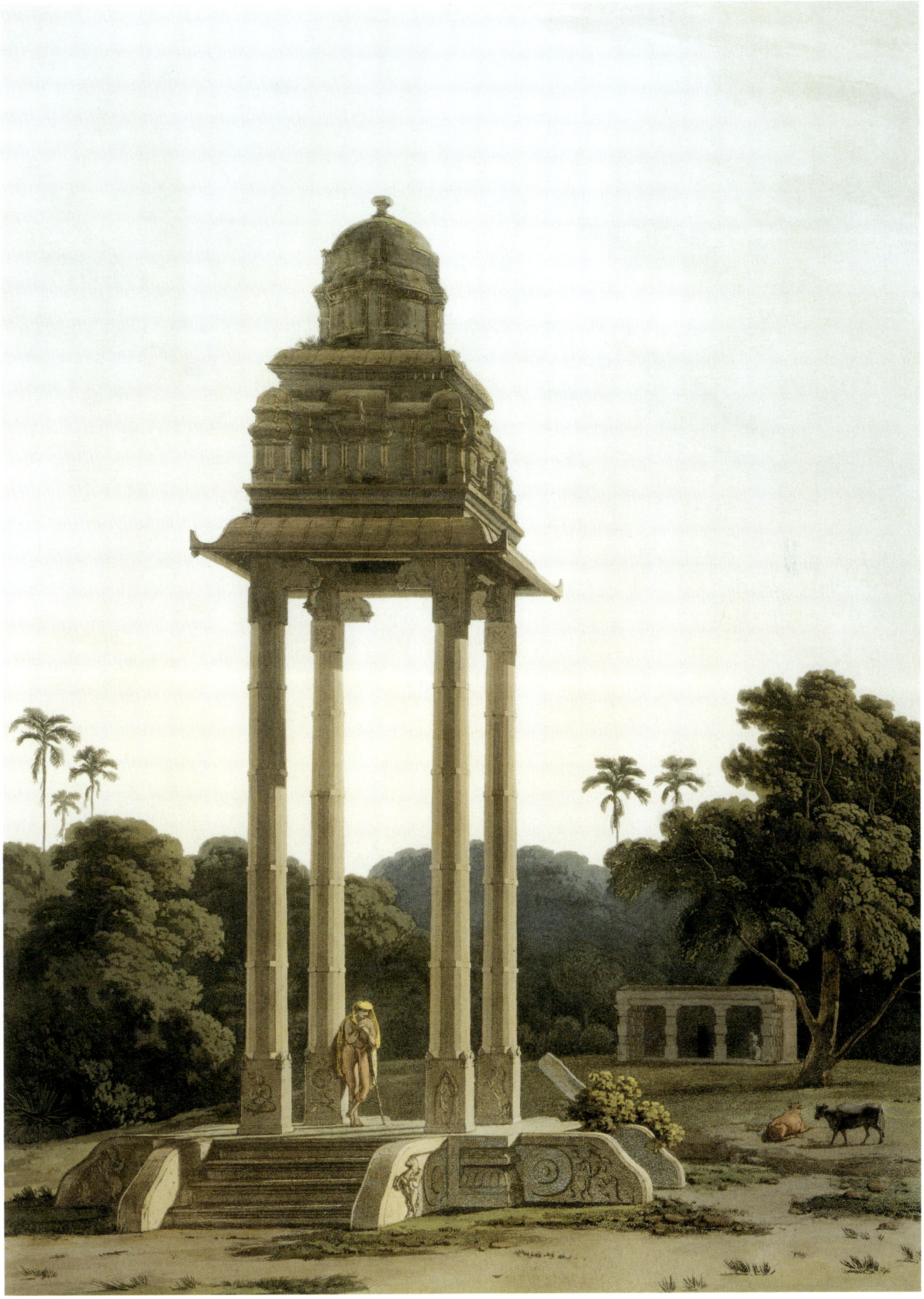

Fig. 148: One of the sources for Lutyens' design for the King George V Memorial was a Hindu stone pavilion from Mahaballipuram (*c.* seventeenth or eighteenth century) that included various small bronze deities.

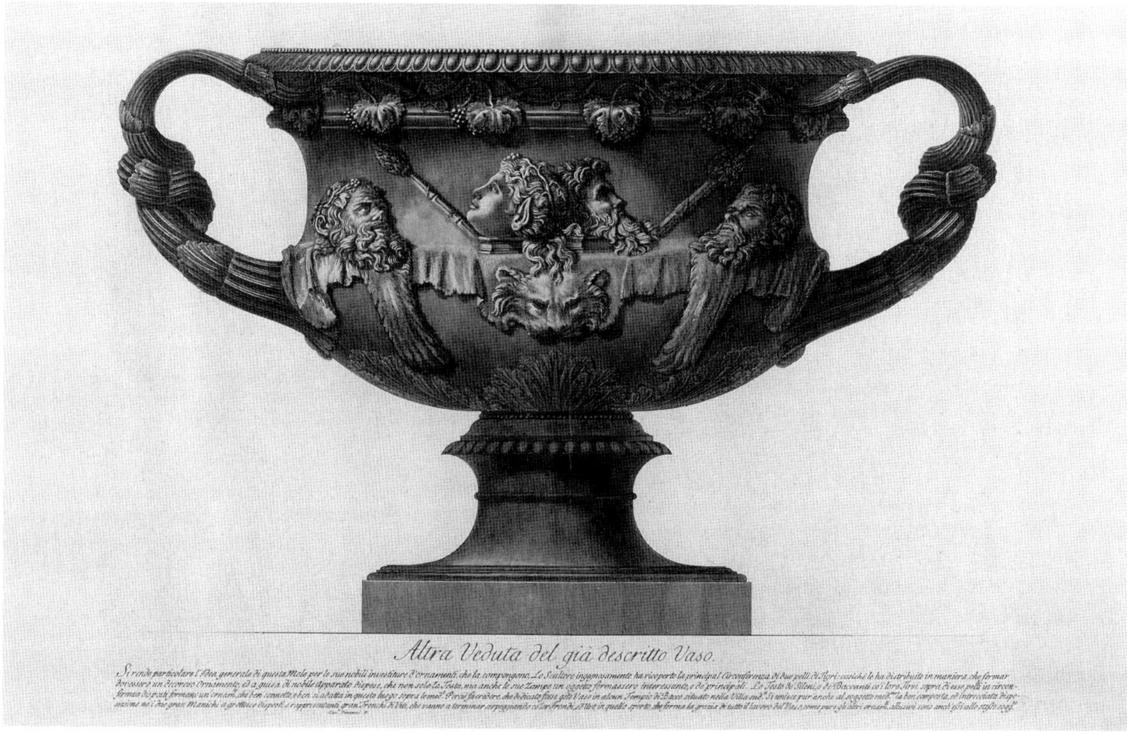

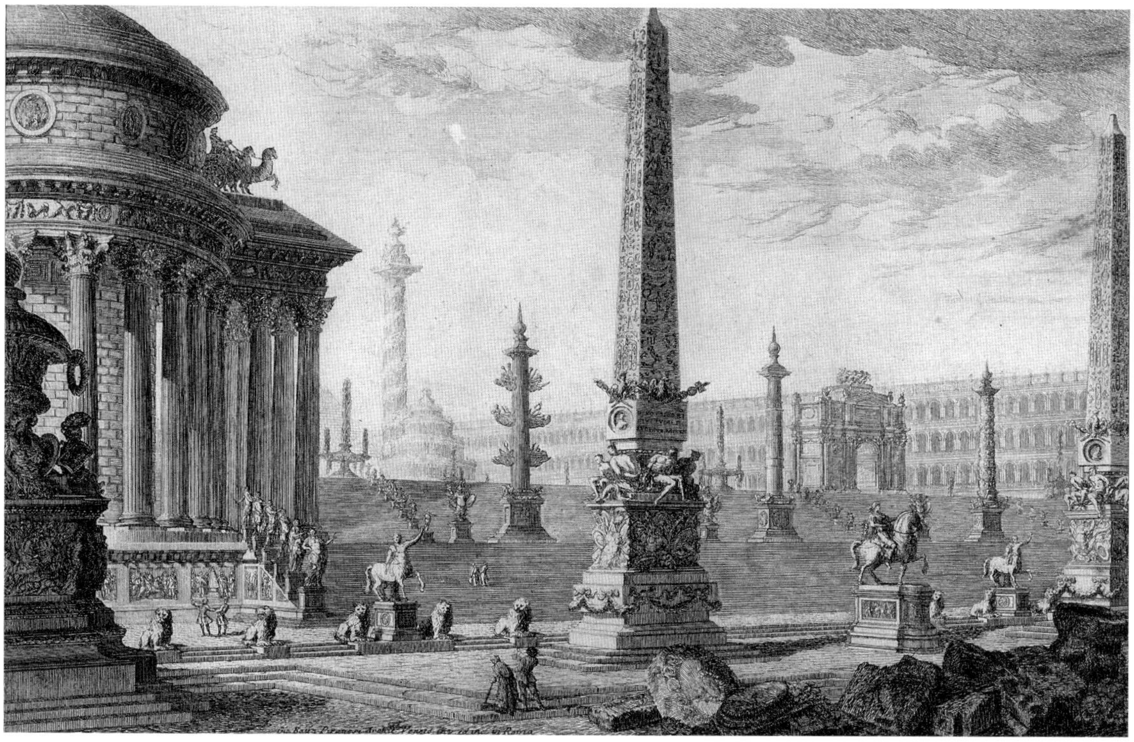

Fig. 149: From Piranesi's inexhaustible repertoire of classical shapes, Edwin Lutyens chose the classical vase (above) and the obelisk (below) as decorative shapes for Hyderabad House.

3.3 European Symbolic Forms: Obelisk, Urn, Vase, Lion and Round Arch

From the first year of the planning of Imperial Delhi into our own time, there has been a protracted conflict between the buildings and symbolic forms of the British Empire on the one hand, and the forms and symbols of the Indian subcontinent, whether they are of Hindu or Islamic origin, on the other. Lord Hardinge, the Viceroy, had originally spoken out decisively for the use of an Indian formal language, but he gradually gave up this aim in the face of continued resistance from Edwin Lutyens and Herbert Baker. Consequently, European symbolic forms appear in equal measure alongside Indian ones.

The **obelisk** made its appearance in the architecture of Lutyens during his search for appropriate symbolic forms for Hyderabad House and Baroda House in Imperial Delhi. Of ancient Egyptian origin, the obelisk had already made its entry into the imperial formal repertoire of ancient Rome as both a symbol of power and of the eternal life of the kings.[75] Lutyens was not only acquainted with the Roman examples through Piranesi's depictions (Fig. 149), but also from his own stays in Rome during the building of the British pavilion for the World Exhibition of 1911. Finally, the great number of obelisks, some genuine and some imitations, in the European architecture of the Renaissance and classical eras was, for Lutyens, a reason to adopt this symbol previously not included in Viceroy's House, Hyderabad House, and Baroda House. In the case of Hyderabad House, obelisks adorn all the important corners of the building. In Baroda House obelisks flank the fireplaces.

Lutyens chose **urns** as adornment for the architecture of Baroda House (Fig. 217) for reasons no longer ascertainable today. They are not to be confused with the Neo-Classical **vases** already represented in Piranesi's work (Fig. 149), which Lutyens again produced on the roofs of Hyderabad House for festive flower arrangements (Fig. 212).

The **lion**, one of the heraldic animals of the British Royal Family, found its entry into the architecture of Imperial Delhi via Piranesi's eighteenth-century depiction of an ancient gymnasium (Fig. 150). Edwin Lutyens, like the Royal Family in London and the English administration in India, was deeply convinced of the humanist task of his country towards its Indian subjects. He therefore adopted Piranesi's allegory of strength and wisdom for the approach to Viceroy's Court.

A visitor to Viceroy's House could hardly avoid going past one of the two symmetrically arranged rows of lions. Thus, he was prepared, as Piranesi had intended, to grasp the strength and wisdom of the British rule over India: "Fate decreed that only two days after new Delhi's inaugural celebrations, Gandhi found himself at the gates of the city's grandest palace for an interview with the King-Emperor's Viceroy. Important constitutional proposals that had been mooted at the recent Round Table Conference now required the assent of Congress nationalists. Consequently, it was in a bold effort to break a political impasse that Lord Irwin had given Gandhi and his colleagues an unconditional release from their year-long internment and then had agreed to meet the Mahatma as 'man to man.'

Punctually at 2:20 on the afternoon of February 17, therefore, Gandhi made his way past the stone gauntlet of Britannic lions guarding Viceroy's Court and was ushered into Lord Irwin's study. His arrival was in vivid contrast to official processions the previous week. A torn woolen shawl, loin cloth, and bamboo stave had replaced the scarlet uniforms and flashing lances of an imperial Body Guard. A prisoner only days before, Gandhi nevertheless came as no humble supplicant, but much more like the plenipotentiary of a sovereign power, on equal terms with the Viceroy."[76]

There are no Islamic keel arches in the architecture of Imperial Delhi; an obvious omission intended to contrast the forms of old Delhi and its Mughal emperors. Already at the planning stage, Lutyens had given up his attempts to include keel arches (see Fig. 1), and none of his partners or successors revised that decision out of principle. **Round arches** modelled after those of ancient Rome, the Renaissance, and later Classicism are objects that represent the political and cultural home of Imperial Delhi, and not just the palace of the British Viceroy. Even for the Muslim Nizam of Hyderabad, Lutyens built a palace that is completely indebted to Palladio

75 Cf. P.A. Memmesheimer: *Das klassizistische Grabmal*, Bonn 1969, p. 127ff.
76 R.G. Irving: op. cit., p. 351

77 Lutyens was so pleased by the capital he developed that he used it again many years later in the baldachin of the high altar of Campion Hall in Oxford and in the facades of many office buildings in London.
78 A.S.G. Butler: op. cit.

and the architectural elements of the Renaissance (Fig. 212). This promptly led to strong protests on the part of the Nizam's two sons, who considered the building style completely "unsuitable for an Oriental house."

Herbert Baker was no less faithful to principles than Lutyens. Even in his conversion of a gateway in front of a grave to an entrance for the Secretariats, he consistently replaced the Islamic arches with round ones (cf. p. 190).

Lutyens and Baker also adhered closely to western models in a great many details. Only the most important rooms in Viceroy's House, e.g. the Porticos, Staircase Court, the Ballroom, State Dining Room and the Durbar Hall were given pillars of the "Delhi Order" conceived by Lutyens himself (Fig. 165).[77] On the other hand, all verandahs and courts had Doric pillars. Furthermore, Baker chose for each of the sixteen outer "temples" of the Secretariats sixteen Corinthian pillars, while in the case of the Legislative Building, 144 pillars for the circular outer layer in the Doric style.

Many detailed drawings by Lutyens have been preserved through fortunate circumstances. Hundreds of works are in the Drawings Collection of the RIBA in London and about a thousand in the Planning Archive of the Central Public Works Department in New Delhi. One of these drawings, edited and published by A.S.G. Butler,[78] shows how closely the architect followed his model, Palladio, right down to the profiles of the base of a pillar (Fig. 156). To quote Lutyens: "Palladio is the game!"

Fig. 150: In the portrayal of a classical gymnasium by Giovanni Battista Piranesi (1720–78), rows of lions guard the entrance to the building. It can be assumed that this imitative classical portrayal of strength and wisdom was Lutyens' inspiration for the rows of lions at both sides of Viceroy's Court.

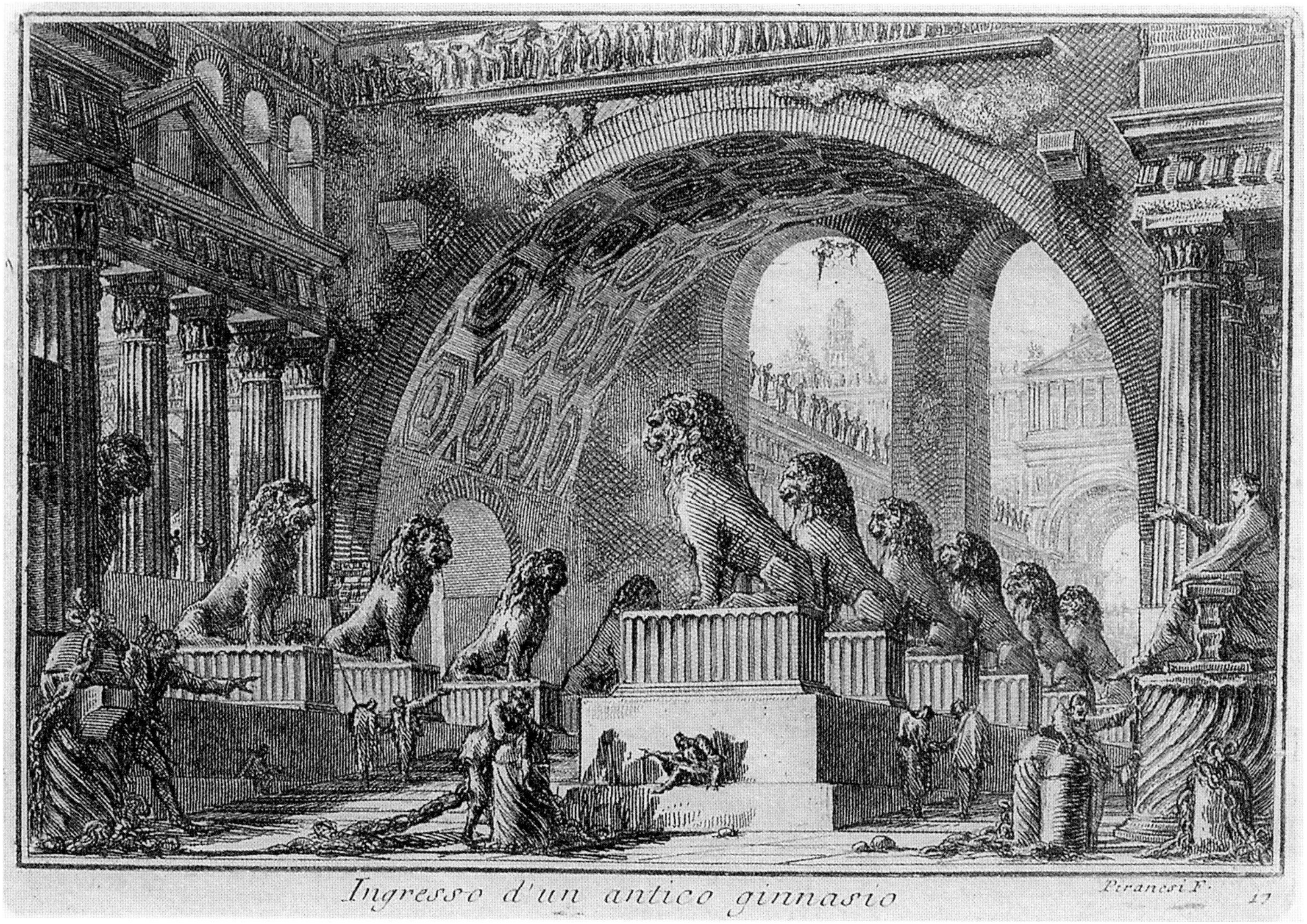

Fig. 151: Viceroy's Court is bordered by a row of lions on the southern and northern sides.

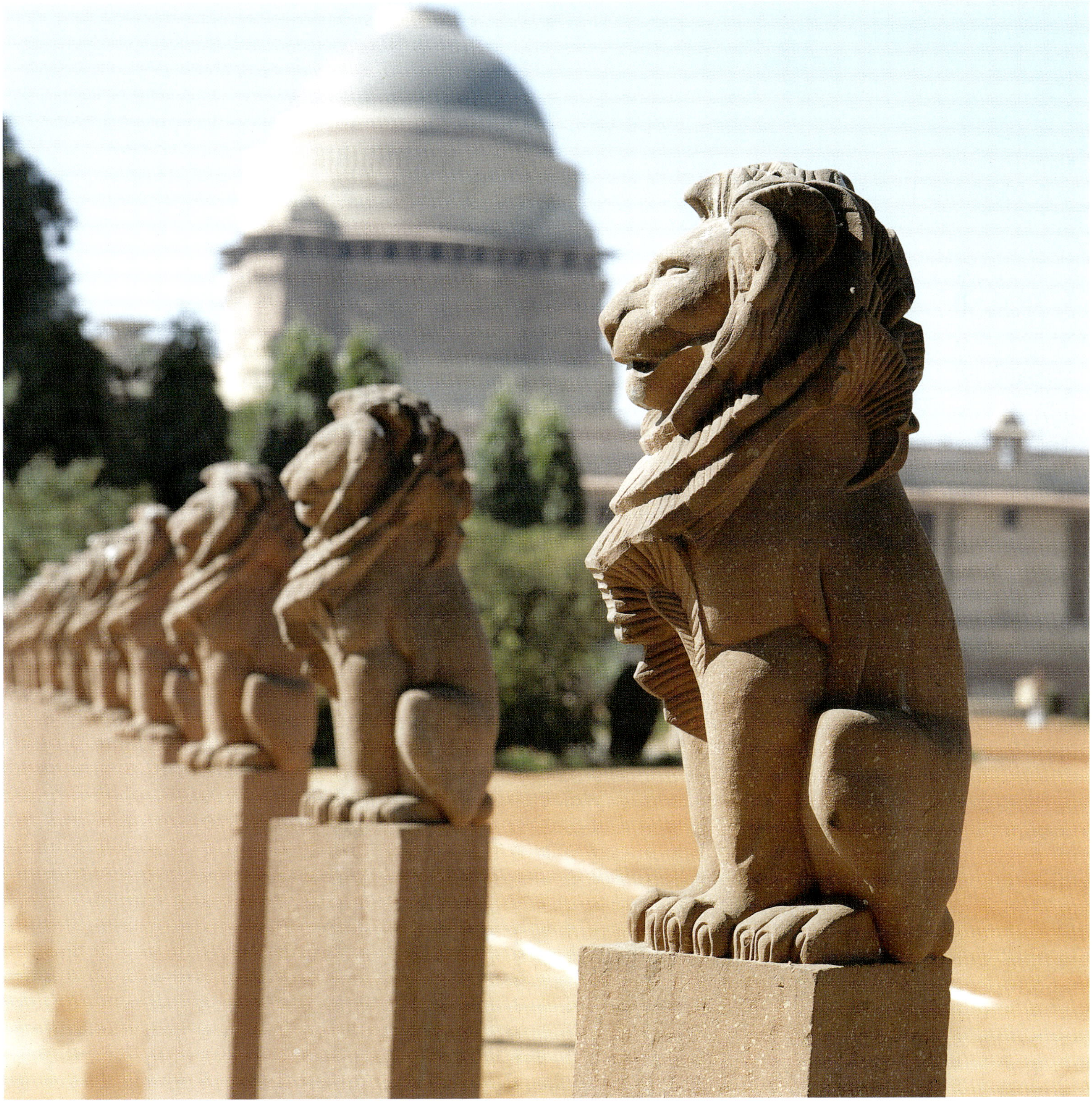

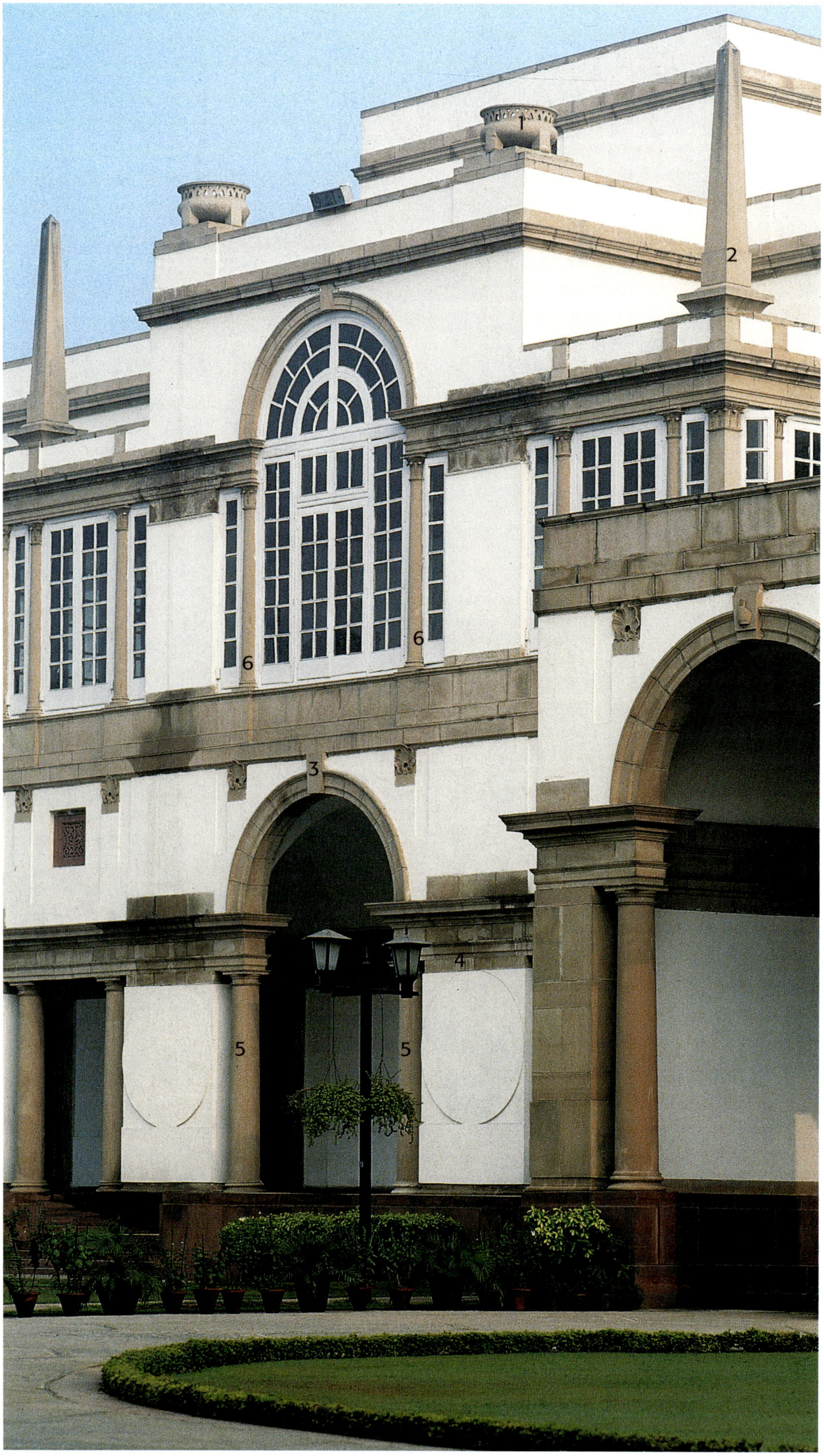

Fig. 152: Hyderabad House by Edwin Lutyens is a veritable dictionary of classical Roman architectural and decorative forms.

1 Vase
2 Obelisk
3 Round arch
4 Architrave
5 Doric column
6 Corinthian column

Fig. 153: Round arch with inset pillars by Palladio.

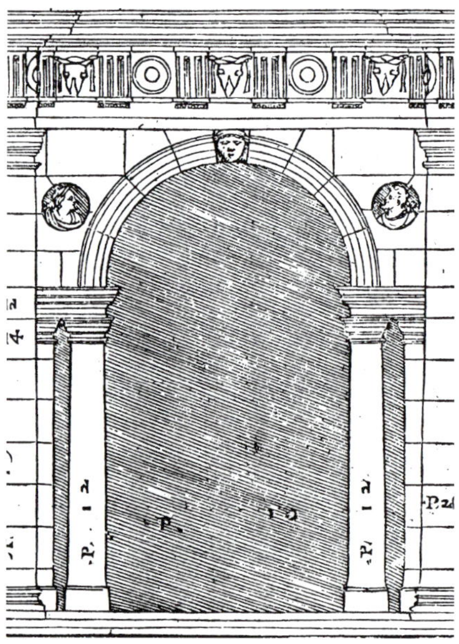

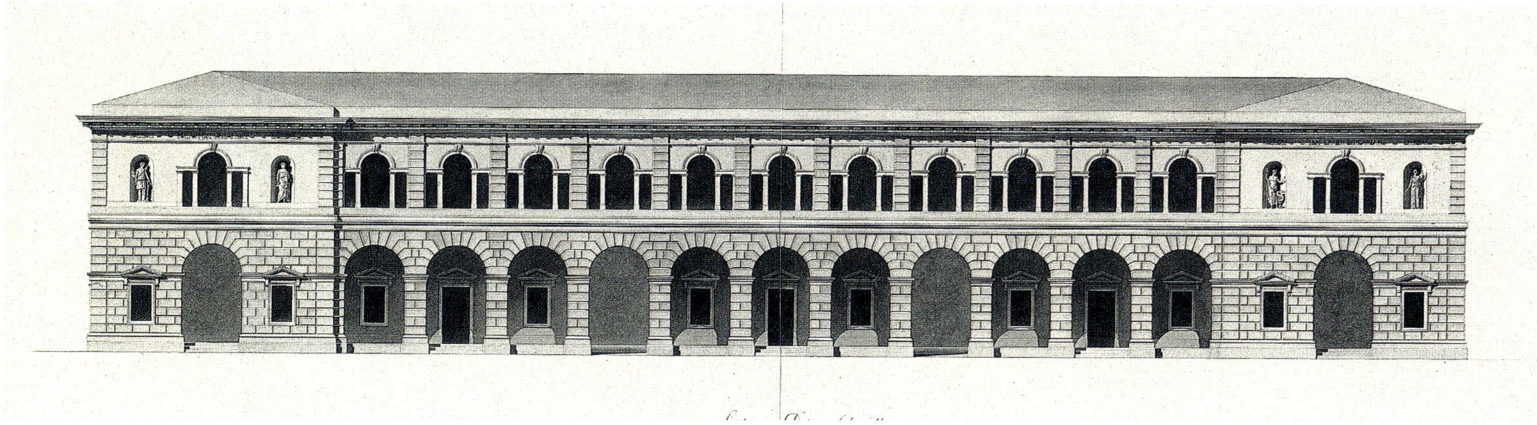

Fig. 154: In 1816, Leo von Klenze designed a corn-market on the Maximiliansplatz in Munich. Its upper storey had the same round arches with rectangular openings at the side that Edwin Lutyens chose almost a century later as the most important formal element in the upper storey of Hyderabad House.

Fig. 155: A model by John Soane for the facade of the Law Courts at Westminster, 1826, adopted the combination of round arches and rectangular windows that often appear with Palladio. This Palladian design was, however, not carried out and was replaced by a Gothic design by John Soane.

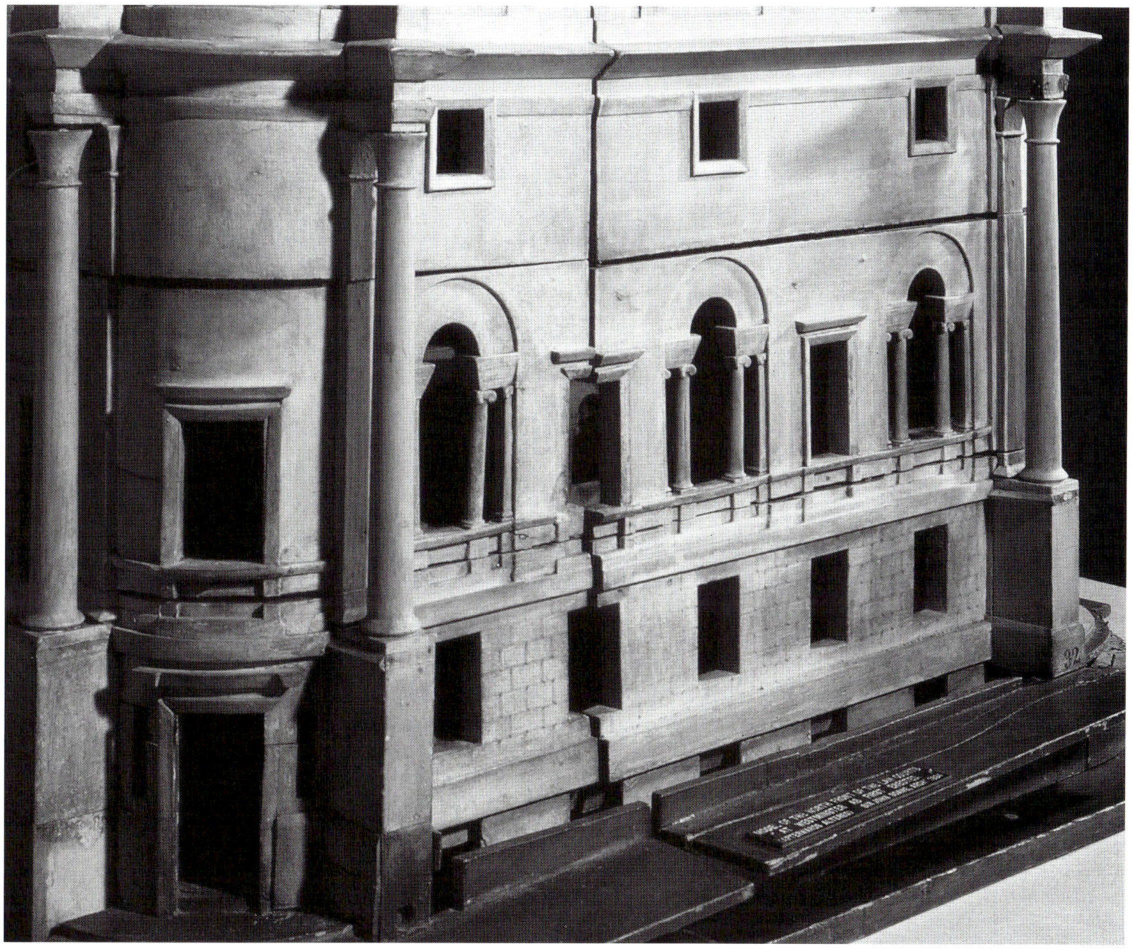

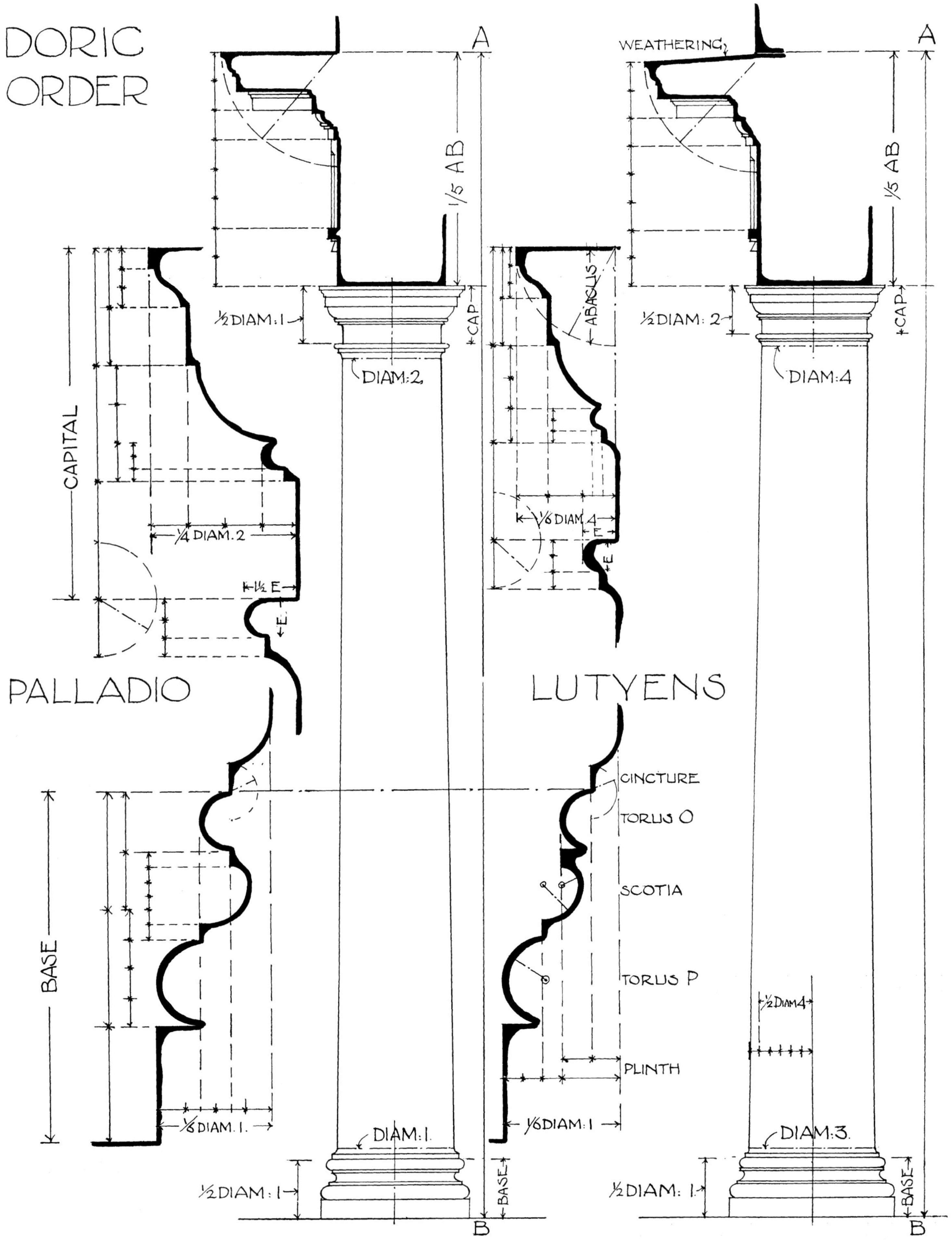
DORIC ORDER
A
WEATHERING
A
1/5 AB
1/5 AB
½ DIAM: 1
CAP
ABACUS
½ DIAM: 2
CAP
DIAM: 2
DIAM: 4
CAPITAL
1/4 DIAM. 2
1/6 DIAM. 4
E
E
1½ E
E
PALLADIO
LUTYENS
CINCTURE
TORUS O
SCOTIA
BASE
TORUS P
½ DIAM 4
PLINTH
1/6 DIAM. 1.
1/6 DIAM: 1
DIAM: 1.
DIAM: 3.
½ DIAM: 1
BASE
½ DIAM: 1
BASE
B
B

3.4 Indian Symbolic Forms: Stupa, Elephant, Nandi (Bull), Snake, Lotus Flower and Keel Arch

In both its town plan and its architecture, Imperial Delhi is laid out in a completely European and Neo-Classical style. This representational schema did not correspond to the preferences of the Viceroy or the King, who had spoken particularly enthusiastically to Lutyens in favour of the style of the Mughal Age as a leitmotif for Delhi, "if it was not so dreadfully expensive." George V was in agreement here with E.B. Havell, who as early as 1911, in a reader's letter to the *Times*, condemned the contemporary historicist style of English official buildings in India and put in a vehement plea for a revival of the architecture of the Mughal Age as an alternative: "In a lecture before the East India Association at Caxton Hall, Westminster, on October 21, 1912, later published in the British Architect and circulated privately to persons of importance, he excoriated the *Times* and other proponents of Renaissance architecture. If adopted for Delhi, he protested, it was a style which spelled 'the ruin of Indian craftsmanship, the intellectual impoverishment of the educated classes, and the strangling of Indian art.' The public buildings of the Government of India exercised a potent influence for good or evil, for Indian craftsmen and aristocratic Indian patrons alike looked to them for models of taste and fashion. In 1913 Havell reserved the entire last chapter of his monumental volume, *Indian Architecture*, for an impassioned polemic against a 'make-believe' capital city of Renaissance or, equally, British-designed Indo-Saracenic architecture. He suggested that intelligent patronage of the indigenous heritage of India, following the example of Akbar, could prove a bridge between the cultures, 'a means of reconciling racial and religious differences.'"[79]

In the spring of 1912, Lutyens and his colleagues were instructed by the Viceroy to examine the Mughal and Rajput buildings of Agra and Jaipur, and later, Dhar and Mandu. Lutyens' comment after the trip was: "Veneered joinery in stone, concrete and marble on a gigantic scale there is a lot of, but no real architecture ... Personally I do not believe there is any real Indian architecture or any great tradition. There are just spurts by various mushroom dynasties with as much intellect in them as any other art nouveau."[80]

Fig. 156: Wherever Edwin Lutyens used columns in the Doric style, he kept closely to the model of Palladio in many details.

In December 1912, after his Mandu visit, he reported, almost despairingly: "The ruins of this once great city, set in wonderful scenery and on a wonderful site, have walls four miles long enclosing jungle with a palace or a mosque here and there, with remnants of great tanks. But behind it all the building is childish, and of that quality of art so dear to the literary mind – work done in a hurry by old war-worn conquerors, ruthless and squalid, with no real nicety as the great Westerners felt it. The Durbar Hall, which seems to have particularly impressed the Viceroy, is a great stone building with sloping buttresses and a series of huge stone pointed arches which once carried a flat stone roof now fallen in. When you consider that the roof 25 ft. wide required 36 to 40 ft. of wall thickness to support it, it becomes ridiculous, and an impossible type to adopt; and when the roof was on it would be quite dark. The other buildings are Mughal – stone treated as timber. A wonderful made picturesqueness but with no intellect. The plans are fine – but quite impractical, except as entertainment rooms for those who wear no clothes, want no furniture, and have no real reason for building except pomp and ceremony, as in, for instance, giant stairways leading to balconies where one man can squat and another precariously stand to wave a flag-fan of peacock plumes."[81]

But despite his condescending, negative attitude towards Indian architecture, Lutyens continually used native architectural forms, whether from his own insight into his task, or in order to follow the Viceroy's wishes and grant him a favour.

The stupa

Lutyens ascribed an especially prominent role to the Buddhist stupa as an architectural form together with the Buddhist stone walls that usually surround it. He chose the form of the fenced-in burial mound (also a Buddhist reliquary and symbol of the axis mundi) for the fashioning of the dome above the Durbar Hall. Even today, the connection in meaning between the burial

79 R.G. Irving: op. cit., p. 104.
80 Clare Percy and Jane Ridley, (eds.): op. cit., p. 250.
81 Christopher Hussey: op. cit., p. 279.

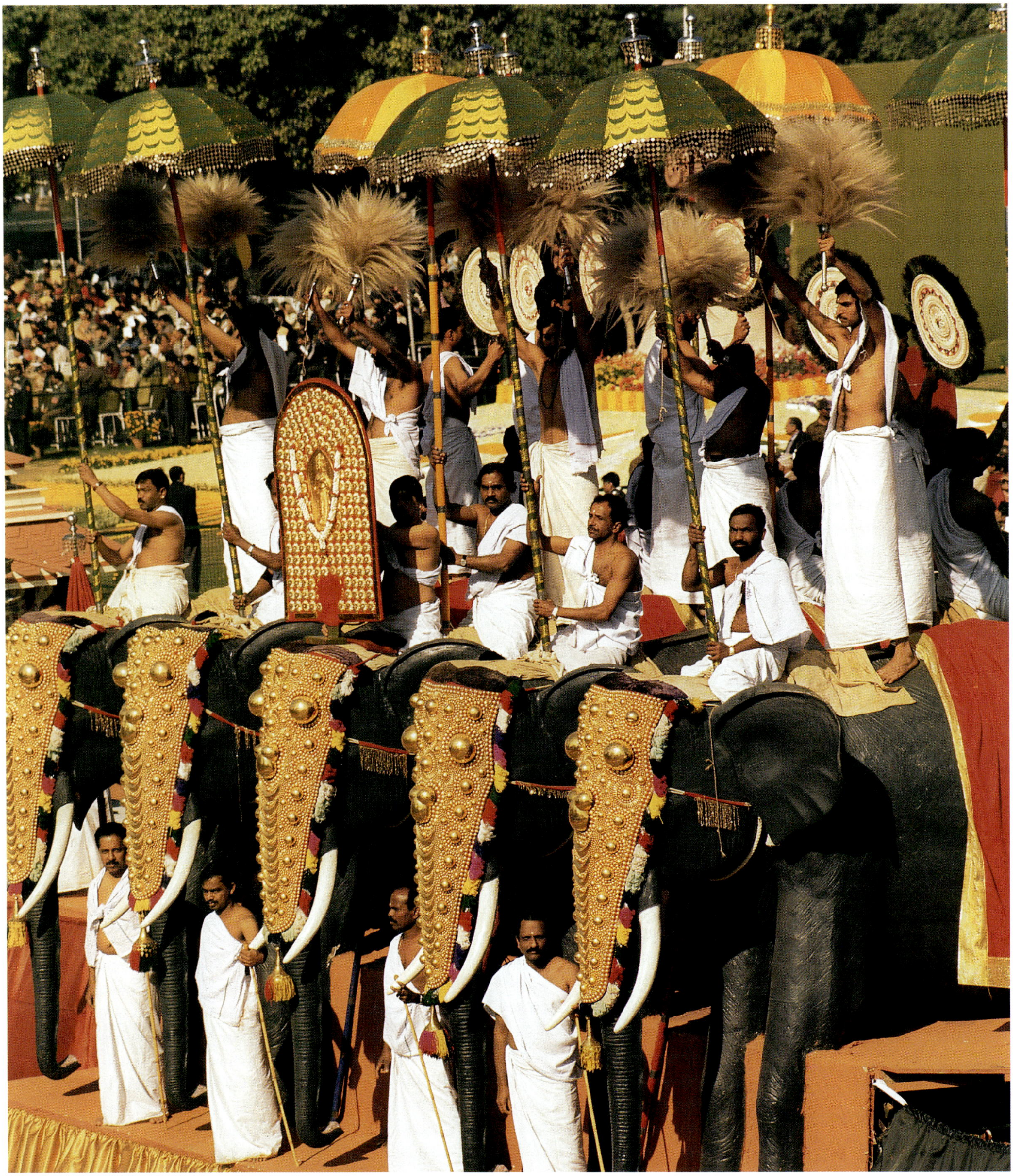

Fig. 157: The military parade on Republic Day, January 26, also shows elephants as symbols of power.

mound and the centre of the government power is almost impossible to work out (Fig. 81). It was presumably the rare, well-preserved stupa at Sanchi, dating from the third century B.C. that was the model for the hall.[82] The shape of its stone surround (vedika) was not only adopted as the tambour for the dome, but also appeared again as the monumental boundary for Prince Edward Place (now Great Place) at the foot of Raisina Hill.

The elephants

Edwin Lutyens placed elephants in various locations throughout Viceroy's House. For the most part, they serve to guard the entrances. Their significance extends far beyond their present-day use as a working animal, and Lutyens understood their significance in Indian mythology. As early as in Mohenjo-Daro,[83] elephants had been found on seals, appearing time and time again as working animals, as well as mythical creatures in Indian mythology: "Elephants are the caryatids of the universe. As such they very properly appear in the rock-cut Shiva-temple at Elura, the temple of the Lord of Mount Kailasa. This is one of the great classic monuments of Hindu religious architecture. It dates from the eighth century A.D."[84]

In the myth of the *Hastyayurveda*, the role of the elephant is defined for the King and his empire: "If they did not pay worship to the elephant, the king and the kingdom, the army and the elephants, would be doomed to perish, because a divinity would have been disregarded. Contrariwise, if due worship is paid to the elephant, they will thrive and prosper together with their wives and sons, the country, the army, and the elephants. Crops will sprout in due time; Indra, the rain god, will send rain in due time; there will be no plague, no drought. They will live a hundred years (a full lifetime) with many sons and many cattle and will have a sturdy progeny. Whoever wishes to have sons will have sons, and longing after riches and other goods will also be fulfilled. The earth will abound in treasures of precious metals and jewels."[85]

The usefulness of the elephant, especially in the arid subtropical landscape of northern India is ultimately linked to its descent: "Elephants are clouds sentenced to walk upon earth. But their cousins like to visit them; hence it is important for a king to have elephants in his stables. They are termed 'the king's clouds' and they guarantee rain for his people in the period of monsoon."[86]

Thus, the stone elephants that Lutyens provided for the entrances to Viceroy's House presumably also held a double meaning for him. First, as relatives of the clouds, they ensured the fertility of the land, and secondly as caryatids of the universe they supported the ruling British Empire.

The fascination that elephants exerted on Lutyens was also reflected in many of his travel sketches and in fantasy tales for his children: "I went for a ride on an Indian dancing horse and was getting along quite nicely until we met a huge elephant and the horse shied and so I nearly came off. Then it swung round, galloped away, and – horror – I found the elephant after me and felt its hot breath between me and the saddle!! Just as I was getting home the elephant caught my horse's tail. But luckily for me the tail came off just as I got home."[87]

In Imperial Delhi, elephants not only guard the palace, as symbols of strength but they are also fixtures in all great processions in India whether religious or political. Even the military parade on Republic Day, held annually on January 26, does not dispense with these important symbolic beasts. Admittedly, in this case, because of the difficulty of coordinating the marching tempos of humans, tanks and elephants, they have recently overcome the problem by using stuffed elephants on a trailer (Fig. 157).

82 Cf. on this point A. Volwahsen: *Living Architecture: Indian*, London and New York 1969, p. 17ff.
83 The Indus Valley Civilization had its high-point in the third millennium B.C.
84 H. Zimmer: *Myths and Symbols in Indian Art and Civilization*, New York 1946 and 1962, p. 105.
85 Andandashrama Hastyayurveda, *Sanskrit Series*, No. 26, Poona 1894, quoted in Zimmer, H., op. cit., p. 108.
86 H. Zimmer: *The Art of Indian Asia*, New York 1955 and 1964, p. 161, Vol. 1.
87 Quoted from Christopher Hussey: op. cit.

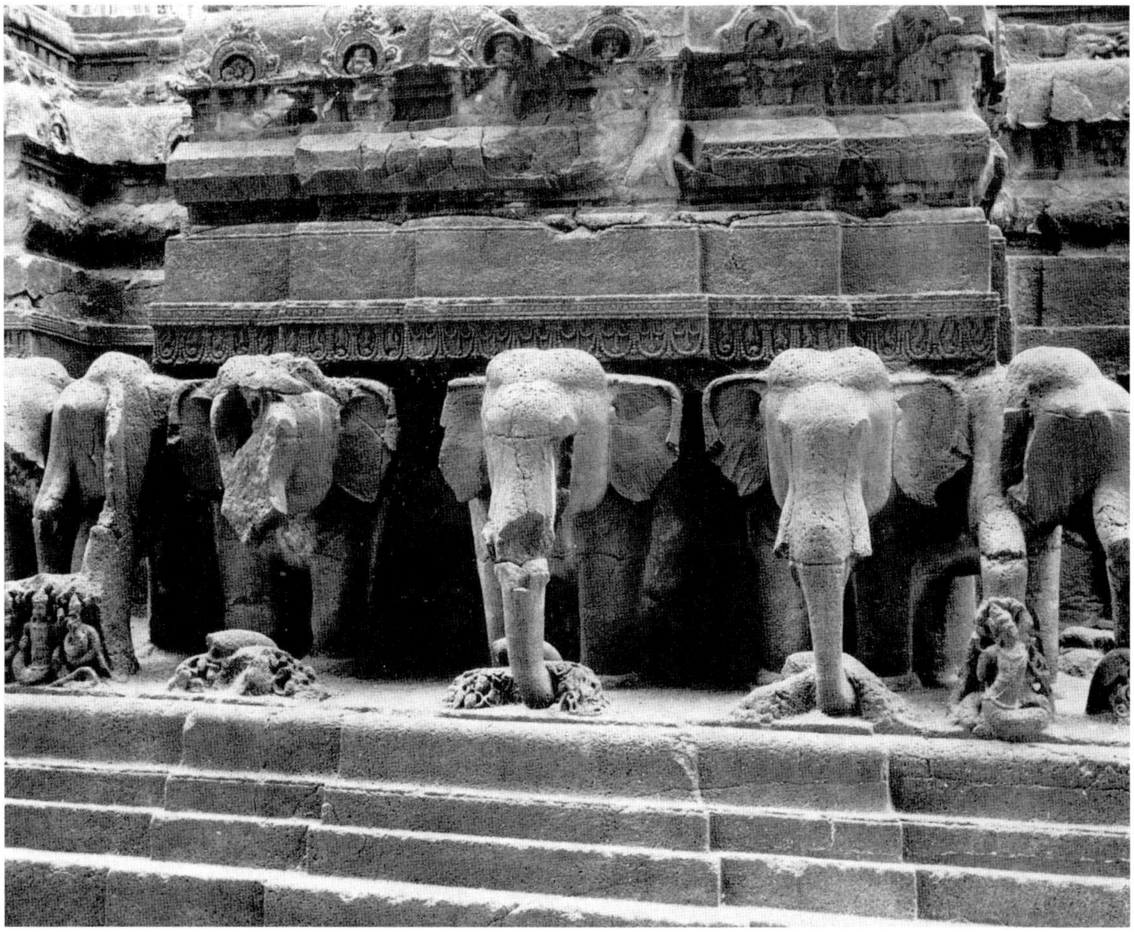

Fig. 158: Elephant caryatids carrying the world mountain Meru at the Kailasa Temple of Elora.

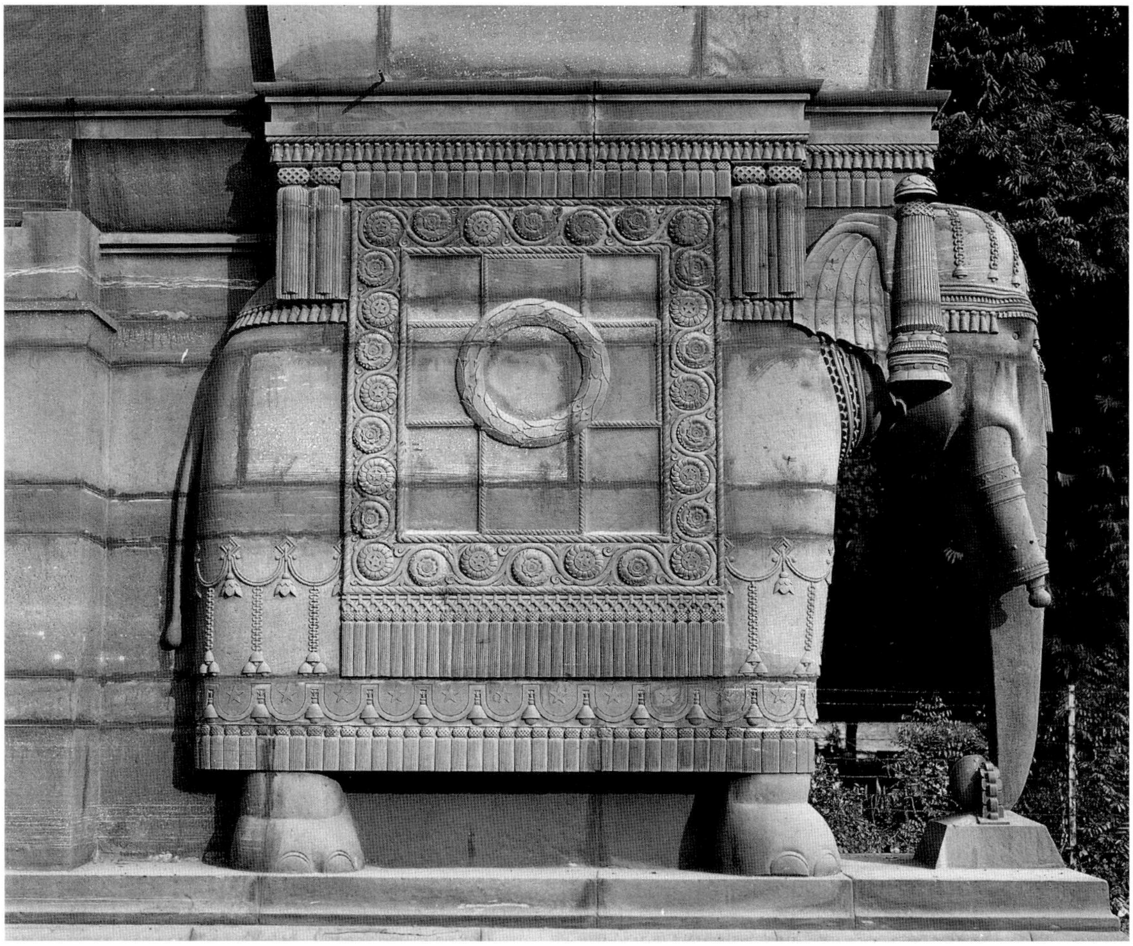

Fig. 159: Splendidly decorated elephants guard the southern entrance to Viceroy's Court, they no longer bear the monogram of the British Emperor.

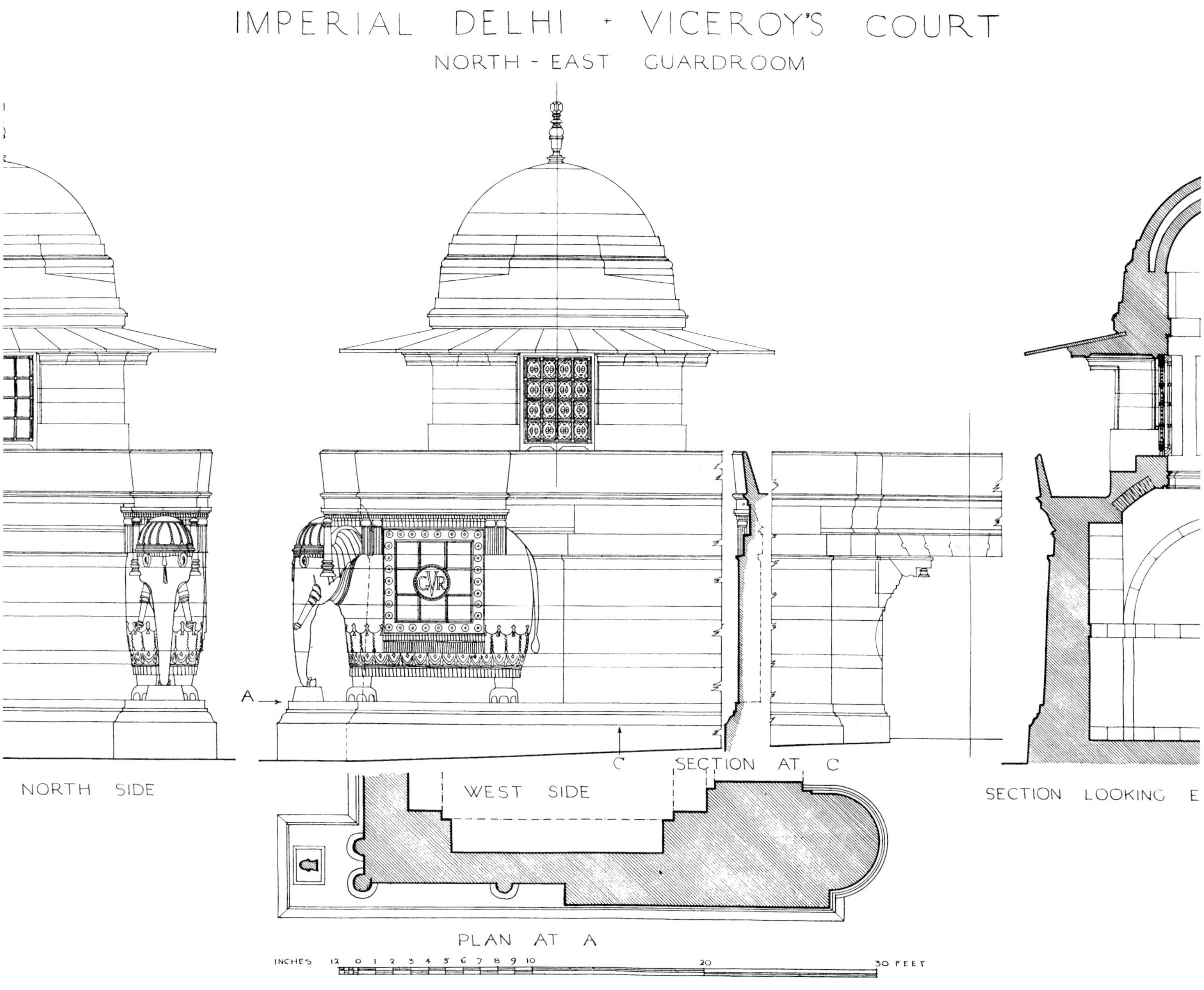

Fig. 160: The British sculptor C.S. Jagger carved the elephants at the entrances to the Viceroy's Court according to Lutyens' designs.

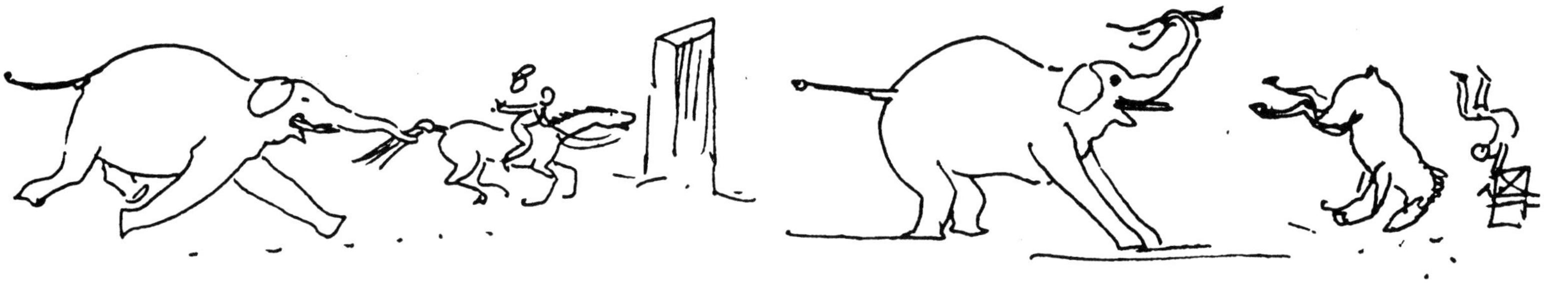

The Nandi (Shiva's bull)

In the portico of Viceroy's House – suddenly and without any relationship to the surrounding architecture – there is a large Nandi bull on a lotus capital. Originally it crowned one of the many monumental stone pillars that Emperor Ashoka (272–232 B.C.) had erected as a sign of his rule over all parts of India. "Ashoka was a convert to the Buddhist belief and an immensely powerful patron. Not only did his domain embrace the whole of northern India, expanding to include Afghanistan, Kashmir and the Dekkan, but he sent out missionaries to the south as far as Ceylon, and westward even into Syria and Egypt."[88]

We find large stone Nandi in Hindu temples in so far as they are dedicated to Shiva. The Nandi is not only the mount of this god, it also symbolizes Shiva's creative power and the righteousness and duty of the Hindu. In a Shiva shrine, the Nandi is placed opposite the actual cella in a separate hall, the Nandi mandapam. Thus, through the Nandi, the portico of Viceroy's House acquired an additional significance as the hall in front of the inner sanctum, the Durbar Hall.

Nevertheless, this symbolic link was arrived at only in the middle of the twentieth century since the Nandi – in the same way as the stone Buddha in the Durbar Hall – is not part of the original concept: "There is a story behind how these two possessions of the Indian Museum, Calcutta, came here. A great exhibition of Indian art was held in London at Burlington House in 1947–48. It was decided that the people of India should also be enabled to see it and so the collection was displayed in the Durbar Hall, forming the nucleus of the National Museum. They stayed here until the Museum's own building on Janpath was ready in December 1960. The Buddha and the Bull were retained while the other exhibits went to their new home."[89]

The Naga snake

Another mythical creature from Hindu mythology was given a particularly prominent place in the architecture of imperial British rule in India: In the South Court of Viceroy's House, two Naga snakes set on high octagonal pillars spout water from a large basin. They are: "serpent kings personifying and directing terrestrial waters of the lakes and ponds, rivers and oceans. Vishnu's shoulders and head are surrounded by nine serpent heads with expanded hoods, he crouches on the mighty coils. Nagas inhabit subaquatic paradises, dwelling at the bottoms of rivers, lakes and seas, in resplendent palaces studded with gems and pearls."[90]

Unlike its place in western mythology, the snake as Naga is not the least bit threatening, nor is it an adversary of goodness. As a divine guardian over the life-giving element of water, it is more a symbol of incomparable and unquestioned power. Therefore, it is not depicted as slithering along the ground, as in western representations. Rather, standing upright, it dispenses precious water for the fountains and waterways of the palace and its Mughal Garden.

In this context, we can be certain that it was not simply a playful use of a well-known animal motif. As in the case of the elephants supporting the world, or the Nandi guarding the portico, the choice of the animal motif and its religious significance was in exact accordance with the mission of the palace and empire. Viceroy's House becomes almost a holy place or even Meru, the World Mountain.

88 H. Zimmer: op. cit., p. 64.
89 H.Y.S. Prasad: Rashtrapati Bhavan, *The Story of the President's House, New Delhi* 1992, p. 58.
90 H. Zimmer: op. cit.

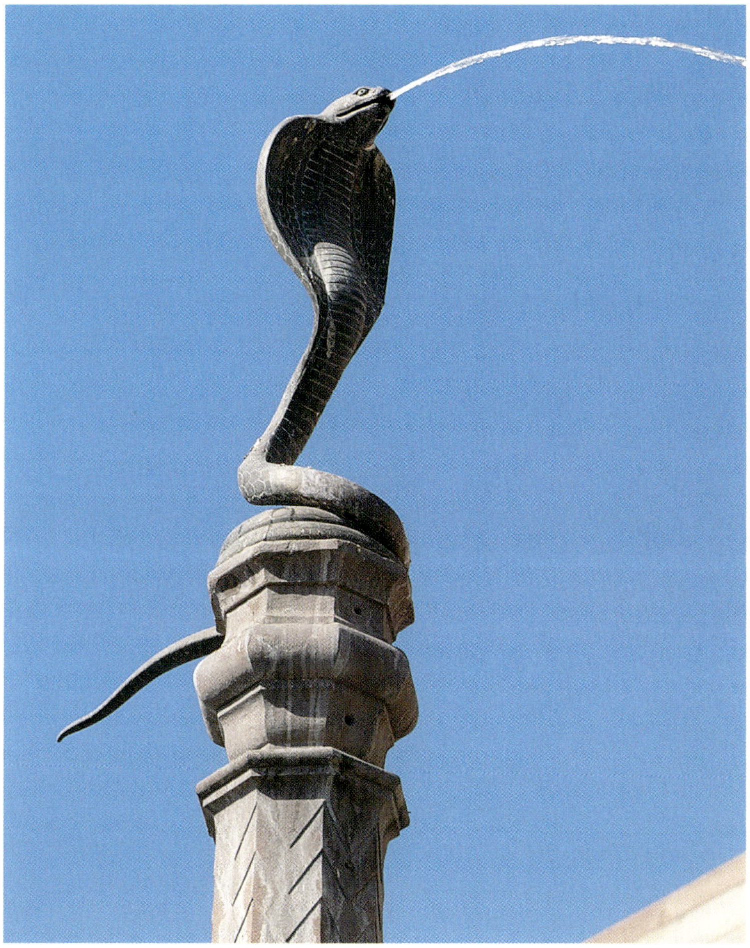

Fig. 161: In the South Court of Viceroy's House, two Naga snakes from the ancient Indian epics rise up out of a wide fountain basin.

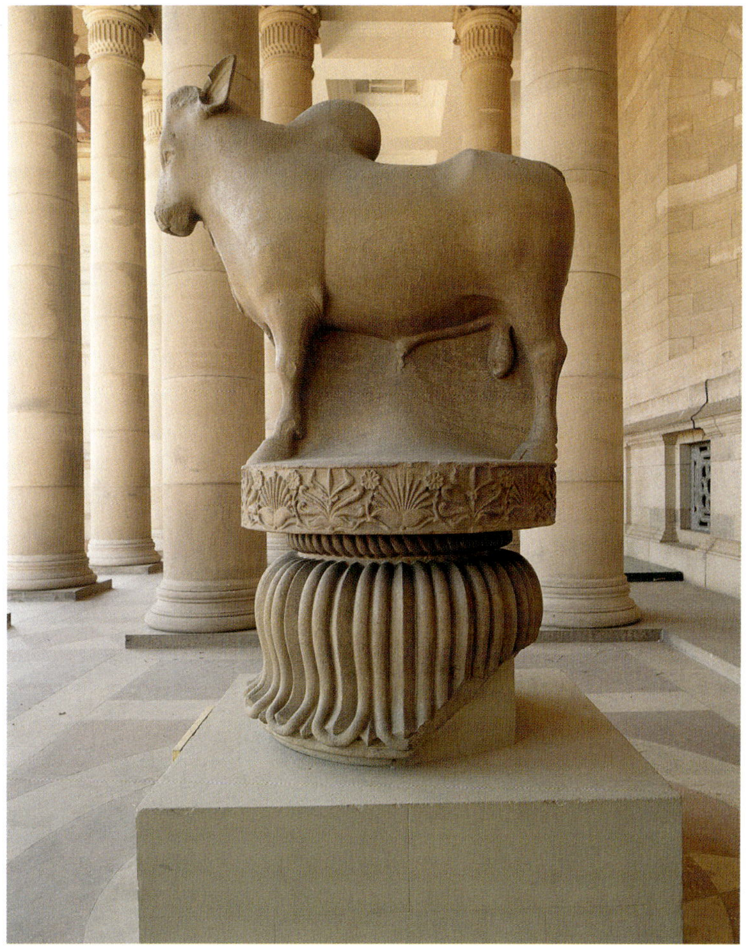

Fig. 162: In the portico of Viceroy's House is the capital of an Ashoka column from the third century B.C. with a sacred Nandi bull.

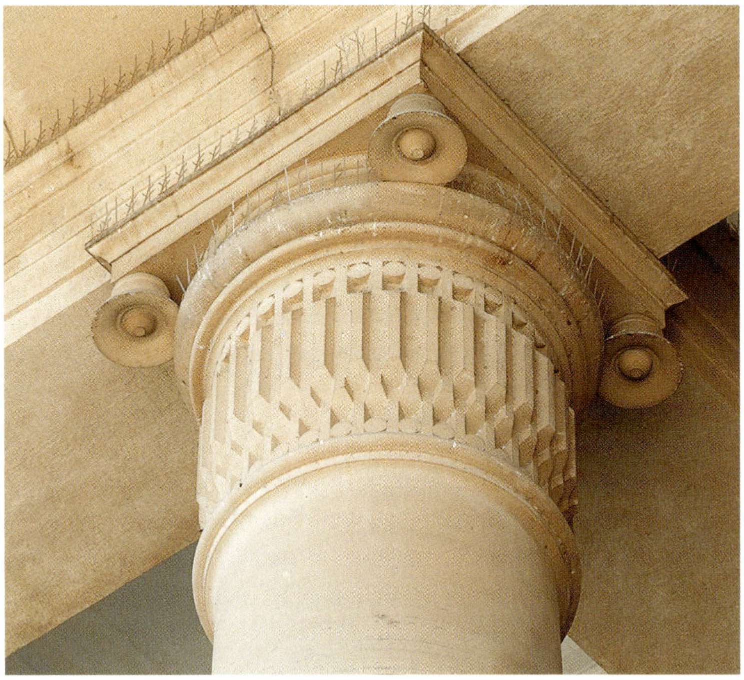

Fig. 163: The capitals of the pillars were developed by Edwin Lutyens especially for Imperial Delhi. The significance of their parts has never been explained.

From today's point of view such meaning may appear blasphemous with regard to the Christian religious affiliations of the Raj. On the other hand, against the background of an undiminished imperial consciousness, every analogy seemed to the Viceroy and his architect to be a demonstration of good will. By the time of the collapse of British rule in India and the entry of the President of the new republic into Viceroy's House, this confident combination of religious symbols and worldly power was sanctioned from an Indian point of view.

The lotus flower

The symbol of the lotus flower often apprears in Viceroy's House. Once at the top of the Jaipur column, where a star grows out of the flower (Fig. 119), and again in the Mughal Garden where four symmetrically arranged fountains each display a hexagonally shaped lotus flower (Fig. 108).

Lakshmi-Shri or Padma is the Lotus goddess and the consort of Vishnu. She represents Vishnu's creative energy: "At the beginning of time (according to the myth of the flowering of the universe), when the waters are to bring forth forms anew, there rises from the navel of Vishnu the golden bud of a lotus, which expands. This cosmic flower is a transformation of a portion of the substance eternally contained within the god's gigantic body. It is an epiphany of those dynamic forces of the creative process, which had been withdrawn into the body (that is to say, into the cosmic waters) at the time of the dissolution. It has now reappeared, to begin its cycle anew; and it will give life again its perennial course. This radiant lotus of the world is the goddess Padma, the *sakti* or divine energy of slumbering Vishnu. She is the awakening of his substance, in dream, as the miracle of life."[91]

Alongside the original connection of the goddess Lakshmi with Vishnu, the lotus flower also appeared later in Hinduism in association with Brahma as "the anthropomorphic symbol of Brahman, the essence of the universe, the cosmic, anonymous Self." The Buddha also is almost always depicted sitting on a lotus flower since the third century, and the lotus position has increasingly become a symbol of divine origin as well as enlightenment: "In Mahayana Buddhism, on the other hand, the lotus seat became a standard element, used as a matter of course to denote the essentially supramundane character and origin of those Buddhas and Bodhisattvas who, having reached enlightenment, refused to pass into nirvana, but instead remained eternally manifest, rescuing souls from every sphere of the universe by their preaching of the enlightening doctrine."[92]

91 H. Zimmer: op. cit., p. 165.
92 Ibid., p. 180.

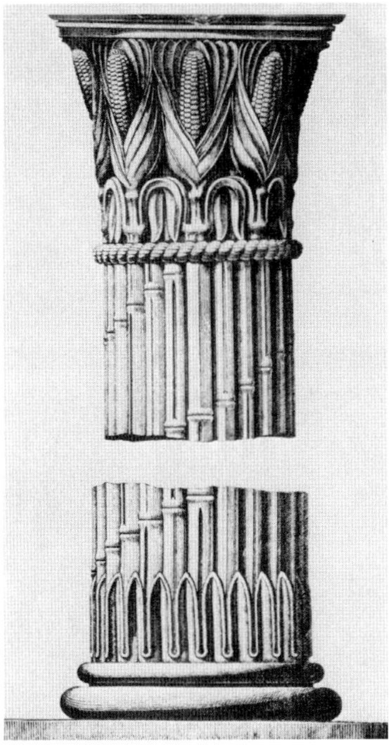

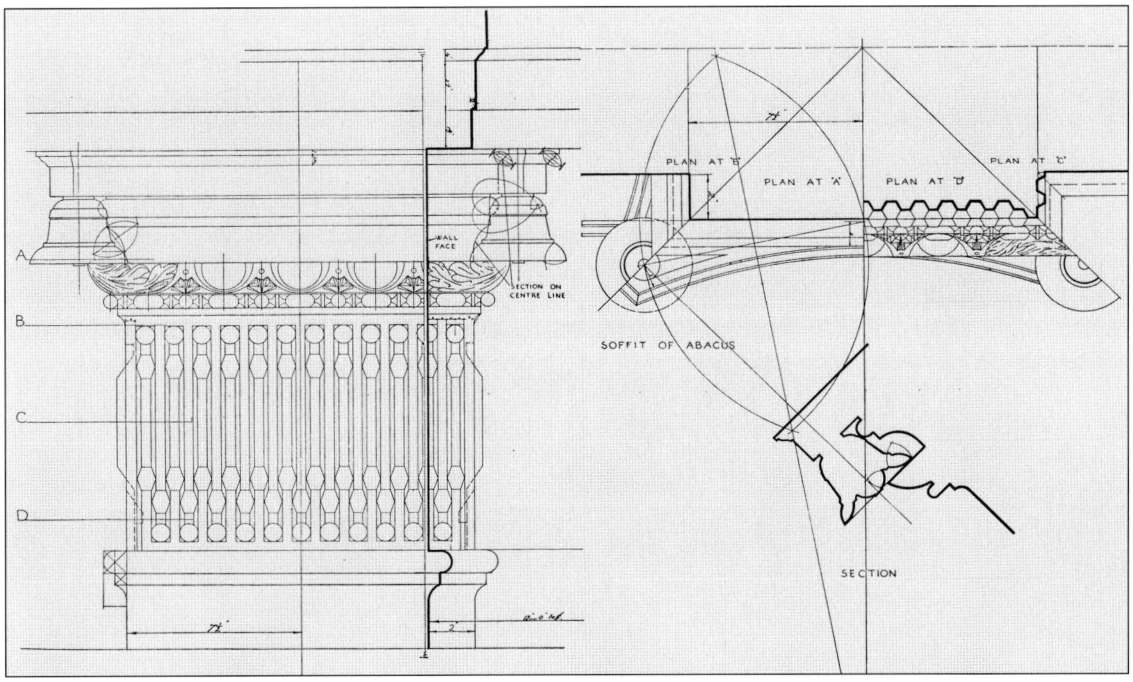

Fig. 164: Elevation of a capital of the "American Order" by Latrobe (1809) for the United States Capitol in Washington, D.C.

Fig. 165: (Right) Ground plan and elevation of a capital of the "Delhi Order" by Lutyens (1914) for Viceroy's House in Imperial Delhi.

In the case of the lotus flower it was not only the beautiful shape which appealed to Lutyens and which prompted him to adopt this Hindu and Buddhist symbol into the formal language of Viceroy's House. It was the association with Indian high culture and symbolic power that assured the lotus flower a place in the imperial palace.

The pillars of the portico of Viceroy's House

Edwin Lutyens very rarely wrote about his own architecture. More than 2,500 letters to his wife, Lady Emily, contain a great deal of information about his everyday life, his professional disputes, and his amusing experiences, but little in the way of his own architectural theory. It comes as no surprise that he made no mention of two of the greatest architectural mysteries in Viceroy's House. The first is the question of the significance of the stupa shape as a dome on the Durbar Hall, and the second is the significance of the capitals that he designed specifically for the portico of this building. Lutyens did not want to refer back to the three Neo-Classical orders (Doric, Ionic and Corinthian) because they had no discernible connection with either the British Empire or with India. He decided on the design of an individual "Delhi Order," as Latrobe had already done for Washington, D.C. in the United States. Whereas Latrobe, at the beginning of the nineteenth century, had incorporated into his capital of the "American Order" the corn cob and the tobacco plant as typical motifs from the southern states, now, at the beginning of the twentieth century, Lutyens chose the Hindu motif of the temple bell: "The capital, at least, is a wholly new invention arrived at after weeks of labour. It is again a kind of synthesis – and one of the usual acanthus leaf type, but strained and restrained to a much greater abstraction while it is, at the same time, touched with an Indian note in its angle bells. There is a prototype of these, in the form of moulded drops, to be found on the columns of the Jaina temple at Moodbidri, and the cultivated bell-form took on a symbolic meaning."[93]

This obvious explanation did not, however, come from the architect himself. According to his son, he once explained the motifs and specific shapes of his plan: "The late Duke of Connaught, who visited Viceroy's House during the building, asked father why he had hung bells from the tops of the columns. Why? – Indeed, why? What reply is possible to such a question? – A question promoted by slightly condemnatory curiosity. How to explain in any communicable terms the treatment of some one factor of design: the joint issue of experience and of something far more personal? Father would never dream of dealing harshly with the

93 A.S.G. Butler: op. cit., p. 35.

ignorant, and would hesitate to give unnecessary offence to useful patronage. In this instance he besought his wit for an answer; and so the legend grew. 'Did you never hear, Sir, of the Mogul superstition that the ringing of bells proclaimed the end of the dynasty?' he asked. 'That is why my bells are made of stone.' The Duke was delighted with the loyalty of the conceit. The rest who heard it were not to know that so circumspect a fiction was without foundation in fact."[94]

The capital developed by Lutyens pleased him so much that he used it again in New Delhi outside Viceroy's House, and in the following decades it also found its way into his plans for the British Embassy in Washington, D.C., Liverpool Cathedral and a grand building at Pall Mall in London.

The Mughal doorways

Like Lutyens, Herbert Baker was also at the mercy of the Viceroy's constant desire to include Indian architectural forms and in this he tried his best. Elephants support the roofs of his pavilions; Hindu overhanging arches terminate many of his entrances (Fig. 133), and Islamic stone lattice work separates external areas in the style of that at Humayun's Tomb in Delhi and the Taj Mahal in Agra.

He took particular care in designing the two main entrances of the Secretariats as seen from Government Court (Fig. 167). In their construction, they are identical with the doorway in front of Humayun's Tomb though rejecting and replacing the Islamic keel arches with western round arches. All the architects of Imperial Delhi were in agreement over the rejection of the keel arch. After all, neither Palladio nor Christopher Wren had ever chosen this kind of arch. The Viceroy was unable to win a single case against the united opponents of the keel arch. Lutyens informed inquirers who were less well-educated than the Viceroy that God had not made the rainbow as a keel arch, but as a round arch.

The shape of the main entrances of the Secretariats, like the construction of the gates (nashiman) of the Humayun Tomb, are direct successors to the deep portal arch of Persia, which again has its prototype in the Neo-Classical exedra common to the Roman bath.

The chattris, chajjas and jaalis of Mughal architecture

Lutyens and Baker were more willing to compromise in the case of the Mughal pavilions or chattris than in the case of the keel arch. An imperial architecture determined by large forms was the very place for these stone pavilions to appear as a welcome stylistic element for the transition to detailed architectural shapes. Thus, chattris are not only found on the tambour of the dome above the Durbar Hall, but also on Baker's domes on the Secretariats.

The chattris mark every imaginable corner and axis thus allowing little room for the Viceroy's criticism. Lutyens even drafted two Mughul chattris, which were never executed (Fig. 50), in front of the gigantic All India War Memorial. In his early sketches for the Viceroy's Palace Lutyens also added windows with keel arches and Mughal chattris. Ultimately, the keel arches were dropped, but the Mughal chattris remained (Fig. 2).

On the subject of the chajjas, which Lutyens as well as Baker frequently used on the facades, Baker explained in his memoirs: "There was wide approval of the general principle advocated in my letter to the *Times* to design in accordance with the eternal principles of the ordered beauty of classical architecture and to graft on appropriate features of Indian architecture. Such we considered were the chajja, the wide projecting shade-giving stone slabs for a cornice – some at the Delhi palace projected seven feet and even more from the wall, and that has made a distinction of all our Delhi buildings. These not only protect the walls and windows from the high sun, but also from any but driving rain, and thus allow the open window."[95]

On the use of the jaalis, Baker continued: "We also made great use of another valuable feature, the pierced stone lattices or window screens called jaalis, on which the old Indian craftsman exhibited his skill in intricate geometrical, and sometimes floral, patterns. They admit the air but not the high sun."[96]

94 R. Lutyens: *Sir Edwin Lutyens, An Appreciation in Perspective*, London, n.d., p. 76.
95 H. Baker: op. cit., p. 71.

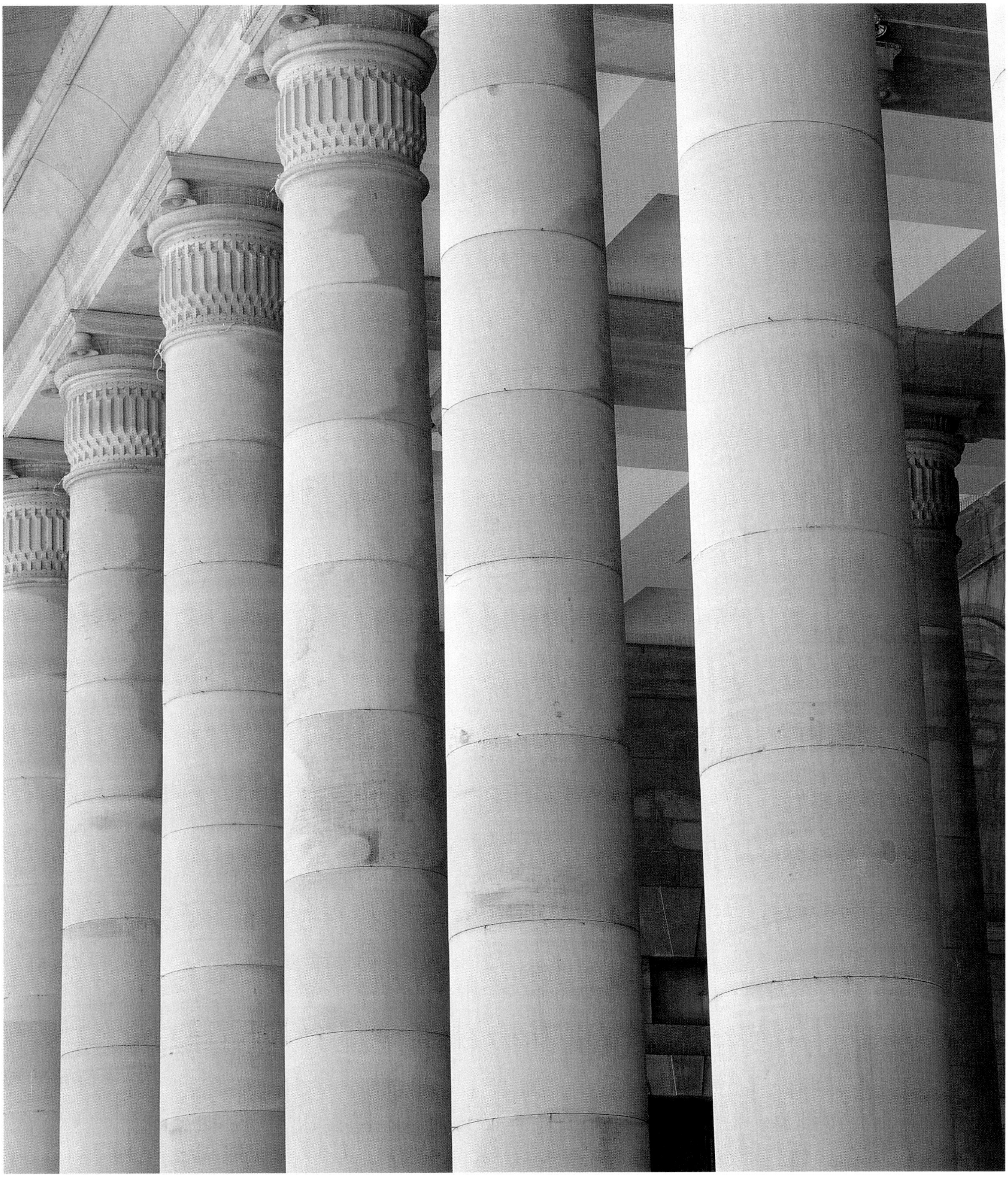

Fig. 166: The unusual height of the portico in front of Viceroy's House underlines the Emperor of India's claim to power.

In many details of his plan for the Secretariats, Herbert Baker tried to accommodate the Viceroy's desire to incorporate Indian motifs. One such opportunity offered itself in his search for the most awe-inspiring entrance for the two Secretariats. His first choice, a portico with a broad protruding staircase was out of the question. Here, this Neo-Classical entranceway would have the effect of a poor copy of the entrance to Viceroy's House.

Herbert Baker, in his expeditions through Delhi's landscapes littered with old mausoleums, finally hit upon an entrance motif which was hardly inferior to those of Classical Antiquity and the Renaissance: the entrance building to Humayun's Tomb from the sixteenth century combined all the elements of Mughal architecture in a grand gateway. Baker took over this model, but replaced the keel arch (that seemed inappropriate to him) with the western motif of the round arch (Fig. 167). The result was a completely novel two-storied entrance derived from varying sources that made a dignified impression on the visitor. Later, in his memoirs, Baker mentioned these unique entrances in Imperial Delhi: "The central entrances on the garden-court side are through high vaulted exedras which are such distinguished features of the Taj Mahal and other famous mausoleums of the Mogul emperors. The openings at the back of the exedras and in the great halls are filled with pierced stone jaalis and right through them can be seen fascinating traceried vistas, as in the Mogul tombs."[97]

96 Ibid., p. 71.
97 Ibid., p. 68.

Fig. 167: In accordance with the wishes of the Viceroy, Herbert Baker adopted a Mughal style for the entrances for the Secretariats. (Left) Entrance to Humayun's Tomb in Delhi, 1565. (Right) Entrance to the northern Secretariat, 1927. The architects all agreed, however, upon rejecting Islamic keel arches.

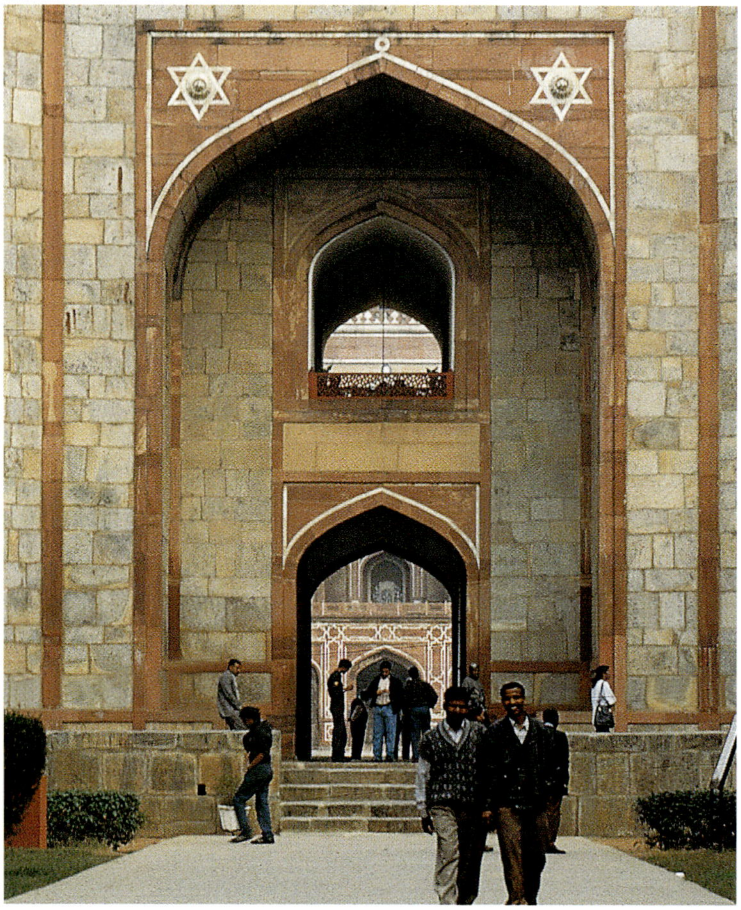

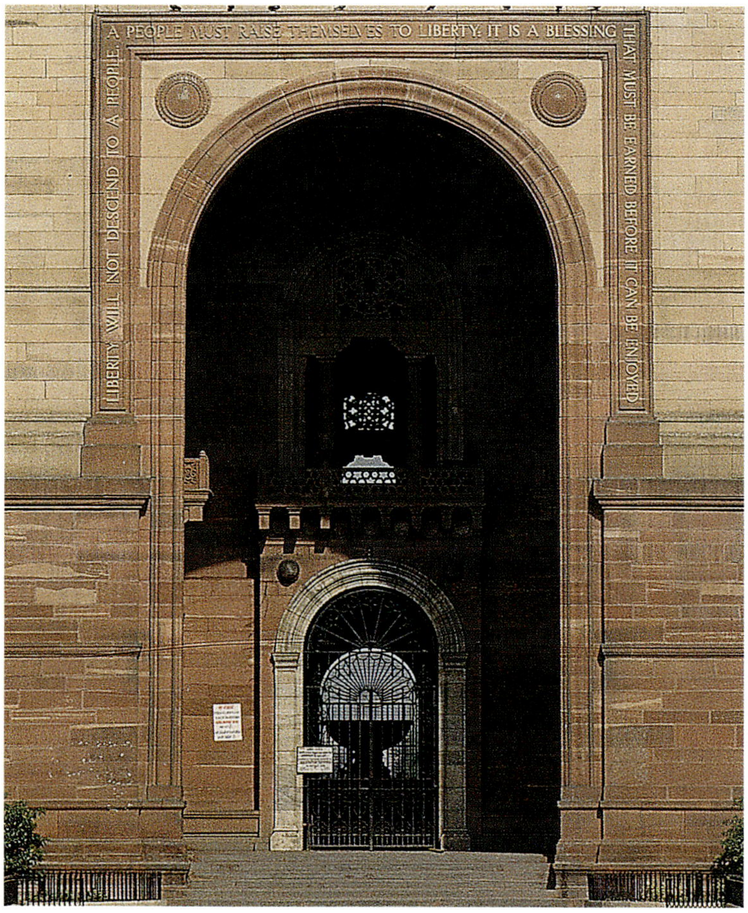

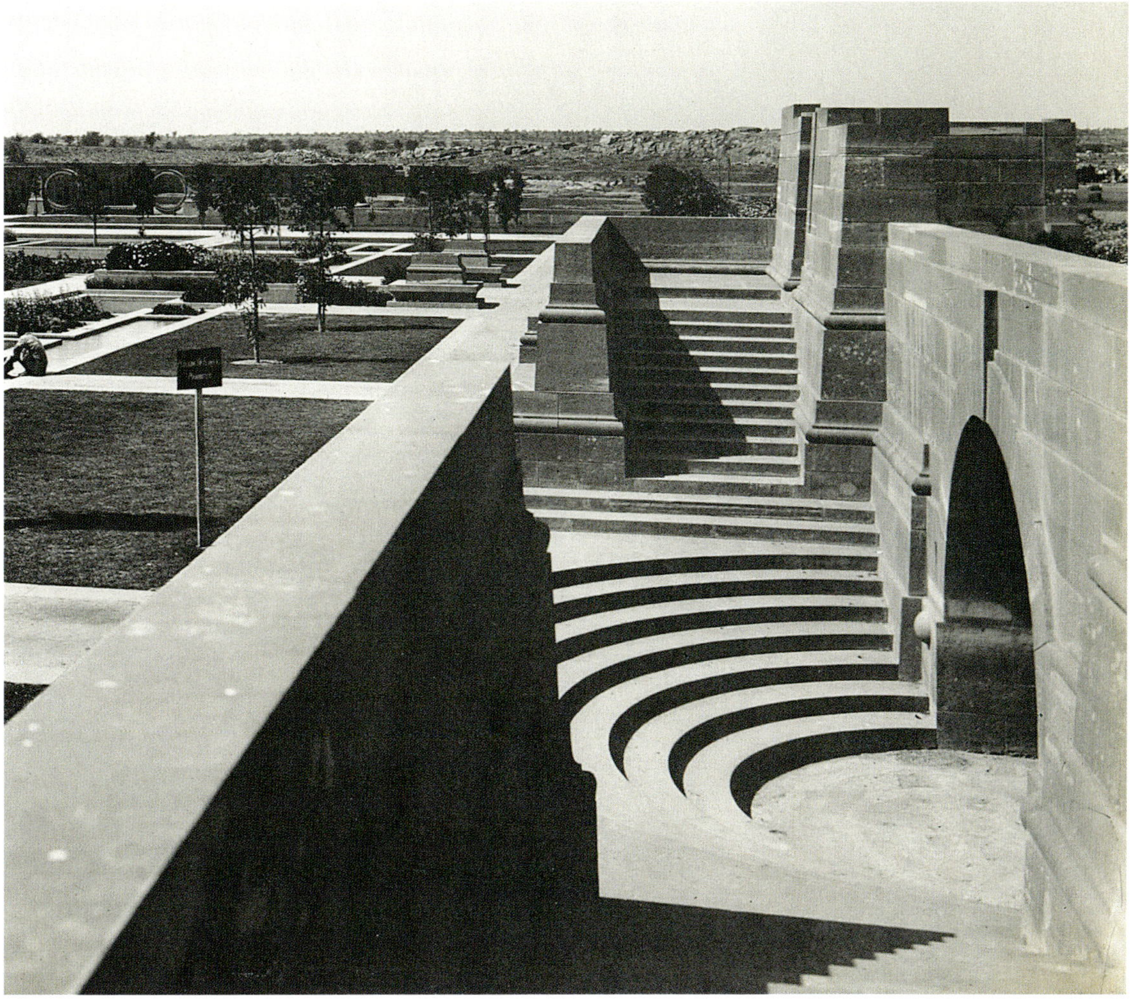

Fig. 168: Entrance to the fountain in the North Fort Garden; historic photograph, c. 1930.

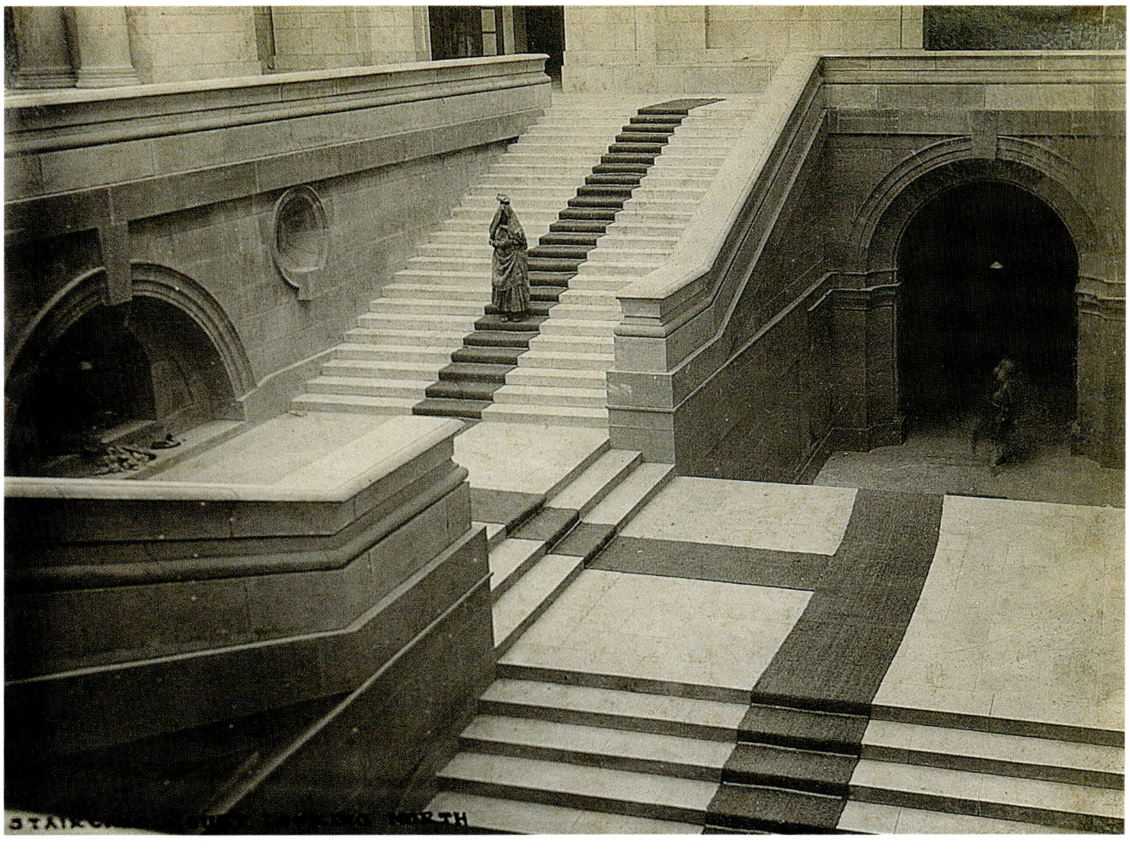

Fig. 169: The open staircase in Viceroy's House; historic photograph, c. 1930.

Fig. 170: Lutyens' desire to experiment with symbolic geometrical forms knew no boundaries.

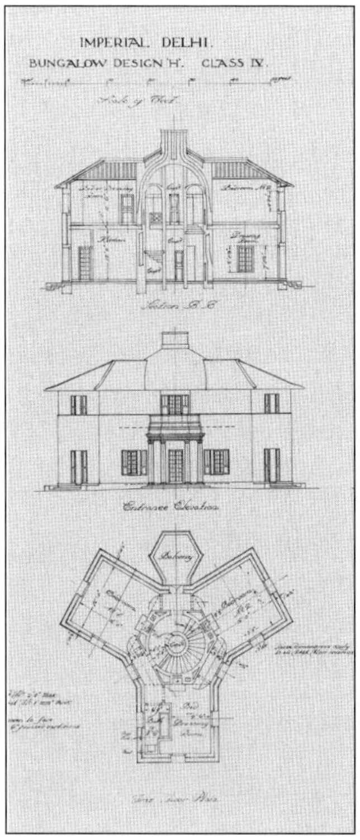

Triangle: accommodation for the servants of the Viceroy, Imperial Delhi.

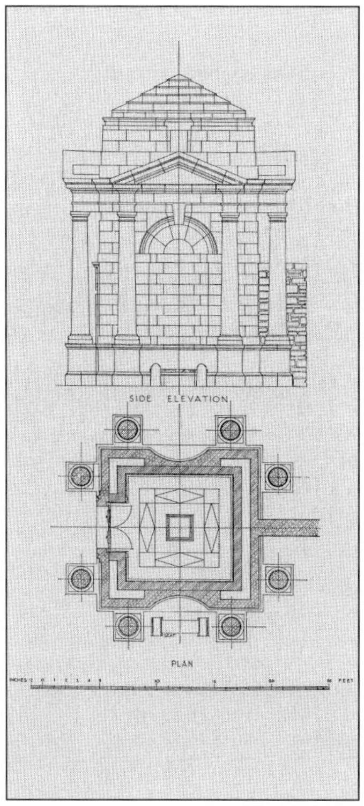

Rectangle: Irish National War Memorial, Book Rooms.

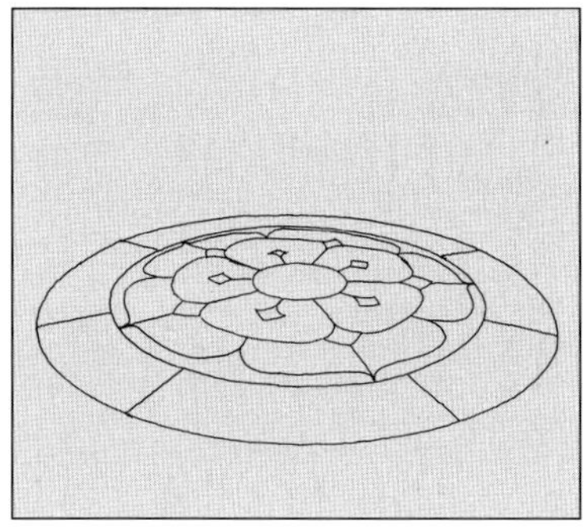

Pentagram: floor pattern in the vestibule of the Durbar Hall, Viceroy's House, Imperial Delhi.

3.5 All Just a Game with Traditional Topoi and Geometric Forms?

The wealth of forms and symbols in Imperial Delhi inevitably leads to the question of whether the architects here were not playing a fanciful game with traditional topoi and with fashionable geometric forms. With regard to the topoi, it is clear from the last chapter that Indian symbolic forms generally are not used indiscriminately, but in a clearly comprehensible and purposeful way. The Nandi stands in the mandappam of Viceroy's House, the elephants, as cousins of the clouds, promise rain and give symbolic support to the "World Mountain" of the British Empire, the Naga snakes watch over the life-giving element of water and the lotus flower marks the seat of cosmic, universal power.

But it remains difficult to explain precisely why a Buddhist stupa forms the dome over the Durbar Hall and why stone walls built in exactly the same style as those two-thousand-year-old walls that mark Buddhist shrines, now surround the "holy realm" of British rule. The architect made no comment. In the many books written since the construction of Viceroy's House, none of the authors finds a plausible, or even a less plausible reason for a formal infringement of this kind.

With the knowledge we have, we can only assume that for Lutyens, the shape of a stupa was as attractive a proposition for the unconventional presentation of a dome, as were the Buddhist stone walls, especially since, enlarged to an imperial scale, they created the perfect motif for the impressive enclosure of the administrative area.

Eclecticism should not be criticized in art and architecture since reverting to well-known forms and symbols is a legitimate way for people to describe and shape their world from already familiar formulae. This path only becomes questionable when the formulae and symbols are not at all familiar, and are only employed for the sake of originality. Thus, the question arises whether, in view of the unexpected conceptual flexibility, the symbolic connections made in the previous chapter go too far with the best intentions and in default of reliable records?

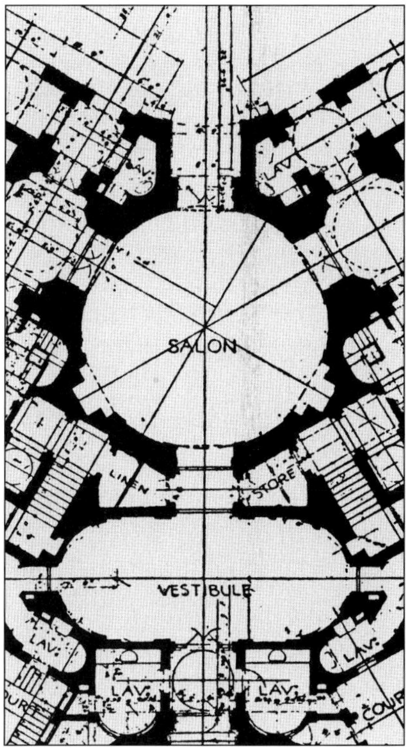

Hexagon: Salon in Baroda House, Imperial Delhi.

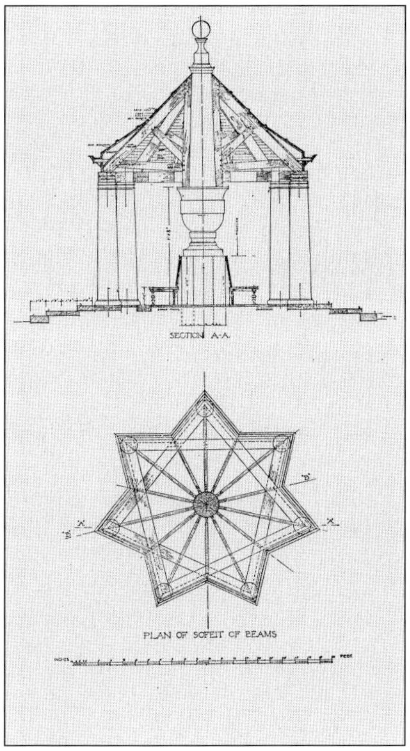

Heptagon: Irish National War Memorial, Temple.

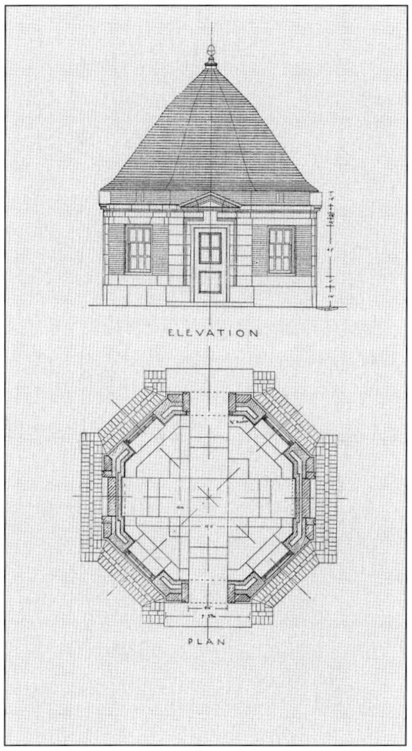

Octagon: Lodges to Egham Entrance, Runnymede.

In Lutyens' architecture and town planning, the expert game with geometric forms also begs further questions. For example, did the comparatively frequent choice of the hexagon and the triangle stem from a whim, or did it arise out of convincing historical reasons? Two possible interpretations are discussed in Chapter 3.1.

A somewhat broader-based view of the building styles of Lutyens is of particular interest: triangle, rectangle, pentagon, hexagon, heptagon, and octagon appear as ground-plan shapes, and square, triangle, and hexagon appear more frequently than the other polygons. What induced the architect to produce a pentagonal lotus flower in the vestibule of the Durbar Hall? Why does the Temple of the Irish National War Memorial have a heptagonal ground-plan?

From what we know, the only answers can be found in the architect's pleasure in experiment, and with his predilection for the unusual and the astonishing as an explanation for the variety of geometric forms. Lutyens only once made reference to these questions in his unpublished writings, but in the final analysis left them open.

Humorously, but also with intense seriousness – and the curious hint (in his references to dignitaries of the Roman Catholic Church) of foresight with which he sometimes chose his words – Lutyens imagined himself as a Pope of Art: "My Cardinals should lay down formulae of beauty as sincere as those laid down for strains and stresses by Engineers. For the only means of solution I see is that some sort of Chair should be founded to search and inquire into the laws of nature's beauty as they affect the eye. I should like to see the curves of tree-stems analysed. The geometry and impulsive forms of crystals, the genial sphere, curves simple and in three dimensions, must be explored, and the facts so obtained be related to the facts known, scientifically or empirically, to architects since Egyptian and Greek times. Codes verified and uttered with authority must influence the critical faculties of the multitudes and give them some consciousness of what they see. Surely God, in His creation, (to small human sense) is blind, a sap within the tree. Yet we, beholding nature, see Him and adore."[98]

98 Christopher Hussey: op. cit., p. 525f.

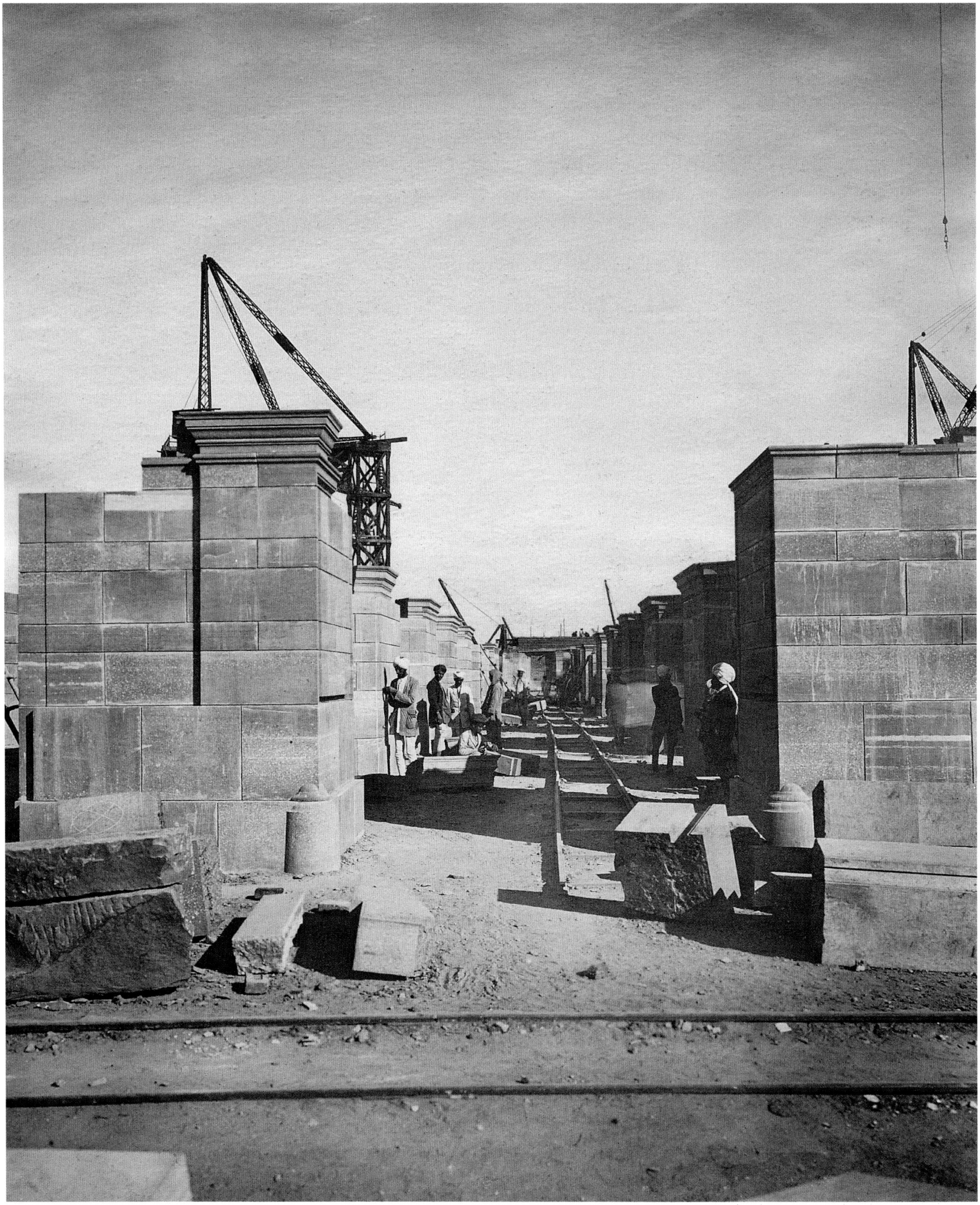

4 Town Plan and Places of Importance in Imperial Delhi

A glance at the history of the founding of towns reveals two basic forms of town plans. Either the new town is laid out in accordance with the particularities of the natural surroundings, such as a merchant town on the bank of a river, or a fort on the summit of a mountain. Or the new town reflects its builders' concept of the order of this world or of the cosmos, such as the Indian town of Jaipur in the pattern of a Hindu Mandala, or the Forbidden City of Peking as a reflection of a concentric, unchanging ruling order.

Unquestionably, Imperial Delhi belongs to this second group. Chapters 3.1 and 3.2 mentioned the way in which the spirit of the age during turn-of-the-century England was moulded by freemasonry as well as the European longing for imperial grandeur. Both influences were factors that determined a strictly hexagonal road network and a colossal axis for processions and parades at its centre.

In a slowly growing settlement, a multitude of successive individual and social decisions determine the cityscape. The foundation of a city such as Imperial Delhi required a consistently grand plan. This was also true for all its secondary functions as well as its system of symbolic elements. The following pages attempt to:

- Give concrete examples of order, symmetry and grandeur as symbolic characteristics of British rule in Delhi.
- Trace the essential secondary functions in the town plan of Imperial Delhi in a sequence of twelve planning stages.

These attempts naturally bring with them the danger of over-simplification and distortion.

Fig. 171: With the simplest technical equipment, the Viceroy's Palace was built to exactly the same size as Buckingham Palace in London.

4.1 Axiality, Symmetry and Size as Symbolic Characteristics of British Rule

Every social community is represented by its buildings, whether it be a Christian community with its churches planned in the shape of a cross, a capitalist economic centre with its skyscrapers, or an absolute monarchy with its centred and symmetrical palaces.

The architects of Imperial Delhi were presented with the rare task of planning an entire city as an image symbolic of the British Empire. Into this bargain, they planned in light of two thousand years of well-documented European architectural history. The British Empire could not be represented by a star-shaped ground plan on the model of Vauban,[1] or by a square ground plan on the model of Bernardo Vittone,[2] or by a strictly hexagonal form after the example of Grammichele.[3] A definite external outline would not be able to reflect the values of British society around the turn of the nineteenth to the twentieth century. Instead, the plan had to be expressed through the forms of construction and their situation in relation to each other. Axiality, symmetry and size were the primary characteristics through which the British Crown represented its imperial claim, its sense of justice, and its military superiority. In this respect, it differed little from French absolutism of the eighteenth century.

Axiality, symmetry and size, however, were only important in Imperial Delhi with regard to government buildings, especially the Viceroy's Palace, and to the central axis of the Empire itself. All other urban functions were grouped according to their purpose around these symbols of political and spiritual power.

1 Sebastian Le Preste de Vauban (1633–1707) built about thirty fortresses and countless defensive walls with a star-shaped ground-plan for his King Louis XIV.

2 Bernardo Vittone (1705–70) with his geometrical town plans especially influenced the town planners in the middle of the seventeenth century in Italy.

3 Grammichele was built at the beginning of the eighteenth century to accommodate refugees from the town of Occhialà in Sicily destroyed by an earthquake.

Fig. 172: A comparison between the size of Viceroy's House (area: 210,430 square feet) with Versailles (area: 198,300 square feet) and the Houses of Parliament in London, Westminster reveals how significant the Raj was for the British crown.

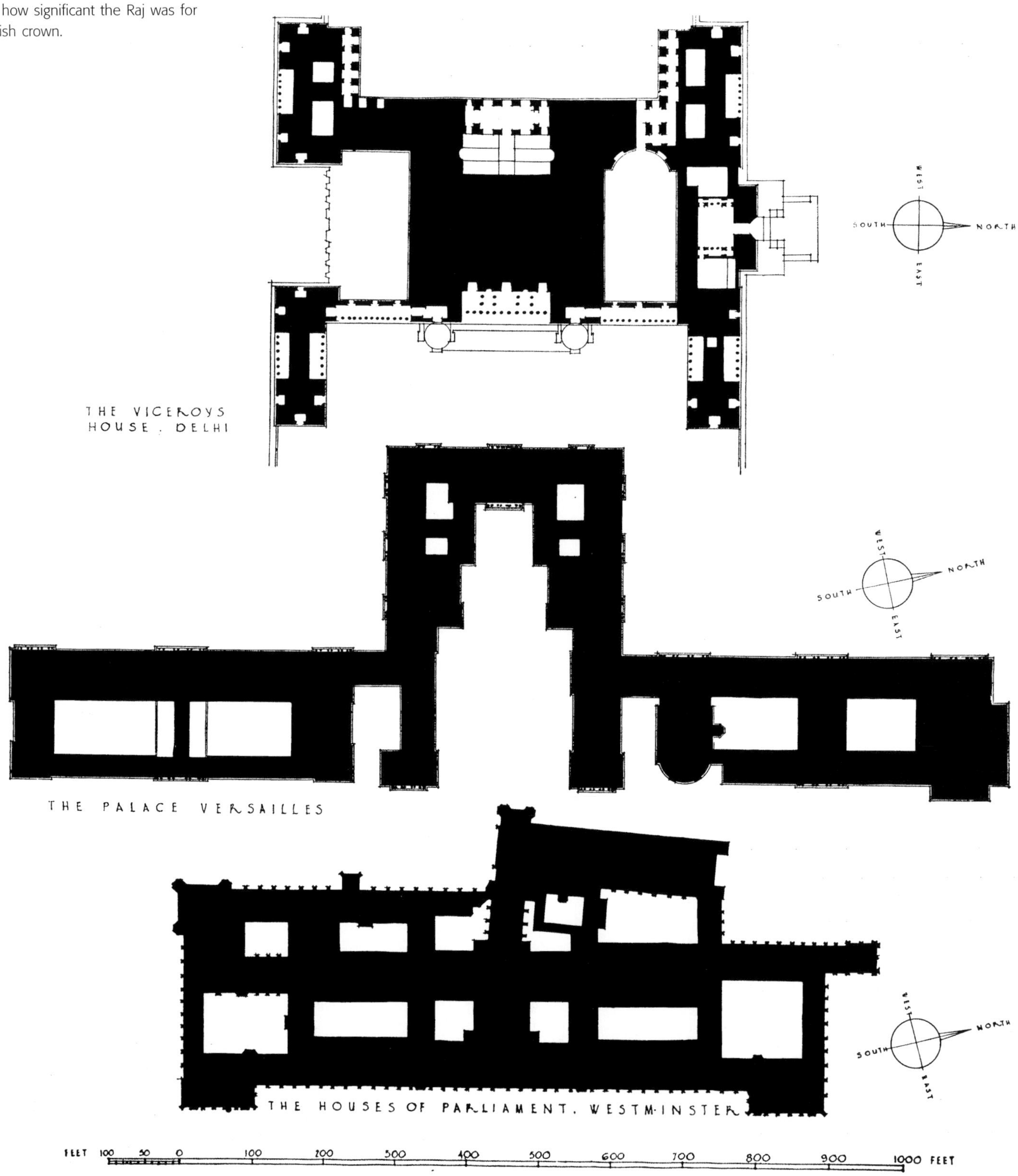

It is no coincidence that the front of Buckingham Palace in London and the facade of Viceroy's House in Delhi share the same width of 630 feet. Furthermore, it was not coincidental when Edwin Lutyens designed a cathedral for Liverpool that, in each of its dimensions, exceeds St Peter's in Rome. There seemed to be no limits for the British Empire.

Axiality, symmetry and size are also encountered as the primary formal characteristics in the architecture and town planning of the thirties in Germany. A typical example mentioned in Chapter 2.7 was Albert Speer's plans for the reshaping of Berlin (see Fig. 49). The obvious parallels and similarities between Speer's plan for a new north-south axis in Berlin with a domed hall at one end and a triumphal arch near the other, and King's Way in Imperial Delhi with the dome of the Durbar Hall at one end and the All India War Memorial near the other end, leave us baffled.

The political systems are certainly not comparable even if both wallow in imperial dreams. As a conceptual way out of the dilemma, one might assume that neither in Delhi nor in Berlin is it a matter of the architectural representation of absolute power structures, but merely of similar misunderstandings of the idea behind the Champs Elysées. Or are both town plans carefully thought-out symbols of the merciless consciousness of imperial mission?

Fig. 173: Size was of great importance in the globally aware and active British Empire. Its importance is apparent in a comparison of size used by Edwin Lutyens between St Peter's in Rome, St Paul's in London, and Lutyens' plan for a cathedral in Liverpool.

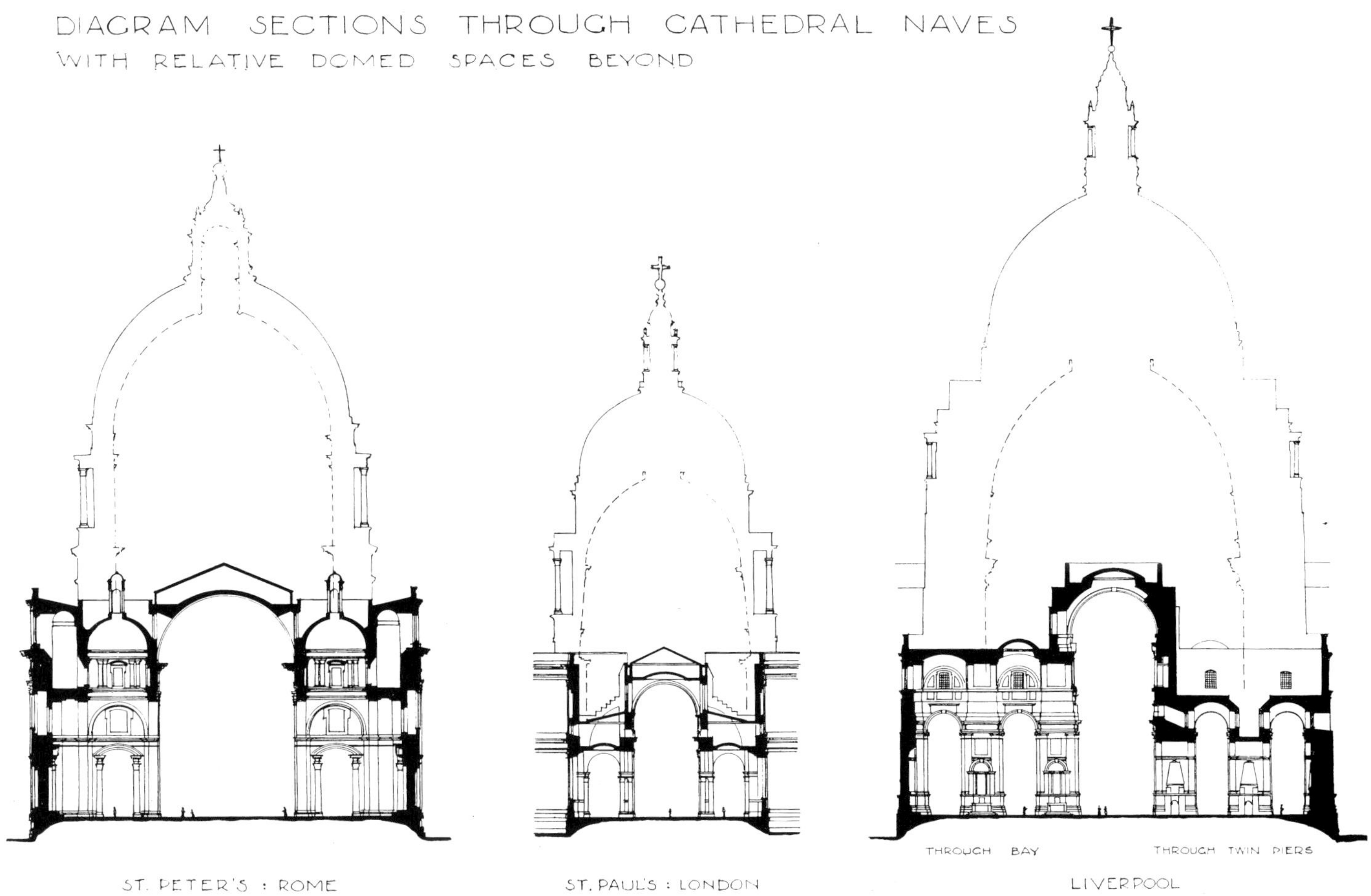

4.2 Basic Conditions and Stages in the Design of Imperial Delhi

The search for a suitable location for the new seat of government near or directly adjoining old Delhi developed into a complex process in which the most varied points of view had to be taken into consideration. Although neither the King in London, nor his India Office intervened from the first draft in July, 1912, to the final plan in March, 1913 (cf. Option 12 on page 207). The experts and the press ensured there would be a rigorous and controversial public debate. This process can – with some admissible generalizations – be represented as a sequence of twelve stages, in which the decision-making process regarding the precise site of the new city as well as that of its essential urban characteristics did not proceed in a linear path, but swayed back and forth.

Option 1: "Champs Elysées" on the North Malcha Site from Government House towards Jama Masjid

In 1912, after the first intensive investigative phase for the three members of the Delhi Town Planning Committee – G.S.C. Swinton (Chairman), John A. Broadie and Edwin Lutyens – the architect, Lutyens, wrote in a letter to his wife: "We have started our preliminary report of the choice of site. This will be a weary quarrelsome affair as Swinton likes embroidery words which mean nothing but Montmorency[4] is all right and will write it and keep us straight. The site is settled and is published – south of Delhi near Malcha. It is a beautiful site – aspects, altitude, water, health, virgin soil etc. right and views across old Delhi and that wilderness of ruined tombs that form the remains of the seven older Delhis."[5]

Ultimately, having studied many other options, the initial considerations of the Delhi Town Planning Committee were established regarding the decision of the site and shape of the new capital: "The origins of the new Delhi of 1931, in its general plan, lay in the tentative layout of the Delhi Town Planning Committee, a design in which the North Malcha site served as a crucial anchor for the central axis of the plan. The principal avenue, designated AB on the tentative layout, ran due northeast from Government House, its long uninterrupted vista crowned by the white domes and spiky minarets of the Jama Masjid, the largest mosque in India. The road followed the inclination of the ground, so that the avenue assumed a slightly concave form in a longitudinal direction, rising by easy gradients to the terminal features, 'somewhat,' the Committee noted, 'on the lines of Champs Elysées in Paris.' (This was not to be the only time a comparison with that famed boulevard would be invoked at Delhi.) At the point where the main avenue was intersected by a line due north from the Jantar Mantar observatory, a low summit served to emphasize a circus introduced at that juncture, a direct antecedent of the present Connaught Place. This vista from Government House to the great Mughal mosque, integral to the earliest conception of the new capital, was preserved in all succeeding plans."[6]

Under the heading *Buildings and Architecture* Lanchester explained in detail the plans being presented: "There can be no question that all buildings in the extension of, or in close proximity to, existing Delhi should be Indian in style. I do not consider that they need necessarily follow the Mogul taste, which is inclined to be too fantastic for modern views, and certainly lacks, to the European mind, a sense of niceties of proportion.

The typical architecture of the earlier Mohammedan periods embodying, as it does, some of the Hindu traditions is in my opinion more restrained and more flexible, while it does not preclude in any way the employment of the capable Indian craftsman for the decorative ornament in which his traditions give him such facility.

The employment of the Indian architect is a more difficult question. Up to the present it is rare to find an Indian who has qualified himself to take entire responsibility of the design and control of important work, and I am inclined to think that the best course would be to retain a competent English architect to exercise these functions and to associate with him such Indian architects who had proved themselves capable of handling Indian architectural forms, and who might, under sympathetic guidance, advance in knowledge of constructional, sanitary and

4 Sir G.F. de Montmorency, secretary and technical adviser of the Delhi Town Planning Committee.

5 Letter of Edwin Lutyens to his wife dated June 9, 1912, in: C. Percy and J. Ridley: *The Letters of Edwin Lutyens to his Wife Lady Emily*, London 1985, p. 253.

6 R.G. Irving: *Indian Summer*, New Haven and London 1981, p. 56.

economic requirements. These Indian architects might in the meantime be valuable as intermediaries between the English building director and the Indian craftsmen."[7]

Option 2: Lanchester's initial layout: Extension of the Indian City

"Lanchester's scheme, elaborated in his second report to the Viceroy under the heading 'The Extension of the Indian City,' provided for wholesale markets for grain and wood, factories and godowns or warehouses on land adjoining the railway lines, and bazaars conveniently close to the residential quarters. The plans incorporated several classes of dwellings, from 3,000-square-foot houses to ten-square-foot, one-room adobe units for the poor. Lanchester, by his own admission, accepted existing Indian traditions. His design denoted sanitary rather than social reforms: sweepers, leatherworkers, brickworkers, and limeburners – the pariahs or untouchable caste – were placed on the outskirts of town, while weavers, cotton stampers, washermen, daily laborers, and keepers of cattle plying for hire were considered 'respectable neighbours.' A progressive feature of the layout was the reservation of open spaces throughout the various districts, to furnish 'adequate aeration' for the more compactly built residences. Sites were set aside for mosques, temples, and a thana, or police station. The gridiron pattern of the contemplated extension comprised five grades of road: a few wide avenues for aesthetic and utilitarian reasons, with the remaining subsidiary streets in proportion to the actual requirements of traffic, lest initial costs and, especially, later maintenance be unnecessarily extravagant."[8]

In this report, Lanchester also reaffirmed his point of view on the desired architectural style: "In my opinion all buildings should be in the Indian vernacular style, as the intrusion of any in the European manner would be destructive to the harmonious effect of the city as a whole. This vernacular being less markedly developed in Delhi than in many other Indian cities, encouragement should be offered to skilled craftsmen to migrate from other districts in order to secure a high quality of design and workmanship which Delhi at present lacks. Probably the best course would be the establishment of a Government Workshop for stone and wood carving with an Art Director (Indian), and a Business Manager. This workshop would be in a better position to obtain supplies of material than the private individual, and could also guarantee permanent employment to skilled craftsmen. It would also, by a system of apprenticeship, ensure the maintenance of a good standard of work on traditional lines."[9]

Option 3: Lanchester's "Revised Layout"

In his "Revised Layout," Lanchester managed to avoid a series of inadequacies recognized in the previous plan. For example, there were some Hindu temples in the location he had planned for a round plaza on the model of the Circus in Bath. Lanchester could not make a detour around them by bending the great avenues because the direct view from Viceroy's House to Jama Masjid would have been lost. He could not simply tear them down without risking massive opposition from Hindus. The great plaza was extended so that the temples were situated at its centre.

Lanchester took the Viceroy's stated aversion to rectangular road networks in the style of military cantonments into consideration by placing greater emphasis on circular and radial roads. Lanchester overlooked one thing: to realize this street plan he would have had to demolish or incorporate one of the small number of settlements on the plain southwest of the old town of Delhi. The settlement of Pahanganj could not be incorporated because the cramped layout of the village was incompatible with the grand avenues of Imperial Delhi. Nevertheless, the British Crown could hardly acquire and demolish this settlement because an early first estimate indicated property costs as high as £ 180,000.

7 DELHI, First Report of H.V. Lanchester, p. 5.
8 R.G. Irving: op. cit., p. 58
9 DELHI, Second Report of H.V. Lanchester, p. 5.

Following pages: The plan for Imperial Delhi was drafted in twelve stages for which Lord Hardinge, Edwin Lutyens, Henry Vaughan Lanchester and Herbert Baker were the main participants. Interim results were presented by the Delhi Planning Committee to the Viceroy and to the Secretary of State for India, Lord Crewe.

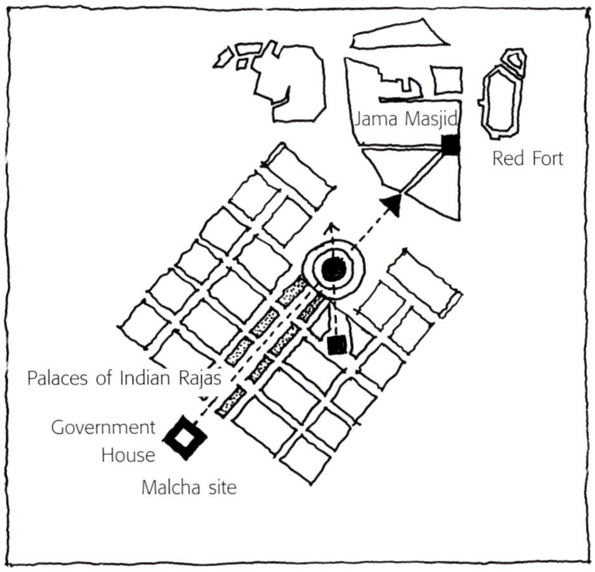

Option 1: "Champs Elysees" on North Malcha Site from Government House towards Jama Masjid
(see Note by His Excellency July 16, 1912)

- Section of Avenue AB slightly concave form in the longitudinal direction somewhat on the lines of Champs Elysees in Paris
- Palaces of Indian Rajas lined up between Government House and a large Circus
- View from Government House to India's largest mosque is the key theme
- Viceroy objected to frequent right-angle intersections, similar to normal layout of grid-pattern cantonments and civil stations in India

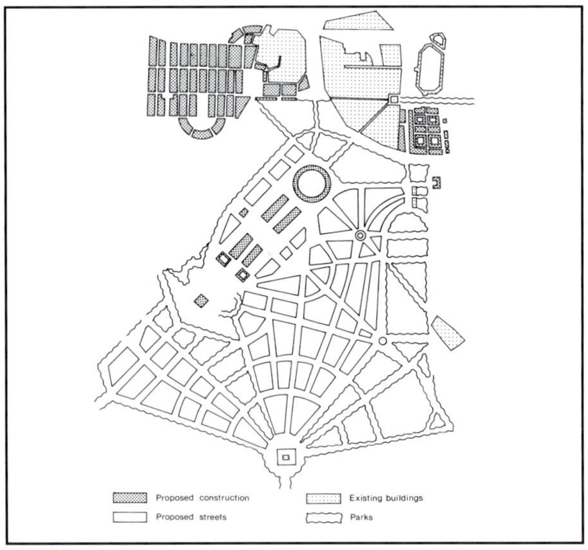

Option 2: Lanchester's initial layout: Extension of the Indian City
(from July 1912)

- Introduction of a cross-axial plaza with two Secretariat blocks in order to avoid a too long main avenue
- Preservation of large areas with historical landmarks as an Archaeological Parc
- Curved streets similar to Regent Street in London to unfold variety
- Gridiron pattern for Indian residential and commercial zone
- Systematically providing open spaces for "adequate aeration"

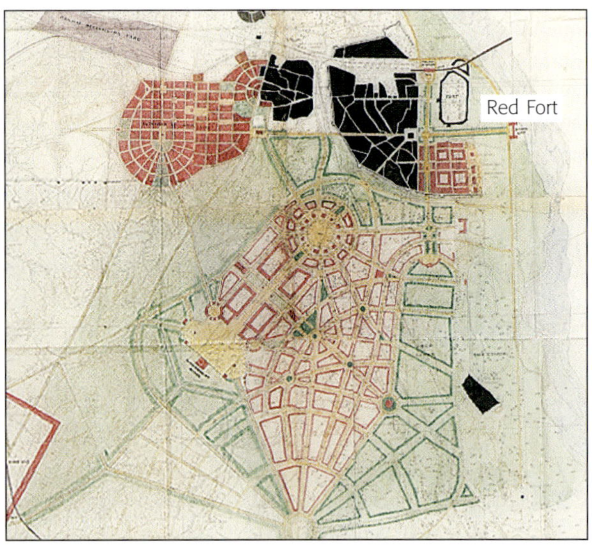

Option 3: Lanchester's "Revised layout"
(also from July 1912)

- Enlarged Circus at the end of main avenue
- Curved streets for the Indian residential and commercial zone
- Village of Pahanganj, across which the main avenue would lead, would incur cost of about £ 180,000 plus transplanting its 15,000 inhabitants

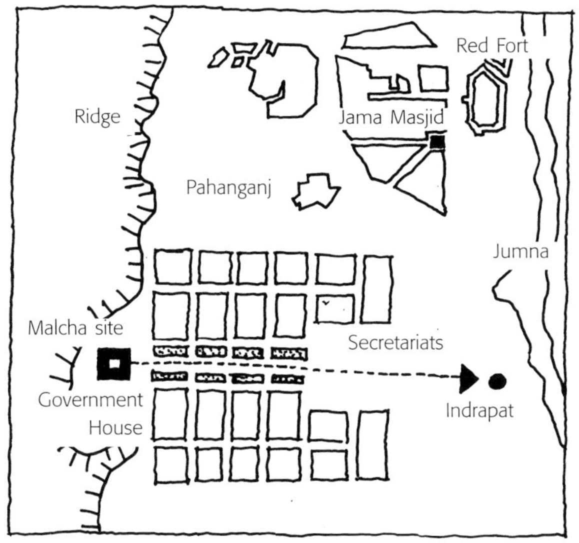

Option 4: Hardinge's suggestion to avoid expensive expropriation of houseowners of Pahanganj
(from August 1, 1912)
– Turn the main axis of the plan 45 degrees southeast towards the ancient fortress of Indrapat (earlier preference of Lord Hardinge anyway)

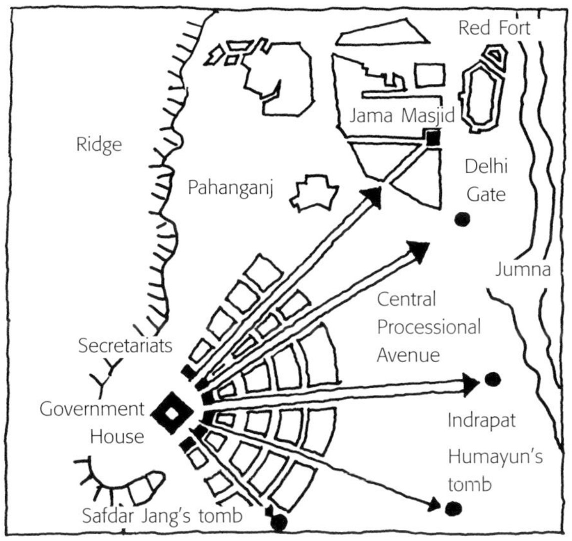

Option 5: Lanchester's "Second revised layout"
(from September 1912)
– Three avenues radiating from Government House (instead of one gigantic one), one towards Jama Masjid, a second towards Indrapat and a third towards Delhi Gate
– Subsidiary avenues to Safdar Jang's tomb and Humayun's tomb
– Design did not fulfil Lord Hardinge's standards "of taste and convenience" with too many curving roads
– Lord Hardinge also felt that the suggested six Secretariats might give undue publicity to activities in front of the Viceregal residence

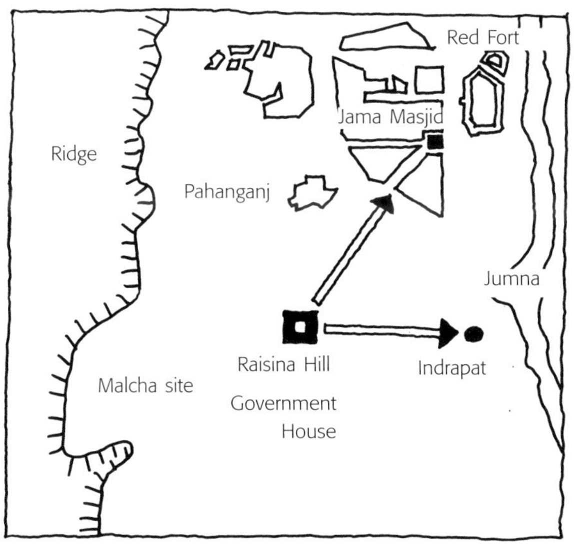

Option 6: Hardinge's "Most beautiful site of all is Raisina Hill"
(from December 8, 1912)
– Move of Government House to back of Raisina Hill (and turn it to face East) thus dominating the entire city
– Lord Hardinge: "I will not listen to any (further) suggestions of Malcha, which is (a site) far too distant"
– Necessary afforestation of Rainina Hill is decidedly possible according to the forest officer consulted

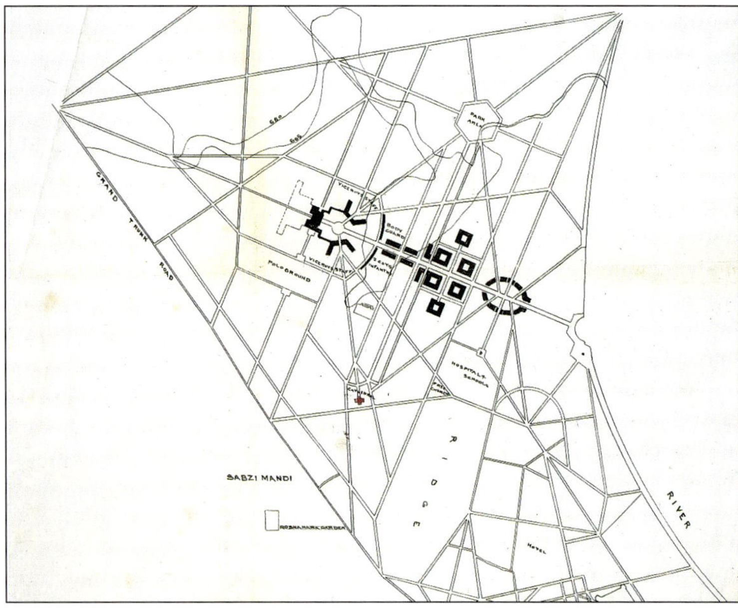

Option 7: Another effort at the Northern Site, "Layout A"
(upon request of Lord Hardinge on January 18, 1913)

- Press campaign in Britain and India for selection of the Northern site forces Lord Hardinge to reconsider his clear preference
- Herbert Baker also argues in favour of a "Via Sacra" on the Northern site
- Result: triangular plan with main avenue northwest to southeast taking up elements of earlier options, e.g. Lanchester's suggestions
- Main avenue leads from Government House to Jumna River with six Secretariats and one Circle defining its rhythm

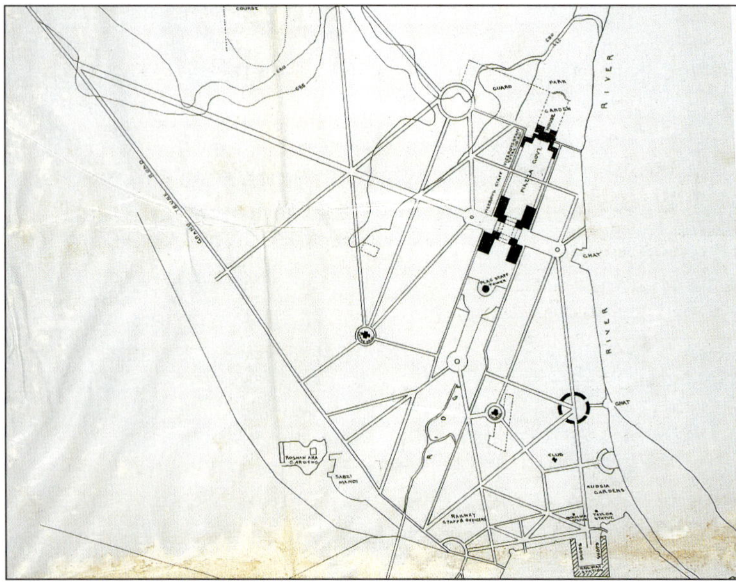

Option 8: Another plan for the Northern Site, "Layout B"
(presented to Lord Hardinge on February 25, 1913)

- Simplified plan with the main avenue in a northeast to southwest direction
- Obviously intended as the 'weaker option' with little effort made regarding a logically consistent street network

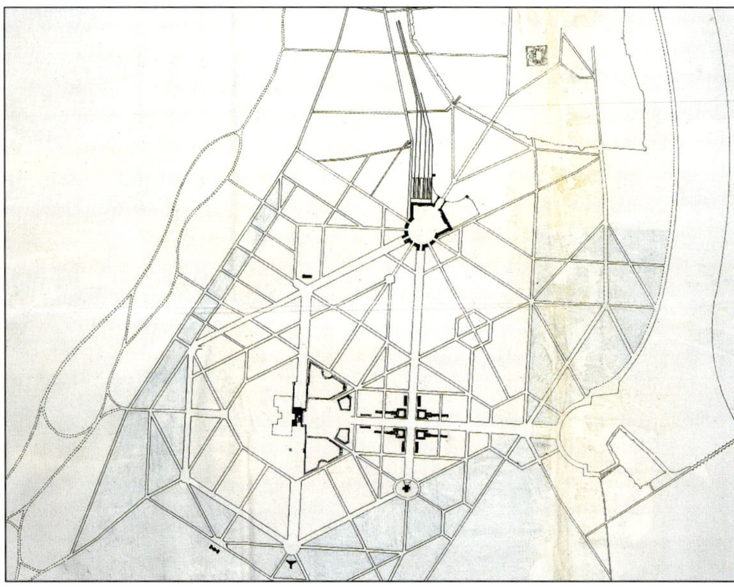

Option 9: Lutyens' new effort for the Southern Site with Government House alone on Raisina Hill
(presented to Lord Hardinge on February 27, 1913)

- Government House back to Raisina Hill
- A street network with all the qualities of the "Layout A" for the Northern site, but now stretching from Raisina Hill to the Jumna River in the East
- Large commercial Circle and train station at the northern end of a cross-axis

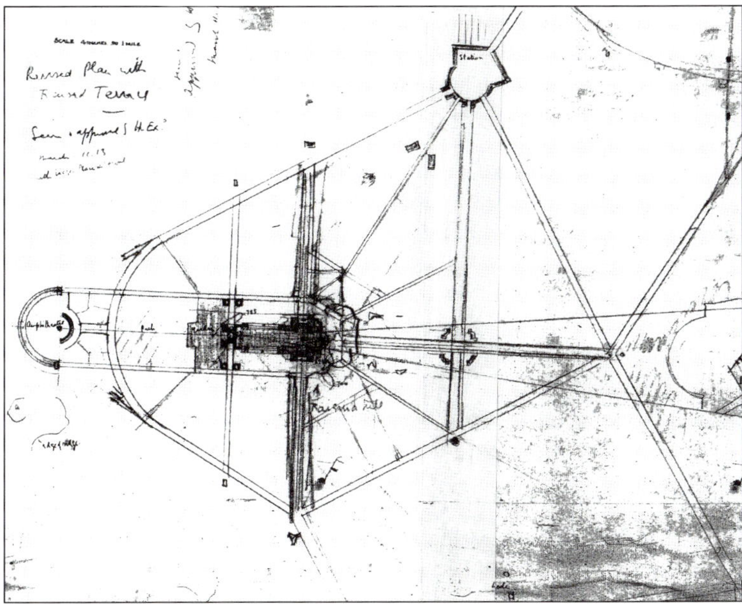

Option 10: Joint effort of Lutyens and Baker with Secretariats joining the Government House on Raisina Hill
(seen and approved by H. Ex. March 10, 1913)

– Main characteristics identical with Lutyens' suggestion from February 27, 1913 except for the new location of the Secretariats on Raisina Hill next to the Government House
– Government House (later: Viceroy's House) moved back in order to allow for sufficient space for the two Secretariats
– Government House looses its view of Jama Masjid

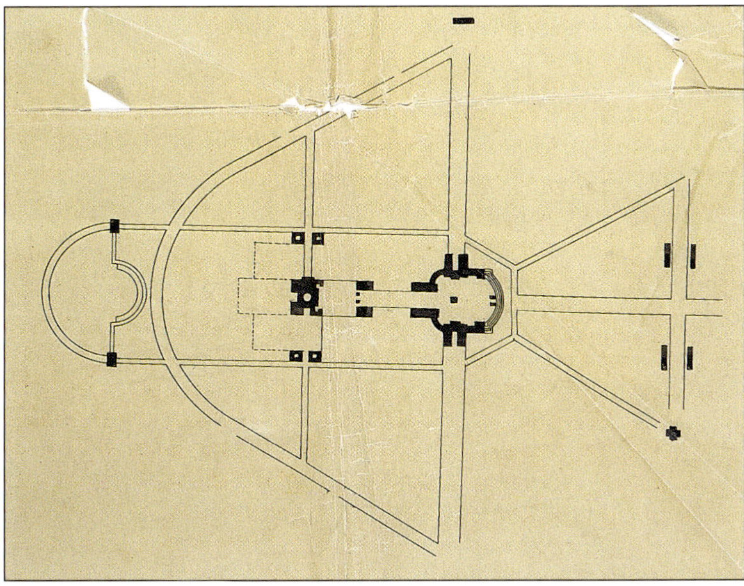

Option 11: Great Plaza between Raisina Hill and Jumna River
(no date)

– Effort to substitute the long processional avenue by a series of different spaces giving more weight to the main crossing of the major north-south and east-west axes

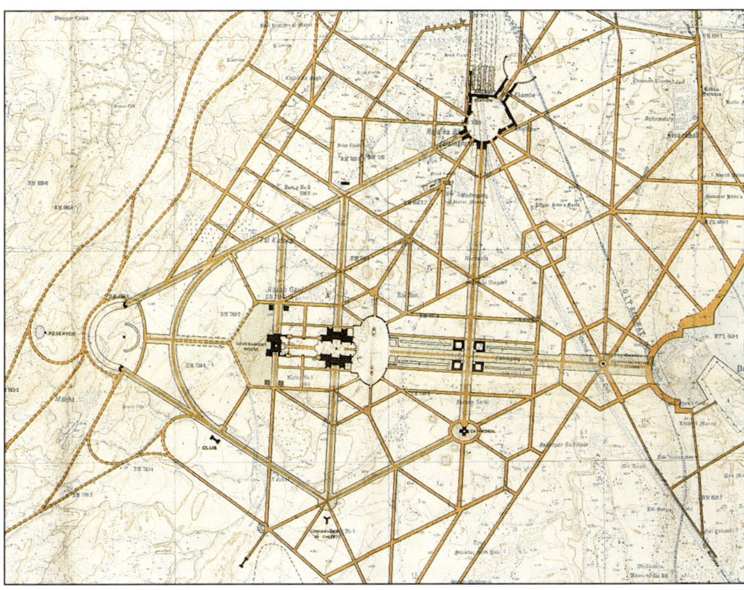

Option 12: Final layout labelled "Accompaniment to the Final Report of the Delhi Town Planning Committee on the Town Planning of the New Imperial Capital"
(from March 1913)

– Large triangular and hexagonal pattern with a square in front of Raisina Hill
– Four archives and museums marking the crossing of the north-south and the east-west avenues
– Jumna River froms a marina at the eastern end of the main processional avenue

Option 4: Hardinge's suggestion to avoid the expropriation of the homeowners of Pahanganj

In this tricky, almost hopeless situation for the town-planners, the Viceroy, who was normally open to the expert advice of his colleagues, took the initiative. In a telegram of August 11, 1912, to Lord Crewe, the Secretary of State, he proposed simply rotating the whole plan of the city – unchanged in its inner structure – by forty-five degrees clockwise. In this plan, although the most important avenue was now no longer aligned with the Jama Masjid, it pointed almost exactly east and was oriented on the old fortress of Indropat, equally rich in symbolism, in the legendary town of Purana Kila on the Jumna river. Thus, the high property acquisition or expropriation costs in Pahanganj would be avoided. "The suburb has been found to contain a population of 35,000 people, and the removal to another suburb and the demolition of the houses is an enormous task, which would have to be undertaken before the avenue through it is made. If the main avenue is shifted, any immediate action to remove this slum is obviated, while its improvement can gradually and tactfully be carried out as an ordinary operation of urban improvement for a few lakhs of rupees."[10]

Option 5: Lanchester's "Second revised layout"

In the following weeks, Lanchester worked feverishly to solve the town-planning problem and take into account the main avenue's new alignment with Indropat. A balanced concept of avenues was worked out that were arranged in accordance with the Viceroy's Palace. Now, instead of one splendid avenue there were additional avenues linking the most important viewpoints of the town. Lord Hardinge, the Viceroy, was still unable to entirely reconcile himself to a large number of curved concentric streets. If in the early plan (option 1) the grid pattern had been too straight and dull for the Viceroy, now the numerous curved streets also appeared to him to go too far in the other direction.

The suggestion of six Secretariat buildings in the direct neighbourhood of the Viceroy's Palace did not seem sensible because this would lead to all kinds of visitor traffic, or even demonstrations directly in front of the palace. The position of the palace in the plain of Malcha was not planned on a particularly favourable site.

Thus, the Delhi Town Planning Committee's search for an acceptable and impressive architectural solution continued. There were now no further contributions by Henry Vaughan Lanchester, who left for London after his temporary contract ran out.

Option 6: Hardinge: "The most beautiful site of all is Raisina Hill"

After Lanchester's departure, Lord Hardinge consulted two independent Senior Government Engineers in his confidence with a comparative analysis of the earlier planning efforts. They confirmed, by and large, the usefulness of the city's ground plan, but suggested a more prominent site for the Viceregal Lodge, such as the range of hills west of the site that had previously been planned for its construction. Lord Hardinge accepted the plan wholeheartedly and immediately had tests carried out for the reforestation of the bare hills.

The King, who now became actively involved, considered this solution to be less attractive, and one of the members of the Delhi Town Planning Committee, George Swinton, was keen on the earlier plan suggested for the palace on the plain of Malcha. After another reconnaissance trip, Lord Hardinge announced categorically: "I will not listen to any suggestions of Malcha, (which) is far too distant."[11] For him it was clear, "The most beautiful site of all is Raisina Hill."

Thus, the final plan for Imperial Delhi, the one eventually realized, had been settled. But an assassination attempt on the Viceroy on December 23, 1912, and continued differences of opinion in London brought new unrest to the decision-making process.

10 Note by H.E. the Viceroy, July 31, 1912.
11 Diary of Lord Hardinge, entry from December 8, 1912.

Option 7: Another effort at the Northern Site, "Layout A"

In London it became fashionable to hold a definite opinion on the Viceroy's new residence. The press took up the subject enthusiastically and came down overwhelmingly on the side of those who – for whatever reason – found a new town to the north of Old Delhi better. Most of those who had opinions were not in the least familiar with the locations. Nevertheless, it suited them that Herbert Baker, the new member of the Delhi Town Planning Committee, was also voting for a "Via Sacra" on the Northern site.

Lord Hardinge, weakened by the consequences of the assassination attempt, renounced his own preferences and directed the Delhi Town Planning Committee to work out a plan for a new imperial seat on the northern site. Two plans were drawn up, the first was known as "Layout A" and it adopted most of the elements of the earlier Option 6, but adapted them to a situation north of old Delhi.

Option 8: Another plan for the Northern Site: "Layout B"

As a variant to "Layout A," the Delhi Town Planning Committee shortly thereafter presented "Layout B." This plan was not worked out in detail and, as the weaker alternative, was possibly only intended to emphasize the advantages of "Layout A." The discussions about the northern site were concluded in February, 1913, with one strong and one weaker alternative.

Option 9: Lutyens' new effort for a Southern Site with Government House alone on Raisina Hill

Individual members of the Delhi Town Planning Committee bemoaned the rejection of the southern site alternative that was also preferred by the Viceroy. Lutyens now seized his opportunity and in February, 1913, presented a particularly well-thought-out plan for New Delhi and the old location where, months earlier, according to the unanimous opinion of all the members, there were the best hygienic, topographical, and scenic conditions. For this new alternative, Lutyens resorted to the essential elements of "Layout A," but now transferred the well conceived system of a boulevard oriented on Viceroy's House together with the large triangle of streets added on both sides, and with only a few changes to the southern location. As in "Layout A," the boulevard ended in the east at the Jumna River and was accentuated by government buildings between the river and Viceroy's House at a spacious crossroads.

Even if, at first glance, no constant principle or objective was recognizable in the long list of town planning options, according to the opinion of all the participants in London and in Delhi, this new effort by Lutyens nevertheless contained a consistent summary of all the positive elements that had emerged from the planning process. The Palace, at that time called Government House, now lay on Raisina Hill. A commercial centre could now be developed on the round plaza north of the boulevard already contained in the first plans by Henry Vaughan Lanchester, especially since Delhi station could now be transferred there. Furthermore, where the boulevard met the river, a new harbour and a promenade along the bank could nicely round off the new town.

Option 10: Joint effort of Lutyens and Baker with Secretariats joining Government House on Raisina Hill

After Herbert Baker and Lutyens had agreed upon a sensible demarcation of their respective areas of responsibility, a new idea by Baker meant new decisions had to be made. He convinced Lutyens of the need to place the Secretariats directly next to Viceroy's House on Raisina Hill. The relevant sketch was explained in a conversation with the Viceroy, who accepted the plan. In order to create sufficient space for the Secretariats, however, Government House had to be moved to the west. The view of the Jama-Masjid was thus lost, but this seemed acceptable to both Lutyens and Baker.

Fig. 174: In a telegram of August 11, 1912, the Viceroy intervened in the planning decisions. To avoid escalating costs, he suggested that the main axis should be oriented to the old Indrapat fort (Option 4).

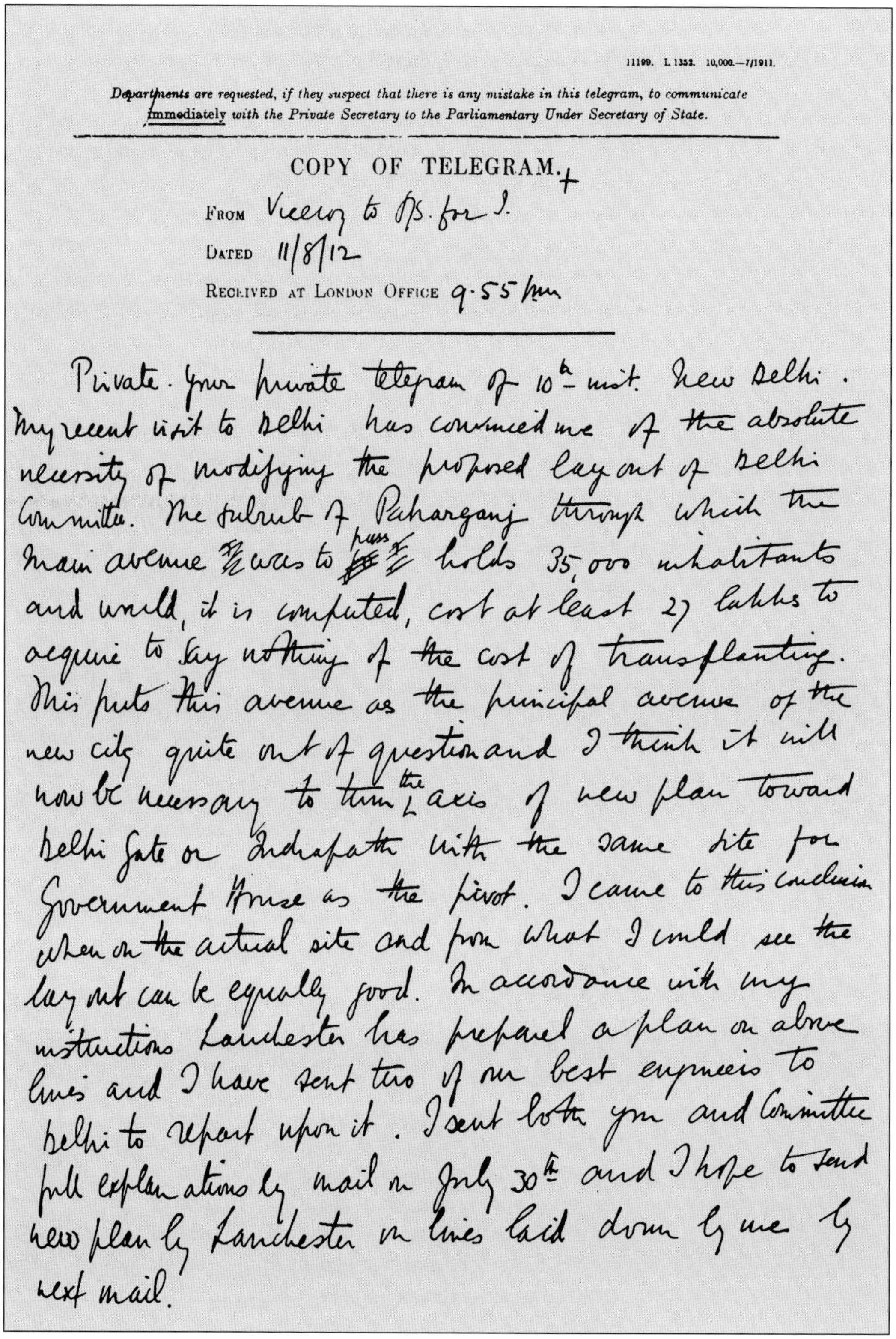

11199. L 1352. 10,000.—7/1911.

Departments are requested, if they suspect that there is any mistake in this telegram, to communicate immediately with the Private Secretary to the Parliamentary Under Secretary of State.

COPY OF TELEGRAM. +

From Viceroy to S/S. for I.

Dated 11/8/12

Received at London Office 9.55 pm

Private. Your private telegram of 10th inst. New Delhi. My recent visit to Delhi has convinced me of the absolute necessity of modifying the proposed lay out of Delhi Committee. The suburb of Paharganj through which the main avenue was to pass holds 35,000 inhabitants and would, it is computed, cost at least 27 lakhs to acquire to say nothing of the cost of transplanting. This puts this avenue as the principal avenue of the new city quite out of question and I think it will now be necessary to turn the axis of new plan toward Delhi Gate or Indrapath with the same site for Government House as the pivot. I came to this conclusion when on the actual site and from what I could see the lay out can be equally good. In accordance with my instructions Lanchester has prepared a plan on above lines and I have sent two of our best engineers to Delhi to report upon it. I sent both you and Committee full explanations by mail on July 30th and I hope to send new plan by Lanchester on lines laid down by me by next mail.

Option 11: Great Plaza between Raisina Hill and Jumna River

A satisfying architectural arrangement of the long processional avenue between Government House (or Viceroy's House) and the Jumna River remained a concern to the two planners. A gigantic plaza, such as in the Italian style, could make an even greater impression than the four government buildings thus far envisaged at the junction with the most important north-south boulevard.

This and many other sensible details continued to demand the careful coordination of all planning procedures. The very sensible idea of the plaza was finally dropped.

Option 12: Final layout labelled "Accompaniment to the Final Report of the Delhi Town Planning Committee on the Town Planning of the New Imperial Capital"

On March 20, 1913, with the "Final Report of the Delhi Town Planning Committee on the Town Planning of the New Imperial Capital" the planners finally presented the town plan for Imperial Delhi that was accepted by all those involved. The appendices to this report not only contain the town plan (cf. Fig. 60), but also a drainage plan and a proposal for the layout of the main and subsidiary streets (Fig. 180).

Naturally, this plan was altered in many details over the years: The station, for example, was not built directly at Connaught Circus and the Cathedral was not built at the place originally envisaged south of the four planned archives and museums. The street plan, however, hardly changed. Today, thanks to the generous layout of all the streets they remain, despite the growing volume of traffic, congested only during rush hours.

Among the striking qualities of the town plan that remain today is the orientation of many avenues along the countless historical buildings from the Muslim and pre-Muslim periods such as the Tomb of Safdar Jang, the fortress of Purana Kila, the Jama Masjid, the Red Fort and the Tomb of Humayun.

Summary

The decision-making process for the architectural design of Imperial Delhi was marked by an unexpected number of turns and diversions. Yet, perhaps for that very reason, the final design was one of unprecedented clarity and unparalleled severity. The hard Neo-Palladian leanings of Edwin Lutyens stood in stark contrast to the desire of a great number of contemporary architectural critics who wanted a link with the earlier age of the Mughal emperors, and was exposed to the continuous criticism of a Viceroy who was as alert as he was determined: "... written in his (Lord Hardinge's) journal at the time of the inauguration of New Delhi, Hardinge belittles the Committee's abilities relative to his own actions: Swinton was one of the three experts sent from England to select a site for new Delhi and after spending six months riding around Delhi on an elephant, they selected a site which, after three hours' examination, I rejected and myself in another, selected the actual site of New Delhi."[12]

However one assesses individual merit in this decision-making process, something unusual is certainly present. A proposal for the geometric explanation of the town's ground plan is contained in Chapter 3.1. A somewhat different suggestion of tempting simplicity was proposed by A. Greenberg in 1969: "The plan of New Delhi is formed by the superimposition of two separate and distinct geometric systems. The one, a narrow rectangular grid, is monumental, and relates to the major scale of the region and government buildings. The other, a hexagonal system, is local and devoted to the residential city (see fig. 175). The outer limits of the symmetrical plan are defined by the two overlapping major hexagons. Their points of intersection coincide with the main east-west axis, the King's Way, and also locate the sites of the War memorial in the east, and the Secretariats in the west."[13]

In mid-1913, with the acceptance of the "Final Report of the Delhi Town Planning Committee, there began, from Edwin Lutyens' point of view, the much more interesting task of

12 Journal of Lord Hardinge, February 7, 1931, quoted in: R.G. Irving: op. cit., p. 367.

13 A. Greenberg: "Lutyens' Architecture Restudied," in *Perspecta* 12, 1969, Connecticut.

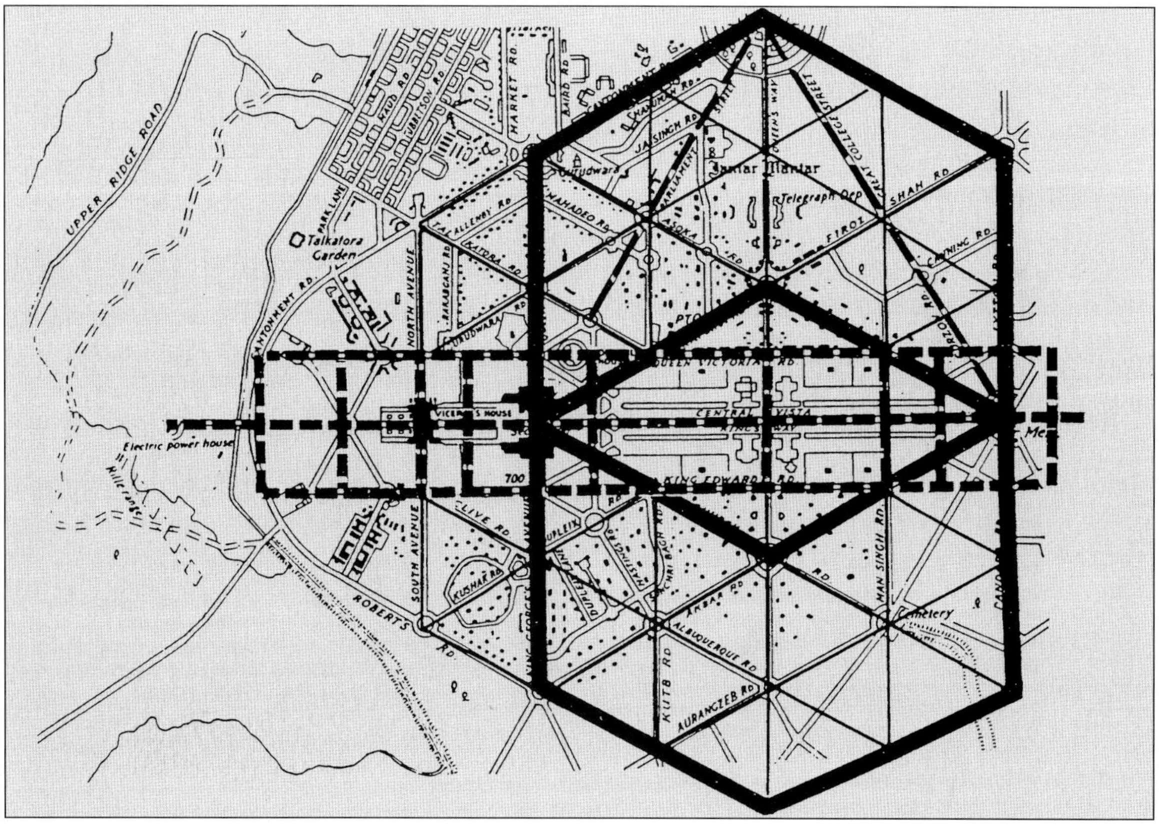

Fig. 175: A. Greenberg suggests a simple and tempting geometric interpretation of the ground plan for Imperial Delhi.

creating the architectural plans: "December to March 1913–14 were the decisive months in the shaping of New Delhi. Lutyens brought out with him complete small-scale plans for Viceroy's House and the designs evolved during the summer embodying his notable synthesis of Eastern and Western architecture. Baker brought similar plans for the Secretariats; and Walcot's perspectives gave an impression of how the great sweep of buildings would be related in appearance. The Government of India was anxious to begin preparations of the site, but the recent pronouncement of the Viceroy that the total cost should not exceed £ 4,000,000 made it certain that there would have to be further modifications of all the plans both of the general layout and of individual buildings, before any works could be put in hand. For the greater part of the time, therefore, Lutyens was plunged in the agonizing occupation of recasting Viceroy's House to accord with Lord Hardinge's demands on the one hand for a slashing of costs but on the other for retaining ceremonial grandeur, whilst he strained to maintain the proportions imposed on the building by its relation to the Secretariats no less than by its site and importance in connection with the city as a whole, and by its own monumental conception. The decision to re-site the building and at the same time reduce its cost were in fact mutually contradictory, indeed it had made the whole Government centre more costly by the immense retaining walls necessitated for the forecourts, as well as for the basements at the sides of Government House (Viceroy's House). But having made his political and financial decisions, Lord Hardinge was inflexible."[14]

14 Christopher Hussey: *The Life of Sir Edwin Lutyens*, London 1950, p. 311.

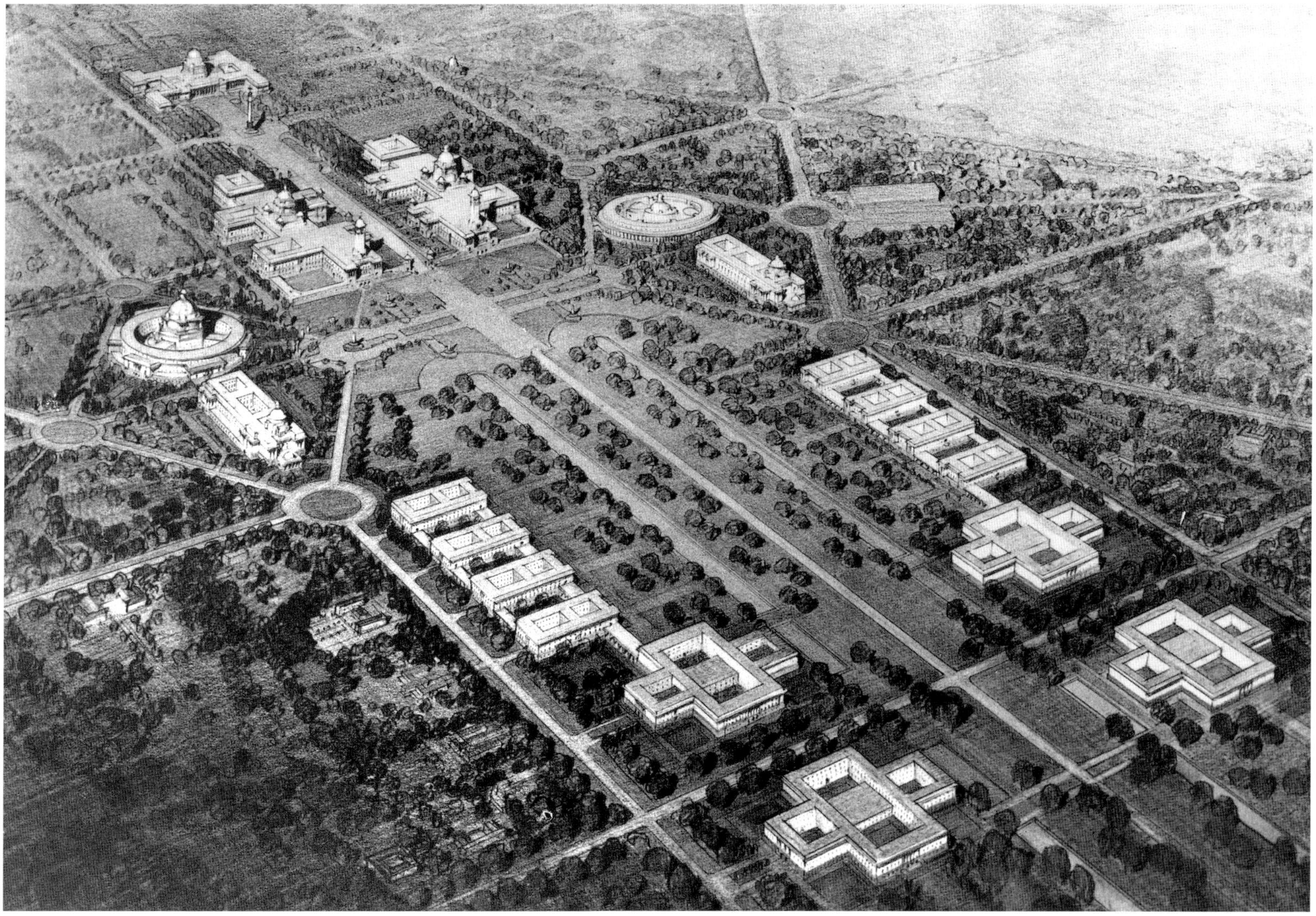

Fig. 176: A survey from the 1920s that covers government buildings in the centre of the new town, shows that the circular Legislative Building (now Parliament House) was to gain an addition with a similar circular building south of King's Way.

Name	Place	Characteristics
Hindi: **Niim** English: Neem Tree Latin: Azadirachta indica	Aurangzeb Road, Janpath	Oil made from seed used as mosquito repellent Natural insecticide, e.g. for rolled-up carpets and crops Used for Indian medicine
Hindi: **Imli** English: Tamarind Tree Latin: Tamarindus indica	Tilak Marg (Hardinge Ave.), Akbar Road	Spice for Indian food prepared from fruit Fruit used for medicine for digestion Also used for candy
Hindi: **Jamun** English: Java Plum Latin: Syzygium cumini	Firoz Shah Road, Raj Path, Janpath	Fruit used to prepare Jamun wine Fruit edible, good for digestion Oil from seed used in Indian medicine
Hindi: **Semul** English: Indian Silk Cotton Tree Latin: Ceiba pentandra	Delhi gardens	Seed gives silky cotton fibre, e.g. for making cushions Very large but slow in growing
Hindi: **Amaltas** English: Golden Chain Latin: Laburnum anagyroides	Public and private gardens, also roundabouts and avenues	Flowers in June, bright yellow Root used for Indian medicine
Hindi: **Mowa** English: Indian Butter Tree Latin: Bassia latifolia	South End Road	Important in early pre-Hindu mythology Roots used in Indian medicine Used by tribal people for brewing liquor
Hindi: **Gulaichi** English: Franjipani, Pagoda Tree Latin: Plumeria alba	In private gardens	White blossoms with exquisite fragrance. Blooms in spring and monsoon season
Hindi: **Morpankhe** English: Laurel Tree Latin: Kalmia latifolia	In private and public gardens	Ornamental, also used as a plant for hedges
Hindi: **Ashoka** English: Ashoka Tree, Ashupal Latin: Polyalthia longifolia	In private and public gardens, temples	Leaves made into wreath Fruit eaten in times of scarcity
Hindi: **Amrood** English: Guava Latin: Psidium guajava	In gardens and orchards	Excellent fruit
Hindi: **Barh** English: Banyan Tree Latin: Ficus bengalensis	Kept at their original sites as landmarks High religious significance	Fodder for elephants Juice of the bark used in Indian medicine Important role in Indian mythology
Hindi: **Shahtoot** English: White Mulberry Tree Latin: Morus alba	In private and public gardens	Fruit used for consumption Leaves used for rearing the silk worm Wood for handles, rackets, etc.
Hindi: **Gul Mohr** English: Gold Mohr Latin: Poinciana regia	In private gardens	Ornamental tree blossoming in summer
Hindi: **Maulsari** English: Maulsari Tree Latin: Mimosops elengi	In private gardens, also roadsides for shade	Evergreen tree with fruit preferred by birds Seed and oil used for Indian medicine
Hindi: **Dhak** English: Flame of the Forest Latin: Butea monosperma	On the Delhi ridge	Bright orange flowers used for dye Cups made from the leaves
Hindi: **Dhauldhak** English: The Coral Tree Latin: Erythrina suberosa	In private gardens	Red flowers in April
Hindi: **Saptparni** English: Dita Bark Latin: Alstonia scholaris	Lodi Gardens	A variety of Ashok (Ashupal), but more stately
Hindi: **Kadam** English: Haldu Tree Latin: Adina cordifolio	In private and public gardens Large, strong and tall trees	With flowers like yellow balls Bark used as an antiseptic
Hindi: **Pipal** English: Bo Tree Latin: Ficus religiosa	Near temples and along avenues	Tree with a very long life Even grows through cracks in buildings Buddha sat under a Pipal during meditation

Fig. 177: Summary of the types of trees chosen by Edwin Lutyens with W.R. Mustoe, Director of Horticulture, for the roads and gardens of New Delhi.

4.3 Town-planning Elements

For Edwin Lutyens, there was not much room to manoeuvre in the town plan of an imperial seat of government for the British colonial administration in India; after all, the essential axial orientation was dictated by protocol (e.g. the processional way to Viceroy's House), and by the Viceroy's preferences (e.g. grouping all the residences of the maharajas together at the other end of this processional way, as far away from the palace as possible). But in the layout of the road network and the assignment of all the offices, churches, living accommodations and commercial services to the central axis there still remained further scope for formal change.

The following section attempts to describe this scope for change and to analyze the following examples in the context of the town plan. The primary examples consist of:

- The road network (Chapter 4.3.1)
- The public buildings and offices (Chapter 4.3.2)
- The residential accommodation (Chapter 4.3.3)
- The tertiary sector (Chapter 4.3.4)
- The residences of the maharajas (Chapter 4.3.5)
- The Christian churches (Chapter 4.3.6)

The sources and models for these plans are numerous and varied. They do not automatically lead to a unified formal representational scheme as in the case of town planning during the Renaissance or the Baroque period.

The road network is oriented primarily on the geometry of the world as seen by British Masonic lodges (for example Fig. 58). The public buildings and offices are given their meanings and forms from the completely opposing creative aims of the two rival architectural stars, Edwin Lutyens and Herbert Baker (Fig. 182). The residences of the British administrative staff express their superior social status through the generous size of each piece of land and by the ever-present pillars (Fig. 201). On the other hand, by being lined up along the avenues, they also document the social distinction of the administrative staff from the centre of power that is Viceroy's House and the Secretariats. Because of the uncompromising persistence of Lutyens, to whom every plan had to be presented for approval, the residences of the maharajas are subordinated to the strict geometry of the town's ground plan around Princes Park. The incredible wealth of the regional rulers was used, as far as possible, in construction thus, for their own self-representation (Fig. 212).

The area for the Tertiary Sector at Connaught Circus was laid out over much too large an area for the originally planned number of inhabitants (75,000). It was only slowly filled up in the first decades of use with businesses and restaurants.

4.3.1 Road Network and Layout

At first the road network of Imperial Delhi resembles the contemporaneously planned road network in Canberra (cf. Chapter 2.6); both towns have spacious avenues connecting the centres of administrative power, commerce and public services. But a closer look shows us one very important difference: the incomparably higher estimation of government power in Delhi, accentuated by only one extremely broad planning axis oriented on Viceroy's House. Only in India was the British Governor General given the title of Viceroy; only in India could the British Crown form an alliance to its own advantage with the existing indigenous ruling families; only in India could the idea occur to elevate the British Queen to an Empress. India, in the last decades before Mahatma Gandhi and the move towards independence from colonial rule, saw the fullest expression of British dreams of military and cultural supremacy.

Under these prevailing conditions it seemed quite consistent that, as far as possible, no exceptions to the geometric regularity of the hexagonal road network would be entertained, and that utilitarian needs were, in the final analysis, always tested against the desire for state occasions, for the outward preservation of supremacy, pomp, and ceremony.

For the timely realization of these aims, a highly qualified team of road-workers, hydraulic engineers, botanists and architects were set to work in Imperial Delhi. Here, they realized their dreams of an imperial city because the prevailing conditions in London, in the face of thousands of attested claims to ownership, had for a long time permitted no innovations in town planning.

"The total mileage of the roads in the lay-out is about 110, the minimum road width being 76 feet for the minor arteries, and as much as 150 feet for the major arteries, whilst the metalled width on all the back service roads is 18 feet. The roads have been planted with trees, both permanent and temporary. The object of putting in the temporary trees is to afford some shade and protection to the roads and pathways whilst the permanent trees are reaching maturity. The time that will be occupied in the latter process is from thirty-five to fifty years, which is, in itself, evidence of the wisdom of the policy followed in this matter."[15]

"The domestic water supply is a joint undertaking for the new capital area, the whole of the old city of Delhi, the civil lines and the new cantonment. There is also an unfiltered water supply, which supplies water for irrigating the parks and gardens in the new city area as well as for the purpose of flushing the sewers and drains. The storm water is carried off in underground drains, which are fed by small open-side drains along the roads. The main run-off from the ridge, which reaches the very considerable volume of 8,000 cubic feet per second, is diverted along the foot of the ridge to the south of the lay-out, and falls into an old channel discharging into the River Jumna, not very far above the headworks of the Agra Canal at Okla.

The sewage is disposed of by a water-borne system. It flows by gravity to the sewage farm at some distance southeast of the lay-out where it is pumped up and discharged on to the surface of the land and used for cultivation purposes. This system has been designed so that it is capable of disposing of not only the sewage of the new capital area but also that of the old city as soon as funds are available for the purpose. The lighting of the new city will be electric."[16]

The geologists and botanists employed by the Delhi Town Planning Committee to select a suitable location for the new capital had undertaken an assessment of the quality of the soil. It was important for them to create the best conditions for the placement of avenues, gardens and parks in the residential areas modelled on the English garden cities.

The gently sloping plain between Raisina Hill and the Jumna River was distinguished by its particularly good soil. The provision of water for the artificial irrigation of the new cultivated areas placed the highest demands on the water suppliers.

The engineers, forestry experts and landscape architects who took part in the preparations for the building of Imperial Delhi worked well with the site: "Before the commencement of the work the major portion of this area was under cultivation; the soil, generally, is a good-class loam. The results of the gardening operations undertaken in the new city to date show the quality of the soil. If in the future, inhabitants in the new capital area pay as much attention to their gardens as many of the inhabitants have done during the period of construction, the results should be a gorgeous blaze of colour and a riot of bloom."[17]

It was not only the quality of the soil that was important for the site of a garden city, but also the correct choice of trees out of the large variety of subtropical vegetation on the Ridge and on the plain of the Jumna River. The most important criteria for selection were first, whether the tree quickly produced a crown that would give shade and secondly, whether it bore useful fruit. In fact, all the avenues were leased to local entrepreneurs for harvesting the fruit and tending to the trees.

"The Committee has already drawn attention to the time for planting trees, and the importance of determining the design of buildings, and the actual entrances to compounds before lines of trees are planted, as the lines of trees and buildings are dependant on one another for effect. Another important point is the kind of trees to be used for avenues. As has been remarked before, the size of the special trees selected for the avenues determine the width of avenues in which they are to stand. For the purpose of getting the right effect from the design of an avenue both the size and shape of trees are of importance; and with this end in view the Committee have picked out thirteen kinds of avenue trees out of a very large number, which will grow in Delhi, and arrangements are being made to grow them in readiness to plant out on the

15 "The New Delhi. The Works of Sir Edwin Lutyens and Sir Herbert Baker," *AR* Vol. LX, July–December 1926, p. 223.
16 Ibid, p. 223.
17 Final Report of the Delhi Town Planning Committee regarding the selected site, London, March 20, 1913, p. 16.

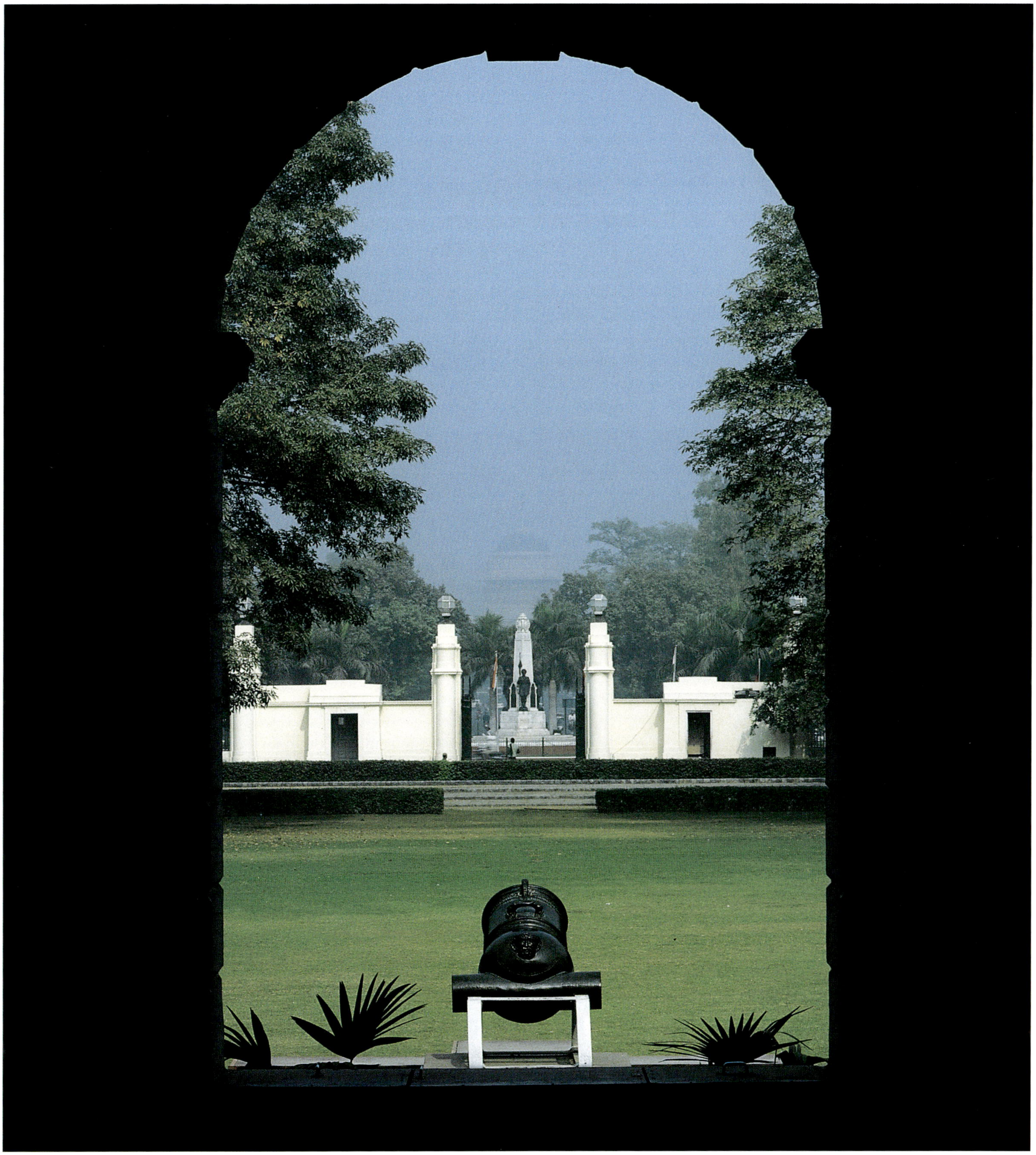

Fig. 178: The Commander-in-Chief's residence was also intentionally aligned with the dome of Viceroy's House (in the background).

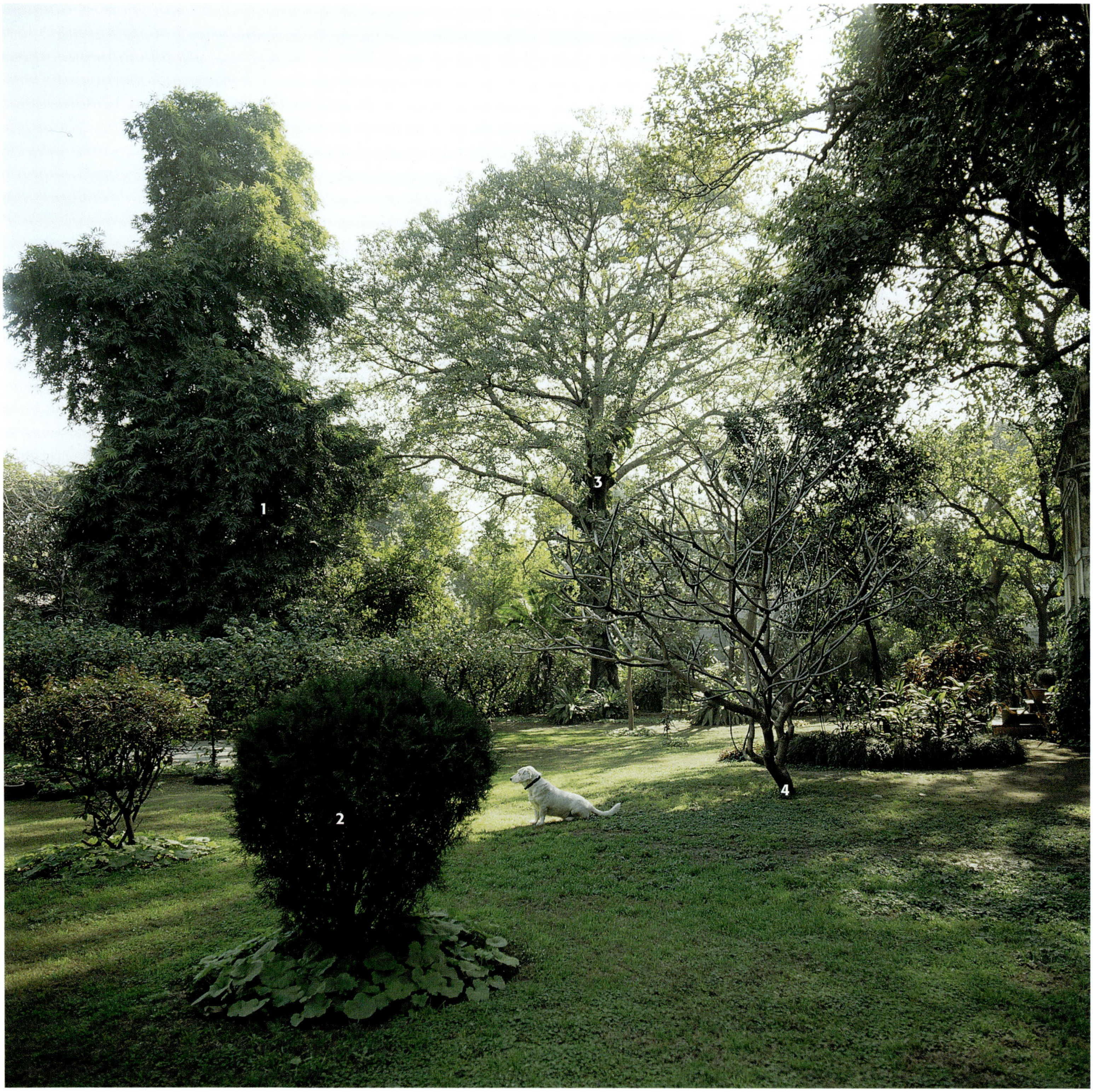

Fig. 179: In his garden, Teja Singh Malik (Chief Engineer for Imperial Delhi) planted an example of each species of local tree chosen for the avenues and gardens by Edwin Lutyens and W.R. Mustoe (Director of Horticulture).

1 Hindi: Ashoka
English: Ashoka Tree
Latin: Polyalthia Longifolia

2 Hindi: Morpankhe
English: Laurel Tree
Latin: Kalmia Latifolia

3 Hindi: Semul
English: Indian Silk Cotton Tree
Latin: Ceiba Pentandra

4 Hindi: Gulaichi
English: Franjipani
Latin: Plumeria Alba

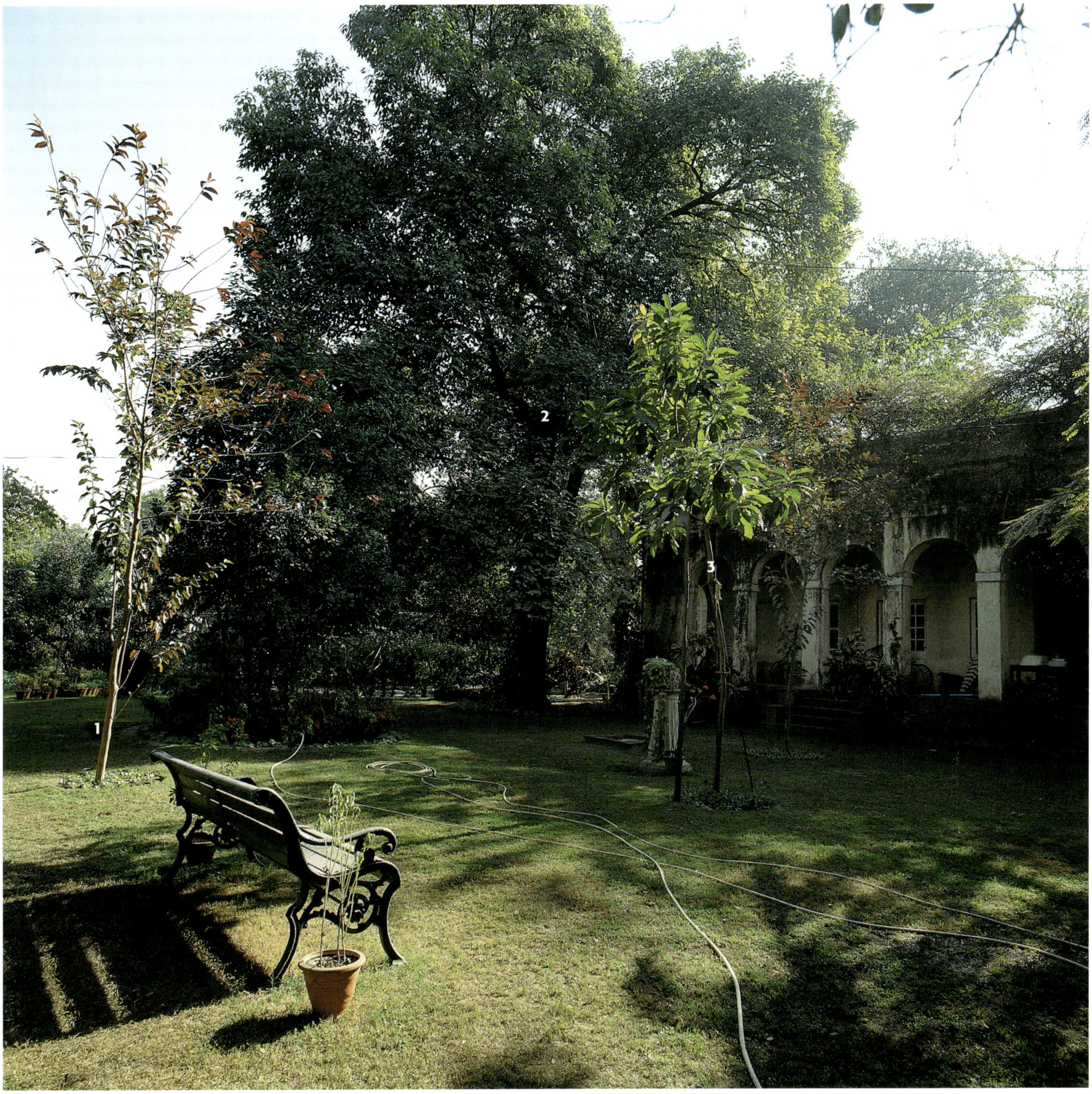

1 Hindi: Amrood
English: Guava
Latin: Psidium Guajava

2 Hindi: Jamun
English: Java Plum
Latin: Syzygium Cumini

3 Hindi: Mowa
English: Indian Butter Tree
Latin: Bassia latifolia

avenues. A deviation from the kind of tree selected to suit each avenue means a loss of a large general effect. The Committee would therefore point out that the matter is one of considerable importance.

In all countries there is a tendency to increase the number of trees in gardens in towns, and in Delhi, where trees give rest to the eye and assist dissipating heat radiation and are quick in growth with irrigation, the afforestation of parks and compounds is likely to proceed apace. This must, however, advance on judicious lines and thought must be exercised to preserve lines of view, and not to conceal intended architectural effects. The general tree effect in New Delhi, it may be safely anticipated, will be very fine: the danger is ... they may be obtained to the elimination of nearly all other effects."[18]

In total around 10,000 trees and over 100 kilometres of hedges were planted in the new royal capital: "The avenues range from 300 feet to 60 feet with the exception of the main avenue east of the Secretariat buildings where a parkway width of 440 feet has been allowed. The widths of the avenues depend on the varieties of trees selected. In all main avenues it is proposed to arrange for running water with fountains at intervals as features."[19]

Because orientation in a hexagonal road system was more difficult for every road user than in a normal rectangular system, it seemed right to give every road an unmistakeable "botanic

Fig. 180: As an attachment to their Final Report of 1913, the Delhi Town Planning Committee made detailed suggestions about the kinds of streets and avenues planned in the new capital.

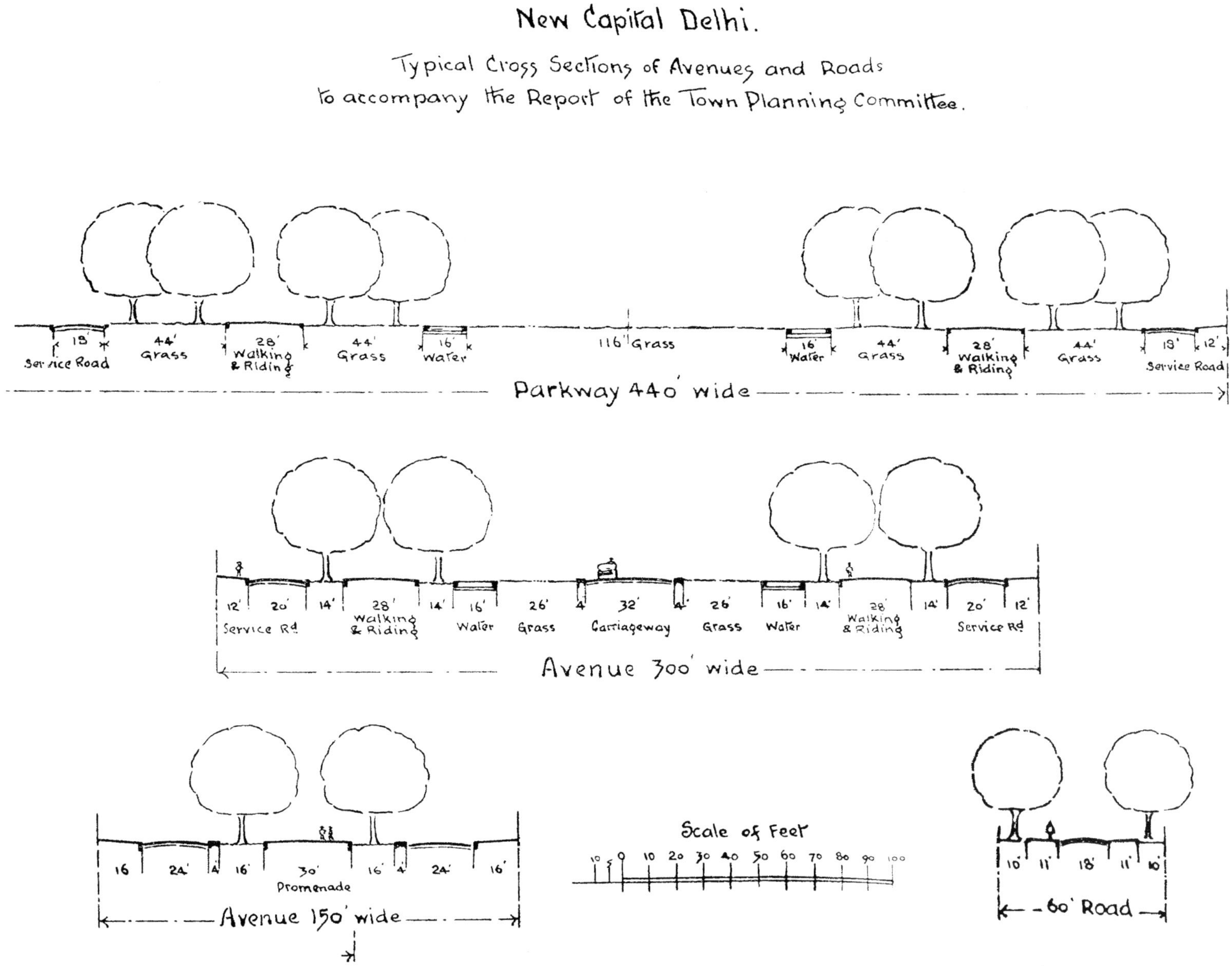

fingerprint." W. R. Mustoe for example had planted only niim trees (artocarpus integrifolia) on the Aurangzeb Road. Insect-repellent is made from their foliage and toothbrushes from their twigs. On the other hand, Akbar Road was planned with the tamarind tree (*tamarindus indica*), and King's Way by the giant Jamun trees (*eugenia jambolana*).

The extremely careful planning of the new royal capital and its attendant issues of geological, climatic, and botanic details, as well as specifics concerning supply, disposal, and traffic,[20] combined with the solid construction of public buildings to create a prosperous and prestigious city structure.

In 1920, Georges Clemenceau, alluding to Delhi's earlier eight foundations continually destroyed by wars, commented sarcastically, "These will be the finest of all the ruins!"[21] He was mistaken – at least, for the time being. The economic benefits, quite apart from the consistently prestigious use of the capital abandoned by the British in 1948, are so great that Delhi today, with its population of 13.78 million[22] and an above-average spending power per inhabitant, has become one of the most stable economic regions of India.

"Lutyens found major historic monuments useful to terminate the main axes of Imperial Delhi and to provide strong visual accents emphasizing his street pattern, in the fashion of contemporary Beaux Arts or City Beautiful planners. He enthroned these sacred landmarks in open spaces, approached directly and without subtlety, albeit with formal dignity, precisely as he was to do thirty years later in the Royal Academy reconstruction proposals for a devastated London ... His instinct for preservation did not extend to the minor tombs dotting the site, relics he deplored as 'nameless uncared-for erections' which would 'interfere everywhere, spoiling avenues and building sites.'"[23]

During Imperial Delhi's long construction period, official opinion in London and in Delhi continued to fluctuate between amazement and disapproval. Thus, it is particularly interesting that H.V. Lanchester, Edwin Lutyens' more or less out-manoeuvred rival whose contributions towards the development of the town plan are described in Chapter 4.2, did not lend his voice wholeheartedly to those of the critics: "As the most important and dramatic Indian building scheme now in progress, and one that is bound to have a considerable influence on future developments, no excuse is needed for including illustrations of the work at Delhi, even though it can hardly be regarded as expressive of the traditional art of northern India.

The problem before the designers of these buildings was not an easy one. The later traditional art of Delhi had lapsed into an enfeebled and expressionless form of Mogul design, which, at its best, could not be considered typical of India as a whole, and which had, therefore, little claim to dominate so important an undertaking.

As the planning of these great buildings was in large measure European in type, the massing, proportion, and much of the detail follow European precedents, while these have been qualified by combination with features prescribed by climatic conditions – features which have inevitably followed the lines predetermined by the Indian tradition. While the purist may object to this combination and might contend that a more complete harmony would have resulted from the substitution of Hindu "classical" for the Greco-Roman, it has yet been possible to achieve, owing to the successful general composition and massing, a consistent and impressive ensemble.

Just here and there, it must be admitted, the harmonization fails, but these details only very slightly derogate from the dignity of whole, which is well maintained throughout by the skilful grouping and placing of the blocks on the slope rising to the low ridge which extends in a south-westerly direction from Shah Jehan's city."[24]

18 Ibid, p. 16.
19 Final Report of the Delhi Town Planning Committee regarding the selected site, Delhi 1913, p. 6.
20 The possibility of building an electric tram was also considered by the Delhi Town Planning Committee but in view of the low returns to be expected from the passengers it was finally rejected.
21 Arthur Llewellyn Basham: *A Cultural History of India*, Oxford 1975, p. 357.
22 Census of India, 2001.
23 R.G. Irving: op. cit., p. 80.
24 H.V. Lanchester: "The Architecture of the Empire. India," in: *Architectural Review* 55, June 1924.

4.3.2 Public Buildings and Offices

A distinction between private residential buildings and public offices is somewhat arbitrary in Imperial Delhi because all the buildings of the British seat of government were planned and erected by public sponsors. Therefore, it is rather the scale and the function of the buildings that, outlined below, deserve particular attention:

- The Legislative Building (now Parliament House) by Herbert Baker for its strange circular shape (Fig. 183).
- The guesthouses for Members of Parliament, Western Court and Eastern Court, by Robert Tor Russel for their unusually clear late Neo-Classicist style (Fig. 193).
- The residence of the Commander-in-Chief, also by Robert Tor Russel, for the attempt to combine motifs from Edwin Lutyens' architecture in the Neo-Classicist building (Fig. 196).
- The Imperial Record Office by Lutyens as the only building to have been built from plans for four similar office buildings at the intersection of King's Way and Queen's Way where a huge plaza had actually been planned (Fig. 198).

One could also include the two Secretariats on Raisina Hill, but they are given special treatment in Chapter three on account of their close conceptual connection with Viceroy's House.

Each of the four buildings mentioned above has a strange history that is of interest in order to better understand the place of administrative buildings and official residences in the building scheme. As a circular structure, the Legislative Building is devoid of orientation and axiality, a rather unfortunate compromise between a jealous Lutyens and a resigned Herbert Baker. Western Court and Eastern Court are the last Neo-Classical buildings in India both in time and in style. The Commander-in-Chief's Residence is not only the residence and official seat of the last British Commander-in-Chief, but also that of the first Indian Prime Minister Jawaharlal Nehru. He was often called "the last of the Viceroys" on account of his feeling for grandeur. The Record Office, now the National Archives, is a comparatively modest wing of one of the four planned monumental archives and museums on an imperial plaza that was never built at the junction of King's Way (now Raj Path) and Queen's Way (now Janpath).

All four architectural examples follow the vertical construction of the period, built on a massive base and a deep verandah with pillars situated above it. In the case of the Legislative Building, however, because of its circular construction, a ring of pillars was built out of the pillared-verandah. Each of the four examples takes up architectural motifs and details from Viceroy's House, but none tries to compete with this indubitably more important building, or to copy its symbols of authority such as the dome.

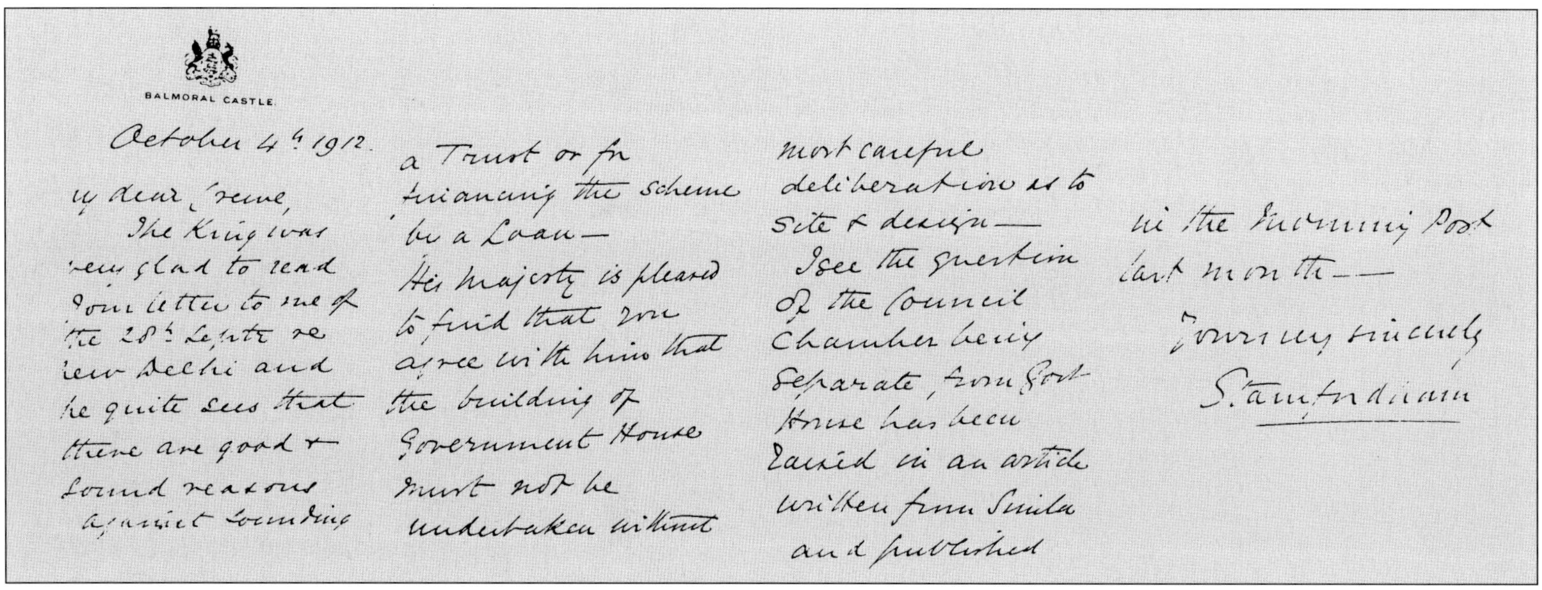
Balmoral Castle.

October 4th 1912.

My dear Crewe,

The King was very glad to read your letter to me of the 28th Septr re New Delhi and he quite sees that there are good & sound reasons against founding a Trust or for financing the scheme by a Loan—

His Majesty is pleased to find that you agree with him that the building of Government House must not be undertaken without most careful deliberation as to site & design—

I see the question of the Council Chamber being separate from Govt House has been raised in an article written from Simla and published in the Morning Post last month—

Yours very sincerely
Stamfordham

Fig. 181: Occasionally, the King intervened through his secretary Lord Stamfordham in the planning discussions. In his letter of October 4, 1912, to the Secretary of State for India, Lord Crewe, Stamfordham drew attention to the need for prudence in the search for the best possible solution for Viceroy's House (at this time still called Government House). The King also intervened in the discussion about an architecturally integrated, or separate, Legislative Building (then called the Council Chamber).

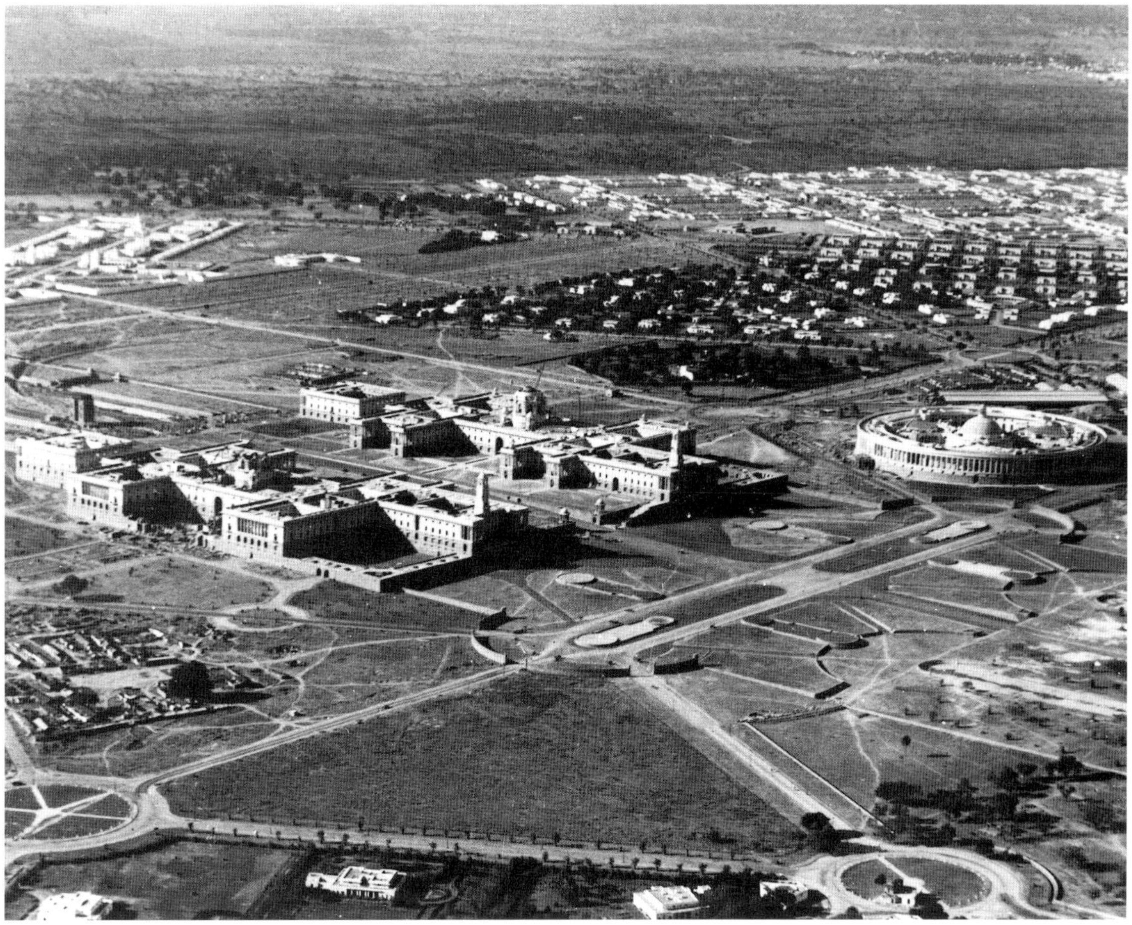

Fig. 182: In an aerial photograph from the 1920s, the unusual site, away from the axis of the capital, and the equally unusual shape of the Legislative Building, a circle without any recognizable axis, appear clearly.

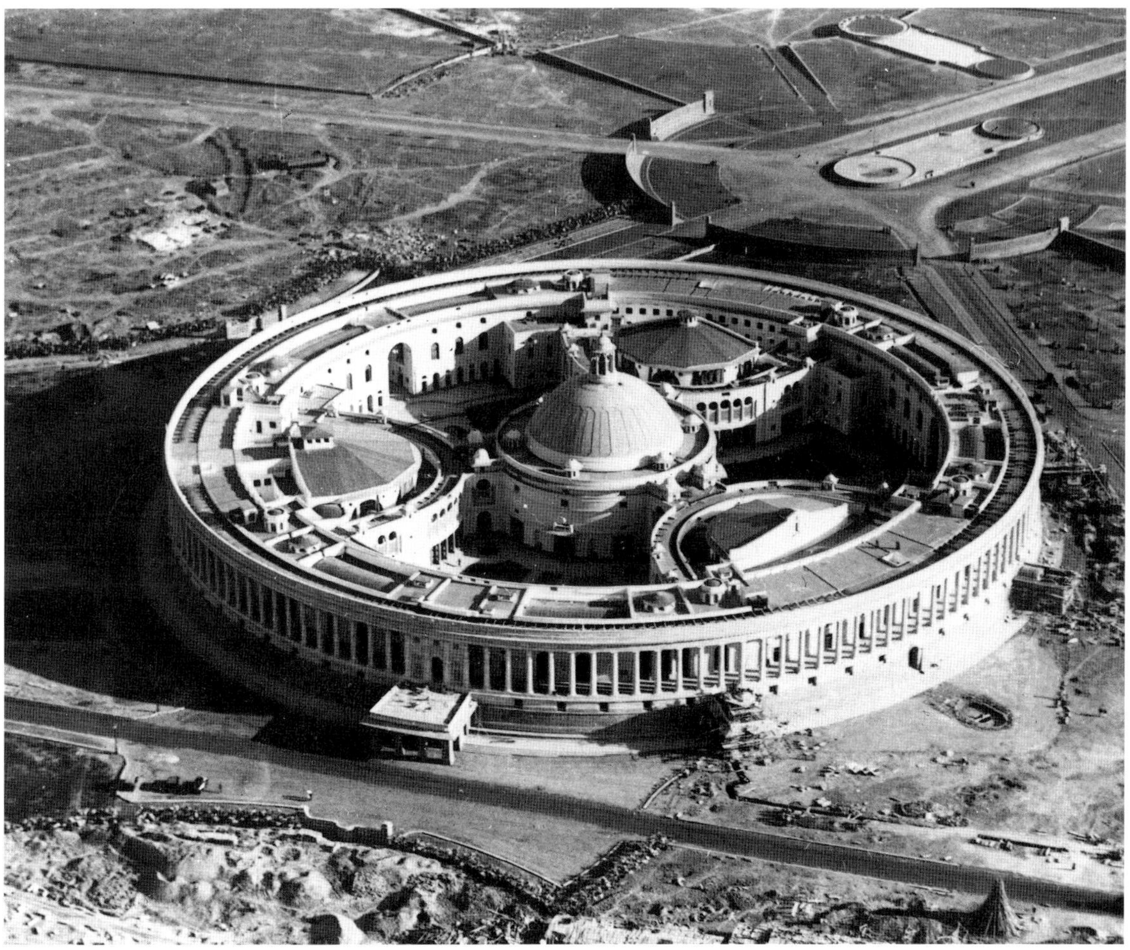

Fig. 183: In this aerial photograph from 1928, the Legislative Building can still be seen without the recessed office storey added the following year.

Legislative Building, now Parliament House (Architect: Herbert Baker), 1919–1928

Even during the earliest planning phase for Imperial Delhi, the question of the appropriate placement and design of a Council Chamber played a special role in the on-going communications between India Office, Buckingham Palace and Viceroy's House. In 1912, the Secretary of State for the India Office wrote: "As a matter of fact, it does not really matter whether the chamber is an annex of Government House, (later the Viceroy's House) or not; the powers possessed by the body that occupies it are what is crucial: but the idea of a range of buildings which would to all appearance be a Parliament House has captivated the minds of some of the advanced Indians ..."[25] But discussions that were to last more than a decade were sparked off about the significance of a Council assigned to the Viceroy, or of an essentially more independent Legislative Chamber.[26]

The Montagu-Chelmsford-Reform of 1919 brought about a turning point in these final critical discussions with the introduction of a three-chamber system of government for India with an Upper House, a Chamber of Princes, and a Legislative Assembly. An independent building with three clearly recognisable chambers now seemed sensible. The task fell to the responsibility of Herbert Baker whose relationship with Edwin Lutyens had, by this time, permanently broken down.

"A very severe strain was put on me and my band of able helpers in designing the Council House with its three chambers, the Legislative Assembly, the Council of State and the Chambers of Princes. The plan had to conform to Lutyens' geometrical layout of the city, which was based on a system of triangulation of angles of thirty and sixty degrees. I struggled along with a three-winged plan in which a central high dome over a great hall in the centre, connecting the three chambers, would have been seen rising from its base. But as the demand for extra accommodation grew I was forced to resort to a circular plan, which Lutyens favoured, embracing the maximum space and still fitting the geometry of the city. With a circular and enlarged plan there could be no high dome, as the outer perimeter wall would have cut in two the view of it from any near standpoint. Even the small chattri, which crowns the present dome, disappears, as one gets nearer to the building, like a Jack-in-the-box behind the cornice of the great perimeter wall.

From the large domed hall in the centre which symbolizes united India, where all the Chambers can meet together in common council, there radiate to the outer perimeter wall and colonnade the three blocks containing the three council chambers, with their attendant lobbies and staircases to galleries above. Three garden courts between, with green turf, orange trees, and fountains, provide a cool colour contrast to the red-stone, interchanged with white walls, colonnades, exedras, and doorways with their inset pierced-stone jaalis. The President's rooms and other offices and committee-rooms range round the outside against the great circular colonnade. There are three chief entrances under *portes cochères* corresponding to each of the three chambers roofed with little domes: they give scale to the large columns above and steady, as it were, the sweep of the great circle."[27]

Of course, a great many possible theoretical reasons for the choice of a circular ground plan might be found. Was it a representation of worldwide British power on whose colonies the sun never sets? Had the wheel of recent Indian history been given concrete form for the first time in architecture with the three chambers as spokes, frame and drive? Or was it simply that the rivalling vanities of two architects prevented any other definite form?

As the result of the disputes between the obstinate Lutyens and a Baker always prone to compromise, there finally arose a remarkably indecisive looking building complex. The Parliament House was now without any perceptible axis and situated on a particularly inconspicuous architectural site. One final change was that its height had been increased by a number of storeys discretely added to provide more office space.

In spite of the unusually difficult circumstances, Baker managed to create a building of amazing originality. The seemingly unending colonnade of the circular building anticipated the formal confusion and imperial arrogance of the Haus der Kunst in Munich. (Fig. 190). The ground plan, in the form of a wheel with three spokes, appears to be a renunciation of any sense

25 Letter of Lord Crewe to Lord Stamfordham dated October 6, 1912.

26 In the Figs. 184–85 Herbert Baker's plan is reproduced for a Legislative Building that, until today, was not clearly assigned to a particular stage. The lavish detailed plan and a north-pointing arrow to the left above the drawing of the ground plan suggest that it was a concrete early sketch which possibly has been overlooked until now by academic research.

27 H. Baker: *Architecture and Personalities*, London 1944, p. 75.

of a clear direction of architectural history. The random aspect of its urban location, away from the order and certainty of the radiating symmetrical axis of the Raj Path, reflects an as yet undefined position of the new Legislatives, caught up in a power struggle between military, political and commercial elements.

"The foundation stone of the Council House was laid by the Duke of Connaught with all the brightness and splendour of Indian ceremonial ... Before the Delhi ceremony the Duke addressed the assembled Members of both Chambers; he spoke with great and affecting earnest, appealing to them as an old friend of India to forgo discord and unite for the common good of India. His secretary, Maffey – now our Minister in Dublin – told me that after the meeting he said to him, 'Do you know, Sir, that many of the Members were in tears?' 'I do not wonder,' he replied; 'I was in tears myself.'"[28]

The architectural uniqueness of the Legislative Building becomes particularly clear in an aerial photograph of 1928 (Fig. 183). Though hemmed in by a restrictive triangle of roads, the circle, rather reminiscent of Kubrick's space station from his film *2001: A Space Odyssey*, appears to hang aimlessly in space. A dome in the centre originally symbolizing India's unity becomes lost in the hub of the rotating circle. The circular lobby, with its seemingly continuous colonnade, may occasionally remind the parliamentarians seeking relaxation and exercise here of the futile efforts in the treadmill of a mouse's cage.

"A shrill fanfare of trumpets pierced the crisp air of a cloudless January day in 1927 as Lord and Lady Irwin arrived at opening ceremonies for India's new Council House. Earlier, hundreds of automobiles had headed towards Raisina, Daimlers and Rolls Royces weaving among bullock carts and idling at railway crossings for scores of freight cars laden with building materials. Now throngs of spectators along King's Way jostled behind impassive soldiers for a view of the Viceregal carriage and six, with magnificent postilions and outriders and the golden umbrella of royalty borne above Their Excellencies by a liveried attendant. Pennons fluttered above two squadrons of cavalry escort and bright sunshine flashed from lances of the impressive Body Guard, clad in scarlet and mounted on silken-black steeds. Hoofbeats resounded on the pavement to the accompaniment of jingling accoutrements. While the pageantry was familiar to the delighted crowds, its setting was novel: it was the first ceremonial use of the Central Vista and Great Place, a long-held dream at last come true.

Within the Council House precincts, a banked amphitheatre seating 2,000 guests encircled a crimson pavilion and English and Punjabi regiments which served as guard of honor. Jewels blazed on the Durbar dress of Indian princes, and colorful military uniforms vied in splendor with parasols and gold-edged saris. The cerise turban of the Maharaja of Patalia towered conspicuously above a sea of topis and grey top hats. As the Second Battalion of the Royal Warwickshire Regiment crashed out the bars of "God save the King," the brilliant company rose at the Viceroy's approach, all under the scrutiny of innumerable coolies precariously perched nearby on builders' refuse heaps. Only the day before, these peasants from the Punjab and Rajputana had held undisputed sway over the site, men and women alike swarming by the hundreds in feverish last-minute efforts to clear rubble, lay turf and gravel, and set out feathery potted palms. Now, while prince and peasant watched, the Union Jack broke for the first time above the Council House and loudspeakers – an innovation – broadcast brave words by Sir Bhupendra Nath Mitra and Lord Irwin, as well as a hopeful message from the King-Emperor himself. Then, at the private entrance for the President of the Legislative Assembly, came the ceremonial climax: Sir Herbert Baker presented a golden key to the Viceroy, who threw wide the door and declared the building duly open."[29]

Herbert Baker was not entirely happy with the results of his efforts but, as a typical Englishman, he did not lose his sense of humour. In his memoirs, Baker mentions as one of the unquestionable deficiencies of semicircular-shaped meeting rooms their acoustic inadequacies and attempts to include supplementary acoustic equipment: "The acoustics have proved, I believe, to be good. But the Governor of one of the Provinces, with a humorous depreciation of the value of Parliaments in India, told me that he did not think much of my Chambers; his was much better, where 'you could not hear a word that was said!'"[30]

28 Ibid., p. 76.
29 R.G. Irving: op. cit., p. 275.
30 H. Baker: op. cit., p. 76.

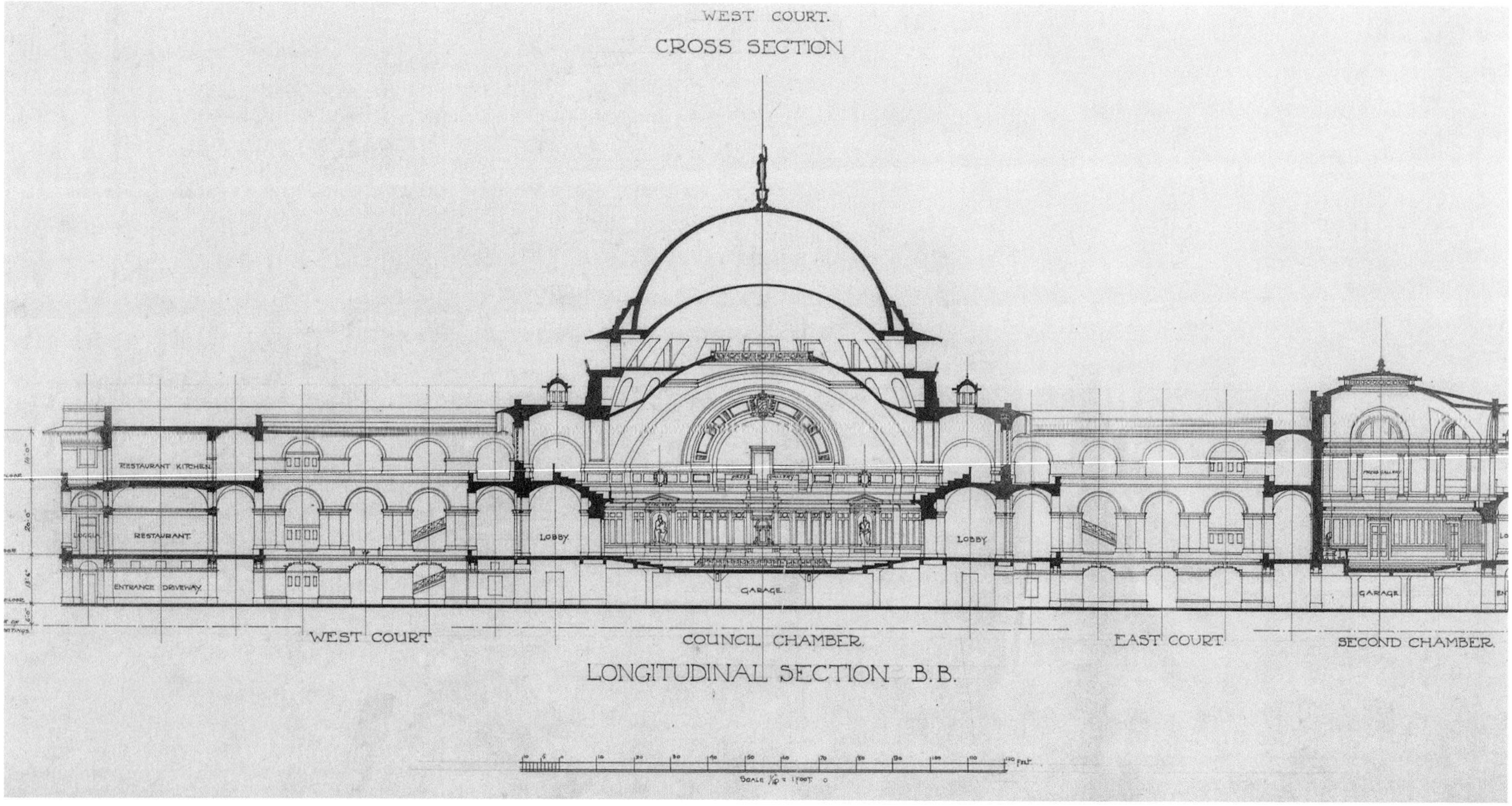

Figs. 184: The first plan by Herbert Baker for the Legislative Building was met by bitter opposition from Edwin Lutyens. Baker yielded and the second stage a building designed in the shape of a three-pointed star assumed a circular plan in agreement with Lutyens' wishes.

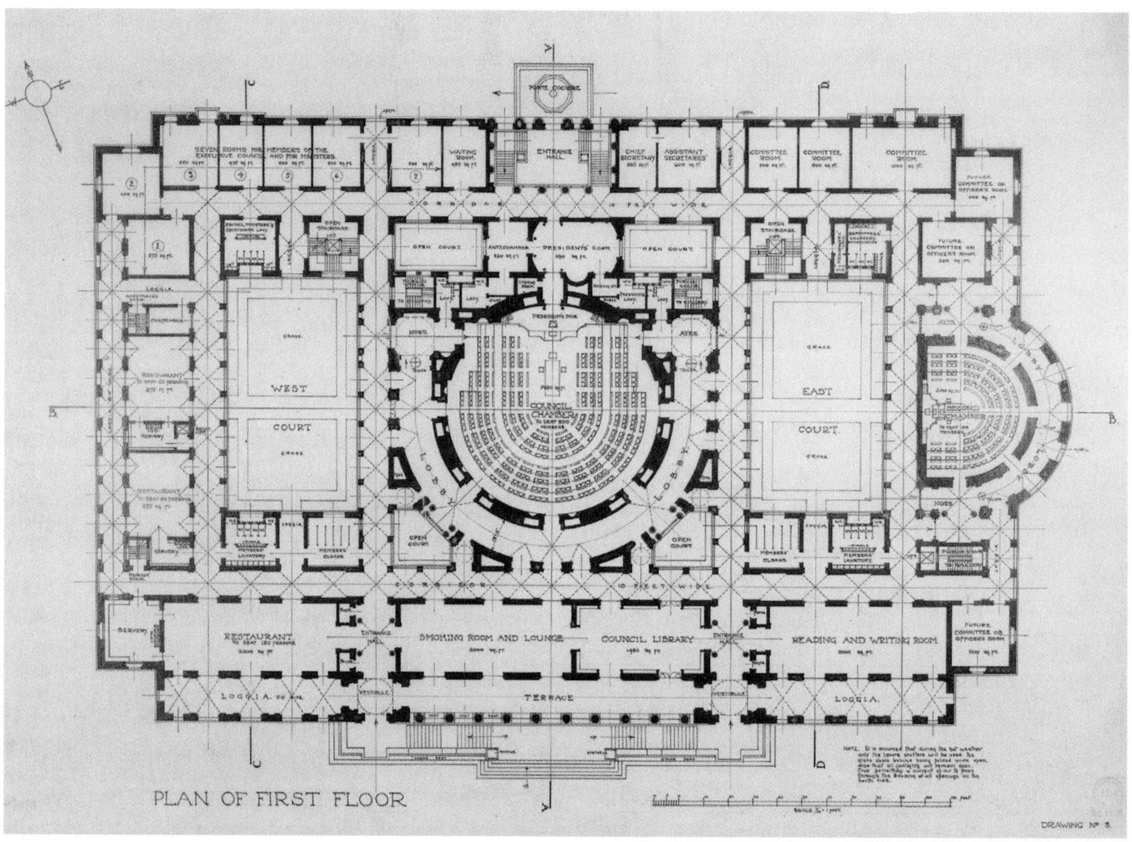

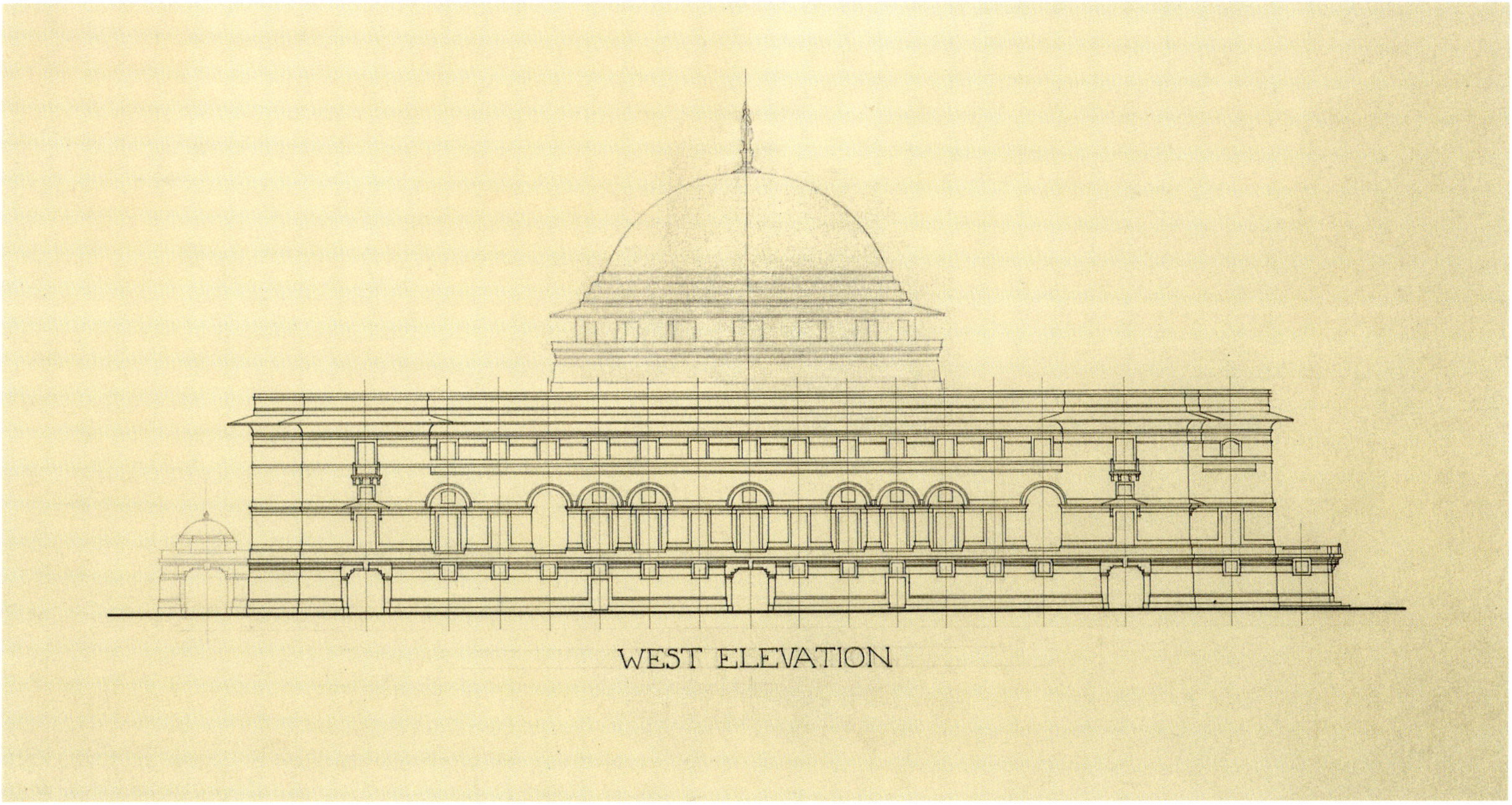

Fig. 185: Elevation of the earliest draft plan for the Legislative Buildings, still without any certain attribution given by architectural historians. The details, such as a protruding *porte cochère* and the deep relief of the Council Chamber, suggest Herbert Baker as the author. But Baker himself made no mention of this plan in his memoirs.

Fig. 186: View of a simpler, two-storied version of the Legislative Building in colour.

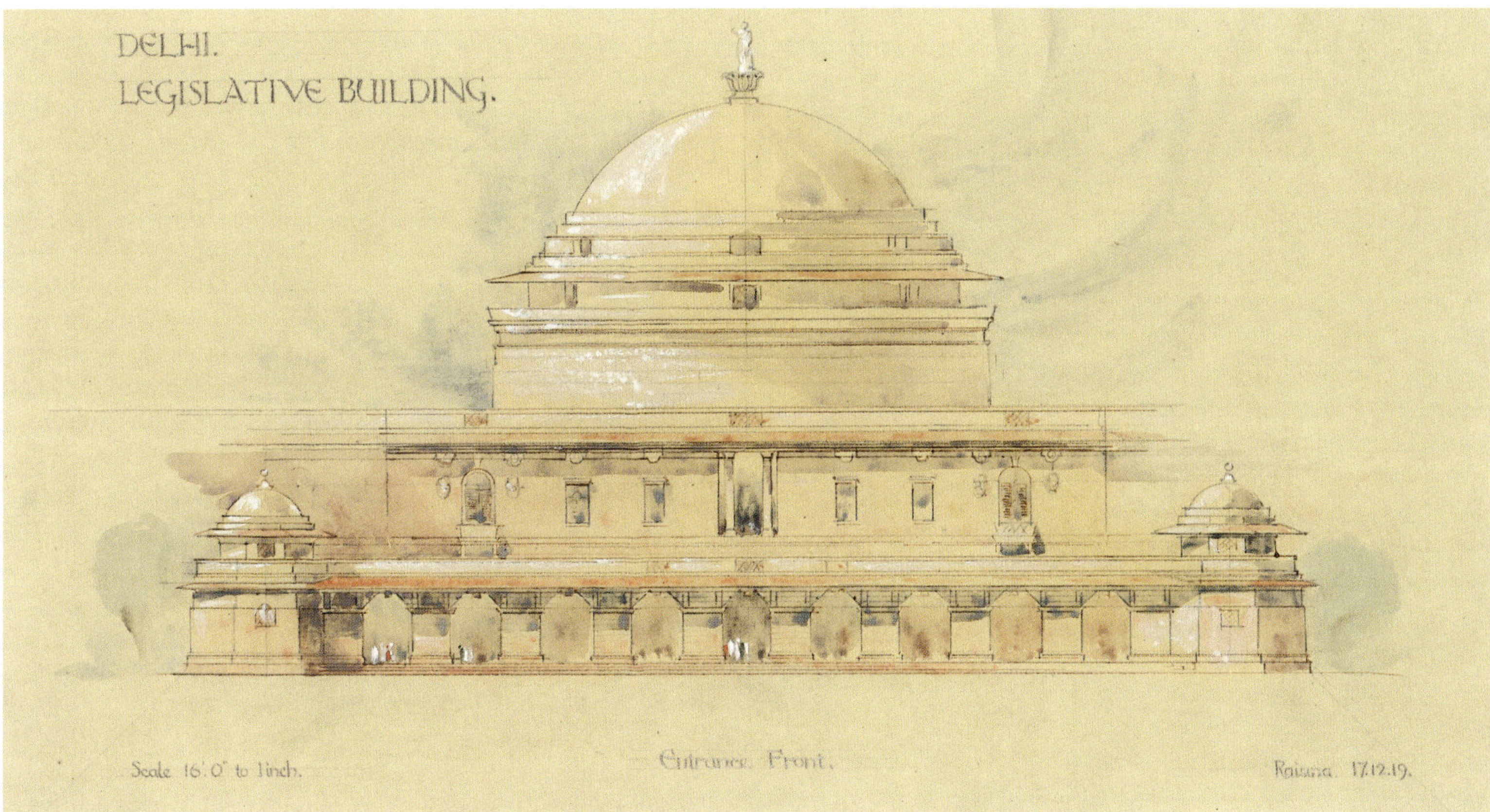

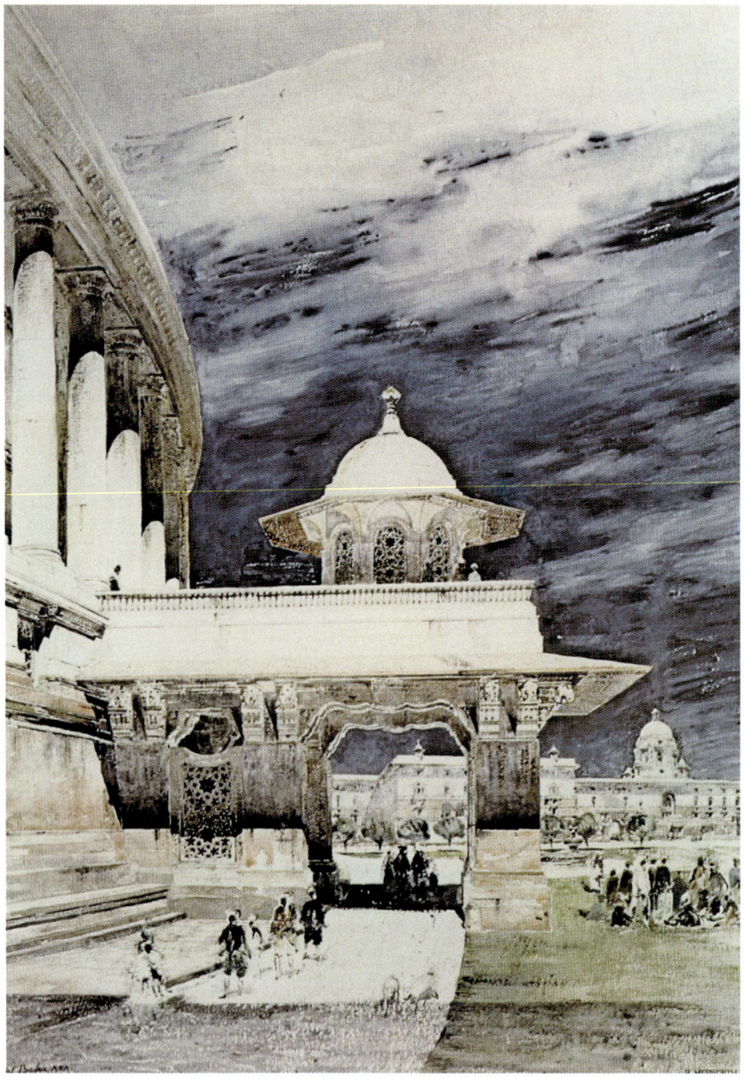

Fig. 187: In a watercolour of 1924 by P.D. Hepworth, the entrance to the Chamber of Princes appears like a dream from *A Thousand and One Nights.*

It was a different India from that of the Durbar in 1911. The building of a grand capital city for the Raj had created a national consciousness that would turn against the British Emperor in the coming two decades: "The House now elected a presiding officer from among its number. To the right of the incumbent President, Vithalbhai Javerbhai Patel of Bombay, were Government officials and nominated Members, to be sure, but in front of him a mere handful of Europeans mingled with Muslim Members, among whom Sir Abdul Qaiyum Khan, 'as rugged as his own frontier hills,' and the tall Sir Zulfiqar Ali Khan stood out in particular. To the left sat the distinguished Motilal Nehru, whose Congress supporters, in rough white homespun, rose behind their leader in tier upon tier ... this monument embodied as none other could the fact of India's progress toward constitutional maturity. The building's massive grandeur proclaimed the dignity and the importance of the Houses it embraced. The Council House expressed, in Lord Irwin's dedicatory words, 'the set purpose and sincere desire of the British people' to establish responsible government in India."[31]

Herbert Baker's contemporaries could not bring themselves to like the strange building. In 1931, Robert Byron complained particularly clearly in his comprehensive report on New Delhi in the *Architectural Review,* that: "... there is all the difference in the world between 'Fusion' and 'Allusion.' The first is the use of diverse architectural inventions and ornamental themes, whatever their dates or racial origins, simply for their practical value in creating an artistic unity and in giving effect to the values of Mass, Space, Line and Coherence in the whole design. The second is the use of these same inventions and themes in a mood of reminiscence – the mood of the nineteenth century – regardless of their relevance to mass, space, line and coherence. The inventions and themes may be virtuous in detachment, but become ineffective and even hideous in conjunction with one another and with the building to which they are attached.

The throwing together of Europe and India has been practised in all the larger buildings of New Delhi, in the Council Chamber, the Secretariats, and Viceroy's House. Under the direction of Sir Edwin Lutyens a fusion has resulted; for he has divined the human greatness behind the 'ideal and fact,' behind the co-existence of England and India, and from this Adam has raised up an Eve whose fig-leaves are applied only to increase the beauty of her natural form. Under that of Sir Herbert Baker the elements have remained separate and allusive: body embryonic; ornament, a writing in symbols.

Once inside the colonnade the effect of a curved gallery, whose massive pillars, divided into black and white by the outward sun, portend that at some remote spot the curve will meet itself and form a circle, and that the zebra'd inner wall of cream plaster will do likewise, produces an impressive sensation of size and novelty. But – and there is a but in every feature of this building – the broad sweep of the gallery is here

31 R.G. Irving: op. cit., p. 311.

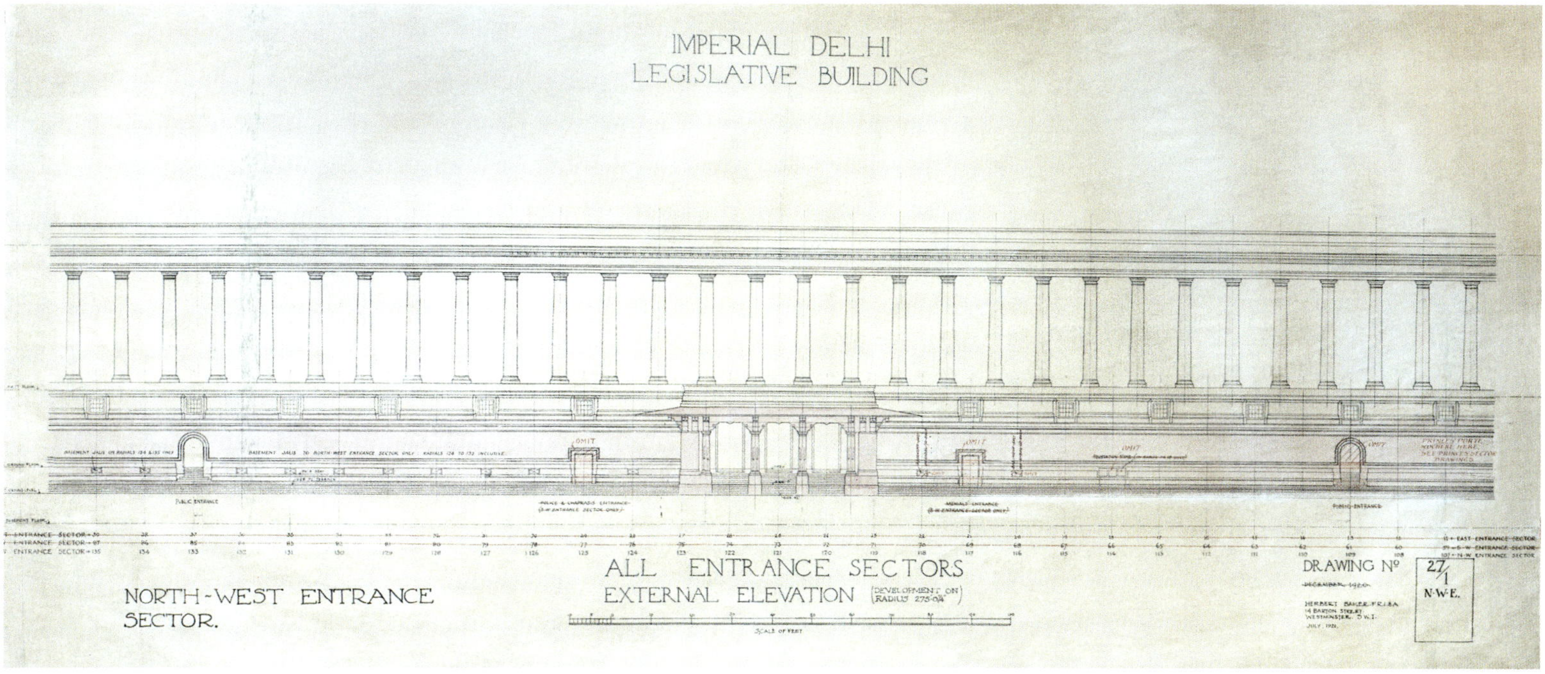

Fig. 188: The elevation of the Legislative Building (the curve of the building is not shown here) demonstrates, through seemingly infinite rows of columns, parallels with the Stoa of Attalos in Athens and the Haus der Kunst in Munich.

Fig. 189: Edwin Lutyens' original 1912 town plan had not included the Legislative Building (now Parliament House). It was added later, in the 1920s, in the town plan for Imperial Delhi and oriented on Viceroy's House.

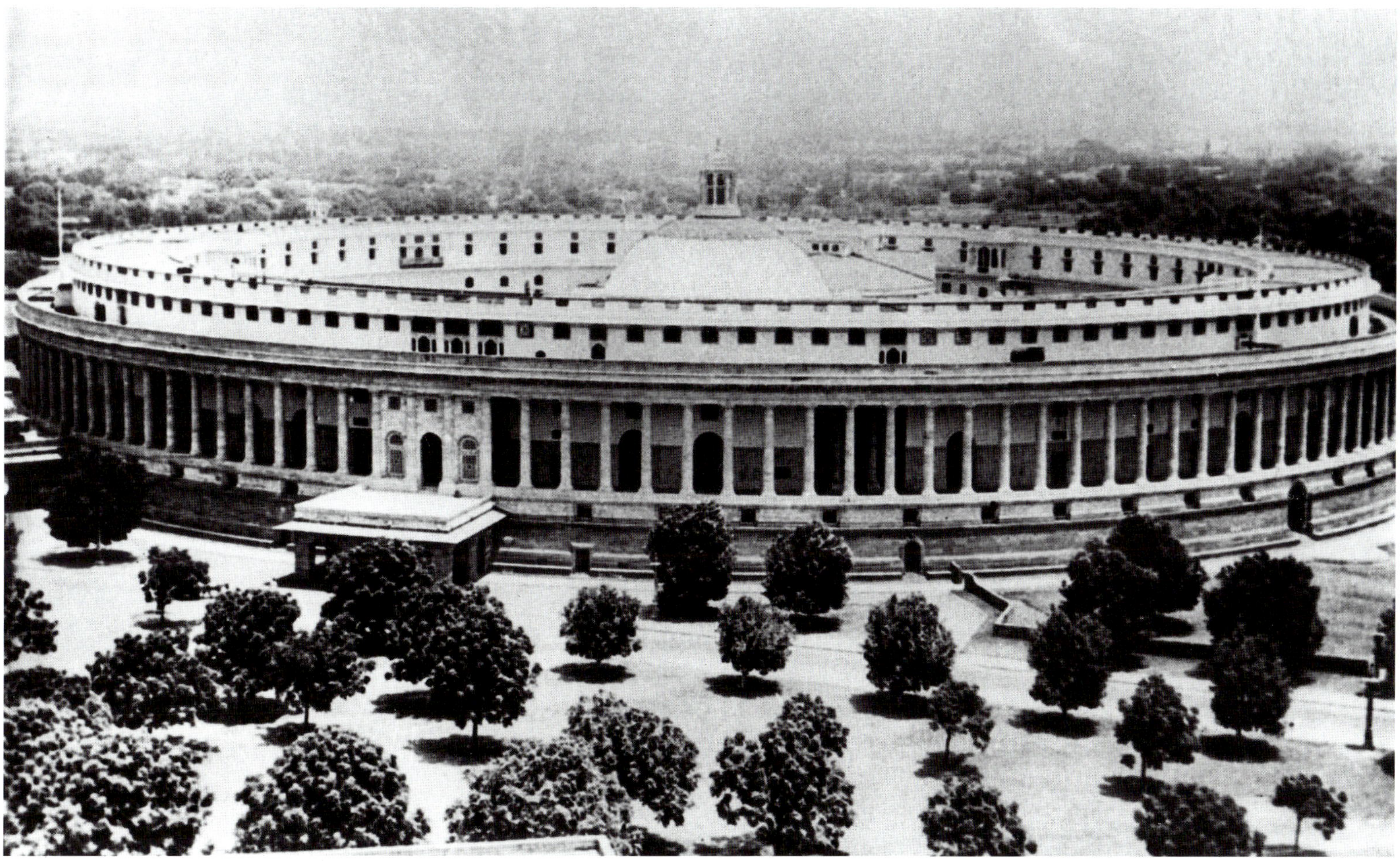

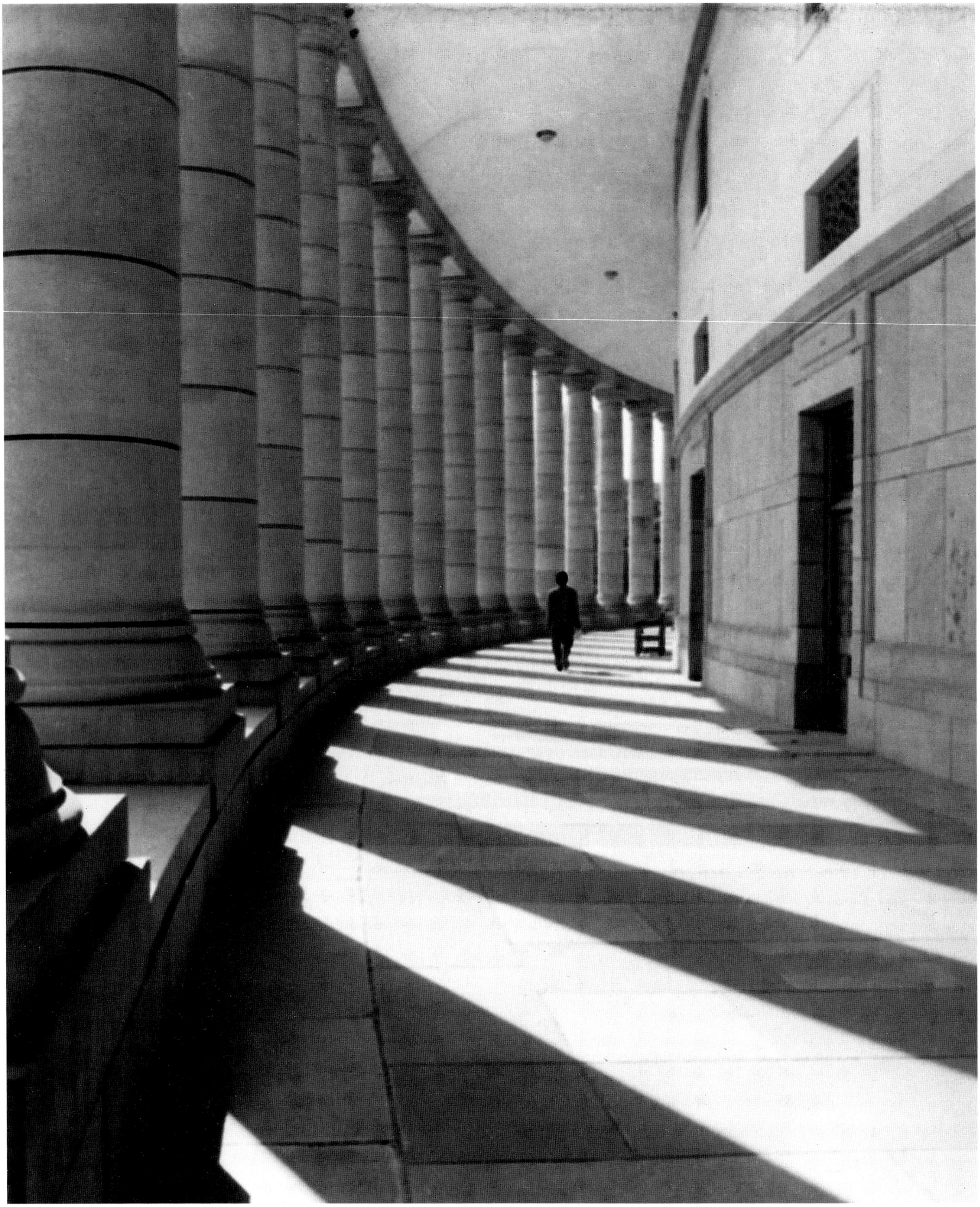

Fig. 190: The colonnade of the Legislative Building anticipates the architecture of the 1930s. Cf. for example the Haus der Kunst in Munich.

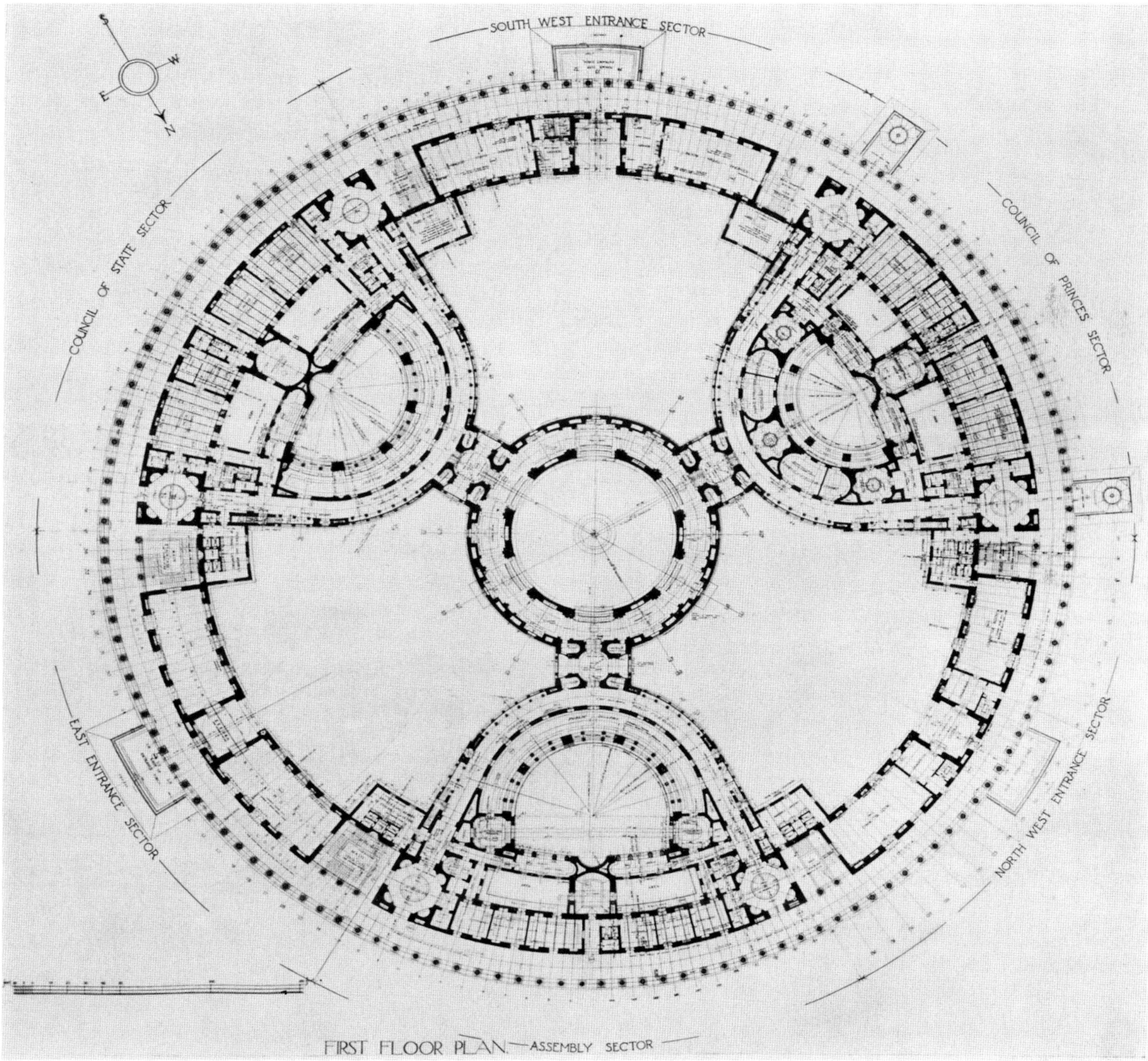

Fig. 191: The plan for the Legislative Building was practically forced by Edwin Lutyens on his former friend and rival Herbert Baker, contrary to Baker's ideas.

and there deliberately interrupted by doorless entrances, entirely purposeless, which consist of two small pillars supporting a lintel, on top of which rests a semi-circle of fretted stone. At points where it is desired to denote a porch without, three or four pillars in the colonnade are joined together by equally absurd screens of masonry which are also adorned with panels of fretwork. The shadow and silhouette effects of these devices resemble the openwork stockings of Edwardian actresses."[32]

The harsh criticism by Robert Byron in 1931 did not refer to the parliament in New Delhi alone. It could equally well have referred to other architectural forerunners, the Stoa of Attalos in Athens, or the Haus der Kunst in Munich. In all three cases, the exaggerated row of enormous pillars diminishes the observer's ability to establish a sense of scale and order between the observational planes of the detail (for example, the base of the pillars), the individual architectural elements (such as the pillars themselves), and aspects of the overall architectural context (the width and length of pillared hall). Ultimately, the visual uncertainty of the observer finds its source in the architecture of the Third Reich, where the effect has been deliberately introduced to demonstrate the powerlessness of the individual confronting the all-powerful empire.

We must assume that the Montagu-Chelmsford Reform of 1919, the reason behind the construction of the Legislative Building, did not aim to further intimidate the people. Instead, it meant to increase participation in political decision-making, yet today, the architecture of the Legislative Building still appears to be a less than ideal reflection of the political situation. To direct this criticism solely at Herbert Baker would be unfair. Baker had already presented two other plans before Edwin Lutyens had finally forced him to accept the circular ground plan.

Unfortunately, the Indian government now restricts access to the Legislative Building as well as to Viceroy's House. The primary reasons being the fear of terrorism and of political assassination attempts. But it is an essential feature of all democracies to provide access to their own decision-making organs for the people as the actual rulers – despite the risks. Therefore, it is to be hoped that this anachronistic separation of Legislative and Executive branches, a remnant of British colonial power, will not last long.

32 R. Byron: "New Delhi," in: *Architectural Review*, Vol. LXIX, No. 410, January 1931.

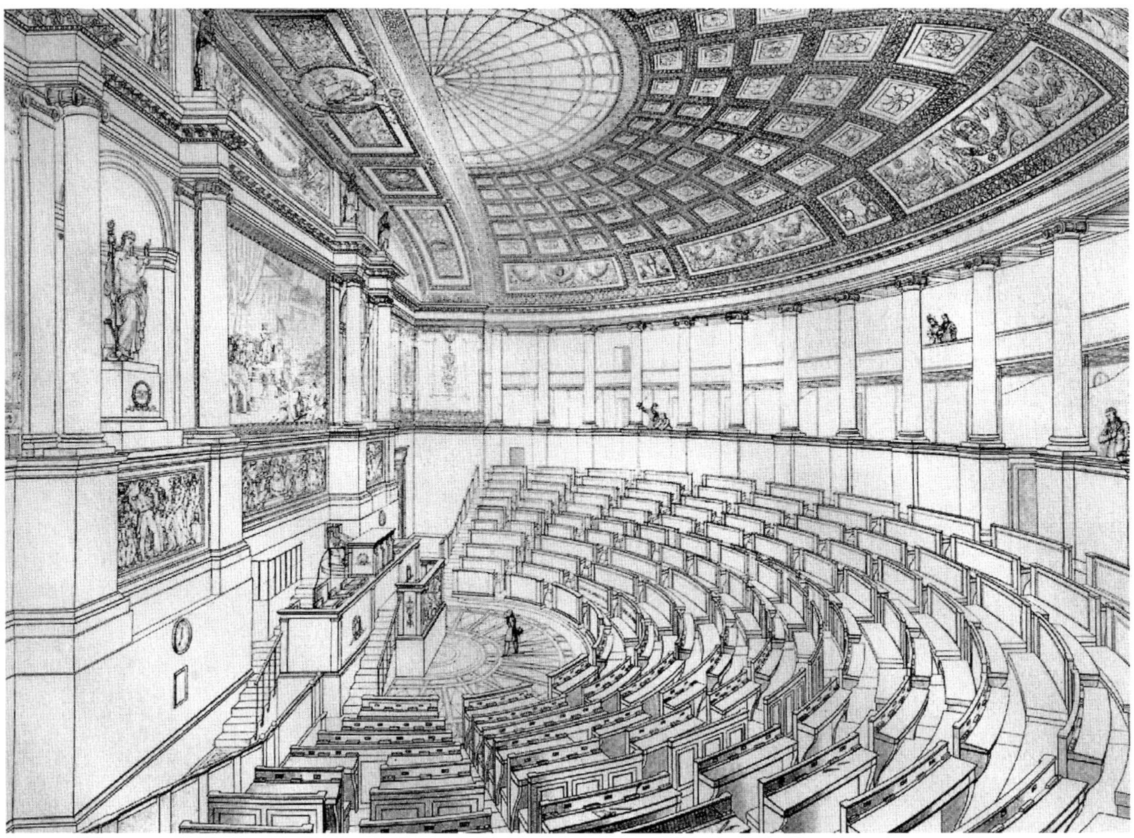

Fig. 192: For Herbert Baker, the assembly room of the Palais Bourbon in Paris (built 1828–33 by Jules de Joly) was a direct model for the three chambers of the Legislative Building (opposite page).

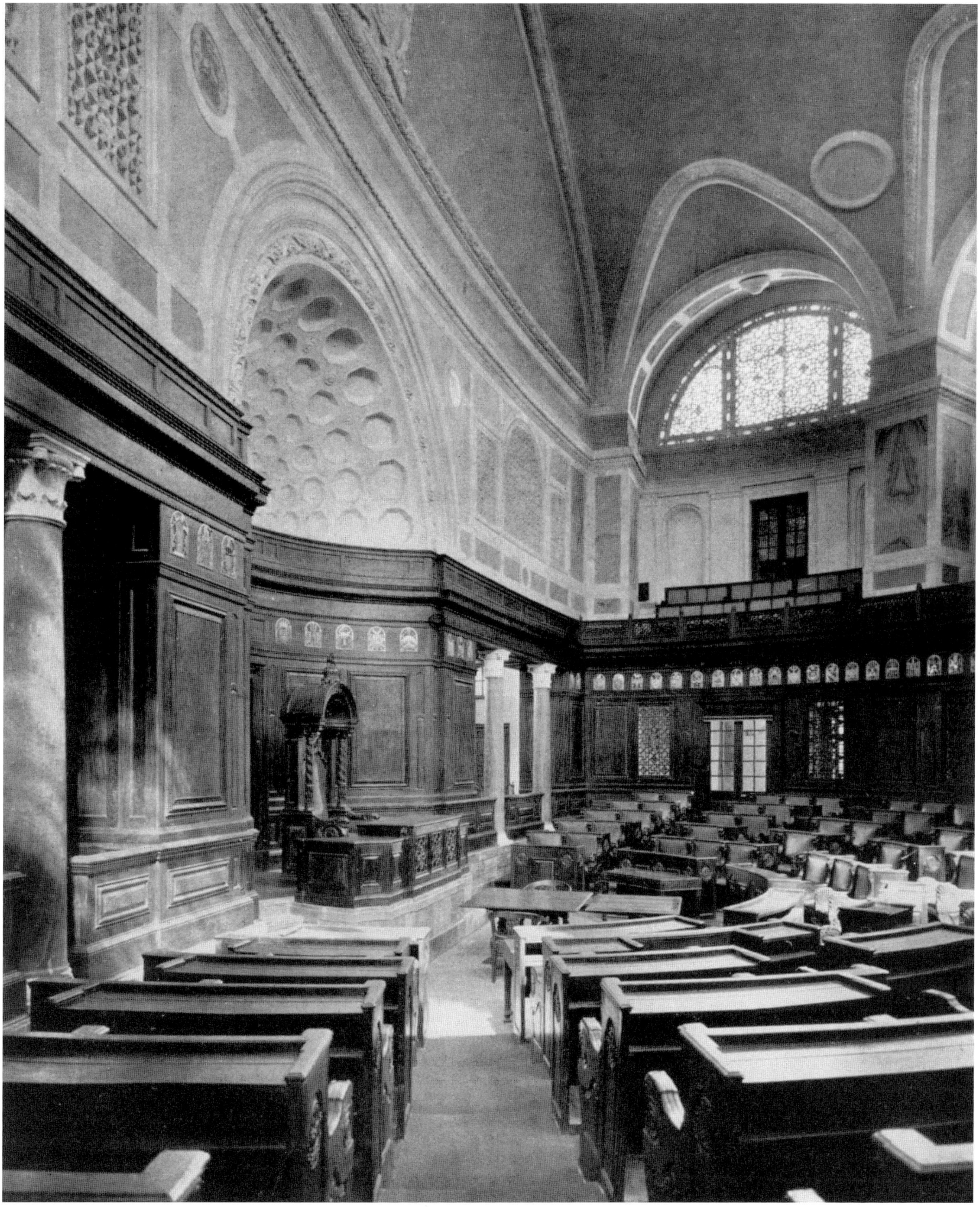

Western Court and Eastern Court (Architect: Robert Tor Russel), 1922

Robert Tor Russel entered the Indian Government service in 1914, but had remained in the shadow of star architects Lutyens and Baker. As the successor to William Henry Nicholls, Chief Architect to the Government of India, he and his team built public buildings all over India. In New Delhi, these not only comprise Connaught Place and about 4,000 bungalows for government employees, but also the two guest houses, known as Western Court and Eastern Court on Queen's Way (now Janpath) for members of parliament.

Although these guest houses are first-class late Neo-Classical designs (Fig. 193), the history of architecture unfortunately makes little mention of them, even less than Connaught Place and Connaught Circus. The reason is obvious: architects all over the world have long since felt determined to set aside the formal repertoire of Classicism. Latecomers to India are in danger of losing contact with the modern age; in the same way as the British Empire risked losing contact with political developments in the western democracies.

Fig. 193: In its central section and in the side wings (here the eastern facade of the northern wing), the facades of the Western and Eastern Courts are constructed strictly according to the formal rules established by Edwin Lutyens and Herbert Baker.

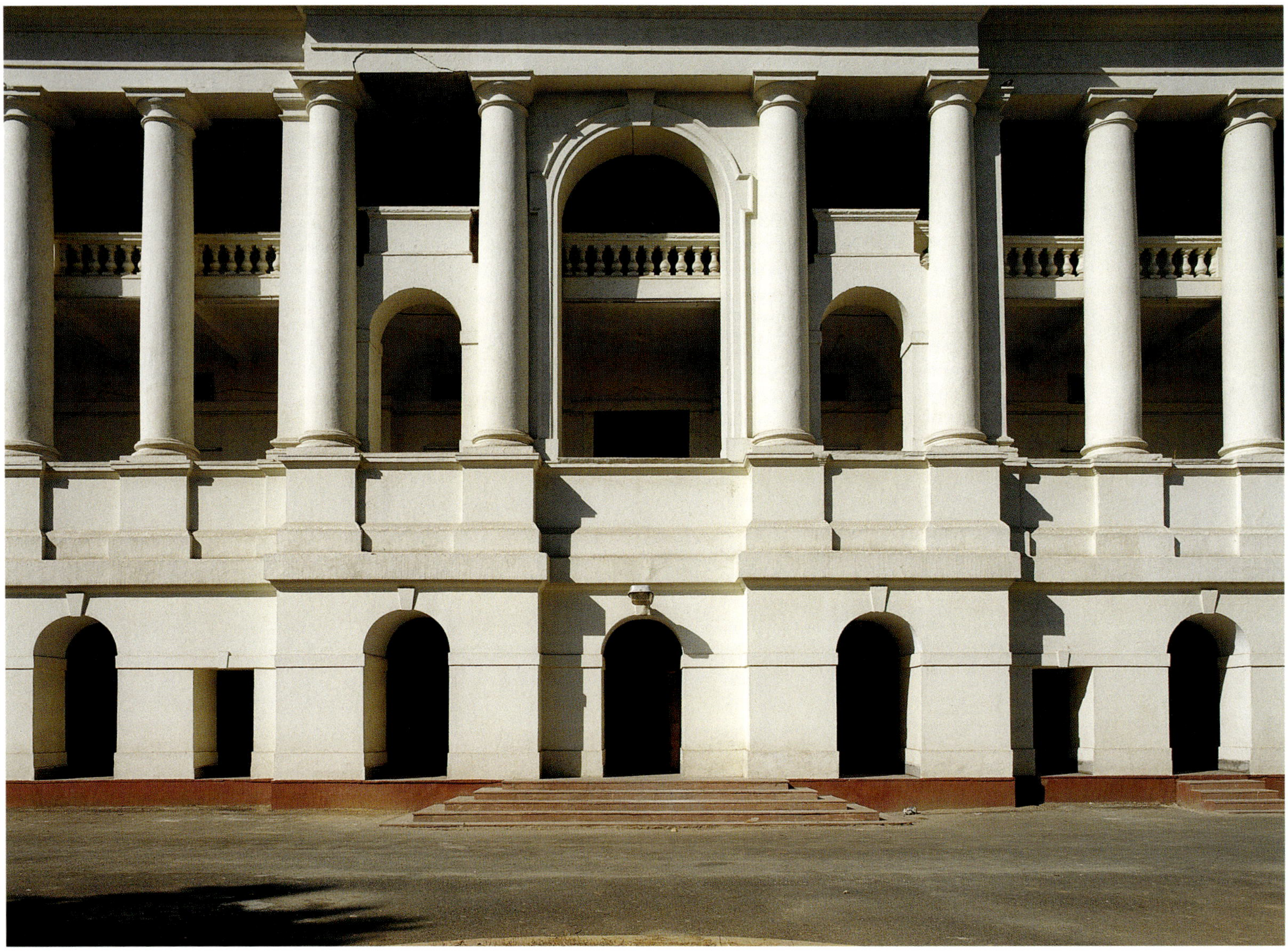

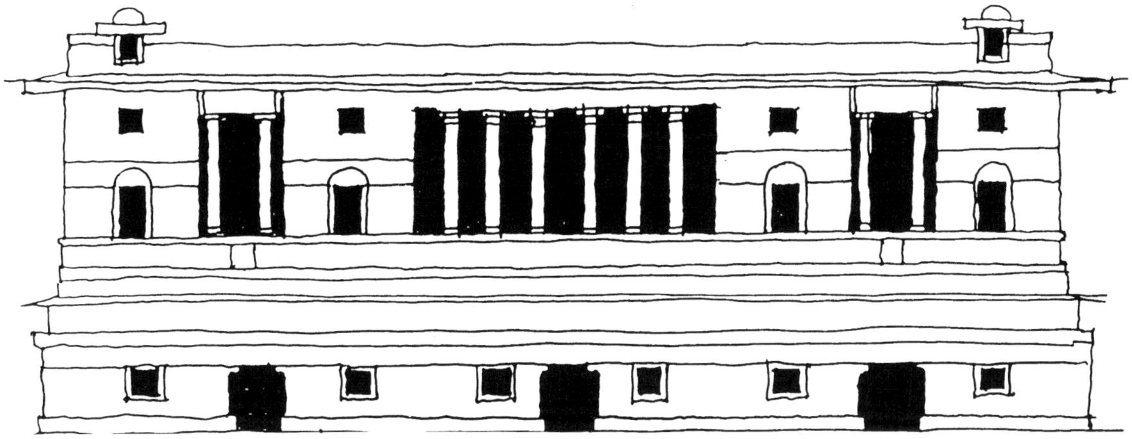

(a) Edwin Lutyens' Viceroy's House

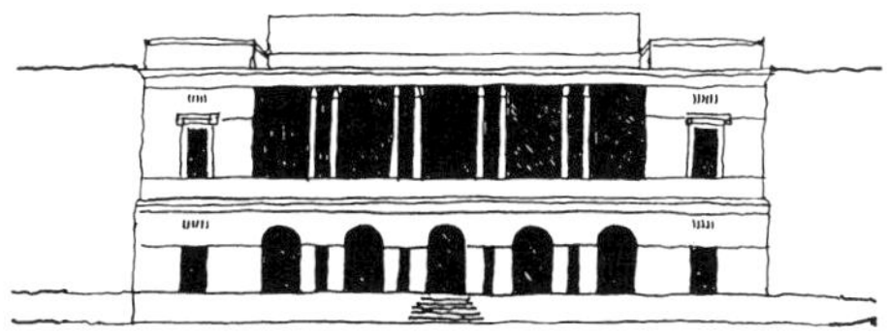

(b) Robert Tor Russel's Residence of the Commander-in-Chief

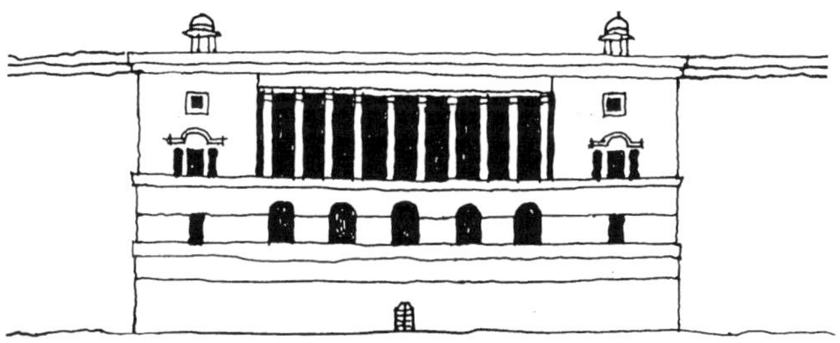

(c) Herbert Baker's Secretariats

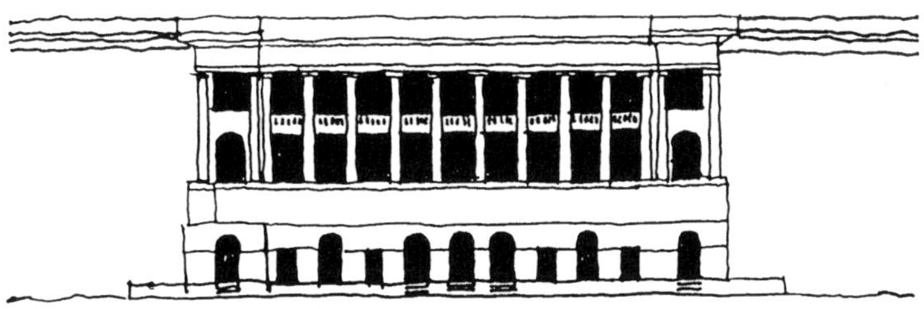

(d) Robert Tor Russel's Western Court and Eastern Court

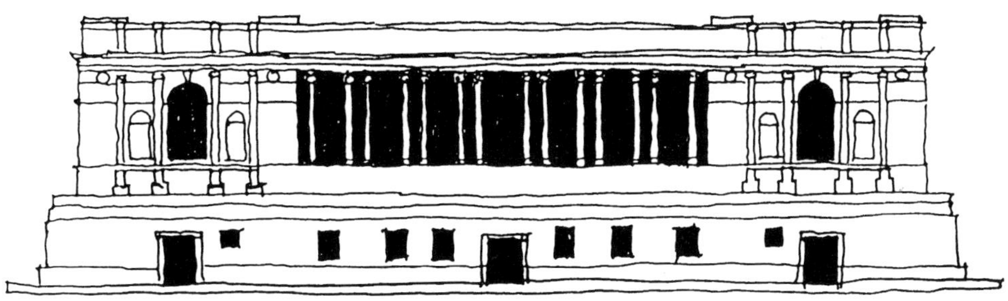

(e) Edwin Lutyens' Record Office

Fig. 194: The motif of the verandah, flanked on both sides by walls with pillars, also appears in Lutyens' plans for the wings of Viceroy's House (a) and the Record Office (e) and in Herbert Baker's plan for the Secretariats (c) and in Robert Tor Russell's plan for the Western and Eastern Courts (d) and the Residence of the Commander-in-Chief (b).

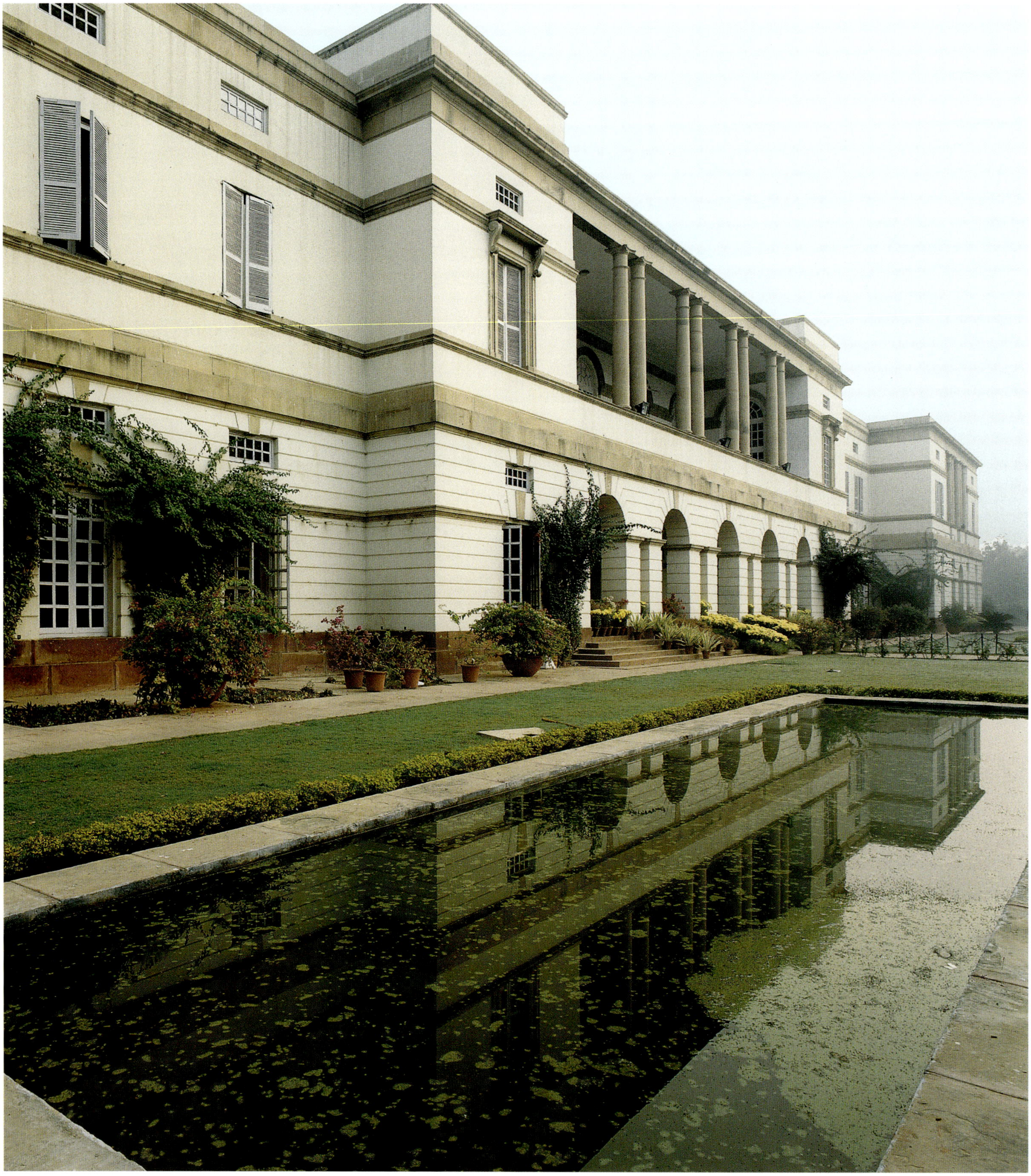

Fig. 195: Garden facade of the Commander-in-Chief's Residence, called Flagstaff House (Robert Tor Russel).

Residence of the Commander-in-Chief (Flagstaff House), now the Nehru Memorial Museum and Library (Architect: Robert Tor Russel), 1930

Securing and extending the British Empire in India required not only an experienced diplomat in Delhi – the Viceroy – but also an experienced Commander-in-Chief for the partly British, partly Indian soldiers and officers. In accordance with his special significance, the Commander-in-Chief was given a magnificent residence known as Flagstaff House. It was built on the axis of one of the avenues radiating outwards from Viceroy's House and therefore, has a direct view of the dome of the Durbar Hall.

The central section of the residence of the Commander-in-Chief is of special interest because for the garden side (Fig. 195), Russel chose an architectural motif that runs like a leit-motif through Delhi's imperial architecture – an enormous verandah with pillars, enclosed with walls and set on a massive base. Figure 194, illustrates the five most impressive examples of this architectural theme. Edwin Lutyens used this theme on a particularly large scale at Viceroy's House (1914) and repeated it at the Record Office (1922), the only one of the four planned buildings to be at least partly realized. These buildings were intended to function as research institutions, museums, and libraries at the junction of King's Way and Queen's Way (see town plan in Fig. 60). Herbert Baker chose the motif for the external southern and northern facades of the Secretariats (1914, cf. Fig. 125). Ultimately, Robert Tor Russel adopted it for the main views of Western Court and Eastern Court (1922, cf. Fig. 193), and for the Residence of the Commander-in-Chief (1930, cf. Fig. 195).

"... Russell's stone and stucco mansion for the Commander-in-Chief appeared to exude the very spirit of Lutyens at his most imperial. Its long symmetrical mass, completed in 1930,

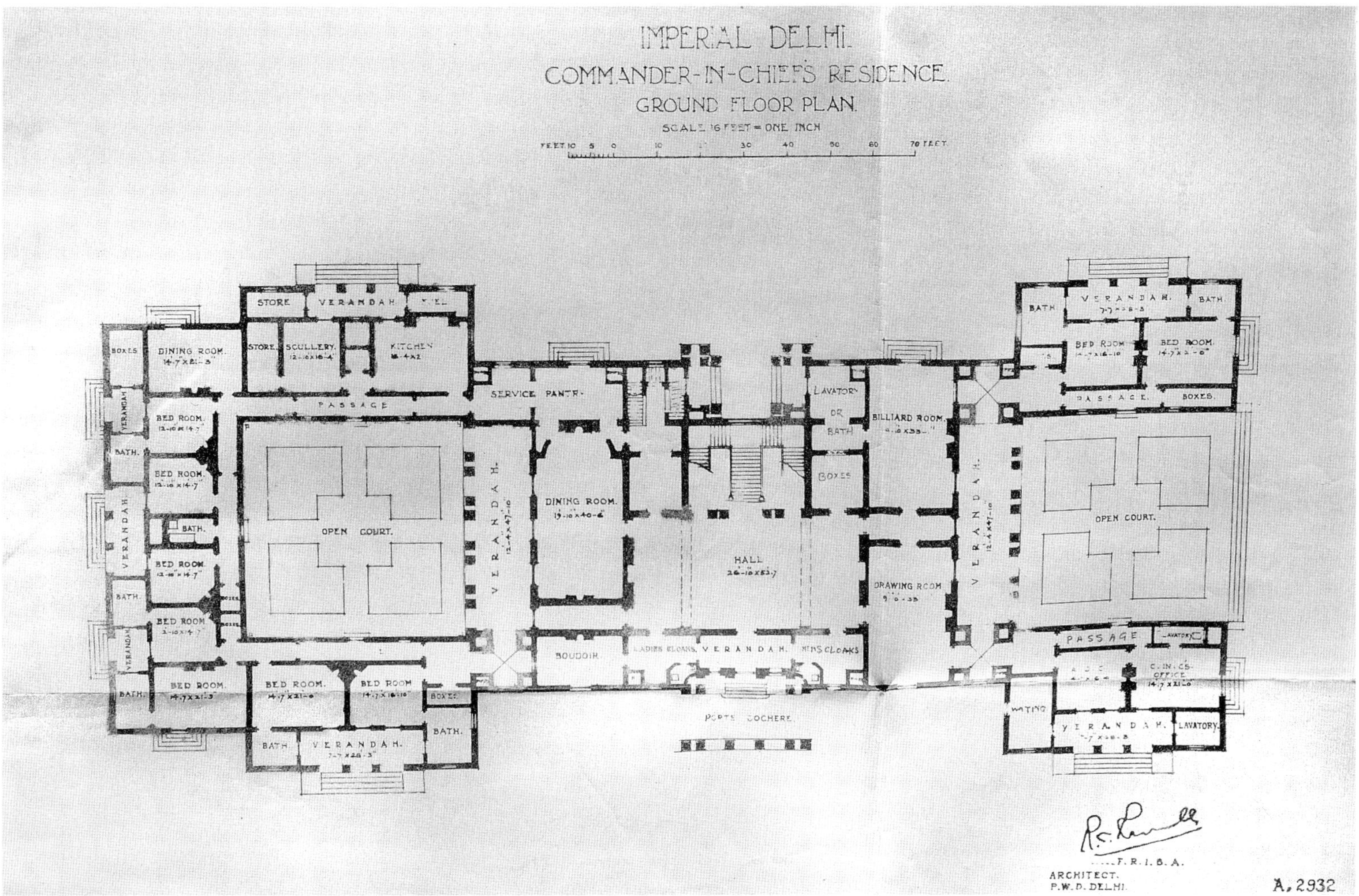

Fig. 196: The Commander-in-Chief's Residence, plan of the ground floor.

echoes motives recalling not only the Viceregal palace, Schedule B, and Hyderabad House, but in particular the cluster of cultural edifices Lutyens designed for the heart of King's Way. Conspicuous string courses, a black ribbon of shadow beneath the cornice, and the rhythm of paired columns in garden loggias all underscored the predominant horizontality. Recessed windows and deep arcades implied massive solidity that would defy the assaults of men and elements. The restrained classicism of the palatial interior, exemplified in the serene and even severe cornice and fireplace details of the barrel-vaulted reception room, admirably befitted a soldier's residence. Later, this austere dignity suited equally well the Anglicised tastes of Jawaharlal Nehru when Prime Minister, and appropriately the house became a museum and library devoted to the man sometimes known as 'the last of the Viceroys.'"[33]

One surviving sketch for the Commander-in-Chief's Residence allows the original architectural concept to be more easily seen than does the present state of the building. Russel obviously intended to build a symmetrical palace with an enormous central section and four additional narrow residential wings. Each of the pairs of these residential wings was grouped, along with a verandah on the main section, around a courtyard. A fourth wing terminates one of the courtyards at the very left of the plan, but this was certainly an unfortunate "last minute" addition to gain extra living space.

If we disregard this last addition, then we can recognize the original conceptual model as Viceroy's House, which is represented here on a more modest scale, and without its symbol of power, the central dome.

Record Office, now National Archives (Architect: Edwin Lutyens), 1922

In 1913, during the course of the development of Imperial Delhi's town plan, it became apparent that it would not be possible to give the main axis – regarded as essential for parades and processions – a city life in the style of the Champs Elysées in Paris (cf. Chapter 2.1) or the Mall in Washington (cf. Chapter 2.4). The spending power of the public employees working in the new seat of government would not be sufficient and the Viceroy, too, would not want to see the main axis flanked by the ostentatious residences of the Indian maharajas in alliance with him. The necessary administrative areas for the ministries were to be situated close to Viceroy's House on the Raisina Hill. Thus, the only alternative was to lay out the large axis, the Raj Path, as parkland and as a recreation area with axial waterways and fountains.

All the options identified in Chapter 4.2 for the future ground plan of the town show, from option 7 onwards (upon request of Lord Hardinge on January 18, 1913), a subdivision of the very long main axis by four large buildings. This subdivision produced a sensible result in the shape of an enormous plaza on the most important junction of the two largest boulevards. In the final sketch of March 20, 1913, the routes were King's Way running from east to west, and Queen's Way running from north to south (from a railway station planned in the north to a cathedral planned in the south – see Fig. 60).

In their Final Report, the members of the Delhi Town Planning Committee emphatically described this intersection known as point B: "The processional route will lead down from the railway station due south to the point where it is intersected by the main east to west axis. Here round a place will be gathered the buildings of the Oriental Institute, the Museum, the Library and the Imperial Record Office which will form what may be termed a centre of intellectual interest."[34]

Of the four large buildings planned only the Imperial Record Office was built in the original arrangement and, even then, only one wing was built (Fig. 198). Thus, King's Way lacked an important focal point at its midpoint compared to the Rond Point of the Champs Elysées.

"Watercolor perspectives depicting Lutyens' monumental grouping of cruciform structures, as exhibited at the Royal Academy in 1922, displayed a pervasive classical vocabulary, skilfully adapted to Indian tradition and weather. The wide expanse of basement walls, their battered red stone punctuated at intervals by shadowy entrances and recessed windows and semi-domes, conveyed a calculated impression of timeless solidity and strength. The

33 R.G. Irving: op. cit., p. 318.
34 Delhi Town Planning Committee: *Final Report regarding the selected site, with plan and two maps*, London 1913, p. 6.

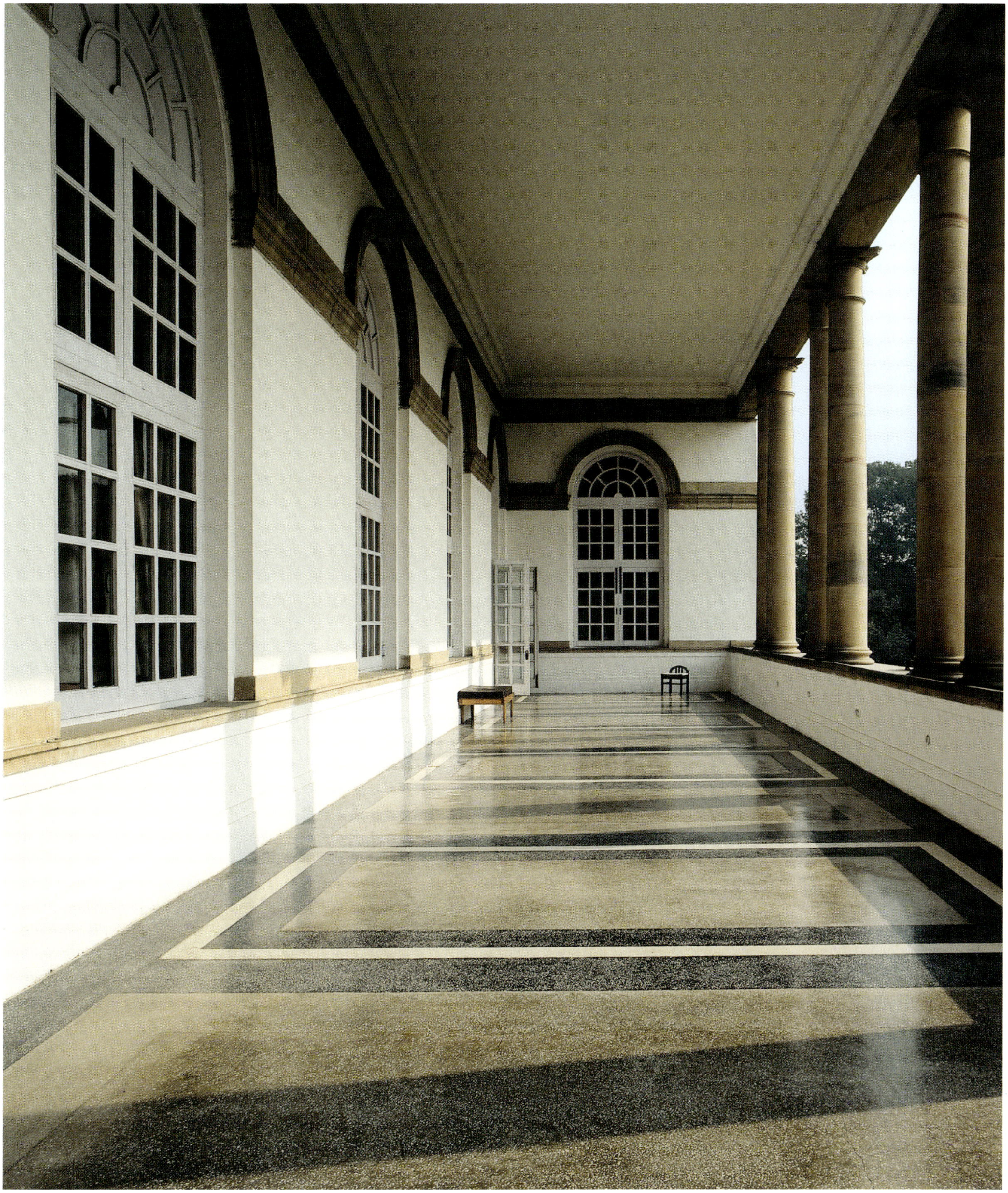

Fig. 197: The Commander-in-Chief's Residence, verandah on the upper storey.

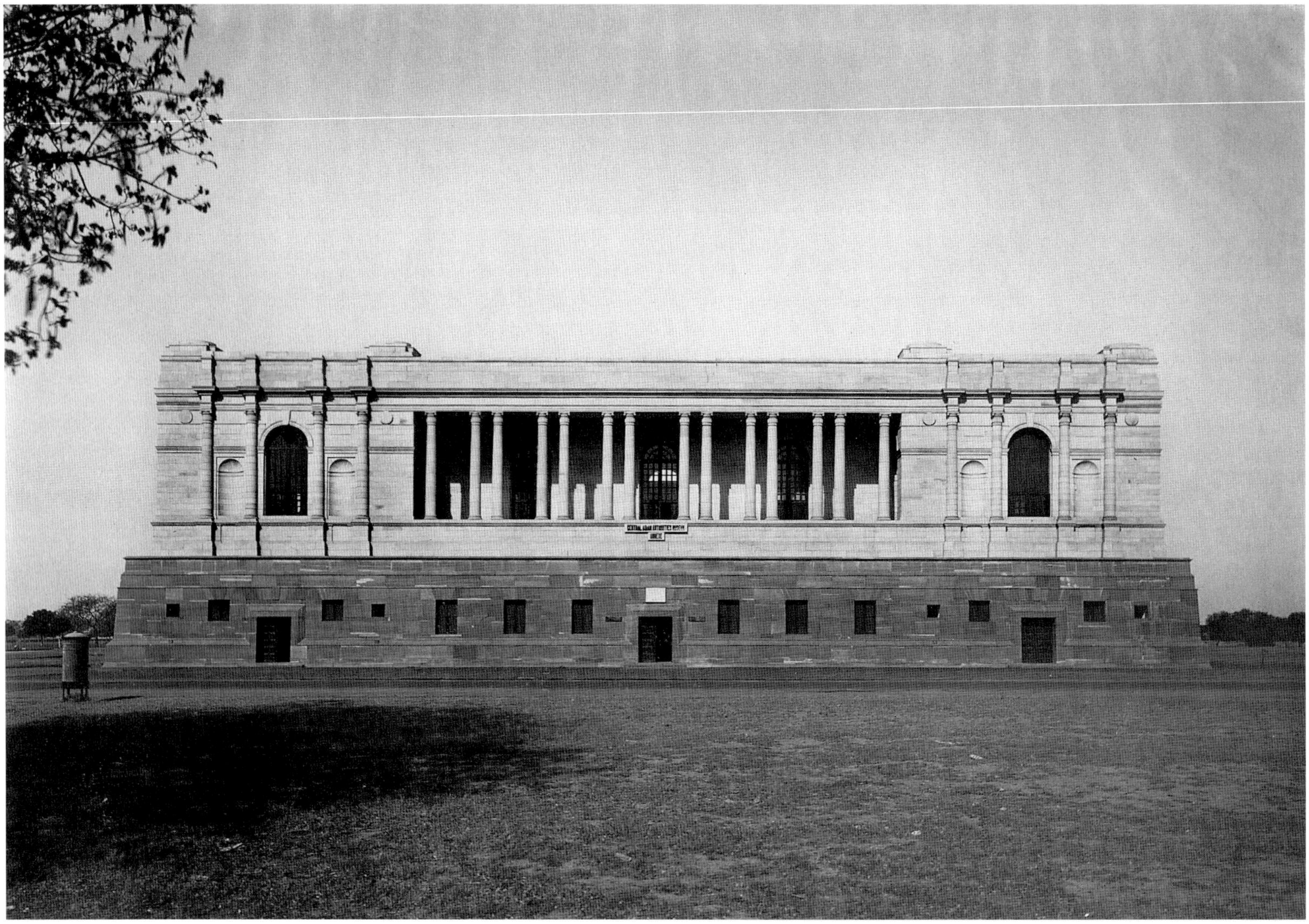

Fig. 198: At the intersection of King's Way and Queen's Way, Edwin Lutyens had planned four national museums and archives. Only one, the Record Office (now National Archives), was realized in 1922–23.

continuous sweep of cornices and string courses and the rhythmic beat of paired columns reinforced a dominant horizontality appropriate to a uniformly flat riverain. The airy central courtyard of each structure, its deep loggias, thick walls, and splashing rooftop fountains acknowledged the preponderantly hot and arid Delhi climate."[35]

In a comparison of the Record Office with other similar buildings in Imperial Delhi (Fig. 194), the unusual quality of its facade is obvious. All the elements stand in a harmonious relationship to each other, that is, the base is neither too high, as in Baker's Secretariat, nor too broken up, as in Russel's Residence of the Commander-in-Chief. Edwin Lutyens was undoubtedly bringing his entire repertoire of Neo-Classical proportions to bear. The facade reflects, with matchless clarity, the two most important architectural clichés of the late Neo-Classical building style in India, namely the hall with columns and the verandah with capitals of the Delhi Order,[36] each with a triple-axis triumphal arch at both sides of this stoa.

The triumphal arches at each side are of extraordinary grandeur and Neo-Classical simplicity. Like the Porte St Denis and the Arc de Triomphe in Paris (Fig. 139), they follow the tripartite geometric division of a square elevation with the central arch in the central field of the resulting nine squares. To illustrate this arrangement, one of these triumphal arches is highlighted in Fig. 141.

Although there appears to be no possible doubt that Lutyens actually had triumphal arches in mind for his design, he appears never to have mentioned it. All the subsequent facades of the same type by his colleagues Herbert Baker and Robert Tor Russel (cf. Fig. 194) do not show this motif and are confined to simpler window openings in the stonework on either side of a pillared verandah.

In the Record Office, the reason behind the significant height increase of the central stoa and with the triumphal side arches on a high base of red sandstone is somewhat puzzling. Its undecorated doorways and window openings were obviously not intended to make their own architectural statement. Thus, the base is to be perceived as part of the similar red earth surrounding the area, rather than belonging to the actual building itself.

With regard to the different treatment of the base and the main storey, some successors to the Record Office clearly differ from their model. By the time Robert Tor Russel's facades for the Western and Eastern Courts were built, and for the Residence of the Commander-in-Chief (cf. again Fig. 194), the base is extremely broken up and merges colourfully with the facade above it. Finally, it is no longer possible to recognize the provenance of the elements as, for example, in the facades of the wings of Western Court (Fig. 193). The isolation of the original triumphal arch (centre of picture in Fig. 193) goes one step further: because it stretches over two storeys, the central arch of the gateway now acquires another balustrade inserted at half height.

One other element becomes quite obvious in the facade of the Record Office: Late Neo-Classicism in India – and also in Edwin Lutyens' offices built later in London – has nothing in common with the contemporary early Fascist architecture in Europe. On the other hand, no features can be discerned in common with the modern architecture of Frank Lloyd Wright or even that of Mies van der Rohe. The imperial expectations of the Britain had produced a totally independent formal canon in architecture.

35 R.G. Irving: op. cit., p. 254.
36 cf. Fig. 165.

Fig. 199: The entrance facade of the House for the Comptroller.

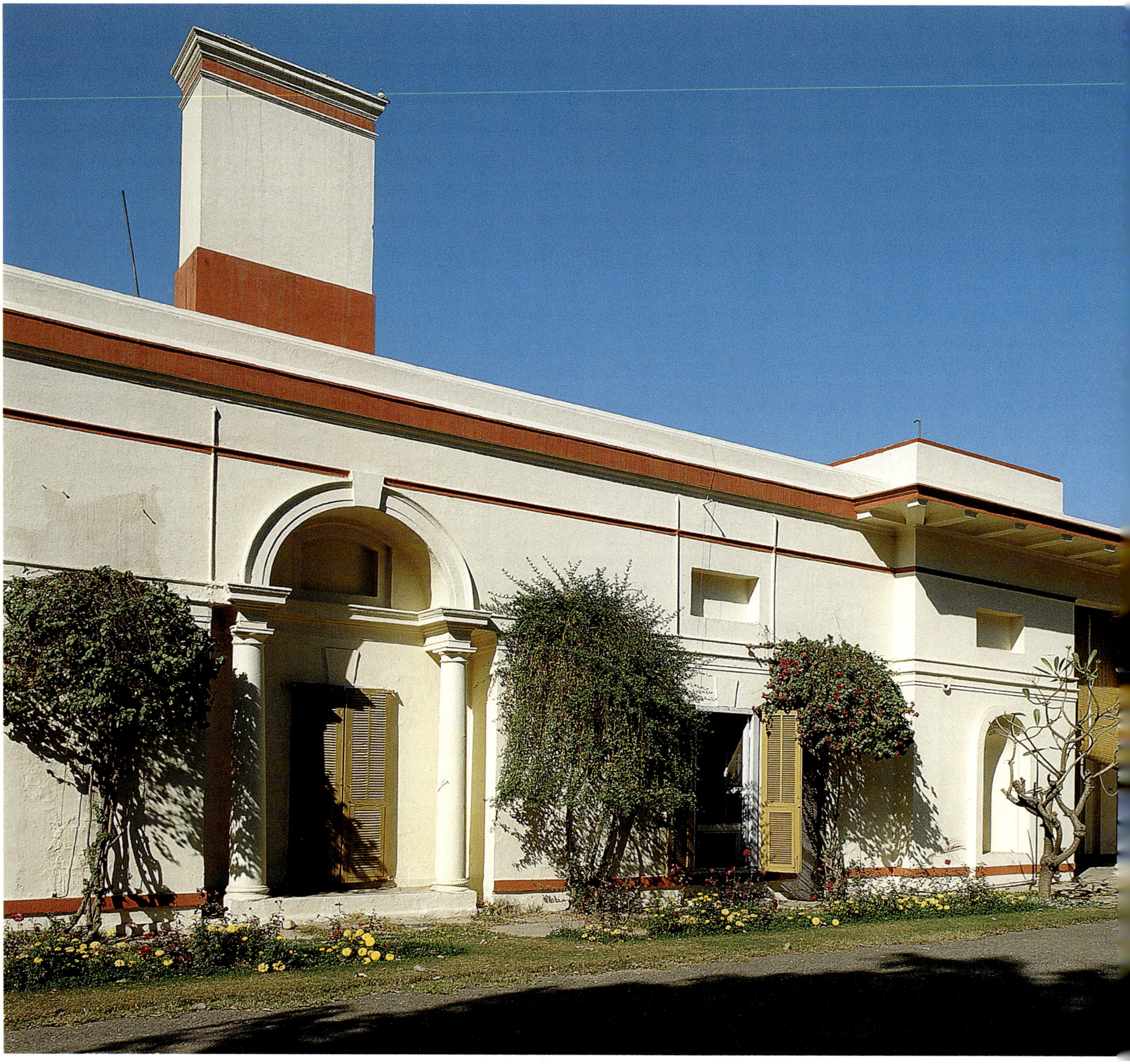

4.3.3 Residences

The architects of Imperial Delhi collectively contributed to the unusually varied architecture of the residences. Edwin Lutyens built the houses for senior officials in the neighbourhood directly west of Viceroy's House, Herbert Baker designed a series of bungalows on King George's Avenue (i.e. south of the Secretariats), and the Central Public Works Department under William Henry Nicholls and Robert Tor Russel built more than 500 bungalows for members of the government and senior officials in New Delhi.

Of the many houses of the twenties and thirties still in good condition today, but often diminished by porches made of synthetic material or tasteless extensions, only three examples are be named here: The House for the Comptroller to H.E. the Viceroy in the prohibited area of the Viceregal Estate, the House of a Justice on the Moti Lal Nehru Marg, and the house of a parliamentarian on Asoka Road.

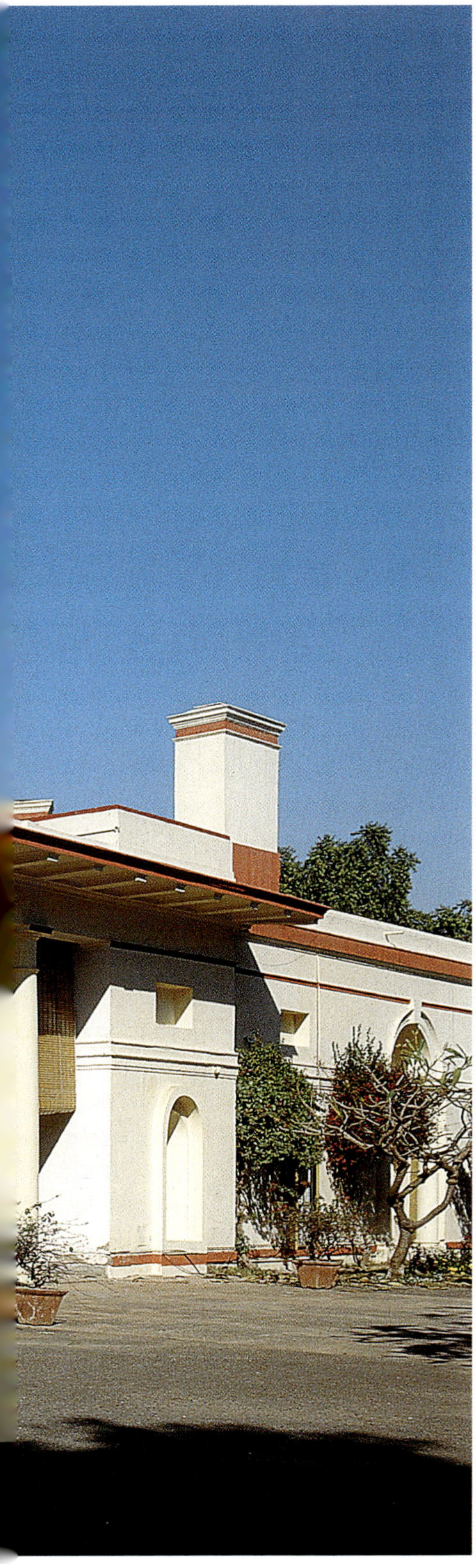

The house on Asoka Road is particularly interesting because it is situated directly at the junction of Asoka Road and one of the typical roundabouts where six roads converge. Here, the property is inevitably shaped like a slice of pie, and the architects of the Central Public Works Department made a logical decision to construct a building of the butterfly type axially oriented on the roundabout. Between the two symmetrical main wings lying at an angle of 120° to each other, there is a prestigious approach (see Fig. 202) and the entrance is emphasized by a curved arrangement of pillars. A few tricks, namely the inviting passageway between the wings of the building and the accentuated entrance, heighten the effect of the building to create a grandiose impression.

The architects of the Central Works Department proceeded no less skilfully with the designing and building of the House of a Justice in the Moti Lal Nehru Marg. Because this residential property lay on the eastern side of an avenue running north-south, the living rooms opened to the west for climatic reasons, hence the separation of the entrance area and the private garden became difficult. The solution was also well conceived: perpendicular to the main axis of the living area, which opened westwards to the garden (see Fig. 201), was the building's entrance along a second axis running perpendicular to it in a north-south direction.

The House for the Comptroller to H.E. the Viceroy, designed and built around 1920 by Lutyens, is one of the few residences for which all the architectural documents have been preserved (see Fig. 200). These records remain intact and complete because it lies in the prohibited area of Viceroy's House (now Rashtrapati Bhavan). This house exemplifies Lutyens' love of symmetry to the extent that, even behind a facade of symmetry, a contrasting spatial disposition was concealed. The type of residence developed here was not modelled on the Neo-Palladian style, nor did it resemble one of Lutyens' British country houses. The essential characteristics are the very different spatial heights designed to aid cross ventilation, a shady porch at the entrance and at the garden side, and high chimneys to ensure the fireplaces were effective in the two or three cold winter months.

All three examples of residences in Imperial Delhi stand out through their surprisingly generous layouts, a characteristic previously only conceivable in England in the country houses of the affluent nobility. In India, where every ambitious official in the service of His Majesty could make a career for himself irrespective of his social background, a luxurious life-style (not only by Indian standards) beckoned the successful man. It is obvious that the great number of officials and military personnel working in all the colonies of the British Crown, without the social restrictions of the homeland, both consciously and unconsciously, contributed to the stabilization of the extremely conservative political system of that time.

There arose a historically unique blend of imperial magnificence and a perception of unlimited power for the Viceroy alongside the unique affluence for the bourgeois supporters of that power. Because this system of rewards was only realized at the expense of a predominantly uneducated native Indian population already worn down by the ruling houses, it finally broke down. A slowly, but steadily increasing number of educated Indians students, most often from Cambridge and Oxford, recognized the laws governing the imperial game and undermined it,

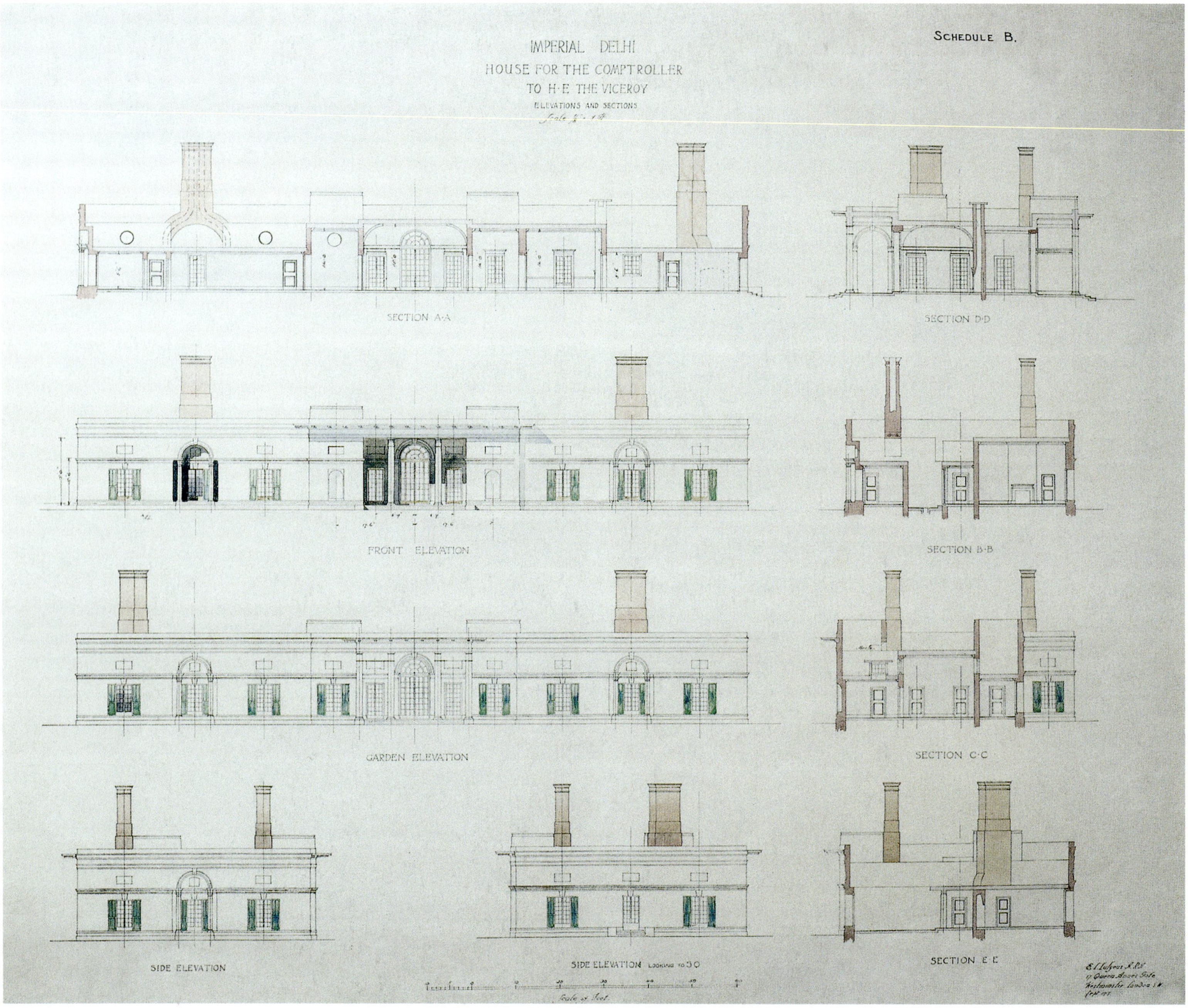

Fig. 200: Diagram for the House of the Comptroller (Edwin Lutyens), *c.* 1920.

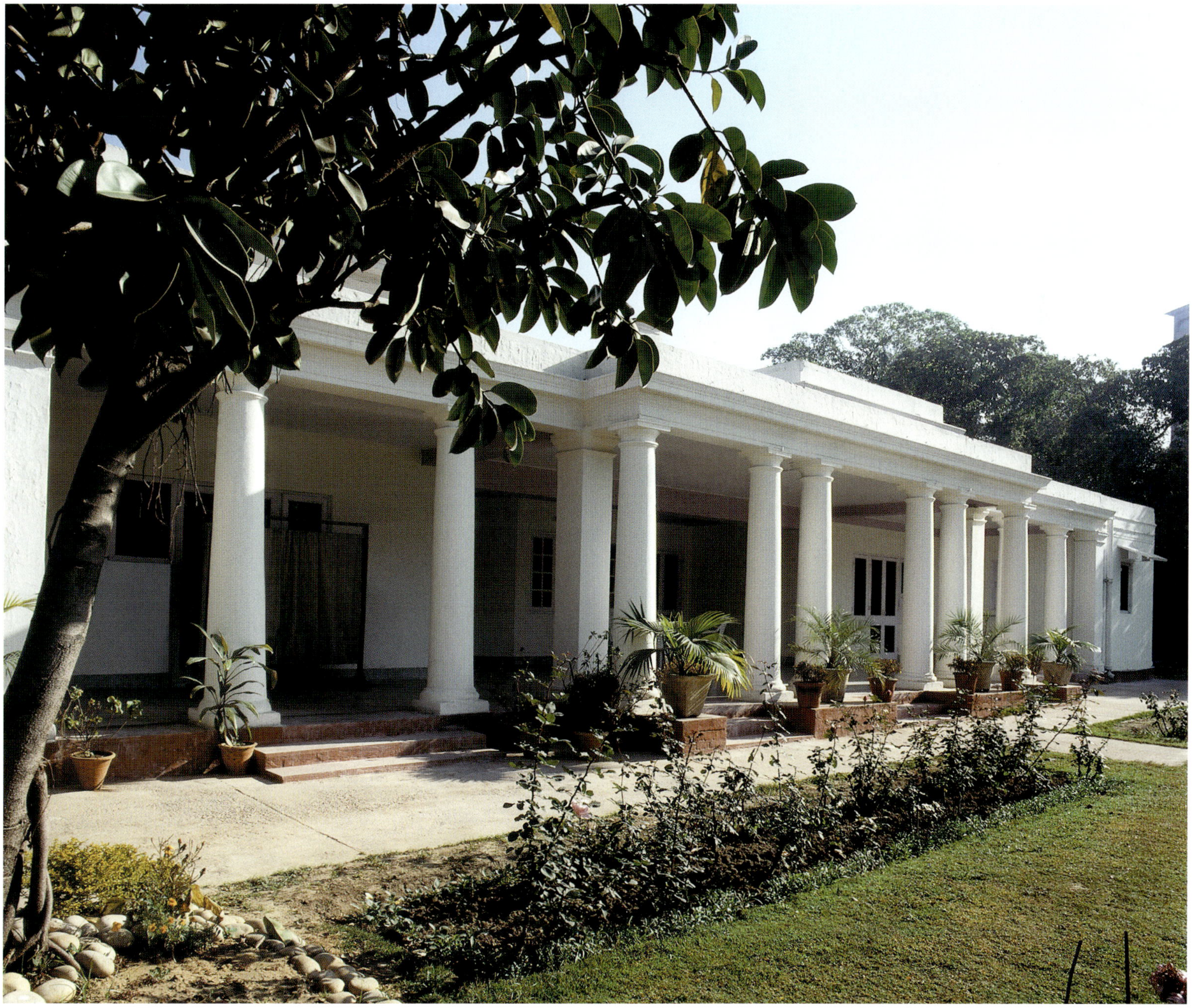

Fig. 201: The House of a Justice from the garden side.

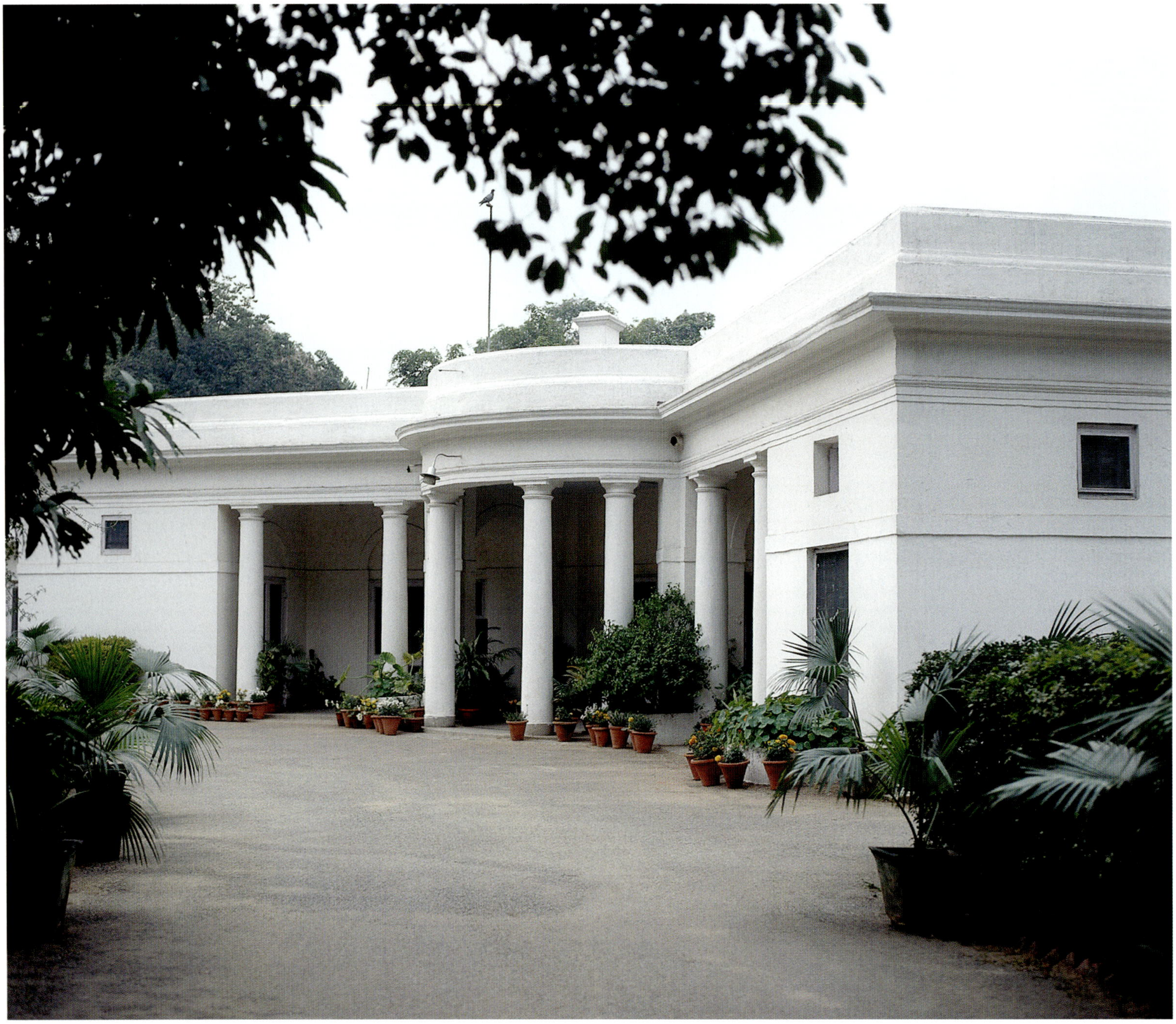

Fig. 202: The house of a parliamentarian on Asoka Road No. 5 built in the butterfly-style around the roundabouts in New Delhi's hexagonal streetplan.

Fig. 203: Town plan with all the residences and offices built up to 1957.

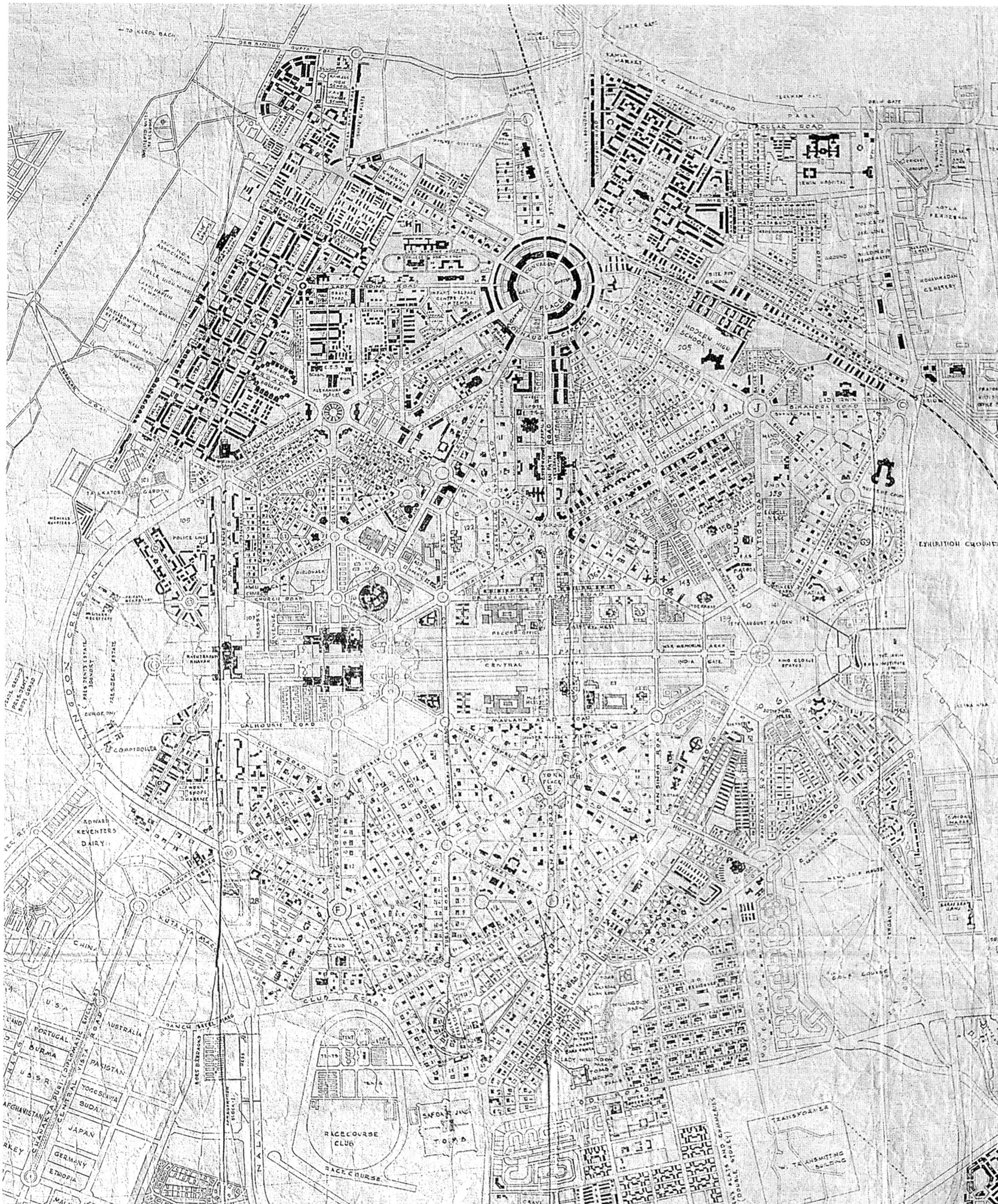

TO KAROL BAGH
CIRCULAR ROAD
IRWIN HOSPITAL
MODERN SCHOOL
TALKATORA GARDEN
POLICE LINES
CHURCH ROAD
CENTRAL
INDIA GATE
DALHOUSIE ROAD
COMPTROLLER
EDWARD KEVENTERS DAIRY
CHINA
U.S.A.
PORTUGAL
BURMA
U.S.S.R.
AFGHANISTAN
JAPAN
GERMANY
ETHIOPIA
AUSTRALIA
PAKISTAN
SUDAN
CLUB ROAD
RACECOURSE CLUB
RACECOURSE
TOMB
SAFDAR JANG AERODROME
TRANSMITTING BUILDING

as Mahatma Gandhi did, through political ideals and practical strategies that while often incomprehensible to the British Crown, also exposed the underlying hypocrisy and injustice inherent in colonial policy.

An unusual system of residential accommodation was built at the same time as Viceroy's House to its northwest and southwest within the extensive Viceregal Estate. Packed together closely, and on the site plan recalling the geometry of English garden cities, lies the houses of the servants to the northwest and those of the bodyguard to the southwest (Fig. 204). Similarly, within the Viceregal Estate – and in the same way that the houses of the servants and the bodyguard are axially oriented on Viceroy's House, stand the much more magnificent official villas of the private secretary and the military secretary to the northwest, and those of the Surgeon and the Comptroller (Fig. 199) to the southwest.

"Quarters were designed and assigned as befitted rank: from single rooms for palace 'menials' and pairs of rooms for 'married syces' or grooms to commodious bungalows, replete with spacious garden and servants' compound, for principals in the Viceroy's Secretariat. The potential monotony inherent in a range of white-plastered bungalows and barracks was skilfully averted in both plan and elevation. Among the predominant quadrangular groupings Lutyens interspersed other basic geometric forms – circuses, crescents, and wedge-shaped designs – at varying distances from common axes. Emphatic axiality, clear-cut symmetry, and focal terminal features gave vigorous expression to imperial preoccupation with order, conformity, and stability. Above a uniform cornice line and consistently flat roofs Lutyens set obelisks, urns, and lantern-capped towers on a dozen and a half buildings to create a picturesque skyline. He employed details such as coining and rustication with accustomed dexterity in the stable blocks to produce lively shadow patterns and surface textures despite the corrosive glare of the sun ... Ranges of menials' cells or modest cottages were dexterously manipulated to look like single large residences, so that, as at Hampstead Garden Suburb, all the houses in a group enjoyed an enhanced grandeur and appeared equally agreeable to inhabit."[37]

37 R.G. Irving: op. cit., p. 231.

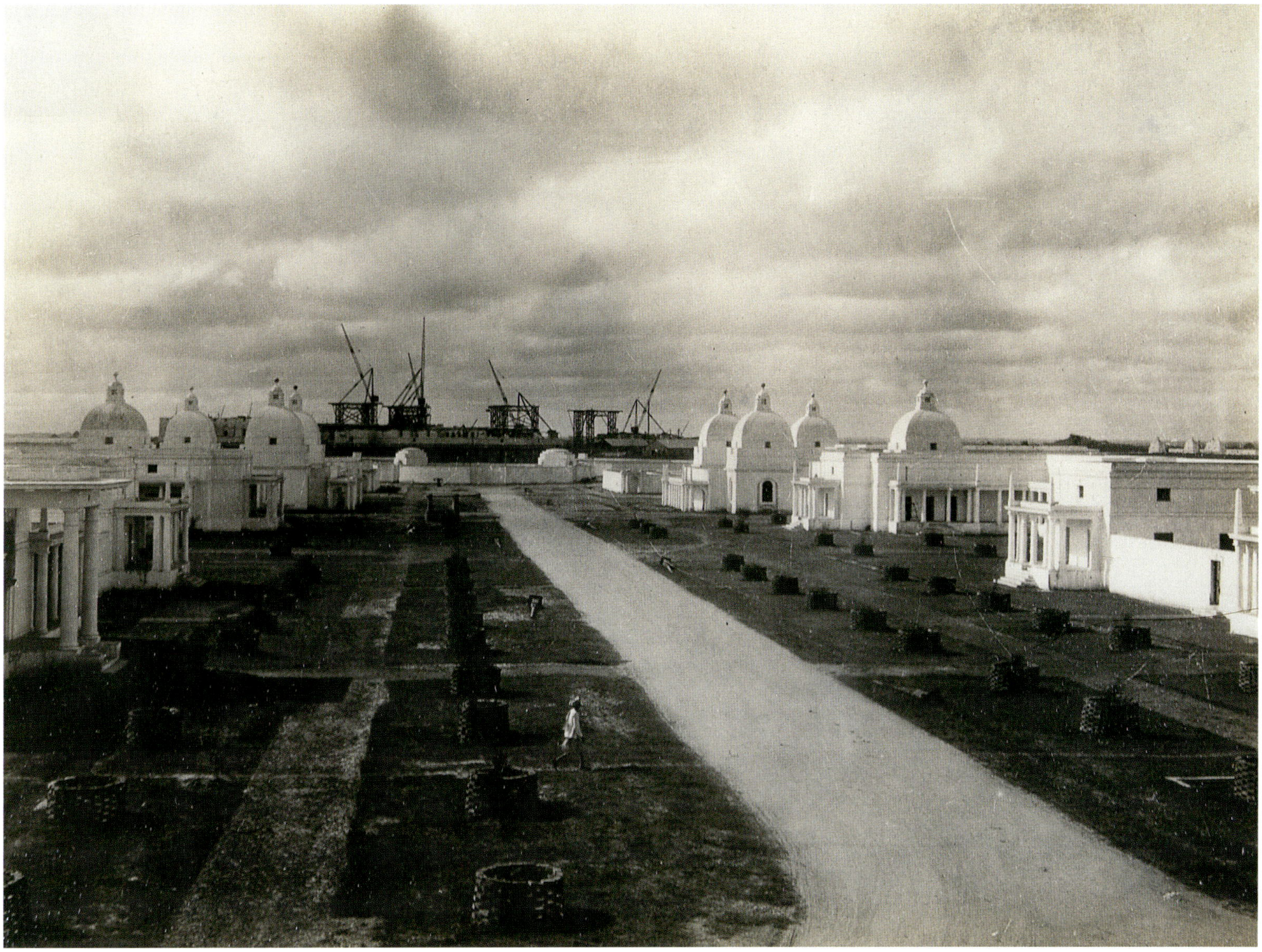

Fig. 204: The Staff Quarters and expansive system of stables were built at the same time as Viceroy's House (in the background). Like the rest of Imperial Delhi, the village was exclusively orientated in the direction of the Palace of the Viceroy.

4.3.4 The Tertiary Sector: Connaught Place and Connaught Circus (Architect: Robert Tor Russel), 1931

Imperial Delhi did not develop from a small market town and did not lie at the junction of important trade routes. Therefore, there is no marketplace in its centre. Instead, the Viceroy's Palace and the administrative buildings for the Raj constitute the centre of the town plan.

Since a seat of government is also inconceivable without businesses and services, these functions were already combined in the early plans at a separate location in the town: Connaught Place. The models for the plans are the eighteenth-century Circus in Bath (see Chapter 2.3), and Park Place in London: "R.T. Russel, Chief Architect to the Government of India, and his office prepared the detailed designs for Connaught Place along the lines which Nicholls[38] had advocated before leaving Delhi in 1917. Airy, stuccoed colonnades, punctuated by Palladian archways, afforded protection to shoppers from sun and rain alike, and the elegant, understated classicism prompted admiring comparisons with terraces at Bath and Cheltenham. Built only two stories high, however, the blocks failed to achieve the intended effect of urban enclosure, even before trees in the central park grew to obscure views across the circus. Furthermore, as Nicholls had feared, the sheer width of avenue entrances interrupted the desired circular continuity and rendered the boundaries of the plaza ambiguous. But these visual defects did not hamper the magnetic popularity of the stylish shops, which eventually eclipsed fashionable Chandi Chauk in Old Delhi. Indeed, forty years after its first bricks were

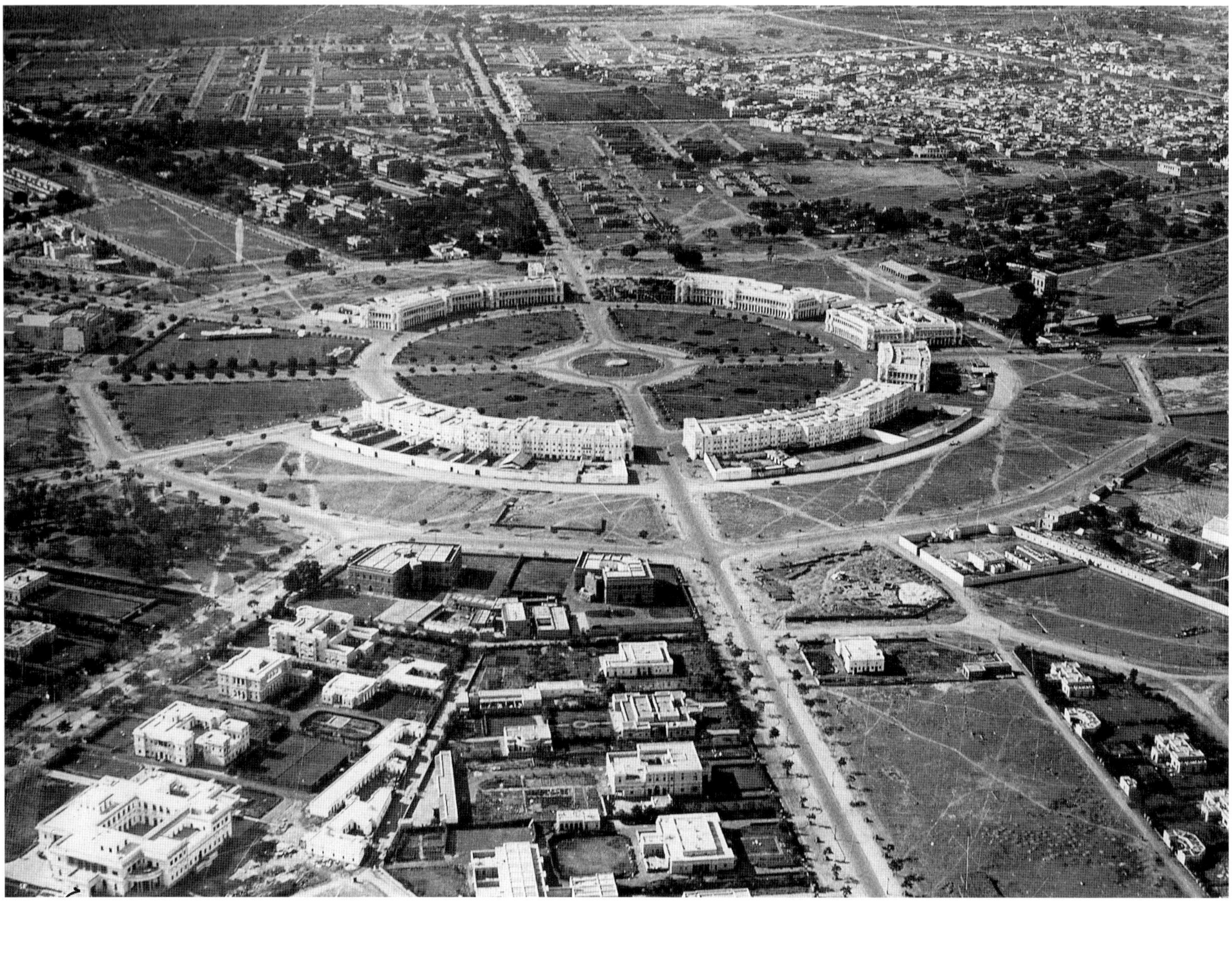

Fig. 205: Connaught Place and Circus, planned by R.T. Russel from 1917 (after suggestions by W.H. Nicholls), and built from 1928 to 1931, is the commercial centre of New Delhi even today. This aerial photograph from the 1930s shows the completed innermost circle of three concentric circles of buildings.

laid, one Indian planner recorded that Connaught Place, full of hustle and glamour, had become the Delhiwallah's abiding image of his city ..."[39]

Connaught Place and Connaught Circus today are in a completely neglected state. Advertising hoardings of every imaginable size conceal the architecture. Filth gathers wherever advertisements or sales do not demand a minimum amount of care for the building structures. Pickpockets, beggars and pedlars fill the arcades and an indescribably hideous underground shopping centre takes up a part of the earlier green area in the centre of the site. Out of an architecturally model and commercially successful shopping area in New Delhi, an increasingly dilapidated area has developed as a result of monuments and buildings not being preserved by the municipal authorities. It is only a question of time before the last vestiges of Neo-Palladian architecture and imperial building are lost beneath cheap restaurants and new office blocks. Sadly, a town is being deprived of its most important economic foundations.

38 William Henry Nicholls, Architect Member of Imperial Delhi Committee 1913–17.
39 R.G. Irving: op. cit., p. 314.

Fig. 206: In the initial plans for Imperial Delhi, a large round plaza with shady arcades was envisaged as a commercial centre. Connaught Place and Connaught Circus are changing today under heavy pressure from speculators and are in the process of losing their original formal compactness.

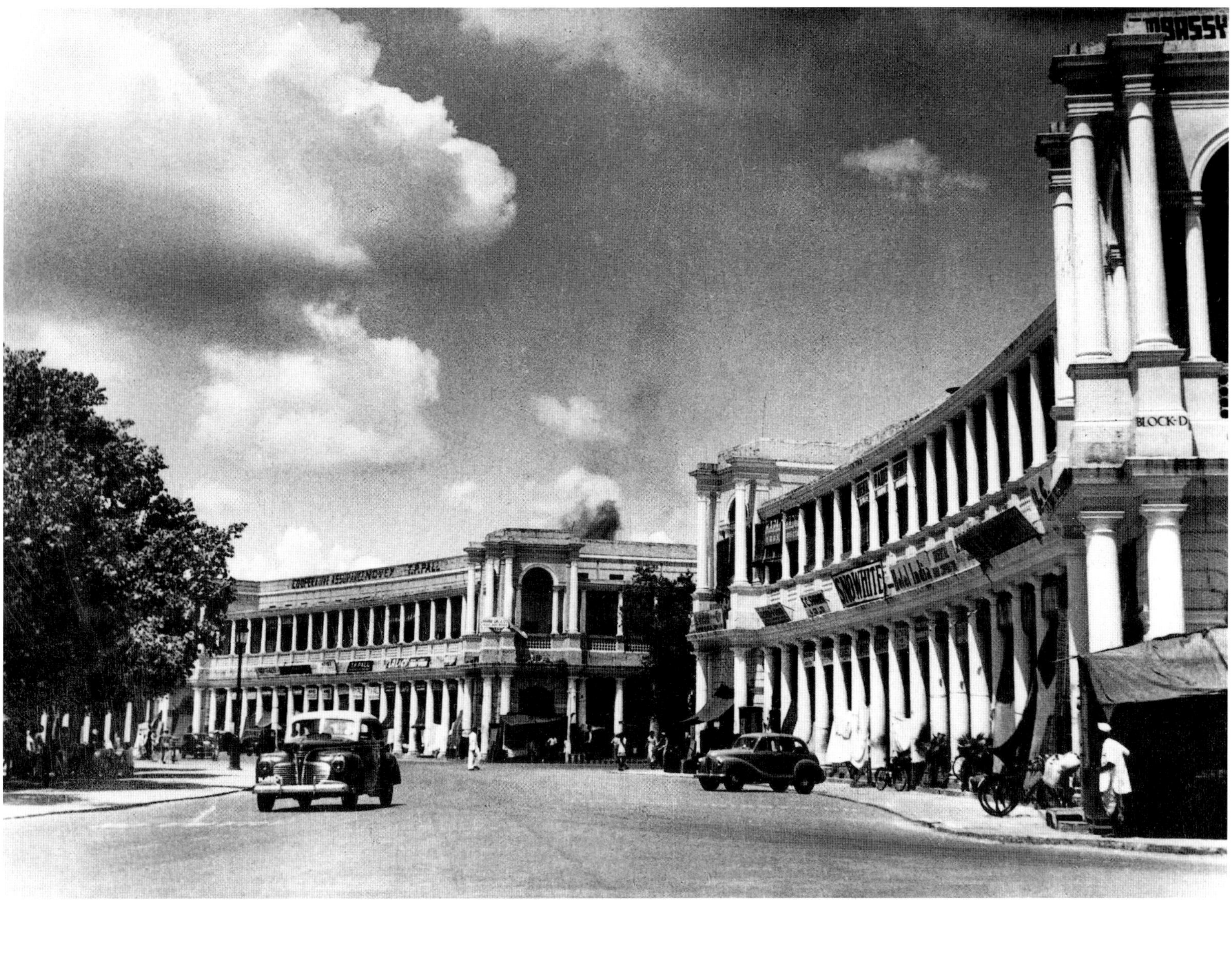

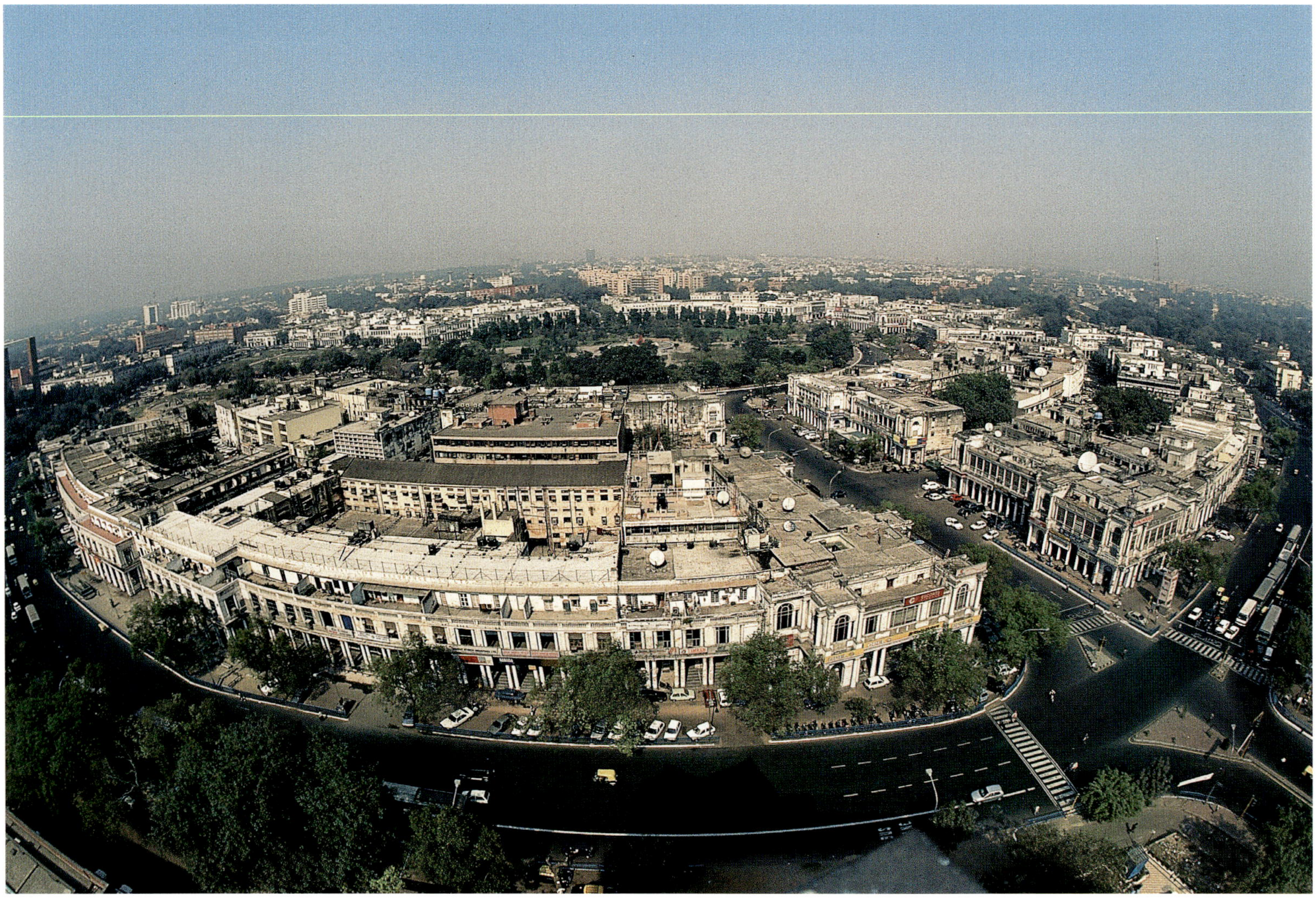

Fig. 207: Connaught Place and Circus today comprise the centre of the business and shopping district of New Delhi.

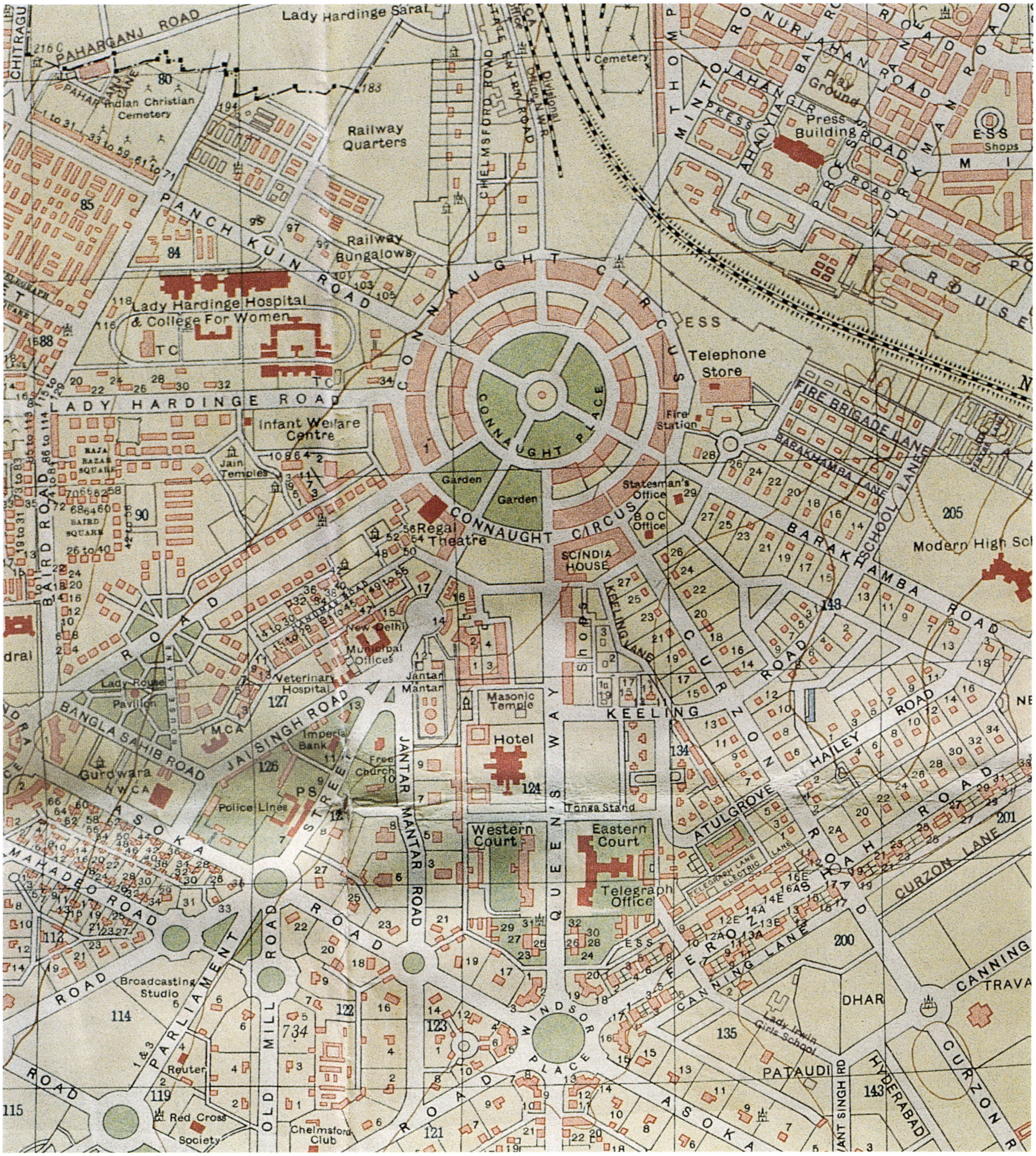

Fig. 208: In the 1931 town plan, it is clear that Connaught Place and Circus are oriented along Parliament Street axially to the Parliament Building situated in the south-east, and now form the terminal point of Queen's Way (now Janpath), the most important commercial street in the city.

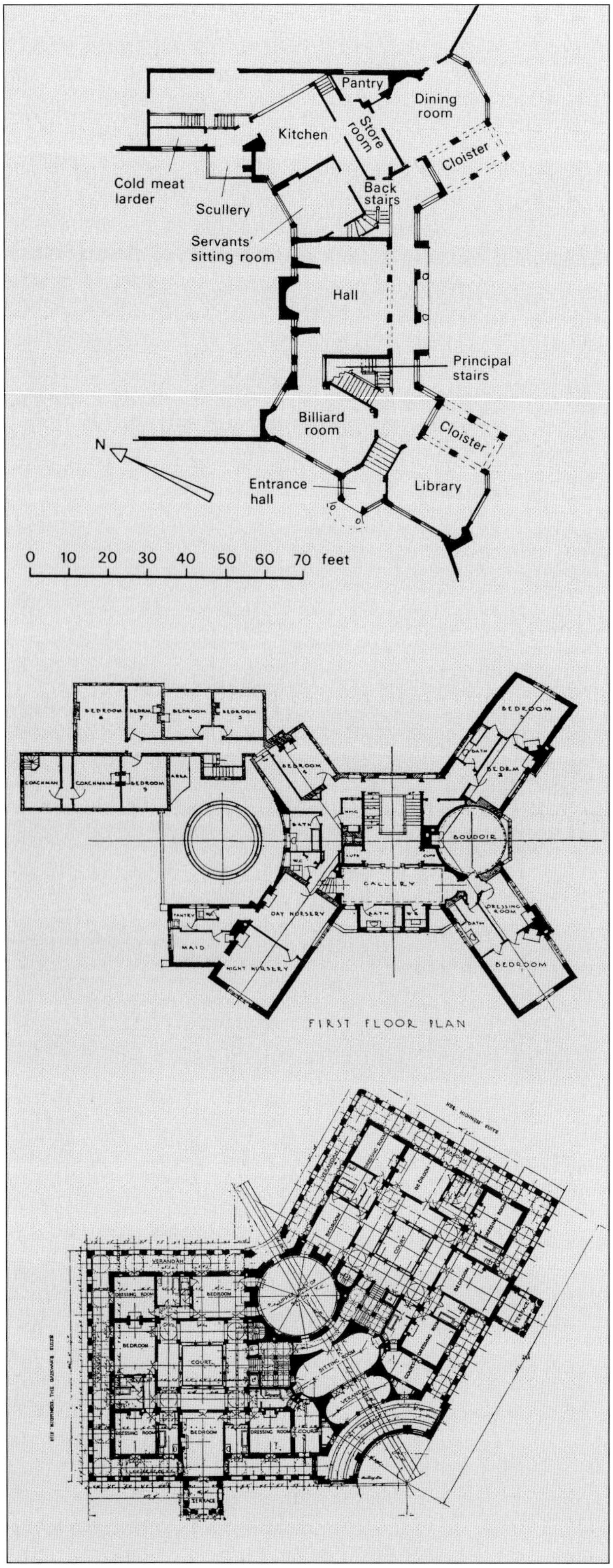

4.3.5 Residences of the Maharajas

The task of maintaining cohesion in British India presented the Raj with several seemingly impossible problems. On the one hand, there had to be a show of unity and closeness between the Crown and the local maharajas. On the other hand, the Viceroy did not want to see the maharajas in their own palaces around Viceroy's House in Imperial Delhi because they were indispensable to him for maintaining order in their native states.

The maharajas themselves sought to be close to the Crown; after all, they had formed an alliance with the British for better or for worse, and in doing so, had brought about a one-sided dependency. They now wanted to safeguard their wealth by showing solidarity with the British colonial power and, at the same time, to profit from the imperial grandeur of the new capital. With the Montagu-Chelmsford-Reform of 1919, a legal framework was created, amongst other things, for their needs. Consequently, splendid palaces with clear formal borrowings from British imperial architecture were built at the end of Raj Path, at a fitting distance from Viceroy's House: "As a rule, palaces in the capital were occupied for scarcely two or three weeks each year. In February, rulers and retinues left their states for meetings of the Chamber of Princes and events of Delhi Week, highpoint of the social season. Nearer twenty than seven days in length, the gala program boasted the Annual Imperial Horse Show and the Annual All-India Polo Tournaments as its central fixtures and numerous other engagements, including the Delhi Hunt Ball, the Freemasons' Ball, a Viceregal ball and garden party, and a State Investiture. Hundreds of officers and wives accompanied regimental polo teams; governors, residents, ministers of state, and Indian gentry deserted their provinces and posts. Princes without Delhi palaces took whole floors at Maiden's or the Cecil Hotel, and lobbies were crowded at cocktail hour with slim equerries in tight-fitting tunics, civilians and their ladies in white silk suits and light summer dresses. At Princes Place, the sound of saxophones wailing the tune of 'I'm Forever Blowing Bubbles' wafted from open loggia windows beneath a floodlit dome."[40]

The political calculation of the division of worldly power and economic advantages between the British Crown and local kingdoms enjoyed success for several decades. This climate of prosperity and privilege gave added impetus to the construction of the town and the architecture in New Delhi. The gearing of all decisions to the standards of the British Empire, however, obscured the view of urgently needed social and economic reform. A young Indian elite, educated at Cambridge and Oxford, recognized and criticized the gap between an elitist administration with a courtly life-style and

Fig. 209: The Edwardian "Butterfly Houses" of Great Britain, such as B.E.S. Prior's Home Place at Holt, 1904–6 (top), and Edwin Lutyens' Papillon Hall, Leicestershire, 1902 (middle) are the models for the residences of the Nizam of Hyderabad, the Maharaja of Jaipur and the Gaekwar of Baroda (bottom).

the exceedingly poor population. Admittedly, between 1919 and 1926, when Edwin Lutyens was building a new palace in Imperial Delhi for one of the maharajas almost every year, none of the politicians and architects of Imperial Delhi suspected how short a time span of only another twenty years was to be granted to the imperial world order.

Lutyens took care not to build palaces for the maharajas which could compete with Viceroy's House. He deliberately aimed at forms and symbols, which were not used in Viceroy's House. And even if his patrons understandably enough did not really know what to do with obelisks, urns and Palladian gates, he nevertheless succeeded time and again in harmonizing his own preferences with the expectations of his patrons. He allowed himself to borrow just one form, namely a comparatively small dome in the centre of a palace, as the symbol of princely power.

In the search for appropriate ground plans for palaces his wide architectural experience with the English nobility stood him in good stead: Edwardian butterfly houses such as, for example, B.E.S. Prior's Home Place at Holt (1904–06), or his own Papillon Hall in Leicestershire (1902), were used as models for several of the maharajas' residences. The butterfly-shaped ground plan was ideally suited to the hexagonal town plan from the point of view of town planning and in addition it had not been previously used up on Raisina Hill.

Hyderabad House (Architect: Edwin Lutyens), 1926

If one wanted to name the four most important buildings that no visitor to Imperial Delhi should miss, then after Viceroy's House, the Secretariats and the All India War Memorial Arch, it would have to be the Palace of the Nizam of Hyderabad. While this is the largest of all the new princely residences in the town, it still cannot be compared with the truly imperial size and splendour of the Viceroy's House.

"As pioneer art historian Ernest Havell repeatedly emphasized, the example set by the Imperial Government in public edifices necessarily had 'a potent influence' not only with Indian craftsmen but also with Indian patrons – princes and aristocrats – who looked to official architecture 'for correct models of taste and fashion.

Lutyens built the biggest and costliest (£ 200,000) of the princes' palaces for the Muslim ruler of Hyderabad, the seventh Nizam, reputed to be the richest man in the world. His main residence in his own state – one of four palaces – was riddled with caches of gold ingots and astonishing gems as well as millions of paper rupees. His psyche was a bundle of contradictions: miserly, averse to personal ostentation, increasingly frugal in the extreme, he nevertheless engaged in periodic bouts of spectacular spending, had a thousand servants, and a harem of some two hundred concubines. His mistresses accompanied him on a special train during his brief visits to Delhi ...

Lutyens' butterfly-shaped plan for the palace was a variant of a design that had been popular in Britain for more than three decades. Lutyens had already devised a three-quarter butterfly in 1902 at the aptly named Papillon Hall, following the example of Norman Shaw, B.E.S. Prior, and Detmar Blow. At Delhi, he halved the butterfly to two wings, and with characteristic wit turned custom on its head to achieve an original orientation. Beneath the dome he set a pivotal entrance hall from which the symmetrical wings radiated at an angle of some fifty-five degrees. These symmetrical blocks, however, did not reach forward like welcoming arms to contain the forecourt but were swept back, as if to shield the zenana (women's quarters) from public view."[41]

The zenana, Lord Hardinge noted on a visit to New Delhi in 1931, comprised: "... a circular court with about twelve or fifteen rooms round it, each the size of an ordinary horsebox & with only one window close to the roof. A rough bed was the only furniture. There were six tiled bathrooms, but no baths, only taps of hot & cold water under which each lady has to sit! There seemed to be no means of mixing the hot & cold water, as it pours on the ladies!"[42]

For the architecture of Hyderabad House, the Nizam obviously did not suggest any formal models to his architect. Only a dome above the circular salon appears as a reflection of the

40 Ibid., p. 270.
41 Ibid., p. 266.
42 Journal of Lord Hardinge, February 15, 1931.

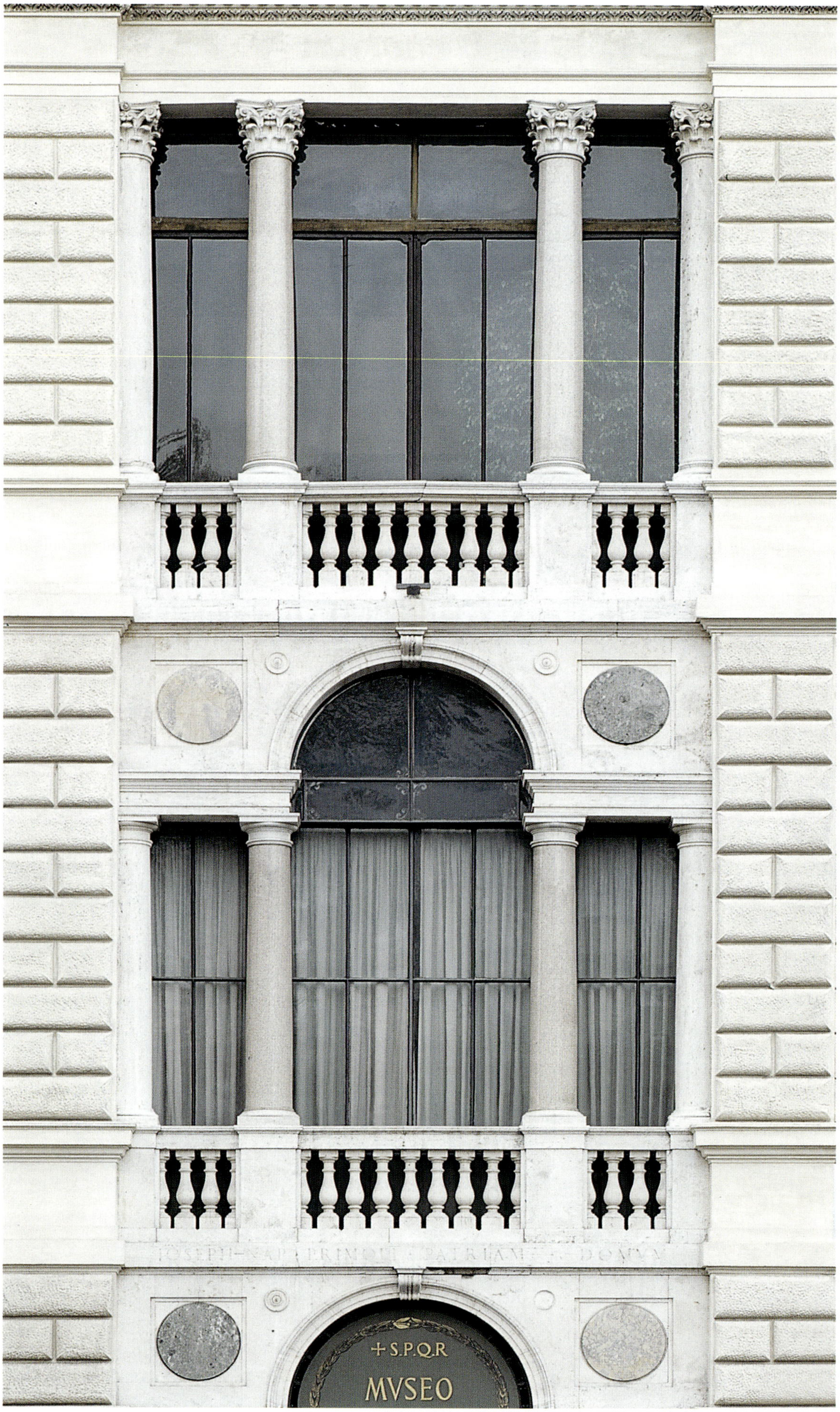

Fig. 210: Not from the facade of the Museo Napoleonico alone, but also from other Roman facades, Lutyens became familiar with the window-shape that he used for the upper storey of Hyderabad House.

Durbar Hall in Viceroy's House and was indispensable as a symbol of domination visible from afar. Edwin Lutyens used the commission of the extremely wealthy prince to introduce the complete repertoire of his experiences in Rome.

The driveway in front of the house is clearly reminiscent of the curving garden facade of the Villa Giulia in Rome by the sixteenth-century architects, Vasari, Vignola and Ammannati. The alternation of round arches and rectangular wall openings, each with inset pillars, is found in Palladio's Teatro Olimpico in Vicenza, also from the sixteenth century[43](Fig. 215). The window facade in the upper storey undoubtedly refers to the Museo Napoleonico in Rome (Fig. 210), and, in the final analysis, like the Durbar Hall, to the Pantheon (Fig. 216) built in the second century.

Hyderabad House is an impressive example of British eclecticism at the turn of the century. Out of the construction set of ancient Rome and its contemporary Neo-Classicist variations, Edwin Lutyens put together an impressive building having no direct model. At first glance, this building seems familiar. Its elements, the round arches with inset pillars, the obelisks, the flower containers on the flat roofs, and the shapes of the windows are all familiar to us.

Meanwhile, in distant America, a contemporary of Lutyens, Frank Lloyd Wright, derived his architecture from the natural features of the environment and integrated his structures back into that environment whereas in Imperial Delhi, Lutyens powerfully demonstrated the supposed independence of the British Crown from *modern* style, time and space.

43 Cf. Fig. 215

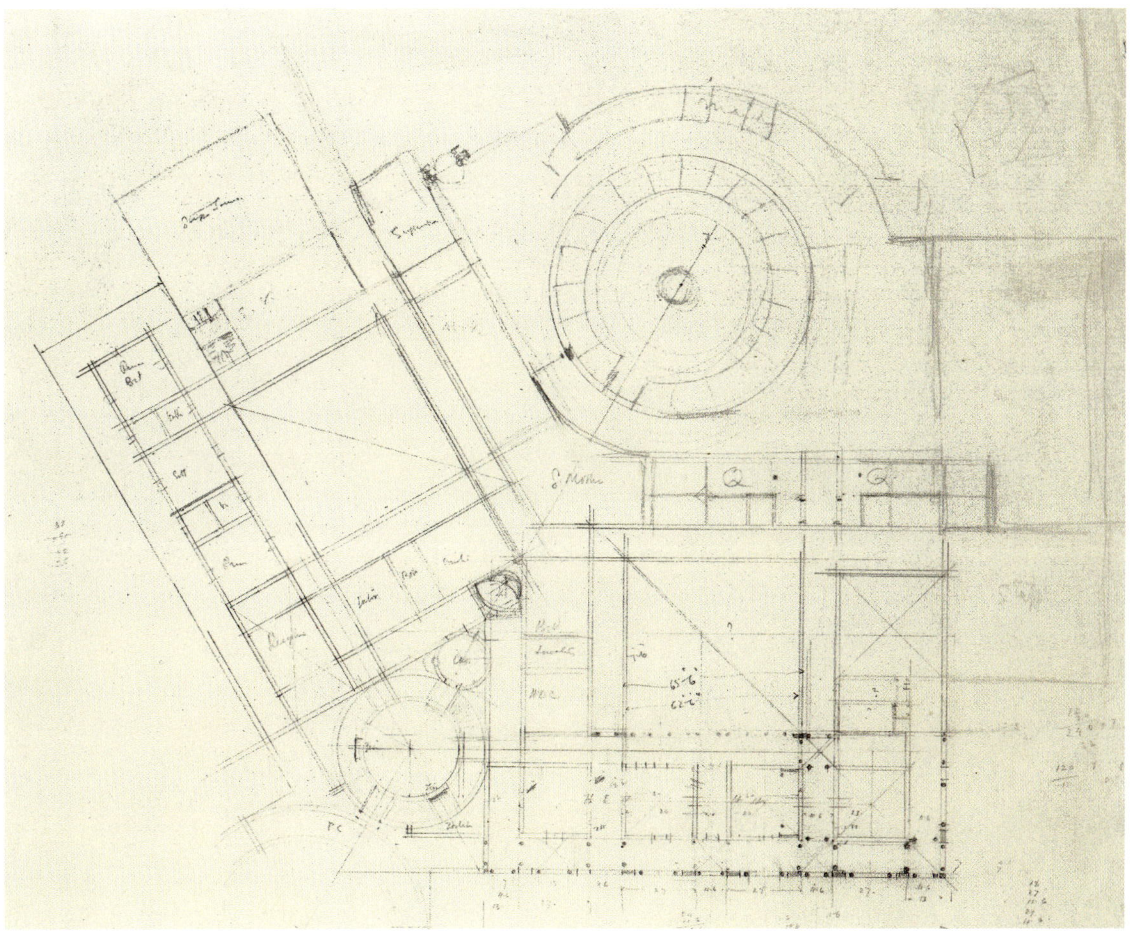

Fig. 211: An early version of the plan for Hyderabad House finally realized, showed an attempt to combine the geometric shapes of the square and the circle in a "butterfly ground plan."

Following page, Fig. 212: The approach to Hyderabad House.

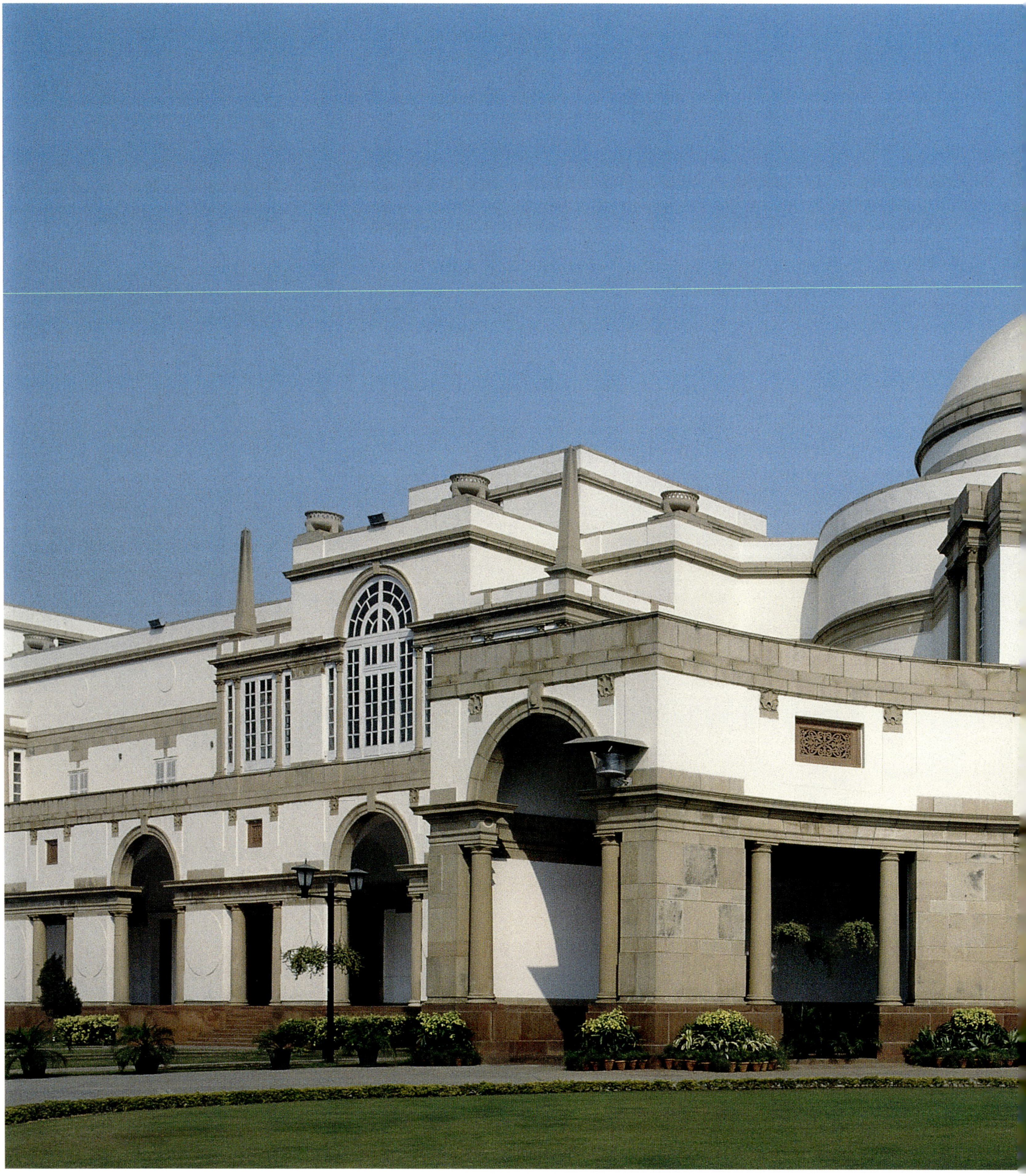

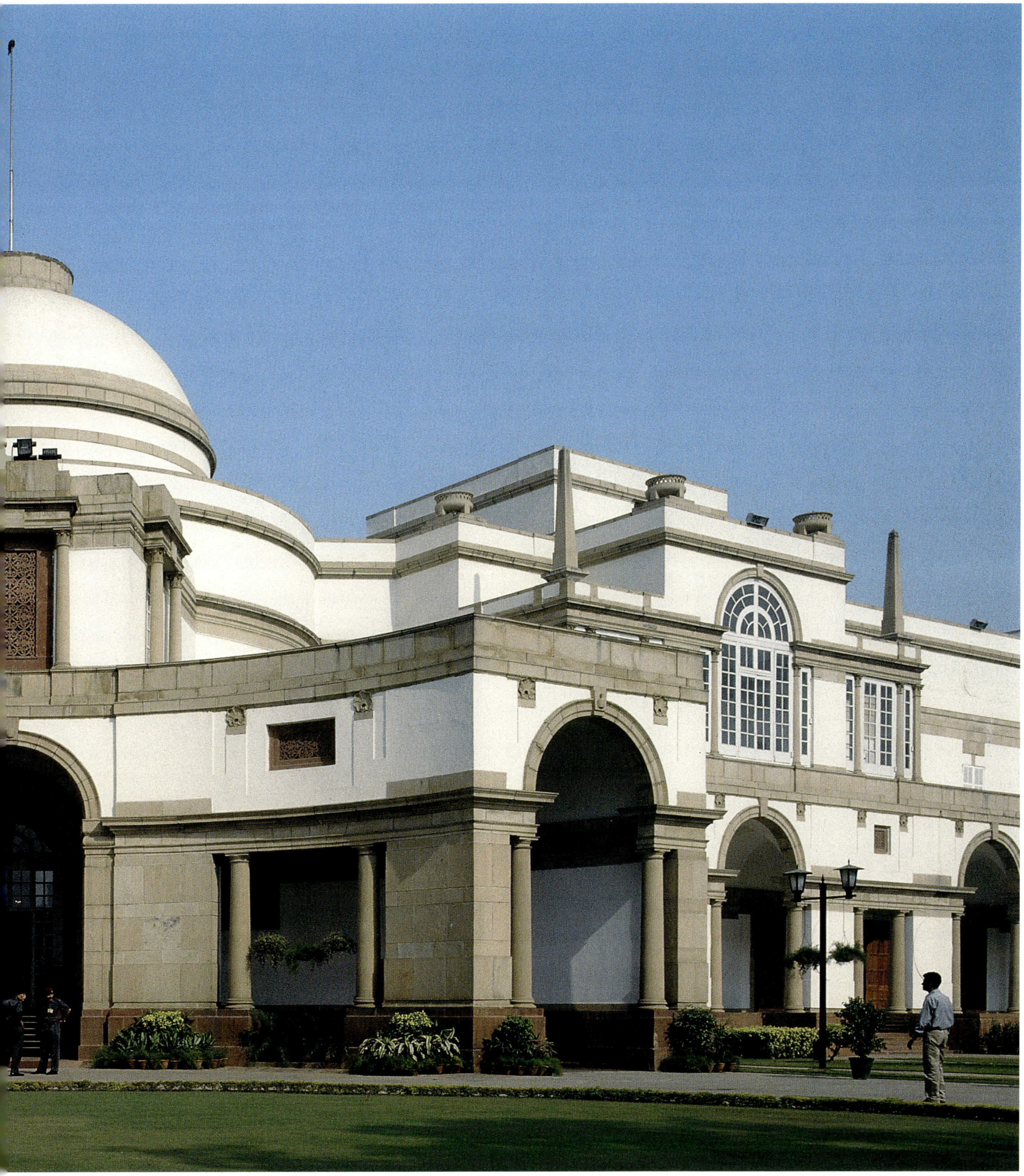

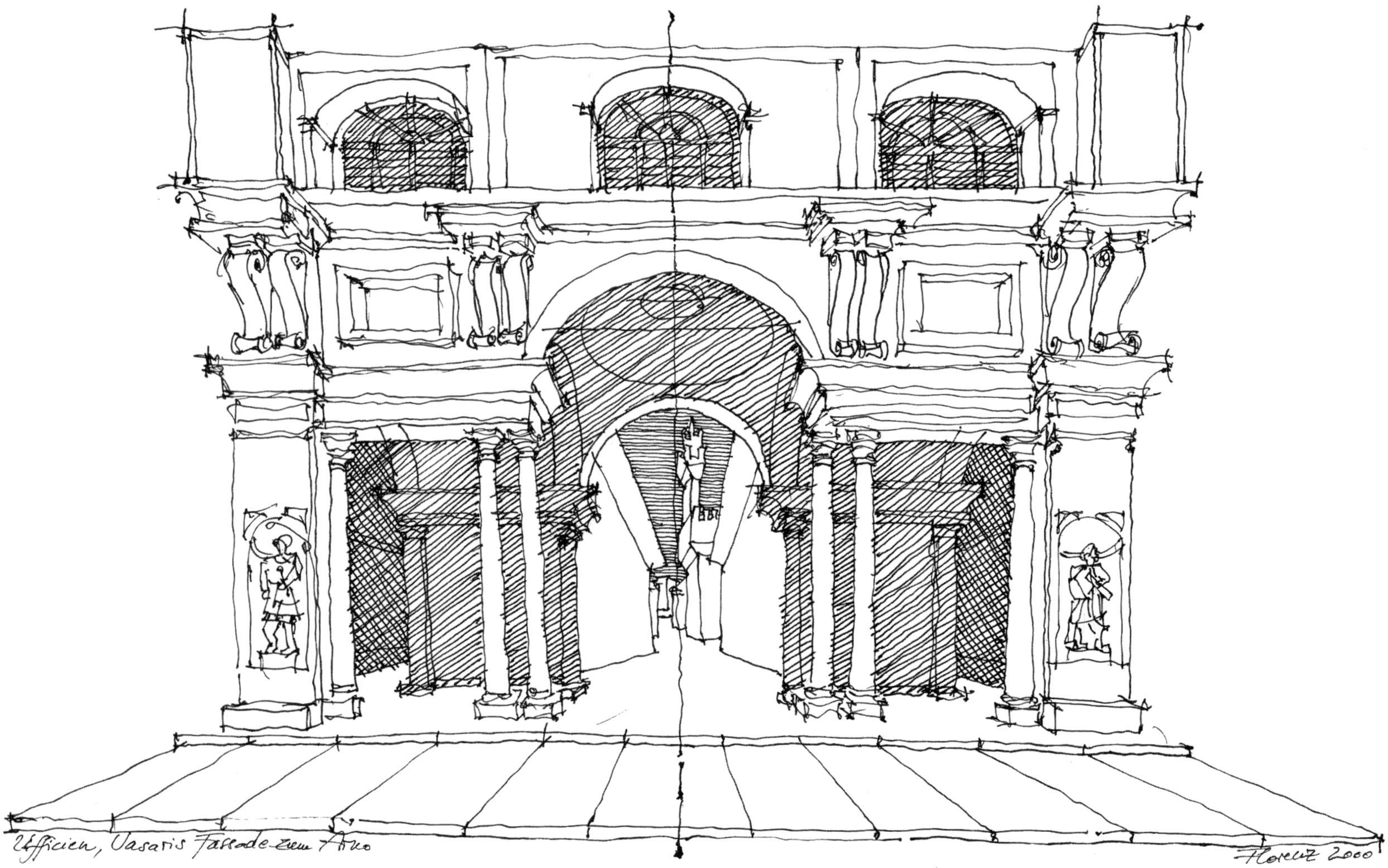

Fig. 213: The passage from the Uffizi to the Arno in Florence shows the combination of rectangular and round arches that Edwin Lutyens chose for the windows in the upper storey of Hyderabad House.

Fig. 214: The main entrance to Hyderabad House.

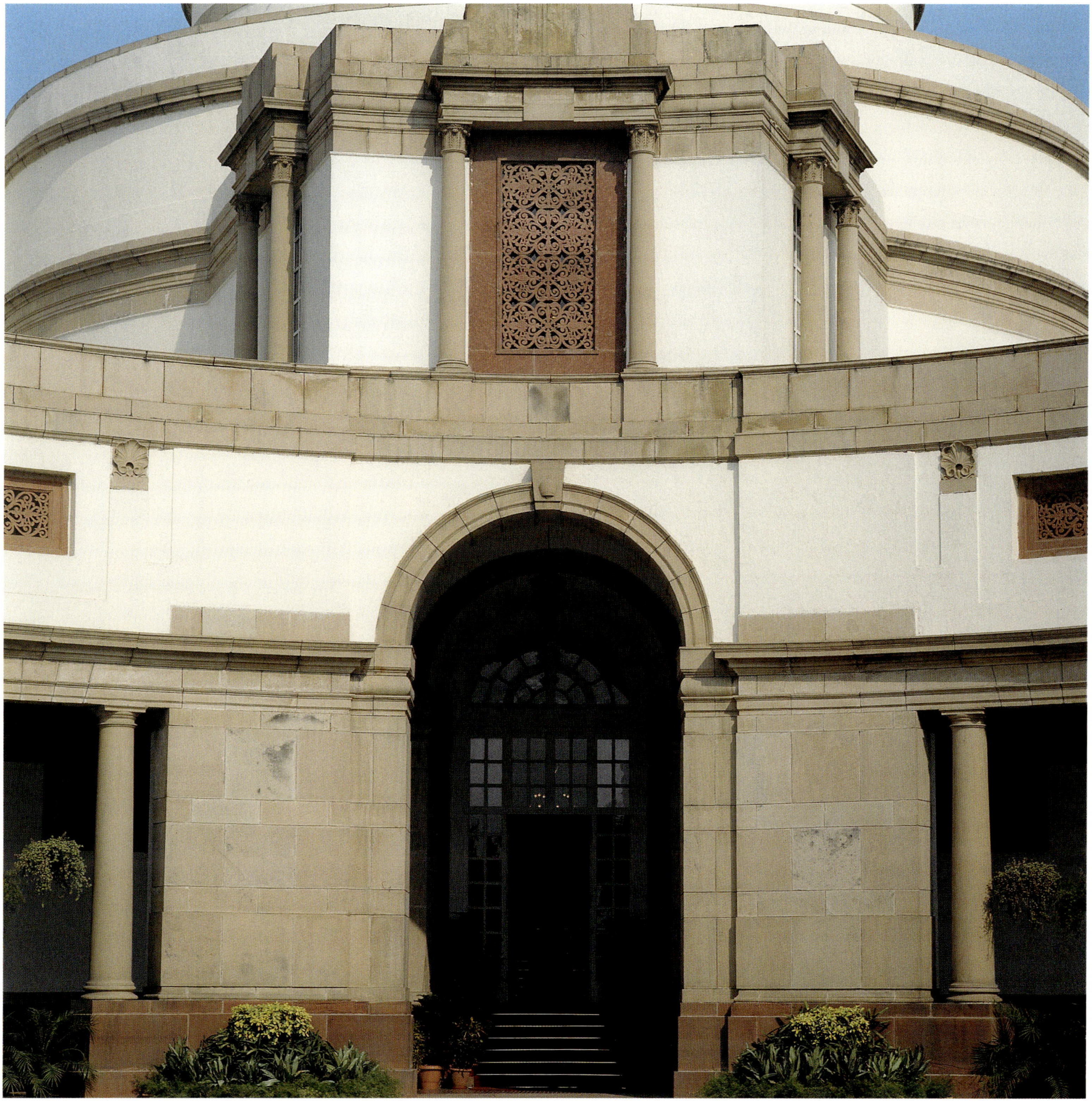

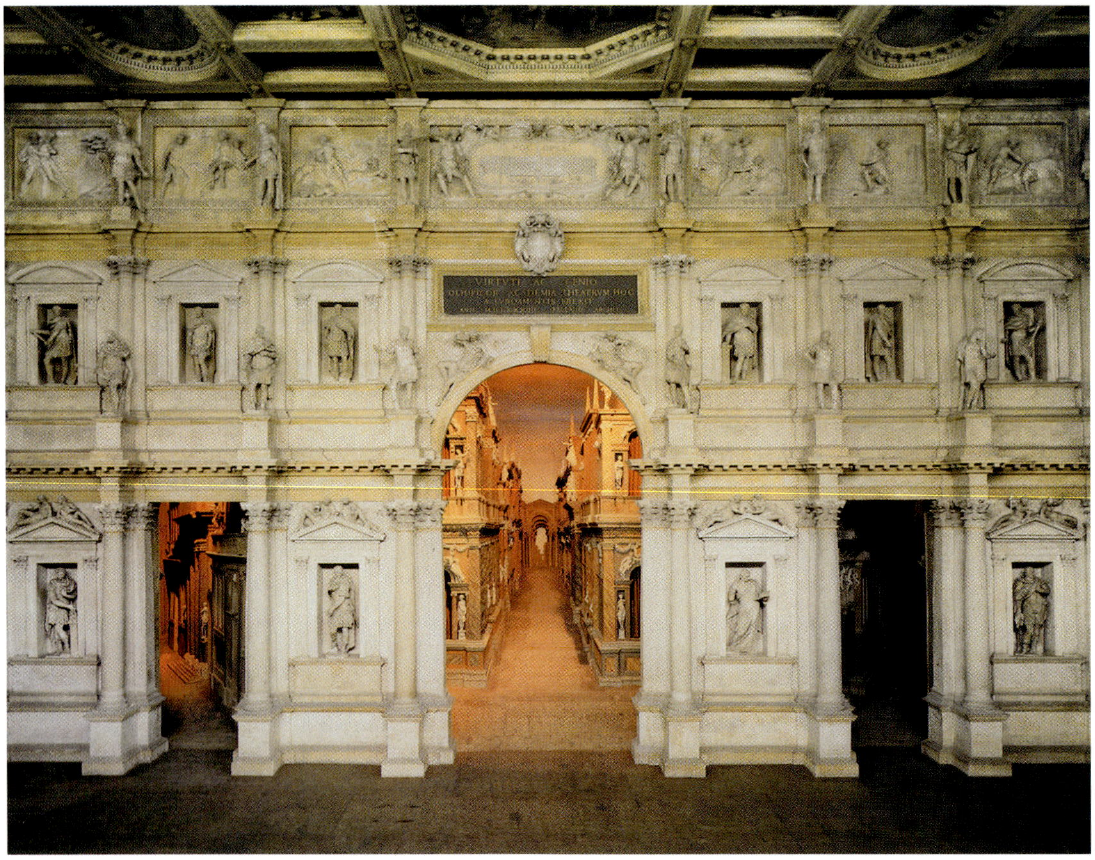

Fig. 215: In the Teatro Olimpico in Vicenza by Palladio (*c.* 1580), the motif from the Pantheon surfaces again: a gateway arch with smaller, rectangular entrances at each side.

Fig. 216: The primary formal motif of Hyderabad House is the round arch flanked by rectangular openings up to the height of the impost. Edwin Lutyens became familiar with this motif in the Pantheon (*c.* 129 A.D.) during his stay in Rome in 1909. Shown here is a drawing by Raphael.

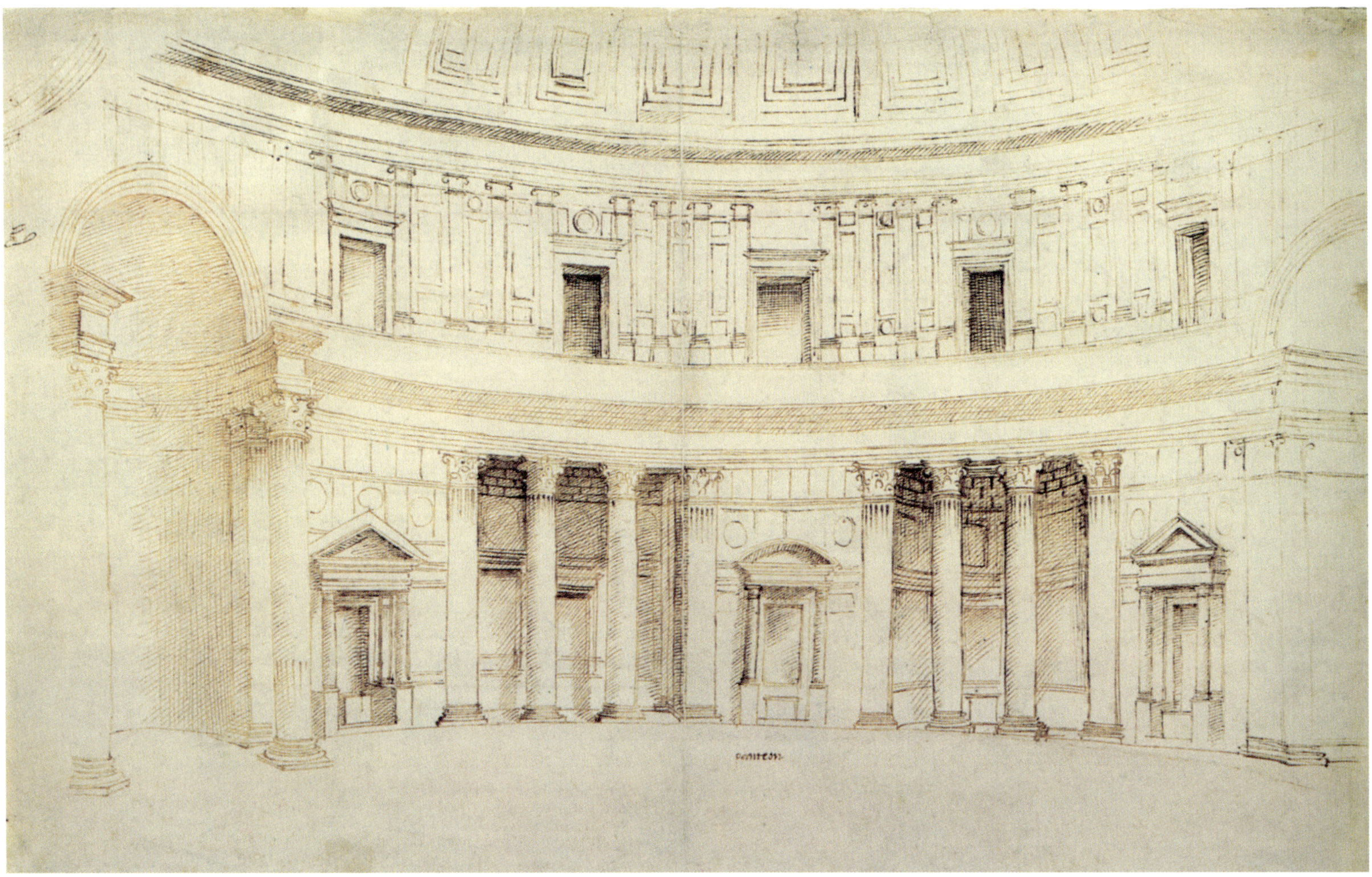

Baroda House (Architect: Edwin Lutyens), 1921

Only a few maharajas and princes were fortunate enough to obtain a building site for their residences in Imperial Delhi directly on Princes Park, around the statue of George V. The rulers of Hyderabad, Baroda, Gwalior, Patalia, Jaipur, Bikaner and Bharatput were the chosen few. But for the rulers of Pataudi, Dhar, Travancore, Faridkot, Mandi, Jind, Sangli, Dholpur, Jaisalmer and Kotha, there were still some first-class sites available on the avenues radiating outwards from the George V Monument (cf. town plan in Fig. 67).

One of the fortunate ones, the Gaekwar of Baroda, commissioned Edwin Lutyens to build a palace with shady terraces, cooling arcades, well-ventilated salons, and refreshing garden views. He was familiar with Lutyens' penchant for Neo-Palladian forms and set no great store by ritual exercises in Hindu or Islamic formal architectural language. His tastes went hand in hand with his unusual life story: "The British had placed the Maharaja on a vacant throne in 1875 at the age of twelve after deposing his predecessor and excluding the descendents from succession. Surrounded by Englishmen, he was educated to be a model of Victorian rectitude and progressive politics. After his first wife died, he married a Maratha noblewoman whose "Brindian" sophistication equalled his own, and they enjoyed fifty years of happy married life. Unlike other native rulers, he kept no mistress and hence Lutyens made no provision for a concubines' zenana. The house at Princes' Place exuded an atmosphere of British affluence: its furnishings were 'comfortably Anglo-Saxon' and its plumbing American, as in the sprawling palace at Baroda. The cook and bandmaster were French, the stablemaster Irish, and the valet and maids English. Table linen was woven to order in Belfast, and the dinner service was fashioned in Bond Street. Scarlet-liveried servants offered guests whiskey or hock with seltzer at breakfast, champagne and port in the evening. The Maharaja hired Britons to run his army

Fig. 217: Baroda House 1921, approach, by Edwin Lutyens.

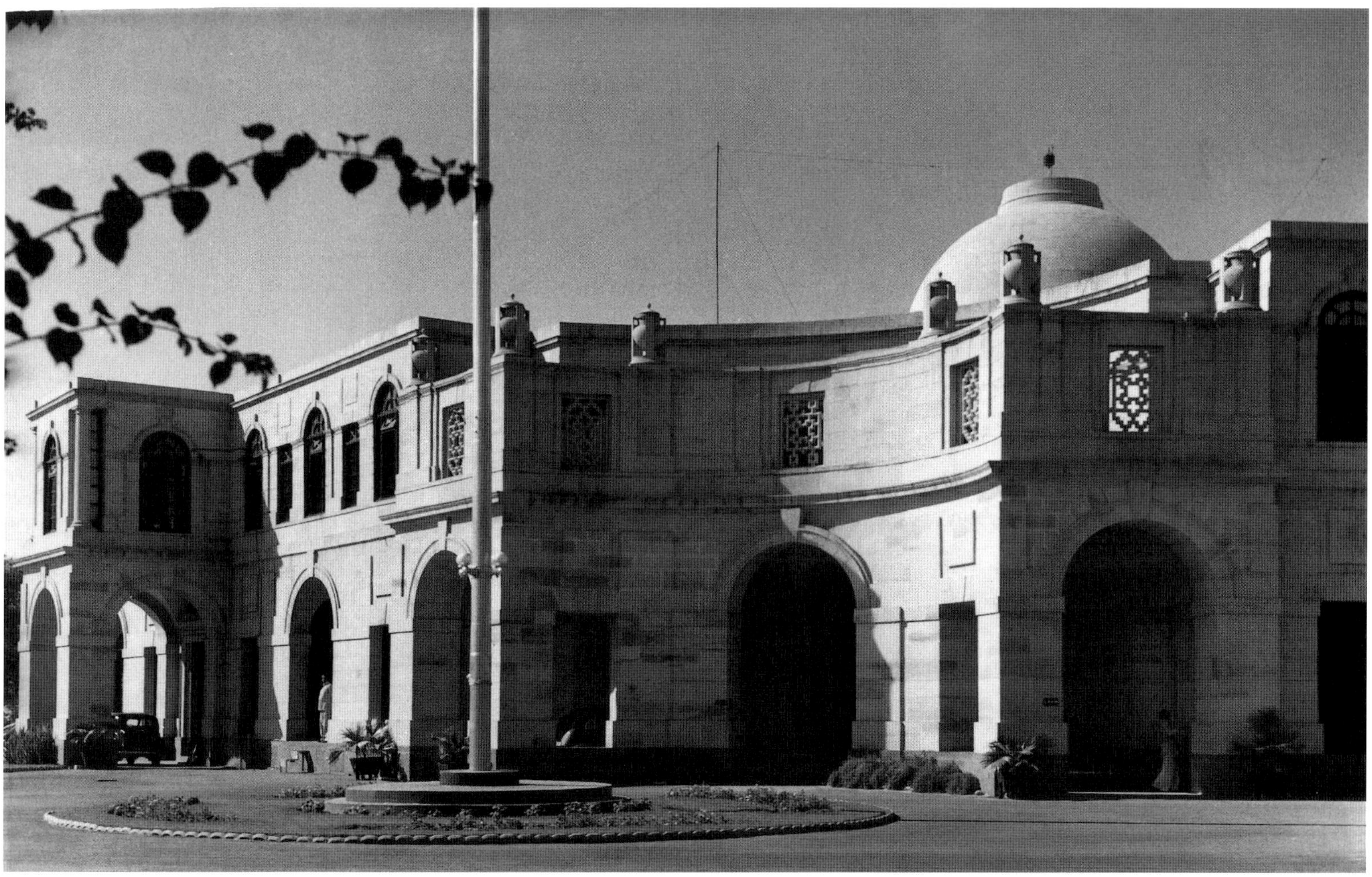

and police force, his hospitals and colleges; it was only fitting that he employed the Viceroy's architect, an Englishman celebrated for his country house designs."[44]

Naturally, Lutyens could not invent a completely new symbolic and formal language for each of his princely Indian patrons. But that was also not a concern for his new clientele. For them, the more a design resembled the Viceroy's Palace, the better. Nevertheless, Lutyens was cautious about that very issue. He knew exactly what the English elite considered appropriate or inappropriate. In case of doubt, as with Baroda House, he decided on a comparatively simple form for the facades and dispensed with symbols of grandeur that were already in use. Understatement in the Viceroy's neighbourhood was a sign of political astuteness, even if everyone in Imperial Delhi was aware of the legendary riches of the maharajas.

"There is, as well, a trace of dullness in the plan of this house. One enjoys the related forms of the curved central porte-cochere, the long Vestibule across the axis and the circular Salon at the pivot of the plan (like Robert Adam's round Saloon at Kedleston). The two principal reception rooms, radiant from this, are delightfully placed with their small domed lobbies bubbling from the larger cupola. But the rest of the wings repeats itself exactly on each side, though reversed. There is none of the pleasure we found elsewhere in discovering different intricacies within balanced and similar shells. Moreover, each wing has on the ground floor three square rooms the same size, together with an open court and a square hall again of similar shape and area."[45]

Baroda House is situated directly next to Hyderabad House. The radial street pattern of the hexagonal Princes Park was suitable for designing both in the butterfly ground plan. The final spatial disposition was attained in the first plan that Lutyens drew in the train from Bombay on December 22, 1921. The building work on the series of courtyards, arcades, corridors, and richly

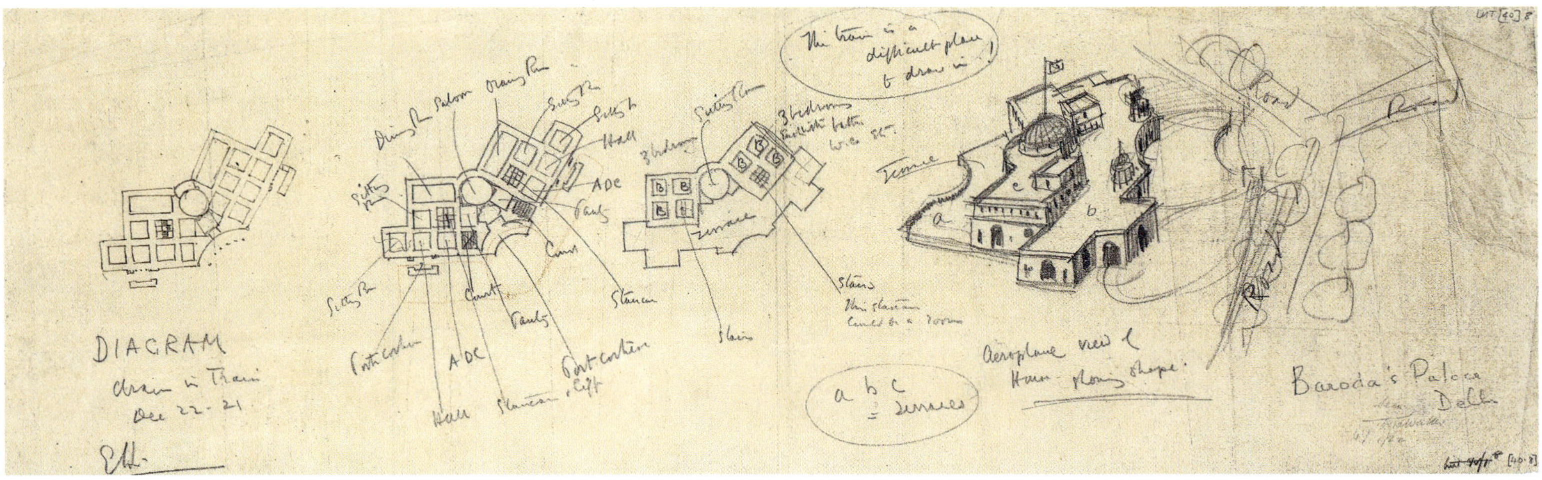

Fig. 218: Diagram of the plan of Baroda House with Edwin Lutyens' comments: "Diagram drawn in train, Dec. 21, " and "This train is a difficult place to draw in!"

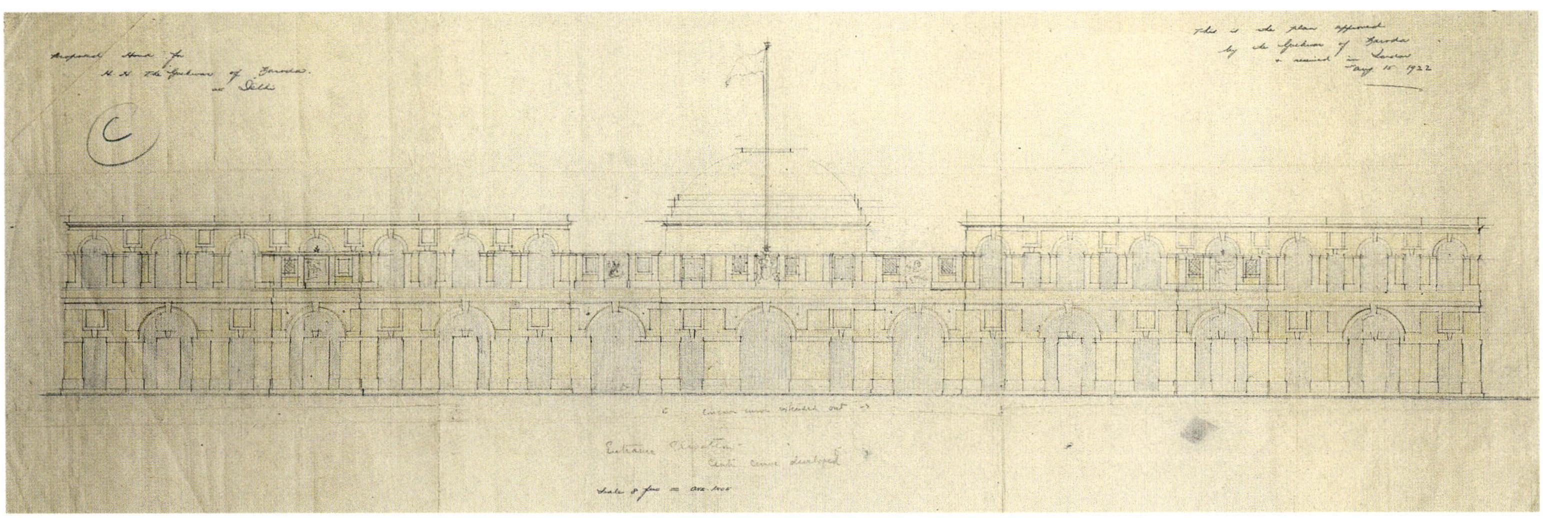

Fig. 219: Baroda House, elevation of the main view.

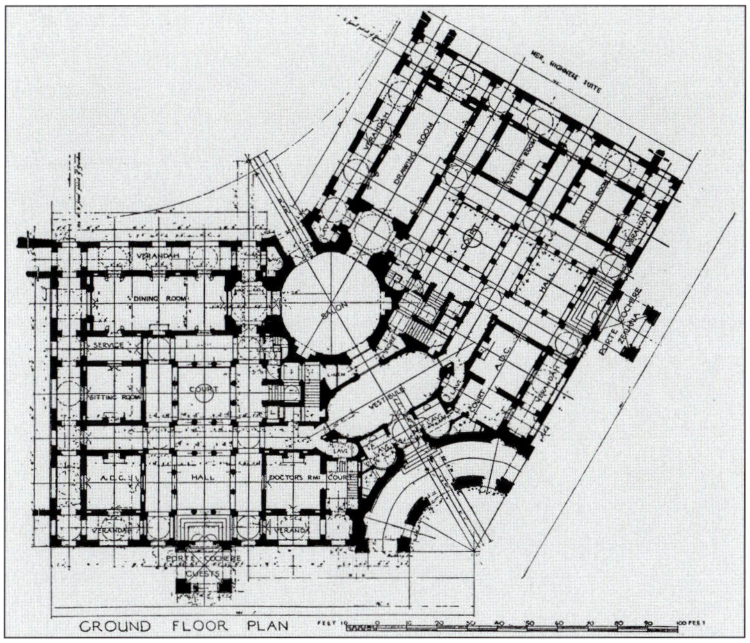

Fig. 220: Baroda House, plan of the ground floor.

decorated living rooms – all conceived in the Renaissance style, began in 1922.

"The plastered brick saucer domes that embellished these palatial corridors, as well as Viceroy's House, were constructed without temporary support or centring by a method ancient in Asia and known to the Byzantines. The Indian contractors' foremen would, in each case, organize a tight ring of laborers at the lip of the circular void they planned to close. Fresh mortar was already laid along the rim. At a given signal – often the beat of a drum which punctuated accompanying music! – every man placed a brick from each hand simultaneously, creating an instant circle. When the mortar dried, the workers repeated the procedure. So they raised a dome, course by course, until it stood entire, its last bricks held in place by callused fingers till the mortar set. Barefoot, scantily clad, covered with dust, braving scorching sun and chilling winds, India's peasants built a princely city."[46]

For the facade of Baroda House, Lutyens chose just one motif that he set on the ground floor to a larger scale than in the lower upper floor. This was a round arch flanked by two rectangular wall openings as it has appeared since Palladio's time in European facades. Lutyens found direct models in John Soane's plan for the staircase at Home House, in Portman Square, London, built in 1775, and in Palladio's Teatro Olimpico in Vicenza built in 1580 (Fig. 215).

44 R.G. Irving: op. cit., p. 268.
45 A.S.G. Butler: op. cit., p. 43.
46 R.G. Irving: op. cit., p. 270.

Fig. 221: An unrealized variant for the facade of Baroda House shows a high central round arch extending to the upper floor. The comment by Lutyens at the top right is: "This is the plan approved by the Gaekwar of Baroda & revised in London August 15."

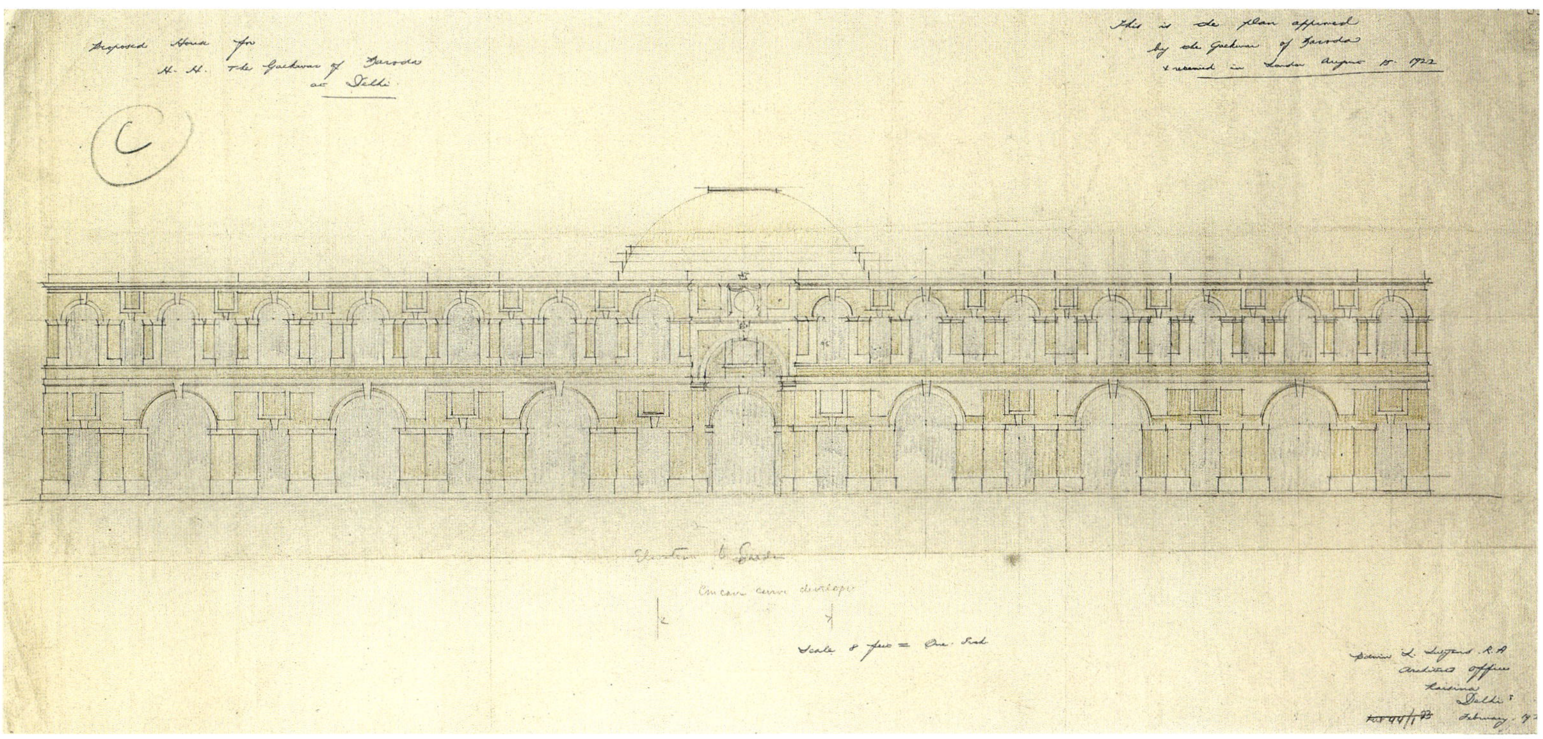

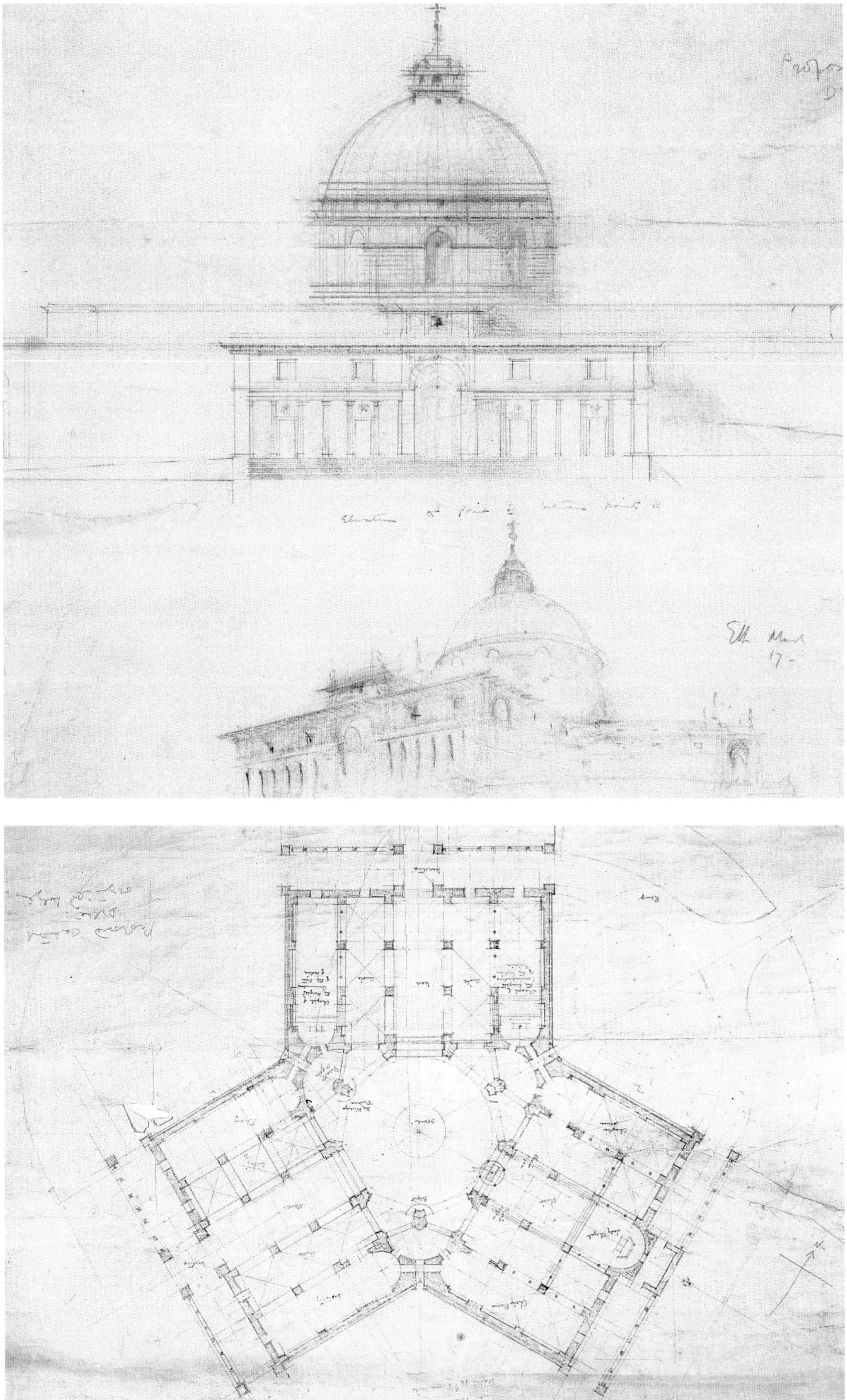

Fig. 222: Edwin Lutyens' plan for a cathedral with three wings in Imperial Delhi would have coincided perfectly with the hexagonal street plan. But the cathedral, replete with Christian symbolism, was never built.

4.3.6 The Christian Churches

In the many documents that have survived from the time Imperial Delhi was built, there is no indication that the British Crown might have considered it one of their tasks to take an active part in missionary work, or to give particular support to one of the Christian churches in India beyond what was expected for all the colonies. It is all the more amazing today that Edwin Lutyens worked on a monumental cathedral for Imperial Delhi in 1917, since the employees of the colonial government and British businessmen in the capital were the only likely churchgoers.

In the plan for the city drawn up on March 20, 1913 (Fig. 222), Lutyens had planned an Anglican cathedral on York Place, a site south of the junction of King's Way and Queen's Way. As might be expected on a hexagonal road junction, he planned – without referring back to Palladio, Piranesi or Wren – a cathedral with a ground plan in the shape of a three-pointed star. Three identical naves terminate in a triangular, domed central area, with the entrance given emphasis by a wide flight of steps.

There is an excellent justification for the boldness of the plan. Was the Trinity not often a reason for unusual ground plans of churches in Baroque times? Moreover, who could seriously have considered placing a rectangular cathedral in the extremely complex system of main and subsidiary triangles and hexagons of the town plan? Admittedly, the Viceroy's Palace itself is rectangular, but it is at the apex of a rectangular road network, waterways, and offices along King's Way. York Place, on the other hand, is devoid of all rectangular references.

"The liturgical problem of a centrally planned church engaged Lutyens no less than it did those Renaissance architects who had pondered its functional complexities. In one wing he fitted the choir stalls and choir room, chapter house, and lady chapel; in another the baptistery and library; and in a third, chapels for the chivalric orders of the Star of India and Indian Empire, underlining the relation between church and imperial state. The aisles of each wing were sufficiently long for ceremonial processions, however, the site of principal ritual activity, the central domed space on which a triad of naves focused, posed the greatest challenge to Lutyens' ingenuity. In the angles of the triangular crossing he placed the Viceroy's tribune (in front of the great organ), a lectern, and, on axis with the main nave, the pulpit. Directly opposite the Viceroy's elevated seat, Lutyens placed the high altar, as if to emphasize the complementary efforts of priest and proconsul amidst an alien culture."[47]

The local chaplain, with whom Edwin Lutyens shared no common ground, showed little understanding of the complexity of the self-imposed task: "When the Chaplain at Raisina began conjuring up visions of an English medieval cathedral, Lutyens promptly denounced any plan for 'a true Christian Gothic Farce.' If such talk persisted, he warned, he would banish the church to an outer ring on the city plan, with the rank of a 'third-rate building.' Despite its beauty, Westminster Abbey with its acres of glass was only fit in India 'for frying bacon.'"[48]

In principle, the plans for a cathedral complied with old wishes of Lutyens. "As a young man, pacing up and down before his mentor Gertrude Jekyll, he had confessed a burning desire 'to build palaces and cathedrals.' Now in 1917, already engaged upon Viceroy's House, he found the prospect of a great church exhilarating and could be heard singing Te Deums throughout the day. But his splendid vision of a cathedral at Delhi, as at Liverpool, was destined for disappointment. Nearly two decades later an elegant church designed by one of Lutyens' disciples rose on a site near Viceroy's House."[49] This was the Cathedral Church of the Redemption, which H.A.N. Medd built between 1927 and 1935.

Roughly around the same time, Arthur G. Shoosmith, who for several years had been Lutyens' representative in Delhi, designed and built another church in the town, rather, in the Delhi Cantonment at the edge of the city. It was the Garrison Church of St Martin, in which Indian late Neo-Classicism was surpassed and modern, post-imperial architecture found its starting-point. There was no portico as at the Pantheon, no more riot of gables as at Il Redentore, no dome, and no more rows of pillars. The radical new beginnings in architecture after World War I attempted to overcome the growing sense of insecurity that now marked the Empire by restricting itself to basic forms, unencumbered by historical precedent (Fig. 225).

47 Ibid., p. 272.
48 Quotation by R.G. Irving, of reports of H.A.N. Medd.
49 Ibid., pp. 271, 272.

St Martin's Church and the Lady Hardinge Serail (Architect: Arthur G. Shoosmith), 1929

The concentration of imperial power in New Delhi was accompanied by an increase in military presence and the need for barracks and facilities for the community. Arthur G. Shoosmith built a garrison church far outside the town that, with a severity hitherto unknown, avoided all associations with the Renaissance and all previous architectural expressions of Crown dominance.

The drought and heat of the outskirts of New Delhi are reflected in the undecorated cubic form. The almost windowless thick walls accord with the responsibilities of the users, and they appear to surround a fortress rather than a consecrated space. To the amazement of contemporary observers, the radical rejection of earlier meaningful forms such as pillars, capitals, and domes did not lead to a feeling of insecurity. Instead, it permitted the representation of military power with an unparalleled dynamism. As a result, St Martin's Church was particularly significant as the last and most severe imperialist structure of the British Empire in India. Thus, just as the comparable fortresses at Verdun announced the end of the German Reich, the fortress-like church of St Martin, with its look of irreconcilability, foretold the collapse of British rule.

With the rejection of European symbolic forms, the question of concessions to the Hindu and Islamic architectural traditions of India was unnecessary. In the end, the question of location and cultural milieu was also altogether unnecessary. The church became an integral part of a social image reduced to attack and defence.

The British sense of mission as a military, cultural, and moral power comparable to that of the Romans could unfold and present itself in a more relaxed way prior to, and during World War I than when it came into dispute with the most varied national Indian movements and the premonition of a global empire's sudden decline.

Even if St Martin's Church broke with all the stylistic proclivities of Edwin Lutyens' generation, the step into a new formal language was comprehensible to Lutyens – especially if this language was derived from contemporary thought and material. In this spirit, Lutyens wrote to Shoosmith on February 13, 1928:

"My Dear Shoo,

Bricks!

A building of one material is for some strange reason much more noble than one of many.

It may be the accent it gives of sincerity, the persistence of texture and definite unity.

The Romans used brick most magnificently, and used bricks three feet long.

I have used bricks three feet long in England. They cost about 5 £ each, the difficulty being to dry them and lift them about prior to burning.

In India there should be no such difficulty in the hot weather and a big brick goes further than a little one.

Q.E.D.

Make your bricks 12in x 6in x 2; 18 x 6 x 2; 24 x 6 x 2; 30 x 6 x 2; 36 x 6 x 2.

If you must cope, use thinner bricks, i.e. tiles.

A cement wash will keep moisture out better than a thick cope of cement which cracks. Then cement is so liable to fissure, and I know if cement ever gets smeared on pavement you can never get it off.

Don't use, whatever you do, bricks on edge or any fancy stuff. It only destroys scale and promotes triviality.

Try bricks of varying thickness. Three inches at the base working up at the top of your tower to 1 in. thick. They are just as easy to make as any other shape, and 5 £ will cover the cost of all moulds.

The Romans did it! Why should not Britons?

You will get a fine wall, and their mass, proportion, with precious fenestration, will do the rest.

Get rid of all mimicry Mary-Ann notions of brickwork and go for the Roman wall.

I hope you get that pavement right in H.E. Council's Court.

Homage to the mem-sahib Shoo."[50]

Historians are not in complete agreement regarding a single architectural classification. While Robert Irving[51] detects elements of a stripped Neo-Classicism, Robert Byron emphasizes

50 Quoted from: Christopher Hussey: op. cit., p. 493.

51 R.G. Irving: op. cit., p. 337.

the fearful form: "... the effect it induces is not so much one of grandeur as one of melancholy – a forgotten example of a style of architecture cut off in its prime by the shifting sands of history. Its atmosphere is forbidding, even frightening, for it is redolent of the great war memorials of Flanders. At the time it anticipated the holocaust yet to come, and the great Pyrrhic victory of 1945 which spelt the end of British Imperial power in India."[52]

No less revolutionary than the Garrison Church of St Martin is the Lady Hardinge Serail by Arthur G. Shoosmith. He built it opposite the new station of New Delhi in 1930–31 for destitute Indian travellers. The idea for that type of accommodation stemmed from Lady Hardinge in memory of the Viceroy's escape from the assassination attempt of 1913. Lady Hardinge, together with many other patrons, endowed the necessary sum for the building shortly before her death. A monumental building was created – hardly noticed today – of unusual simplicity and dignity.

52 Ph. Davies: *Splendours of the Raj, British Architecture in India*, 1660 to 1947, London 1985, p. 241.

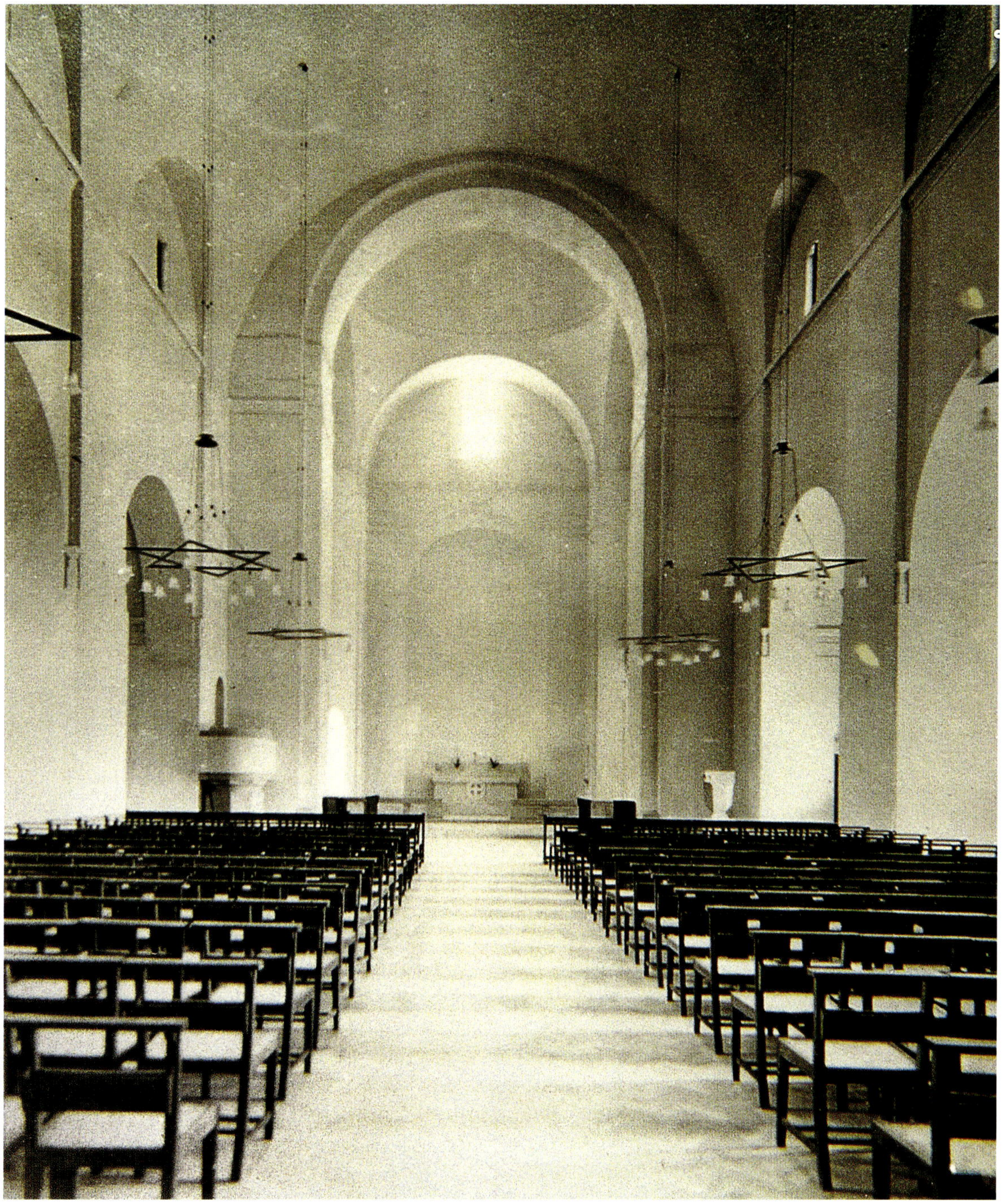

Fig. 223: The interior of St Martin reflects the austerity as well as the monumentality of its exterior.

Fig. 224: In the early 1940s, Arthur G. Shoosmith, who had been in charge of Edwin Lutyens' office in Delhi for several years, designed and built the garrison Church of St Martin for the Delhi cantonment.

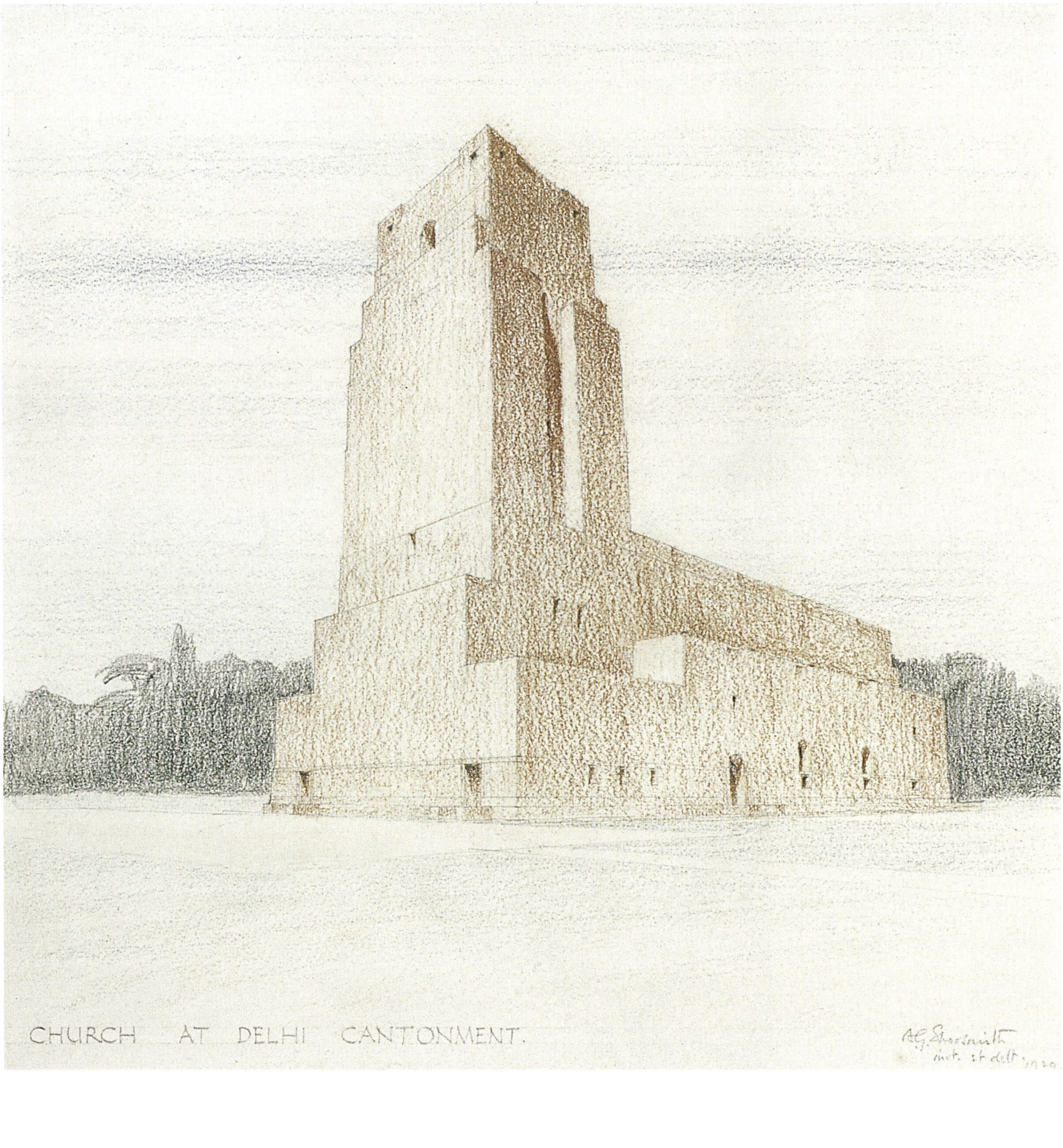

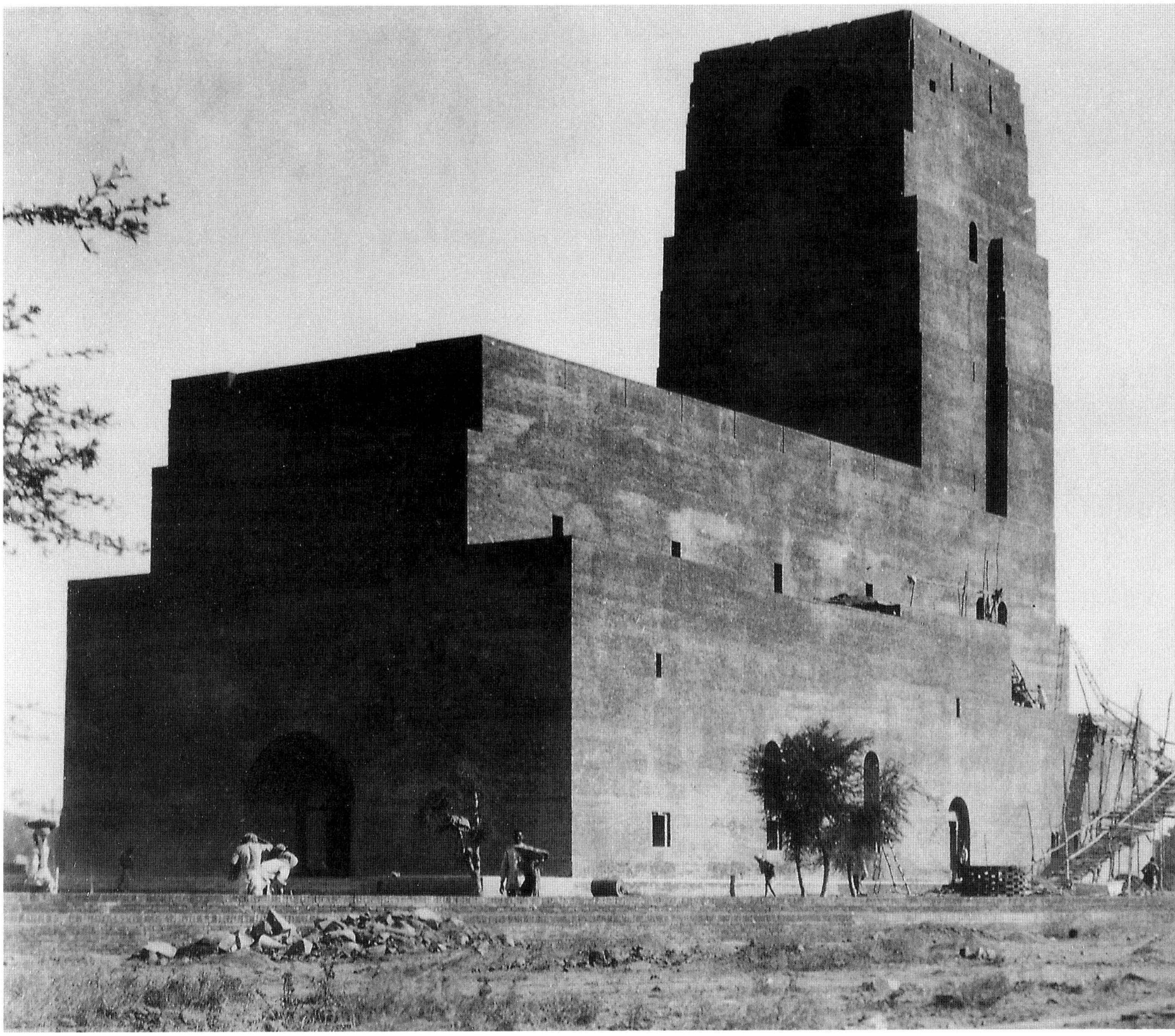

Fig. 225: St Martin's Church did not endorse the imperial architecture of Edwin Lutyens and Herbert Baker. It stood for radical new beginnings in architecture after World War I.

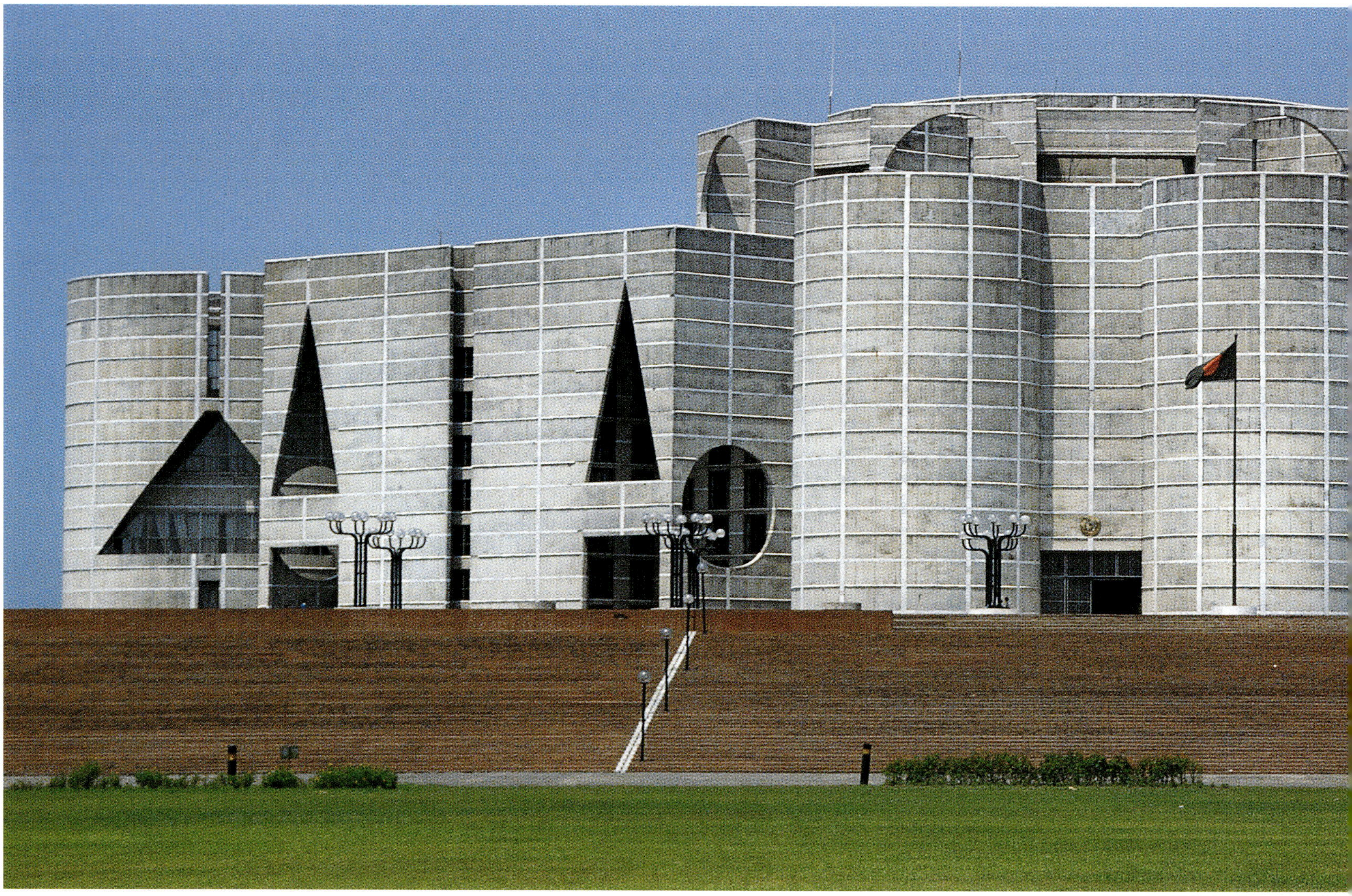

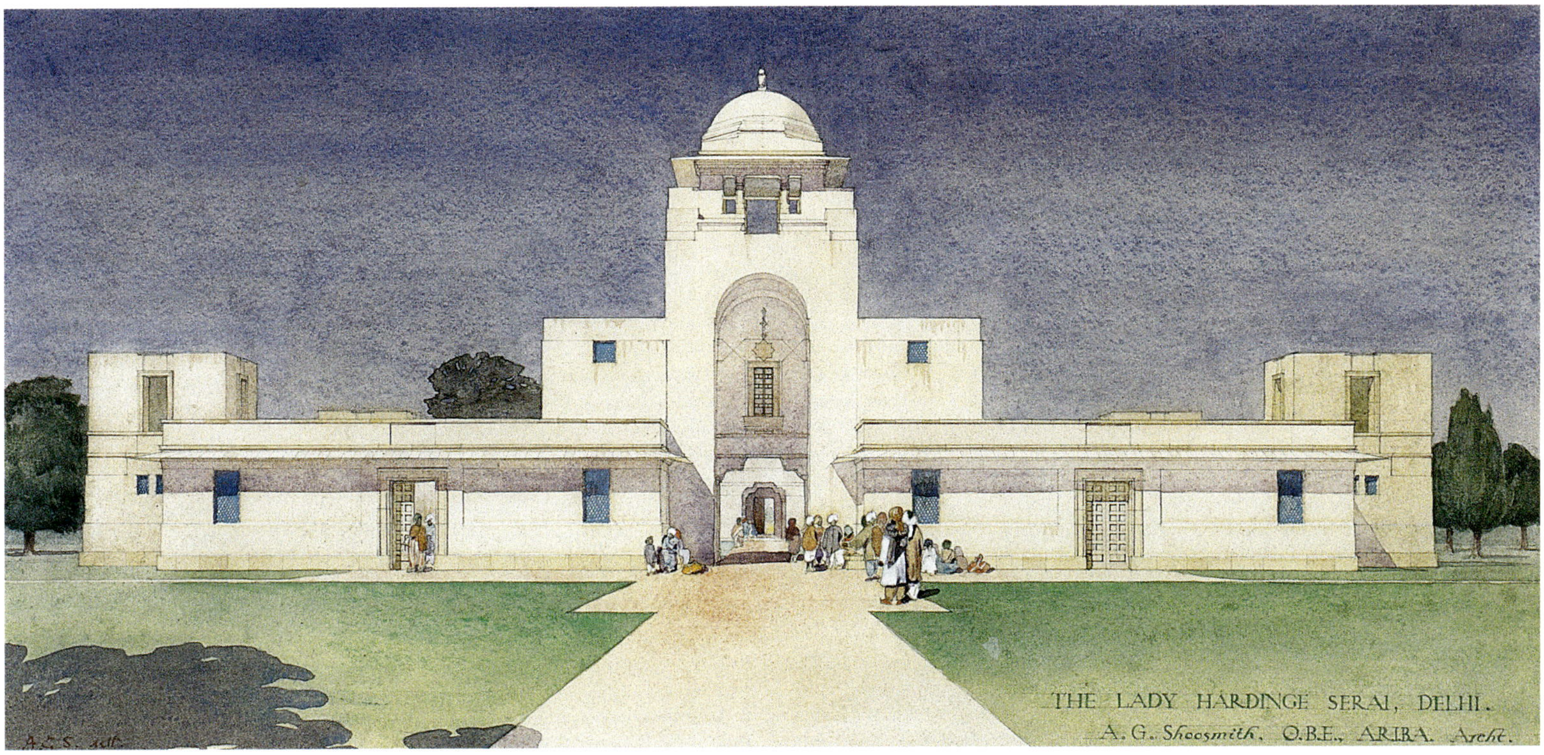

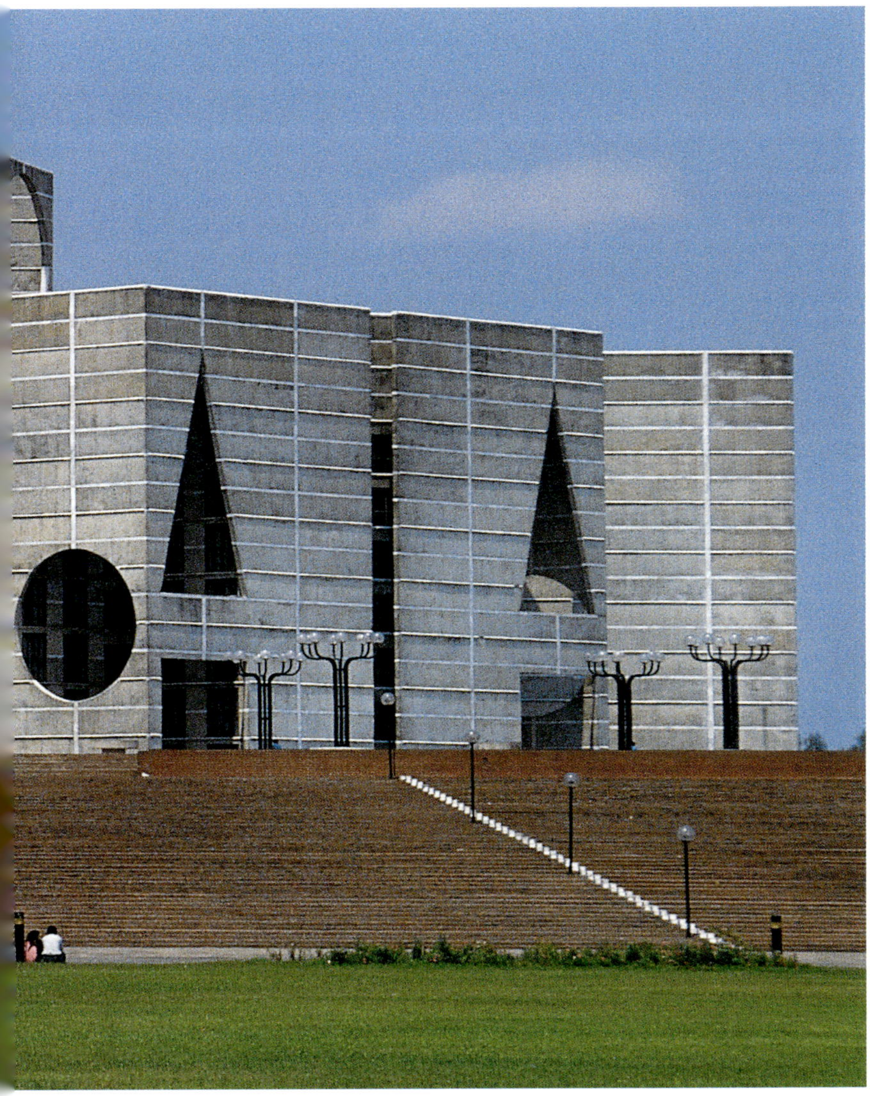

Fig. 227: In his plan for the Lady Hardinge Serail (New Delhi), Arthur G. Shoosmith combined various elements of Mughal architecture with a simple, but monumental architectural style

Fig. 226: From Arthur G. Shoosmith's design for the garrison Church of St Martin (1929) it was only a small step to Louis I. Kahn's buildings for Dhaka (1962–83), capital of Bangladesh.

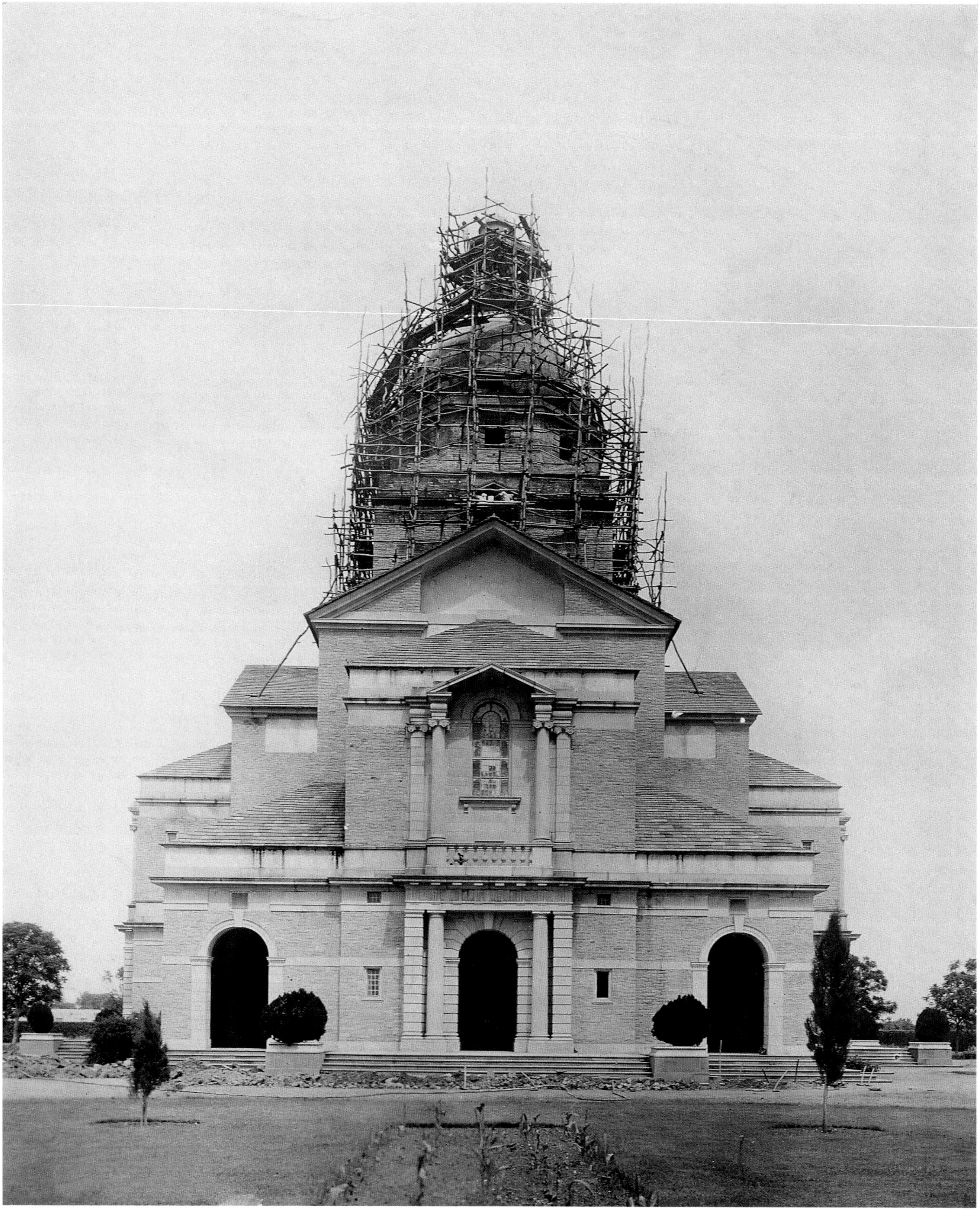

Cathedral Church of the Redemption (Architect: H.A.N. Medd), 1927–1935

Directly next to Viceroy's House is the Cathedral Church of the Redemption at the northern end of Brassey Avenue that leads out from the Jaipur Column (see town plan on pp. 76/77). The prominent site on an important town-planning axis led H.A.N. Medd to conceive a special architectural form. In general, every church is oriented to the east on its main axis. However, this church lies on an important north-south town-planning axis. Therefore, Medd chose a cruciform ground plan with two symmetrical axes. Viewed from the Jaipur Column (see left view in Fig. 230), this architectural solution fit the town planning requirements by producing the symmetrical view that functioned as a terminal point for the road axis going from south to north. Yet the axis of the main nave pointing eastwards from the church entrance in the west (see Fig. 228) was not disrupted by taking the town plan into consideration.

The decision to hold an advertised competition and to build the Church of the Redemption was made in 1925. The Chaplain of Raisina had convinced the appropriate Bishop of Lahore of the need for a church in close proximity to the Secretariats because this was where most of the members of the congregation worked. Edwin Lutyens, at this time at the height of his importance in respect to all architectural and town-planning problems in Imperial Delhi, was the only judge in the competition entries. He decided in favour of Medd.

When Lord Irwin (a particularly pious Anglo-Catholic) assumed his office as the new Viceroy in 1926, the designs for the Church of the Redemption were given special priority: "Medd designed a high central tower, possibly too tall, instead of the modest dome of his competition drawing, which had strongly echoed Lutyens' Free Church of 1910 at Hampstead

Fig. 228: In 1935, the construction of the Cathedral Church of the Redemption was nearing completion, view from west.

Fig. 229: Cathedral Church of the Redemption, view from the southwest.

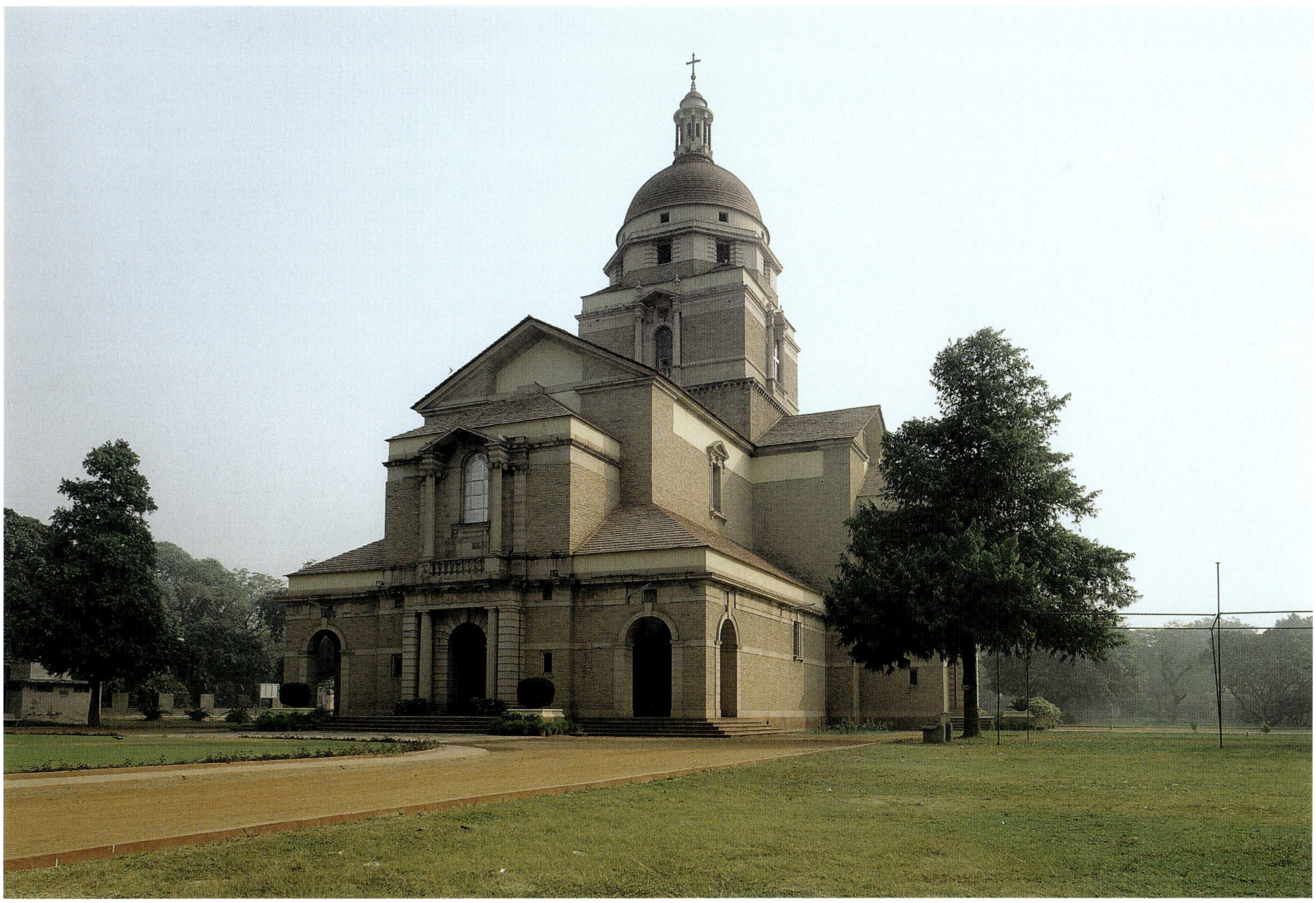

Garden Suburb. Immense foundations for this lofty feature were laid deep on stable soil, but no tower was completed until 1935, when a third design by Medd, of an intermediate height, was built during his absence from India."[53]

One of the reasons Medd's plan was an appropriate choice was the obvious formal borrowings from Palladio, Lutyens' great model. These elements are revealed particularly clearly in the entrance facade: the vertical and three-dimensional staggering of the pillars, gables and rooftops of Medd's design correspond to the Mannerist staggering and interlocking of pilasters and gables on the facade of Il Redentore in Venice (Palladio, 1577–92).

In both places, the crossing is supported by interior Corinthian pillars, and in both places a semicircle concludes the transept.

It was not possible to finance the church building simply with money from the local Anglo-Catholic community. That it was built, nevertheless, was first due to Lord Irwin receiving substantial subscriptions in Britain and, secondly, because the builders did not use expensive natural stone. Finally, in London, the King also helped: "In addition to his earlier subscription of £100, the King-Emperor gave the silver cross, a token of his personal interest in the new city and its buildings. Lord Irwin, a Yorkshireman, prompted the gift of the altar and the altar rails, the figures above the reredos and the pulpit by York Minster, as part of its celebration of thirteen centuries of Christianity from the baptism of King Edwin of Northumbria in 627... Lord Irwin's devoted concern never flagged, and often in the evenings, he could be seen at the site on Church Road, inspecting the progress and discussing details with Medd. The Viceroy was genuinely delighted with the result, and he recorded his enthusiastic approval of its consummate unity, especially the way the interior scheme carried the eye forward naturally to the high altar ... Irwin's well-known interest in the building, and its final location close to the palace, led to a popular misnomer, 'Viceroy's Church,' which has persisted for half a century.

The actual name of the church (later, a cathedral in 1947) was in fact the subject of prolonged debate. Lutyens and Irwin favoured dedication to God the Father. But the Metropolitan, the Bishop of Calcutta, expressed doubt about a title for which there was little or no precedent in the Western Church. The example of Palladio's Il Redentore suggested the Redeemer, or Holy Redeemer, to Medd, but eventually the building was consecrated as the Church of the Redemption, which the architect and others considered exotic for an Anglican edifice."[54]

The Cathedral Church of the Redemption – in spite of the unquestionable originality of its concept in relation to the particularly difficult site – fits into the long succession of unwavering formal and conceptual discussions for Imperial Delhi's architects about relating Italian Mannerism to the British tradition, in this case, the Anglican church. All this took place in the

53 R.G. Irving: op. cit., p. 326.
54 Ibid., pp. 326, 327

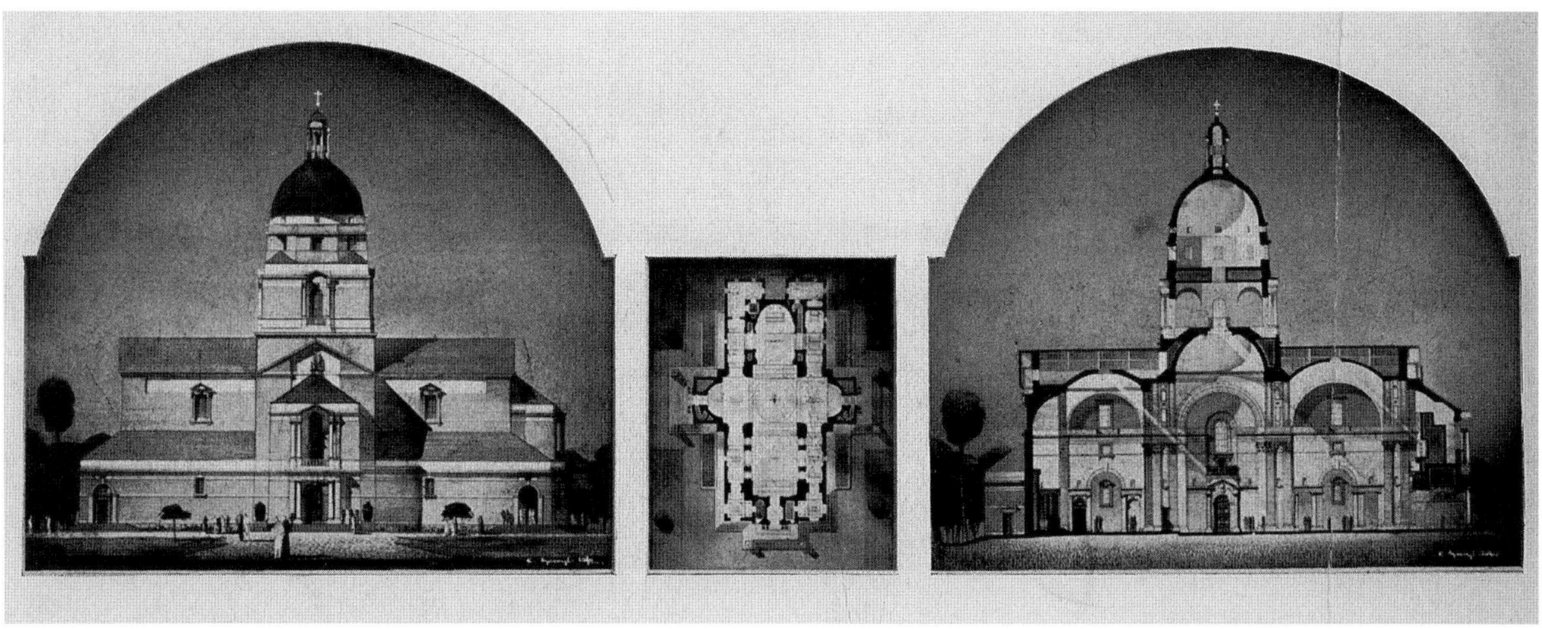

Fig. 230: An early drawing of the Cathedral Church of the Redemption, view from the south, ground plan and east-west section.

centre of the Indian sub-continent already characterized for centuries by rivalry and exchange between Islam and Hinduism, where foreign conquerors constantly tried to make their mark both militarily and culturally.

The British Crown's dream of a world order pleasing to God collapsed after little more than a decade after the new cathedral's opening. The important question here, is not whether Palladio and the Anglican church in India were well-suited to each other, but rather what role the non-Christian religions would play in the growing independence movement in the formation of a non-British and non-Palladian identity.

Fig. 231: Cathedral Church of the Redemption, main nave.

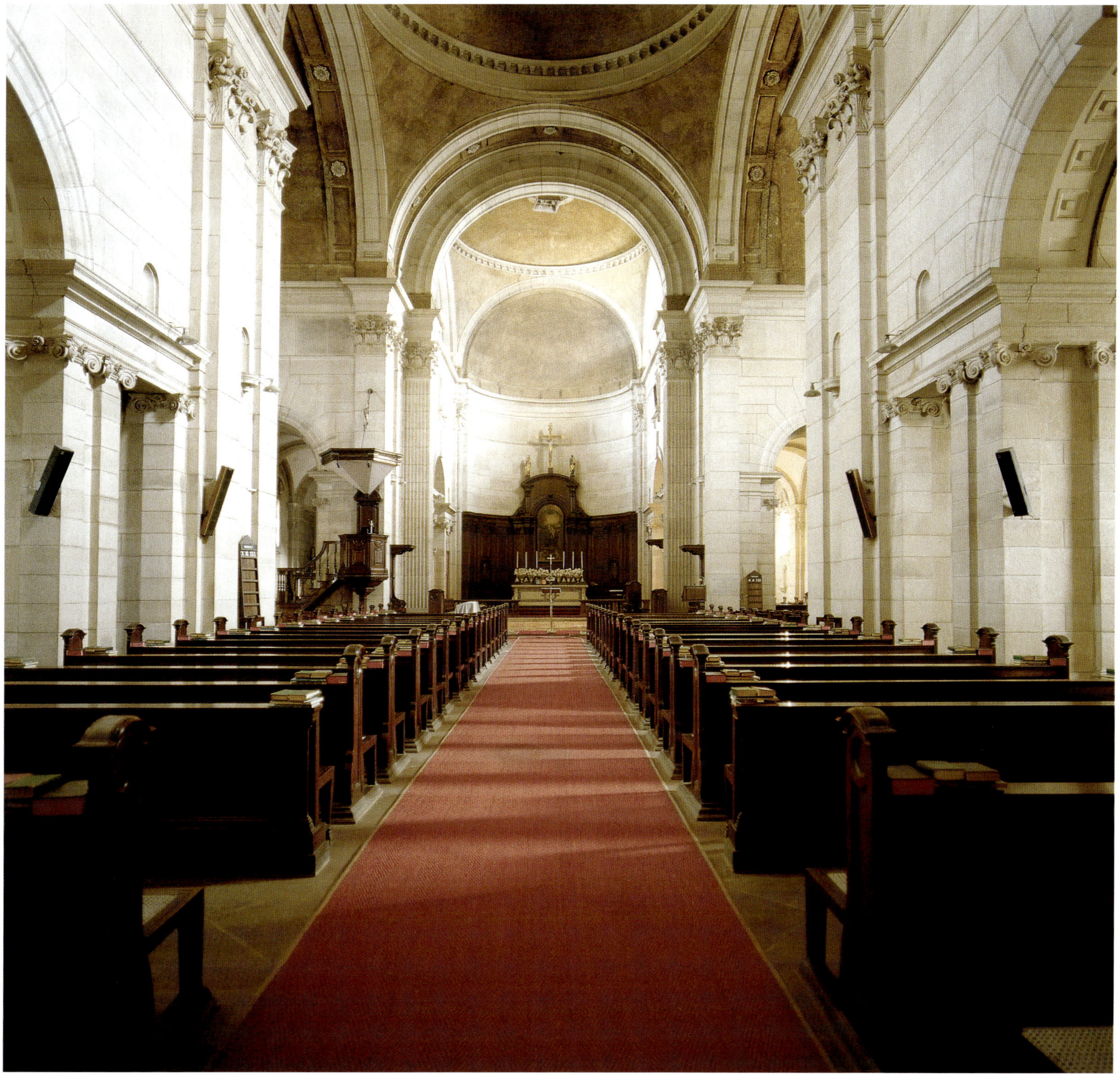

4.4 Realization of the Plans and Utilization as the Capital of the Raj

In December, 1911, a few days after the historic Coronation Durbar of King George V as Emperor of India, the foundation stone for the new capital was laid.

"A visit to the Government of India Camp on the 14th of December showed that the Public Works Department was working day and night to have everything in readiness for the important ceremony. By the morning of the 15th, a wall seven feet high, running some fifteen feet from east to west, had been built. Two blocks of dressed stone were slung by pulleys over the masonry, and these stones were two and a half feet wide and one and a half feet deep. A platform with a wide approach completed the arrangements ...

Only five hundred persons, including the residents of the Government of India Camp, received invitations to be present at the laying of the foundation stones by Their Imperial Majesties. The Ruling Chiefs, Heads of Governments, High Military Officers, and Provincial Representatives who did homage at the Durbar were invited – and that was all ...

The route from the King-Emperor's Camp was lined with troops, the Gordon Highlanders extending their line to the dais where, under a small shamiana, two thrones had been placed. His Imperial Majesty was in Field-Marshal's uniform, and the Queen-Empress wore a cream dress, a magnificent crimson velvet cloak that had been specially embroidered in Kashmir, and a large hat with black feathers."[55]

The laying of the foundation stone for the capital of the Raj was accompanied by the following speech by the King: "It is a matter of supreme satisfaction to the Queen-Empress and myself that it has been possible for us before leaving Delhi to lay the first stones of the Imperial Capital which will arise from where we now stand. This is the first step to give material effect to the important announcement which it was my pleasure to make on that magnificent and to us, deeply impressive occasion of my Coronation Durbar three days ago. I earnestly hope that the anticipation of the beneficial and far-reaching results from the great changes now to be effected may be amply fulfilled, securing to India improved administration and to its peopled increased happiness and prosperity. It is my desire that the planning and designing of the public buildings to be erected will be considered with the greatest deliberation and care so that the new creation may be in every way worthy of this ancient and beautiful city. May God's blessing rest upon the work which is so happily inaugurated to-day. "[56]

With these words one of the largest building projects in the history of humanity was set in motion. The realization of the project led to a construction period of some eighteen years (1913 to 1931) on paper, out of which one can count out five years (1914 to 1918) due to the interruption in building during World War I.

Logistical demands

The logistical and organizational demands on the engineers and architects involved were without precedent. Town-planning, details of architecture and construction were coordinated partly in London, and partly in the location offices set up for that purpose in Delhi.

There were 700 million bricks that were produced in twenty-seven brickworks specially built for the construction project. 100,000 cubic feet of Indian marble for the floors in Viceroy's House had to be brought from various quarries by specially built railway lines. An incalculable amount of red and buff-coloured limestone was broken in the very quarries of Northern India from which the Mughal Emperors had already extracted building materials for their palaces.

"The sandstone used was of the same strata as that used by Akbar and Shah Jehan. The stoneyard was one of the largest in the world, employing 3,500 men, who dressed over 3½ million cubic feet, and about 350,000 cubic feet of marble."[57]

"Besides it virtues of workability and endurance, this stone has been put to most astonishing uses, including beams up to 30 feet span; and lintels and slabs of 16 feet span are common. The quarries originally selected were to the south of Delhi, in Dholpur State for the white and buff varieties, in Bharatpur for the red ... The scene of operations was a rocky desert, miles

55 The Imperial Publishing Company: *The Imperial Coronation Durbar*, Delhi 1911, pp. 89, 90.
56 The Imperial Publishing Company, op. cit., p. 90.
57 Sir Edwin Lutyens: Speech made at a meeting of the India Society on February 2, 1933.

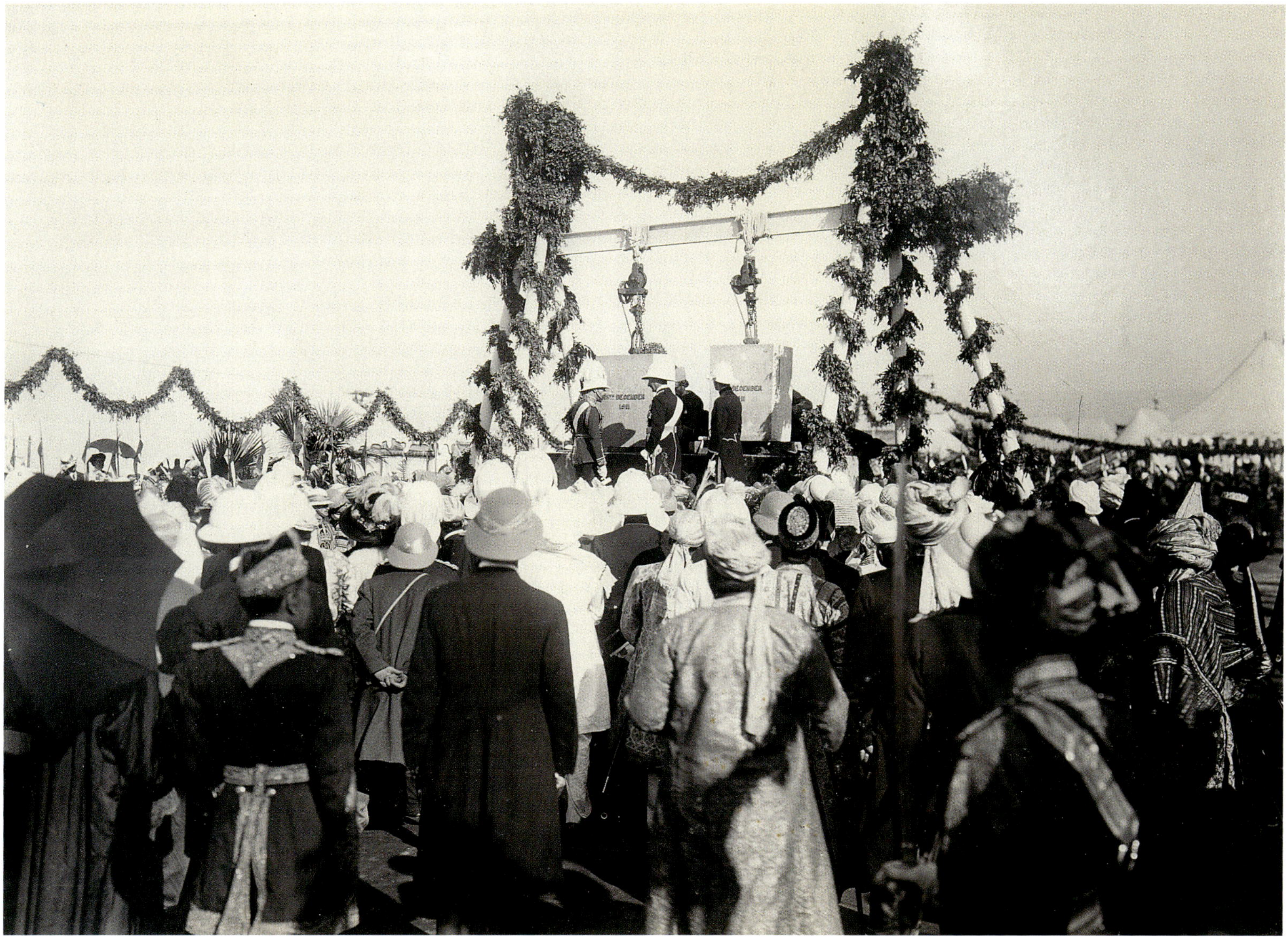

Fig. 232: Laying the foundation stone of New Delhi on the morning of December 15, 1911.

from civilisation, infested with outlaws, and a veritable inferno in hot weather. The difficulties of labour supply were enormous. No less than eleven quarries had to be abandoned after heavy development expenses, owing to the quality of the stone not coming up to expectations ...

By 1922, a third of the stone had been delivered, approximately a million cubic feet. The Committee's recommendation for expediting work therefore meant that a plant could be purchased and the number of railway wagons increased. By these means the output gradually rose to 40,000 cubic feet of dressed stone per month, reaching a peak of nearly 60,000 in 1926 when 3,500 stonemasons were being employed. The total quantity of three million cubic feet of dressed stone used in the Central Buildings involved the actual transport of nearly 6 million cubic feet weighing 400,000 tons for some 200 miles in all. The stoneyard at New Delhi was the largest in the world. From one end where the rough stone was delivered, to the other where it passed, still by rail, to the site, measured some 2,000 feet, its buildings covered 22 acres and at the period of maximum activity it was turning out 2,500 cubic feet of dressed stone a day ...

The only stone imported, with the exception of the Royal Foundation Stones, that for the floor of the Durbar Hall, in particular the Rosso-Porforico marble procured from Italy since it was found impossible to obtain stone from India of the size and colour specified. The marbles of India are of an infinite and beautiful variety, and were used extensively in Government House (Viceroy's House). But most of the quarries were underdeveloped or inaccessible, and of the many samples submitted, it was found that no pieces larger than the sample were obtainable. The white marble used most was that from Makrana in Jodhpur State, also from Alwar. The green was procured from Baroda and Ajmere, the grey from Marwar, and the yellow for the columns of Durbar Hall from Jaisalmer. The latter had to be carried slung on camels for forty miles over sandy desert, which limited the size of the blocks. When the camel struck work, lorries were employed, but their carrying capacity was small over the trackless desert and their life short. Pink marble was obtained from Alwar, Makrana and Haripur.

The whole constructional responsibility for the new city remained with Sir High Keeling, whose knighthood in 1923 acknowledged the outstanding technical services, established by the Committee's investigations, which he had rendered to New Delhi since its inception, and continued till his retirement in 1925. He was then succeeded as Chief Engineer by Sir Alexander Rouse, previously Superintending Engineer in which capacity he was followed by Mr J. L. Sale, with Mr T.S. Malik as Executive Engineer for Government House. The latter, a stalwart Sikh who never flinched from assuming responsibilities, eventually became Sadar Bahadur Sir Teja Singh Malik and Chief Engineer of the Central Public Works Department."[58]

Teja Singh Malik recorded the progress of the building work in many photographs, and his albums today make an important contribution to the reconstruction of individual phases of the building process (Fig. 236).

The engineers, forestry experts, and landscape architects involved in the preparations for the building of New Delhi were noted to have performed their duties well: "Before the commencement of the work, the major portion of this area was under cultivation; the soil, generally, is a good-class loam. The results of the gardening operations undertaken in the new city to date show the quality of the soil. If in the future, inhabitants in the new capital area pay as much attention to their gardens as many of the inhabitants have done during the period of construction, the results should be a gorgeous blaze of color and a riot of bloom."[59]

The following passage characterizes the execution of the building and its progress: The top of Raisina Hill was removed to create a level surface for Viceroy's House, the Mughal garden situated behind it, and the Secretariats in front. The gravel that was removed was used for building the sloping driveway and for enlarging the level surface at its edges: "The Viceroy's House stands on rock which involved blasting, but saved very deep foundations. The great masses of its structure are built in ordinary bricks, made locally. These are entirely faced externally with stone from the Dholpur quarries a hundred and twenty miles distant. It is the same material as was used by the Mogul Emperors. Two shades of it were quarried – a dull tomato red and a creamy buff. It is a durable sandstone with a texture midway between the British variety and our

58 Christopher Hussey: op. cit., p. 427ff.
59 "The New Delhi. The Works of Sir Edwin Lutyens and Sir Herbert Baker," *AR* Vol. LX, July–December 1926, p. 223.
60 Christopher Hussey: op. cit., p. 345.
61 A.S.G. Butler: op. cit., p. 32–33.

Portland stone. The floors and roofs are reinforced concrete – the latter covered with stone slabs laid on asphalt. The floors of all rooms of any importance are paved with marble, and the heating comes from panels between this and the concrete. The fuel used is coke. Nearly all the joinery is executed in teak to resist attacks by the white ant. Most of it is painted in light colours. These are a few of the practical points in connection with this palace which, we understand, cost between £ 900,000 and £ 1,000,000. That cannot be said to be expensive because two-thirds of the London County Hall, built about the same time, cost almost three times as much. Labour in India, was, of course, very cheap."[60]

World War I brought with it a clear decrease, indeed at times a halt, to all building activity. "Lutyens described the position as 'estimating goes on; schemes gradually get sanction, and then go on as money provides.' Work already undertaken continued but no new operations were sanctioned unless in some way contributing to war potential. One result was that Lutyens could apply himself immediately to some of the important matters of detail and organisation for which there had hitherto been little time. The eventual need of architectural sculpture raised questions of the forms and symbols to be employed, which required to be determined or designed; and of finding or training sculptors, out of which issued the much larger question of forming the centre for the training of craftsmen which was laid down in the architect's agreement with the government."[61]

Fig. 233: Chief Engineer Teja Singh Malik (front and centre of picture) with his team of engineers from the Public Works Department was responsible for the construction work of Viceroy's House and the two Secretariats, photograph from *c.* 1925.

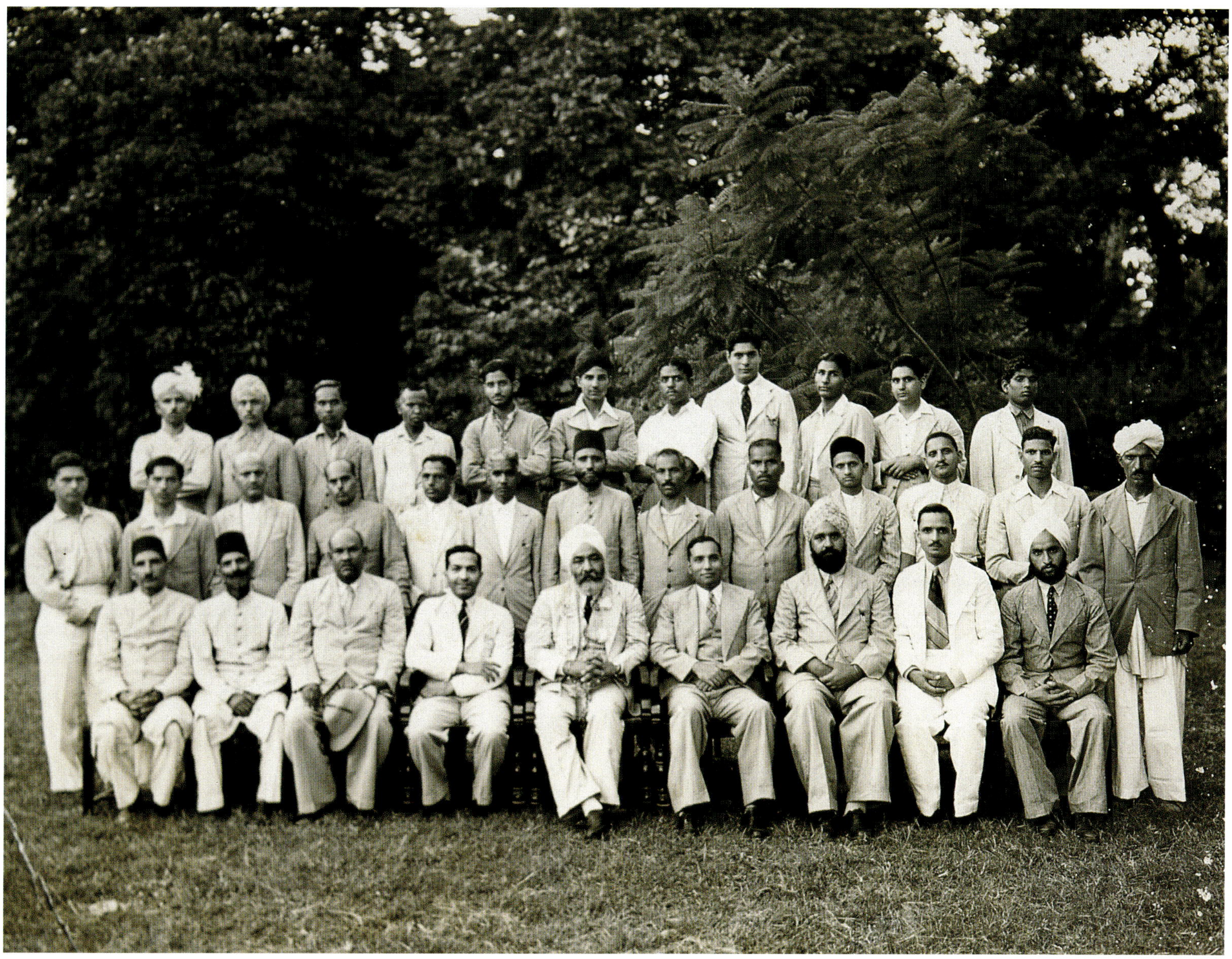

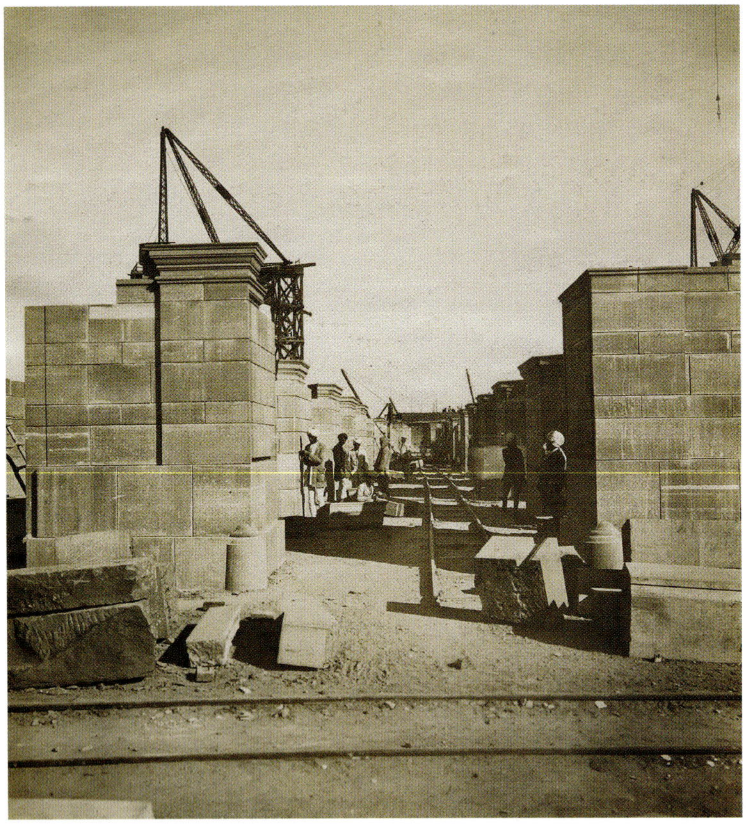

Fig. 234: The Viceroy's Palace was built to exactly the same size as Buckingham Palace in London.

The construction of Viceroy's House progressed as it became increasingly clear that the initial budget would have to be exceeded. The Viceroy was worried, but in London, the King was quite relaxed. On November 4, 1916, Lutyens provides details of the King's view of the costs incurred by Viceroy's House's construction: "As to the costs, it did not matter how long the Palace took to build, so long as it was, when built, worthy of India and of its purpose, and if money was not forthcoming now, parts might for the time being be omitted and facades left unfinished as is usual in Italy, until such time as money was available to complete them."[62]

After the shell of the building was completed the difficulties, far from decreasing, increased. During work on the interior it became clear, for example, how difficult it was to acquire technical components and pieces of quality furniture on the Indian market whether they were door locks, heating components, or carpets.

"Lutyens was especially anxious that the weaving of the carpets for Government House should revive the standard of design and technique of the great Persian period. It was partly in this connection that he had gone to Kashmir, where some of the finest carpets were made.[63] For the Durbar Hall the design selected was a copy of a Persian Royal Garden carpet of the sixteenth century, fragments of the original of which were lent by Mr H.D. MacLaren (now Lord Aberconway). Similarly, for the other State rooms, sixteenth and seventeenth-century Persian originals were loaned so that not only the patterns but the dyes and materials should be reproduced and so revive standards of the age of Shah Abbas. The carpets occupied 500 weavers two years. It was estimated that those for the Durbar Hall, dining-room and drawing-room alone contain 279,000,000 knots and that 7,000 miles of wool was used."[64]

In 1926, the *Architectural Review* reported in detail for the first time about the progress of the building: "It is not, however, possible to publish views of the completed works; first, because Government House (Viceroy's House) is not yet completed, and the Viceroy is not likely to be in residence there until 1928; and, secondly, because the Secretariats, though now being occupied, are not yet complete in respect to the two large domes. Nor will it be possible to complete the gardens surrounding the principal buildings until such time as the workmen have quite finished their task on the outside of the building."[65]

62 Letter of E. Lutyens to Lord Chelmsford.
63 The leading makers were Hadow's of Srinagar and Stavides of Lahore.
64 Christopher Hussey: op. cit., p. 497.
65 *Architectural Review*: The New Delhi (no author), Vol. LX. July–December 1926, London.

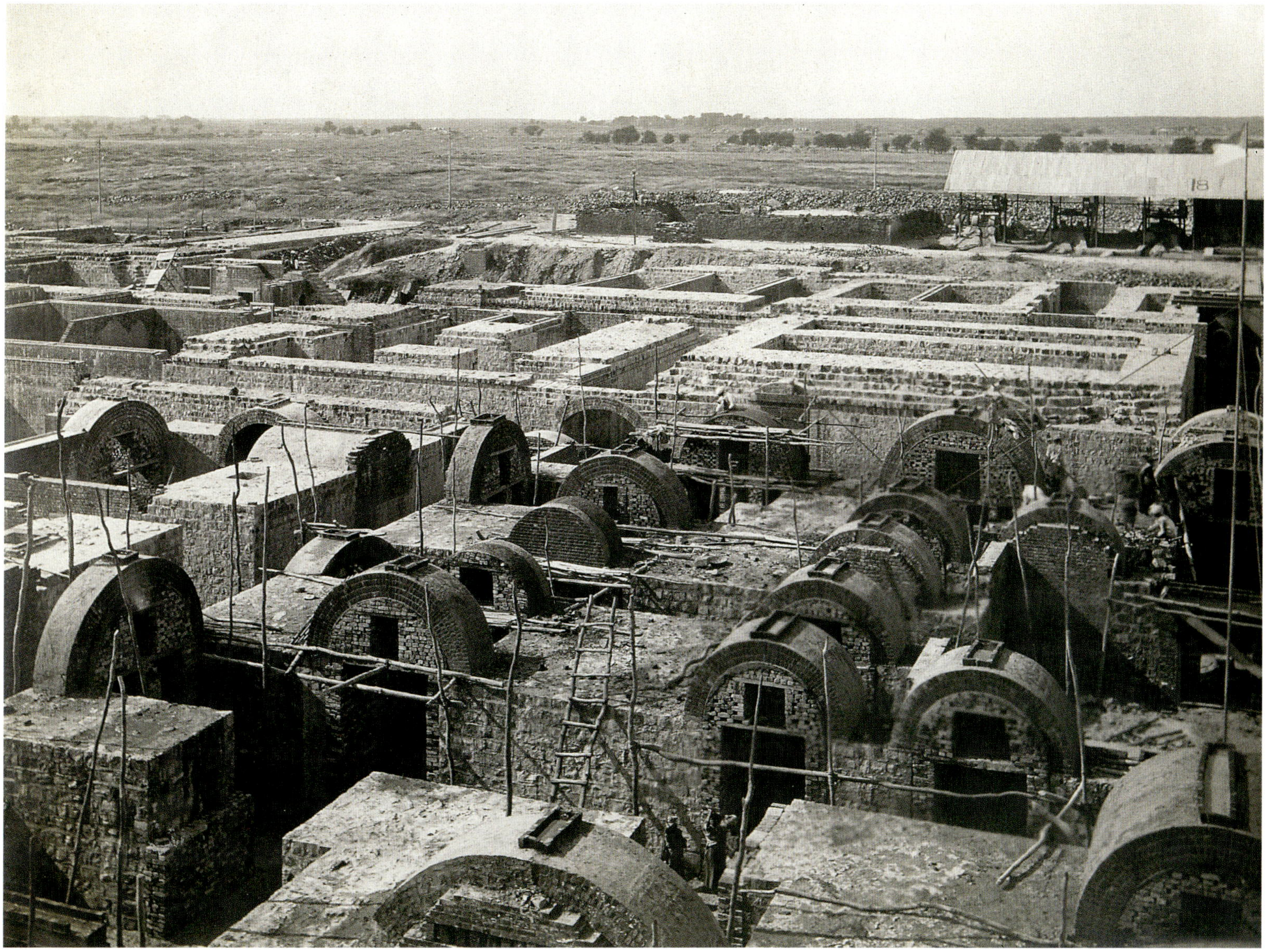

Fig. 235: Round arches, barrel vaults, and cross vaults in the upper basement of Viceroy's House support the Renaissance-style halls and domes of the *piano nobile*. Photographed during construction, *c*. 1925.

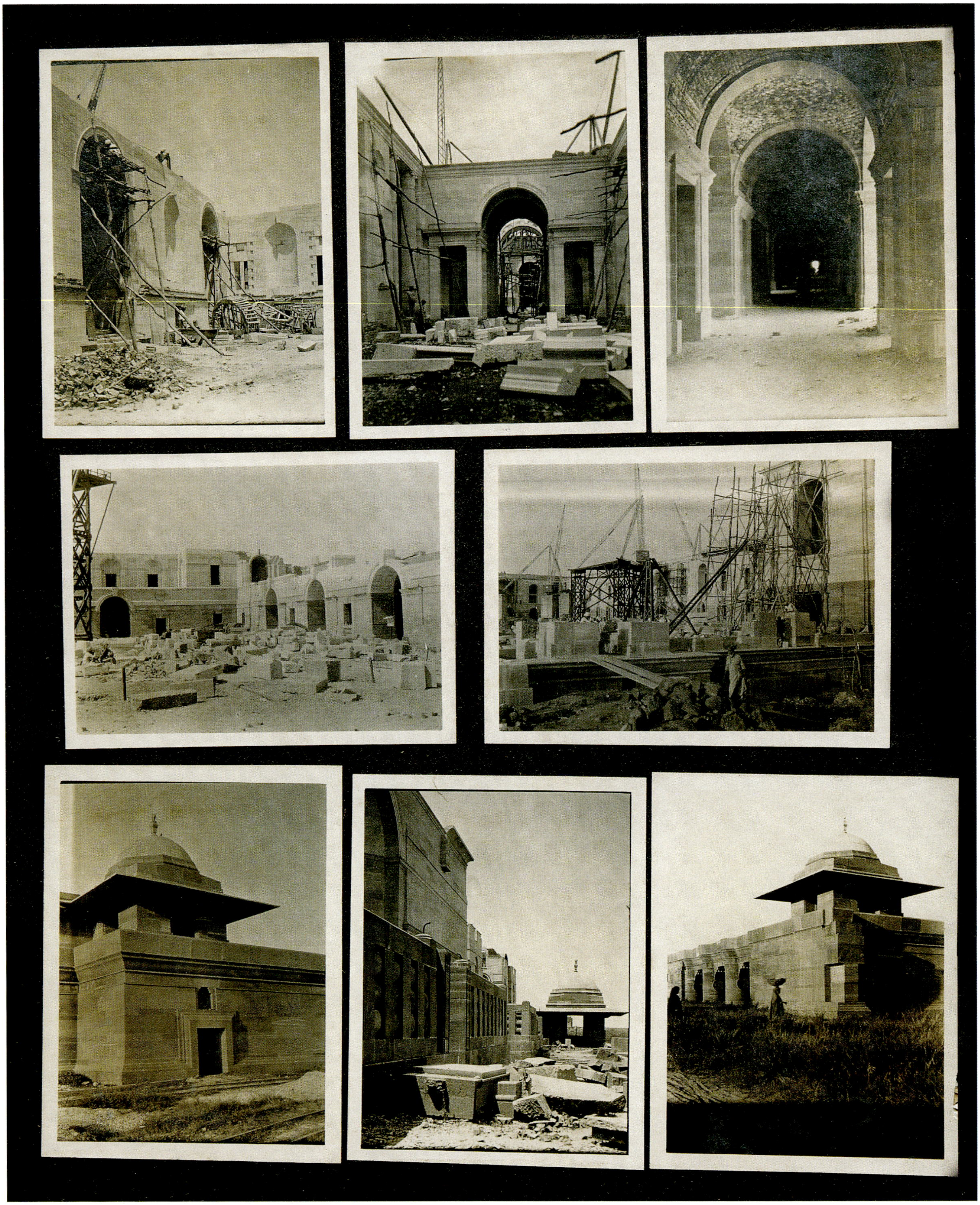

Inauguration of the new capital

After seventeen years of construction Delhi was inaugurated as the capital of Imperial India in February, 1931, by a series of festivities held over two weeks. But receptions, garden parties, festive dinners, and speeches could not deceive many of the guests that the age of imperialism and racial prejudice would soon be approaching its end.

"Not surprisingly, little was heard in 1931 of New Delhi as embodiment of imperium, but instead much was made of its perceived role as emblem of a new era. The very week of its inaugural ceremonies, delegates returned to India from the first Round Table Conference, which had been convened in London to chart the course towards Indian self-rule. Leading British newspapers agreed that the coincidence was 'almost miraculous,' for it was now possible to regard Raisina as representing the government's 'altered spirit.' History would associate New Delhi with the beginning of real self-government; its buildings would not be seen as 'vainglorious gestures' of dominion and the trappings of imperial power, but rather as the offices and council chambers where India would plan and direct her own future ...

Commemorative ceremonies for the new capital could not hope to rival the Delhi Durbar of 1911. While the inauguration in 1931 was, in Lord Irwin's words 'a landmark in the history of India,' economic depression and consequent financial stringency made impossible the lavish expenditure of nineteen years before. Even the sum of £22,000, the cost of bringing a representative Indian army to Delhi and supplying the essentials of a simplified pageant, raised protests from the European community. Their heightened concern about the future of British interests following the Round Table Conference undercut any festive sentiments. One English journalist reported glum descriptions of inaugural events as 'the funeral of our Indian Empire.'"[66]

Edwin Lutyens had travelled to the new capital's inaugural celebrations with his wife, Lady Emily. After years of estrangement and misunderstandings, both agreed that not only had the building of New Delhi been an unparalleled historic opportunity for Lutyens, but also that its overwhelming success had made them put aside all their past differences.

Fig. 236: A page out of Teja Singh Malik's photograph album shows the building progress at Viceroy's House in the mid-1920s.

"The apogee of British New Delhi was 1931, when the new capital was inaugurated with pomp and ceremony. Lutyens was there with his wife, Lady Emily, who, despite her earlier flirtation with Indian nationalism, was impressed. She wrote to her children that 'this remains a colossal and most wonderful achievement and should make father's name go down in history as one of the architects of all time. Hudson[67] is so moved that he can hardly keep from tears. He said to me yesterday Poor old Christopher Wren could never have done this!' Hudson was probably right."[68]

"The undeviating geometry of the city plan had appeared symbolic of Britain's efforts to impose order and unity on the subcontinent, while the monumental scale of the avenues and principal buildings had implied a permanence that challenged time itself. As the domes and towers fashioned by Lutyens and Baker rose on Raisina Hill, bright against the sky above city and plain, they had seemed to proclaim the success of British discipline and power. By February 1931, however, many persons acknowledged that Delhi's inaugural celebrations were but a requiem for that dream of abiding dominion ..."[69]

"The days preceding the formal opening of the House,[70] when everybody would be in top hats to receive their Excellencies, and the Municipal Council would present an address, were chaotic. Lutyens, with a heavy cold, described it: '... like an Exhibition. It is impossible to conceive they have been at it seventeen years. Contretemps follow each other from hour to hour. The English foremen work day and night. If it had not been for this handful of trained craftsmen I cannot imagine what would have happened. The Indian foremen agree there is not nearly enough supervision. 3,000 panes of glass have been broken and 500 keys stolen, besides doorknobs and window-fastenings. I keep on exploding and stopping to blow my nose.'

Monday the 23rd was a morning of white mist, in which the booming of distant salute guns heralding the Viceroy's arrival marked another explosion. An attempt, echoing that on Lord Hardinge when enacting the transfer of the capital to Delhi, but mercifully ineffective, had been made to bomb Lord Irwin's train. The ceremony proceeded, 'then H.E. went up the

66 R.G. Irving: op. cit., p. 340ff.
67 Edward Hudson, proprietor of *Country Life* and devoted friend of Edwin Lutyens.
68 G. Stamp: op. cit., p. 42.
69 R.G. Irving: op. cit., p. 340.
70 Lord Irvin moved in on January 23, 1931.

stairway to the great portico, where I and others were presented to him. At a given signal the doors were opened (there was no key, as there was no lock). They went into the House, and for the first time in seventeen years the House was closed on me.'"[71]

Imperial Delhi was to serve the British Viceroy as his residence for less than two decades. Many visitors at the official inauguration ceremonies already suspected that the end was nigh for British colonial rule in India, but the city enchanted all those taking part with its palaces, gardens, boulevards and monuments.

Robert Byron's description of the city in 1931, when it could be seen, more or less, as Lutyens envisaged is particularly telling: "Since first turning up the King's Way, the traveller has come two miles. Returning to the iron screen across the front of the courtyard, he can look back across the park and waterways to the great white arch in the distance. On all sides radiate the avenues of the new city, lined with bungalows in spacious woody gardens, and carved into merry-go-rounds at points of intersection. Every thoroughfare conducts the eye to some more ancient monuments, looming in grey silhouette from the horizon of the imperial plain. Even the great Pearl Mosque, four miles off in the heart of the Old City, has its approach set at an angle of sixty degrees to the axis of the central design. Beyond the Arch, a hump of walls proclaim the old Fort (Purana Kila, the sixth city). A side avenue discloses the clustered domes of the tomb of Safdar Jang. Far away Q'tab is visible, an extravagant chimney on the south horizon. The English quarter presents the aspect of a forest. Each house is set in a compound of two to three acres, whose trees have matured in ten years and become enormous in twenty. At one or two points only are the buildings beginning to congregate in close formation."[72]

All descriptions of the new capital of the Indian Empire during the remaining sixteen years of British rule (1931–47) bear witness to the grandeur of the appearance of the city, to the elegance of the festivals, and above all, to the relaxed protocol at the Viceroy's court: "The Irwins in fact had relaxed Court etiquette at Delhi. The requisite curtseys at dinner, as many as seven in an evening under the Reading regime, were reduced to three. Guests were still shepherded into a drawing room by a platoon of aides-de-camp and ranged in two solemn lines, men opposite women, to bow and curtsey as Their Excellencies swept past. But then various dogs who tumbled all over the house would scamper in behind the Irwins, giving a reasuring impression that the Viceroy was, after all, a country squire."[73]

All these are qualities that, for various historical reasons, occurred with relative ease far from the court in London and the spatial, social, and economic restrictions of Europe. Yet it was here in India that during these years the bell tolled signalling the end of the British Empire. The differences and difficulties between the British Raj and the traditions of Indian society were too great. The Crown's strategies of preserving power and extending it were too arrogant vis-à-vis the determined efforts of the native elite and their tactics of non-violence and civil disobedience.

When in the face of a large demonstration in Amritsar in 1919, General Reginald Dyer lost his nerve and ordered his soldiers to shoot indiscriminately into the crowd, the British Crown in India lost whatever good faith had remained. The fall of the British Empire in India was only a matter of time.

Yet precisely in view of the futility of all British attempts at stabilizing their colonial policies, we are still amazed today at the imperial architecture that outlasted all the political turmoil. No alterations or additions diminish the powerful statement of Viceroy's House, no auto-routes cut through the hexagonal street-system. Only at Connaught Circus does the wall of late Neo-Classical facades crumble under the pressure of property speculation in the tertiary sector (cf. Chapter 4.3.4).

71 Christopher Hussey: op. cit., p. 520f.
72 R. Byron: *New Delhi*, reprint of: *Architectural Review*, Vol. LXIX, January 1931, New Delhi 1977, p. 11.
73 R.G. Irving: op. cit., p. 342.

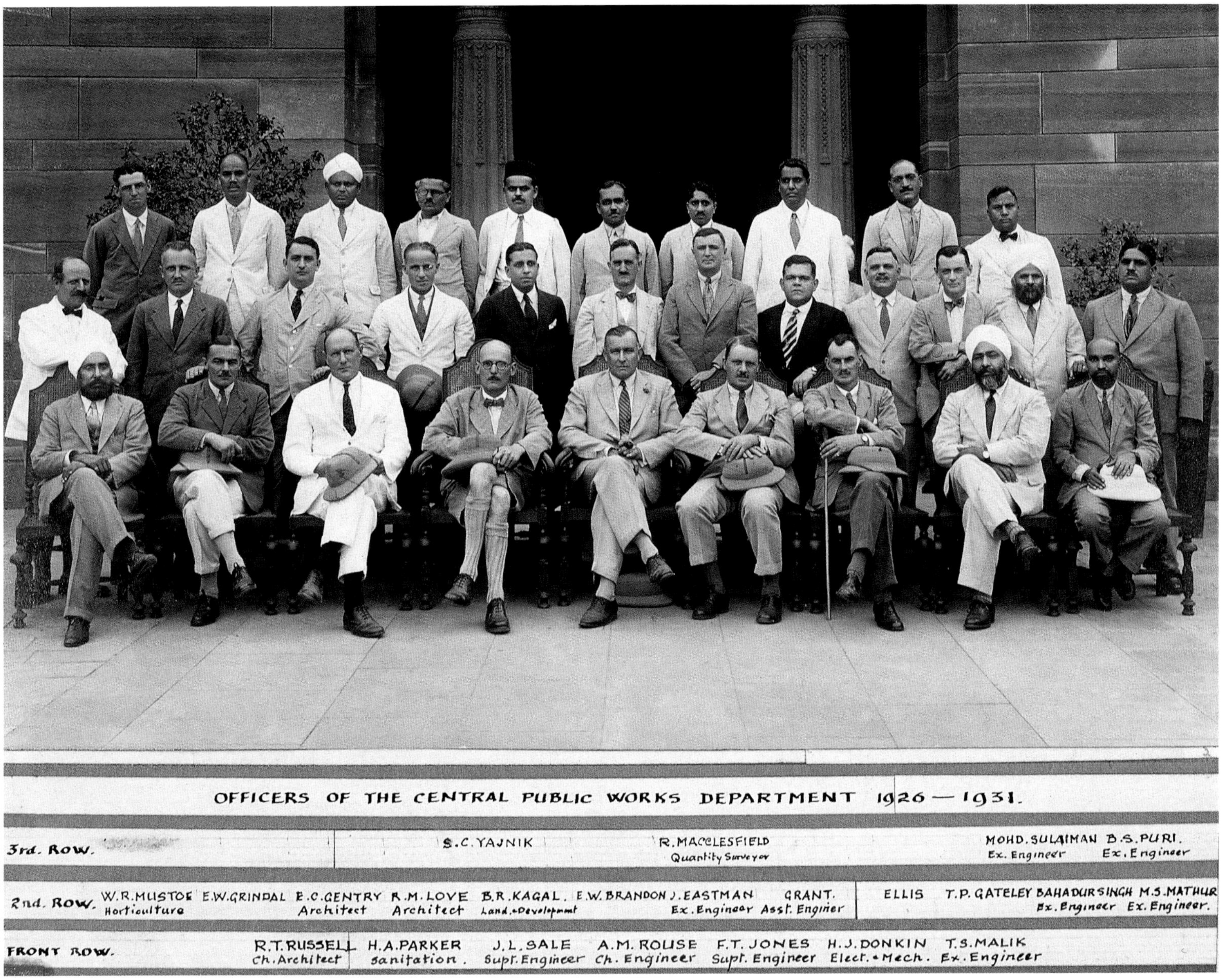

Fig. 237: As expected, in Teja Singh Malik's photograph album there is also a group photograph of the officers of the Public Works Department 1926–31 with the most important executives in the front row: R.T. Russel, A.M. Rouse and T.S. Malik.

4.5 Architecture and Town Planning as a Flexible Service for Different Social Groups

It is the fate of many great architects that, because of their special achievements for a certain type of patron, they are always offered similar commissions. Palladio's villas were such a success in sixteenth-century northern Italy that only rarely was the master given the opportunity to develop other styles of building to the same perfection. It is even possible that Frank Lloyd Wright would have liked to have built some churches and offices in the United States; only his reputation as a first-class architect of luxurious residences prevented him from doing so.

A similar fate also threatened the young Lutyens who was, undoubtedly, the most successful architect of British country houses at the turn of the century. But the surprisingly flexible attitude of the English nobility in the administration of the empire, and a no less flexible Royal House, finally made it possible for him to test his obvious talents on other architectural commissions. The result in India confirmed just how right his patrons' opinions were.

With hindsight we can see that it was not only the patrons of Lutyens who combined flexibility with far-sightedness. Lutyens himself also did justice to the ever-changing tasks he performed through his readiness to experiment. He was not committed to any fixed architectural style because, after all, workers' houses, a bank and a castle did not have to be built in the medieval, Neo-Palladian, or Louis XVI style.

How explicitly and informally Lutyens responded to the social background of each patron can be briefly explained by the examples assembled here in Fig. 238:

a) In 1906, he built a Neo-Classical villa called **Heathcote** near Ilkley in Yorkshire for a rich Yorkshireman, "who could not spend his money – until he met me ..."

"The full Neo-Classical orchestra of a Doric Order – bases, columns, friezes, cornices, with their correct mathematical ratios is martialled in Heathcote ... His Heathcote concerto, though using the same instruments as the hundreds of so-called Palladian compositions produced in eighteenth-century England, differs radically from them because, to continue the metaphor, whereas they are more or less clear echoes of one Italian composer's, Andrea Palladio's, variations on Vitruvian airs, Lutyens here goes straight for his basic theme, to the Doric Order itself as used by Sanmichele, working out his harmonies and intervals from the proportions inherent in that Order, and weaving them into the orchestrations of his melody – namely a country house for a particular man, with particular requirements, on a particular site."[74]

Fig. 238: Lutyens' flexibillity allowed him to respond to every clients' wishes:

a) A villa in the Neo-Palladian style (Heathcote, Ilkley, Yorkshire),1906.

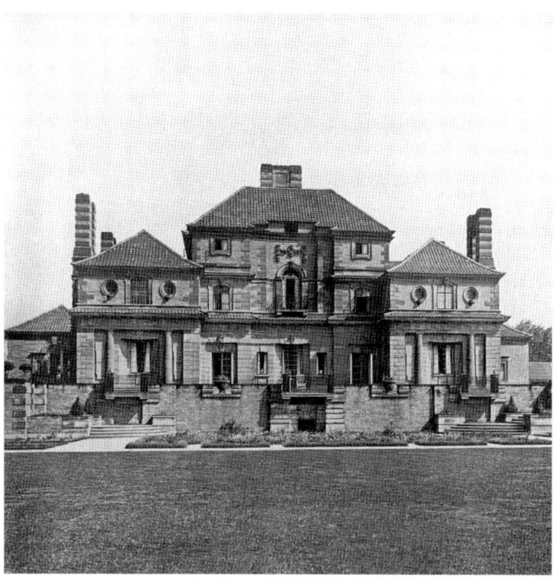

b) A medieval castle (Castle Drogo, Devon), 1910.

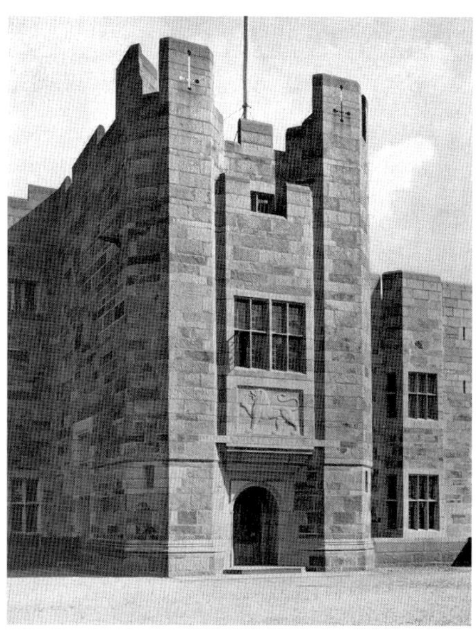

c) Workers' flats (Westminster Housing Scheme), 1930.

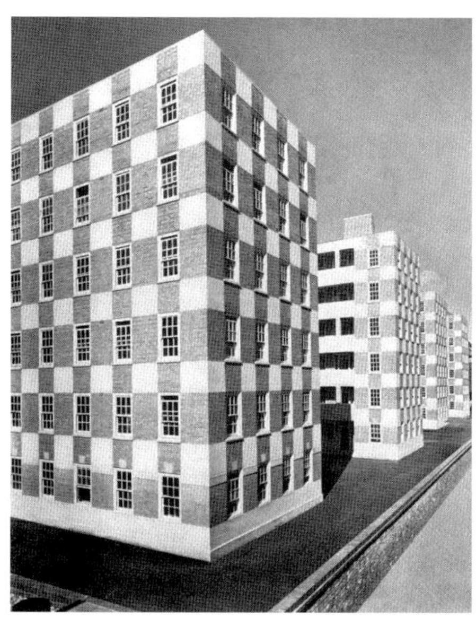

b) The medieval **Castle Drogo** in Devon dating from the year 1910 was built on a rock 900 feet above sea level and 200 feet above a nearby river for the affluent Mr. Drewe in memory of his ancestors in Devonshire.

"As it is, Drogo is even more of a castle, even more dramatic, for being thus an unresolved fragment. The seeming obscurity and wilfulness of its groupings and plan thus have much the same cause as the sublime irrationality produced in medieval castles by forgotten military needs, catastrophic truncations, and the domestic accretions of centuries ... One cause of the 1911 design being drastically reduced was that, at the time of the laying of the foundation stone, the owner decided that the thickness of the walls should be doubled in order to produce more completely the character aimed at."[75]

c) The simple workers' houses of the **Westminster Housing Scheme** in London's West End dating from 1928 were commissioned by London City Council. They replaced a slum area and offered the very poorest families flats with one to four rooms. Each flat had at least one south-facing window so that the cheerless area was made less so by the sunlight streaming in. The facades – even if there were no borrowings from Palladio – were made of light Portland stone, light grey bricks and white Portland cement assembled in a checkerboard design, and with gradually decreasing window height as they moved upwards. Edwin Lutyens, at the peak of his fame at this time, accepted this rather unusual commission with commitment. He did not cling to his dream of capital and Acropolis in the period of a slowly collapsing British Empire.

d) The palace-like villa in **Middleton Park** near Bicester was a commission by Lord Jersey in 1935 for Robert and Edwin Lutyens. In their joint offices, the father and son designed a courtly architecture in the French style full of symmetries and axes that was not disrupted by a single asymmetrical bathroom or kitchen window. The extremely severe external form reminds us of Viceroy's House in Imperial Delhi. In both structures, the architecture harmonizes a complex internal functional layout and a strictly geometric external form without any discrepancies.

e) The **Headquarters of the Theosophical Society** in Gordon Square, London, was commissioned in 1911. Lutyens received this commission in part, because of the active role of his wife, lady Emily, in the Theosophical Society, but also because of his childhood acquaintance with the English Theosophist leader Mrs. Annie Besant. After the interruption of the construction during World War I and because of the financial difficulties of the Theosophical Society, the unfinished building was completed by another architect and for a new owner, the British Medical Association. But the structure of the facade still corresponds, to a large extent, to the ideas of Edwin Lutyens: a base with round arches, above that a *piano nobile* with axial Corinthian columns and, on the roof storey, a crowning triangular gable.

f) In 1923, a branch of the **Midland Bank** was built in Piccadilly in London in the exact style of a small Renaissance palace. Bosses, symmetry, and stone garlands signalled to the bank's

74 Christopher Hussey: op. cit., p. 128.
75 Ibid., p. 219.

d) A castle in the French style (Middleton Park, Bicester) 1935.

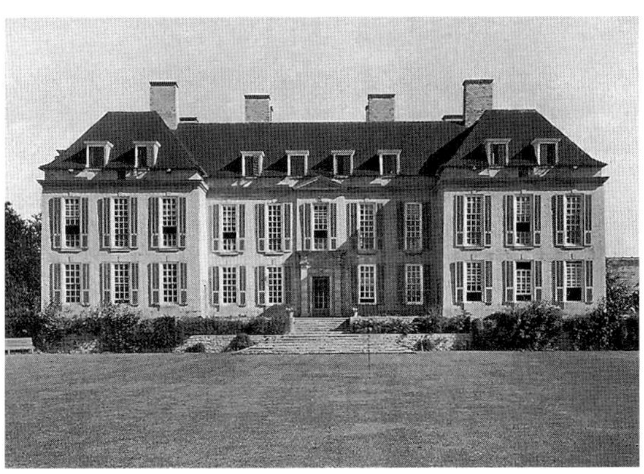

e) A prestigious Neo-Classical building (Theosophical Society, London), 1911.

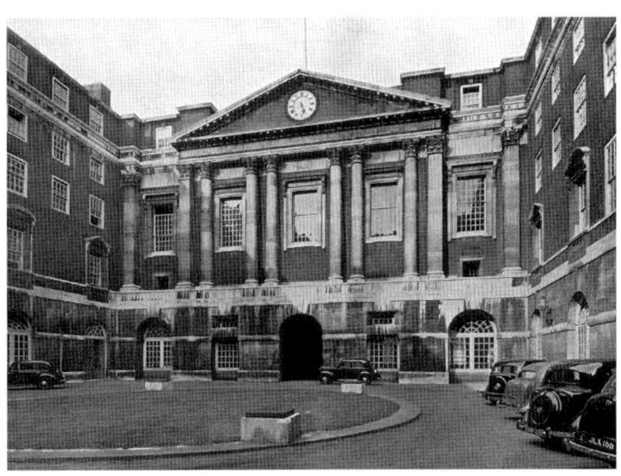

f) A bank in the Renaissance style (Midland Bank, Piccadilly, London), 1923.

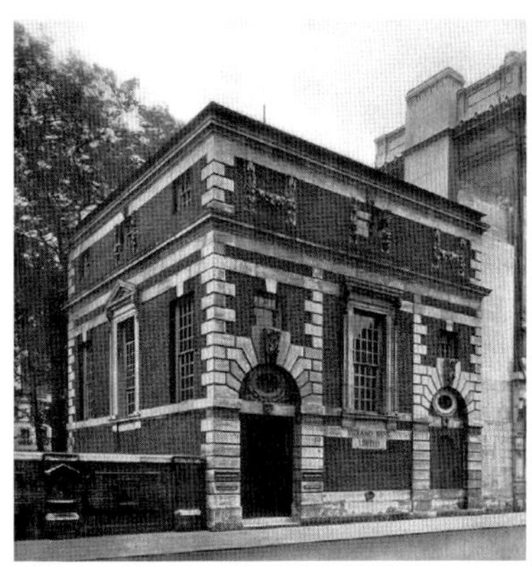

clientele security for their deposits. The cubic body of the building was reminiscent both of a treasure chest and a guardroom.

The surprising variety of architectural forms and style must not be misunderstood as being a disoriented eclectic mix. Rather, it arises from the serious attempt of an architect not plagued by the vanities of self-portrayal to find, as far as possible, an appropriate formal image for the intellectual world and the social milieu of his current patron.

A glance at the ground plans and elevations in Fig. 239 of the large variety of both early and later plans shows the limits of flexibility drawn by the architect himself. In so far as topography, road networks or other given determinants, Edwin Lutyens always chose a symmetrical ground plan, irrespective of the use and the size of the building. Thus, in the same way as a Roman town planner, before the precise measurement and layout of a new town, establishes the *decumanus* and *cardo* as the geographical, even cosmological framework of the town, so Lutyens – at least in a first attempt – chose an axial entrance with a corresponding outside room and an inside room as a reception area. One encounters this *cardo* in his buildings every bit as much in a small country house as in the huge Viceroy's Palace. Even in the case where two houses, each a mirror image of the other (cf. example c. in Fig. 239 from Hampstead Garden Suburb), come together without any internal symmetry, he planned a side entrance to the garden as a symmetrical axis between them.

Let us return to the example of Viceroy's House. Lutyens not only designed the largest and most splendid building in the British Empire, he also went through the whole range of formal sophistication as found in classical antiquity and the Renaissance. A good example is the arrangement of pillars on the entrance side (the eastern side) of the palace (Fig. 242). "At first glance, the portico appears to be a wide shadowed space behind a row of twelve equally spaced columns. But the intervals between these are by no means regular. It is not the delicate and almost invisible variation in spacing practised by the Greeks in their subtlety, but a deliberate widening of the intercolumniation opposite the three entrance doors from a standard 9 feet between centres to as much as ten feet six inches. And, again, in the spacing of the pillars of the long lateral loggias there is a similar widening where they occur over the three arched openings to the North and South Courts – a widening of two feet over the standard seven feet ten inches. Nowhere, then, do the centres of the columns on this front correspond with the centres of the dentils of the cornice, except in the case of the pair flanking the statues of the King and Queen. These are 9 feet 8 inches apart. Yet few people would notice this trifling with the orthodox ..."[76]
The ideas put forward here on:

- The unusual flexibility of Edwin Lutyens in the choice of an appropriate architectural style
- His preference for traditional types of ground plan
- His love of a highly differentiated proportioning of details

are attempts to understand at least the individual components of his uniquely monumental architectural style. Every observer of the facade of Viceroy's House (see Fig. 242) feels a respectful perplexity in the face of many familiar elements.

They are, for example:

- The Buddhist stupa as a dome and as a reminder of the Maurya Empire of Ashoka in the third century B.C.
- The Islamic chattris of north Indian Mughal architecture for accentuating the roof surface and for demonstrating the British claim as successors of the Mughal dynasty.
- The fountains on both sides of the dome, here as sacrificial basins reminding us of the high cost of heroism.
- The Roman pillar arrangements as a visible preparation for the centre of power and the Durbar Hall as representative of this centre.
- The open staircase reminiscent of the Capitol in Rome for demonstrating the distinction between the power of the British Viceroy and the position of his visitors.

These familiar elements have not been pulled indiscriminately out of the magic box of eclecticism and then arranged in an original way. Rather, each element has the task of declaring and consolidating the historic legitimacy of British power over India.

76 A.S.G. Butler: op. cit., p. 35.

Fig. 239: Irrespective of the size and function of the building, Edwin Lutyens used axiality, symmetry and courtly entrances as formal elements, whether for a small country house (a), or for the Emperor of India's Palace (f).

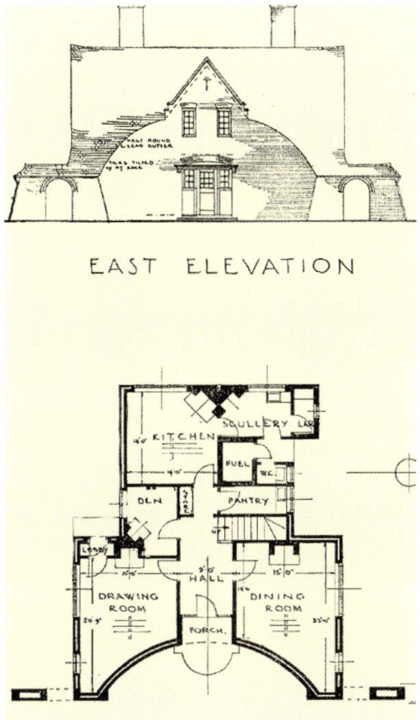

a) Witwood, Camberley, Surrey.

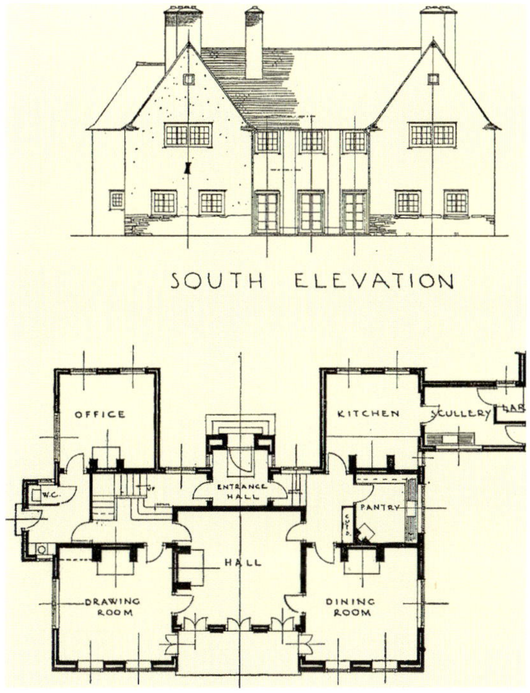

b) Ashby St Ledgers, Northants.

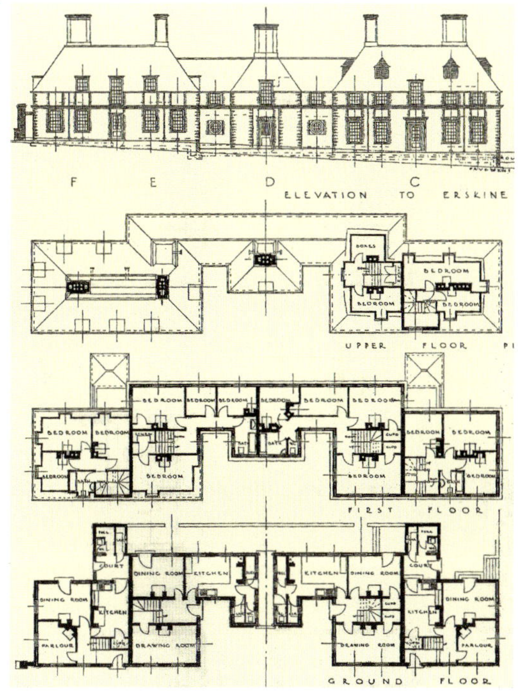

c) Hampstead Garden Suburb.

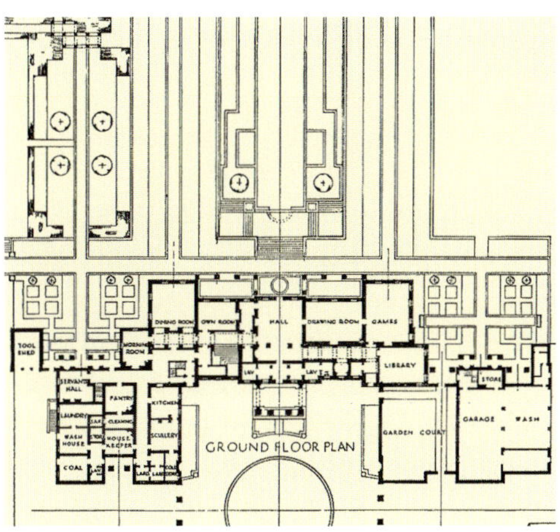

d) Gledstone Hall, Yorkshire.

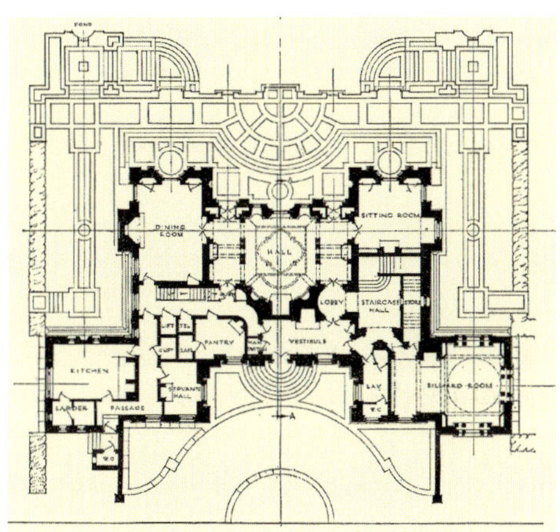

e) Heathcote, Ilkley, Yorkshire.

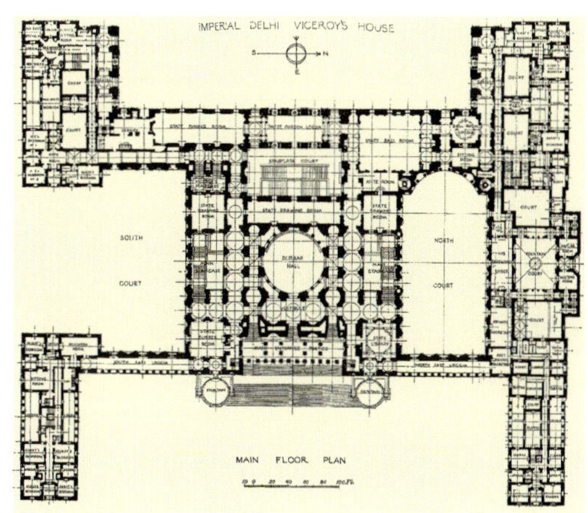

f) Viceroy's House, Imperial Delhi.

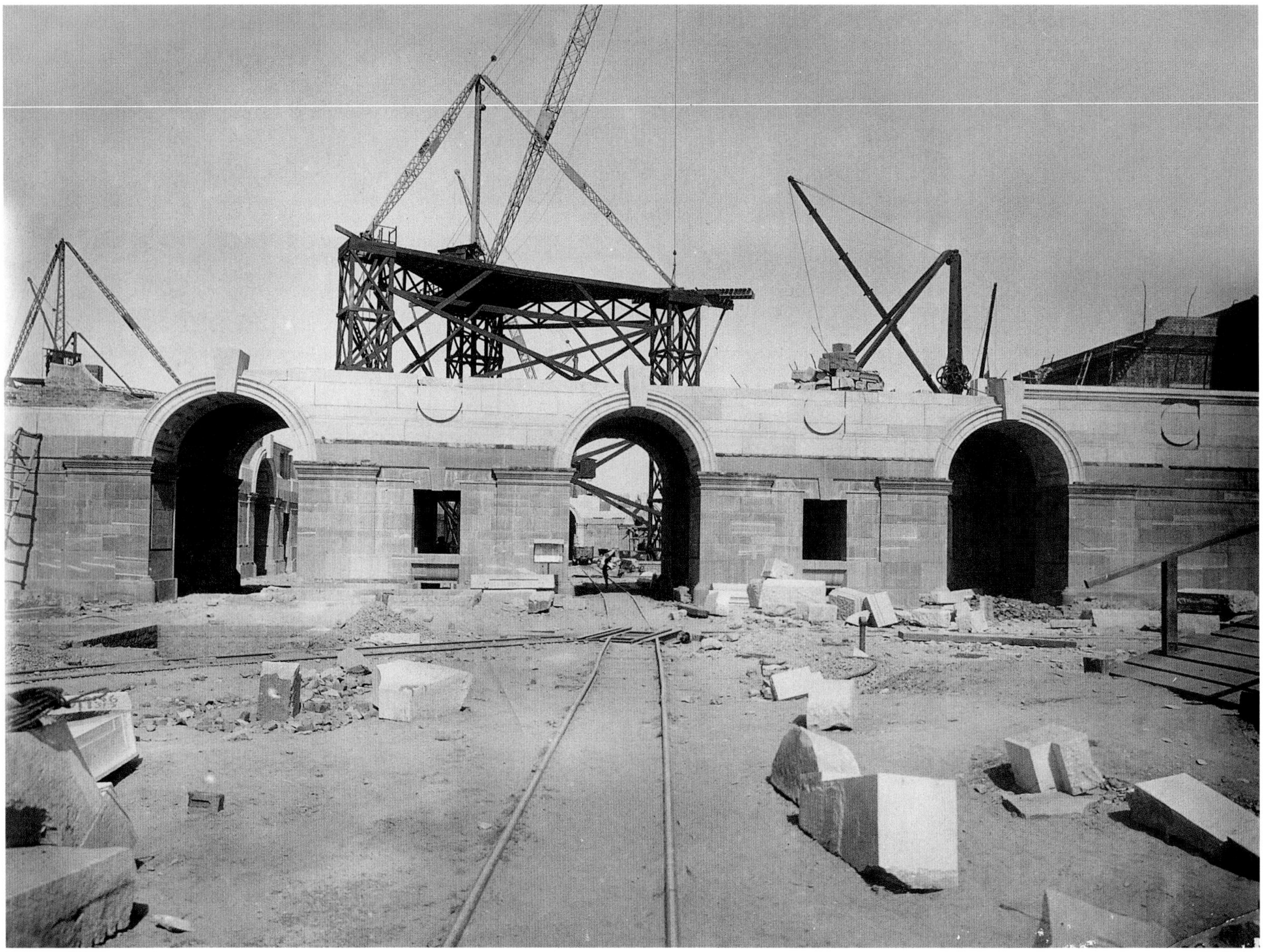

Fig. 240: The upper basement of Viceroy's House from the east, during construction in 1924.

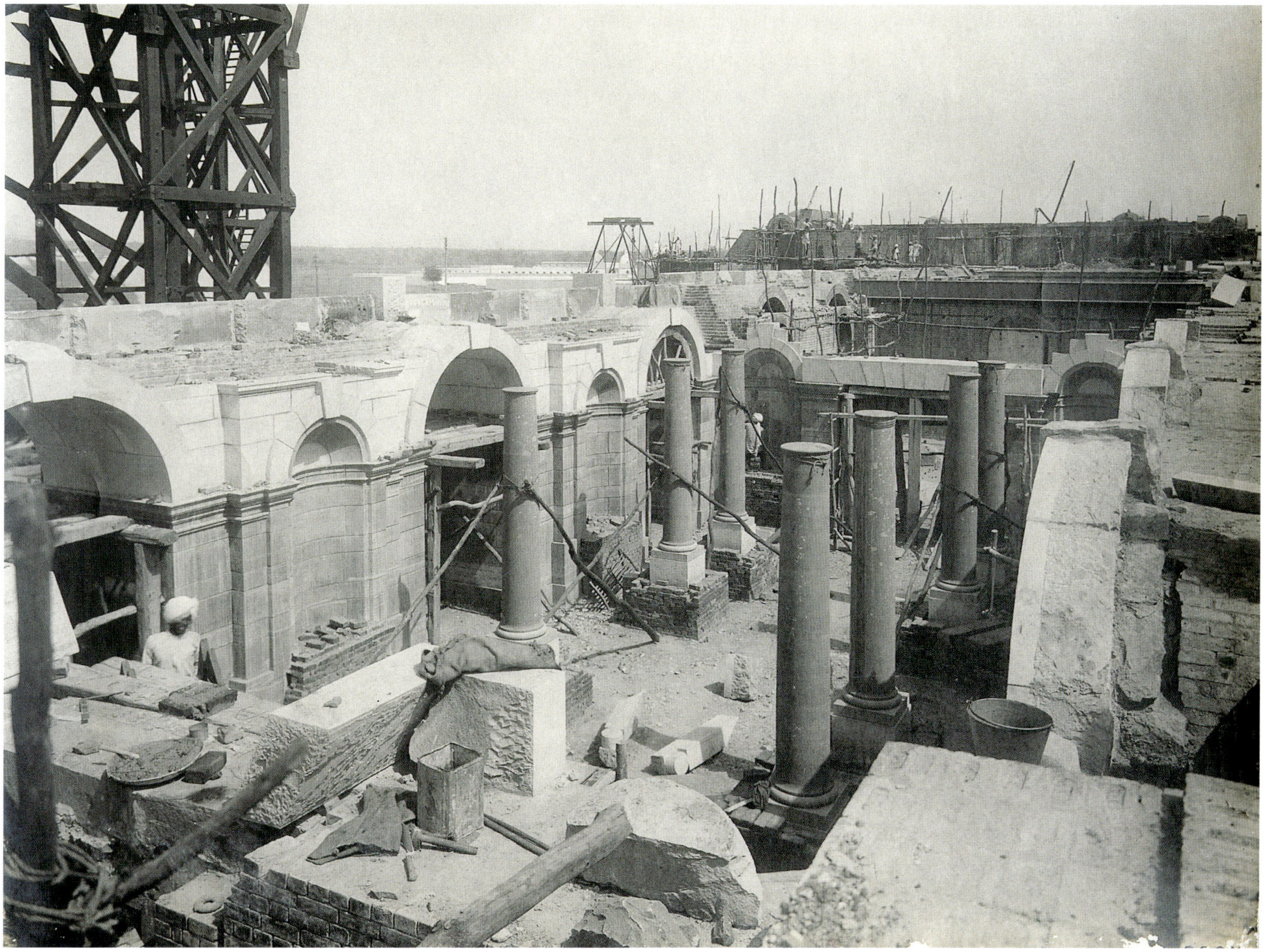

Fig. 241: View into the lower west garden loggia, from the southeast to the northwest corner, during construction of the upper basement floor in 1924.

Following page, Fig. 242: View of Viceroy's House from Jaipur Column.

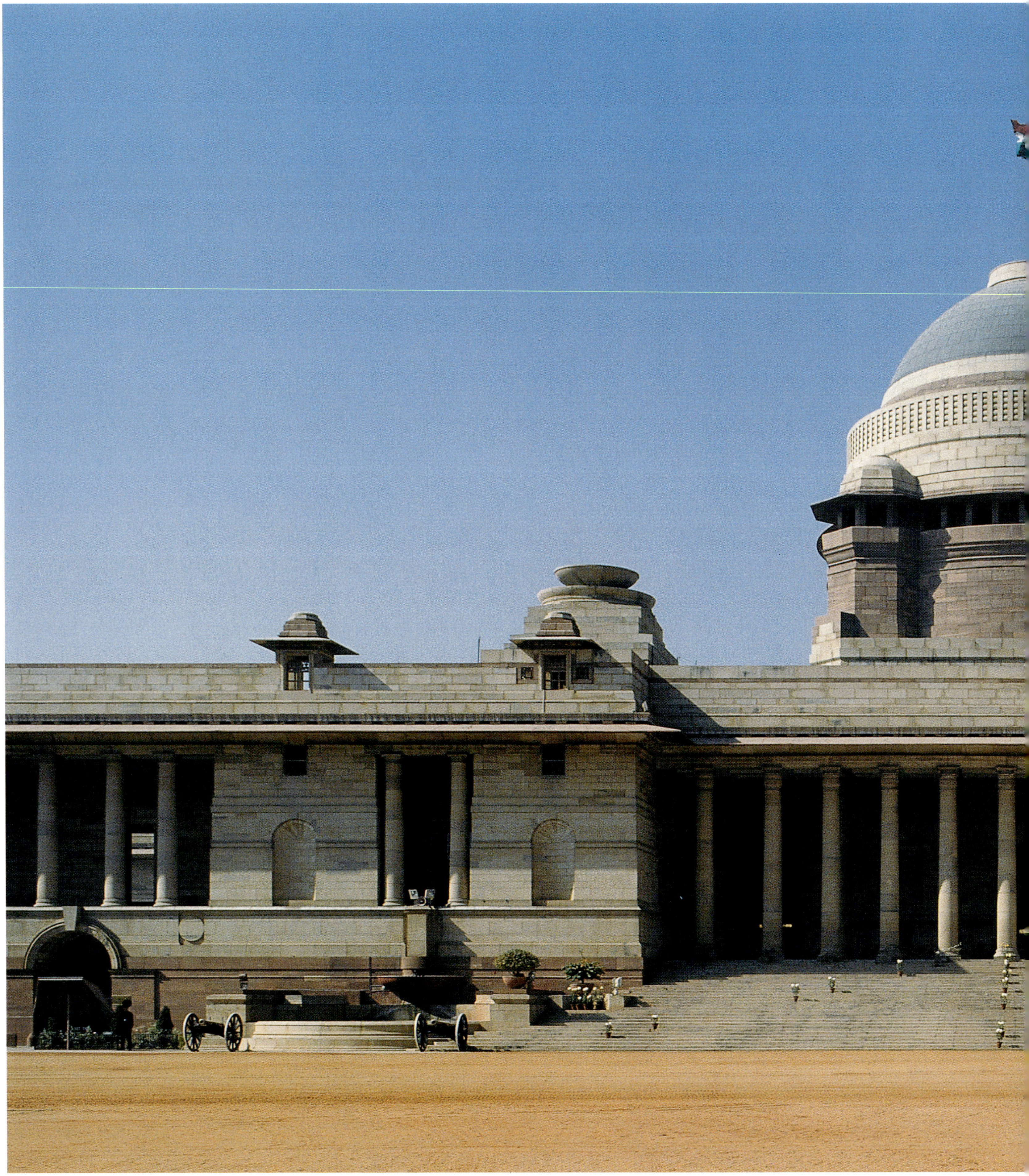

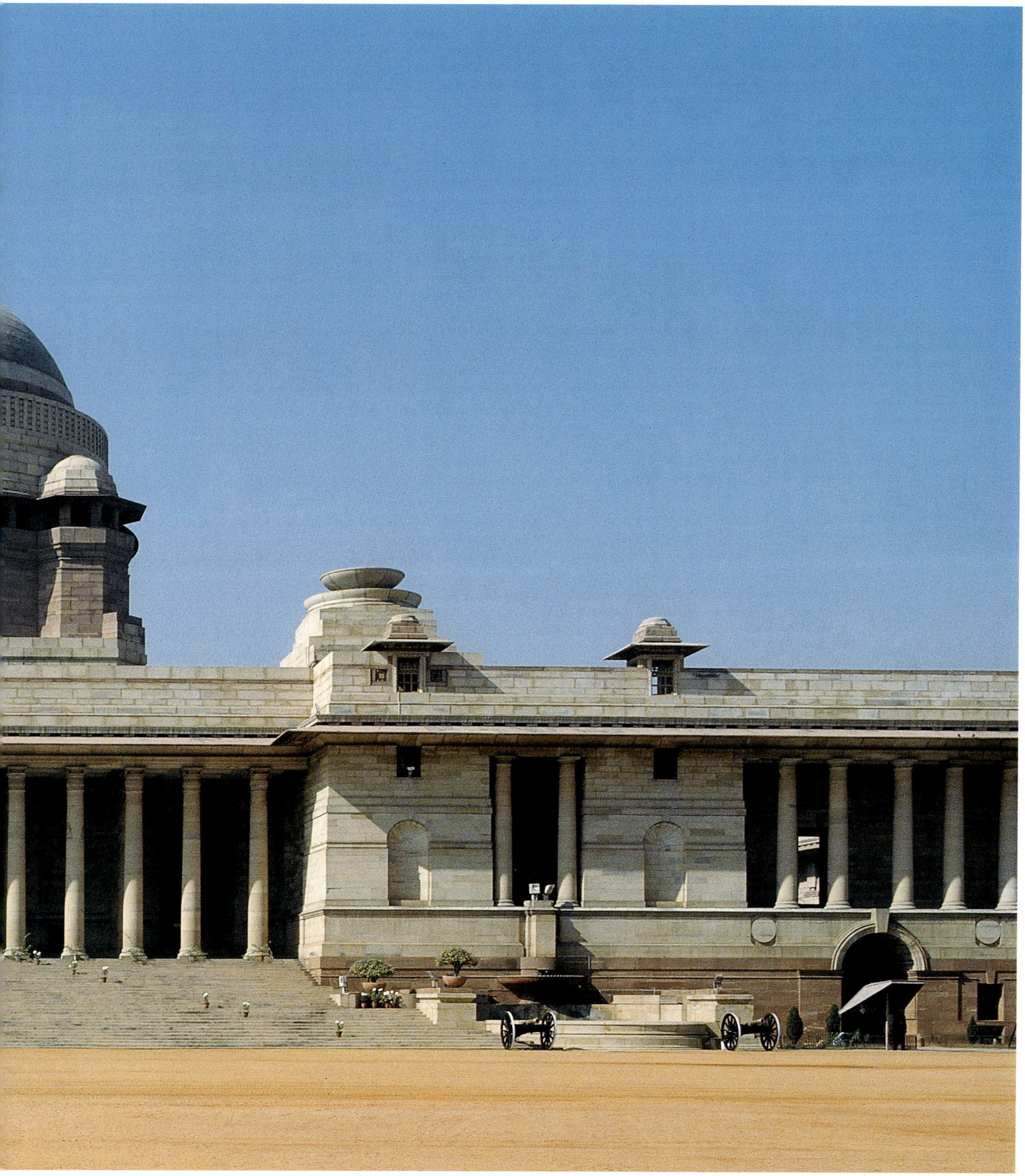

4.6 The Collapse of the Raj

In February, 1931, whilst receptions, dinner parties and garden parties were taking place in quick succession in Imperial Delhi and the Raj appeared to be at the peak of its power, leaders of the Congress Party in Allahabad were meeting to mourn the death of their leader, Pundit Motilal Nehru, and to draw the first plan from the Round Table Conference.

Uncertainty on the side of the British administration, and the premonition of historic changes, led to the capital appearing rather like an army camp. The Duke and Duchess of York cancelled their planned visit to the inaugural celebrations for security reasons. Assassination threats by militant nationalists made things all the more uncertain, worsened by the fact that they did not fit the unyielding but peaceful negotiating tactics of Mahatma Gandhi.

Motilal Nehru's son, the later Prime Minister Jawaharlal Nehru, commented scornfully in his diary on the arrogant self-portrayal of the colonial power: "Their court ceremonies, their durbars and investitures, their parades, their dinners and evening dress, their pompous utterances.

Viceroy's House in New Delhi was the chief temple where the high priest officiated, but there were many other temples and priests. All this ceremonial and display of imperial pomp was designed to impress our people in the old days, for Indians are also given to ceremonial observances. But new standards had arisen, different values had been created, and now this elaborate show was the subject of jest and ridicule. Indians are supposed to be a slow-moving people, but even they had developed a certain speed and vigour in their work, so strong was their desire to get things done. The Congress provincial governments, whatever their failings might have been, were anxious to achieve results and worked hard and continuously, disregarding their many old-established routines. It was irritating to see the passivity and slowness of the Government of India and its many agents in the face of grave crisis and peril."[77]

In London, Winston Churchill was one of the first to recognise the extent of the approaching dangers for the British Empire. He took every opportunity to stress that if India were ever lost the gradual disintegration of the whole Empire would be only a matter of time. He mistrusted above all the chief Indian negotiator: "It is alarming and also nauseating to see Mr Gandhi, a seditious Middle Temple lawyer, now posing as a fakir of a type well-known in the East, striding half-naked up the steps of the Viceregal palace, while he is still organizing and conducting a defiant campaign of civil disobedience, to parley on equal terms with the representative of the King-Emperor."[78]

The relationship of the Viceroy, Lord Irwin, with Gandhi was quite different. He reported to the King in London about the enigmatic charm of his negotiating partner: "I think most people meeting him would be conscious, as I was conscious, of a very powerful personality, and this, independent from physical endowment, which indeed is unfavourable. Small, wizened, rather emaciated, no front teeth, it is a personality very poorly adorned with this world's trimmings. And yet you cannot help feeling the force of character behind the sharp little eyes and immensely active and acutely working mind."[79]

From a trust in personal integrity, a sort of friendship developed between the two, which absolutely amazed people in London.

"The two men did not kneel together in prayer, as was reported, but they did laugh over Churchill's lurid description of the 'half-naked fakir.'"[80] The two very different chief negotiators finally succeeded in creating, with the Delhi Pact, the foundations for a transitional period in India. It was now no longer a question of if there would be a handover of governmental power but only of settling how and when. Both deeply regretted that Lord Irwin's period in office expired in April, 1931, and that they would no longer together be able to continue to shape India's path to independence.

The path from the Delhi Pact in 1931 to independence in 1947 was difficult and lined with many disappointments. One particular difficulty, the incompatibility of the persistent demands of the Muslim League for a separate Islamic state with a peaceful transference of the Raj into a democratic nation, stood out more clearly with each passing year.

77 J. Nehru: *The Discovery of India*, New Delhi 1981, p. 450ff.
78 W.S. Churchill: *India: Speeches and an Introduction*, London 1931, p. 81f.
79 Quotation from: R.G. Irving: op. cit., p. 352.
80 R. Bernay: *Naked Fakir*, New York 1932, p. 184.

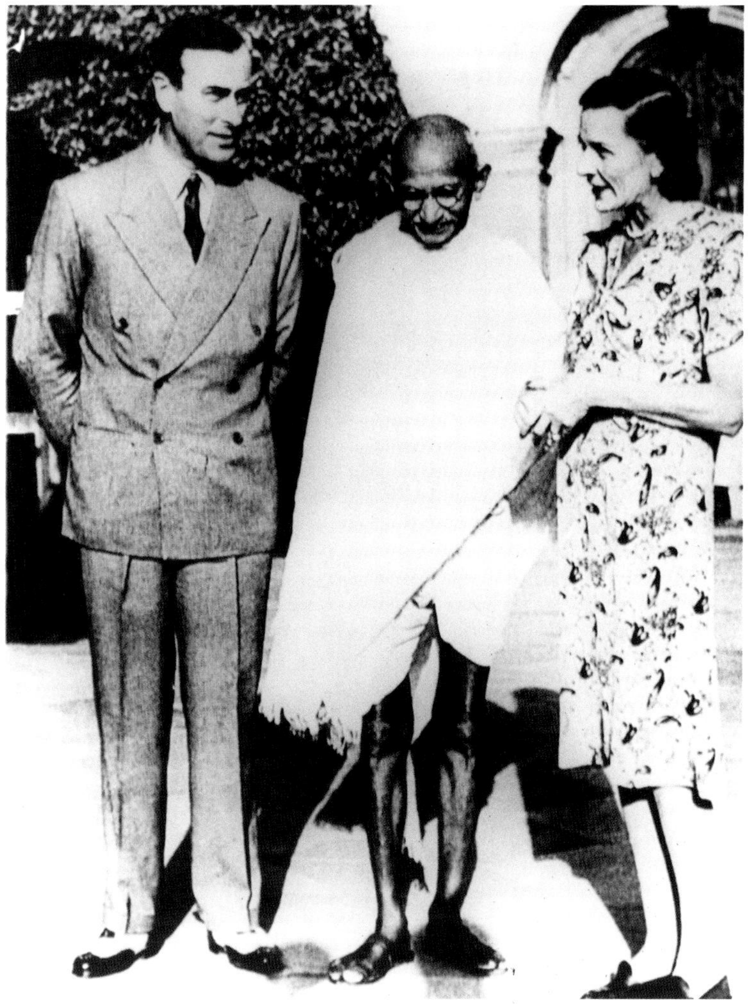

Fig. 243: Lord Mountbatten, the last British Viceroy and Governor-General, together with Mahatma Gandhi, agree on the orderly transfer of governmental power. At right is Lady Mountbatten.

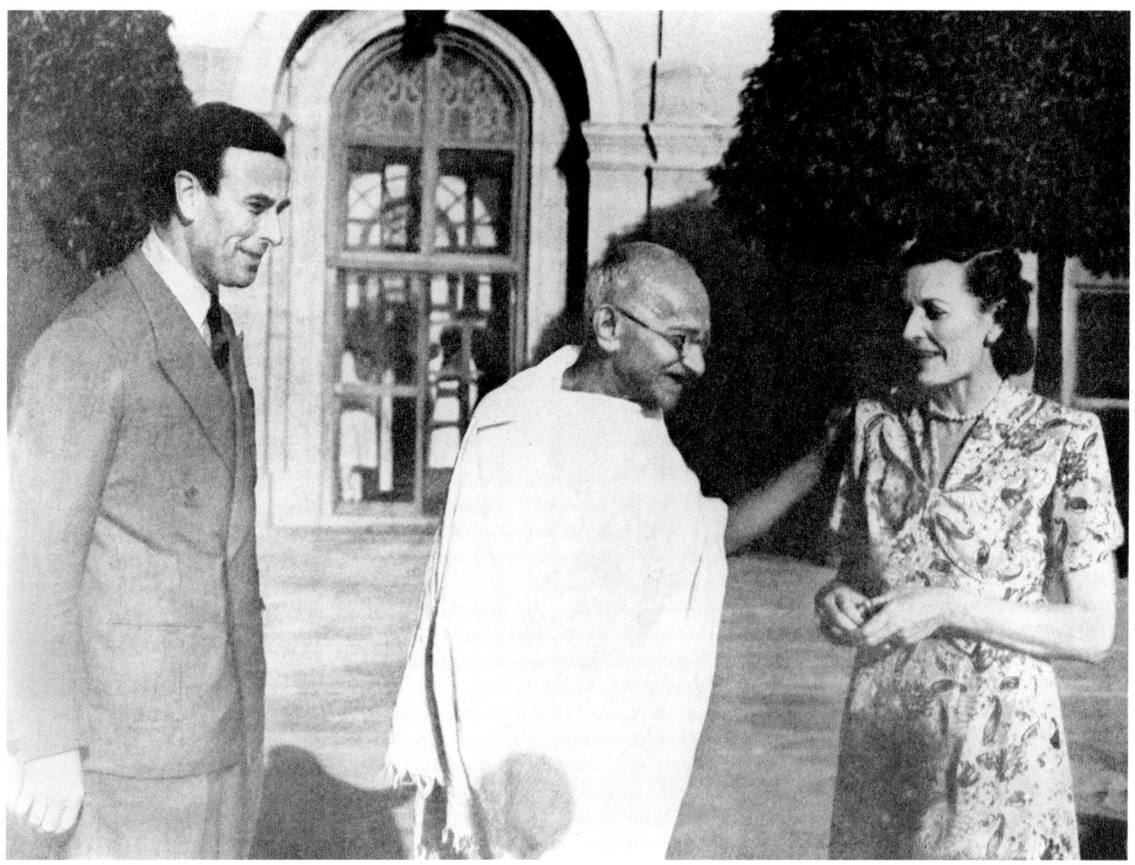

"On February 20, 1947, the British government announced its intention of leaving India by June, 1948 and appointed Lord Mountbatten as Viceroy to carry out the transfer of power. The Muslim League once more embarked on 'direct action.' Violence, murder, and arson convulsed the Punjab and the North-West Frontier Province. Congress reluctantly accepted the fact that, if independence were to be achieved, India must be divided.

On June 3, the new Viceroy broadcast a declaration of British government policy. Its substance was: (1) if Muslim majority areas so desired, they should be permitted to form a separate dominion, and a new constituent assembly would be set up for that purpose. In that case, however, Bengal and Punjab would have to be partitioned if the representatives of Hindu-majority districts in the legislatures of those provinces so demanded. (2) A referendum would be carried out in the North-West Frontier Province to ascertain whether or not it wished to join Pakistan. (3) The district of Sylhet would be joined to the Muslim area of Bengal after the people's views had been discovered by a referendum. (4) Boundary commissions would be set up to define the boundaries of the Hindu and Muslim provinces in Bengal and the Punjab. (5) Legislation would be introduced in the current session of parliament at Westminster to confer immediate dominion status on India (or on the two countries, if partition was decided upon), without any prejudice to the final decision of the constituent assembly (or assemblies) in this respect.

Both Congress and Muslim League finally accepted this plan, and the India Independence Act passed through parliament on 1 July 1947.[81]

Fig. 244: On Republic Day, January 26, the government of India holds a grand parade on Raj Path (previously King's Way) with a grandeur and authority reminiscent of the collapsed British Empire.

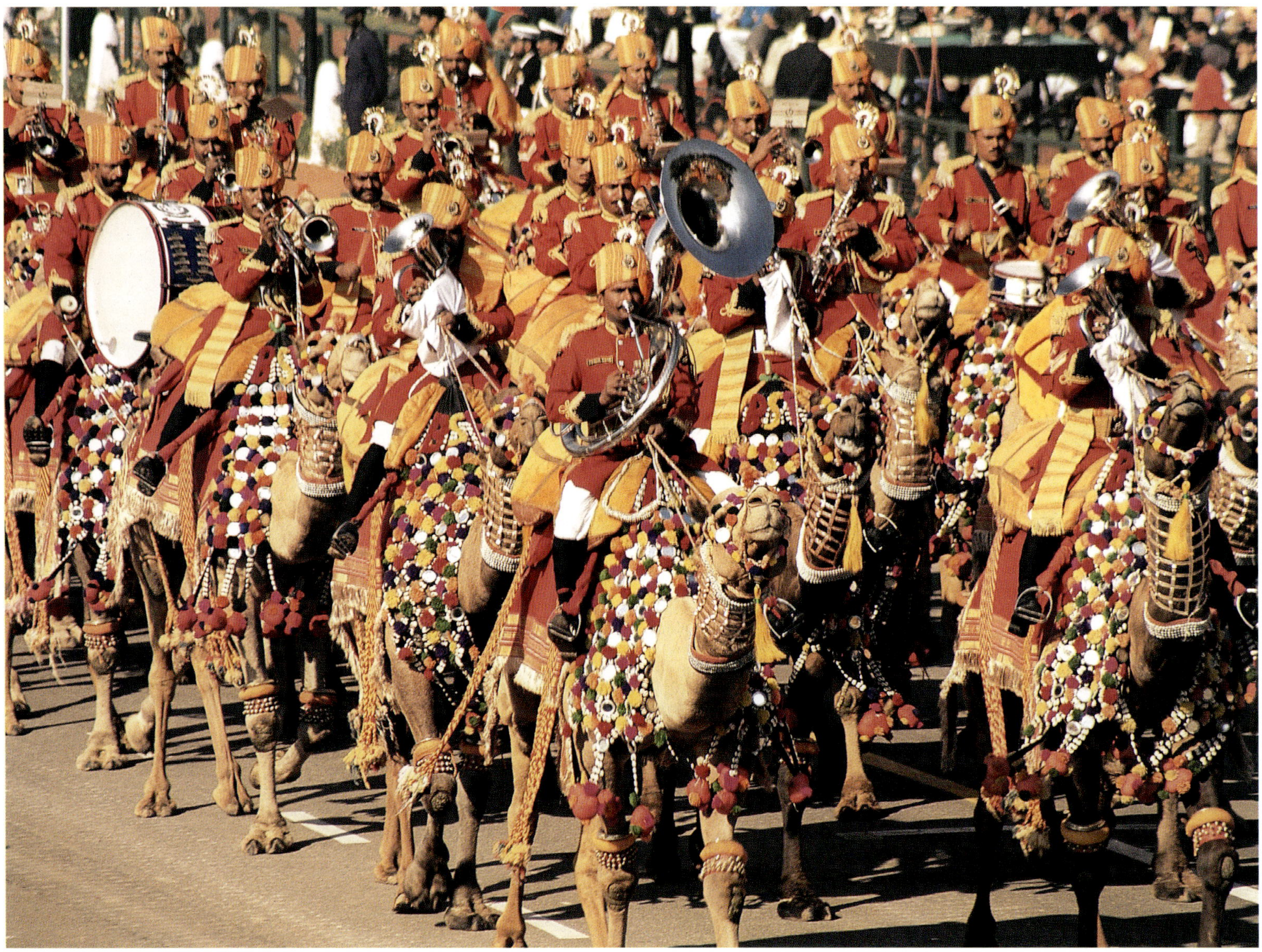

81 M. Edwardes: *British India 1772–1947*, New Delhi 1967, p. 163ff.
82 Muhammad Ali Jinna became First Governor General of Pakistan.
83 M. Edwardes: op. cit., p. 206.
84 G. Stamp: op. cit.

On August 15 of the same year, the constituent assembly in New Delhi declared India an independent dominion within the British Commonwealth with Lord Mountbatten as its first Governor General. "In Karachi, the capital of the new dominion of Pakistan, and in New Delhi, the capital of the new and truncated India, the words of the last Emperor of undivided India were read out by the new governors-general[82]: On this historic day when (India/Pakistan) takes her place as a free and independent Dominion in the British Commonwealth of Nations I send you my greetings and heartful wishes. With this transfer of power by consent comes the fulfilment of a great democratic ideal, to which the British and (Indian/Pakistani) peoples alike are firmly dedicated."[83]

Thus, the British Empire came to an end.

In 1981, in his foreword to an exhibition about the work of Edwin Lutyens, Gavin Stamp summarized the fate of the British royal seat in India as follows: "The story of New Delhi is one of tragedy as well as one of triumph. The triumph was remarkable: for an architect of genius to realize his grand, humane conception in the face of implacable opposition of Anglo-India and despite the ingrained philistinism and meanness of British government. But the triumph was short-lived: New Delhi took nineteen years to build, it was occupied by the British for a mere sixteen."[84]

The history of Imperial Delhi, however, went farther than the history of the capital of a democratically constituted Indian society, still today searching for a balance between power

Fig. 245: The President's bodyguard in the Republic Day parade.

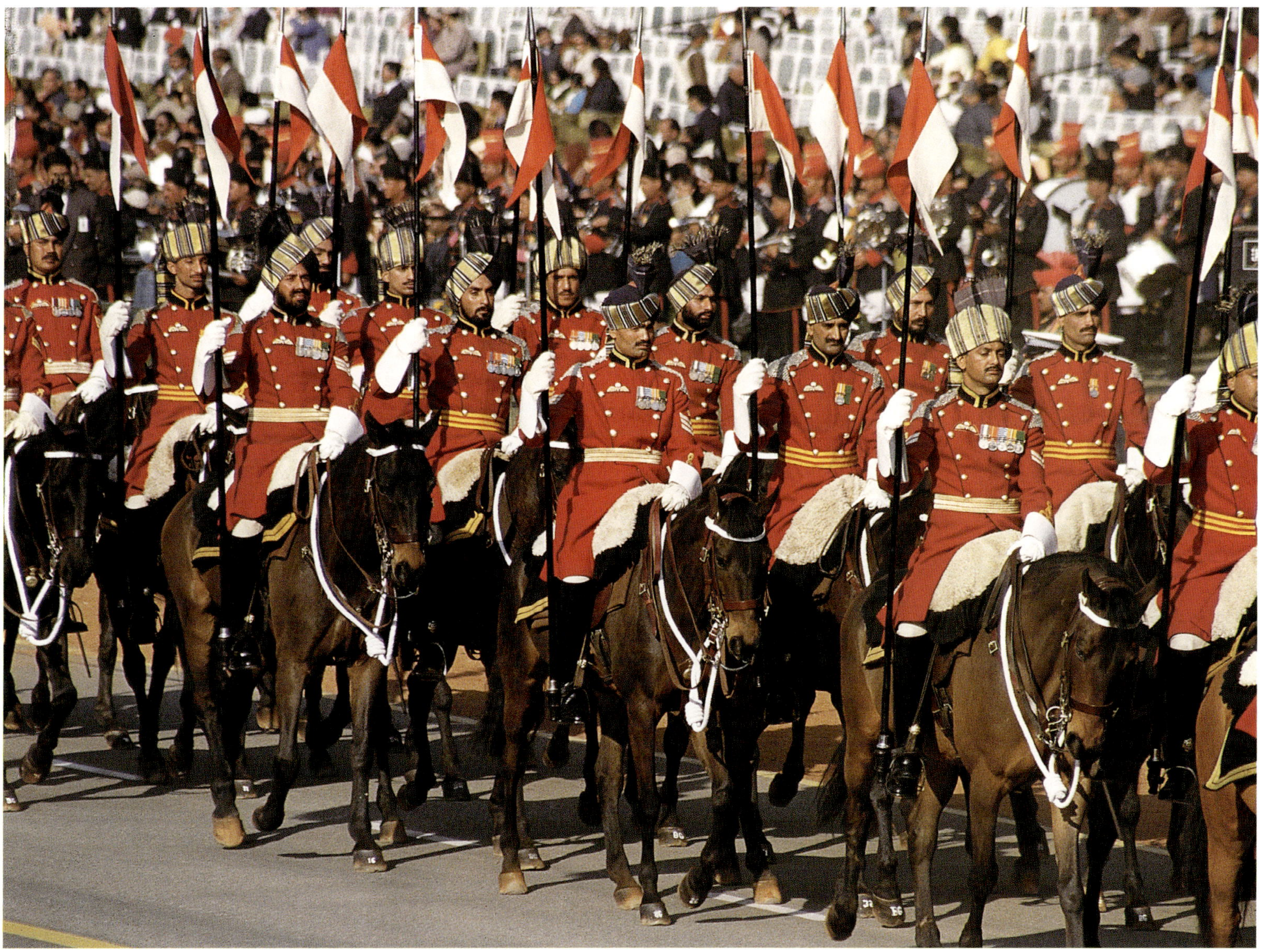

politics towards its rival, Pakistan, and the memory of the ideals of her first modern political leader Mohandas Karamchand Gandhi (1869–1948), known as Mahatma – the Great Soul.

On June 21, 1948, Lord Mountbatten handed over the government administration to C. Rajagopalachari: "No two persons could be more unlike than Dickie and Rajaji, as they were popularly known – the British military personage of picture book handsomeness with his chest full of medals and golden epaulettes adorning his right shoulder, and the small, birdlike, bald elder clad in white handspun with an *angavastram* thrown over his left shoulder, and a pair of dark glasses perched on his aquiline nose. Dickie was an imperial admiral and had held many commands; Rajaji was a general in Gandhi's non-violent army, known for his philosophical mind and his polemical powers. Dickie had grown up in palaces, indeed Queen Victoria was present at his christening; Rajaji had aged in jails and *ashrams*. Dickie was known for his love of ceremony. Rajaji's life was simplicity personified."[85]

In the following decades the new parliamentary democracy consolidated its political framework and its importance in the international community. Only once a year, on Republic day, does the old imperial splendour resurface to bring life to the axis of King's Way, now known as Raj Path.

"The Republic Day Parade, which takes place on the morning of every January 26, is a pageant of great color and liveliness. Originally intended as a march-past of the defence forces to salute the president, who is their Supreme Commander, and to reassure the nation of their ability and willingness to defend its integrity, it has developed, in addition, into a cultural display in which the magnificent and many-hued heritage of the numerous regions of the land is presented. The different states send groups of folk dancers and tableaux depicting events from their history or architectural landmarks. Besides, hundreds of Delhi schoolchildren sing and dance their way down Raj Path and into the hearts of the million or more spectators. Special attractions are the sowars on horses, the camel units which guard the desert border in the west, the caparisoned elephants and the veterans – some from World War II – marching smartly in civilian clothes and displaying their decorations without any medal fatigue. It is also a great day for the bands with their brasses and cymbals filling the air and gleaming in the morning sun."[86]

85 H.Y.S. Prasad: *Rashtrapati Bhavan*, New Delhi 1992, p. 90.
86 Ibid., p. 14.

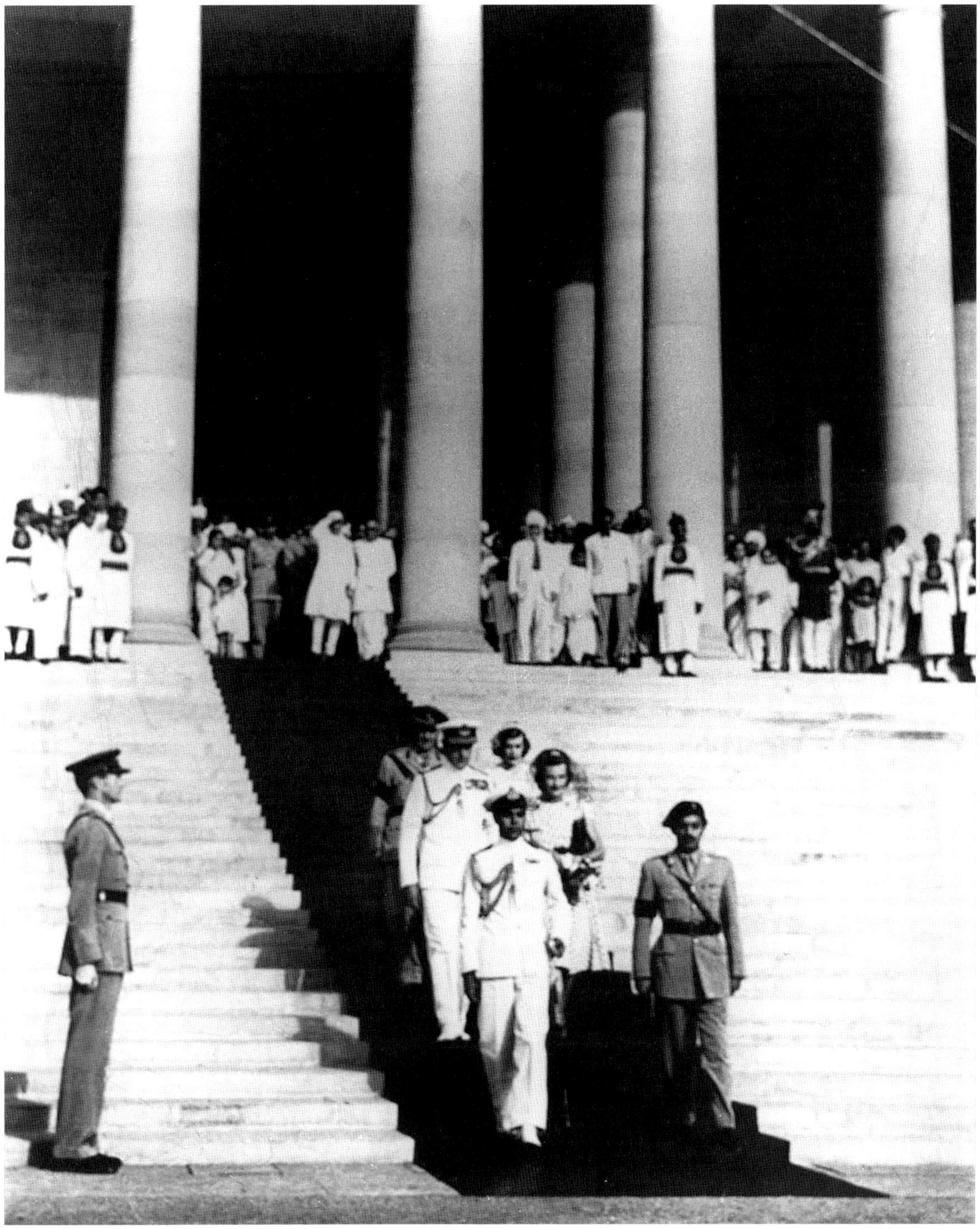

Fig. 246: In June 1948, in a festive act, the last British Viceroy Lord Mountbatten and his wife left Viceroy's House. British reign in India thus came to an end.

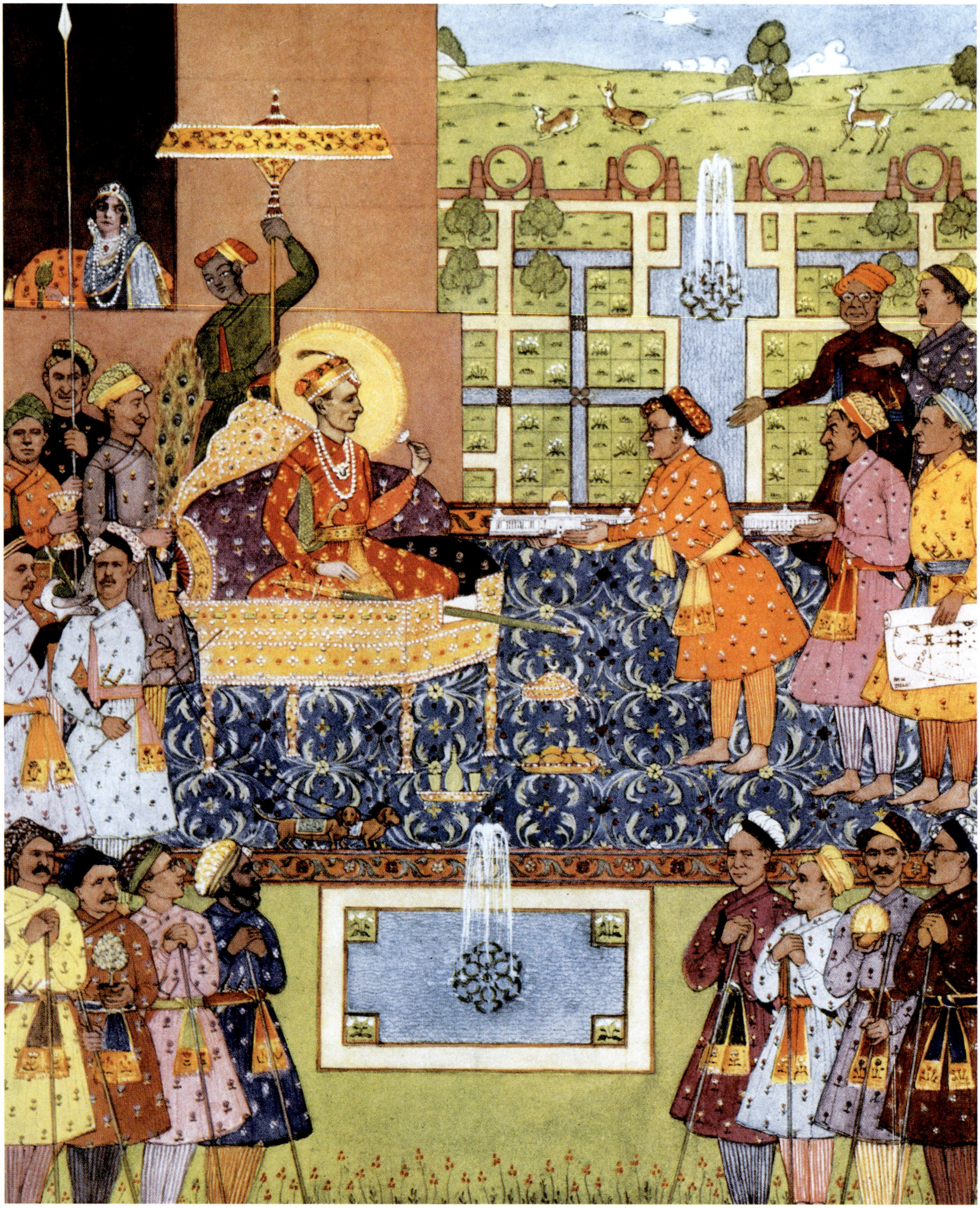

CV Edwin Lutyens 1869–1944

Sir Edwin Landseer Lutyens was born in London in 1869, the son of Captain Charles Lutyens, a painter of horses, and Mary Lutyens, formerly Gallway. His early education provided at home, he became a student at the Royal College of Art, South Kensington in 1885. In 1887, he joined the office of Ernest George and Peto, where he met Herbert Baker. Two years later he set up an independent practice and worked on many country houses with the garden designer Gertrude Jekyll. Soon after establishing his practice, Edwin married Lady Emily, third daughter of the 1st Earl of Lytton, and moved office and home to No. 29 Bloomsbury Square. In 1898, he was commissioned to design the British Pavilion for the Paris Exhibition of 1900. In 1906, he became a Fellow of the Royal Institute of British Architects (R.I.B.A.). From 1908–1909, he served as the consulting architect to the Hampstead Garden Suburb and to the Royal Commission for the International Exhibition at Turin and Rome. In 1911, he received the commission for the Rand Regiment's memorial and the art gallery in Johannesburg. One year later, he was appointed as advisor to the Delhi Planning Committee only to become the architect of New Delhi, along with Herbert Baker. Edwin was elected to the Academy of Royal Architects (A.R.A) in 1914 and received a knighthood four years later. In 1921, he received the Gold Medal from R.I.B.A. and the gold medal of the American Institute of Architects in 1924. He became Vice-President of the R.I.B.A. that same year. In 1928, he received the honourary degree of LL.D. from Liverpool University. During the 1920s he designed more than ninety war memorials. Then from 1928–1930, he worked on the Westminster housing scheme on Page Street. During this time, Edwin also began work on the Liverpool Metropolitan Cathedral. In 1932, he was appointed as an officer of the Legion of Honour and in 1933 he was named a Master of the Art Workers Guild. In 1934, he was appointed as consultant, with Sir Charles Bressey, to the Highway Development Survey of Greater London, which resulted in the Royal Academy Plan for London. He became the President of the A.R.A. in 1938.

CV Herbert Baker 1862–1946

Sir Herbert Baker was born at Owletts, Cobham, Kent in 1862. In 1879, he was articled to his cousin Arthur Baker, a London architect, and attended classes at the Royal Academy Schools and the Architectural Association. In 1882, he transferred to the office of Ernest George and Peto, and was a senior assistant there when (Sir) Edwin Lutyens became a pupil. In 1890, Baker was named an Associate of the Royal Institute of British Architects (R.I.B.A.). In 1892, he went to Cape Town, South Africa, where Cecil Rhodes became his patron. In 1896, he rebuilt Groote Schuur Hospital with Francis Masey, at the Cape, for Rhodes. In 1899, Masey became his partner and F.K. Kendall his chief assistant. Soon after, he was sent by Rhodes on a tour of the Mediterranean countries to study classical architecture. In 1900, he was elected as a Fellow of R.I.B.A. In 1902, he began practice in the Transvaal at the invitation of Lord Milner, the governor. In 1903, Ernest Willmott Sloper became his partner in Transvaal. By 1904, he had three practices, one in Johannesburg where Frank Fleming worked with him, one in Cape Town under the direction of Masey and one in Bloemfontein under Kendall. In 1911, he became the Vice President of the Transvaal Association of Architects. In 1912, he returned to England, only to depart for New Delhi in 1913, to collaborate with (Sir) Edwin Lutyens. In 1922, he was elected to the Academy of Royal Architects (A.R.A.). He was knighted in 1926 for his services to the Empire in India. In 1927, he received the Royal Gold Medal for Architecture followed by his election as Royal Architect five years later. In 1937, he was awarded the honourary degree of D.C.L. by Oxford University.

Fig. 247: Mrs A.G. Shoosmith, in a Mughal-style miniature, sketched the handing over of the keys of Viceroy's House by Lutyens to the Viceroy. Depicted from left to right in the centre of the image is Lord Irwin, the Viceroy; Edwin Lutyens and Herbert Baker, the architects; and Alexander Rouse, the Chief Engineer. Lady Irwin is in purdah.

Bibliography

Alastair Service (ed.), *Edwardian Architecture and its Origin*, London 1975

Arts Council of Great Britain, *Lutyens* (Exposition Catalogue), London 1981

Baker, H., *Architecture and Personalities*, London 1944

Basham (ed.), *A Cultural History of India*, Oxford 1975

Baumgart, F., *Stilgeschichte der Architektur*, Cologne 1969 from the RIBA Archive: *The Lutyens Family Papers*

Bence-Jones, M., *Palaces of the Raj*, London 1973

Birrelly, *Walter Burley Griffin*, Brisbane 1964

Biver, M.L., *Le Paris de Napoleon*, Paris 1963

Bracker, J., *Bauen nach der Natur, Palladio, Die Erben Palladios in Nordeuropa*, Stuttgart 1997

Brenner, H., *Die Kunstpolitik der Nationalsozialisten*, n.p. 1963

Brown, G., *History of the United States Capitol*, Washington, D.C. 1900, reprint 1970

Brown, J., *Lutyens and the Edwardians*, London 1996

Burnham, D.H., *Plan of Chicago*, n.p. 1909

Butler, A.S.G., *The Architecture of Sir Edwin Lutyens*, 3 vol., London, New York 1950

Byron, R., "New Delhi," reprint from: *The Architectural Review*, Vol. LXIX, January 1931, New Delhi 1997

Castells, W. Bro. Rev. F. de, *Arithmetic of Freemasonry*, London 1925

Chapman, J.M., *The Life and Times of Baron Haussmann*, London 1957

Chipkin, C.M., "Lutyens and Imperialism," in: *RIBA Journal*, July 1969

Coen, L. and l'Institut Claude-Nicolas Ledoux, *A la recherché de la cité idéale*, Arc et Senans 2000

Coleman, B.I., *The Idea of the City in the 19th Century in Britain*, London 1973

Curl, S.J., *The Art and Architecture of Freemason*, New York 1991

Curzon of Kedlestone, G.N., *British Government in India, The Story of Viceroys and Government Houses*, London 1925

Daniell, T. and W., *Oriental Scenery. One Hundred and Fifty Views of the Architecture, Antiquities, and Landscape Scenery of Hindoostan*, London 1816

Dehio, G., *Untersuchungen über das gleichseitige Dreieck als Norm gotischer Bauproportionen*, Stuttgart 1894

Deutsches Archäologisches Institut, *Berlin und die Antike* (Catalogue), Berlin 1979

Dyer, C.F.W., *Symbolism in Craft Masonry*, London 1983

Edwardes, M., *British India 1772–1947*, New Delhi 1967

Ehrenkranz, E.D., *The Modular Number Pattern*, London 1956

Fishman, R., *Urban Utopias in the Twentieth Century*, New York 1977

Forssmann, E.(pub.), *Palladio, Werk und Wirkung*, Freiburg 1997

Franklin, *Edwardian Butterfly Houses*, n.p. n.d.

Frazer, J.B., *Views of Calcutta and its environments*, London 1824–1828

Frommel, C.L. et al., *Raffael, Das architektonische Werk*, Stuttgart 1987

Gaehtgens, T.W., "Napoleons Arc de Triomphe," in: *Abhandlungen der Wiss.*, Göttingen, No. 90, 1974

Gibbs, J., *Book of Architecture*, London 1728

Goodwin, G.B., *The Geometric Symbols of Masonry*, London 1920

Gradidge, R., *Edwin Lutyens, Architect Laureate*, London 1979

Gray, A.S., *Edwardian Architecture, A Biographical Dictionary*, London 1985

Greenberg, A., *Lutyens' Architecture Restudied*, n.p. n.d.

Griffin, W.B., *The Federal Capital*, n.p. n.d.

Gromort, G., *Histoire Abregee de l'Architecture en France au XIXe Siecle*, Paris 1924

Gutheim, F.A., *Worthy of a Nation. The History of Planning for the National Capital*, Washington, D.C. 1977

Hale, J., *Dictionary of Subjects and Symbols in Art*, n.p. 1979

Hall, T., *Planung Europäischer Hauptstädte*, Stockholm 1986

Hamill, J., *The Craft. A History of English Freemasonry*, London 1986

Hardinge, C., *My Indian Years, 1910–1916*, London 1948

Havell, E.B., *The Building of New Delhi*, Guilford 1912

Havell, E.B., *Indian Architecture*, London 1913, reprint 1927

Hussey, C., *The Life of Sir Edwin Lutyens*, London, New York 1950

Hussey, C., "The Personality of Sir Edwin Lutyens," in: *RIBA Journal*, April 1969

Hussey, C., "An Early Lutyens Castle in the Air," in: *Country Life*, January 22, 1959

Irving, R.G., *Indian Summer, Lutyens, Baker and Imperial Delhi*, New Haven, London 1981

Johnson, D.L., *Canberra and Walter Burley Griffin, A bibliography of 1876 to 1976 and a guide to published sources*, Melbourne n.d.

Judd, D., *The Life and Times of George V*, London, 1993

Lanchester, H.V., *The Art of Townplanning*, New York 1925

Lanchester, H.V., "The Architecture of the Indian Empire," in: *Architectural Review* 55, June 1924

Larsson, L.O., *Die Neugestaltung der Reichshauptstadt*, Stockholm 1978

Lennhoff, E., *Die Freimaurer*, Vienna 1932

Library of Congress, *The Grand Design*, Exposition Catalogue, Washington, D.C. 1967

Loosen-Frieling, J., *Architektur zwischen Norm und Geschmack, Studien zur Kunstgeschichte*, Hildesheim, Zurich, New York 1992

Lutyens, Sir E., "Notes regarding the building of New Delhi and Viceroy's House, taken from a speech made by Sir E. Lutyens at a meeting of the India Society," February 2, 1933

Lutyens, E., *Candles in the Sun*, London 1957

Lutyens, M., *Edwin Lutyens, by his daughter*, London 1980

Lutyens, M., *The Lyttons in India*, London 1979

Lutyens, R., *Sir Edwin Lutyens, an Appreciation in Perspective*, London 1942

Lutyens, R., *Six Great Architects*, London 1959

Lytton, V.A.G.R., *Pundits and Elephants*, London 1942

Mackay, A.G., *Encyclopedia of Freemasonry*, Chicago 1946

Martinelli, A., Michell, G., *Voyage en Inde*, Paris 1998

Mead, J.C., "Mathematical Symbolism in Freemasonry," paper prepared for *Langport Lodge* No. 8072, September 17, 1986

Mitra, A., *Delhi Capital City*, New Delhi 1970

Naredi-Rainer, P.V., *Architektur und Harmonie*, Cologne 1982

Nehru, J., *The Discovery of India*, Calcutta 1946

Nicolson, *King George V*, Munich 1954, reprint 1984

Nilsson, S., *European Architecture in India 1750–1850*, London 1986

Oliver, G., *The Pythagorean Triangle*, London 1875

O'Neill, D., *Sir Edwin Lutyens, Country Houses*, London 1980

Oliver, D.D., *The Pythagorean Triangle*, London 1875.

Palladio, *Four Books on Architecture*, Venice 1570

Percy, C., Ridley J., *The Letters of Edwin Lutyens to His Wife Lady Emily*, London 1985

Pevsner, N., *Funktion und Form*, Hamburg 1998

Prasad, H.Y.S., *Rashtrapati Bhavan, The Story of the President's House*, New Delhi 1992

Rao, V.K.R.V., *Greater Delhi*, Bombay 1965
Reinborn, D., *Städtebau im 19. und 20. Jahrhundert*, Stuttgart 1996
RIBA, *The Baker Papers*
RIBA, *The Lutyens Letters*
Richardson, M., *Sketches by Lutyens*, London 1994
Rollo, J., "Metiendo Vivendum: By Measure We Must Live," in *arq*, Vol. 3, no 2, 1999, p. 147ff.

Scholfield, P.H., *The Theory of Proportion in Architecture*, Cambridge 1958
Sekler, E., *Wren and His Place in European Architecture*, New York 1956
Serlio, *Five Books on Architecture*, n.p. 1547
Shoosmith, A.G., "Reminiscences on Sir E. Lutyens," in: *AAJ*, LXXIV, 1959, p. 234
Smithson, P., "The Viceroy's House in Imperial Delhi," in: *RIBA Journal*, April 1969
Smollet, T., *The Expedition of Humphrey Clinker*, London 1771, reprint 1967
Spar, T.G.P., *Delhi, Its Monuments and History*, Bombay 1945
Spear, P., *A History of India*, New Delhi 1965
Speer, A., *Inside the Third Reich*, London 1971
Speer, A., *Architecture 1932–1942*, Brussels 1935
Spence, R., "The Griffin Plan for Canberra," in: *AR*, Vol. CLXXXIV, No 1100, October 1988
Stamp, G., *Edwin Lutyens, Country Houses*, London 2001
Summerson, J., *Architecture in Britain 1530 to 1830*, Melbourne, London, Baltimore 1953, reprint 1977
Sutcliffe, A., *Metropolis 1890–1940*, London 1984

Tillotson, G.H.R., *The Tradition of Indian Architecture*, New Haven, London 1989

Venturi, R. and D. Scott Brown, "Learning from Lutyens," in: *RIBA Journal*, August 1969
Volwahsen, A., *Living Architecture: Indian*, Fribourg, London, New York 1969
Volwahsen, A., *Living Architecture: Islamic Indian*, Fribourg, London, New York 1970
Volwahsen, A., *Cosmic Architecture in India, The Observatories of Maharaja Jai Singh of Jaipur*, Munich, London, New York 2001

Walls, A.G., *Geometry and Architecture in Islamic Jerusalem*, Buckhurst Hill, Essex 1980
Wells, R.A., *Freemasonry in London*, London 1984
Willms, J., *Paris, Hauptstadt Europas 1789–1914*, Munich 1988
Wittkower, R., *Architectural Principles in the Age of Humanism*, n.p. 1949
Woods, J., *The Origin of Building*, n.p. 1741
Woods, J., *Towards a Description of Bath*, n.p. 1742
Wren, C., *Parentalia*, Farnsborough, Hants 1965
Wundram, M. et al., *Palladio*, Cologne 1988

Zanten, Van D., "Walter Burley Griffin's Plan for Canberra, the capital of Australia," in: Zukowski, J., *Chicago Architecture 1872–1922* Munich 1988

Illustration Credits

All numbers refer to figures

Blondel La Rougery: 24, 27
Butler, A.S.G.: 70, 81, 82, 87, 94, 102, 108, 109, 114, 145, 146, 156, 160, 165, 170, 172, 173, 209, 220, 239
Cambridge University Library: 10, 11, 13, 14, 17, 21, 22, 60, 135, 174, 181, 211
Cape Institute of Architects, South Africa: 131
Central Public Works Department, New Delhi: 92, 106, 124, 125, 126, 130, 180, 184, 185, 186, 188, 190, 200, 203
Central St Martins College of Art and Design, London, UK/Bridgeman Art Library: 32
Centre of South Asian Studies, University of Cambridge: 36, 62, 83, 100, 101, 110, 112, 115, 136, 147, 168, 169, 176, 182, 183, 189, 191, 198, 204, 205, 217, 225, 228, 230, 232
Christie's Images, London, UK/Bridgeman Art Library: 104
Daniell, T. and W. from a private collection: 148
Daniell, T. and W. from a private collection/Bridgeman Art Library: 63, 64
Gast, K.: 226
Imperial Hotel, New Delhi: 3, 4, 5, 6, 7, 9, 15, 20
Library and Museum of Freemasonry, London: 52, 54, 55, 107
Malik, B., New Delhi: 44, 67, 91, 93, 95, 132, 171, 208, 233, 234, 235, 236, 237, 240, 241
National Library of Australia: 45
Nehru Memorial Museum, New Delhi: 196, 243, 246
Pandey, A., New Delhi: 66, 134, 157, 207, 244, 245
Photo Division, Govt. Of India: 206
Publications Division, Ministry of Information and Broadcasting, Govt. Of India: 96, 97, 98, 99, 103
Royal Institute of British Architects Library Drawings Collection, London: 1, 16, 50, 51, 69, 71, 75, 76, 78, 80, 84, 90, 137, 138, 192, 218, 219, 221, 222
Soanes Museum, London: 155
Staatsgalerie Stuttgart: 72, 73, 149, 150
Volwahsen, A: Frontispiece, 2, 30, 31, 40, 43, 53, 56, 57, 58, 59, 65, 79, 86, 111, 116, 117, 118, 119, 120, 121, 122, 128, 129, 133, 139, 140, 141, 142, 143, 144, 151, 152, 159, 161, 162, 163, 166, 167, 177, 178, 179, 193, 194, 195, 197, 199, 201, 202, 210, 212, 213, 214, 227, 229, 231, 242

The author and the publisher would like to thank those copyright owners who have kindly given their permission to reproduce their works in this volume. The publisher would be pleased to hear from any copyright holder who could not be traced.

Index